ADULT EDUCATION:
ISSUES AND DEVELOPMENTS

ADULT EDUCATION: ISSUES AND DEVELOPMENTS

PATRICIA N. BLAKELY AND ANNA H. TOMLIN
EDITORS

Nova Science Publishers, Inc.
New York

For permission to use material from this book please contact us:
Telephone 631-231-7269; Fax 631-231-8175
Web Site: http://www.novapublishers.com

NOTICE TO THE READER

The Publisher has taken reasonable care in the preparation of this book, but makes no expressed or implied warranty of any kind and assumes no responsibility for any errors or omissions. No liability is assumed for incidental or consequential damages in connection with or arising out of information contained in this book. The Publisher shall not be liable for any special, consequential, or exemplary damages resulting, in whole or in part, from the readers' use of, or reliance upon, this material.

Independent verification should be sought for any data, advice or recommendations contained in this book. In addition, no responsibility is assumed by the publisher for any injury and/or damage to persons or property arising from any methods, products, instructions, ideas or otherwise contained in this publication.

This publication is designed to provide accurate and authoritative information with regard to the subject matter covered herein. It is sold with the clear understanding that the Publisher is not engaged in rendering legal or any other professional services. If legal or any other expert assistance is required, the services of a competent person should be sought. FROM A DECLARATION OF PARTICIPANTS JOINTLY ADOPTED BY A COMMITTEE OF THE AMERICAN BAR ASSOCIATION AND A COMMITTEE OF PUBLISHERS.

LIBRARY OF CONGRESS CATALOGING-IN-PUBLICATION DATA

Adult education : issues and developments / Patricia N. Blakely and Anna H. Tomlin (editor).
   p. cm.
  ISBN 978-1-60456-272-9 (hardcover)
  1. Adult education. 2. Learning, Psychology of. 3. Cognitive styles. I. Blakely, Patricia N. II. Tomlin, Anna H.
LC5225.L42A32 2008
374--dc22
                    2007049740

Published by Nova Science Publishers, Inc. ≃ New York

CONTENTS

Preface   vii

Chapter 1   Minimizing The Stress of Accelerated
               Adult Education: A Descriptive Study
               Mary T. Boylston and Anthony L. Blair   1

Chapter 2   How Teachers Change: A Study of Professional
               Development in Adult Education
               Cristine Smith, Judy Hofer, Marilyn Gillespie,   25
               Marla Solomon and Karen Rowe

Chapter 3   The Development of Knowledge Structures in Adulthood
               Gabriel Bukobza   175

Chapter 4   Learning Styles and Higher Education: No Adult Left Behind
               Karen Burke and Laura Shea Doolan   205

Chapter 5   Teaching Adult Learners Through a Learning
               Styles Approach: An Anecdotal Reflection
               on 44 Years of Teaching Experience
               Bill Purkiss   217

Chapter 6   The Field Dependence/Field Independence
               Learning Styles: Implications for Adult Student
               Diversity, Outcomes Assessment and Accountability
               Blue Wooldridge and Melanie Haimes-Bartolf   231

Chapter 7   Evidence on the Impact of Adult Upper
               Secondary Education in Sweden
               Anders Stenberg   253

Chapter 8   Adult Learners in Higher Education:
               Barriers to Success and Strategies to Improve Results
               Elaine L. Chao, Emily Stover DeRocco and Maria K. Flynn   271

Index   355

PREFACE

Adult education is the practice of teaching and educating adults. This often happens in the workplace, through 'extension' or 'continuing education' courses at secondary schools, at a college or university. Other learning places include folk high schools, community colleges, and lifelong learning centers. The practice is also often referred to as 'Training and Development'. It has also been referred to as andragogy (to distinguish it from pedagogy). A difference is made between vocational education, mostly undertaken in workplaces and frequently related to upskilling, and non-formal adult education including learning skills or learning for personal development.

Educating adults differs from educating children in several ways. One of the most important differences is that adults have accumulated knowledge and experience that can add or hinder the learning experience. This new book presents recent studies on this topic from several perspectives.

Chapter 1 - Student stressors in higher education are not confined to those of traditional college age. Working adult students experience unique stressors due to their multiple roles as students, providers, and employees, and institutions of higher learning have not always been adept at recognizing and responding to these pressures. This descriptive study examines adult students in two accelerated higher education programs (nursing and management) at one institution. Students in both programs were surveyed regarding the degree to which the university addresses the context (as opposed to merely the content) of the learning environment for these students. The data derived from the survey process indicates significant areas of positive feedback and other areas in which universities can better serve their adult students. The essay concludes with a reflection on the degree to which the faith identify of the institution is responsible for its student support ethos.

Chapter 2 - The NCSALL Professional Development Study investigated how adult education teachers changed after participating in one of three different models of professional development (multisession workshop, mentor teacher group, or practitioner research group), all on the same topic of learner persistence. The study also investigated the most important individual, professional development, program, and system factors that influenced the type and amount of teacher change. This study was conducted primarily to help professional development decision-makers plan and deliver effective professional development, and to understand the factors that influence how teachers change as a result of professional development.

Chapter 3 - This study examined the ways by which individuals construe knowledge in adulthood. 80 participants between the ages of 17-70 were interviewed regarding their personal knowledge of self and culture. Content analysis of the interviews revealed four fundamental structures of knowledge, or *epistemes*, that consistently appeared in both domains. These were named Monolithic-Monoformal, Relativistic-Relational, Dialectical-Deconstructive, and Integral-Inclusive. The results suggested that these epistemes can be positioned along a developmental trajectory that is continuous and spiral. The implications of the findings to the areas of self, culture, post formal cognition, and wisdom are discussed.

Chapter 4 - A basic premise of this chapter is that the quality of teaching in many colleges and universities is perceived as unacceptable. Additionally, in higher education, teaching and learning practices need to be vastly improved to meet the needs of its diverse learners. The world of higher education and the world in which higher education plays a significant role are changing. With these premises as a backdrop this chapter will address the theory, practice, and research on the Dunn and Dunn Learning-Style Model. The authors will suggest specific strategies to identify and accommodate college students' individual learning styles.

Chapter 5 - Exploring selected events and themes developed over forty-four years of teaching at a number of educational levels, the chapter discusses the movement from an intuitive approach to learning styles-based teaching, into one that reflected a studied and strategized approach to learning styles. Comparing the teaching theories of Viola Spolin and David Kolb, it shows how the explorational techniques utilized in teaching theatre proved to be a perfect entrée into a more academic discipline and its traditional classroom. Also discussed are the ways in which forms of student diversity are positively addressed in the learning styles-based classroom.

The way we process the possibilities of each new emerging event determines the range of choices and decisions we see. The choices and decisions we make, to some extent, determine the events we live through, and these events influence our future choices. Thus, people create themselves through their choice of the actual occasions they live through. . . . Human individuality results from the pattern or 'program' created by our choices and their consequences. (Kolb, 1984, p. 64)

Chapter 6 - In this chapter the authors define and describe the Field Independence-Dependence (FI/FD) Cognitive Learning Style as developed by Herman Witkin. The evolution of FI/FD is described and discussed, along with significant research findings. Special emphasis focuses on research that demonstrate individual differences in students, and that suggest alternative instructional strategies for maximizing the achievement of learning outcomes. The chapter suggests that the integration of the results of such research into instructional design and delivery demonstrates the willingness of instructors to be held accountable for their efforts.

Chapter 7 - This chapter gives a brief survey of the literature on earnings effects of adult education at upper secondary level in Sweden (AE) and presents new estimates based on more detailed information than previous studies. The data concern all individuals born in 1970 and residing in Sweden from 1988 to 2001. One third was at some point registered in AE and among them 44 per cent went on to higher education. Regression results indicate that credits equal to one year of AE increase annual earnings by five per cent. The positive returns are mainly associated with vocational studies such as health related subjects and computer science while general subjects like Mathematics, Swedish or English are linked to insignificant estimates. Of those that went on to higher studies, the payoff to another year of education is essentially similar between individuals with and without AE prior to enrolment. The results thus imply that AE works well as a preparation for higher education but individuals who have no interest in further studies should choose vocational courses.

Chapter 8 - All materials that are copyrighted and protected by The Copyright laws are marked with a copyright Notice. Permission is granted to quote that material for noncommercial instructional, personal or scholarly use. Any material quoted must include a complete reference citation including the author and this publication. Prior written permission from the author(s) is required for any other use of the material submitted by author(s). However, those portions of this publication authored by employees of the U.S. Department of Labor or any other federal agency, are in the public domain, and may be quoted or reproduced without permission, with reference citations.

This series presents research findings and analyses from papers prepared by research contractors, staff members and individual researchers.

In: Adult Education: Issues and Developments
Editors: P. N. Blakely, A. H. Tomlin, pp. 1-23

ISBN: 978-1-60456-272-9
© 2008 Nova Science Publishers, Inc.

Chapter 1

MINIMIZING THE STRESS OF ACCELERATED ADULT EDUCATION: A DESCRIPTIVE STUDY

Mary T. Boylston and Anthony L. Blair
Campolo College of Graduate and Professional Studies
Eastern University, St. Davids, Pennsylvania

ABSTRACT

Student stressors in higher education are not confined to those of traditional college age. Working adult students experience unique stressors due to their multiple roles as students, providers, and employees, and institutions of higher learning have not always been adept at recognizing and responding to these pressures. This descriptive study examines adult students in two accelerated higher education programs (nursing and management) at one institution. Students in both programs were surveyed regarding the degree to which the university addresses the context (as opposed to merely the content) of the learning environment for these students. The data derived from the survey process indicates significant areas of positive feedback and other areas in which universities can better serve their adult students. The essay concludes with a reflection on the degree to which the faith identify of the institution is responsible for its student support ethos.

INTRODUCTION: REVOLUTIONS IN HIGHER EDUCATION

Within the past fifteen years Western institutions of higher education have experienced multiple, simultaneous, intertwined revolutions to a degree not experienced since the founding of the first universities in the high middle ages.[1] In that initial revolution the

---

[1] The use of the word "revolutions" here, while seemingly hyperbolic, is actually derived from another source written a full decade ago: "A revolution...has been slowly unfolding during the past several decades transforming the landscape of higher education, not only here in the United States but also throughout the world. This transformation in education is often referred to as the 'Adult Student Revolution.' Sparked by social, cultural, economic and technological factors, this sea-change is rightly called a 'revolution' since it is causing astute educators, like scientists undergoing a paradigm shift, to assume pioneering attitudes and adopt

cathedral schools morphed into degree-granting institutions with professional scholars, paying students, established curricula, and an administrative structure not entirely separate from but also not directly controlled by the Church. Later changes saw the expansion of academic disciplines beyond the *trivium* and *quadrivium*, the beginnings of state-sponsored lower and higher education, the creation and ascendance of the Doctor of Philosophy degree for professional scholars, the secularization of the academy and, most recently, the politicization and commercialization of the American university (Bok, 2003). Each of these has exerted a powerful influence on the nature and character of higher education in the early twenty-first century, yet there are other revolutions that have the potential to entirely remake and redefine higher education in the quarter century ahead. And such remaking and redefining may not necessarily be a bad thing.

As indicated, the revolutions are multiple and intertwined but may be defined as consisting of four distinct strands. The first of those strands is the large, unprecedented influx of adult students into institutions of higher learning. Adult students represented a miniscule fraction of the total enrollment in the 1980s but Richardson and King (1998) suggested that the adult learner population has soared with a 144% increase over the past 33 years, whereas the number of students younger than 25 years has reflected only a 45% increase (Anderson, 2003). The National Center for Education Statistics (NCES) reports that 39% of all postsecondary students were 25 years or older in 1999, compared with 28% in 1970. Moreover, the 1999–2000 statistics report that there was an additional increase of nontraditional students with women comprising more than half of the collegiate population (NCES, 2002). Indeed, it is appropriate to argue that while higher education programs for adult students may be yet "non-traditional," they are certainly "mainstream."

The second strand concerns the deliveries developed to provide access to these students. Even those institutions of higher learning that had adopted a congenial approach to the adult student (through re-entry programs, for example) had not necessarily made their educational offerings more accessible to those with career and family responsibilities (Fungaroli, 2000). Previous to the 1980s, "adult education" consisted largely of non-credit or non-degreed courses in job training or skills development for employment or in recreational learning (e.g. arts for the senior citizen or homemaker). In the 1980s one began to see a proliferation of for-credit programs offered through evening and weekend classes, primarily through "continuing education" or "extension" units within the colleges and universities. Finally, in the early 1990s one began to see the growth of "accelerated programs" for working adults. These programs are based on two controversial premises: that "seat time" is not, by itself, a sufficient measure of the quality of learning that takes place, and that students are more likely to succeed if the learning takes place within a consistent and supportive social network known as a "cohort." Many of these programs were and are labeled "degree completion programs" and were designed for adult students who had previously earned an associate's degree or its equivalent and need to complete their baccalaureate. A typical format consisted of creating a cohort of 10-14 students who would together take a series of five-week courses in sequence, meeting one night a week for four hours.

The third revolutionary strand involves the changes in teaching roles and instructional design as a result of these new deliveries. The new adult education programs in the 1990s

---

unprecedented methods which the influx of adult students onto college campuses demands" (Naugle, 1995, 24ff).

relied increasingly on non-professionals to teach their courses. These non-professionals were practitioners—individuals who had usually earned at least a master's degree (sometimes a doctorate) within their discipline but who preferred full-time practice in the workplace over full-time teaching or scholarship (Wachs, 1993). The utilization of practitioners as the primary instructors in these programs permitted the professional studies programs (which represented the majority of the market) to provided "just-in-time" learning. The immediacy of such learning was attractive to adult students. Further, it permitted these programs to operate with a fairly high profit margin.

The fourth and most controversial revolution was the proliferation of online programs. On the one hand, online learning is merely the latest form of "distance education," which has been in existence in various forms for quite some time. On the other hand, online learning challenges some basic assumptions of the instructional task and the learning process, assumptions that have undergirded the academy for quite some time. Therefore, while for some online learning is yet another "delivery method," for others it is a threat to traditional understandings of the primacy of the instructor in the learning process and the means by which the transmission of knowledge occurs.

All four strands have created tensions, all have been controversial, and all are still new enough to be regarded by many as unwelcome intrusions into a somewhat calcified academic culture in the West.

Faith-based institutions have responded to these revolutions in adult education more quickly than many others (Wlodkowski, 2003). This is doubtless due to both practical and ideological motives. Practically speaking, faith-based universities do not usually have either the endowment funds or public investments that other, more secular institutions enjoy, and adult professional programs have proven themselves effective profit centers for such financially strapped institutions. In an ideological sense, institutions that perceive their objectives within a comprehensive mission to redeem humanity are perhaps more likely than others to seek a broader audience for their educational services.

Of note, however, is that adult students, whether attending secular or faith-based institutions, have reported significant amount of pressures or stressors while attempting to complete a degree (O'Connor and Bevil, 1996; Sutherland, 1999). According to Kobasa (1979), "A life event is defined as stressful if it courses changes in, and demands readjustment of, an average person's normal routine" (p. 2). O'Connor asserts, "Stress has been identified as an important psychosocial factor in the educational process because it may influence both academic performance and student well-being" (p. 246). It can be argued that the addition of college or university studies to the multiple daily activities of an adult can be construed as overwhelming as the individual struggles to balance competing roles. Therefore, the combination of academic pressures and existing adult stressors may intensify and can impact academic performance and the student's ability to persist until graduation. By determining the adult student's professed items of academic importance and the concomitant levels of satisfaction derived from the institution's attempt to create an "adult-friendly" environment, faculty, staff, and administrators may acquire valuable information that can be used to provide programs and services desired by this population. Moreover, the recognition and creation of services as deemed important by the adult student may serve to minimize the stress inherent in the role of a student. Therefore, analyzing the target university's attempt to provide services to ultimately minimize these stressors are the focus of this research.

NEED FOR THE STUDY

Sissel, Hansman, and Kasworm (2001) put forth that adult students, while emerging as the new majority in higher education, may unfortunately be viewed by faculty, staff, and administrators as less important than the traditional student. There is insufficient research to identify the unique stressors of adult students; therefore, attempts to define modalities to support them through the educational process, may be insufficient (Brown and Eggert Linnemann, 1995; Hadfield, 2003; Simonite, 1997; Viechnicki, Bohlin, Milheim, 1990). Without knowledge of how to support this vital population, officials appear to make educated assumptions on what the students' needs might be; hence, conclusions may be made about creating learning environments that presume an enhanced academic experience. There is need, therefore, for additional studies of accelerated learning environments to determine the degree to which they address the unique stressors of their students.

STATEMENT OF THE PROBLEM

The hypothesis of this study is that the learning environment created for adult students in two accelerated undergraduate programs (one in Nursing, the other in Business) in an institution with significant experience in adult education adequately addresses the unique stressors of the students enrolled therein. It is assumed that this success in responding to stressors is due primarily to two factors: 1) the intentionality of design of the programs (derived from the institution's experience), and 2) the institution's faith commitment (which compels a holistic understanding of the student). This hypothesis is tested through the administration of a nationally-normed survey instrument among these two student populations and the interpretation of the data thus gathered.

DEFINITION OF TERMS

Accelerated RN to BSN Program: The Baccalaureate of Science in Nursing (BSN) is offered to Registered Nurses (RNs) in 16 to 24 months, a shorter time period than that of traditional programs. The students are more independent in achieving their goals. The courses are offered sequentially during the same time and day each week until the student has met program requirements.

Adult Learner: A college student over the age of twenty-five years and distinguished by the NCES (2002) criteria. Defined by the NCES, the "nontraditional" student will have one or all of the following characteristics: delays college enrollment after high school, attends postsecondary education part-time for at least part of the academic year, works full time, is considered financially independent, has dependents other than spouse, is a single parent, and/or does not have a high school diploma.

Faith-Based Institution: An educational institution with an explicit faith commitment that is apparent in both the content and the context of the learning environment.

Management Programs: A broad-based business program designed for students in the for-profit, not-for-profit, and public sectors. In this essay, undergraduate programs leading to a Bachelor of Arts (BA) in Organizational Management or Bachelor of Arts (BA) in Management of Information Systems and graduate Master of Business Administration (MBA) tracks in Management and Health Administration were employed as case studies.

Professional Studies: In general terms, any academic program designed to prepare students for the professions; in specific terms, any academic program designed to provide academic qualifications for existing professionals.

Registered Nurse: A member of the health care profession who has successfully completed the requirements and passed the National Council Licensure Examination for Registered Nurses (NCLEX-RN).

Stress: any noxious stimulus that affects the sympathetic nervous system.

REVIEW OF LITERATURE

The Unique Status of Adult Students in Higher Education

The NCES (2002) reports that an increase in adult students may be due to the influence of the changing employment requirements, which seem to be demanding new skills and knowledge. Interestingly, an adult student is considered "nontraditional" by institutions and faculty in higher education. However, Richardson and King (1998) purport that the "nontraditional" students or adult learners should not be treated as a homogenous group since they are more diverse than the traditional students. Thus, while this essay identifies certain unique stressors of adult students, it is important to note here that such identifications are not intended to be universal; they serve merely as generalizations to assist in the distinction between traditional and nontraditional learning environments.

In addition, Hadfield asserts that it is essential to have an appreciation for adult learners as customers of higher education as they return to college in preparation to meet new employment demands. And as the numbers of adult students proliferate, institutions are beginning to count on the revenue generated by this population (Hadfield, 2003). Presumably, administrators depend on the matriculation of "nontraditional" learners to help balance the budget and perhaps create some additional revenue for the institution to fund other programs. Furthermore, Hadfield contends that since most services in higher education focus on the traditional student, a change in culture and concomitant services would potentially benefit all students. Therefore, the goal ought to be to develop a comprehensive program to evaluate the areas of importance to adult students as they choose a higher education setting (Boylston, Peters, and Lacey, 2004).

As the adult student population rises, issues have emerged that pertain to how to recruit, educate, and retain this "nontraditional" group (Beeman, 1988; Boylston, Peters, and Lacey, 2004; Brown and Eggert Linnemann, 1995). Services in postsecondary institutions, grounded in a traditional student paradigm, often set hours in business offices, financial aid offices, bookstores, and offices of registrars that are convenient for traditional students, but completely inaccessible for the adult who has personal and professional commitments during the day (Hadfield, 2003). This pattern is shortsighted, for as Hadfield states, "Except for the quality of our academic offering, excellence in customer service is the single most important factor in determining the future of our programs for adult learners, now and for the foreseeable future" (p. 19). The lack of services may create unneeded stress for the adult learner and ultimately cause the student to drop out of the university. Furthermore, Hadfield suggests looking at the business model of customer service to attract and retain this population. Presumably, this model would include a service guarantee, formal promises made to the consumer about the services received, and the assurance of a quality educational experience (McCollough and Gremler, 1999). In addition, consistent inquiries regarding their needs and desired services can promote open communication between students and campus officials. In return, administrators can offer services that the adult student desires, thereby increasing the students' satisfaction with the educational process.

Presumably, this satisfaction data can be gleaned by periodically administering satisfaction surveys. These assessments will prospectively invite students to rate their experiences and determine whether the institution has provided the educational services needed to achieve personal and professional goals. Furthermore, students can be queried regarding their satisfaction of instructional effectiveness, registration, financial aid processes, campus climate, security, and safety. Equipped with data from a survey, administrators can strive to make changes in existing programs to enhance service and address needs of this growing population of students. El Ansari (2002) reports that student satisfaction can be an important quality indicator, with respect to teaching and learning. However, it seems that the majority of satisfaction surveys are completed at the end of the students' academic experience in the form of exit interviews. The question is then posed to the student as "Were you satisfied with your college experience?" (Elliott and Shin, 2002). This data offers a retrospective depiction of the students' experiences, thereby negating opportunities that the institution would have to create a more conducive adult-oriented environment for the responding student.

Historically, colleges and universities have provided services for the traditional student who matriculates immediately after high school (Bowl, 2001). However, with the metamorphosis of collegiate demographics there apparently has not been a concomitant change in the services that institutions of higher education offer to adult learners (Sissel, Hansman, and Kasworm, 2001). Without the benefit of accessible campus services, the "nontraditional" student may find it too difficult to achieve personal and academic goals (Zuzelo, 2001). This can ultimately affect retention (Fralick, 1993).

Characteristics of Adult Learners

Arguably, the profile of adult learners is multifaceted. Incorporating adult education theories is only one way that colleges and universities may employ to provide a holistic and meaningful educational experience. Moreover, institutions and faculty are encouraged to know the demographic data and personal distinctiveness of students who now compose the majority in their classes. The NCES (2002) characterizes 73% of undergraduates as "nontraditional" (aged 25 years or greater with part-time enrollment status). Additional defining characteristics of adult "nontraditional" students according to the NCES include an initial delay of enrolling in postsecondary education, full-time employment, perceived financial independence, support of dependents, single parenthood, or lack of high school diploma. Similarly, Horn, Peter, Rooney, and Malizio (2002) define the "nontraditional" student on a continuum based on the number of aforementioned characteristics that the individual possesses. Students can be minimally "nontraditional" to highly "nontraditional" if they have four or more of the aforesaid characteristics. According to government data collected for 1999 to 2000, 27% of all undergraduates were traditional, and 28% were highly "nontraditional", with 28% moderately "nontraditional" and 17% minimally "nontraditional" (NCES). According to the research of Horn et al. on persistence and attrition, the "nontraditional" students who enter postsecondary education seeking a degree are less likely than traditional students to attain a degree or remain enrolled after five years.

The NCES data assists in defining the "nontraditional" student; however, there are additional features that distinguish the adult student. Typically, the adult student is self-supporting, mature, and responsible (MacKinnon-Slaney, 1994). Adult students can lead lives filled with responsibilities, such as families, mortgages, and careers, and may be independent citizens. They may also be motivated to learn more readily from internal motivators, such as self-esteem, recognition or a better quality of life (O'Brien and Renner, 2000). Moreover, they can be task directed and pragmatic (Bohlin, 1994). Presumably, they cope sufficiently well with life's stressors, including child-rearing, elder care, working full-time and balancing career and education (Fairchild, 2003). In addition, they may feel compelled to return to school to update their skills for the job market (Kerka, 2001). Most adults enter higher education voluntarily (Vichnicki, Bohlin, and Milheim, 1990), whereas a vast number of adults have returned to school to cope with change in their personal lives, stretch their minds, and facilitate career change or advancement (Fishback and Polson, 1998). Moreover, adult students can present a challenge to faculty and administrators because of their personal, educational, and professional histories, along with their lack of familiarity with the university community and policies (Green, 1987). The aforementioned characteristics can assist in creating a depiction of the "nontraditional" as the higher education community attempts to recruit this population for a variety of academic programs.

Another feature that characterizes adult learners is that they appear to more effectively manage time. This may be a function of the myriad of roles that consume their lives and their ability to juggle these roles (Grupe and Connolly, 1995; Knowles, 1978; Richardson and King, 1998). Reportedly, adults are challenged to balance adult careers and family roles with college schedules (Fralick, 1993). O'Connor and Bevil (1996) argue that the balancing of all adult responsibilities while attending college can lead to stress and role overload. This can have a detrimental affect on this population's ability to persist until graduation or achieve their academic goals.

Another defining trait of adult students (in addition to their age and their level of responsibility) is their level of motivation, which Richardson and King (1998) counter-intuitively suggest may be more intrinsic than vocational. In all probability, the adult has a purpose for attending college. The reasons can be numerous, from seeking a new position to promotion in the place of employment to personal gratification. Therefore, they have a range of backgrounds and a variety of interests (Grupe and Connolly, 1995). The NCES (2002) reports that no matter how "nontraditional" the respondents were, 73% reported that personal enrichment or interest in the subject, gaining skills to advance in their jobs or career, and completing a degree or certificate were important considerations in returning to postsecondary education.

According to Fralick (1993), "programs need to be developed to increase retention. Adults will drop out if they are unsuccessful academically or unable to balance school, career, home and family" (p. 36). In response, academic programs may create course schedules conducive to adult time pressures and many provide adequate student services, as well as other programs for this population to achieve their goals. In addition, Bowl (2001) alleges that institutional and financial barriers can generate numerous stressors. With the barriers torn down by the institutions, the adult learner can focus on achieving academic goals.

Richardson and King (1998) argue that adult learners have been consistently stigmatized in terms of the ability to benefit from higher education, with faculty and administration sharing in the creation and dissemination of negative stereotypes. In addition, they have "prior life experience, which promotes a deep approach to studying in higher education" (Richardson and King, p 73). Because of this, faculty ought to address the practical and unique needs of adults. Due to the "nontraditional" heterogeneity, an attempt to meet the needs of this population can appear to be a daunting task for faculty and administration. Fishback and Polson (1998) determined that the educational process for adults can be full of emotion and the learning ought to take place in a supportive, interactive environment. Creating a milieu that addresses the uniqueness of this population may become a top priority of higher education personnel in order to recruit, retain and graduate the adult learner and minimize the stress one may face as a student.

Unique Stressors of Adult Learners

The particular stressors presented by the adult learner may pose a challenge for counselors, faculty, and advisors. According to Reed and Beaudin (1993), "Institutions of higher education need to welcome adult learners and provide processes, systems and learning environments to meet adult needs in order to survive economically in the upcoming decades" (p. 2). MacKinnon-Slaney (1994) adds that adults have concerns at home that affect their academic performance. Conversely, a disappointing grade may affect relationships at home. This may distract the student from achieving academic and personal goals. "Services for traditional college students cannot meet the needs of adult learners" (MacKinnon-Slaney, p. 269). Therefore, counseling departments can include a series of services that focus on the issues that the adult may face in order to encourage retention among this population.

An area of uniqueness explored by researchers is the fact that adults expect to immediately apply newly learned knowledge (Knowles, 1978; MacKinnon-Slaney, 1994). Theoretically, adult learners want new knowledge to be applicable and appropriate for life and work experiences. Adults want to build upon the current skills, usually focusing upon a problem or current need that must be addressed (Grupe and Connolly, 1995; Knowles, 1978). Thus, case study learning is particularly effective.

An important facet for educators to contemplate is the notion that adult learners may bring considerable knowledge to the learning process. This can potentially enhance any classroom setting (Grupe and Connolly, 1995). Hypothetically, adults can be active learners (Bohlin, Milheim, and Viechnicki, 1994). Experts concur that adults seek independence and self-direction while learning and implementing new concepts (Grupe and Connolly). This can lead to dynamic classroom discussions regarding the application of new concepts. Presumably, this can affect the quality of the class and educational experience for all beneficiaries and serves to motivate the student to stay in the program until graduation.

Creating a learning community that is open to the needs of the "nontraditional" student may assist the population in achieving its academic goals. A program that is designed to be supportive, that fits into the busy adult lifestyle, and that has a predictable structure may serve to attract and retain the "nontraditional" student (Kasworm, 2003). This can promote the student's overall success in higher education.

The stressors that the adult student may face can precipitate a physiological reaction (Selye, 1976). Hans Selye described a "fight-or-flight" response. He conceptualized three phases of his general adaptation syndrome theory. The first phase is the alarm phase, characterized by the individual's perception of a stressor. The body prepares itself for a physiological response. The second phase is the resistance stage, in which the organism or body fights the stressor. The third phase, called the exhaustion phase, occurs when the body is no longer able to fight the stressor. It is here when the individual may become ill or even death can occur.

O'Connor and Bevil (1996) researched academic outcomes and stress in full-time day and part-time evening baccalaureate nursing students. The researchers suggested the evening students' anxiety increased by mid-semester. Additionally, the participants were able to achieve academic outcomes despite the anxiety and stress. Similarly, Lee (1988) studied RNs who returned to higher education for a BSN. The research disclosed that the stress of returning to school was a deterrent to the student's success in school.

Success and Failure in Higher Education

The success and failure of adult learners in higher education can depend upon a multitude of factors. According to MacKinnon–Slaney (1994), adults must have a "robust sense of self" (p.72) in order to succeed in college. Presumably, individuals who lack a positive sense of academic self-concept may not continue their education. This is especially prevalent among women and adult learners of color (MacKinnon-Slaney, 1994). Advising implications may include support and counseling to assist the student in overcoming the multitude of hurdles and stresses that they encounter on a daily basis.

Another concern for adults is the clarification of goals, expectations, success and the meaning of education. Adult learners must commit to goals and believe that education is a pathway toward the achievement of these goals (MacKinnon-Slaney, 1994). Interestingly, success for the adult learner can be defined as "the student's subjective judgment about college achievement rather than more traditional, institutionally defined measures of college success" (Fralick, 1993, p. 30). Fralick researched college retention and found that the more academically successful students are more likely to return to complete a degree program. Consequently, the author suggests periodic satisfaction surveys be distributed to this population at regular intervals. This will help to identify the "at risk" dropout students.

Due to the complexity of adult life, there can be a number of additional factors that can lead the adult to leave postsecondary education without completing the degree program. Fairchild (2003) states, "The basic needs of the family, like food and rent or mortgage, take priority over educational outlays" (p. 12). Threats to the new role can be caused by multiple personal demands and institutional barriers. In order to combat the attrition of the adult learner or "nontraditional" student, institutions of higher education can seek to provide services that will eliminate stressors and build connections among the student, faculty, and program. This can be done with careful thought and consideration and by treating the adult learner as a unique student. Bowl (2001) admonishes, "Financial, institutional, and class-based barriers impede the progress of non-traditional students" (p. 157). These barriers seem to emerge early as the student attempts to move forward despite a commitment to education as a way to a better life. Students may be highly motivated but may remain frustrated participants unable to gain access to support and constructive advice (Bowl, 2001).

Responsiveness to the Adult Market in Higher Education

According to Havarnek and Browdin (1998), a new focus is needed to produce higher education institutions that are more responsive to students' needs by providing access to quality support services. Additionally, "colleges and universities are extraordinarily slow to change in the face of new realities that make change necessary for their continued survival" (Havernick and Browdin, 1998, p. 116). Bohlin, et al. (1994) concur: "In order to effectively teach learners with a different set of needs, motives, and backgrounds, we need a new set of techniques and instructional strategies" (p. 4). By asking the students what they value in an educational experience through qualitative and quantitative measures, a pool of data can be developed that may provide answers and solutions and direct administrators toward innovation. Interestingly, Bowl (2001) purports that institutions tend to "problematize" the nontraditional student rather than seek ways to promote success among this population.

For the adult learner, the role of student is one of multiple responsibilities and commitments that compete for their time (Kerka, 1995). Stressors such as child care, family problems, and job demands can cause withdrawal from higher education. Furthermore, Kerka asserts that the institution cannot control personal problems, but the university and faculty can influence student's satisfaction with the program through personal attention to the needs of the student. Attention to the "nontraditional" student and the creation of flexible, user-friendly models of education can serve to attract and retain the role overloaded adult (Ayer and Smith, 1998).

METHODOLOGY

To determine the effect of the campus services and their effect on minimizing academic stressors, the researchers employed the following research methodologies. A nationally-normed survey instrument was employed to compare results between two different academic departments (Nursing and Management Studies) within the same institution of higher learning. They are presented here in tandem as Survey A (Nursing) and Survey B (Management).

For each survey, the authors gained university permission to conduct the study, and the informed consent of the student after describing the research. All subjects were anonymous and data were coded to maintain confidentiality. Respondents to Survey A were invited to participate in an additional interview process, consent for which was indicated by signing one's name and providing an email address at the bottom of the consent form to be contacted at a later date. The researcher and participant discussed a mutually agreed upon time to meet. The researcher selected students for interviews until the discussions yielded a saturation of themes. An audiotape was used to capture the participant's mood or strength of feelings on raised issues. Respondents to Survey B also responded to unique questions regarding stressors in their own academic experience.

SUBJECTS

The sources of data for Survey A (Nursing) were volunteer students who were enrolled in an accelerated RN to BSN program in a relatively small faith-based institution of higher learning. All of the matriculated students in the program were recruited for the study. There was a 100 percent return for a total of 53 students. Ten of the respondents were interviewed in person.

The accelerated nursing program has been in existence for six years with steady enrollments. The university offers a twenty-month, 48-credit baccalaureate in nursing science (BSN). In accordance with the university's mission, a Bible course is mandated for graduation. Students take this course at the end of the program.

The average age of a practicing nurse is 45.2 years (AACN, 2003) as compared to the age of the studied population at the university, which is 35 years or older. The majority of the sampled BSN population was female (94.34%). The ethnicity/race of the students was Caucasian/White (58.49%), African American/Black (13.21%), and Asian (18.87%). All students were attending classes full-time with the majority (67.92%) also employed full-time.

The sources of data for the Management survey were volunteer students who were enrolled in an accelerated management program in the same faith-based institution. A total of 407 students participated in the survey; 76% of respondents completed the survey in-class and 23% online. Fifty-nine percent of respondents were female and 41% male. Sixty-two percent were between the ages of 25 and 44. The ethnicity of respondents was as follows: African American (32.90%), Asian (2.33%), Caucasian (52.85%), Hispanic (2.59%), and "Other" (3.89%).

The sources of data for Survey B (Management) were students enrolled in accelerated undergraduate and graduate programs in the Management or Business disciplines. These programs were the first offered of their delivery by any institution of higher education in the market area. Begun in 1989, they had graduated over 450 cohorts of adult students by early 2005. The average age of the students is 33 years (slightly higher for undergraduate students). The programs enjoy a wider ethnic/racial diversity in their student demographics than does the university as a whole. Nearly 95% of the students are employed full-time while maintaining a full-time, accelerated academic load.

Options for Management education include an undergraduate Organizational Management major (offered in an accelerated degree completion program format), an undergraduate Management of Information Systems major (delivered in the same format as the Organizational Management program and designed for a niche market), two tracks (Management and Health Administration) in an accelerated ("Fast-Track"®) Master's of Business Administration, and a Master of Science in NonProfit Management (delivered via a distance education/residency model). Instruction is offered in over twenty sites throughout the market area, including campuses of corporate partners. Respondents to the survey were from all five Management programs.

SURVEY INSTRUMENT

To obtain an in-depth depiction of "nontraditional" student satisfaction in the selected accelerated programs, the researcher analyzed survey responses and employed qualitative interview techniques to triangulate the data. The proposed research design called for a tool that could measure adult learners' expectations within an academic program along with the concomitant level of satisfaction with existing university services, curriculum, and personnel. To accomplish this, the Noel Levitz Adult Student Priorities Survey[TM] (ASPS), a three-part instrument, was used to gather data on student satisfaction.

The ASPS consisted of 50 items that cover a full range of college experiences as well as demographic characteristics of the respondents. Students were asked to rate each Likert-like statement on a seven-point scale ranging from one (1), not very important at all or not satisfied at all, to seven (7), very important or very satisfied. The ASPS is designed to measure students' perceptions along eight dimensions, which include academic advising effectiveness, instructional effectiveness, service excellence, registration effectiveness, campus climate, service excellence, admissions and financial aid services, and safety and security. Three summary questions were identified: levels of satisfaction with overall educational experience, levels of expectations met by the institution, and whether the respondent would enroll again in the selected baccalaureate program.

Noel-Levitz[TM] (2003) reports that the ASPS's reliability is high. For example, "Cronbach's coefficient for the importance scores was .93 and .90 on items of satisfaction, and the test-retest reliability estimate was .82 and .81 for the mean satisfaction scores" (p. 3). In addition, the validity was assessed both quantitatively and qualitatively. The quantitative assessment was .74 for importance and .67 for satisfaction ($p<.0001$). Qualitatively, the instrument validity was conducted by correlating respondents' scores on the ASPS with their interview responses on a qualitative protocol reflecting the content of the instrument. All scale correlations were significant ($p = .05$) (Noel-Levitz[TM]), thereby indicating that the instrument reflects the construct that it was designed to measure.

To triangulate the findings, an interview portion of the Nursing student survey was employed with the additional use of four prepared questions. The posed questions were as follows:

- What made you choose this program to complete your BSN?
- What services do you seek in an academic program?
- What would cause you to withdraw from this program?
- What services do you need the university to provide to keep you in the program?

The Management student survey contained two unique questions:

- Being a student was a stressful experience for me.
- My stress was lowered as a result of the support I got from my instructors, other staff members, and fellow students.

RESULTS

The findings of the Nursing Program study (Survey A) were delineated by using the Noel-Levitz Adult Student Priorities Survey[TM] (ASPS) and personal interviews that identified the levels of importance that accelerated RN to BSN students place on aspects of their student experience. The experiences were included in the analysis of eight inventory composite scales from the ASPS, which were identified as academic advising effectiveness, academic services, admissions and financial aid effectiveness, campus climate, instructional effectiveness, registration effectiveness, safety and security, and service excellence. Data results represent areas of importance and potential levels of satisfaction among the sampled population.

Figure 1 depicts a graphic representation of the RN to BSN students' responses to the ASPS questions. Instructional effectiveness and advising effectiveness were the highest areas of importance.

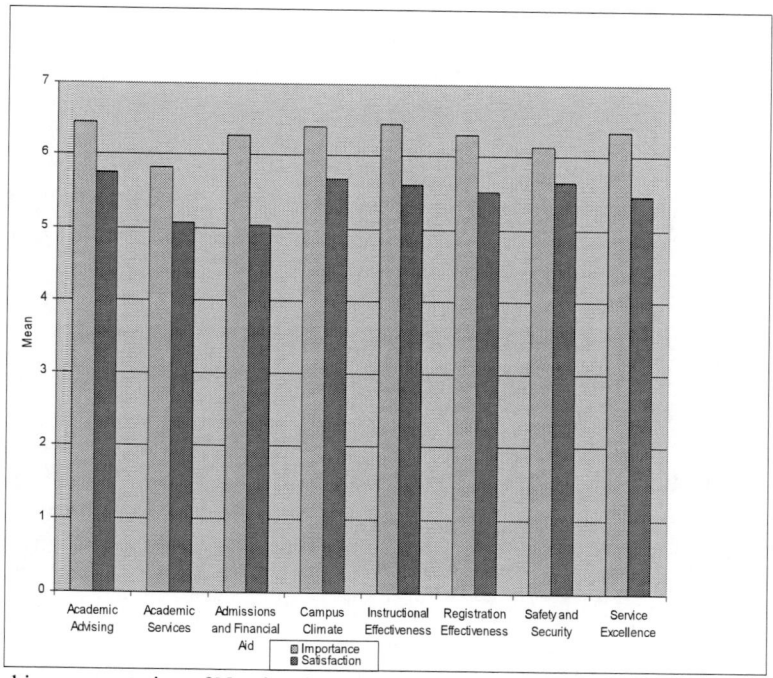

Figure 1. Graphic representation of Nursing department's composite scales.

Table 1 demonstrates a statistical summary of the participants' responses in relationship to the composite scales. Academic services were rated at the bottom of the eight scales with a higher performance gap (0.75) indicating a satisfaction with services despite the lower rating in importance (5 81).

Table 1. Nursing Survey: Institutional Means of Composite Scales

Scale	Importance	Satisfaction	Gap
Instructional Effectiveness	6.44	5.60	0.84
Academic Advising	6.43	5.74	0.69
Campus Climate	6.40	5.74	0.73
Service Excellence	6.34	5.45	0.89
Registration Effectiveness	6.29	5.51	0.78
Admissions and Financial Aid	6.26	5.51	1.22
Safety and Security	6.14	5.65	0.49
Academic Services	5.81	5.06	0.75

Specific items pertaining to university services were extrapolated from the data. Of the top ten items of importance rated by the students, five of ten focused on the relationship between the professor, advising process, and quality of the educational experience. The other more notable items of importance determined by the sampled population were as follows: (a) classroom locations are safe and secure for all students; (b) classes are scheduled at times that are convenient for me; (c) tuition paid is a worthwhile investment; and (d) I am able to complete most of my enrollment tasks in one location.

The interviews gleaned additional data for analysis. When questioned about the reasons for choosing the program, all respondents stated the convenience of the classes as important. The dominance of the convenience theme as articulated by all subjects was evident with comments such as "I like the convenience of staying in my own area." Other statements verified the need to be in close proximity to home or work. "I have a large family, a lot of responsibilities, and so forth, so it was the flexibility that was the major aspect and my primary goal" was voiced by another student.

Thirty percent mentioned the number of transfer credits accepted by the institution was instrumental in selecting the program. The more credits accepted, the fewer courses the student would have to take to complete the degree and the less time spent in class. One student purported, "I came to an open house and they would accept my high school chemistry; that was important to me."

In addition, twenty percent noted the Christian worldview and the supportive cohort model as instrumental in enrolling and staying at the university. "I like the cohort setting of going in with the same women through the whole program." Another student suggested, "I like being in a group….we really support one another."

The second question posed to the students, "What services do you seek in an academic program?" yielded additional information. Fifty percent mentioned the advising and support offered by faculty as important variables needed by the students to minimize the pressures of attending the university. According to one student, "It's hard to feel that you are out there on your own. This program does not have that…you have support." Another student volunteered, "The services that I seek in an academic program are that you have one person and have them help you or facilitate contact with other people. It's frustrating when you go to one person then you are sent to another, and then you are sent to another. I don't have time for that. Give me the person to contact and she can help with the problem."

Another theme that emerged from the data was the need for financial aid. Students clearly stated the expense of the program and their unwillingness to incur additional debt that could compromise their family financial solvency were indicators of their need for some type of financial assistance that could help them with the stresses of tuition and book fees. One student verbalized, "The family comes first."

The third question, "What would cause you to withdraw from the program?" generated two themes. Theme number one was a family crisis. According to one student, "It would take a family problem....this has been hard on my family." Theme number two emerging from the data was a "major life crisis." "It would take something cataclysmic for me to leave the program" was verbalized by a student. "Family stressors...just not having the time that you want to have spend doing the work and just being okay with that but where's the point where okay I'm not spending enough time doing school work. It's hard to balance family and family comes first" was stated by another student. "To withdraw I would have to feel totally overwhelmed with what is going on in my life, it is difficult going to school full time and working fulltime

Question number four, "What services do you need the university to provide to keep you in the program?" revealed a need for a financial aid infrastructure to complete the program. Several students commented, "I need financial aid to stay in school." Otherwise, students described the current university services were adequate to address the stressors in their situations. One student reported, "The ongoing support is already there."

Figure 2 depicts a graphic representation of the Management students' responses to the ASPS questions. As with the Nursing survey, instructional effectiveness and advising effectiveness were rated the highest areas of importance.

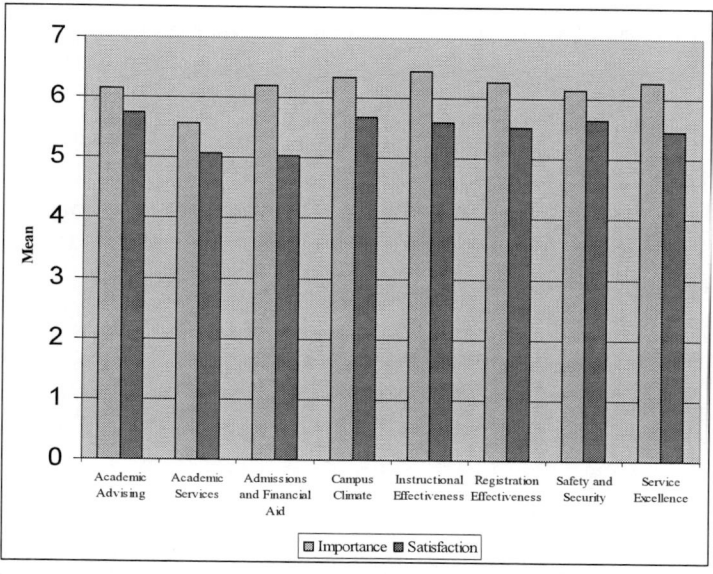

Figure 2. Graphic representation of Management programs' composite scales.

As for the Management survey, it generated no scale in which the performance gap exceeded 1.00, indicating a rather positive evaluation of program's effectiveness. Indeed, the scores for the eight scaled items exceeded national norms for the Noel-Levitz survey in every category except academic services, which is not surprising. One of the features of many adult education programs (and of the Management programs of the studied institution) is that classes are held at off-campus sites. Of the two dozen or so classroom sites utilized by these Management programs, only six are staffed. The inevitable result is occasional frustration at not being able to resolve issues with a live person at the moment those issues arise. It is important to note that the students do regard this as a stressor in their academic experience, however, and to work creatively to find ways to address it.

Table 2 demonstrates a statistical summary of the participants' responses in relationship to the composite scales. As with the Nursing survey, academic services were rated at the bottom of the eight scales in terms of both importance and performance. The performance gap of 0.99 was the highest in this survey.

Table 2. Management Survey: Institutional Means of Composite Scales

Scale	Importance	Satisfaction	Gap
Instructional Effectiveness	6.45	5.74	0.71
Academic Advising	6.15	5.36	0.79
Campus Climate	6.34	5.74	0.60
Service Excellence	6.27	5.45	0.82
Registration Effectiveness	6.28	5.71	0.57
Admissions and Financial Aid	6.19	5.35	0.84
Safety and Security	6.15	5.36	0.79
Academic Services	5.86	4.87	0.99

The two unique questions addressed how the institution explicitly addressed the issue of stress in the life of the students. Students agreed strongly that "being a student is a stressful experience for me" but also agreed that their stress was lowered as a result of the support received from instructors, other staff members, and fellow students. It appears that the structures created by the studied institution have been effective to some degree in minimizing the unique stressors of the adult student.

It is interesting and instructive that the responses to the two surveys were quite similar; this indicates a consistency from one program to another throughout the institution in addressing the learning environment of adult students. The stressors are not discipline-specific and neither are their remedies.

DISCUSSION

While research has already established that student satisfaction improves retention (Brown and Eggert Linnemann, 1995), it also contributes to academic, personal, and professional achievement (Bean and Bradley, 1986). In addition, by monitoring items of importance to students, the institution can scrutinize areas of weakness and strength, and seek to fortify areas of satisfaction. "By collecting information from students that asks not only how satisfied they are with aspects of the campus but also how important these aspects are, a college can prioritize its interventions" (Juillerat and Schreiner, 1999, p. 4). The findings of the both studies suggest the subjects identified several items of importance related to teaching and academic services needed to stay in college in an attempt to complete a degree. From the ASPS data, students identified advising and instructional excellence as the most valued items of importance in both departments. The program advisors are typically full-time faculty or staff members who advise the entire cohort. In other words, the individual faculty member is known by all of the students in one cohort as the primary advisor who begins the relationship in orientation and ends it at graduation. Part of the workload of faculty members is to advise students. One student stated, "I can contact my advisor at any time."

Due to the nature of accelerated education, the need for quality faculty has been identified by the students as high in importance with a concomitant level of high satisfaction. Students articulated that they want knowledgeable and available instructors who are master teachers and will not repeat content and concepts. Students desire faculty who can assist them in applying newly learned knowledge (Knowles, 1978). According to one student, "Professors need to recognize that we are adult learners and that we bring experience to the program. We want this to be an additional growth experience and not repeat everything that we have already learned."

Interestingly, participants rated service excellence high in importance and relatively high in satisfaction. This scale assessed the university staffs' attitude toward students as a positive one. Staff friendliness and ability to be responsive to students' inquiries resulted in positive responses by the subjects.

Presumably, the nature of higher education can be service oriented. Students need to navigate through a complicated system to enroll, register, purchase textbooks, attend classes, and communicate with financial aid and registrar's offices. As adult learners, the majority of the sampled population are employed and have spouses and children, which adds layers of complexities and responsibilities. These multiple roles may threaten their academic success (Fairchild, 2003). The research suggests that having positive contact with staff correlates with increased satisfaction with the campus, climate, and personnel, and university. "From the perspective of adult students, access to higher education institutions sensitive to their developmental, academic, and logistical needs will maximize the outcomes from their educational investments" (Brown and Eggert Linnemann, 1995, p. 11). In addition, it is suggested that student satisfaction has a positive impact on student motivation, recruiting efforts, and fundraising (Elliott and Shin, 2002).

Registration effectiveness, an integral component of the higher education process, was rated lower in importance and higher in satisfaction. Billing and registration processes comprise this scale. At the studied institution, the students register once at the beginning of the program and there is no need for additional paperwork. Interestingly, students reported convenience as the dominant feature for enrolling in the program. With the streamlining of the registration process, the convenience of completing university formalities within the classroom generated overall satisfaction with this process.

For the Nursing population, seven of the eight composite scales had performance gap scores of less than one (1.0) and for the Management population, all eight of the composite scores had performance gap scores of less than one (1.0), indicating an overall satisfaction with the student experience and services offered by the university. Of interest, only admissions and financial aid were reflected a gap score of greater than 1.0 (1.22), indicating dissatisfaction among Nursing students with these services. The items of dissatisfaction, focused on the variety of payment plans for adult students, adequate financial aid, and admissions representatives responding to the students' needs. Further, these findings were validated by the interview responses. When questioned what services students needed in order to stay enrolled at the university, the most frequent response was the need for financial aid.

With private school tuition, textbook and fees, the amount of money spent on tuition was an expressed concern for participants. Subjects' reactions corroborate the findings of Wlodkowski (2003), who suggests that the use of financial aid strengthens adult student persistence. "Adults who received financial aid were three times more likely to persist, than adults who receive no financial aid" (p. 11).

In contrast, safety and security were rated low in importance yet high in satisfaction (particularly among Nursing students, who are more likely to take classes at the main campus). The scale measured the effectiveness of security personnel and campus facilities. Presumably, the safe location of classrooms with close parking while not considered essential was well received by participants. With panic boxes for emergency use located in strategic positions in each of the parking lots, low crime statistics were reported in the surrounded vicinities. In other words, students feel safe at this institution.

Interestingly, the lowest rated (in terms of importance) of eight composite scales was academic services. The services had a concomitant high satisfaction rating and a fairly narrow performance gap, which suggested that students were satisfied with quality service and personal concern, demonstrated by faculty, staff, and administration. This was also reflected in the highly rated advising effectiveness. From data gleaned from interviews, students verbalized that the faculty and staff at this institution consider students with a customer focus since the faculty work diligently to return phone calls and e-mails within a short time frame. In addition, support personnel have been reported as accessible and responsive to student questions and concerns. According to one participant, "I think the staff are easily available and are more than willing to be helpful."

Moreover, at the participants' university, academic services available for traditional and nontraditional students and even maintain extended hours to accommodate their needs. However, given the nature of the modern university, which fosters computerized literature searches and the use of a personal laptop computer, the need to come to campus on a regular basis except for class has been minimized. One student's comment, "I have never been to the library" may reflect the nature of the university's computerized informational resources. In addition, since the university subscribes to an interlibrary loan service, which is a computerized retrieval system, students can send a request to the librarian and have articles, research studies, dissertations, or books sent to their homes. Presumably, this ease of facilitation via the Internet and campus Intranet had a positive impact on satisfaction with the university, program, and services, as reflected by data from interviews. Upon reflecting on this university's services, one participant responded, "The ongoing support is already there."

The service departments within the university have been designated as responsive and proactive. Because all books and syllabi are delivered to the students' classrooms, one week before the beginning of the next class, the student does not need to use the bookstore to purchase textbooks. With service focus on students, support staff attempt to create an environment of assistance that leads to effectively educating the student. An interviewed student commented, "I don't need the services that I needed when I was younger." Further, another interviewee suggested, "It's nice to have everything delivered to you. You do not have to run to the bookstore." Another student concurred, "It's hard to feel that you are out there on your own. This program does not have that...you have support." Lastly, a student verbalized, "I like the support."

Of the ten top rated items, delineated from eight composite scales, six implicated the value of qualified faculty. These items included the following: (a) "nearly all faculty are knowledgeable in their field;" (b) "the quality of instruction that I receive in my program is excellent;" (c) "faculty are fair and unbiased in their treatment of students;" (d) "faculty provide timely feedback about my progress;" (e) "my academic advisor is knowledgeable about requirements in my major;" and (f) "my academic advisor is accessible by telephone and email." The scores reinforced the importance of faculty knowledge, approachability, advising, and treatment of students as adult learners. Furthermore, data indicated that quality of instruction was rated as highly important and with correlated satisfaction. Since the goal of the academic process is to educate students with a quality, flexible, and effective program, students' satisfaction rating was one of high significance for the administration and university. The high ratings also provided positive feedback to the faculty, whose attention to detail was appreciated by the students. Interviewees corroborated survey results; that is, students appreciate the quality of instruction and responsive nature of the faculty to questions and concerns. One student said, "I feel that the faculty have done real well." Another student concurred, "The instructors are supportive." Lastly, one student responded, "I enrolled because I wanted a program to be all inclusive in terms of providing the best nursing related education that it can; provide a well-rounded school; and a school that has a high academic standard."

As demonstrated in the academic advising composite scale, two items involved the quality of the advising process and faculty student interactions. The importance and continued significance of advising had been implicated as one of the dominant themes of this study, and interestingly, was supported throughout the interview process. One student stated, "You have one person and have them help you or facilitate contact with other people." Another student concurred with the value of quality advisement, "Give me the person to contact and she can help with the problem." Lastly, one student stated, "I have a fabulous advisor."

As suggested by related research (Beeman, 1988), convenience emerged as another dominant theme, based on the high rating of classes being scheduled at suitable times. Presumably, this also reflected satisfaction with the predictable class schedule that remains unchanged until graduation. Designed for adult students, the classes meet the same night each week at the one location for the duration of the program. Students know where and when the classes are scheduled, up to 24 months in advance. A busy adult can plan his or her schedule based on this knowledge. Similarly, the item "I am able to complete most of my enrollment tasks in one location" was rated high in importance and satisfaction. Therefore, based on the design of an adult friendly system, the student can complete important educational transactions from registration to advisement sessions in their classroom. Participants' responses supported the theme of convenience, as highly valued, and listed it as one of the reasons for enrolling in the program.

CONCLUSION

Based on the findings of these studies, which sought to identify the items of importance and areas of satisfaction for the adult students, relevant implications were presented.

1. The adult students value quality academic advising and the collegial relationships that are forged with this experience. The university should continue to incorporate

the use of competent and available faculty who understand the program and the needs of the adult student. This model can minimize the stress of returning to higher education.

2. The students value quality faculty. They appreciate faculty who are unbiased, approachable, knowledgeable, committed to excellence, and provide timely feedback.

3. Students are concerned with the quality of instruction and interactions with faculty as a measure of satisfaction and importance. Hiring procedures should focus on individuals who are academically and clinically qualified and are comfortable with working with the accelerated format and adult learners.

4. The institution should focus on cohort orientations to include advisement procedures, service access, technology and use of online databases. By focusing on minimizing time spent on campus, students can be assured that the university values their time.

5. The university ought to work with financial aid services to improve communication about programs, loans, scholarships, and grants. In addition, this information needs to be published in catalogs and student handbooks, posted online, and included in admissions packets.

6. External forces, such as family commitments, job responsibilities, and loss of financial aid, impact the students' ability to persist until graduation. Therefore, advisors may seek to remove institutional barriers while assisting students to identify methods to complete the degree.

7. Students look for convenience as a determining factor for enrolling in a program; therefore, the placements of cohorts and classrooms should be strategic in a dense population of potential students.

8. Students value and appreciate a safe learning environment. This aspect should be preserved.

9. Students favor the convenience of an accelerated program and camaraderie of the cohort model. Maintaining this model is suggested.

10. Despite a shortened time frame to complete assignments, students are able to perform well academically in the program and are motivated to complete the program as evidenced by interviews and high grade point averages.

Presumably, the sampled population responded positively and honestly when asked to participate in a study with specific research questions. With a high return of the ASPS, the indications are that students were ready and willing to voice their needs and suggestions on improving the entire educational process. Participants articulated what was and was not important to them in their academic experience. These data can assist in empowering faculty, staff, and administration at this institution to make changes, and to be more proactive in meeting students' needs and expectations. Additionally, these findings can help to create an academic environment conducive to preparing the adult learner to succeed in a professional environment. The focus on the adult student and program excellence may yield dividends undiscovered by the university.

SUMMARY

Stress can manifest itself in a number of physiological and psychological ways in each individual (Jacobs, 1999). By providing academic services for the burden-laden adult, the university may minimize the number or trips to campus, bookstore, registrar's office and library thereby diminishing the stress levels. In addition, with online libraries and databases, combined with technological support, the student may perform research from home and remote locations thereby decreasing the number and times on campus to complete assignments. According to one student, " I enjoy the services such as the books delivered to the classroom."

Adult students face unique stressors as they attempt to balance their life roles. Returning to school may be construed as a stressful event (Holmes and Rahe, 1967). One student commented, "If I couldn't balance it anymore I would quit the program."

Institutions that wish to establish programs designed for adult students must take these stressors into consideration when designing a supportive learning environment. As one student verbalized, "It's hard to feel that you are out there on your own. This program does not have that…you have support."

Students in the studied institution rate it highly in terms of providing that learning environment, and that satisfaction exists in two very different academic disciplines. "It's nice to have everything delivered to you…you're not running to the bookstore."

Based on the findings of these studies, further research may focus on the use a pre- and post-assessment of stress and anxiety to ascertain whether the services were instrumental in diminishing student stressors. Additionally, by treating the adult student as a customer of higher education, the university may increase the interpersonal support provided to each individual.

REFERENCES

Anderson, E. (2003). Changing U. S. demographics and American higher education. *New Directions for Higher Education, 121*, 3–12.

Ayer, S., and Smith, C. (1998). Planning flexible learning to match the needs of consumers: A national survey. *Journal of Advanced Nursing, 27*, 1032–1047.

Beeman, P. (1988). RNs' perceptions of their baccalaureate programs: Meeting their adult learning needs. *Journal of Nursing Education, 27*(8), 364–370.

Bohlin, R. M., Milheim, W. D., and Viechnicki, K. J. (1994). The development of a model for the design of motivational adult instruction in higher education. *Journal of Educational Technology Systems, 22*(1), 3–17.

Bok, D. (2003) *Universities in the marketplace: The commercialization of higher education.* Princeton: Princeton University Press, 2003.

Bowl, M. (2001). Experiencing the barriers: Nontraditional students entering higher education. *Research Papers in Education, 16*(2), 141-160.

Boylston, M. T., Peters, M. A., and Lacey, M. (2004). Adult student satisfaction in traditional and accelerated RN-to-BSN programs. *Journal of Professional Nursing, 20*(1), 23–32.

Brown, C. D., and Eggert Linnemann, R. (1995, Spring). Services for adult undergraduate students in a four-year college. *The Journal of Continuing Higher Education, 2*–13.

El Ansari, W. (2002). Student nurse satisfaction levels with their courses: Part I – effects of demographic variables. *Nurse Education Today, 22*(2), 159–170.

Elliott, K. M., and Shin, D. (2002). Student satisfaction: An alternative approach to assessing this important concept. *Journal of Higher Education, 24*(2), 197–209.

Fairchild, E. E. (2003/Summer). Multiple roles of adult learners. *New Directions for Student Services, 102,* 11-16.

Fishback, S. J., and Polson, C. J. (1998). *The cognitive development of adult undergraduate students.* In *Proceedings of the 17ᵗʰ annual Midwest research to practice conference in adult, continuing, and community education.* Edited by G. S. Wood, Jr. and M. M. Webber, p. 81-86. Muncie, Indiana: Ball State University (ED 424 419) Retrieved January 28, 2004, from
http://www.bsu.edu/teachers/departments/edld/conf/cognitive.html

Fralick, M. (1993). College success: A study of positive and negative attrition. *Community College review, 20*(5), 29-36.

Fungaroli, C.S. (2000) *Traditional degrees for nontraditional students.* New York: Farrar, Straus, and Giroux, 2000.

Green, C. P. (1987). Multiple role women: The real world of the mature RN learner. *Journal of Nursing Education, 26*(7), 266-271.

Grupe, F., and Connolly, F. (1995, January – February). Grownups are different: Computer training for older adult learners. *Journal of Systems Management,* 54-68.

Hadfield, J. (2003, Summer). Recruiting and retaining adult students. *New Directions for Student Services. 102,* 17-26.

Holmes, T., and Rahe, R. (1967). Social readjustment rating scale. *Journal of Psychosomatics Research, 11,* 213-218.

Horn, L., Peter, K., Rooney, K., and Malizio, A. G. (2002). *Profile of undergraduates in U. S. postsecondary institutions 1999-2000: Statistical analysis report* (NCES 97-578). Retrieved July 5, 2004, from http://nces.ed.gov/pubs2002/2002168.PDF U. S. Department of Education, NCES. Washington, DC: U. S. Government Printing Office.

Jacobs, G. D. (1999). The physiology of mind-body interactions: The stress response and the relaxation response. *The Journal of Alternative and Complementary Medicine, 7*(1), S-83-S-92.

Kasworm, C. E. (2003, Spring). From the adult students' perspective: Accelerated degree programs. *New Directions for Adult and Continuing Education, 97,* 17-27.

Kerka, S. (1995). *Adult learner retention revisited.* Washington, DC: Office of Educational Research and Improvement. (ERIC Document Reproduction Service No. ED 389880)

Kerka, S. (2001). *The balancing act of adult life.* Washington, DC: Office of Educational Research and Improvement. (ERIC Document Reproduction Service No. ED 459323)

Knowles, M. (1978). *The adult learner: A neglected species (2ⁿᵈ ed).* Houston, TX: Gulf Publishing Company.

Lee, E.J. (1988). Analysis of coping methods reported by returning RNs. *Journal of Nursing Education, 27*(7), 309-313.

MacKinnon-Slaney, F. (1994). The adult persistence in learning model: A road map to counseling services for adult learners. *Journal of Counseling and Development, 73*(2), 268-275.

McCollough, M. A., and Gremler, D. D. (1999). Guaranteeing student satisfaction: An exercise in treating students as customers. *Journal of Marketing Education, 21*(2), 118–130.

National Center for Education Statistics (NCES) (2002). Special analysis 2002: Nontraditional undergraduates. Retrieved January 29, 2004, from http://www.nces.ed.gov/programs/coe/2002/analyses/nontraditional/index.asp

Naugle, D. (1995). The Christian college and adult education. *Faculty Dialogue* 24 (Spring, 1995), 24ff.

O'Brien, B. S., and Renner, A. (2000). Nurses on-line: Career mobility for registered nurses. *Journal of Professional Nursing, 16*(1), 13–20.

O'Connor, P. C., and Bevil, C. A. (1996). Academic outcomes and stress in full-time day and part-time evening baccalaureate nursing students. *Journal of Nursing Education, 35*(6), 245–251.

Reed, N., and Beaudin, B. (1993). Adult students and technology in higher education: A partnership for participation. *Collegiate Microcomputer, XI*(1), 1-4.

Richardson, J. T. E., and King, E. (1998). Adult students in higher education: Burden or boon? *Journal of Higher Education, 69*(1), 65-88.

Selye, H. (1977). *The stress of life.* New York: McGraw Hill.

Sissel, P. A., Hansman, C. A., and Kasworm, C. E. (2001). The politics of neglect: Adult learners in higher education, *91*, 17–27.

Viechnicki, K. J., Bohlin, R. M., and Milheim, W. D. (1990, Fall). Instructional motivation of adult learners: An analysis of student perceptions in continuing education. *The Journal of Continuing Education,* 10-14.

Wachs, M. (1993). *The case for practitioner faculty.* Los Angeles: Graduate School of Architecture and Urban Planning.

Wlodkowsi, R. J. (2003, Spring). Accelerated learning in colleges and universities. *New Directions for Adult and Continuing Education, 97,* 5-15.

Viechnicki, K. J., Bohlin, R. M., and Milheim, W. D. (1990, Fall). Instructional motivation of adult learners: An analysis of student perceptions in continuing education. *The Journal of Continuing Education,* 10-14.

ABOUT THE AUTHOR

Matthew M. Martin (Ph.D., Kent State University, 1992) is a Professor, Communication Studies Department, West Virginia University, Morgantown, WV, 26506, (304-293-3905), *MMartin@wvu.edu*. Jacob L. Cayanus (Ed.D., West Virginia University, 2005) is an Assistant Professor at Oakland University. Keith Weber (Ed.D., West Virginia University, 1998) is an Assistant Professor at West Virginia University. Alan K. Goodboy (M.A., West Virginia University, 2004) is a doctoral student at West Virginia University.

In: Adult Education: Issues and Developments
Editors: P. N. Blakely, A. H. Tomlin, pp. 25-173

ISBN: 978-1-60456-272-9
© 2008 Nova Science Publishers, Inc.

Chapter 2

HOW TEACHERS CHANGE: A STUDY OF PROFESSIONAL DEVELOPMENT IN ADULT EDUCATION[*]

Cristine Smith, Judy Hofer, Marilyn Gillespie, Marla Solomon and Karen Rowe

SUMMARY

The NCSALL Professional Development Study investigated how adult education[2] teachers changed after participating in one of three different models of professional development (multisession workshop, mentor teacher group, or practitioner research group), all on the same topic of learner persistence. The study also investigated the most important individual, professional development, program, and system factors that influenced the type and amount of teacher change. This study was conducted primarily to help professional development decision-makers plan and deliver effective professional development, and to understand the factors that influence how teachers change as a result of professional development.

The research question that guided our inquiry was:

How do practitioners change as a result of participating in one of three different models of professional development, and what are the most important factors that influence (support or hinder) this change?

---

[*] Excerpted from NCSALL Reports #25, November 2003

[2] In this chapter, "adult education" refers to the broad range of basic and literacy education services for adults, including adult basic education, adult secondary education, and English for speakers of other languages.

The study design was based on the overall hypothesis that teachers change in different ways and amounts as a result of participating in professional development, and that multiple factors influence the type and amount of change practitioners experience as a result of professional development, including:

- Individual factors—their experience, background, and motivation as they come into the professional development
- Professional development factors—the quality and amount of professional development attended
- Program and system factors—the structure of and support offered by the program, adult education system, and professional development system in which they work, including teachers' working conditions

Methods

The sample consisted of 106 women and men from three New England states (Maine, Massachusetts, and Connecticut). One hundred of these teachers participated in up to 18 hours of professional development in either a multisession workshop, a mentor teacher group, or a practitioner research group; the other six people were nonparticipant teachers who served as a comparison group. Representing a traditional professional development activity, the workshops were organized in multiple sessions and included experiential, active learning activities. Mentor teacher groups and practitioner research groups are considered "reform" types of professional development. As conducted for our study, the mentor teacher groups blended together features of study circles and peer coaching and observation. Practitioner research groups allowed teachers to investigate their own classroom practice by collecting and analyzing data to answer a question of concern to them. As noted previously, in all three models and across all three states, the topic was the same: learner motivation, retention, and persistence. From the 100 participants, 18 teachers were randomly selected (six from each model) to serve as a subsample. Participants were listed as completers if they attended at least two thirds (12 of the 18 hours) of the professional development required. If they completed less than 12 hours, they were considered dropouts. Total dropouts equaled 16 out of 100. Participants provided data to researchers through questionnaires and interviews before, after, and one year after participating in the professional development.

Our goal was to develop high-quality professional development in three different models appropriate for adult educators. The research team designed all three professional development models, using the best methods and accepted principles of adult learning and effective professional development. Experienced teachers or professional development leaders in each state, recruited and trained by the research staff, facilitated the professional development.

Findings

We had two measures of change (our dependent variables): 1) Overall amount of change (thinking and acting on and off the topic of the professional development—learner persistence), and 2) Type of change (thinking and acting on the topic of learner persistence).

How much did teachers change? Most teachers, even dropouts, changed at least minimally through gains in knowledge or actions in their classrooms; relatively few experienced no change at all. Almost all (90% of the whole sample, 95% of completers) gained some knowledge on the topic, but for many it consisted of only one or two concepts. The majority (78% of the whole sample, 87% of completers) took some action, on or off the topic, but for many it was very minimal.

In what role did teachers change? Changes were most often seen in teachers' roles as classroom teachers (53%), rather than their roles as program members (20%), learners (7%), or members of the field (1%).

In what ways did teachers change? The research identified four types of change: 1) no to minimal change, 2) thinking change (changes in thinking were greater relative to changes in acting), 3) acting change (changes in acting were greater relative to changes in thinking), and 4) integrated change. The four types of change represent the direction of "preferred change": from "no or minimal change" at one end of the spectrum to "significant integrated" change at the other. However, we made no qualitative distinction between "thinking change" and "acting change"; both are preferable to "no change," but less preferable than "integrated change."

Therefore, we combined these four types of change into a three-category spectrum of change: (1) no change, (2) nonintegrated change (thinking or acting changes), and (3) integrated change. The majority (72%) of the 83 completers demonstrated change, most of which was nonintegrated change reflected in their thinking. Teachers who fell into the "integrated change" type (24%) also demonstrated a higher overall amount of change. They showed more sustained change, and in more arenas (classroom, program, and field).

What factors influenced teacher change? Multiple factors interacted to influence teacher change as a result of participating in professional development. The most important individual factors that related to change in our study included teachers' motivation to attend the professional development, years of experience in the field of adult education, venue of first teaching experience, and level of formal education. To a somewhat lesser extent, teachers' level of commitment to the field played a negative role in change.

The most important professional development factors included hours of professional development attended, and the quality of the professional development (both as rated by researchers and as perceived by teachers). Model of professional development in which the teacher participated was not a significant factor, although there were differences in patterns of change among the models. Whether teachers participated in professional development with other teachers from their program was another somewhat important factor that affected change.

The most important program and system factors included teachers' access to benefits and prep time through their adult education job, and program's history in addressing learner persistence coupled with teachers' access to decision-making in the program. To a lesser but still important extent, other factors influencing teacher change included teachers' access to paid professional development release time, collegiality, number of working hours, and freedom to make changes to the curriculum used.

Recommendations

While there are limitations to the generalizability of these findings outside of the New England area, professional developers should consider these findings and advocate for teachers to spend a greater number of hours participating in well-designed professional development. Program directors should consider how to: provide access to professional development, allow teachers greater say in decision-making, provide more opportunities for teacher sharing, and create well-supported jobs for their teachers.

Specifically, we propose the following recommendations, for policymakers in programs and states, for professional developers, and for teachers themselves.

For *program directors and states:*

- Improve teachers' working conditions, including access to decision-making in the program.
- Pay teachers to attend professional development.
- Increase access to colleagues and directors during and after professional development.
- Establish expectations at the state and the program level that all teachers must continue to learn.

For *professional developers:*

- Ensure that professional development is of high quality.
- Offer a variety of professional development models for teachers to attend, including program-based professional development.
- Help teachers acquire skills to build theories of good teaching and student success.
- Add activities to each professional development session to help teachers strategize how to deal with the forces that affect their ability to take action.

For *teachers:*

- Expect high-quality professional development.
- Recognize the need to develop a philosophy and theory of good teaching and student success.
- Work to increase opportunities for collegiality and teacher decision-making in their programs.
- Advocate for paid prep time, professional development release time, and benefits as part of their adult education jobs.

This study is important to the field of adult education because, unlike K–12 research on professional development, it provides information about factors unique to adult education, such as program and working conditions, that influence teacher changes in thinking and acting after participating in professional development. Professional development is necessary but not sufficient by itself to help teachers learn about and adopt new practices that promise to improve the quality of service, and policymakers at the federal, state, and program level will need to understand and address these factors in an era of accountability that stresses improved student outcomes.

OVERVIEW OF THE PROFESSIONAL DEVELOPMENT STUDY

Introduction

This study was one of many sponsored by the National Center for the Study of Adult Learning and Literacy (NCSALL) during its first five-year phase (1996–2001). The goal of NCSALL is to improve the quality of practice in adult basic education, English for speakers of other languages, and adult secondary education programs through basic and applied research.

The NCSALL Professional Development Study was conducted with 106 adult education teachers in three New England states (Connecticut, Maine, and Massachusetts) between 1998 and 2000. Teachers participated in one of three 18-hour professional development activities (either multisession workshop, mentor teacher group, or practitioner research group), and they provided data to researchers through questionnaires and interviews before, after, and one year after participating in the professional development.

The research question that guided the NCSALL Professional Development Study was:

How do practitioners change as a result of participating in one of three different models of professional development, and what are the most important factors that influence (support or hinder) this change?

This study was conducted primarily to help professional development decision-makers— adult education administrators and professional developers at the program and state level— plan and deliver effective professional development, and understand the factors that influence how teachers change as a result of professional development. This full research report details the study and its findings and is written primarily for researchers. Other articles and reports of interest from this study, tailored for nonresearchers, include:[3]

- *The Working Conditions of Adult Literacy Teachers* (Smith, Hofer, & Gillespie, 2001)[4]

---

[3] All articles and reports on the NCSALL Professional Development Study are available for downloading from NCSALL's Web site (Hhttp://ncsall.gse.harvard.eduH).

[4] *Focus on Basics*, Volume 4, Issue D. (April 2001). National Center for the Study of Adult Learning and Literacy.

- *Pathways to Change: A Summary of Findings from NCSALL's Staff Development Study* (Smith and Hofer, 2002)[5]
- *The Characteristics and Concerns of Adult Education Teachers* (Smith & Hofer, 2003)[6]

The study design was based on the overall hypothesis that teachers change in different ways and amounts as a result of participating in professional development, and that multiple factors influence the type and amount of change practitioners experience as a result of professional development, including:

- **Individual factors**—their experience, knowledge, and attitudes about teaching as they come into the professional development
- **Professional development factors**—the quality and amount of professional development attended
- **Program and system factors**—the structure of and support offered by the program, adult education system, and professional development system in which they work, including teachers' working conditions, which we define as their access to resources, professional development and information, colleagues and directors, decision-making, and well-supported jobs.[7]

The main activities of the study were:

1. Developing and testing three models of professional development activities appropriate for adult education.
2. Gauging the change (differences in thinking and acting) for teachers who participated in one of these professional development activities.
3. Identifying the most important factors that influenced whether and how teachers changed.

Structure of this Report

In this first chapter, we discuss the focus and foundation of the research, including its guiding question and a review of the relevant professional development literature that provides the rationale for this study. We then describe the study design: the sample, research context and implementation, and data collection and analysis. Finally, we outline the limitations of the study. In the second chapter, we present the findings of the study, beginning with the results of how and why teachers participated, followed by how they changed as a result. We then outline the factors that influenced and explain such change. The final chapter

---

[5] *Focus on Basics,* Volume 5, Issue D. (June 2002). National Center for the Study of Adult Learning and Literacy.

[6] NCSALL Reports # 26. (November 2003). National Center for the Study of Adult Learning and Literacy.

[7] We define "well-supported jobs" as full time, relatively well-paid and stable jobs that include benefits (medical coverage, paid vacation and sick time, pension plans, etc.), paid preparation time, and paid professional development release time.

makes recommendations based on these findings for policymakers, program directors, professional developers, and teachers themselves.

Rationale and Literature Review

Our earliest conception of this study's design included the goal of discovering the relative effectiveness of different models of professional development. Since very little research on professional development for adult education teachers has been conducted, we needed to first determine what information about approaches to professional development exist in the K–12 literature. However, while there are principles of effective professional development derived from research and theory in K–12 professional development (American Federation of Teachers, 1995) that can be useful to adult education professional developers, K–12 research is limited in its usefulness to adult education professional development for two reasons, and both are related to the differences in context between K–12 and adult education.

First, the research in K–12 has, by and large, studied professional development models that are not replicable in adult education because of differences between the two systems in funding and teacher status. Much of the research on K–12 professional development is related to evaluations of professional development that have been done in connection to large-scale adoption of specific curricular interventions or to ensure compliance with preferred routines or methods of operation. Often, the professional development in these studies is designed as intensive, multiyear professional development with small numbers of teachers receiving hundreds of hours of professional development. Holderness (1993) and Swafford, Jones, Thornton, Stump, and Miller (1999) are examples of projects where small groups of teachers received intensive professional development (up to 15 full days) over extended periods of time (several weeks to several years) on the same topic using multiple models or design features (training plus technical assistance plus peer coaching, etc.). Such professional development models are probably not replicable on a wide scale even in K–12 with greater resources, and school districts will have to choose between providing average-quality professional development for all teachers or high-quality professional development for fewer teachers (Porter, Garet, Desimone, Yoon, & Berman, 2000). The problem in adult education is even more acute because many teachers do not receive preservice preparation in teaching adults and the turnover rate seems to be at least as high as in K–12[8] and possibly higher. Therefore, in adult education, those who fund and plan professional development need to choose from realistic and doable models (less than 20 hours) of professional development. They need information about which models are most effective in promoting teacher change, and which models can be used to reach the largest number of teachers in the least amount of time. In most cases, neither teachers nor programs nor states can afford much more.

The second reason that K–12 professional development research is limited in its usefulness to adult education decision-makers is that K–12 and adult education operate in vastly different contexts and structures. The factors that may influence the effectiveness of professional development are different in adult education, where teachers are mostly part time

---

[8] The most recent national survey of K–12 teachers indicates a turnover rate of 14.3% per year, but half of these are "migrators" who move to another K–12 school; the other half are retirees and those who leave the field of teaching entirely (Ingersoll, 2001).

and teach without prep time, paid professional development release time, or benefits in multisite programs with limited resources. Because so little research on professional development has been done specifically related to the effectiveness of professional development in this context, those who make decisions about professional development in our field also need to know who adult education practitioners are and the conditions under which they work, because these factors may influence the outcomes of different models of professional development on teacher change.

The effectiveness of different professional development approaches is an issue of much debate in the literature on professional development. Professional development decision-makers need to decide between competing models of professional development—traditional and "reform"—based on new philosophies about the purpose of professional development: helping teachers acquire a "change orientation" rather than just adopt new techniques (Richardson, 1998). Traditional activities, such as workshops, are very common in the adult education field because they are usually shorter in duration, making it easier for part-time adult education teachers to attend. Reform activities, such as study circles, practitioner inquiry, and mentoring, are less common but they may also be appropriate for adult education because they can be based in the program, making it more convenient for teachers with limited time for travel and participation. However, we do not know whether reform activities are more effective than traditional activities (workshops) within our field, and even in K–12, "there is a clear need for new, systematic research on the effectiveness of alternative strategies for professional development" (Garet, Porter, Desimone, Birman, & Yoon, 2001).

Key stakeholders in the adult education field supported our idea of designing this study as a comparison of appropriate models of professional development. At the beginning of our design phase, we organized a one-day meeting of 22 professional development experts and providers, teachers, and policymakers in Washington, DC in February 1997, cosponsored with Pelavin Research Institute. We asked the participants to discuss and prioritize the key needs for information and research about professional development in the field of adult education. The results indicated four main questions for research around professional development:

1. What impact can we expect from professional development?
2. How can impact be measured?
3. Which approaches to professional development are most effective in achieving this impact?
4. Which professional development systems best support effective professional development?

The synthesis of responses from this group of experts confirmed our intention for the study to compare different models (or approaches) of professional development. Although we did not feel we had the resources to measure student achievement as a result of professional development, we were able to investigate the impact on teacher change. Therefore, we felt that the immediate and most important research question for our field concerned the design of professional development and the factors that influence its effectiveness. The research question that drove the NCSALL Professional Development Study is:

How do practitioners change as a result of participating in one of three different models of professional development, and what are the most important factors—individual, professional development, and program/system factors—that influence (support or hinder) this change?

After further discussion with stakeholders in the field, we decided to test three models of professional development[9] appropriate to adult education:

1. **Multisession workshops**—a traditional professional development activity, but organized in multiple sessions and including experiential, active learning activities
2. **Mentor teacher groups**—a "reform" type of professional development activity, blending features of study circles with features of peer coaching and observation
3. **Practitioner research groups**—a "reform" type of professional development activity where teachers investigate their own classroom practice by collecting and analyzing data to answer a question of concern to them

To aid us in designing the highest quality professional development to test, and to help us understand the type of data we should collect about the individual, professional development, program and system factors that might influence the effectiveness of the different models, we conducted a literature review of the existing research on professional development in both K–12 and adult education.

A Review of the K–12 Research on Teacher Change and Professional Development

With this rationale and research design in mind, we began a review of the research literature. We wanted to know what research existed about the effectiveness of professional development in helping teachers change in preferred and substantial ways, whether these changes are lasting, and whether they make a difference in student achievement. We also wanted to learn more about how professional development "works" and under what circumstances. Our review of the knowledge base about professional development and teacher change necessarily focused largely on the K–12 research, since there has been little research specifically related to the adult education field. We learned that, over the past 30 years, the research has focused on discovering different perspectives on what drives good instruction and determining how to design effective professional development for teachers.

The existing research shows that philosophy about professional development has evolved from a focus on training teachers to adopt particular, expert-recommended behaviors in the classroom to a focus on helping teachers adopt a critically reflective stance that allows them to determine for themselves what is effective. In the 1960s and 1970s, for example, the primary focus of teacher education and professional development research was on **teacher behavior** and how professional development could help teachers to change their behaviors and adopt innovations (particularly new interventions developed through research and development); such research focused on the "transfer" of training back to the classroom. In the 1980s, the focus shifted toward **school improvement** and the role of professional development in supporting school reform or restructuring. In the early 1990s, the focus shifted toward **student achievement** and the role of professional development in improving student learning, perhaps because of increased emphasis on educational accountability (Elmore, 2002). Finally, in the late 1990s, the focus shifted to **teacher quality** (defined variously as teachers' years of experience, level of education/certification, and knowledge of subject matter), its importance as a key predictor of student achievement, and the role of professional development in helping teachers develop into high-quality teachers (Wenglinsky, 2000). Although individual research studies based on these different foci still continue to appear, the trends are clearly visible when looking at the evolution of professional development and teacher education philosophies over the years.

Models for Professional Development

One of our purposes for reviewing the K–12 literature was to better understand recent trends regarding the most effective models for professional development. Researchers have categorized and studied a range of approaches. Sparks and Loucks-Horsley (1987) list five models: individual/self-directed, observation/assessment, school improvement, training, and inquiry. Pelavin Research Institute (1996) lists four approaches: workshop/presentation, observation/feedback, inquiry-research, product/program development. Feiman-Nemser (2001) argues that different types of professional development should be offered on a "continuum" over the teacher's career, starting with formal education (courses offered by the college), then induction (pairing with a master teacher or mentor when beginning to teach, offered by the school), then ongoing inquiry activities while teaching (practitioner research or study circles, organized by the school), supported by a learning environment in the school, and opportunities for professional development (workshops, institutes offered by the district). Coaching (whether peer or mentor) has strong advocates within the K–12 professional development field (Joyce, 1983; Joyce & Showers, 1995).

Through our review of the literature we learned that professional development could be successful *if* it took place over time (not one session only), was integrated with the school context, and focused on helping teachers not just acquire new behaviors but change their assumptions and ways of thinking (reflectiveness) as well. The difficulties of trying to meet all these demands through one-shot, traditional professional development such as workshops prompted professional development experts to recommend "alternative" or "reform" types of professional development, such as study circles, mentoring, collaborative problem-solving groups, practitioner inquiry, and so on, that can be organized as part of teachers' daily work to help them acquire a reflective stance as much as to acquire new knowledge of content and practices (Ball & Cohen, 1999; Guskey, 1999; Richardson, 1998). Professional development, these experts contended, should have as its goal increased reflectiveness and an inquiry stance among teachers, rather than simply adoption of new practices. Adoption of new practices, they believed, would come about as teachers reflected and systematically tested "what works" in their own context (Richardson & Anders, 1994).

By the 1990s, much of the writing on professional development emphasized this paradigm shift, as Sparks (1994) termed it, in thinking about professional development: away from an emphasis on teachers adding new skills or fixing "bad" practice and toward an

---

[9] For more information about the design and development of the three models investigated in this study, please see Appendix A.

emphasis on teacher reflectiveness and problem solving as a result of professional development (Arlin, 1999; Olson, Butler, & Olson, 1991; Rueda, 1997). Richardson and Placier (2001) describe this shift as a move from the "empirical-rational" model of change (where academic researchers study and decide on most effective practices and then teachers are trained to understand and implement these practices) to a "normative-reeducative" model of change (where teachers and administrators build their capacity to solve problems by looking at their own beliefs and practices, and through dialogue and collaboration with other practitioners). Teachers should adopt a "change orientation," seeing themselves not as teachers who master and then replicate instructional tasks dictated from outside but as *learners* who must constantly grow from their own practice, through experimentation, problem solving, and reflection on their work (Richardson, 1998). Professional development models that focus on teacher knowledge and inquiry are preferred to those that deliver expert knowledge and expect teachers to adopt specific practices (Lytle, Belzer, & Reumann, 1992a, 1992b).

In addition to teacher reflectiveness, this new vision of professional development emphasized professional development that was "results-driven" (focused on students learning rather than teachers teaching), "systems-related" (focused on organizational rather than individual change), and "constructivist" (focused on professional development embedded in practice and driven by teachers, rather than knowledge and skills transferred from expert to teacher) (Guskey, 1997; Sparks, 1994, 1995). Since the goal of improving student outcomes is the central objective (Elmore, 2002), other researchers (Ball & Cohen, 1999; Darling-Hammond &Ball, 1997) advocate making student work the center of professional development, promoting strong content-based and practice-based professional development models, where groups of teachers use an inquiry process to look at "artifacts" of teaching— samples of student work or samples of other teachers' teaching—to analyze what this "data" tells them about how to solve problems of practice. Helping teachers to look at how students think and reason generates teachers' knowledge and self-sustaining ability to learn (Carpenter & Franke, 1998).

Educators promoting the new paradigm of professional development advocate for schools to be organized as learning communities for teachers and school leaders, with opportunities for teachers' continuous learning and reflection built into their jobs and into the structure and culture of the school (Langer, 2000; Stein, Smith, & Silver, 1999; Valli, 1997). When universities partner with local school districts to support such learning communities, the result is a "professional development school," where professional development linked with ongoing research projects is integrated into the work, culture, and structure of teaching and the school. Simultaneously, researchers began to use the term "professional development" (rather than "staff development"), since "professionals" are developed through the self-sustaining process of learning from one's own practice, whereas "staff" are developed through training processes aimed at school improvement and adoption of new innovations.[10]

Based on the research in K–12, we decided that our study would investigate the relative contribution of one traditional (workshop) and two "reform" models (mentoring and practitioner research) for professional development. Understanding whether one model was

---

[10] Over the course of this five-year study, we as researchers have used both of these terms and have decided to use the term "professional development" based on our field's use of the term (even though the original title of the

superior to another in promoting teacher change would be helpful to a field (adult education) that has historically relied on traditional professional development models. We next needed to understand theories of teacher change, so that we could base outcomes for our study on what has been learned previously about the connection between professional development and teacher change.

Research on Teacher Change

In reviewing the broad and varied research on teacher change, we needed a frame within which to describe the relevant knowledge base. We chose to use, for this review, the three types of research on teachers identified by Stein and Wang (1988); that is, research on:

- **Teaching and teaching effectiveness**—to determine what types of teacher background and preparation lead to student improvement
- **School change**—to determine the factors that support school improvement and teacher change, such as leadership and school culture)
- **The social-psychology of teachers**—to determine factors that influence teacher change, such as teachers' motivation, self-efficacy, and attitudes

The first category covers much of the research on the connection among professional development, teacher change, and teacher effectiveness; the second two categories cover much of what is known about the contextual (school) and individual teacher factors that influence how effective professional development can be.

Professional Development and Teacher Effectiveness

When considering the topic of teacher change, it is important first to understand the literature related to teacher effectiveness. Ultimately, the measure of teaching effectiveness is whether students learn better. If students achieve, then teachers are assumed to be effective. The idea that teachers themselves (rather than class size, specific curriculum, or student socioeconomic background) are important to student achievement has recently been supported by a landmark study on teacher quality in Tennessee. Sanders and Rivers (1996) used achievement data for all teachers in one school in a given year to determine who the "effective" teachers were, then tested and followed students over several years. They found that students who performed equally well in second grade, but had different teachers over the next three years, performed unequally by year five. Fifth graders who had "effective" teachers in third, fourth, and fifth grades scored in the 83rd percentile in grade five, but those students who were studied in the third, fourth, and fifth grades under the "ineffective" teachers scored much lower (the 29th percentile, a 54-point difference) by the end of fifth grade. Similarly, Sanders and Rivers found that the most effective teachers could boost the scores in one year of low-achieving students an average of 39 percentile points more than similar low-achieving students with ineffective teachers. This study is often cited to illustrate the proposition that teacher quality is the single best predictor of student success.

---

study included the term "staff development") and based on our investigation of individual teacher development and change rather than changes in "staff" of particular programs.

The link between teacher effectiveness and teacher preparation is being established using large, aggregate state and national databases. Researchers such as Darling-Hammond, 2000, Darling-Hammond & Youngs, 2002) have matched indicators of teacher preparation and background—such as certification, level of formal education, degree in the subject in which the teacher is teaching (i.e., a degree in math rather than a degree in education), and teachers' verbal ability—with student test scores. Such research consistently has found that the formal preparation of the teacher (specifically, certification and subject matter degree) predicts higher student achievement. Teachers' general intelligence and knowledge of subject matter are not as important to student achievement as teacher completion of a formal degree in subject matter and knowledge of teaching and learning.

If teacher preservice preparation predicts higher student achievement, then it follows that professional development may also have similarly positive effects. Since virtually all K–12 teachers receive some form of ongoing professional development annually,[11] the exact contribution of ongoing professional development to student achievement, while considered important, is less well known. Demonstrating that participation in professional development is the direct cause of better student achievement is difficult (Adey, 1995), because teachers don't all change the same way as a result of professional development. However, a recent large-scale survey (Wenglinsky, 2000) attempted to look specifically at the various contributions of teacher background, classroom practice, and professional development on student achievement (math and science test scores of over 7,000 eighth-graders). Students of teachers who received professional development in higher-order thinking skills, in working with special populations, or in laboratory skills significantly outperformed their peers. Wenglinsky concluded that professional development can change teaching practices, and that if teaching practices focus on higher-order thinking skills, hands-on learning activities, and monitoring tests, student performance will improve.

Professional Development and Teacher Change

Despite Wenglinsky's promising finding, a variety of quantitative and qualitative studies over the years indicate that change, at least as promoted by an "external" factor such as professional development, is a complicated process.

Change is slow. Even when professional development extends over several years, with multiple opportunities for learning (Short & Echevarria, 1999), change is a process occurring over time that requires support (Imel, 2000; Joyce, 1983).

Change requires support. Change requires much more intensive learning support than teachers generally receive in the type of professional development they usually experience: "mandated district-sponsored staff development, consisting of a menu of training options (workshops, special courses, or in-service days) designed to transmit a specific set of ideas, techniques, or materials to teachers" (Stein et al., 1999, p. 239).

Change is not always linear. Fullan (1990) argues that there is an "implementation dip" as teachers try new actions, before they have fully integrated the new idea, and this is a period of stress and anxiety for teachers.

---

[11] Ninety-nine percent of K–12 teachers participated in some staff development over the past year, according to a recent national survey (Lewis et al., 1999). In another national survey, 85% reported having attended some staff development in the past year (National Education Goals Panel Report, 1999); however, another study reported that 50% of teachers in one national survey attended less than two days of staff development per year (Wenglinsky, 2000).

Change is not easy. Bridges (1991) sees it as a three-step psychological transition process with an ending (for old ways), neutral zone (rethinking stage), and beginning (with a purpose and plan). Change comes about through reflection, and the heart of reflection is first challenging one's assumptions (Garmston, 1997; Lewis, 1992)—a difficult task. Change can also be threatening to the larger institution: if teachers, through professional development, learn to be "change oriented" and reflective, their autonomy will increase, which may cause problems within the program or school as students move from teacher to teacher (Richardson, 1998). Therefore, individual teacher change sometimes leads to new challenges unless teachers and administrators work together to discuss consistency of goals and curriculum across the program.

Change is not always direct or guaranteed. Practice may not change just because something new was learned. In one study, teachers attending a three-day training on "effective teaching" implemented only 3 out of 18 concepts and strategies, and were more likely to just "bolt on" new strategies to existing practices ("horizontal" integration of new ideas), rather than to really change their existing beliefs and practices ("vertical" integration) (Gardner, 1996). Joyce, Wolf, and Calhoun (1995) found that only 10% of practices were adopted, even after 10–15 days of training, unless followed by coaching or action research, and Meyer (1988) found only 15% implementation of new practices after a one-shot training. Even then, implementation of new practices can drop off over the long term if teacher excitement and momentum is not maintained (Stallings & Krasavage, 1986). One recent longitudinal study of professional development (Porter et al., 2000), using self-reports of change among 287 teachers, found "little change in overall teaching practice" after three years: "teachers changed little in terms of the content they teach, the pedagogy they use to teach it, and their emphasis on performance goals for students," even though individual teachers did sometimes show moderate change. Porter et al. felt that their findings "add support to the concept that both teaching and professional development are typically individual experiences" (p. ES-10). Even though teachers may have learned about or even espouse a new theory or practice, they may not, for other reasons, adopt it. Teachers make judgments about whether or not to actually implement a practice based on **instrumentality** (how well the new practice was described and presented), **congruence** (how well new practices conform to teachers' current philosophy and practice), and **cost** (how much benefit there might be in using the new practice, weighed against the time and energy required to enact it) (Doyle & Ponder, 1977). Lortie (1975) proposed that there is a culture of school teaching, directed by three norms, that makes it harder for teachers and schools to change: the norm of conservatism (teachers teach as they themselves were taught in school), the norm of presentism (teachers focus on the short term, uncertain of the future), and the norm individualism (reliance on self for knowledge and skills, practice driven by trial and error and personality).

Elmore (1996) provides a good summary of the change process:

> Changing teaching practice even for committed teachers takes a long time, and several cycles of trial and error; teachers have to feel that there is some compelling reason for them to practice differently, with the best direct evidence being that students learn better; and teachers need feedback from sources they trust about whether students are actually learning what they are taught. (Elmore, 1996, p. 24)

However, another perspective on teacher change is that teachers change all the time (Richardson & Anders, 1994); they are just more resistant to externally driven change (as opposed to change that they initiate on their own) or change that goes against their existing beliefs and values. We may not always be able to see the change if it is masked by the difference between a teacher's espoused theory and actual practice. Most research on teacher change relies on teachers' self-reports of change, and the attitudes, beliefs, and knowledge that teachers express are not always played out in what they actually do in the classroom (Magnusson, Borko, & Krajcik, 1994).

Some current research has also looked at whether the model of professional development makes a difference in teacher change. Porter et al. (2000) found that when change happened, it was more often the result of reform type (nontraditional) professional development that was longer in duration and included "collective participation" (several teachers from the same school), active learning, and "coherence" with teachers' goals and district standards. A recent large-scale survey (Garet et al., 2001) lends support to the idea that *model* of professional development is not as important to teacher learning and change as are the *features* of the professional development. This survey randomly sampled 1,027 teachers who had participated in a range of activities sponsored under the Eisenhower program of funding for math and science professional development. Outcomes were self-reports of changes in knowledge and practices. Researchers specifically looked at three "structural features" promoted in the literature as features of quality professional development (Loucks-Horsley, Hewson, Love, & Stiles, 1998): the *form* of the activity (reform or traditional), the *duration* of the activity (contact hours and span), and degree of *collective participation* (how much it involved teachers from the same school or grade). Other independent variables included "core features" of the professional development activity: the *content* of the activity (how much it focused on content knowledge in math and science), how much the activity included *active learning*, and how much the activity was in *coherence* with other activities the teachers had participated in, or with state or district standards. School (percent of minority enrollment, percent of students eligible for free lunch) and teacher characteristics (gender, subject [math or science], grade level, certification, and years of teaching experience) were also considered. Researchers found that three fourths of all Eisenhower professional development activities were traditional, and half of all activities (traditional and reform) focused strongly on content. Reform-type activities were more likely to have active learning and coherence, but some traditional activities had active learning and coherence, and some reform activities did not. "Many staff development activities do not have features of high quality, whether they are structured as reform or traditional" (p. 935). Reform activities (study groups, mentoring) were of longer duration and span: longer activities were related to positive effect on knowledge, to content, to active learning, and to coherence. Teachers reporting knowledge gain were also more likely to report changing practice. Coherence exerted a strong influence. However, type of professional development was important only indirectly, in that reform activities had more of the structural and core features, and these factors influenced knowledge and practice outcomes. Researchers found that the most important of these features of professional development (for increasing knowledge and practice) were a focus on content; opportunities for hands-on, active learning; and greater coherence of the professional development to school and district standards. The authors conclude: "to improve professional development, it is more important to focus on the duration, collective participation, and the core features (i.e., content, active learning, and coherence) than type" (Garet et al., p. 936).

Overall, researchers seem to agree that, for teacher change to happen, professional development should:

- **Be of longer duration.** Professional development is more effective in changing teachers' practice (at least as self-reported) when it is of longer duration (Porter et al., 2000). Longer-term professional development permits more time for teachers to learn about their own practice, especially if it includes follow-up (Joyce & Showers, 1995; Stein et al., 1999).

- **Make a strong connection between what is learned in the professional development and the teacher's own work context.** This is especially relevant if the professional development is organized outside of the school (as the majority is). Fingeret and Cockley (1992) found that the effectiveness of any given professional development activity depended upon how well a teacher could tie what they learned in professional development back to their own work situation. Professional development needs to help teachers plan for application and to identify and strategize barriers to application that they will face once back in their programs (Ottoson, 1997): "devoting no time or little time for synthesis, integration, and planning beyond the (professional development) program is inadequate preparation for application. Helping participants anticipate and plan for barriers may facilitate practice changes" (p. 105).

- **Include a strong emphasis on analysis and reflection, rather than just demonstrating techniques.** Asking teachers to explain and defend what they currently think and do contributes to reflectiveness and change in teaching practice (Bollough, Koachak, Crow, Hobbs, and Stoke, 1997). Arlin (1999) argues that professional development cannot, in and of itself, help teachers become "wise," unless it has a focus not just on "external" knowledge (new practices and techniques) but on helping teachers acquire the "internal" knowledge of a wise teacher: (1) factual knowledge of teaching and their subject matter, (2) procedural knowledge of teaching strategies and when to use them, (3) a sense of context for instruction, (4) an awareness of relative values of and priorities of their peers and students, and (5) an uncertainty about teaching decisions and a willingness to take risks when participating with students. Arlin claims that the final three of these are what differentiate the "wise" teacher from the "expert" teacher, and that a sense of context, relativism, and uncertainty is evidence of "mature, adult thought." Joyce (1983) maintains that teachers need "executive control" over a new approach: knowing *when* and *why* to use a strategy, not just *how* to use it. Guskey (1997, 1999) and Sparks (1994, 1995) advocate professional development that focuses on learning rather than on teaching; on problem-solving and reflectiveness rather than on acquiring new techniques; and on embedding change within the program rather than on individual change.

- **Focus on helping teachers to study their students' thinking,** not just try new techniques or even listen more to their students. One study found that change was sustained over longer periods of time when math teachers were trained and supported to really understand what their students were thinking, and teachers had a base from which to generalize practices to other situations and continue learning (Carpenter &

Franke, 1998). In another study, teacher inquiry about student learning, student work, and the conditions that support better performance was a powerful tool for changing teacher practice and ultimately changing school structure (Ancess, 2000).

- **Include a variety of activities,** such as theory, demonstration, practice, feedback, and classroom application (Joyce & Showers, 1995; Joyce et al., 1995; Mazzarella, 1980). If professional development is short-term or one-shot, it needs to be followed by assistance to help teachers implement (Stein & Wang, 1988), because "teachers are more likely to learn from direct observation of practice and trial and error in their own classrooms than they are from abstract descriptions of teaching" (Elmore, 1996, p. 24). Professional development should also follow principles of adult learning: establish a supportive environment, acknowledge teachers' prior experience, , help teachers consider how new learning applies to their specific teaching situation, and encourage teachers to make their implicit knowledge about teaching (their "craft knowledge") explicit (Gardner, 1996; Tibbetts, Kutner, Hemphill, and Jones, 1991).
- **Encourage teachers from the same workplace to participate together.** "Professional development is more effective when teachers participate with others from their school, grade, or department" (Porter et al., 2000, p. ES-9).

The research on teacher effectiveness and teacher change provided important background information to help us understand teacher change for our study. We saw that we needed to gauge teachers' thinking and acting over time, not just before and after the professional development, since change can be slow. In our study, we decided to define teacher change as differences (before and after professional development and over time) in teachers' thinking and action, so as to allow the broadest possible range for what "counts" as change.

We also became aware that we needed to plan a professional development intervention that, regardless of the model of professional development in which teachers would participate, included effective features, as indicated by the research. The professional development activity should: be of longer duration (not one session), focus on a variety of active learning activities, help teachers to be reflective about their practice, help teachers focus on students' needs, and involve teachers in thinking about how they could apply what they learned once back in their classrooms.

Factors That Contribute to Teacher Change

Another area of interest for our research team was school and individual teacher factors that play a role in influencing the effectiveness of professional development on teacher change. If teacher change is not an automatic outcome of even the highest-quality professional development, what is known about the factors that mediate between professional development and teacher change?

Evaluating the effectiveness of professional development requires researchers to collect data not just about the teacher but also about the teacher's context. This is especially true if researchers want to understand the connection between professional development and student learning because, while the teacher is always the link between professional development and student achievement, teacher practice is only one of many factors affecting student learning. Researchers call this the "dilution" effect of professional development: the actual impact of the professional development is diluted by all of the other factors that support or hinder teachers from making change. The dilution effect is the primary criticism behind arguments against judging professional development according to "process-product" research (i.e., the process of professional development does not always result in the product of student achievement) (Adey, 1995).

Several researchers have come up with categories of factors that mediate the influence of professional development. Gusky and Sparks (1996) discuss three categories of factors:[12]

1. **Content characteristics**—"what" the professional development covers; the credibility and scope of the practice or concept being conveyed
2. **Process variables**—the "how" of professional development, the models and type of follow-up
3. **Context characteristics**—the "who," "when," "where," and "why" of the professional development; the organizational or system culture; and expectations and incentives for using new practices

Ottoson (1997) names five factors that affect "application" of what is learned in training:

1. **Educational**—the characteristics of the professional development, including quality of facilitation, organization, and methods
2. **Innovation**—the ideas, practices, and strategies taught or suggested to teachers during the professional development
3. **Predisposing**—the characteristics of the teacher, including their motivation for attending, background knowledge, and pre-existing attitudes
4. **Enabling**—the teacher's skill in applying the new strategy; factors in the context of the teacher's program, including resources, authority, and opportunity to apply
5. **Reinforcing**—the factors in the context of the teacher's program that support the teacher in applying knowledge, such as help from colleagues, the director, and students

For our study, we found it useful to separate the factors that influence the effectiveness of professional development into individual factors and contextual factors. In the section below, we first review the research on individual factors: who teachers are and what they bring to the professional development. We then discuss the research on school factors that support change after professional development.

Individual Factors

A significant body of research exists on the social psychology of teachers, some of which is relevant to the question of whether teachers' experience, dispositions, and motivations support or prevent them from learning and changing.

Teachers' motivation to attend professional development is a key factor in change. Stout (1996) poses four motivations teachers have for participating in professional development:

---

[12] Guskey and Sparks also consider administrator knowledge and practices, plus parent knowledge and practices, which are important factors mediating teacher change and student learning, because parents and administrators affect curriculum policies that dictate the types of changes teachers can make.

salary enhancement, certificate maintenance, career mobility (building their resume to move up the ladder into administration or pursue other careers), and gaining new skills/knowledge. Livneh and Livneh (1999) surveyed 256 K–12 educators in Oregon to gauge their motivation to learn, background characteristics, and the amount of professional continuing education they had attended in the previous year. They identified three factors that predicted participation: (1) high internal motivation to learn, (2) high external motivation to learn (wanted career advancement or to network with others), and (3) lower levels of formal education. The researchers argue that this finding:

> ...lends support to the notion that people with comparatively lower educational levels in professional fields often recognize the need to upgrade their educational skills and abilities. They may also be beginning their professional career, a time when they recognize the need for additional information and skill building. (Livneh & Livneh, 1999, p.100)

Strong motivation may mitigate other factors that are not supportive of change. Ottoson's research (1997) with 27 participants in a health education program indicates that strong predisposition (motivation to attend, background knowledge, and attitudes) may be especially important: "strong predisposition has the potential to overcome some of the rough terrain of context and can compensate for the relative absence of enabling and reinforcing factors...reinforcement with predisposition supported application but reinforcement without predisposition was not likely to lead to application" (p. 104). In other words, teachers strongly motivated to take action on the topic may be able to overcome a school or program situation that doesn't encourage them to do so. Based on the belief that motivation is key to the effectiveness of professional development, Jones and Lowe (1985) argue that teachers need individual plans for ongoing professional development, built on self-evaluation of their own needs (including reflection questions, case studies of learners, and input from peers).

Joyce (1983) studied teachers' motivation to participate in professional development and categorized teachers as learners and consumers of professional development. Based on teachers' participation in (a) formal systems (courses, workshops, coaching/supervision), (b) informal systems (exchanges with other teachers and professionals), and (c) personal activities (reading, leisure activities), Joyce proposes five categories to describe teachers' states as learners:

1. **Omnivores** are teachers who "actively use every available aspect of the formal and informal systems available to them" (p.163).
2. **Active consumers** are teachers who keep busy in one or more of the domains or systems.
3. **Passive consumers** are teachers who go along with professional development opportunities that arise but don't seek them out.
4. **Entrenched** teachers are suspicious of change and take courses only in areas where they already feel successful; they may actively or surreptitiously oppose new ideas.
5. **Withdrawn** teachers are actively opposed to engaging in one or all three domains.

Joyce claims that omnivores generate energy for the system in which they are engaged, while entrenched and withdrawn teachers consume energy from the system. An entrenched or withdrawn teacher with influence within the school—even informal power—can act as a "gatekeeper," preventing any type of collective action, change, or improvement from occurring. Even the best professional development will not have an impact if there is a poor culture in the school, one in which there is a poor fit between teachers' states of growth and the culture that could support growth and new ideas from professional development. Another thread in the literature relates to what Fuller and Bown (1975) call teachers' "concerns." They propose that teachers have three types of concerns: (1) **self-survival** (controlling classes, having adequate knowledge, finding one's place in the school, satisfying others' expectations of them); (2) **task** (planning instruction and handling the administrative work), and (3) **impact** (meeting students' individual needs and increasing students' motivation). Ghaith and Shaaban (1999) argue that these concerns change over time; new teachers are more concerned about classroom tasks and experienced teachers are more concerned about impact. Kagan (1992) supports the idea that beginning teachers are more concerned about self-survival. Hord, Rutherford, Huling-Austin, and Hall (1987) expanded on this theory to explain that as teachers change by adopting new attitudes and practices, they have different types of concerns: personal concerns about how change will affect them, task concerns about how to manage new practices, and impact concerns about how new practice will affect students. Differing concerns may dictate what types and subjects of professional development teachers will participate in. A 1999 NCES survey on K–12 teacher participation in professional development found that experienced teachers are less likely to participate in professional development on topics of classroom management and new teaching methods; newer teachers are more likely to participate in mentoring than more experienced teachers (Lewis et al., 1999). Other researchers challenge the notion that new teachers are only interested in classroom management and techniques, claiming that new teachers are concerned with content and teaching ethics as well as with classroom management (Grossman, 1992).

Another individual factor well studied in relation to teacher change is teachers' level of self-efficacy, a concept first outlined by Bandura (1995). Bandura defined self-efficacy as "beliefs in one's capabilities to organize and execute the courses of action required to manage prospective situations" (p. 2). Stronger self-efficacy among teachers has been related to student achievement (Goddard, Hoy, & Hoy, 2000; Tschannen-Moran, Hoy, & Hoy, 1998). Professional development researchers then tested hypotheses about whether teachers' level of self-efficacy was related to how much they changed. Overall, they found that:

- **Self-efficacy is related to individual factors.** Ross (1994) found that new teachers had high levels of general self-efficacy[13] but low levels of personal self-efficacy (i.e., a strong belief in the power of education but a weak belief about whether they personally could be successful as teachers), whereas experienced teachers felt just the opposite (i.e., a strong belief in their own competence as teachers but a weak belief in education's power to reach all students; that success is "limited by factors beyond school control," p. 382). Ross feels that this research confirms that teachers' sense of self-efficacy is more stable among more experienced teachers and that "to change it

---

[13] "General" self-efficacy is the belief that education itself can be successful with all students, regardless of background and abilities. "Personal" self-efficacy is the belief that teachers themselves are "instrumental to the learning of their students" (Smylie, 1988, p. 23). "Collective" self-efficacy is the common belief held by groups of teachers that together they are successful.

in a material way (would) likely take something more substantial (e.g., a dramatic shift in teaching assignment that often comes with a change of school or an involuntary alteration of curriculum) than a routine in-service program" (p. 391).

- **Stronger self-efficacy going into professional development affected teacher change.** Smylie (1988) found that teachers were more likely to change as a result of professional development if they had high personal self-efficacy. Guskey (1988) found that teachers with high levels of self-efficacy were more likely to adopt new practices, but that high self-efficacy was also associated with effectiveness (although how "effectiveness" was measured is not defined), and so teachers with high self-efficacy least *needed* to adopt new practices. Tschannen-Moran et al. (1998) concluded that teachers with strong self-efficacy may be less motivated to learn and try new things.

- **Professional development in turn affected self-efficacy.** Stein and Wang (1988) found that those who implemented a new practice showed an increase in self-efficacy; Ross (1998) found that teachers who did try new strategies initially showed a drop in self-efficacy but that self-efficacy increased again when they saw that the new strategy worked. Roberts, Henson, Tharp, and Moreno (2000) found that teachers who entered professional development with high levels of self-efficacy didn't change their feelings of self-efficacy much, no matter how long the professional development was, but that teachers who entered professional development with low levels of self-efficacy increased their sense of self-efficacy, proportional to the length of the professional development.

Other characteristics of teachers as individuals that researchers believe relate to teacher change include cognitive "style." Joughin (1992) proposes that some teachers have an analytic ability to understand a strategy and how to use it, whereas other teachers lack this ability and need more structure to grasp and then apply a new strategy. Similarly, developmental theory (Helsing et al., 2001) holds that all adults have "ways of knowing" that they bring to a learning task; specifically, a learner with an **instrumental** way of knowing would tend to see the trainer as an expert and look for the "right" answer; a learner with a **socializing** way of knowing would learn from others and see the trainer as a mentor; and a learner with a **self-authoring** way of knowing would want to bring their own knowledge to the learning process and understand that there may be no one right answer. Theories of cognitive style or development have implications for the fit between individual teachers' ways of knowing and the style of the professional development in which they participate; for example, teachers with an instrumental way of knowing may feel more comfortable in workshops lead by experts, whereas teachers with a self-authoring way of knowing may feel more comfortable in professional development activities (such as practitioner research) that allows or asks them to generate knowledge of their own.

Perhaps one of the largest subareas of investigation in the professional development and teacher education literature concerns teachers' reflectiveness. Schon (1983) began the discussion of how to help teachers develop a "stance" of looking at their own practice (reflection-in-practice, reflection-on-practice), by analyzing, adapting, and always challenging their assumptions, in a self-sustaining cycle of reflecting on their own theory and practice. Ferry and Ross-Gordon (1998) found that a reflective stance was not automatically related to years of teaching experience; some new teachers demonstrated a cyclical approach to problem solving, learning from one problem to inform the next, while some very experienced teachers used a sequential (noncyclical) approach to problem solving: when faced with a problem, they summon up their existing knowledge and choose the "best fit" solution from what they already know.

Based on what we learned from research on individual factors, we determined that we would ask questions about teachers' background (demographics, educational background, years of teaching in K–12 and adult education), their motivation for attending the NCSALL Professional Development, and their level of professional development "consumption." While we felt we could reliably obtain that information through questionnaire from all participants and analyze the data quantitatively, we knew it would not provide us with a full picture of teachers' motivations, dispositions, and reflectiveness as learners, teachers, program members, and members of the field. Therefore, we decided that more qualitative data, collected through extensive interviews with a subsample of the teachers in the study, might allow us to gain greater insight into how the teachers perceived themselves as learners and teachers.

School Factors

In addition to individual teacher factors, the literature on K–12 contains research on school factors that may also influence teacher change. Factors identified by researchers as mediating (hindering or supporting) teacher change include:

- **Leadership.** The school leadership has a role in readying teachers for change by creating a positive culture that lets teachers' attitudes change naturally when they see how and whether a new practice helps students' learning (Sparks, 1995). Principals that were too controlling and principal turnover negatively affected teacher education programs (Bollough et al., 1997).
- **Coherence.** Coherence is defined as the match between school adoption of particular reforms and individual professional development of teachers in that school; i.e., the school is working to improve the same problem or issue addressed by the professional development. The match can either be required (by the district) or voluntary (the school or teachers sought professional development related to the school-improvement issue). Recent research by Garet et al. (2001) indicates that teachers gain more knowledge and change practices when there is a match between school or district standards and goals. When change is voluntary (i.e., there is no concurrent reform effort at the school level), then leadership or supportive school factors (such as teachers' access to decision-making) were not as important in promoting change as the teachers' own beliefs (Smylie, 1988).
- **Collegiality within the school.** The movement for teacher professional communities within schools grew from the belief that one can't take individual teachers out of their environment, train and change them, then put them back into the same environment and expect them to change that environment; rather, teachers need a community of teachers within the school, so they can learn together about their work as they apply that learning (Calderón, 1999; Grossman, Wineburg, & Woolworth, 2000). Most professional development researchers view collegiality as a necessary organizational support to professional development (Sparks & Loucks-Horsley,

1990). In a review of previous research about the relationship between school culture and the effectiveness of professional development, Olson et al. (1991) found that collegiality emerged as a key indicator. Interactions with colleagues seem to help teachers develop a "body of technical knowledge about what teaching practices are likely to be effective" (p. 23) and a sense of their own competence (Smylie, 1988). Other research suggests that more collaboration within a school increases teachers' commitment to teaching (Rosenholtz, 1986), which may in turn support openness to new knowledge and practices. When teachers don't have opportunity to talk to colleagues about strategies learned during professional development, they are less likely to implement them (Gardner, 1996; Huberman & Miles, 1984); the greater the communication, the more likely teachers were to adopt the new practice (Adey, 1995). By contrast, Joyce (1983) found that professional development was less effective when there was an entrenched teacher who acted as gatekeeper to spoil/prevent other teachers from adopting new strategies. In short:

Teaching practice is unlikely to change as a result of exposure to training, unless that training also brings with it some kind of external normative structure, a network of social relationships that personalize that structure, and supports interaction around problems of practice. (Elmore, 1996, p. 21)

Our review of the K–12 research on individual and school factors that mediate between professional development and teacher change provided valuable insights for the development of our study. We recognized that, if we wanted to understand whether a particular professional development intervention was effective, we could not collect information only about the quality of and teacher's participation in the professional development. We would also need to collect information about individual teacher and adult education program factors that research has indicated will help or hinder teachers from making change. Specifically, we needed to collect information about individual factors such as teachers' educational background, length and type of teaching experience, and motivation to attend the NCSALL Professional Development. We also needed to collect information about teachers' program situation: size and type of program, leadership within the program, amount of collegiality within the program, whether other teachers from the same adult education program also attended the professional development, and whether the adult education program where they worked was also simultaneously addressing (through program reforms) the same topic as covered by the professional development.

Before concluding our review of the research on teacher change and professional development, we needed to review any specific literature related to adult education teachers. Our review is presented below.

A Review of the Adult Education Literature on Professional Development and Teacher Change in Adult Education

A search for primary research in adult education on professional development and teacher change is a short one. We found a few surveys and evaluations of professional development activities and systems, and several technical reports related to evaluating the state of adult education overall. Much of this information focuses on the characteristics of adult education teachers and the programs and situations within which they work, rather than on the effectiveness of professional development for teacher change. This review, however, helped us to identify some of the factors specific to the adult education context that may influence teachers' abilities to change.

Professional Development in Adult Education

Professional development in the adult education field is organized primarily through statewide professional development systems, rather than through school districts as it is in K–12 (Belzer, Drennan, & Smith, 2001; Tolbert, 2001). Beginning with the passage of the National Literacy Act in 1992, and the establishment of State Literacy Resource Centers, more states attempted to build comprehensive statewide systems, rather than rely on programs to offer what professional development they could. At least one researcher, however, has claimed that such a delivery system itself reduces the likelihood that professional development will affect teacher change: because most states do not have a common curriculum for adult education programs to use, statewide professional development by necessity must focus on broad teaching and adult learning topics, leaving individual teachers to attempt the difficult task of adapting such general information to their specific classroom situation (Leahy, 1986). It is also more difficult to create "coherence" between program improvement efforts and professional development activities when the majority of activities are delivered at the state level; a recent evaluation of adult basic education (ABE) professional development found a continuing division between professional development and program development (RMC Research Corporation, 1996). Also, one of the realities of the adult education field is that professional development receives far less funding than K–12 professional development.[14]

Perhaps because of the predominance of statewide systems for planning and conducting adult education professional development, much of the professional development attended by adult education practitioners is offered at centrally organized workshops and conferences rather than in the teachers' own program (Wilson & Corbett, 2001). The predominant form of professional development in ABE is short-term training and single-session workshops (Crocker, 1987; Kutner, Herman, Stephenson, and Webb, 1991; Tibbetts et al., 1991). Even with the advent of alternative forms of professional development, this reliance on one model of professional development persists: the most recent national evaluation (RMC Research Corporation, 1996), which surveyed all states' use of federal monies for professional development, by conducting interviews with state administrators, trainers, and more than 1,000 adult educators, found that single-session workshops accounted for 38% of all

---

[14] The federal government spent $619 million on K–12 professional development in 1993, and additional "state investments in professional development probably range from less than 1 percent to over 3 percent of total state spending on public education" (p. 3, Center for Policy and Research in Education Policy Brief, 1995, available at http://www.ed.gov/pubs/CPRE/t61/t61c.html). It is interesting to note that more federal dollars were allocated in 1993 for professional development of K–12 teachers than were allocated in 2002 by the federal government for the entire adult education budget, which was approximately $500 million. Stout (1996) estimated staff development spending in K–12 at an average of $1,700 per teacher per year in 1994 dollars. According to the Department of Education Adult Education Human Investment Impact report 1994–1998, combined federal and state funding divided by total enrollment for 1996 calculated out to an adult education per *pupil* spending of approximately $249 per adult student (Hhttp://www.ed.gov/offices/OVAE/9499hinvest.htmlH). We could not find figures for per teacher spending on adult education professional development.

professional development activities, followed by institutes or courses (24%), and statewide or regional conferences (11%). Twenty-seven percent of activities were less structured, or "reform," activities (study groups, technical assistance, independent study). Conferences accounted for 40% of the money spent, even though they accounted for only 11% of the activities. Eighty percent of practitioners surveyed attended at least some professional development the year prior to the survey (1994); of these, 57% attended a conference. There was no difference in participation between full-time and part-time practitioners, but those 20% who received no training were more likely to be younger, have fewer academic degrees, and be less experienced. When polled, almost half of teachers surveyed listed an activity that had an impact on their work, but 30% said no activities they attended had an impact on them and 18% didn't respond.

In recent years, some states and projects have begun to promote "reform" types of professional development, such as practitioner research, mentoring, and study circles. Experimentation with practitioner research has happened at the state level (Virginia), the university level (University of Pennsylvania PALPIN project), and the project level (Georgia/Literacy South, System for Adult Basic Education Support Math Team, NCSALL's Practitioner Dissemination and Research Network) level, with groups of teachers from different programs working together to do research, either individually or collectively. At least one national organization has made an attempt to document the findings of these practitioners so that others can learn from them (Sherman, Green, Taylor, and Greenberg, 1997). However, the predominant form of professional development remains workshops (Tolbert, 2001).

In a recent survey of 423 adult education teachers (Sabatini et al., 2000), which was aimed primarily at more full-time, "professionalized" adult education teachers, teachers reported that their primary purpose for professional development was learning techniques they could use immediately. Effective instructional techniques for teaching reading and writing were a top content priority. Their top two priorities for participating in professional development were to "add to my instructional skills" and "add to my knowledge of teaching adults." Researchers found that teachers with five or fewer years of experience more often wanted knowledge about how to teach adults than did more experienced teachers. The survey also found that teachers who participated in collaborative working groups were more satisfied with that type of professional development than with workshops.

Although individual states and projects have evaluated their professional development efforts (Drennon, 1994; Fingeret & Cockley, 1992; Foucar-Szocki et al., 1997; Kuhne, Weirauch, & Doyle, 1997; Lytle et al., 1992b) and a framework for evaluating the effectiveness of adult education professional development has been proposed (Kutner & Tibbetts, 1997) and is being adopted in some states (e.g., Pennsylvania), no larger-scale or longitudinal studies of the outcomes of professional development for adult education teachers existed at the time we began our study.

Teachers in Adult Education

Young, Fleischman, Fitzgerald, and Morgan (1995), through the National Evaluation of Adult Education programs (more than 2,600 local programs), found that:

- Adult education program staff are heavily part time: 36% of programs do not have any full-time staff (teaching or administration); 59% do not have even one full-time instructional staff member; and the ratio of part-time to full-time teachers is 4 to 1.
- Forty percent of full-time and 33% of part-time instructors have master's degrees or higher.
- Eighty percent of full-time and just under half of part-time instructors have taught in adult education for more than three years (meaning a little more than half of all part-time instructors have taught for less than three years).
- More than 55% of teachers teach more than one instructional component (ABE, preGED, GED, ESOL,[15] etc.), rather than specializing in one, making the need for more professional development on a broader range of topics desirable.

The difficulty of providing high-quality professional development in adult education is exacerbated by the structure of the system itself. Teachers in adult education are hindered by factors that make it hard for them to simply know what professional development opportunities are available, and then to participate (Burt & Keenan, 1998). Wilson & Corbett (2001), after interviewing 60 adult education "decision-makers" and practitioners from 10 states, categorize these hindering factors as:

- **Distance**—professional development is not offered locally through the program but at state-organized, centrally located venues, which requires practitioners to travel
- **Time constraints**—working part time, as the majority of adult education teachers do, makes it hard for them to participate, and they are generally not paid to do so
- **Information gaps**—infrequent contact with other practitioners in and out of the program means that program directors and other supervisors serve as "gatekeepers" through which new information must pass
- **Goal mismatch**—the mismatch between the programs' goals and individual practitioners' professional interests, particularly evident where the program's goal is for students to pass the GED and practitioners are interested in preparing students for lifelong learning
- **Lack of face-to-face interaction**—teachers rarely have a chance to meet and talk, resulting in a "disjunction" between how they would like to learn and the opportunities for learning open to them

Wilson and Corbett conclude:

Currently, the conditions of the ABE occupation are such that those in the field will never be able to participate systematically in the very activities they see as necessary to doing their jobs well. Educators claim the desire for professional development is present;

---

[15] ABE stands for adult basic education; these adult learners are typically defined by their grade level reading equivalency of 0–5. GED stands for General Educational Development; these adult learners are typically defined by their grade level reading equivalency of 8–12 and by their stated goal of passing the GED test. PreGED stands for pre-General Educational Development; these adult learners are typically defined by their grade level reading equivalency of 5–8. ESOL stands for English for speakers of other languages; these adult learners are typically defined by their limited oral English skills, which may or may not be related to their reading and writing English skills.

readily accessible opportunities to fulfill that desire are most notably not. (Wilson & Corbett, 2001, p. 26)

Turnover of adult education teachers may exacerbate the challenge of professional development, with new teachers coming into the field regularly. The exact rate of turnover, however, is not well documented. Darkenwald (1986) reports on one study of retention (Boggs and Travis, 1982) of 145 adult education teachers; after 7 years, 45 (31%) of 145 remained, most having left for full-time K–12 jobs or having left education entirely. The Sabatini et al. (2000) survey of 423 adult education teachers[16] indicated that about 40% had taught in the field less than five years, from a sample that consisted of almost 60% full-time teachers; in their sample, 43% of part-time teachers (which constitute the bulk of the national population of adult education teachers[17]) had been in the field less than five years.

This same survey found that the majority of adult education teachers in their sample were at one time K–12 teachers and they typically have K–12 certification (Sabatini et al., 2000). However, adult education teachers also need professional development focused on teaching adults. One survey of states (Tolbert, 2001) found that only nine states require adult education teachers to get preservice training specifically related to teaching adults. The 1995 National Evaluation of Adult Education programs (Young et al., 1995) found that only 18% of full-time staff and 8% of part-time staff were specifically certified in adult education.

The review of adult education literature related to teachers and professional development underscored for the research design team the fact that the adult education field, and perhaps the teachers who work within it, has some unique structural features that may mediate (support or hinder) teacher change. Together with our experience as adult education teachers, professional developers, and administrators, we hypothesized that these factors might influence how teachers change as a result of professional development:

Individual factors:

- **Type of teaching** (ABE/GED/preGED/ESOL) teacher does. In addition to any differences in teachers' perspectives as a result of teaching these different learner populations, many adult education teachers teach multiple populations.
- **Whether teacher ever taught in K–12.** Some adult education teachers may never have taught before they began working in adult education (and some of these teachers may not be certified or have a bachelor's degree, unlike K–12 teachers).
- **Full-time/part-time status.** The majority of adult education instructors are part time, unlike K–12 instructors.

---

[16] This was a self-response survey study, which specifically attempted to target "professional" teachers; sampling was done by mailing surveys to state-identified "quality" programs in large states with greater numbers of full-time teachers, making the self-selected sample deliberately skewed toward more full-time teachers. The final sample was 59% full time, 41% part time (Sabatini et al., 2000), a full-time/part-time ratio substantially different from the U.S. Department of Education estimates (see footnote 16).

[17] 1998 DOE data on numbers of part-time and full-time adult education personnel: 13% of state-administered adult education program personnel (including administrators) are full time, so the percentage of full-time teachers is probably considerably less than 13%. Thirty-nine percent of personnel were part time, 48% were volunteer (see www.ed.gov/offices/OVAE/98personnel.html).

Program factors:

- **Enrollment policies.** Unlike K–12, adult education programs often allow adults to enter at any time during the semester or year, which may affect how teachers deliver instruction.
- **Access to prep time.** Many adult education teachers are paid by the hour and do not, unlike their colleagues in K–12, receive paid prep time.
- **Access to benefits.** Since most adult education instructors are part time, many do not receive benefits (paid sick time, vacation, pension, medical insurance) as part of their adult education job.
- **Paid professional development release time.** Part-time instructors, particularly, may not receive paid time to attend professional development.
- **Required use of curriculum.** Unlike K–12, where states and school districts often require teachers to follow a specific curriculum or framework (usually geared to test requirements), adult education is much more varied; programs may have a required curriculum, and some GED teachers teach only to the GED test, but other teachers are free to develop their own curriculum for their own classes.
- **Teaching situation (class vs. individualized).** Many adult education classes are organized as "individualized group instruction," where adult learners "drop-in" to learning centers, instruction is organized via workbooks, and students work individually while sitting among other adult students also working on their workbooks; the teacher rotates among students providing one-on-one assistance or checking answers. Other adult educators (more so in ESOL instructional settings) teach within a traditional class structure.

Results of the Literature Review

Overall, this review of the literature on professional development in both K–12 and adult education provided us with a rationale for the design of the study (testing multiple models of professional development that could be appropriate for the field of adult education), and the elements of professional development that make it most effective for teacher growth. It also informed our understanding of what is already known about how teachers change and about the factors that have been shown to affect change, and the review confirmed the factors related to adult education context that should be investigated in our study. We then used the knowledge gained from our review to design the study methodology: the professional development models, the list of expected and preferred outcomes, and the data collection protocols that would allow us to gauge such outcomes among the teachers who participated. The methodology of the study is presented in the next section.

Methodology

Research Context

We conducted the study in Massachusetts, Connecticut, and Maine in order to make data collection cost effective yet allow us to achieve a sample size of 100 teachers, large enough for quantitative analysis of data. Locating the study across three states also provided the advantage of including a wider range of program and system factors. All three states offered the full range of services to adult basic education, ESOL, and GED learners, and in all states the administrative home of the adult education system was the state education agency. Key differences among states include type of program (Maine and Connecticut programs were primarily school-based local educational agencies, or LEAs, whereas Massachusetts has a mix of LEAs and community-based organizations, or CBOs) and type of curriculum (Connecticut is a CASAS[18] state; curriculum in Massachusetts is program-driven but influenced by state curriculum frameworks; curriculum in Maine is program-driven but influenced by the Equipped for the Future standards[19]).

Sample

The sample consisted of a total of 106 women and men from these three New England states. One hundred of these teachers participated in up to 18 hours of professional development in one of three models of professional development (multisession workshop, mentor teacher group, or practitioner research group); the other six people were nonparticipant teachers who served as a comparison group.[20] From the 100 participants, 18 teachers were randomly selected (six from each model) to serve as a subsample.

In each state, there were five different professional development groups (one multisession workshop, two mentor teacher groups, two practitioner research groups), so that a total of 15 different professional development groups across three models and three states were conducted between July 1998 and June 1999. The number of participants who enrolled in and completed each activity, by state, is included in Table 1 below.

Participants were listed as completers if they attended at least two thirds (12 of the 18 hours) of the professional development required. If they completed less than 12 hours, they were considered dropouts. Total dropouts equaled 16 out of 100.

To be eligible to participate in the NCSALL Professional Development, participants had to be an adult basic education teacher, adult English for speakers of other languages teacher, or adult secondary education teacher who taught at least one class or tutored at least one student. Each state recruited participants as they would for any other professional development activity. Interested teachers were not assigned to a particular model; they were free to participate in any model they wanted to attend. In most cases, because of geography, teachers participated in the model offered closest to them. We paid participating teachers a stipend for their participation,[21] which was less than what they would have been paid hourly for the same number of teaching hours but adequate for the time they spent providing us data

---

[18] Comprehensive Assessment System for Adult Students.

[19] Equipped for the Future (EFF) is a system reform initiative of the National Institute for Literacy, designed to provide learner content standards.

[20] These were teachers who had originally registered for one of the professional development activities but then either did not show up or confirm their registration, thus constituting a very small "comparison group" for this study.

[21] Each participant who completed more than 12 hours of professional development *and* completed three questionnaires received $200. The 18 subsample teachers received an additional $150 for allowing us to interview them three times and visit their classroom. Practitioner research group participants who submitted a final write-up of their practitioner research project received an additional $125, to compensate for this extra time.

Table 1: Number of Participants in Professional Development, by State and Group

Number of Participants, by Model	Conneticut		Maine		Massachusetts		Total	
	Enroll	Complete	Enroll	Complete	Enroll	Complete	Enroll	Complete
Multisession Workshop	15	15	11	11	9	9	35	35
Mentor Teacher Group	9	8	10	8	9	8	28	24
Practitioner Research Group	12	6	12	9	13	10	37	25
Totals	*36*	*29*	*33*	*28*	*31*	*27*	*100*	*84*[22]

We collected data from participants at three points in time: (1) Wave One, before the professional development started; (2) Wave Two, immediately after the professional development was finished; and (3) Wave Three, one year after the professional development was finished. Of the 106 individuals for whom we collected data in Wave One, we were able to collect usable follow-up data in Wave Three from 99 individuals.[23]

Individual Characteristics of Teachers in the Sample

Table 2 provides information on the basic individual characteristics of respondents in the sample.

As the table shows, the overwhelming majority of participants were white females. The age groups ranged from 26–30 to more than 60 years old. About two thirds of the teachers (67%) were in the 41–60 age groups. The composition of teachers, by role, was approximately even among teachers of ABE/preGED students (lower literacy levels), ESOL students, GED students, and those who taught multiple types of students (ABE/preGED/GED).

Approximately half of the teachers had completed formal education higher than a bachelor's degree (either a master's or doctoral degree) and less than 8% had either an associate's degree or a high school diploma or GED. More than half of the sample (53%) reported that they had not completed any *formal* coursework in adult education (undergraduate- or graduate-level courses in adult education, adult basic education, adult literacy, or English for speakers of other languages). More than 80% of the respondents in this study had participated in minimal coursework (up to three formal courses) in the field of adult education.[24]

---

[22] Even though 84 teachers completed the study, we only have final and complete data from 83 teachers; one teacher who completed the workshops never returned the second and third questionnaires.

[23] Out of 104 individuals who gave us such data, 13 individuals reported they had left the field sometime between Wave One and Wave Three. Of the 91 still in the field, 82 reported that they were still teaching in a program and the remaining 9 were still working in an adult education program or in an adult education-related organization but not teaching. This equals a teacher turnover rate of 21% over approximately 18 months.

[24] Massachusetts teachers on average reported having taken more courses (*M*=2.8) than either Connecticut (*M*=2.0) or Maine (*M*=1.1) residents; however, these differences were not statistically significant.

Table 2: Individual Characteristics of Teachers in the Sample

Characteristics	n	Percentage
Gender (*n*=106)		
Female	88	83%
Male	18	17%
Race (*n*=106)		
White	97	91.5%
Black	4	3.8%
Hispanic	5	4.7%
Age (*n*=99)		
26–30 years	6	6.1%
31–40 years	17	17.2%
41–50 years	32	32.3%
51–60 years	34	34.3%
61+ years	10	10.1%
Formal Education (level completed) (*n*=106)		
< B.A.	8	7.5%
= B.A.	46	43.4%
> B.A.	52	49.1%
Teaching Role (*n*=102)		
ABE (0–4)	14	13.7%
PreGED (5–8)	4	3.9%
ESOL	26	25.5%
Combination (ABE/preGED/GED)	23	22.5%
GED/Adult Secondary	28	27.5%
Other (e.g., vocational ed)	7	6.9%

Sixty-five percent reported that they had, at some point, taught in the K–12 school system, while 30% of respondents indicated that adult education was their first teaching experience.[25] Of the 62 teachers in the sample who had experience teaching in the K–12 system, the median years teaching in K–12 was four. At the time of Wave One data collection, 10% of the teachers reported that they were still involved in teaching in the K–12 system. Massachusetts teachers were the least likely to have ever taught in the K–12 school system (47%), compared to three quarters of the teachers from Maine (74%) and Connecticut (73%) who had taught in K–12; differences among states was statistically significant (χ^2=6.5, df=2, p<.05).

Combining their experiences in K–12 and adult education, teachers in this study ranged from teaching less than one year to teaching for 34 years. We asked participants to tell us in Wave One how long they had been *teaching* in the field of adult education. The mean number of years teaching in adult education was 6.83; one third (32.4%) of the teachers reported they had taught in adult education for two years or less. The median number of years teaching in the field was five. Differences by state were not significant. Age correlated with both years

---

[25] We assume that the other 5% of the sample gained initial teaching experience outside these two arenas (e.g., church, overseas programs).

teaching in adult education and in K–12. Those who participated in the practitioner research group model had been teaching in the field significantly longer on average (M=11 years, $SD =$ 6.9) than individuals in the workshop (M=8.5 years, SD =6.3) or mentor teacher group (M=7 years, SD=6) (F=3.38, df=2, p<.05) models. Since we subsequently found that some of the participants had worked in the field (as administrators or counselors) for perhaps longer than they had been teaching, we asked in Wave Three how many years they had *worked* in the field of adult education. The mean number of years working in adult education was 8.8 (SD=6.4), and the median number of years was seven.

Eighty-five percent of the respondents reported that teaching was their primary role. The remaining 15% reported their primary role as administrator (9%), counselor (2%), professional developer (1%), or equal part teacher and counselor or teacher and director (3%).

Twenty-four percent of the sample was full time (full time being defined as working across all adult education jobs 35 hours or more a week). The mean number of hours *worked* per week across the sample was 23.5 (in Wave One, the mean was 23 hours, SD=11.5; in Wave Three, the mean was 24, SD=12.6). The mean number of hours they *taught* was 16.5 hours (M=17, SD=9.9, Wave One; M=16, SD=10.9, Wave Three). Age was negatively correlated with hours worked (r=-.20, p<.05); the older the teacher, the fewer hours she or he worked.

The majority of the teachers (80%) reported that their primary teaching situation was a classroom setting while 17% of the sample reported teaching individual students. Forty-eight percent of the teachers still working in the field by Wave Three received benefits as part of their adult education job, and 54% received paid prep time. Twenty-three percent of the sample reported receiving no paid professional development release time during the previous year; about three quarters of the sample (73%) reported that they received fewer than three days a year to participate in professional development activities. On average, individuals from Massachusetts reported receiving more hours of professional development release time (M=28, SD =21) than either Maine (M=15.6, SD=16.7) or Connecticut (M=10.8, SD=14), a statistically significant difference (F=8.83, df=2, p<.001).

There were no significant differences among teachers participating in the three professional development models in: venue of their first teaching experience (adult education or K–12); access to paid prep time; opportunities for collegiality; age; number of annual hours of paid professional development release time; access to benefits as part of their adult education job; teaching situation (ABE, GED, ESOL, etc.); or program type. The only significant difference among teachers by model was in number of hours per week working in adult education (mentor teacher group participants worked significantly fewer hours in adult education on average than did teachers in the other models) and number of years working in the field of adult education (practitioner research group participants had been working in adult education for longer, on average, than teachers in the other models).[26]

---

[26] Teachers who participated in mentor teacher groups worked an average of 15 hours a week in adult education (n=27, SD=9.4), compared to 26.6 hours per week for workshop participants (n=34, SD=10.86) and 23.6 hours per week for practitioner research group participants (n=36, SD=10.71), and this difference was significant (ANOVA F=9.10, df=2, p<.001). Teachers who participated in practitioner research had been working in adult education an average of 11 years (n=31, SD=6.94), compared to 7 years for mentor teacher group participants (n=28, SD=6.0) and 8.5 years for workshop participants (n=34, SD=6.25), and this difference was significant (ANOVA F=3.4, df=2, p<.05).

Program Characteristics of Teachers in the Sample

Table 3 on the following page provides a few of the general characteristics of the programs in which teachers in this study worked.

Table 3: General Program Characteristics of Teachers in the Sample

Problem Characteristics	Percentage Of Sample
Location	
Urban	52%
Suburban	27%
Rural	19%
Category	
Local Education Agency	53%
Community-based Organization	27%
Corrections (jails or prisons)	7%
Workplace	4%
Library	3%
Homeless Shelter	2%
Community College	2%
Other	3%
Size	
Fewer than 5 paid staff	11%
5–20 staff	60%
21–30 staff	9%
30+ staff	19%

Overall, about half of the programs were urban, half were based in school district settings (local education agency), and more than half had between five and twenty staff members.

Designing the NCSALL Professional Development

The topic of the NCSALL Professional Development—learner motivation, retention, and persistence[27]—was the same across all models and across all states. After much discussion with professional development leaders in the three states about a range of possible professional development topics for the study, they decided that the topic of learner persistence—how to help learners persist in reaching their educational goals—would be most likely to interest a large number of adult education teachers in each state.

Our goal was to develop high-quality professional development in three different models appropriate for adult educators. The research team designed all three professional development models, using the best methods and accepted principles of adult learning and effective professional development. Experienced teachers or professional development

---

[27] Sometimes referred to in this report as LMRP: learner motivation, retention, and persistence. We define "learner motivation" as learners being engaged in learning while in class. "Retention" refers to learners attending class regularly and staying enrolled in the program until they reach their goals. We define "persistence" as learners seeing themselves as successful, lifelong learners, even if they "stop out" or drop out at any given point.

leaders in each state, recruited and trained by the research staff, facilitated the professional development. The common and unique elements of the professional development models tested in this study are included in Table 4.

Table 4: Common and Unique Elements of the Three Professional Development Models (See Appendix A for more information about our Professional Development models.)

Common Elements (Each Model Included)	Unique Elements
	Different numbers of participants in each model • *Multisession workshop*: up to 16 teachers • *Mentor teacher group*: up to 5 teachers • *Practitioner research group*: up to 7 teachers
Same 3 objectives Participants would: • increase knowledge of the topic (learner motivation, retention, and persistence) • critically reflect on their learning and make plans for taking action • take action to increase learner persistence	**Additional objectives specific to the following groups:** • *Practitioner research group:* learn basic principles of research, conduct practitioner research, help one another with research, draw conclusions about practitioner research as a professional development model • *Mentor teacher group:* learn about the process of peer coaching, get feedback from observation by mentor, draw conclusions about mentoring as a professional development model
All models designed for 18 contact hours, over multiple sessions	**Different time spans for each model** • *Multisession workshop*: three full-day sessions over 1–3 month span • *Mentor teacher groups*: four 2–3 hour sessions, plus two individual 4-hour mentor observation sessions, over 4-6 month span • *Practitioner research group*: six 3–hour group sessions over 6–9 month span
Common activities to build collegiality among participants Examples include: • sharing experiences, trouble-shooting, group brainstorming for action plans • Expectation that practitioners would try things out in classroom/program between sessions	**Different activities and amount of time studying the topic** • *Multisession workshop*: approximately equal time in activities for learning about the topic, activities for gathering information, and activities presenting strategies for addressing learner motivation/persistence • *Mentor teacher group*: learning about topic through brief activities and discussion of readings; time for learning about peer coaching; more than one third of time devoted to individual mentor observation sessions

Table 4: Continued

Common Elements (Each Model Included)	Unique Elements
	• *Practitioner research group*: learning about topic exclusively through discussion of readings; most of time devoted to learning about, designing, and conducting own classroom research project on topic
Trained facilitators deliver the highest-quality professional development	**Type and role of facilitator varied by model** • *Multisession workshop*: run by former adult education teacher who was also a qualified trainer/professional developer; "facilitated" learning through activities and discussion among participants • *Mentor teacher group*: carried by current adult education teachers trained and supported by research staff; facilitated group learning but also mentored or coached each participant individually, providing specific feedback based on classroom observations • *Practitioner research group*: conducted by previous or current teachers with professional development experience and experience conducting and/or facilitating practitioner research; guided teachers through the research process, and facilitated the group to learn from their own and each other's research rather than from activities
All participants received the same readings and handouts	**Amount of exposure to reading and discussing literature on topic varied.** • *Multisession workshop*: devoted least time to reading and discussing the literature; much of the learning about the topic was done through workshop activities • *Mentor teacher group*: devoted a moderate amount of time to discussing readings on the topic, along with one or two workshop-type activities • *Practitioner research group*: spent most of the time discussing readings, with a full hour of discussion of readings in sessions 2-6

Table 4: Continued

Common Elements (Each Model Included)	Unique Elements
Used an inquiry approach/cycle for studying the topic. Participants would:	The origin of knowledge is different, philosophically, in each model.
	• *Multisession workshop*: knowledge primarily from research on the topic or from published accounts of teachers' experiences related to the topic; learning from activities that demonstrate strategies and allow teachers to practice and discuss
• learn about topic and strategies for addressing the problem	• *Mentor teacher group*: knowledge partly from the literature or published accounts of teachers' experiences, partly from mentor as more experienced colleague, and partly from experiences of other teachers in group; learning from interaction between mentor and participant, via observation and feedback
• gather information about the specific supports and barriers to persistence experienced by the learners in their own classrooms	• *Practitioner research group*: knowledge somewhat from research and the facilitator (through discussion of readings) but most knowledge generated by teachers themselves through their own classroom research; learning from analyzing one's own data and experience in classroom and hearing about the research of other teachers in the group
• think about the implications of this information or data for choosing a specific strategy for addressing the problem	
• take action (implement strategy)	
• think about how the strategy worked and repeat the inquiry cycle	

Defining and Measuring Teacher Change

In order to gauge change as a result of professional development, we had to define "change." We defined "change" as differences in thinking and acting, on and off the topic. Change "on the topic" included increased knowledge about the topic and reported action taken to address learner persistence in the classroom, in the program, or in the field. Change "off the topic" included increased awareness of the field of adult education, increased confidence in teaching, decreased feelings of isolation, or use of a new teaching technique. In order to differentiate levels of change and to acknowledge that change, in itself, may not always be change for the better, we defined the "preferred direction" of change as: thinking integrated with acting in multiple arenas (in one's own learning, in the classroom, in the program, and/or in the field).

To gauge such changes, we developed a set of outcomes (differences in thinking and acting) on and off the topic that we expected to see in teachers as a result of participating in these three models of professional development. In other words, any of these outcomes, based on the objectives and design of the professional development, would "count" as change,[28] as presented in Table 5:

Table 5: Outcomes That "Counted" as Change

	Changes *ON* the Topic	**Changes *OFF* the Topic**

Thinking Changes	Learning about the topic and learning strategies for addressing learner motivation, retention, and persistence(LMRP)	• Gaining general teaching knowledge
		• Learning strategies (tools) for research
		• Expressing importance of collegiality in program or in field
		• Becoming more aware of and/or critically analyzing the weaknesses or strengths of:
		  • The community within which they or learners live
		  • Their program
		  • The field of adult basic education
		  • How they best learn

Acting Changes	Taking action to: • Find out about forces affecting the motivation and persistence of the learners with whom they worked • Address LMRP in the classroom • Address LMRP in the program • Address LMRP in the field	Making a general change, without intention to affect LMRP: • In class, using a new teaching technique • In the program, initiating a policy change • In the field of adult education, contribution to field or community

Data Collection

Our goal was to collect data that would help us see the change (differences in thinking and acting) for each participant, on and off the topic, in their roles as learners, teachers, program members, and members of the field, as a result of their participation in the professional development. To do this, we needed to collect a range of data related to their thinking and acting, both before and after they participated in the professional development. We collected data through questionnaires from the whole sample (106) and through questionnaires and interviews from the subsample (18 teachers from across the three models and three states).

All data are self-reports from the teachers; however, we didn't just ask: "did you take any action?" We asked for specific examples of action they had taken (before and after participating in the professional development) related and unrelated to the topic, what exactly they did, for how long, and what the outcome of their action was. To measure whether they changed their thinking on the topic we asked them to state specific strategies that could be

---

[28] By looking at the range of outcomes emerging from preliminary analysis of the second wave of data, we confirmed and organized the set of outcomes shown here.

used to address the issue of learner motivation, and specific concepts related to the topic that they remembered from the professional development. To see if, over the course of the professional development, they changed the way they thought they learned best, we asked them (in each wave) to tell us how they best learn to improve their teaching and why. Although self-reports in no way substitute for multiple and repeated observations and documentation of teachers' behavior change (which would have been beyond the resource scope of our study, given the sample size), we do feel we were able to gauge changes in thinking and acting by looking at the details of their self-reports over time (before, after, and one year after).

The data we collected to gauge change included:

- **Questions about their thinking and acting on the topic.** What helps or hinders learners to persist, what strategies are effective for increasing persistence, what is the main concept on the topic you got out of the professional development, what have you done to address learner persistence (with individual learners, in the class, in the program, in the field)?
- **Questions about thinking and action off the topic.** Besides the topic, what is the main concept you walked away with and what did you do with this?

For the whole sample, then, we had two measures of change (our dependent variables):

1. Overall amount of change (thinking and acting on and off the topic)
2. Type of change (thinking and acting on the topic of learner persistence)

To collect data about factors influencing teacher change as a result of professional development, we created a set of hypotheses from the literature, and built questions into both the questionnaire and interviews to collect data about these factors for each teacher. There were three categories of factors for which we collected data: (1) individual factors, (2) professional development factors, and (3) program and system factors, including working conditions of teachers. Table 6 provides an overview of the kinds of data we collected from teachers about themselves and their programs.

We conducted class observations, but only to understand the teacher's teaching situation and program context, rather than to collect data about teacher performance. Similarly, the purpose of the interview with the program director or coordinator was to get a better understanding of the program context, not to ask the program director to comment on the individual teacher.

In addition to the data collected from participants, we audiotaped each of the 15 different professional development group sessions, with a note taker in attendance; we also kept attendance records, audiotaped conversations between facilitators and note takers after each session was over, and took notes during a reunion of facilitators a few months after the professional development concluded. Using this data, the research team developed a rating of group quality based on the quality of the group dynamics, quality of facilitation, and the integrity of the model (the extent to which the professional development was conducted as designed). For a more complete description of how the quality of the groups was rated, please see Appendix C.

Table 6: Overview of Data Collected from Teachers and Programs

	Whole Sample	Subsample
Number of Teachers	106 in whole sample	18 out of the 106 in the sample
Method	Three questionnaires (one at each wave, ranging from 20-38 pages per questionnaire)	Three 2-3 hour interviews with teacher(one at each wave), one 1-hour interview with program director, one class and program visit
Timing of Data Collection	Wave One: Before participating in PD[29] Wave Two: After completing PD Wave Three: One year after completing PD	Wave One: Before participating in PD Wave Two: After completing PD Wave Three: One year after completing PD
Focus of Data	• Teachers' backgrounds (gender, race, level of formal education, years teaching in adult education type and amount of teaching currently being done, their reasons for working in adult education, etc.) • Program information (location, size, staffing, curriculum and attendance requirements, preparation time allowed, professional development release time allowed, etc.) • Amount and type of other PD attended before and after NCSALL PD • Views about teaching • Thinking about the topic • Self-reports (detailed examples) of action on and off the topic • Opinions about the professional development	• How they became an adult education teacher • Experiences as a *learner* (professional development activities, learning style), *teacher* (goals of teaching, roles of teachers, and views about learners), *program member* (participation in program decisions and change), and *member of the field* (promoting adult literacy or advocating for students' needs) • Self-reports of action on and off the topic • Opinions about the professional development
Types of Questions	Closed-ended and open-ended	Open-ended questions (delivered in structured interview)

Data Analysis Strategy

We analyzed the data from the whole sample quantitatively, and the additional data collected from the subsample was analyzed qualitatively. The analysis plan called for using the data from the whole sample (quantitative) and the data from the subsample (qualitative) iteratively to understand the types and amount of change among participants. For example,

---

[29] PD=professional development

`after Wave Two, we began analyzing the data qualitatively, looking for patterns and types of change. This informed our quantitative coding scheme. Once all data had been collected, we analyzed the quantitative data, and then used the results of the quantitative data to test against the qualitative data for important factors that emerged in both types of data.

Analysis of the data included the following steps and timing:

Examining the quantitative data:

- We entered all data from the closed-ended questions in the questionnaire from all three waves using SPSS, a statistical software program (after each wave of data was collected).
- We compiled all data from the open-ended questions in the questionnaire in an Excel table, one for each teacher (after Wave Three), and then coded and tabulated change (see Table 5 on page 38 for what "counted" as change, and see "Criteria for Change" in Appendix B for a full description of how we coded this data). We used the "types of change" that evolved from the qualitative analysis to assign type of change to each teacher in the whole sample (after the qualitative analysis had produced the four types of change; see below).
- We ran frequency tests to gauge change for the whole sample, and performed statistical tests to test our hypotheses about factors that could influence the amount and type of change among teachers (after Wave Three). Specifically:

  - *One-way ANOVA tests* were used when one variable was categorical (such as the level of formal education) and one variable was continuous (such as amount of overall change).
  - *Bivariate correlation tests* were used when both variables were continuous (such as years of experience working in the field and amount of overall change).
  - *Chi-square tests* were used when both variables were categorical (such as model of professional development and type of change).
  - *Multivariate analysis* was done with each dependent variable (amount and type of change) and those factors that emerged from the statistical tests cited above as most influencing amount and type of change.

Examining the qualitative data:

- Three members of the research team independently read through all of the data for each of the 18 subsample teachers—from the interviews with teachers and program directors, class observation, and program visit—and created a "summary profile"[30] of all the salient outcomes and factors as a *learner*, as a *teacher*, as a *program member* and as a *member of the field* for each subsample teacher (after Wave Two, with additional information added after Wave Three).

---

[30] What Miles and Huberman (1994) call *interim case summaries*: "a provisional product of varying length (10–25 pages) that provides a synthesis of what the researchers know about the case and also indicates what may remain to be found out…The summary is the first attempt to derive a coherent, overall account of the case" (p. 79).

- We used the profiles of each subsample teacher to create a matrix of all change and factors across the subsample (after Wave Three).
- We then analyzed the matrix for patterns in change and factors ("pattern coding"), from which our four types of change emerged (described in the "Findings" chapter).
- We then used these four types of change to code the data from open-ended questions from the rest of the sample (after Wave Three).

Combining the quantitative and qualitative data:

- Using the results from the quantitative analysis, we then returned to the summary profiles to create short case studies of teachers representing the four types of change and verify how the factors that were important in the whole sample were or were not also important among the subsample teachers (after all quantitative and qualitative analysis was completed).

Producing results:

- Using the information both from the whole sample and the subsample teachers (quantitative and qualitative), we developed a final list of the most important individual factors that influenced teacher change.[31]

To ensure rigor in our analysis, two or more members of the research team looked independently at the data when coding, summarizing, or rating. Whenever a question of interpretation or a difference in ratings among coders arose, we returned to the raw data for verification. Finally, we held two-day analysis meetings among researchers at each stage of completed reduction/display.

Limitations

Two (sometimes competing) priorities influenced the design of this study: one, the need for a rigorous and high-quality research design, and, two, the need for the professional development we offered to be as realistic as possible. In order for the findings to be valid, we felt that the professional development should be offered through the existing professional development systems in our test states so that findings would be most relevant to the actual contexts in which adult education professional development is offered. In most cases, the "research" and "reality" priorities did not conflict; however, there were instances when

---

[31] In general, we identified as the most important those factors that emerged as strong in *both* the quantitative and qualitative analysis. However, we also identified several factors that were especially strong in one type of analysis (either the quantitative or qualitative) but for which we have no corresponding data, or the data was not as strong, in the other type. For example, there is one factor (access to benefits) that emerged from the quantitative analysis as important in influencing change, but this did not emerge in the qualitative (interviews, observations) analysis. Similarly, one factor (participating in professional development where all members of the group are from one program) was especially strong in the qualitative analysis but the numbers are too small and data not clear enough in the quantitative analysis to support that in the whole sample. However, we still identify these factors as important and worthy of future research because they were particularly strong in one type of analysis.

decisions made to uphold research or data collection rigor may have affected the quality of the professional development, or when decisions made in order to offer the most realistic professional development may have affected the research design.

For example, for the sake of fair sampling across the models, we chose to keep recruitment uniform for all three models: all potential participants received the same type of flyer announcing the professional development activity. However, since mentor teacher groups and practitioner research are less familiar formats for professional development than are workshops, teachers may not have had as much information about what to expect from the practitioner research group, for example, than we now know they need before participating in this type of professional development. On the other hand, the uniform recruitment may have reduced selection bias into the three models, and thus permitted us to learn lessons about recruitment.

Another example of the need to balance research design with professional development principles—an example where research was favored over realistic professional development—is our request to facilitators to be faithful to the model as designed, and to follow the guide, with some flexibility, so that there was less variation among groups within a particular model. Some facilitators felt constrained to stick to the guide, knowing that they were in a research study and comparability of professional development experiences within the same model across states was important. In some cases, this constraint may have prevented the facilitators from adapting the professional development activities to the specific needs or interests of the practitioners in their group, as they may have done had they not been involved in a research project.

Another design limitation was that the data used to determine change is all based on teachers' self-reports. Although most K–12 professional development research also relies on self-reporting, researchers understand its limitations. In this study, we do feel that the repeated collection of data over time, plus—for the subsample teachers—the classroom observation and triangulation of the data (through program director interviews and tapes of professional development activities) allowed us to make realistic judgments about the differences between espoused theory and actions, and, to a lesser extent, about the accuracy of these self-reports.

A third design limitation is that, because of the desire for quantitative data to support the qualitative data and to provide a broader view of professional development outcomes, we decided to recruit larger numbers of teachers to participate in professional development on the same topic than would ordinarily be expected in naturally-occurring professional development within a state or region. In some cases, this meant that either program directors or state literacy resource center staff encouraged teachers to participate, when they ordinarily might not have either self-selected or had access to such professional development. Also, because all completing teachers were given a stipend for their participation to compensate for their time in providing us with data, some of the participants in the study who would not have ordinarily participated in professional development of this length felt they could because the stipend partially compensated them for their time. How this affected the sample of teachers in our study is unknown, but receiving payment may have played a role in the composition of the sample.

The size of the sample limits generalizability of quantitative results. While large from a qualitative point of view, it is small from a quantitative point of view. On some data points, cell sizes were too small to run statistical tests comparing practitioners across models.

Another limitation is that all of the research was conducted in New England, and, although the three participating states have different adult education and professional development systems, there may be similarities in the learner and teacher populations within this region that would not be applicable in other regions of the country. Care should be taken before generalizing these findings to practitioners in other systems, states, and regions.

Another design limitation, although common enough in how teachers usually choose professional development, is that not all participants had the choice, because of geography, to participate in a particular professional development model. Although technically any practitioner could have registered to participate in any of the models in their state, realistically, most practitioners registered for the model that was offered closest to their home or program.

We believe that the tape recording and observation of professional development sessions may, for some participants, have influenced the level of openness in their discussions about program conditions or other barriers that would prevent them from making changes based on what they learned in the professional development. Although some subsample teachers reported forgetting that the tape recorder was running, others did say that they were conscious of it and that it may have influenced what they shared during the professional development sessions. Obviously, practitioners in the study, some more than others, were aware that they were participating in a research study and this may have affected responses about the quality of the professional development and the amount of change they said they experienced as a result.

Finally, the research design team and research director/coordinator primarily come from a background as teachers and professional developers in adult education. As such, we each have formed beliefs about the purposes of literacy, the best approaches to instruction in adult education, and the quality of some types of professional development activities over others. While there were minor differences in viewpoints about how the professional development research and activities should be designed, based on these belief systems, the researchers shared a common view of the value of learner-centered professional development and adult education instruction. We recognize that this view may not be common throughout the field of adult basic education. Our views may have biased us toward designing professional development activities and interpreting findings that are consistent with a learner-centered approach to education, as we define it.

FINDINGS

In this chapter, we present our findings in response to the research question: How do practitioners change as a result of participating in one of three different models of professional development, and what are the most important factors that influence (support or hinder) this change? We first present information about who participated in the professional development, why, and for how long. The rest of the chapter is divided into two main sections: how teachers changed, and what factors influenced that change. In each section, we first discuss the amount or type of change experienced by the teachers, and then we provide some snapshots from the subsample participants to demonstrate, beyond the numbers, what change looked like for them.

Participation in the Professional Development Activities

The hours of participation among the sample of 100 participants ranged from 2.5 to 18. The average number of hours that teachers participated in the professional development activities was 15 (median number of hours equaled 17.25) and that was consistent across the three states. However, teachers in the practitioner research group model participated fewer hours on average (mean [M]=13.7, standard deviation [SD]=5.6) than teachers in either the workshops (M=16.4, SD=2.7) or the mentor teacher groups (M=14.6, SD=4.4). Statistical tests indicate that the differences in number of hours attended across the professional development models were statistically significant (ANOVA, F=3.4, p<.05).

Sixteen out of the original 100 participants left the NCSALL Professional Development before completing two thirds (12) of the required hours. Chi-square tests show a significant difference among the three models in dropouts (χ^2=14.2, df=2, p<.001): 12 out of 37 (38%) participants dropped out of practitioner research groups; 4 out of 28 (14%) dropped out of mentor teacher groups; and 0 out of 35 dropped out of the multisession workshops. Dropouts were evenly distributed across the states, with no significant differences: Maine had 5 dropouts out of 33; Massachusetts had 4 dropouts out of 31; and Connecticut had 7 dropouts out of 36. We asked dropouts (in the Wave Three questionnaire) the reason they left the professional development before completing the full 18 hours; 11 of the 16 dropouts responded to this question. Five dropouts indicated "lack of time, other commitments" as the primary reason; three reported health problems; two indicated a change of job; and one reported not liking the professional development as the primary reason for dropping out.

Another factor related to attendance in our professional development was hours of paid professional development release time a teacher received annually, which was positively correlated with number of hours attending (r=.299, p<.01, n=100). Hours attended was also significantly related to the rated quality of the professional development groups (as rated by the researchers) (r=.345, p<.001, n=100), but not to perceived quality (how the teachers rated the professional development after they had participated in it). In other words, if the professional development was of low quality (according to our rating), they attended for fewer hours, but how many hours they attended was not related to teachers' perception of its quality afterward. (Please see Appendix C for more information about the criteria used by researchers to rate group quality.) Finally, number of working hours was related to completing the professional development: all dropouts were part time, with a mean number of hours worked per week of 16.79 (n=14, SD=10.3), compared to completers as a whole, who averaged 23.28 hours worked per week (n=83, SD=11.2). In other words, teachers who worked part time were more likely to drop out than teachers who worked full time. This is statistically significant (χ^2=6.8, df=2, p<.05, n=97).

Another factor affecting attendance was the level of priority the teacher assigned to this particular topic (LMRP), compared to other topics on which she or he could seek professional development, but interestingly, it was negatively correlated (r=-.21, p<.05, n=100). The less of a priority it was, the more hours the teacher attended the NCSALL Professional Development; we can't explain why that would be significant.

Discussion of Participation

Our qualitative data offer three reasons for the higher number of dropouts from the practitioner research groups. Although most of the dropouts reported relatively benign reasons (health, lack of time, change of job), their reports may have been colored by their desire not to express negative opinions of the professional development to us. From other data (interviews with subsample practitioner research group participants, feedback from facilitators, and the notes/tapes from the professional development activities) we believe there may have been other reasons for dropping out, beyond what teachers gave as their primary reason, and these reasons are related to (a) recruitment information, (b) teachers' developmental level, and (c) quality of the group (facilitation, group dynamics, flexible adherence to the model).

Recruitment was the same for all three models. We did not advertise the practitioner research groups differently from the way we advertised the workshops or mentor teacher groups (feeling it might somehow affect the results of the study by skewing the uniformity of the recruitment process). However, we now feel, based on the feedback from participants and facilitators, and based on the data, that teachers should have been given a better description of what they were signing up for before they participated in the practitioner research group—a model that was new to many practitioners. The concept of "practitioner research" is still less familiar in general than the other forms or models of professional development in the field. Clearer expectations beforehand about the type and amount of work involved may have influenced the dropout rate from this model. One teacher who participated in a practitioner research group recommended:

> More clarity when describing the research project so people don't think that they're just going to sit there (in the professional development) and listen. Explain to them that we expect X, Y, and Z from you. Are you willing to…?

— Beth,[32] Wave Three interview

Practitioner research may also interact with a teacher's particular learning style or developmental level, perhaps negatively. Participation in a research study requires teachers to play a more active role, with more self-initiative, than merely attending a workshop. Although each of the models asked teachers to read or conduct activities in the time between one session and the next, more "homework" was certainly required of practitioner research group participants. In addition, the style of the practitioner research group is substantially different: the facilitator doesn't give "the answer"; rather, the "answer" comes from teachers' own investigation into what is going on in their classrooms. We heard from facilitators that dropouts tended to be the teachers who often asked, during the course of the practitioner research group, "what's the right thing to do?" or "what exactly am I supposed to be doing here?" While some of that confusion could undoubtedly have come from poor facilitation, completing practitioners seemed more able to grapple with a professional development design where they had to form their own question and design their own research project. Further research should investigate how teachers at different developmental levels (different ways of knowing) respond to various types of professional development that call on them to play roles beyond that of just listening to or being exposed to new teaching techniques.

---

[32] In this report, the names of all teachers have been changed to protect their confidentiality.

A final reason for the greater dropout rate from the practitioner research groups may have been the quality of these specific practitioner research groups: three of the six practitioner research groups were rated by the researchers as low in quality, compared to two out of six low-quality mentor teacher groups, and no low-quality workshops. Information from facilitators' notes and interviews with participants and facilitators indicated a reciprocal relationship between dropouts and quality: the lower the quality initially, the greater the dropouts; the greater the dropouts, the worse the group dynamics and thus the lower the quality.

How Teachers Changed

In this section, we present the findings about how much teachers changed, and in what ways and roles. As discussed in Chapter One, what "counted" as change included changes in thinking and acting on and off the topic. We used two indicators of change:

1. **Amount of change**—a measure of overall level of change in thinking and acting, on and off the topic.
2. **Type of change**—a measure of the kind of change in thinking and acting on the topic.

We looked at change in four roles: as a learner, as a teacher, as a program member, and as a member of the field. We judged change within the context of what the professional development covered and recommended for knowledge and action, specifically:

- Teachers' *thinking changes* (on and off the topic of learner motivation, retention, and persistence), including learning about the topic of LMRP and strategies for addressing LMRP; gaining general teaching knowledge; learning strategies for research; expressing importance of collegiality in program or in field; becoming more aware of and/or critically analyzing weaknesses or strengths of communities, programs, field of adult basic education; or how they best learn.
- Teachers' *acting changes* (on and off the topic), including taking action to find out about forces affecting the persistence of learners; addressing LMRP in the classroom, program, or field; or making a general teaching change such as using a new teaching technique, initiating a policy change, or taking action in the community or field.

For more information about what was covered in the professional development and how we judged change, please see Appendix A and Appendix B.

How Much Did Teachers Change?
When coding teachers' open-ended answers on the questionnaires, we assigned scores for amount of change for each teacher, according to the different outcomes (thinking and acting, on and off the topic). This gave us an overall amount of change[33] for each teacher, plus some

---

[33] Total possible change score was 51. For overall amount of change, scores ranged from 0–30 out of a possible 51. The total possible score for thinking changes was 30, for acting changes was 21; total possible score for change

indication of whether change occurred mostly in thinking or in acting, on or off the topic. (For more information about coding of the data, please see Appendix B.) Overall, we found that:

- Most teachers, even dropouts, changed at least minimally through gains in knowledge or actions in their classrooms; relatively few experienced no change at all.
- Almost all (90% of the whole sample, 95% of completers) gained some knowledge on the topic, but for many it was only one or two concepts.
- The majority (78% of the whole sample, 87% of completers) took some action, on or off the topic, but for many it was very minimal.

Among the whole sample (completers, dropouts, and comparison group), amount of overall change was a mean of 7.5, on the lower end of the 51-point scale Only 8 out of the 101 in the whole sample and only 2 of the 83 completers no change at all, either on or off the topic.

Table 7 below breaks down the means for all variables of change, by level participation.

Figure 1 below shows amount of overall change by professional development model in the dropout and completer groups.

Dropouts, overall, made significantly less change than did completers. Mentor teacher group dropouts (*n*=4) demonstrated more change than practitioner research group dropouts (*n*=12) but these numbers are too small to test for any statistical differences among the groups. The difference in amount of change by model of professional development among completers was not statistically significant. (This finding will be discussed in more depth later in the chapter under "Factors Influencing Teachers' Change.")

Table 7: Change by Level of Participation (*n*=101)

	Overall Amount of Change (Range 0-51) Mean (SD)	Change in Thinking or Acting		Change On or Off Topic	
		Thinking Range (0-30) Mean (SD)	Acting Range (0-21) Mean (SD)	On Topic Range (0-15) Mean (SD)	Off Topic Range (0-36) Mean (SD)
Comparison (*n*=6)	1.33	.67	.67	.00	1.33
	(1.63)	(.82)	(.82)	(.00)	(1.63)
Dropouts (*n*=12)	2.58	2.00	.58	1.67	.92
	(1.98)	(1.48)	(.99)	(1.37)	(.99)
Completers (*n*=83)	8.65	5.59	3.06	4.76	3.87
	(5.93)	(3.93)	(2.49)	(3.88)	(2.80)
Totals	*7.50*	*4.87*	*2.62*	*4.11*	*3.37*
	(5.97)	*(3.93)*	*(2.48)*	*(3.83)*	*(2.80)*

on topic 15, and for change off topic 36. For someone to score the maximum, they would have had to demonstrate significant change in thinking and acting both on and off the topic.

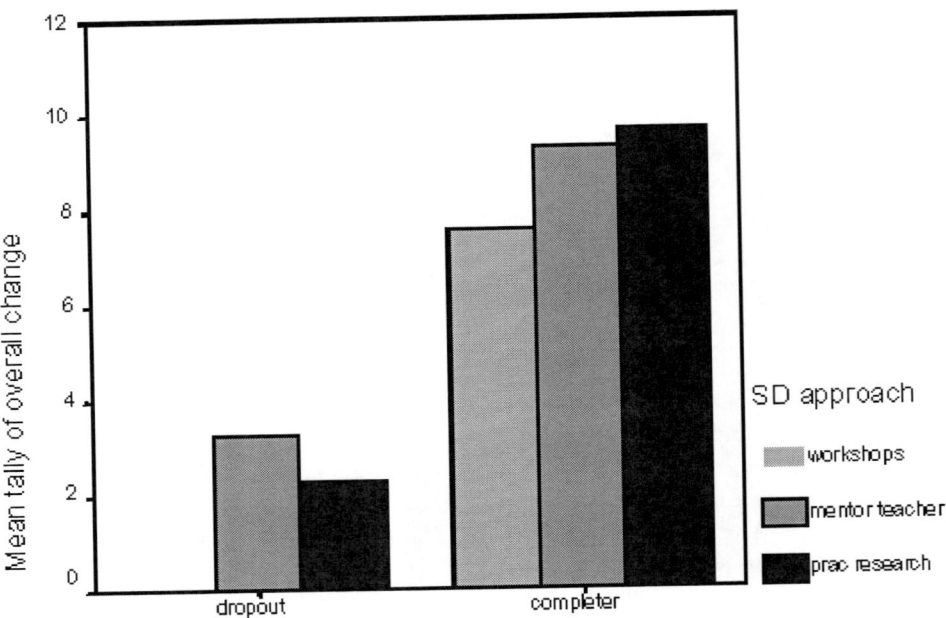

Figure 1: Amount of Change by Professional Development Model (n=101)[34]

Changes in Thinking

Only 10 (9.9%) out of the 101 completers, dropouts, and comparison group members for whom we have complete data demonstrated no change in thinking, either on or off the topic. Among the 83 completers for whom we have data, only 4 (4.8%) demonstrated no change in thinking.

Table 8 provides information about the percentage demonstrating changes in thinking on topic (one measure) and off topic (eight measures). For a more detailed description of these measures, see Appendix B.

Table 8 below shows that, not surprisingly, the most common change was learning on the topic; most teachers in the study gained some knowledge about learner motivation, retention, and persistence. Eleven of these 83 gained significant knowledge, and 20 gained moderate knowledge; the remaining 52 demonstrated minimal knowledge gain. Most seemed to have gained (or at least retained) a concept or two including, for example, the ideas that some students "stop out" rather than "drop out," or that persistence is affected by "turbulence" (students coming and going in the classroom, new students entering at any time, etc.).

---

[34] This number includes completers, dropouts, and comparison group members for whom we have complete data. There was a teacher who attended all workshops but provided us with no data, so we dropped him completely from the sample; therefore, no dropouts from the workshop model appear.

Table 8: Changes in Thinking, On and Off the Topic
(*n*=101, *indicates missing data for one respondent)

	On/Off Topic	Percent Changed	Demonstrated Change	No Change	Too Vague to Judge[35]
Learned about the topic	On	82%	83	14	4
Increased general teaching knowledge*	Off	38%	38	54	1
Increased awareness of:	Off				
the field of adult education		44%	44	53	4
how best they learn to teach		34%	34	57	10
program strengths and/or weaknesses		25%	25	76	0
own or learners' community		5%	5	95	1
Expressed importance of:	Off				
field collegiality		49%	49	51	1
program collegiality		24%	24	77	0
Learned research tools and strategies	Off	18%	18	81	2

If a teacher demonstrated some change in learning about the topic, we coded specific types of learning (see below); teachers often expressed or demonstrated knowledge in multiple ways (which is why numbers below add up to more than 83). Out of the 83 who learned about the topic:

- 74 expressed broader understanding of the topic and/or learners, including knowledge of the forces that affect learners' motivation and persistence, and strategies for addressing LMRP.
- 35 expressed the need to get to know learners better (which we recommended as a step in the process of addressing learner motivation, retention, and persistence).
- 25 expressed a change in their thinking about sphere of influence as a teacher (a feeling that they could have some effect on learners' motivation), while 6 expressed a negative sphere of influence[36] (the feeling that it was beyond their control because learner retention is based solely on the problems learners face in their lives).
- 23 expressed the need to broaden their instruction based on learners' needs or forces that affect learners' retention.

---

[35] These were cases where the information provided by the respondent was too confusing and insubstantial to merit a clear judgment about whether a change in thinking in this area had occurred.

[36] A positive sphere of influence is characterized in the following comment: "*It made me realize that unless there are major problems at home that would stop my student from continuing, the responsibility for his continuing lies with me.*" Negative sphere of influence is characterized by these types of comments: "*All adult educators are faced with absenteeism and it should not be internalized. There are an overwhelming number of student reasons for lack of retention.*" "*Is there really anything I can do to improve retention, or should I just accept the reality of a max of 50% who finish?*" "*We can't fault them for not attending class because of sick kids, working overtime, no transportation, etc., or resolve these issues for them—or blame ourselves.*" "*Why do we spend so much time worrying about the early dropouts?*"

- 8 expressed an understanding that learners' motivation and teachers' motivation are connected (e.g., if there is teacher turnover, there will be learner turnover).

Interestingly, the next two highest areas of thinking change (after changes in thinking about the topic) relate to the field of adult basic education: the importance of collegiality in the field and an increased awareness of the field. These are changes that one would expect to occur when teachers have time to share experiences during discussions that are part of the professional development activity. It is an indication that teachers experience changes in thinking about issues unrelated to the topic of the professional development itself. Of the 44 who expressed an increased awareness of the field:

- 30 became more aware of the field in general (e.g., expressing the idea that they didn't know other programs and teachers also faced the same issues, or an awareness that research, publications, and other professional development activities existed when they thought there was none).
- 16 expressed a critical awareness of the professional development or adult education system's strengths or weaknesses (e.g., expressing the realization that funding was too limited to offer learners the support services they needed, or that the nature of the field contributed to teachers' lack of training and isolation).
- 5 expressed a change in their own identity as a member of the field (i.e., they realized this was the field within which they wanted—or didn't want—to continue to work).

Thirty-four teachers demonstrated changes in how they feel they best learn to improve their practice. Most of these changes (20) were minimal, and a larger proportion of mentor teacher group participants (14 out of 25) and practitioner research group participants (11 out of 27), as compared to workshop participants (9 out of 33) changed how they feel they learn best, but differences among models were not statistically significant ($\chi^2 = 8.95$, $df=6$, $p>.05$, $n=85$). Typically, mentor teacher group participants talked about the benefits of being observed, while practitioner research group participants talked about the value of conducting and reading research.

Of the 25 people who expressed a critical awareness of program strengths and weaknesses:

- 18 expressed the realization that their program was weak (e.g., the program would not take action to address LMRP as they hoped it would, or it did not provide enough opportunities for teachers to meet and share).
- 8 expressed a new awareness that teachers and/or learners should be involved in program decision-making.
- 5 expressed the realization that the program was fine (i.e., that the program was "on the right track" about how to address the problem of learner retention).

Changes in Acting

The professional development encouraged teachers first to ask learners about the forces supporting and hindering their persistence, and then to take action in their classroom, program, or in the field based on what learners told them. We collected information from teachers to help us gauge how much and what type of action they took. We also collected information about actions teachers may have taken not related to the topic of the professional development (learner persistence), such as trying out a new teaching technique or initiating change in the program unrelated to learner persistence.

Of the sample for which we have data on this question (n=101), 78% took some action on or off the topic. Out of the group who completed the professional development (n=83), 87% took action.

Table 9 provides information about the percentage of teachers that demonstrated changes in acting on topic (four measures) and off topic (three measures). For a more detailed description of these measures, see Appendix B.

The table shows that the three top actions were related to taking action on the topic, but that, in general, fewer teachers took action than made changes in their thinking (see Table 8): while 83 demonstrated increased knowledge on the topic, only 57 took any action and 34 of these were coded as having taken "minimal" action, usually making one or two changes in their classroom that were not sustained over time, such as calling an absent learner once or twice or trying a technique once and then abandoning it.

Of the *57 teachers who took some action in their class to address the issue of LMRP*, most (34) took minimal action; 17 took moderate action and 6 took significant action (multiple types of action):

- 37 made a formal change (used a specific technique or activity) in their class to address learner motivation, retention, and persistence (e.g., goal-setting activities, evaluation of class, project-based learning to address one of the forces identified by learners as hindering their persistence).
- 24 made an informal change in their class (i.e., not adopting a formal activity but changing a facet of the classroom atmosphere, such as "lightening up" to allow students time during class to talk to one another or the teacher about aspects of their daily life that affect their persistence).
- 14 made an informal change outside of the classroom (e.g., calling learners who had been absent to urge them to return to class, talking with individual learners about their goals).

Of the *43 teachers who took action within their programs to address LMRP*, most (28) took minimal action, while 9 took moderate and 6 took significant action:

- 38 took action to improve the overall program (e.g., setting up meetings to discuss LMRP or share techniques/activities learned during the training with other teachers, initiating changes in intake process to better identify learner goals).

- 12 took action in the program to improve their own classrooms (e.g., changing the way intake was done for their own classes, asking the director for resources to do different activities in their class).

Table 9: Change in Acting, On and Off the Topic
(*n*=101, *indicates missing data for one or more respondents)

	On/Off Topic	Percent Changed	Demonstrated Change	No Change	Too Vague to Judge
Took action to:					
find out forces related to LMRP with learners*	On	42%	42	55	3
address LMRP in class*		57%	57	36	7
address LMRP in program		43%	43	49	9
address LMRP in field		6%	6	95	0
Took general action in:					
class, teaching technique*	Off	26%	24	67	2
program, initiate policy change*		7%	7	90	1
field, contribution to field or community*		7%	7	87	1

Of the *42 teachers who took action to find out about the forces that affect the learners* with whom they work, most (31) took minimal action, 8 took moderate action, and 3 took significant (often multiple) actions:

- 29 took a formal action (used a technique or activity) to learn about the forces affecting learners (e.g., initiated a class discussion, used a "force-field analysis,"[37] had learners interview each other, conducted an activity where learners could write about the forces that affect their motivation, retention, and persistence).
- 16 took an informal action in the classroom to uncover forces (this almost always involved an unstructured discussion with learners during a break in the work to simply ask them what supported them or hindered them from attending class).
- 4 made an informal change outside of class (e.g., talked with individual students before or after class to discover forces affecting them).

It is interesting to note that 42 teachers took action to learn about forces affecting learners, and 57 teachers took action to address learner persistence. This means that 15 fewer teachers took action to find out about the forces affecting learners than teachers who addressed the problem, indicating either that these teachers underreported "finding out" activities or that they took action without first talking to the learners with whom they work. These are examples where teachers did not undertake the whole process for addressing the

---

[37] A force-field analysis is a strategizing technique where people first list factors that prevent them from reaching a particular goal (in this case, persisting in their education), then list the factors that help them reach the goal, then strategize how to reduce the hindering factors and increase the helping factors.

topic (which asked teachers first to determine the specific forces affecting the learners in their own classes and programs); instead, it is likely that these teachers took action based on their assumptions about what forces affected learners.

Most (18) of the 24 teachers who made a general change in practice in the classroom made a minimal change, and this was usually the addition of a new technique or activity learned during the professional development (e.g., force-field analysis, discussion activity) that they used to teach other content in their class. For example, one activity conducted at the end of each workshop had teachers make a paper "quilt" about their plans to take action to address learner persistence; several teachers mentioned in Wave Two and Wave Three questionnaires that they had used this technique with learners as an activity in the class, but on another topic (such as health). The 24 teachers who made a change in their general teaching practice were almost evenly spread across models, but the 2 teachers who made significant change in this area were practitioner research group participants.

Action taken within the program off the topic usually involved an effort by the teacher to initiate more opportunities for collegiality in the program, through teacher-sharing meetings. We did not see much reported change in the type or amount of interactions with colleagues within the program as a result of this professional development, although some practitioners in the sample did talk about how they shared the information from the professional development with colleagues during their regular interactions.

Action taken within the field on the topic usually entailed providing professional development in other programs or at a conference about what changes teachers or their program had made to address learner persistence, or action within the local community to support the needs of learners (such as seeking funding support for new facilities). Action taken within the field off the topic, for the few teachers who undertook such action, was usually related to seeking more contact with colleagues or providing professional development for other teachers on a topic other than learner persistence. Regardless of whether the actions taken by teachers were on or off the topic of learner persistence, the teachers who reported them attributed them to their participation in the professional development.

In What Roles Did Teachers Change?

For each respondent, two researchers independently made a judgment about the primary arena of change (as a learner, as a teacher, as a program member, or as a member of the field), based on the arena of thinking and action where most change occurred. In some cases, the change seemed equally distributed between two of these arenas, usually as a teacher and a program member. The data indicate that:

> Changes were most often seen in teachers' roles as classroom teachers (rather than their roles as learners, program members, or members of the field).

Figure 2 shows the percentages of teachers (*n*=101) by primary arena of change.

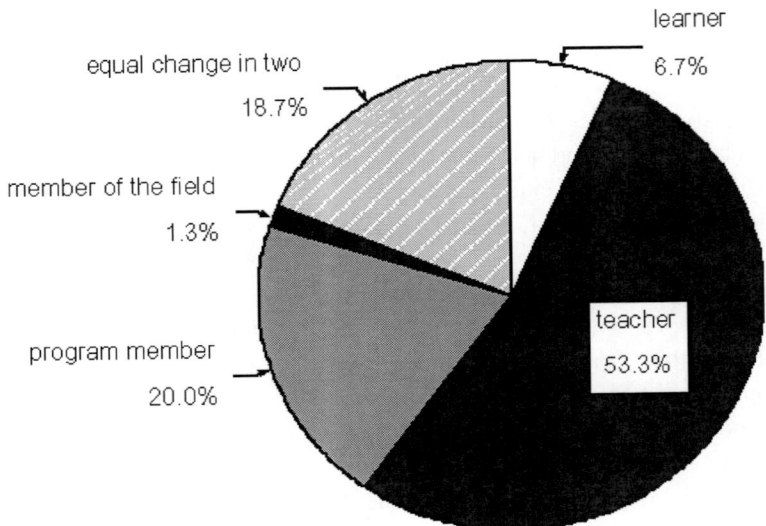

Figure 2: Primary Arena of Change

In What Ways Did Teachers Change?

Using the categories developed by looking at patterns in the qualitative data, and then coding the whole sample, we found that:

Change fell into four types:
   •   Integrated
   •   Acting
   •   Thinking
   •   No or minimal
 	
 The most common type of change was thinking change.
 The percentage of *completing* teachers (*n*=83) in each type was:
   1.   Integrated Change: 24%
   2.   Acting Change: 13%
   3.   Thinking Change: 35%
   4.   No or Minimal Change: 28%

The characteristics that emerged for these four types of change are presented in Table 10.

The four types of change described above represent the direction of "preferred change":[38] from "no or minimal change" at one end of the spectrum to "significant integrated" change at the other. We made no qualitative distinction between "thinking change" and "acting change"; both are preferable to "no change," but less preferable than "integrated change."

---

[38] "Preferred change" is defined as thinking integrated with acting in multiple arenas (in one's own learning, in the classroom, in the program, and/or in the field).

However, there is a natural dividing line between the types, based on the key factor of whether or not demonstrated changes in thinking and acting were integrated: that participants—regardless of the amount of change—reached all three objectives of the professional development in an integrated way and/or used the inquiry process/cycle.

Table 10: Characteristics of Types of Change

Types of Change	Characteristics
Integrated	<ul><li>Demonstrated thinking *and* acting changes, which were balanced and integrated: actions tied to new thinking, expressed theories and critical reflection related to topic and to existing theories.</li><li>Made changes: – that were not haphazard or random: thoughts and actions linked and integrated into teachers' understanding of the topic and theories of good teaching and student success. – that were sustained over time. – on one of two levels: (1) minimal-to-moderate integrated and (2) significant integrated. – that were limited overall and that usually occurred in one arena (i.e., as a teacher), if they showed minimal-to-moderate change. – that were "transformational": significant overall and occurred in multiple arenas (i.e., as a learner, teacher, program member), if they showed significant integrated change.</li><li>Most often used an inquiry approach[39] and achieved all three objectives of the professional development.[40]</li></ul>
Acting	<ul><li>Demonstrated change (at least minimally) in thinking and acting, but acting changes outweighed thinking changes.</li><li>Scored minimally in a few thinking categories but scored minimally or moderately across more acting categories.</li><li>Took actions that didn't have significant link to thinking change: limited rationale for action, actions not tied to thinking on topic or theories of teaching.</li><li>Took actions (trying new techniques or implementing different strategies) that appeared random in nature, and did not appear to lead in any particular direction (either to a next step or another insight).</li><li>Took actions that were typically not sustained over longer periods of time.</li></ul>
Thinking	<ul><li>Demonstrated change (at least minimally) in thinking and acting, but thinking changes outweighed acting changes.</li><li>Scored minimally or not at all in acting categories but scored minimally or moderately across more thinking categories.</li></ul>

---

[39] Inquiry approach/cycle: (a) learn about topic and strategies for addressing the problem, and (b) gather information from learners about the specific supports and barriers to persistence experienced in the learners' classrooms; (c) think about the implications of this information for choosing a specific strategy for addressing the problem; (d) take action (implement strategy); (e) think about how the strategy worked and repeat the inquiry cycle.

[40] (1) Increase knowledge of the topic (learner motivation, retention, and persistence); (2) critically reflect on their learning and make plans for taking action; and (3) take action to increase learner persistence.

Table 10: (Continued)

Types of Change	Characteristics
	• Took actions not linked significantly with changes in thinking; any actions small or short-lived.
	• May have demonstrated a clear idea about an inquiry approach to addressing the topic but took little or no action either to find out about forces affecting their own learners or to choose a strategy for addressing the problem.
No or minimal	• Demonstrated little change in thinking or action.
	• Scored minimally in a very few categories (on or off the topic).
	• Showed little breadth or depth of thinking or acting change over time: gained a concept or two, tried out an activity when directed to as part of the professional development, but little indication that any of three objectives of the professional development achieved.
	• Showed no connection between even minimal thinking and acting changes; any changes not sustained.

Therefore, we combined these four types of change into a three-category spectrum of change: (1) no change, (2) nonintegrated change, and (3) integrated change. This allowed us to use larger cell sizes for further quantitative data analysis to test hypotheses about factors influencing type of change. This spectrum of change, including the percentage of *completing* teachers in the sample who demonstrated change in each type, is presented in Figure 3 below:

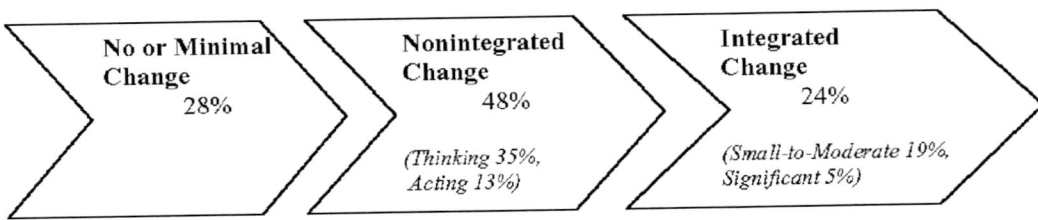

Figure 3: Spectrum of Change by Type (Among Completers) (n=83, completing teachers)

The majority (72%) of the 83 completers demonstrated change, most of which was nonintegrated (thinking or acting) change. Teachers who fell into the "integrated change" type also demonstrated a higher overall amount of change; amount of overall change is significantly related to type of change (ANOVA, $F=33.42$, $df=4$, $p<.001$, $n=83$), as shown in Table 11. Those who demonstrated integrated change also demonstrated change in more arenas (classroom, program, and field), more sustained change, and change off the topic.

Participation in the professional development was a factor in type of change. Most of the dropouts and comparison group members demonstrated "no change." Two of the 18 dropout/comparison group members for whom we have data demonstrated what could be called "integrated" change, and three demonstrated nonintegrated change. This may be a result of their participation in other professional development; the numbers are too small, however, to make any judgment about contributing factors.

The next section describes the change demonstrated by teachers in our subsample, according to the type of change they experienced.

Table 11: Amount of Overall Change by Type of Change (Completers, *n*=83)

Type of Change	n	Mean Overall Change	SD
No or minimal	23	3.04	1.97
Acting	11	8.64	2.50
Thinking	29	8.17	3.10
Minimal-to-moderate integrated	16	14.88	5.14
Significant integrated	4	19.50	9.15
Totals	*83*	*8.65*	*5.93*

Integrated Change

In our study, the category of teachers who showed the most change were those we described as "integrated change" teachers. These teachers changed both their thinking and their acting and were able, to a greater or lesser degree, to integrate these two kinds of changes. "Thinking" changes are differences in knowledge and attitudes; for integrated change teachers, we saw evidence of their ability to reflect critically on what they were learning in the professional development, their existing theories about what good teaching is like, and what it means for students to be successful. "Acting" changes have to do with applying new knowledge or ideas, by using a new technique, for example. The teachers in this category were able to make significant, concrete changes in their classrooms or programs based on the changes in their thinking. Moreover, these changes appeared not to be haphazard or random changes, and in most cases, they were sustained over time.

> *The language of persistence and motivation and retention is much more in the center of my mind when I think about these steps that I take. It helps to be thinking about these actual aspects of learners' lives when I'm taking the steps because that makes it more of a forefront issue: it's something new that I'm doing for a reason. I can articulate that with students.*

> — Erica, Wave Three interview

There were five teachers in our subsample who demonstrated "integrated change." These five teachers all understood and used an inquiry approach/cycle for studying the topic outlined in the professional development: they gained knowledge about the topic, connected this knowledge to action in order to find out about learners' needs and the forces that affect learner motivation, and then took action in line with the theories and learners' needs. In their interviews, each teacher expressed growth in their conceptual understanding about the topic. They chose strategies to address the issue of learner persistence based on what learners told them, and took action to implement those strategies. Those with minimal change demonstrated limited integrated change in one arena (learner, teacher, program member, member of the field), whereas those with significant integrated change demonstrated more change within multiple arenas.

Only two of these teachers—Esther and Meg—experienced changes in their thinking and acting as a result of their participation in the NCSALL Professional Development that we characterized as "significant." Both had thinking and acting changes in multiple arenas (as learners, as teachers, and as program members). Both teachers also made a strong connection between learner retention and teacher retention; both expressed the opinion that a critical strategy for enhancing learner persistence was for programs to provide teachers with more support to alleviate teacher turnover. The other three of the five "integrated change" teachers had thinking and acting changes mostly limited to one arena (the classroom).

All five teachers also had an outcome related to a broadened and more critical understanding of their own program's strength or weakness: four realized that their programs were weak, and the other received confirmation that her program was indeed on the right track with respect to LMRP. To varying degrees, all five teachers also had an increased critical awareness of the field, having entered the professional development with a fairly limited awareness of the field beyond their own local area. Finally, four of the five teachers increased their confidence as teachers, some through a better understanding of learner dropout they could and could not control and some based on the feedback from the mentors with whom they worked. The specific outcomes for each teacher are presented below; teachers are ordered from least amount of integrated change to most significant integrated change.

Erica: Erica, a first-year adult education teacher, worked full time as a one-on-one teacher in a rural family literacy program, and she attended the first 12 hours of the workshops (but missed the final 8 hours). Erica demonstrated minimal-to-moderate integrated change. Like the other teachers of this type, Erica changed her thinking, expanding the depth and breadth of her understanding of the issue. She also learned the terminology for the kinds of forces and barriers learners faced that affect retention. Erica gained a deeper understanding of the factors she could and could not control, recognizing that there might be instances of learner dropout that were beyond her control but others where either she or the program could have an effect. Rather than rejecting the issue (as some of the "no or minimal" change teachers did), this new understanding helped her to depersonalize discussions she had with learners about dropping out and increased her overall confidence as a teacher.

The actions she took derived directly from this more complex understanding of why learners drop out: after first trying out a technique to help learners identify forces that affect their persistence (which she learned in the workshops), she continued over the next year to ask students directly, in each class session, about forces affecting their participation. She also discussed with another staff member in her program how to change the intake process so that intake included collecting information from learners about forces.

Her other program-level changes were simply "getting on board" and getting involved in activities to increase persistence—open houses for learners, coffee hours for learner sharing—that her program was already doing. Even though potentially she would have been supported to take other actions, she did not do so, perhaps because another outcome for Erica was her realization that, relative to others, her program was already doing a good job with LMRP. Similar to Pamela and Debbie, discussed below, she also increased her awareness of the broader field of adult literacy education and her role within it.

Debbie: Debbie, a part-time (14 hours a week) ESOL teacher who had taught for three years, divided her time between two urban programs; she participated in all 18 hours of a multisession workshop. Like Erica, Debbie demonstrated minimal-to-moderate integrated change. She also became more aware of social and contextual factors that affect learners and, to her relief, better understood what was and was not within her control as a teacher. Her first action was to use several techniques she learned in the workshops (force-field analysis, class discussions) to find out what barriers learners faced. She learned that many of them would be able to attend class more frequently if it were held on Saturdays. She then took action by proposing this to her program director, but her proposal was rejected.

Based on her discussions with learners and the discussions in the workshops, she began to shift her thinking from an exclusive skills-based focus:

> My focus had always been, "How do I teach the language skills?" It [the professional development] started getting me to look in a more holistic way towards teaching, shifting the focus to "How do I improve the lives and the situations of the learners?" ... I've got this real intrigue now for project-based learning. Things that are a little bit more relevant for a natural approach to teaching as opposed to what our program involves, which is teach to the curriculum using these books and these binders.
>
> —Debbie, Wave Three interview

This thinking shift included generating ideas for improving learner support and involvement in the program, such as establishing a student welcoming committee and creating a student buddy system. However, she reluctantly forfeited the idea of taking action in these areas because of the response she got from the director about her proposal for Saturday classes.

When Debbie found herself blocked from making program-level changes, she focused more on the classroom level. The workshops had presented, as a strategy for addressing persistence, the idea that learners need a good idea of the scope and sequence of what will be learned in the class, so she began to present the various content components as units, reviewing at the end of each class what they had covered that day and what they would cover on that same unit in the next classes. Based on the theory of increased learner support through strong class community, she took action to "lighten up" the tight lesson plans she had; she allowed time for the class to chat with her about what was going on in their lives.

Debbie also broadened her awareness of the field of adult literacy education. She learned about the kinds of supports teachers with more ideal working conditions enjoyed, as well as about the limited avenues for professional growth within the field. Within this context she became more cognizant of the lack of support her own program provided, both to her as a teacher and to her students. By the last interview Debbie had decided to leave the field, partially attributing this to her own lack of interest in teaching and partially to frustrations with the system, which, in her state, required testing and a required curriculum; such a structure limited, in Debbie's new perspective, the possibility of meeting learners' overall needs rather than just their language-skill needs.

Pamela: Pamela, a part-time ESOL teacher who had been teaching for 14 years, taught in a community-based program and participated in a mentor teacher group, missing the last two-hour session. She demonstrated minimal-to-moderate integrated change. Pamela's changes also began with a focus, in thinking and acting, on increasing her understanding of learners' needs, then changing the curriculum based on those needs.

Intrigued by the idea of goal-setting discussed in the professional development, she conducted activities in her classes to involve learners in goal-setting. Instead of just giving students a goal-setting form to fill out, she created a case study and scripted dialogue to model the goal-setting process for her learners. This activity helped her discover forces that hindered and helped them; she came to understand that discussing learner needs was not peripheral to the learning process, but an integral part of it.

We talked about what their goals are, we talked about whether or not our program was meeting those goals, and what their expectations are, and their evaluation of it. ... We talked about what's preventing you from coming here?
What makes it easy for you to come here? I changed the whole format. We have a questionnaire that we give students, and the way I did it this time was to break them into groups. I made it several steps rather than a one-shot deal. ... It gave them a springboard and that's what we had been missing before.

— Pamela, Wave Three interview

She then began to add other classroom activities to bring learners' daily lives into the lessons. She asked them to bring in problems they had in everyday life and then she wrote scripted dialogues about how they could deal with such problems (e.g., having a conversation with the landlord about faulty heat) that the students practiced orally with each other in the classroom and that they could take home to practice.

I learned a lot about dialogue this year, to tell you the truth, how important this is. ... I've done a continuous stream of writing my dialogues, because I did it for our thing [being observed as part of the mentor teacher group]. It worked well and I got input from them that it's one of the best things they can have.

—Pamela, Wave Three interview

Through this activity, she slowly began to learn more about students' lives and about other ways to bridge the gap between classroom and community. For example, when the learners talked about not fully understanding the way their children's schools worked, she and the learners together planned a field trip to the local elementary school.

The changes in her thinking and her actions in the classroom increased her desire to discuss curriculum with other teachers in her program; she proposed sharing one of the case study stories she had written but there was no venue for teacher sharing in her program. Her commitment to the field of adult education deepened, though, as she thought about ways for teachers to work together more collaboratively. She felt that the positive experience of the professional development increased her motivation to stay in the field and, although she was still testing the waters in terms of her role as more than just a teacher, she began to think about how she could work to increase the opportunities for teachers to learn from one another.

Esther: Esther, a second-year ABE and ESOL part-time teacher (18 hours per week), taught in a rural LEA; she participated in 18 hours of the mentor teacher group. She demonstrated significant integrated change. Through her participation in the professional development, Esther increased her self-confidence as a teacher and became a respected member of her team. The discussions with her mentor and with other teachers in her group (all of whom were from her program) reassured her that she was on the "right track" and that her colleagues valued her opinion. Esther's thinking broadened on the topic; she was particularly intrigued by the definitions of the three terms (motivation, retention, and persistence).[41] She also realized the importance of sharing theories of learner persistence with students, so that students can think proactively about the issue. She sought to find out about

---

[41] We define "learner motivation" as learners being engaged in learning while in class. "Retention" refers to learners attending class regularly and staying enrolled in the program until they reach their goals. We define "persistence" as learners seeing themselves as successful, lifelong learners, even if they "stop out" or drop out at any given point.

the forces affecting the learners in her classes by asking them to interview one another, but she didn't feel that this gave either her or the students the information she wanted about what might prevent students from staying in the program. So she tried another activity presented in the professional development: she and the learners all told the stories of their schooling experiences. This worked very well, and the students expressed their desire to share their stories with others in the community in order to encourage other learners to attend classes. Esther then adapted her curriculum; she and the class decided to approach the local media (television and newspaper) to broadcast and publish their stories. During class, Esther helped learners write and rehearse the script that then aired on a local television program, and she invited and made class time available for a newspaper reporter to come into the classroom to interview learners. She specifically connected these actions to two of the strategies— "creating safety" and "building community"—suggested by the professional development for addressing learner persistence.

> I think it affected motivation. I think the students have been very motivated this semester. The biggest thing they got out of this was that they actually can take control and what they want to do can happen.
> —Esther, Wave Two interview

Reflecting on this process, Esther felt that she became more aware than she had been prior to the professional development of the importance of listening to students, and she changed her lesson plans to add time for hearing about and responding to students' needs. As she did this, she learned of other needs expressed by the students: the desire to learn more about nutrition and the desire to get extra help with their difficulties/disabilities in reading.

In response to these student desires, she added a nutrition component to her curriculum. She sought and received permission from the director for the class to schedule a special lunch in the cafeteria, together with other classes, where students could talk about nutrition concepts. She requested and received permission from the director to attend an Orton-Gillingham learning disabilities training, so that she would know more about how to help students with learning disabilities. Even though Esther's actions were abruptly interrupted when she moved to Oregon with her family, she continued to think about the topic. One year after the professional development, she was still pondering the connection between learner motivation and assessment, feeling that assessing student progress should also involve assessing their motivation and persistence.

Meg: Meg, a veteran teacher in her sixth year of teaching, worked full time as a family literacy and ESOL teacher in a rural LEA; she completed all 18 hours of the mentor teacher group. Meg was the teacher in our subsample who demonstrated the most significant change. This professional development was truly transformative for her, in that it challenged and changed both her assumptions and her practice. Overall, she became very active in responding more to learners' needs through curriculum and program improvement, and advocating for better working conditions within programs. These outcomes were sustained; one year after the professional development, she was still pondering the issues and taking new actions following the trail she started in the professional development.

Meg used the inquiry process/cycle for addressing learner persistence. She first conducted a force field analysis with learners and was surprised to learn that the class wanted to meet more often. Based on learners' requests, she changed her own class schedule to add an extra class each week. The process of talking to students about the forces that affected their persistence led her to realize that she was not as learner-centered as she had thought, and she became more strongly convinced that teachers and programs should listen more in order to better address learners' needs. She wanted to hear, on a regular basis, learners' ideas for improving the class, so she added an evaluation journal and reflection time to the end of each class. She herself also began to regularly keep a journal about the class and began to view classroom situations more objectively, thereby decreasing her tendency to personalize issues and blame herself for lags in learner motivation, retention, and persistence. In response to learners' desire to have a more interactive curriculum and move beyond the workbooks she had been utilizing, she ordered and used a new curriculum, Crossroads Café. To make the class more interactive, she conducted two project-based learning activities. The first was a class project to create a student newsletter; the second was a project to create a new recruitment flyer. Changing the classroom structure and curriculum produced new questions about her practice; she pondered how much students' personal lives should affect classroom instruction and how much students were learning the skills they had wanted to acquire as she implemented project-based learning. At the program level, she began a support group for learners. She became an advocate for the students, twice supporting them to take their concerns about scheduling and poor classroom space to the director and helping them see the importance of advocating for program change as a group.

> *I think my teaching has shifted to this point [of taking learners' needs more into account] because of that professional development. If I hadn't asked the students what they wanted to learn, I would have continued doing it more [in a] teacher-directed [fashion].*
> —Meg, Wave Three interview

The second major change in Meg's thinking and acting stemmed from her realization of the connection between teachers' retention and learners' retention. She felt that teacher turnover, stemming from poor working conditions, would increase learner dropout. She found that other participants in the mentor teacher group, all of whom were teachers in her program, also shared this perception, and she acted to advocate within her program for pay increases, teacher access to budgetary information, and increased resources in their classrooms. Her desire for collegiality also increased, and she and the other teachers advocated with the program director for regular teacher meetings (which they got). She also encouraged her colleagues to advocate as a group for program improvements, but she learned that teachers fear losing their jobs as a result of speaking up. Her belief that teachers needed to have a strong voice in program decision-making was strengthened. Based on her new thinking about teachers' poor working conditions, she took action in the field by informally surveying other teachers, administrators, and/or professional developers in the state when meeting them at workshops and conferences. She asked them about teachers' working conditions and talked with them about common concerns, especially regarding teachers' low salaries. She came to believe that programs are in large part responsible for the marginalized conditions of teachers and students.

> *... [I]f the teacher's not motivated, then learners will not be. [Teacher] retention is also a problem, teacher persistence. As ... teacher[s], we are always looking toward making*

sure that learners' needs are met. I can't do that if my needs are not met. If I'm going to teach students to voice their opinions and to make changes, I need to do it also.
                                                                    —Meg, Wave Three interview

During our last conversation with Meg, one year after the professional development, she was still taking new actions and developing her thinking based on the changes she had already made as a result of the professional development. For her, more than any other teacher in our subsample, her thinking and practice had been transformed.

Acting Change

Acting change involves applying techniques and ideas learned in the professional development to the classroom. These changes can consist of actions made both on the topic studied in the professional development (LMRP), or they can be general (off topic) changes—using a new teaching technique, attempting to improve programs, or making contributions to the field of adult education.

I'm a copycat.. I'm the kind of person that if you tell me it might help, them I'm going to try this...if it doesn't work, it doesn't work, but I have to try it.
                                        —Emmanuela (native language literacy teacher)

There were four teachers in our subsample who demonstrated "acting change." The "acting change" teachers demonstrated more change related to the topic of the professional development (learner persistence) than did "thinking change" teachers, but also exhibited a number of action outcomes that went beyond the topic: three of the four added techniques from the professional development to their repertoire, using them off the topic. In other words, they took a technique they had seen in the professional development and used it in their classroom to address other content (such as health).

The use of the term "acting change" does not imply that the teachers' actions were not informed by thought; in fact, they were, and oftentimes by new ideas learned from the professional development. The teachers in this category experimented or tinkered with some ideas, but typically without active reflection and consideration for how these new ideas and actions contributed to or challenged their existing ideas about teaching or about the topic. Rather, these teachers' new actions appeared random in nature, or fairly inconsequential to the mainstay of their practice, and the changes typically were not sustained. Many of those who tried a technique to uncover forces affecting learners' persistence did not use this information to select a strategy for addressing the problem. Brenda, who will be discussed below, provides a good example of this. She used several techniques she acquired in the professional development to elicit information from her students, but did not follow up on the things she had learned.

Emmanuella: Emmanuella was a full-time native language literacy teacher in her first year of teaching, working in a uniquely community-centered program and, like a number of staff there, she was a former learner. She attended and completed the 18-hour multisession workshop. The main change she made was to try three techniques she learned in the professional development: she tried the force-field technique with students around their motivation to be in school, but found that it did not work, as the barriers students mentioned far outweighed the supports, leading students to become discouraged; she later used the technique in a health lesson. She used a form to help students break up long-term goals into a series of weekly goals. Emmanuella talked to the director and counselor about adding life-skills assessments to their intake process.

Emmanuella did learn about LMRP as a result of participating in the professional development, particularly about students' need for internal motivation. However, she did not tie this realization to any of the actions she took in the classroom; she did not express any theoretical reason for using these techniques, other than that she heard about them in the workshops. Outside of the program, she shared information that she gained from the workshops with other community service providers. She also, for the first time at any professional development, advocated for her own language needs during the workshop; since English was her second language, she explained to the facilitator and the other participants that she would appreciate some consideration of her need to ask for definitions or to have something repeated.

Emmanuella made one main thinking change, which was a dawning realization about the realities of teaching: teachers are not magical and cannot do everything for learners. In short, she took a good deal of action, but we found little critical reflection about the connection between her theories of persistence or student success and her actions.

Monica: Monica, a full-time adult education and pre-GED teacher with less than one year of experience, taught in a small urban library program; she participated in a multi-session workshop for the full 18 hours. She demonstrated "thinking changes" on several, unconnected fronts: the realization that her program was on the "right track" in its struggle with attendance problems; increased confidence in her teaching; and an awareness of the lack of options and career paths for teachers in the field, leading her to doubt that she would stay in the field. Her primary action was to "lighten up" in class, allowing more informal student-to-student interaction, although she couldn't say whether this action was prompted by the professional development. Her other actions took place on a program level. Monica persuaded her initially resistant fellow teachers to try a technique from the professional development that asked students to talk about their learning histories. Monica also advocated for a more stringent program-wide attendance policy; however, the idea was one that she held prior to the professional development and the program had already been discussing the new policy. None of these actions, however, was connected with an expressed theory that students needed to bond or that negative learning histories were a cause of dropout.

Brenda: Brenda, a new, part-time teacher, worked in two different programs: an ABE class in a site-based volunteer program where she was one of the few paid teachers, and a GED class in another program, both located in an urban area. She participated for the full 18 hours in a multisession workshop.

Brenda did exhibit a thinking change—a realization that there are many ways to teach.

If I learned nothing else, I learned that every teacher teaches differently. ... It helped me a lot to be working with other professionals ... we kept moving around in these different groups and trying different techniques. ... I think that some of that stayed with me, the differing teaching styles, different people...

—Brenda, Wave Three interview

Brenda's acting changes involved experimenting with several techniques she had seen in the professional development, such as varying her instruction format. She tried using small group and individualized instruction, and adding demonstrations to her standard straight large-group lecture format. She took at least three actions to find out more about learners: she tried a force-field activity asking students to list the "positives" of coming to class versus not coming to class; she asked learners to keep logs at the end of class explaining what worked and did not work for them; and she allocated a very limited portion of class time, at least once, for students to discuss "the negative things" interfering with the classroom.

You have to get them talking a little bit about some of these negative things. You can't let it overwhelm the class, but you need to let them have some outlet to talk a little bit.
                                                    —Brenda, Wave Two interview

However, Brenda did not understand what to do with the information elicited; she viewed these activities as peripheral to instruction, detached from any next step or direction. In addition, her use of the activities was short-lived: by the third interview, she no longer asked students about their lives, restricting any "dialogue" to their academic needs.

I wouldn't necessarily want to know personal information, whether they have four kids and they're divorced ... you can waste too much time getting into talking about personal problems. I would want to talk more about learning strategies, what works for them or [does] not work for them.
                                                    —Brenda, Wave Three interview

She glimpsed the importance of goal-setting but did not take action to find out about students' goals. She did ask her program director for pretest information on students, which he never provided. When she suggested that he institute course evaluations for each class, he recommended that she do it herself in her own class. In short, while Brenda took actions to vary her teaching, she expressed little to no theoretical understanding of why she took each action or how they fit together to improve student persistence or achievement.

David: David, an experienced, part-time (15 hours per week) GED instructor who worked in an urban multisite program, participated for the full 18 hours in a practitioner research group with teachers, all from his own program. He took action, through his practitioner research project, to persuade administration to change intake procedures: for one semester in his own classes, he rescheduled intakes to the beginning of class. redesigned the intake to find out students' postGED goals, followed up with the "supportive other" in learners' lives if they failed to attend class, proved that this process increased learner retention, and took this evidence to the director to make his case. When the idea of applying it to the whole program was rejected, he stopped doing it in his own classroom.

There was no evidence that David had added to a cohesive theory of what adults need to succeed; in fact, he came into the professional development with one idea, used it for one purpose, then abandoned it even though it was successful with his own learners. In his thinking, all changes were off the topic: he professed a preference for practitioner research and an interest in reading field-based publications such as *Focus on Basics*. He presented, when encouraged, for the first time at a state conference. We almost rated David as "no or minimal change," given that all of his changes were short-term, but because he took a significant though unsustained action, we placed him in this group.

Thinking Change

Thinking changes involve the acquisition of new ideas. Participants learned not only about the topic presented in the professional development, but many also increased their general teaching knowledge. Others gained increased awareness of issues in the field of adult education or in their learners' lives. They also gained insights into how they best learn and into the strengths and weaknesses of their programs.

> *Rather than changing techniques, it [the professional development] has changed attitudes. It didn't change the way that I taught as much as it changed the way I supported or tried to support students.*
>
> —Lucy, Wave Two interview

There were four teachers in our subsample who demonstrated "thinking change." Each of these teachers demonstrated a range of different types of thinking change, while action was limited. All four teachers gained knowledge of learners and LMRP but, for three of the four, their major outcome was a thinking change *off* the topic. They felt that what they gained most from the professional development was support from other practitioners, support that would help them deal with difficult program situations, ones in which they felt marginalized and powerless or isolated and burned out. For some in this type, the thinking shift was profound and may have an important impact on the teachers' long-term change trajectories, but they took very little or no related action during the course of our study.

Lucy: Lucy, a full-time experienced EDP,[42] ESOL, and college-prep teacher who taught in an urban union-funded workplace-based educational program, participated in practitioner research and attended all the sessions. Her attitude and role as a program member changed as a result of participating in the professional development. Lucy felt she got support from other participants in the practitioner research group to influence program management that she felt was creating a negative atmosphere in the program. She was intrigued by the concept of increasing student involvement in the program, and she was interested in initiating activities such as having current students act as recruiters of new students, having students do the orientation for new students, and having students serve as classroom aides. Lucy felt she gained a new awareness of the causes of LMRP, especially the "stopping out" phenomenon, and she applied this understanding to one of her students: Lucy realized that she was mistaken in thinking this student had dropped out. She also became interested in practitioner research and applied the analytical framework used in the professional development to her reading of other adult education articles. However, her actions were minimal compared to her ideas; she did take steps to improve program atmosphere by being as encouraging as possible to the learners in her own classes.

Caroline: Caroline, a part-time GED teacher who had been teaching for two years in a large multisite program before she participated in a mentor teacher group for the full 18 hours, changed her view about her program as a result of the professional development. She realized that the program's treatment of her was not acceptable and that her current situation was untenable. She was not teaching a class of her own, but instead had been assigned as a

---

[42] External Diploma Program, a type of adult secondary education program where high school dropouts complete specific course requirements and are then entitled to a standard high school diploma, rather than a GED.

coteacher, based on her program's assessment of her as a poor teacher. When she realized that she couldn't continue to work that way, she persuaded her coteacher to let her conduct a class activity that would respond to learners' desires. Her confidence in her own teaching ability was buoyed as a result. Caroline realized that mutual support among staff was critical, and she began to think about the importance of teachers' involvement in the program. She felt the professional development also made her think about the importance of knowing more about learners and their personal lives and about how that knowledge might fit in with teaching GED. Despite these new realizations, she did not (or could not) take much action to address the issue of learner persistence.

Gail: Gail was a full-time job skills teacher who had been teaching preemployment training and vocational skills for three years in a large urban multisite adult education program; she participated in the workshops and attended for 16.5 hours (she attended one of the workshop sessions in a neighboring state, because she couldn't attend that workshop on the date it was offered in her own state for 4 of these hours). She felt she reconnected to the field of adult education and to teachers in her own and another state as a result. Her main change was reflected in how she thought about herself, her work, and the field.

I really think it's given me a bigger awareness, more so than everything else, and [I identify] myself more as an adult education instructor.

—Gail, Wave Three interview

Gail resolved to continue working in the field, and she set up a "support group" of similar adult education teachers in her region to provide an avenue for sharing (and venting).

We all work for adult education, we seem to all be in the same boat. One person referred to us as the lone rangers, which kind of feels that way, but we have more of a support system that we've developed, we feel better about it. That there's somebody we can call if we're frustrated or have an idea of sharing different things.

—Gail, Wave Three interview

Realizing that teaching and LMRP are more complex than she'd previously thought, Gail felt she listened more to learners after the professional development, but this had no real effect on her teaching practice aside from trying, randomly, a few new techniques she learned in the professional development.

Andrea: Andrea was an experienced full-time GED teacher with a background in vocational education who taught in an urban program. She participated in all 18 hours of a practitioner research group. She felt she learned about the topic of learners' motivation, and she started to consider the connection between brain research, learning math, and learner motivation. By the time of the last interview, she indicated that she would like to apply this knowledge to the classroom but had not yet done so; according to her, her classroom practice had changed little.

I did learn some things. I've just put them into my being and then gone on and lost the labels for them somewhere. ... Right now I'm still doing it the way I've [always] done it. I know there are some things that are different, but I couldn't tell you where or when or why.

—Andrea, Wave Three interview

Andrea thought about shrinking topics to smaller units that would fit within one class session, in response to students' irregular attendance. One action she did take—presenting with other practitioners at a conference on her practitioner research—was discounted by her as insignificant. She stated that she became more aware of how program structures and issues affected LMRP but hadn't taken any action to influence such structures.

> *I became aware of the systemic problems that could come up because, as someone who just stayed in my classroom and minded my business, I wasn't aware of some of these other problems and how they can interfere with retention and students' progress.*
> —Andrea, Wave Three interview

She also increased her awareness of and interest in professional journals in the adult education field, and felt she was reading slightly more learning theory.

No or Minimal Change

At the other end of the spectrum from those who exhibited integrated change are those who made no or minimal change. These participants demonstrated little change in thinking or action. While they may have tried a few techniques learned in the professional development, there was no evidence of any sustained change. Overall, there was little indication that any of the three objectives of the professional development were achieved.

> *I don't think my thoughts about the subject of learner motivation have changed a lot. There were some specifics that I remember…that students don't necessarily drop out, they stop out. I feel that, as a result of this professional development, if I lose students, it's not my fault; it's to be expected.*
> —Beth, Wave Two interview

Four out of 17 participants in our subsample exhibited "no or minimal change." Although these teachers acquired a new concept or two, there were no real changes in thinking or acting on or off the topic.

Penny and Elizabeth: Two of the four teachers in this group could be characterized as "rejecters." Penny, a part-time (five hours a week), experienced GED teacher who teaches in a 12-week GED-prep course, where all instruction is individualized and workbook-based, participated in and completed the mentor teacher group development. Elizabeth, a part-time (22 hours per week), experienced ESOL teacher, participated in the mentor teacher group, missing one session and one observation. These two teachers came away from the professional development believing that it was the learners' chaotic lives (rather than something that could be changed within the classroom or program) that accounted for lack of persistence; the professional development seemed to confirm their belief that there is nothing practitioners can do to influence learner persistence, and teachers should neither blame themselves nor spend time working on or worrying about it as an issue.

> *[The retention problem comes from students'] lack of interest, present job demands, present family demands, peer pressure—(our students are younger than some), inability to do the work, [and] present economy [which] allows people to be hired despite lack of*

education. I am still not sure if the data [information in the professional development] we've discussed has any significant import since we can't change previous problems and upbringing of so many. I really feel that nothing's going to keep some of these people.

—Penny, Wave Three questionnaire

Now we can put labels on it (dropping out) and we can look at things we've read, and maybe categorize them, you know, this one's leaving because of such-and-such. ... I have come to the conclusion (and probably because of this study group) that you will never motivate some people. You just can't interest them. ... some people who are just overwhelmed with life that they can't handle ... you're always hearing excuses, with kids, with this and that, my job...

—Penny, Wave Two interview

Deirdre: Deirdre, a part-time (about 20+ hours a week), experienced ESOL teacher, participated in a practitioner research group, but dropped out after nine hours, only attending the first, second, and fourth sessions. She strongly disliked the professional development, feeling the facilitation was poor and the purpose of the practitioner research unclear. She did change her thinking off the topic related to her negative experiences in the professional development; she reflected on her expectations for well-designed professional development, and began to define the elements of good facilitation. Recognizing that clear structure is important in professional development, she thought about the implications both for the professional development she facilitates and for her classes, but she admitted that she gained little from the professional development itself, walking away with no new strategies and implementing none:

I understood how important a really good facilitator is to the process and progress of the group, how important it is to have some structure for the work that's supposed to be done. Those are the kinds of things you can keep in mind for yourself because they related to being a teacher, too ...

—Deirdre, Wave Three interview

Beth: Beth, a part-time (16 hours per week), experienced ESOL teacher who participated in a practitioner research group and completed it, also demonstrated change off the topic: from visiting a learner's home as part of the practitioner research project she conceived, she came away with a feeling that she would like to work in family literacy, and she successfully negotiated with her director for a new position in the family literacy component of the program. Although it may seem that clarifying one's vision as a professional would be a big change, Beth demonstrated no change in any other way; her thinking on the topic did not change, and she demonstrated no acting change relevant to her role as a teacher, program member, or member of the field.

I am convinced that we, as educators, can do our very best and still not be able to affect learner motivation. So many factors cannot be changed.

—Beth, Wave Three interview

Discussion of How Teachers Changed

The majority of teachers who completed the professional development (attending at least 12 of the 18 hours) did report some change; relatively few experienced no change at all. For most, however, the primary change was thinking change (learning more about the topic). About a quarter of those who finished the professional development demonstrated integrated thinking and acting change, but only a few of these teachers experienced major or transformational change.

We identified four types of change resulting from participation in the professional development: (1) no or minimal change, (2) thinking change, (3) acting change, and (4) integrated change. According to the objectives of the professional development, we "preferred" to see change where thinking was integrated with acting, where teachers achieved all three objectives (learn more about topic, critically reflect on your work and plan for action, take action to address the topic) and where teachers utilized an inquiry approach/cycle to addressing the topic (learn about the issue, hear from learners about forces affecting them, select a strategy based on forces heard from learners, take action to implement strategy, reflect on results of the action).

The evidence indicates that, with only 25% demonstrating integrated change, it was difficult for teachers to integrate thinking and acting change. Those teachers who did demonstrate integrated change also changed more overall, even in thinking and acting not related to the topic of the professional development. While some teachers in the sample may have actually changed more than they indicated through their questionnaires, or may have had changes in thinking and acting later than one year after the professional development was completed, it still appears that there were teachers who participated in the professional development who did not make as much immediate change as we would have hoped.

The largest percentage of teachers changed within their role as teachers. Many teachers also made changes in thinking and acting off the topic of learner persistence, such as improved self-confidence as a teacher, increased appreciation of importance of collegiality, greater awareness of the field and of program and system strength and weaknesses, and increased understanding of research.

Overall, far fewer teachers changed in ways that we would have preferred, even when they attended up to 18 hours of professional development, but almost all gained at least some knowledge on the topic. It is possible that teachers who took limited action may put their new knowledge into play many months or years later, perhaps after attending future professional development that triggers some motivation to act. However, it is also possible that teachers who changed little experienced some combination of individual, program, and system factors that prevented them from changing more. We next investigate the factors influencing (supporting or hindering) the amount and type of change demonstrated by the teachers in our sample. Identifying the most important factors (from both whole sample and subsample data) will, we hope, allow us to understand why some teachers didn't change more as a result of participating in professional development.

Factors Influencing Teachers' Change

In this section, we answer the second part of our research question: "What are the most important factors (individual, program, system) that influence (support or hinder) teacher change as a result of professional development?" First, we outline the factors that we hypothesized would influence teacher change. Then, we present data and findings from the whole sample and from the subsample that indicate which of these factors are most important in influencing change.

We developed a set of hypotheses, gleaned from the professional development literature and from our experience in the field of adult basic education, about the individual, professional development, and program or system factors that were most likely to support or hinder teacher change:

1. Individual factors:
    *   Motivation to attend the professional development
    *   Level of formal education
    *   Years of experience in adult education
    *   Level of professional development consumption
    *   Level of commitment to working in adult education
    *   Belief in purpose of literacy instruction
    *   Venue of first teaching experience (K–12 or ABE)
    *   Type of teaching (ABE, ESOL, GED)
    *   Teaching situation (one-on-one, small class, large class)
    *   Teaching experience in K–12
    *   Age of teacher
    *   Belief that knowledge about the learner is important
2. Professional development factors:
    *   Model of professional development
    *   Amount (hours) of participation in professional development
    *   Quality of professional development group (as rated by researchers)
    *   Quality of professional development (as perceived by participants)
    *   "Coparticipation" in professional development with other teachers from same program
3. Program or system factors:
    *   Enrollment policy
    *   Program concurrently working on same issue (learner persistence)
    *   State in which participant worked
    *   Required use of curriculum
    *   Access to prep time
    *   Access to resources
    *   Number of hours teacher works each week in adult education
    *   Access to benefits
    *   Program type
    *   Teachers' perception of leadership in the program
    *   Opportunities for collegiality among teachers
    *   Perceived freedom to decide what and how to teach
    *   Amount of paid professional development release time
    *   Program situation (decision-making in the program)

We characterized factors as important when there was evidence in both the whole sample (quantitative) data and the subsample (qualitative) data to support their connection to either amount or type of change, or when the evidence for the factor was particularly strong in either the quantitative or qualitative. Table 12 below outlines all the factors we examined in this study by their *level of importance*. **Most important** factors are those for which we have strong evidence, either through statistical significance found in that variable in the whole sample (quantitative data) or through clear, consistent findings in the subsample (qualitative data). Factors that are **somewhat important** are those for which there are trends but no strong statistical confirmation in the whole sample or those for which there are emerging but not conclusive trends in the subsample. **Not important** factors are those for which there is no statistically significant relationship with change and no clear trend in the qualitative data.

In other words, teachers who gained the most from the NCSALL Professional Development were those who:

- Had a strong motivation to learn about the topic or about theories of good teaching and wanted to integrate new learning with their actions.
- Began their teaching in the field of adult education, had fewer years of experience in the field, and did not have a post-graduate degree.
- Participated in high-quality professional development (as rated by the researchers), for more hours, and perceived it to be of high quality.
- Worked in programs where they had a voice in decision-making *and* where strategies suggested in the professional development had not yet been implemented.
- Received benefits as part of their adult education jobs and had access to prep time.

To a lesser extent, teachers tended toward more change when they were not required to use a particular curriculum, worked more hours in adult education, had more paid professional development release time, expressed a weaker level of commitment to staying in the field of adult education, participated in professional development groups where all participants were from the same program, and had access to opportunities to share ideas with colleagues during and after participating in the professional development. Model of professional development was not one of the most important factors, although there were different patterns of change related to model.

In the sections below, we explain our hypotheses and present the evidence related to each of the important individual, professional development, and program or system factors investigated in our study. Since we already know that the level of participation in the professional development activities is significant (the more a teacher participated, the more she or he was likely to demonstrate change), the findings presented here are for the completers only. (We note the few variables in the analyses where it made more sense to examine the whole sample.)

Table 12: Factors That Influence Teacher Change, by Level of Importance

Factor Type	Most Important	Somewhat Important	Not Important
Individual(out of 12 factors)	• Motivation to attend the professional development • Years of experience in adult education • Venue of first teaching experience • Level of formal education	• Level of commitment to working in adult education	• Level of professional development consumption • Belief in purpose of literacy instruction • Type of teaching (ABE, ESOL, GED) • Teaching situation (one-one-one, small class, large class) • Teaching experience in K–12 • Age • Belief that knowledge about the learner is important
Professional Development (out of 5 factors)	• Hours of NCSALL PD attended • Quality of PD (as rated by researchers) • Perceived quality of PD (as rated by teachers)	• Type (model) of professional development • "Coparticipation" in professional development (with teachers from the same program)	
Program or System(out of 14 factors)	• Access to prep time • Program situation[43] • Access to benefits	• No required curriculum • Number of working hours • Amount of paid professional development release time • Opportunities for collegiality among teachers	• Student enrollment policy • State in which participant worked • Access to resources • Program working on the same issue • Teachers' perception of leadership in the program • Perceived freedom to decide what and how to teach • Program type

[43] "Program situation" refers here specifically to how much programs were already addressing problems of learners' persistence *and* how much voice teachers had in decision-making in their program.

How Much Did Individual Factors Matter?

We found that the *most important individual* factors influencing change among theteachers in our sample included:

- **Motivation to attend the professional development.** Those teachers with a strong need to learn, either on the topic or about good teaching and student success, changed more.
- **Years of experience in adult education.** Those teachers with fewer years of experience changed more.
- **Venue of first teaching experience.** Those teachers who began their teaching career in adult education (not K–12) changed more.
- **Level of education.** Teachers with a bachelor's degree or less changed more.

Among the *most important* individual factors were the following:

Motivation to attend the professional development

Our hypothesis was that teachers without a strong motivation to learn would change less, based on theories of adult learning, and we concluded that this hypothesis was supported. Teachers in this sample who responded to a question about their primary reason for attending the professional development (n=87) reported a variety of reasons for attending the professional development:

- 30% to learn more about the topic.
- 22% to participate in a particular model of professional development.
- 20% to learn more about teaching in general.
- 8% because their director asked them to attend.
- 5% because they wanted to be part of the research study.
- The rest because they wanted Continuing Education Units (CEUs), thought the facilitator would be good, a colleague was attending, or wanted to meet other teachers.

The qualitative data also supports the finding that teachers had a variety of motivations for attending the professional development, and that an interest in the topic (although it was the most-cited reason) was not the primary reason for the majority of teachers who participated.

In Wave One, we asked teachers to rate, on a scale of 1–6, to what extent they considered learner motivation, retention, and persistence to be a priority topic, compared to other topics on which they have sought or would seek professional development. The mean score for the completers (n=83) was 5.07 (SD =.93), which indicates a strong interest; on the other hand, it was not a score of six across the board, indicating that some of the teachers in our sample had other topics of equivalent or greater importance to them. Statistically, a teacher's higher rating on this question of LMRP as a priority topic was not associated with either measure of change.

However, we had much richer information from the subsample teachers on the question of motivation to attend the professional development, and within the subsample we saw a definite pattern: teachers who had reasons for wanting to attend *other than* to learn about the topic or about teaching (i.e., their director urged them to attend, the professional development was convenient in time and location, they wanted continuing educational units or credits, or they were interested in a particular professional development model) more often demonstrated limited or nonintegrated change. The teachers who demonstrated integrated change expressed strong motivations, coming into the professional development, to solve the problem of learner dropout or to learn more about teaching. The connection between motivation and change was strong enough in the subsample that we identify it as an important factor influencing change.

Years of experience in adult education

Our hypothesis was that teachers who have been teaching in this field longer would change less (perhaps because they feel they have greater knowledge about teaching and, consequently, weaker motivation to learn on any given topic). For completers of the professional development, we found that the hypothesis was supported, for both amount of change ($r=-.245$, $p<.05$, $n=81$) and for type of change, as seen in Table 13 below:

Table 13: Type of Change by Years of Experience in Adult Education (Completers only, $n=81$)

Type of Change	n	Mean Years of Experience	SD
No or minimal	21	13.19	6.10
Nonintegrated	40	7.65	6.96
Integrated	20	8.35	5.87
Totals	*81*	*9.26*	*6.83*

$F=5.270$, $p<.01$

In our subsample, the pattern was also supported: all of the "no or minimal" change teachers had more than three years of experience in the field of adult education, whereas three of the five integrated change teachers were relatively new teachers. Although the sample size is small, we concluded that teachers who had been teaching for more years in the field were less likely to demonstrate greater overall change and change in a preferred direction.

Venue of first teaching experience

We were not surprised to find that most teachers (69%) in our sample began their teaching career in a non–adult-education venue. We hypothesized that a teacher who first started teaching in the adult education field, rather than in K–12, would be more likely to change as a result of participating in professional development, because they would be eager for ideas and confirmation that they were in fact doing a good job as a teacher. This hypothesis was supported.

In our sample, teachers whose first teaching experience was in adult education were more likely to change. This factor was significantly related to both overall amount and type of change. For completers (n=81) whose first teaching experience was in adult education, the mean score for overall amount of change was higher (M=10.92, SD= 7.82) than those whose first teaching experience was K–12 or other (M=7.89, SD =4.62), a statistically significant difference (ANOVA F=4.85, p<.05). Also, those whose first teaching experience was in adult education were more likely to show integrated change. Among those who completed the professional development, 11 of the 25 (44%) whose first teaching experience was in adult education demonstrated integrated change, compared to 9 of the 56 (16%) whose first teaching was in K–12, also a significant difference (χ^2 = 7.3, df=2, p<.05, n=81). This finding was supported among subsample teachers, where three of the four "no or minimal change" teachers started teaching in K–12 but three of the five "integrated" change teachers began their teaching in adult education.

The multiple regression analysis also highlighted the importance of this factor. One of the two variables that most predicted change in a preferred direction (integrated change) in our study was whether teachers' first teaching experience was in adult education.[44] Those teachers who reported that their first teaching experience was in adult education, rather than in K–12, were more likely to demonstrate both overall change and change in a preferred direction as a result of participating in this professional development.

Level of formal education

Based on the belief that teachers with more formal education have better-developed philosophies of education and theoretical schema upon which to "hang" new learning, we hypothesized that more formal education overall would correspond to more change. Our hypothesis was *not* supported: those participants who had more than a B.A. (master's or doctorate) were *less likely* to demonstrate both overall change and change in a preferred direction.

In our questionnaire, we asked teachers to list their highest level of formal education completed; we did not, however, ask them in what field they held a degree. Among the completers (n=83), those with a bachelor's degree *or less* had a higher mean score for amount of overall change of 10.69 (SD=6.5), compared to those with a master's degree or higher (M=6.24, SD=4.1). Thus, those with less formal education were significantly more likely to change (ANOVA F= 13.37, p<.001). Level of formal education completed was also significantly related to the type of change teachers made: of the 20 completers who demonstrated integrated change, 14 of them (70%) had a bachelor's degree or less. The subsample supported the rejection of our hypothesis that more education would be associated with more change, since all of the four teachers who fell into the "no or minimal" change category had master's degrees, but three of the five teachers who demonstrated "integrated change" did not have a master's or a teaching certificate.

---

[44] The other factor that predicted change in a preferred direction (integrated, as opposed to thinking or acting, change) was teachers' access to benefits as part of their adult education job.

Level of education also emerged from multiple regression analyses as one of the strongest predictors of two types of change: (1) overall amount of change, and (2) any change at all (as opposed to no change). Out of nine variables run in an analysis of factors related to amount of overall change, education was the strongest predictor of change; those teachers with a bachelor's degree or less were more likely to demonstrate higher amounts of change than those teachers with a master's or doctoral degree. Out of ten variables tested to determine their relation to demonstration of any change at all, only the education variable was significant: those with a bachelor's degree or less were 11 times more likely to change than those with a master's or doctoral degree. No other variables were significantly associated with whether a teacher demonstrated any change (as opposed to no or minimal change). Education was not a predictor of whether teachers made more "preferred" change (integrated change, as opposed to thinking or acting change).

To ensure that change among those with higher levels of formal education was not restricted by the fact that these teachers entered the professional development with more knowledge about learner motivation, retention, and persistence (although few teachers in our sample had participated in any formal courses specifically related to adult education, so they were not likely to have acquired specific information on the topic by virtue of a master's degree), we reviewed their level of knowledge about the topic in Wave One. There was no relation *before* participating in the professional development between higher levels of education and more knowledge or acting change on the topic: many teachers with master's degrees reported little knowledge of strategies for addressing LMRP and no previous action taken to address the issue, and other teachers without master's degrees sometimes demonstrated some knowledge and previous action prior to with the professional development. Therefore, we feel confident that amount of change was not a function of more or less knowledge and action before the professional development began, but rather a function of differences in thinking and acting as a result of the professional development.

One individual factor emerged as *somewhat important* in influencing teacher change. Level of commitment to working in adult education was a factor that emerged as important in the quantitative but not the qualitative analysis. We do not have good data from the subsample on this variable, as we did not probe in depth about a teacher's commitment to working in the field of adult education. We did, however, ask several questions about commitment on the questionnaire, but it is unclear whether these questions are an accurate gauge of commitment and we are not sure how to interpret the results. Our hypothesis was that teacher change as a result of participating in professional development would be related to their level of commitment to working in the field of adult education: the stronger the commitment, the more change. We hypothesized that teachers who felt more strongly that adult education was their long-term career would be more likely to take in and use new knowledge, but this hypothesis was *not* supported.

In the Wave Three questionnaire, we asked teachers to what extent (using a scale of 1–6) they considered the field of adult education to be their long-term career; to what extent they desired to be teaching/working in the field of adult basic education one year from now; and to what extent they desired to be working in the field five years from now. We then created a composite score for each participant who answered all three questions, which averaged their ratings on all three questions. While means for commitment by type of change were not significantly different, there was a negative and significant correlation ($r=-.33$, $p<.01$, $n=70$) between commitment and overall amount of change for those who completed the professional development.[45] In the multiple regression analysis of overall amount of change, level of commitment to working in adult education emerged from nine variables tested (along with level of education and number of hours attending the NCSALL Professional Development) as a significant predictor of overall amount of change. (Level of commitment was not a significant factor in multiple regression analyses of whether teachers demonstrated any change at all or more preferred [integrated] change.) Thus, the higher their commitment to the field, the lower the overall amount of change; commitment level was not related to type of change.

However, since we did not explore level of commitment during interviews with teachers in the subsample, it is difficult to say how reliably these three questions gauge actual commitment to the field. There were strong positive correlations among age, more experience in the field, and strength of commitment, such that older teachers tended to have been in the field longer, and teachers with more years in the field expressed a stronger desire to stay in the field and see it as their career. Perhaps it is the case that teachers with more years of experience are more settled in the field and more confident in their teaching, and thus have less motivation to change. Since we do not have good information from subsample participants to back up this finding from the whole sample, we see it as a "somewhat important" variable worthy of further research, if researchers can determine a reliable measure.

Individual factors that were *not important* (not related) to type or amount of change for those teachers who completed the professional development included:

Level of professional development "consumption."

We collected information from participants about both the amount of professional development, on any topic, attended in the year before participating in our study and the amount of professional development attended on the topic (whether and how much other professional development on the topic of learner motivation they attended before, during, or after participating in the NCSALL Professional Development). Neither of these was related to amount or type of teacher change.

Belief in purpose of literacy instruction

As the professional development endeavored to help teachers act on issues important to students' lives, we hypothesized that teachers who believed the purpose of literacy is social change, rather than improvement of basic skills, would change more. We measured whether teachers believed the purpose of literacy instruction was primarily the acquisition of basic skills or social change. Their beliefs on the purpose were not related to whether they demonstrated change or not.

---

[45] Correlations between each individual question and change are as follows: The correlation between seeing adult education as their long-term career and overall change was -.243 ($p<.05$, $n=70$). The correlation between "working in the field one year from now" and overall change was -.328 ($p<.01$, $n=70$), and the correlation between "working in the field five years from now" and overall change was -.341 ($p<.01$, $n=70$).

Type of teaching (ABE, ESOL, GED)

We asked teachers to identify their primary type of teaching, and there were roughly equal numbers of teachers who taught ABE (0-8), GED, ESOL, and an equal combination of ABE/GED or other (vocational, family literacy) in our sample. However, primary type of teaching was not related to either amount or type of change among those who completed the professional development.

Teaching situation

We asked whether teachers taught learners in a one-on-one situation, a small class, or a large class setting; teaching situation did not appear to be related to teacher change.

Teaching experience in K–12

Sixty percent of respondents in our study had taught in the K–12 system. Teachers who taught in K–12 at one point in their career were less likely to have demonstrated change compared to teachers who had not taught in K–12; however, the difference was not statistically significant.

Age

Age was not a factor directly influencing change.[46]

Belief that knowledge about the learner is important

Since the professional development asked teachers to find out about the forces affecting learners' persistence, and some of these forces related to learners' lives, we asked teachers how important they felt it was for adult education teachers to know about their learners' lives and backgrounds. A stronger belief in knowing who learners are was not related to change.

For a further explanation of the hypotheses underlying these factors, and the findings of these analyses, please see Appendix D: Additional Information on Factors.

---

[46] Age, however, was positively correlated with number of years teachers had worked in the field of adult education. The more years in the field, the less likely a teacher was to demonstrate change.

How Much Did Type, Amount, and Quality of Professional Development Matter?

We found that the *most important professional development* factors that influenced change among the teachers in our sample included:

- **Hours of NCSALL Professional Development attended.** Those teachers who participated for more hours demonstrated more change.
- **Rated quality of professional development groups (as rated by researchers).** Teachers who participated in professional development groups of higher quality demonstrated more change. (Higher quality groups had good facilitation, good group dynamics, and a good model with flexibility to adapt to the needs of the group.)
- **Perceived quality of professional development (as rated by teachers).** Those teachers who gave the professional development activity a higher rating demonstrated more change.

Among the *most important* professional development factors were the following:

Hours of participation in NCSALL Professional Development

The first hypothesis related to professional development factors was that attending the professional development for more hours would lead to more change. Across the whole sample, this hypothesis was supported, with more hours of participation (from 0-18 hours) positively and significantly associated with both overall amount of change ($r=.25$, $p<.05$, $n=95$) and type of change, as shown in Table 14:

Table 14: Type of Change by Mean Hours of Participation

Type of Change (N=95)	n	Mean Hours of Participation	SD
No or minimal	32	13.64	5.54
Nonintegrated	42	16.33	2.73
Integrated	21	15.67	3.26
Totals	95	15.28	4.13

$F=4.252$, $p<.05$[47]

Teachers who completed at least two thirds of the professional development experienced more change than dropouts or those who did not participate at all; for those who attended at least 12 of the 18 hours, the number of hours above 12 was not significant to amount or type of change.

Additional support for the importance of attending more hours of the professional development came from the multiple regression analysis of factors related to overall amount

---

[47] The significant difference between groups was between the "no change" group and the "nonintegrated change" group ($p<.05$). Differences between the "integrated change" group and either "no change" or "nonintegrated change" were not significant.

of change. Attending more hours emerged as one of three (out of nine) significant factors predicting change.[43]

Rated quality of professional development group (as rated by researchers)

Of the 15 groups, researchers rated 6 as high quality, 4 as medium quality, and 5 as low quality.[49] For completers ($n=83$), the mean score for amount of overall change went up as the rated quality of the group went up: mean for low-quality groups was 5.6 ($SD=4.6$), mean for medium-quality groups was 9.0 ($SD = 6.3$), and mean for high-quality groups was 9.6 ($SD= 6.3$). While this difference was not significant, the trend is clear, and we feel with a larger sample size these differences would be statistically significant.[50]

The rated quality of the groups was, however, significantly associated with the type of change. Of the 20 completers who demonstrated integrated change, 12 of them (60%) were in the high-quality group, compared to 6 (30%) in the medium-quality group, and only 2 (10%) in the low-quality group. Even with the small sample size ($n=83$), this difference was statistically significant ($\chi^2=12.6$, $df=4$, $p<.05$). These findings indicate that better quality of facilitation, better group dynamics, and flexible adherence to the professional development model[51] were associated with more change in a preferred direction.

Perceived quality of the NCSALL Professional Development (as rated by the participants)

The third hypothesis in this category was that the higher the participants rated the professional development quality, the more likely they would be to make changes. To test this hypothesis, we asked participants a series of questions, using Likert scales (1=weak or low quality, 6=strong or high quality) about how they would rate the overall quality of the NCSALL Professional Development in which they participated. We also asked them to rate particular elements of the professional development, such as facilitator/presentation, group dynamics, length of the activity, session organization, and readings/materials. (See Appendix C for data tables of participants' ratings of key aspects of the NCSALL Professional Development and of how they feel it affected them.)

We averaged the individual responses to the 13 questions we asked about the quality of the professional development. We then used this combined average (a number between 1 and 6) as a measure of each subject's perception of the quality of the professional development.

---

[48] The other two factors predicting overall amount of change were level of education and level of commitment to working in adult education. See Appendix D for a full description of the multiple regression analyses.

[49] Please see Appendix C for a complete description of the process of rating the professional development groups.

[50] Post hoc analyses show that the difference in the mean score of the low-quality group as compared to the high-quality group at the 95% confidence interval is approaching significance ($p>.05$).

[51] Flexible adherence means that the facilitator neither omitted significant activities planned in the professional development design, nor stuck to the design like a script; rather, high-quality groups were characterized by completion of all of the activities in the design but with discussions adapted to the needs and questions of the participants.

Teachers' perception of the quality of the professional development was positively and significantly correlated with overall amount of change (r=.246, p<.05, n=81). Their perception of quality was also positively and significantly associated with the type of change they demonstrated, as shown in Table 15 below:

Table 15: Type of Change by Teachers' Perception of Professional Development Quality (Completers, n=81)

Type of Change	n	Mean Combined Quality Score	SD
No or minimal	21	3.90	.710
Nonintegrated	40	4.57	.625
Integrated	20	4.44	.533
Totals	81	4.37	.681

F=8.047, p<.01

Interestingly, there was not a significant relationship between the rated quality of the group (as rated by the researchers) and perceived quality of the group (as rated by the teacher participants). Teachers in the lowest-quality groups (n=21) gave their professional development a mean rating of 4.23 (out of 6); teachers in medium-quality groups (n=29) gave their professional development a mean rating of 4.51; and teachers in the highest-quality groups (n=42) gave their professional development a mean rating of 4.33. Since both rated quality and perceived quality were associated with type and amount of change, but not with each other, it is an indication that teachers in our study experienced professional development differently from one another[52] and, in some cases, differently than how we as researchers rated it.

Professional development factors that were *somewhat important* to type or amount of change included:

Type (model) of professional development

Although all three models were designed to be high quality, and all three offered sustained exposure to concepts (18 hours over 3–6 different sessions), with encouragement to try activities and take action between sessions, the mentor teacher group and practitioner research group models offered slightly more one-on-one support for making direct changes in teachers' classrooms and programs. Therefore, we hypothesized that teachers participating in the mentor teacher groups and practitioner research groups would demonstrate more change overall and more change in a preferred direction (toward more integrated change) than would teachers in workshops. (Please see Table 4: Common and Unique Elements of the Three Professional Development Models in Chapter One or Appendix A: Professional Development Models and Objectives for more information about the three different professional

---

[52] Correlations also show that years working in adult education field (r=-.23, p<.05) and years teaching adult education (r=-.22, p<.05) were both significantly and negatively correlated with the teachers' perception of the quality of the professional development, indicating that the longer the participant had been working and teaching in the field, the less she or he liked the professional development.

development models.) However, the model of professional development—whether the teacher participated in a multisession workshop, a mentor teacher group, or a practitioner research group—was not significantly related to type of change. We did, however, identify different patterns of change among the models, and a larger sample size might have produced significant differences.

Teachers who participated in and completed practitioner research groups and mentor teacher groups demonstrated slightly more change overall than did workshop participants. Practitioner research group completers had a mean amount of change of 9.67 (n= 24, SD=7.66), and mentor teacher group completers had a mean amount of change of 9.25 (n=24, SD=6.71), while workshop completers had a mean amount of change of 7.52 (n=35, SD=3.53). Although this difference was not statistically significant, practitioner research group and mentor teacher group completers demonstrated more awareness of the field, a greater appreciation for learning with other teachers, and increased knowledge of research.

A slightly higher percentage of teachers who participated in the mentor teacher group model demonstrated integrated change; the three subsample teachers who demonstrated the most significant integrated change all attended mentor teacher groups. Overall, percentages of teachers demonstrating integrated change were higher in the two "reform" models of professional development: 29% of mentor teacher group completers (n=24), and 25% of practitioner research group completers (n=24), as compared to 20% of workshop participants (n=35), demonstrated integrated change. However, this difference was not statistically significant, as shown in Table 16 below.

When looking at amount of overall change by type of change, the model of professional development comes into play only for those teachers demonstrating integrated change (the most preferred direction of change). Figure 4shows that teachers in mentor teacher groups and practitioner research groups who demonstrated integrated change also demonstrated relatively higher overall amounts of change, as compared with workshop participants who demonstrated integrated change.

Table 16: Type of Change by Professional Development Model (Completers only; n=83)

Professional Development Model	n	Type of Change			
		No Change	Non-Integrated	Integrated	Totals
Workshop	35	8	20	7	35
Mentor teacher group	24	7	10	7	24
Practictioner research group	24	8	10	6	24
Totals	*83*	*23*	*40*	*20*	*83*

χ^2=2.1, df=4, p>.72, not significant

In fact, no workshop participant had an "overall amount of change" score over 15 (in a range of 0–30), whereas four mentor teacher group participants and five practitioner research group participants had scores between 16 and 30.

We also asked participants what their first choice for type of professional development model would have been; participating in a model preferred by the teacher was not associated with type or amount of change.[53]

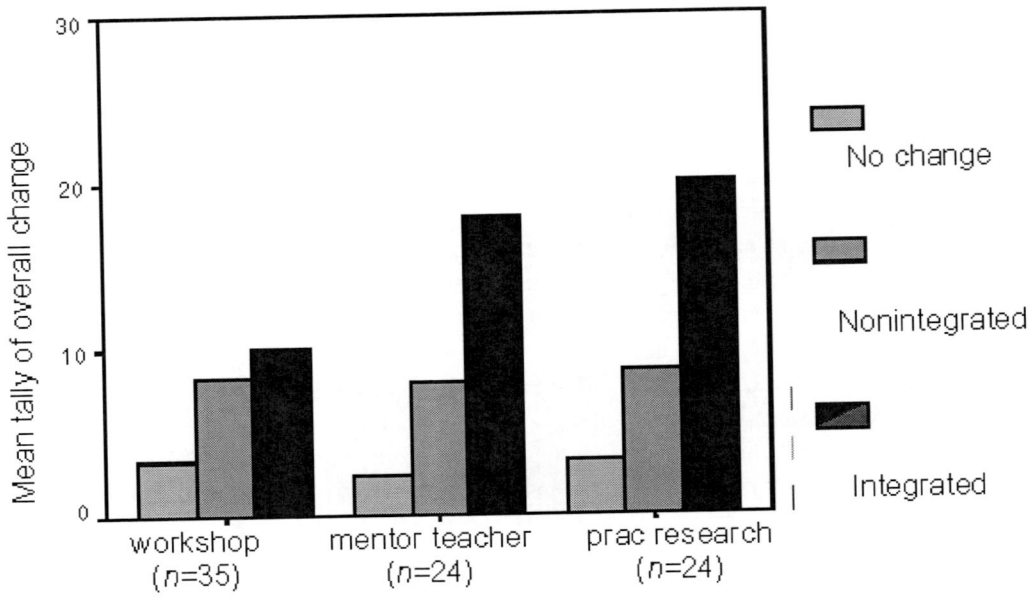

Figure 4: Type and Amount of Change by Professional Development Model (Completers only; *n*=83)

Being in professional development with others from the same program ("coparticipation")

In adult basic education, where most professional development is offered through a state system, teachers often participate in centrally located workshops or training where the other participants are teachers from different programs. On occasion, however, more than one teacher from a program participates in the same professional development activity. When the program itself organizes the professional development, all of the participants would be teachers from that program. In these instances, teachers would have a colleague or colleagues from their program as a "coparticipant" in the professional development, and these teachers might be able to share ideas between and after professional development sessions about what they learned and how they might take action. If this were the case, would teachers change more?

This factor emerged from the qualitative analysis by accident. We did not pose a hypothesis about this before the professional development, because teachers from each of the states self-selected to participate; we did not control who would join each professional development group. Therefore, we did not think to collect data from the whole sample about

---

[53] In other words, teachers who participated in a mentor teacher group and said their first choice would have been a mentor teacher group were not more likely to change than teachers whose first choice was mentor teacher group but actually participated in a workshop or practitioner research group.

multiple participants from the same program participating in the same professional development group. However, it happened that there were teachers in our subsample for whom one of these three types of "coparticipation" applied:

1. Another teacher or teachers from the subsample teacher's program were participating in *other NCSALL Professional Development groups* studying learner motivation, retention, and persistence.
2. Another teacher from the subsample teacher's program was participating in the *same professional development group* (i.e., same workshop, same mentor teacher group) as the subsample teacher.
3. All of the teachers (including the subsample teacher) in the professional development group were from the same program.

The incidence of this "coparticipation" in professional development among the subsample teachers is presented in Table 17, where we present information about the type of professional development, the type of "coparticipation," the quality of the professional development group, the relative amount of ongoing teacher sharing in the program, and the type of change the subsample teacher demonstrated.

Overall, coparticipation was varied as a factor supporting change, but the pattern suggests that, when it is combined with higher-quality professional development and moderate-to-high levels of opportunities for teacher sharing, it can support change. Some teachers (Monica, Penny) did not attribute much importance to it or even downplayed it as a contributing factor when asked. Other teachers (Meg, Esther) stressed how critical it was to have another teacher interested in the topic whom they could talk to when they thought about trying out new activities; these two teachers demonstrated the most significant change and participated in mentor teacher groups where all of the other participants were from their program.

This was so new to us, we were able to talk as a group. Otherwise, we would have felt lonely. It was so exciting to be together and be able to voice our issues: "This is what I'm going through and what should I do?" ... That really brought a positive into the program.

—Meg, Wave Three interview

The change in these two teachers was strong enough that we propose a hypothesis for further research: coparticipation, coupled with more opportunities for teachers to share ideas between and after professional development sessions, supports change. Although this did not emerge as one of the most important factors, it lends support to the idea of program-based professional development in cases where the program can also provide real opportunities for participating teachers to have ongoing discussions about what they are learning and applying from the professional development.

Table 17: Extent of Coparticipation in NCSALL Professional Development Among Teachers in the Subsample

Sub-Sample Teacher	Model of Professional Development	Type of Coparticipation	Quality of PD group	Level of In-Program Teacher Sharing	Type of Change
Meg	Mentor teacher group	All other teachers in group were from her program	High	Moderate	Significant integrated
Esther	Mentor teacher group	All other teachers in group were from her program	Medium	Moderate	Significant integrated
Erica	Workshop	Another teacher from program in same group	High	High	Minimal-to-moderate integrated
Debbie	Workshop	Another teacher from program in same group	High	Low	Minimal-to-moderate integrated
Monica	Workshop	Another teacher from program also in same group	High	High	Acting
David	Practitioner research group	All other teachers in group were from his program	High	Low	Acting
Brenda	Workshop	Another teacher from program in practitioner research group, third teacher in program in mentor teacher group	High	Low	Acting
Penny	Mentor teacher group	Another teacher from program also in same group	Low	Moderate	No or minimal
Beth	Practitioner research group	Another teacher from program also in same group	Low	Low	No or minimal

How Much Did Program or System Factors Matter?

We found that the *most important program and system* factors that influenced change among the teachers in our sample included:

- **Access to prep time**. Those who received prep time were more likely to change.
- **Program situation.** Teachers who worked in programs that were not already taking action to address learner persistence *and* where teachers had a voice in decision-making were more likely to change.
- **Access to benefits.** Those teachers who received one or more benefits from their adult education job (health or dental insurance, vacation, etc.) were more likely to change.

Access to prep time

Whether a teacher had paid time to prepare for classes was another in the constellation of working condition factors we investigated, the hypothesis being that teachers with prep time would be better supported to make changes in thinking and acting. In Wave Two, we asked those teachers who were still teaching (n=78) if they received paid preparation time. Of these 78 teachers, 38 (54%) reported that they had received paid preparation time in the past year. Of the 18 completers who made integrated change, 13 (72%) of them had received paid preparation time. Those who received paid preparation time were more likely to make integrated change and this difference was statistically significant (χ^2=6.66, df=2, $p<.05$, n=78). Mean overall amount of change was also higher (9.0 out of 30) for those with prep time (n=38, SD=5.78) than for those without prep time, who had a mean of 7.9 out of 30 (n=40, SD=5.11), but this difference was not statistically significant.

Program situation

We hypothesized that teachers working in programs that proactively encouraged their actions in addressing learner persistence would demonstrate more change after participating in professional development. On the questionnaire, we asked several questions to determine (using a scale from 1 to 6) how strongly teachers felt supported by their directors, believed they had a voice in program decisions, and felt that their voice was used in program decision-making. None of these factors was related to type or amount of change. On the hypothesis that teachers would make more change if their programs were simultaneously working on addressing the same issue they were learning about in the professional development (in this case, learner motivation, retention, and persistence), we asked each teacher if their program chose to try to improve one issue each year and, if so, what issue had been chosen that year. Of the 106 teachers in our sample, 60 teachers indicated that their program chooses a program improvement issue each year; of those 60, 11 teachers indicated that the issue was learner persistence. However, there was no pattern of change associated with programs' decisions to focus improvement on LMRP.

However, the information gleaned from the subsample interviews painted a very different picture. Teachers talked long and eloquently about the support they did and didn't receive from the director and leadership in their program, on this and on other topics. Through the stories of the changes in their thinking and acting, we deciphered a clear connection between program structure and teacher change in particular circumstances: where the program was not already working on this topic *and* where the teacher had a voice in program decision-making, teachers made more change inside and outside of their classrooms, related to the topic. However, if either one of these circumstances did not obtain (program already addressing the topic, teacher did not have a voice in decision-making), change was less. For example, in cases where the program had already taken action to address learner motivation, retention, and persistence, teachers made less change. In cases where the teacher had no access to decision-making in the program, the teacher made less change. But where work was needed in the program related to the topic AND the teacher had the ability to make suggestions about how to do that work, more change happened.

When teachers didn't have a voice in decision-making in the program, they often made thinking changes, recognizing strategies and developing ideas for addressing the issue, but since they did not feel that they had the ability to influence the director, they initiated far fewer actions. Teachers felt they had learned new knowledge and strategies but did not feel they could or should initiate change when there were either real barriers (director rejected an idea presented by the teacher) or perceived barriers (teacher didn't know how to influence the director or felt it was hopeless to try). The profiles of subsample teachers in the "Support from Subsample Data about Important Factors" section provide examples of this factor. We conclude, therefore, that program situation was an important factor, in that the program was a supportive influence for change when the program had been inactive on this topic *and* when the program had mechanisms for and an environment conducive to teachers' having a voice in decision-making.

Access to benefits

We hypothesized that teachers working under good conditions and in well-supported jobs would be in a better position to take action. The configuration of working condition factors included access to paid prep time, paid professional development release time, more working hours, benefits, and stability on the job.[54] (We did not ask about salary.) We discovered that access to benefits was related to type of change, but not to overall amount of change. Although the mean amount of overall change was higher for those with benefits than for those without, the difference was not statistically significant. However, access to benefits seemed to be an important factor supporting more integrated change. Of the 18 completers who demonstrated integrated change, 14 of them (78%) reported that they received benefits as part of their adult education job, while only 4 (22%) of those who demonstrated integrated change did not receive benefits, and this difference was statistically significant, as shown in Table 18.

On the multiple regression analysis of factors related to type of change (integrated change as opposed to thinking or acting change), benefits emerged as one of two factors that predicted more "preferred" (integrated) change.[55] Those who received benefits as part of their adult education job were five times more likely to demonstrate integrated change than to demonstrate thinking or acting change.

Table 18: Type of Change by Benefits (Completers for whom we have data; *n*=69)

Access to Benefits	Type of Change			
	No Change	Non-Integrated	Integrated	*Totals*
Yes	8	13	14	*35*
No	10	20	4	*34*
Totals	*18*	*33*	*18*	*69*

χ^2=7.3, df=2, *p*<.05

Program or system factors that were *somewhat important* to type or amount of change included:

---

[54] Benefits were strongly correlated with type of program (those who work in CBOs were more likely to receive benefits as part of their adult education job), but program type itself was not a direct predictor of change.

[55] The other factor predicting integrated as opposed to thinking or acting change was venue of first teaching experience (whether the teacher first taught in adult education rather than K–12).

Required use of curriculum.

In some programs, teachers were required to use a specific curriculum, one that was developed by the program or by the state. In other programs, teachers developed their own curriculum. Our hypothesis was that teachers who had the ability to develop their own curriculum would make more changes than teachers who were required to use an established curriculum. We collected information to test this hypothesis by asking teachers whether or not they were required to use a curriculum. Fifty-six (about 58%) of the teachers were not required to use a curriculum by their program or state. Those participants who *were* required by their program or state to use a curriculum were less likely to change in a preferred direction. Of the 18 completers who showed integrated change, those who could choose their own curriculum were twice as likely to show integrated change (12 of 18, or 67%) compared to those who were required to use a curriculum. However, this finding was not statistically significant, and use of a required curriculum was not significantly related to overall amount of change. However, when analyzing this factor among subsample teachers, we concluded that GED teachers who taught in programs designed to "teach to the test" demonstrated less change than did teachers who had more flexibility to develop their own curriculum.

Number of working hours

Our hypothesis for this factor was that teachers who work more hours or work full time in the field of adult education would be more motivated to make change and have more time and support to take action based on what they learned from the professional development. We collected information from the participants about the number of hours they worked (across all adult education jobs) each week, and we found that 24 participants worked more than 35 hours a week (which we designated as full time); this equals roughly one quarter of the participants.

Number of working hours was not a significant factor in either overall amount of change or type of change. However, teachers with more working hours were more likely to demonstrate integrated change: teachers demonstrating integrated change worked an average of 26.27 hours per week ($n=22$, $SD=11.71$), while teachers who demonstrated nonintegrated (thinking or acting) change worked 22.27 hours ($n=41$, $SD=10.91$) and teachers who demonstrated no change worked an average of 21.83 hours a week ($n=36$, $SD=12.00$). Of the 24 full-time (more than 35 hours per week) practitioners who participated in the professional development (and for whom we have data), an equal number fell into each of the three types of change. Since there were fewer teachers overall who demonstrated integrated change, the proportion of teachers within the integrated change type who were full time is higher (36%) than the proportion of full-time teachers within the nonintegrated (20%) or the no change type (22%).

Although the quantitative data did not show a significant relationship between more hours of work in adult education and change, the qualitative data indicated a much stronger trend. Among our subsample, all four teachers who made no or minimal change worked part time. Not having enough time was a common theme in interviews with the 10 subsample teachers who were part time,[56] and it was frequently cited by participants in their questionnaires as a barrier to change.

Amount of paid professional development release time

The final factor we examined is the number of hours annually a teacher is paid to attend adult-literacy-related professional development. In our sample, which may not be representative of the field as a whole since it is made up of teachers who chose to come to professional development, the mean paid professional development release time was 18.6 hours (n=98, SD=22.639) per year. Almost one quarter of the teachers in the sample report that they received no paid professional development release time. The amount of paid professional development release time was not directly a significant factor in either amount or type of change, although the trend was that those completing teachers who demonstrated more preferred (integrated) change had an average of 24 hours of paid time per year (n=19, SD=20.5), whereas teachers demonstrating thinking or acting (nonintegrated) change had an average of 16.3 hours (n=39, SD=16.9) and teachers demonstrating no change had an average of 20.2 hours (n=22, SD=22.5).[57] Similarly, when asked how they would rate (on a scale of 1–6) their access to professional development, there was no significant relationship to amount or type of change, but teachers demonstrating integrated change felt their program was stronger in this aspect; the average rating given by teachers who demonstrated integrated change was 4.8 (n=20, SD=1.21), compared to a mean rating of 4.3 for teachers demonstrating nonintegrated change (n=39, SD=1.2) and a rating of 4.3 (n=21, SD=1.4) for teachers demonstrating no change. In addition, those who dropped out of the professional development had half as many annual hours paid professional development release time: dropouts averaged 9.44 hours per year (n=16, SD=8.6), whereas completers, as a whole, averaged 18.8 hours per year (n=81, SD=19.4), and relationship between number of hours participants attended the NCSALL Professional Development and their annual professional development release time was significant (r=.30, p<.05, n=97).

Opportunities for collegiality among teachers (inside and outside of the program)

We hypothesized that teachers who feel they have more opportunities to meet and share with or talk to colleagues, either inside or outside of the program, would feel more supported to change. We asked teachers several questions about their level of collegiality (the opportunities they have for meeting and sharing with other teachers), then formed a composite score for collegiality overall. We also asked teachers how many times per year,

---

[56] Working full time was also significantly related to having paid prep time (χ^2=7.1, df=1, p<.01, n=77), which was related to change among completers.

[57] There were nine cases that could be considered outliers (teachers who reported high numbers of hours of paid professional development release time); one teacher reported paid release time of 150 hours a year, which is equivalent to almost four weeks of paid professional development release time. Taking out these outliers does not change either the trend or the significance: teachers demonstrating integrated change still have more paid hours of professional development release time (17.83 hours per year, n=18); however, this mean was still not significantly different from teachers demonstrating no change or nonintegrated change.

within their program, teachers meet to share ideas for teaching (not just to talk about parking policies or paperwork). Across the whole sample, neither collegiality nor frequency of teacher sharing meetings was associated with type or amount of change.

However, this factor appears to be similar to program situation: while it was not significant as measured by the indicators above, it surfaced as a strong factor for many teachers within the subsample analysis and in the open-ended questions of the survey. In our subsample, there were teachers who had adequate opportunities for collegiality in their programs and those who did not. For those who felt isolated in their programs, there was a clear pattern in the qualitative analysis that showed that they felt this lack of collegiality affected their initiative to take action based on what they had learned in the professional development. Lack of opportunities for collegiality operated as a barrier to change for those who valued collegiality. Teachers felt that sharing ideas with colleagues, even colleagues who had not participated in the professional development, helped them to continue thinking about what they had learned and prompted them to take action. Therefore, we identify opportunities for collegiality as a somewhat important factor because it was voiced so strongly by teachers in the subsample interviews and open-ended questions as a barrier (to those who lacked opportunities) and a support (to those who had opportunities) to taking action. However, because it did not emerge in the quantitative analysis, further research could investigate exactly how collegiality supports change for those teachers who value it. These findings tentatively support the use of program-based professional development models, especially if the program also organizes opportunities for teachers to share ideas during and after the professional development.

The following program or system factors that were *not important* to type or amount of change included:

Enrollment policy (closed, rolling, or open)

We hypothesized that closed enrollment would support change, and open enrollment would hinder change, based on the assumption that open enrollment contributes to more turbulence in the classroom, making it more difficult for teachers to implement their planned lessons, including new activities. If the teacher is constantly dealing with new students, then she or he may not have as much time, energy, or freedom to adopt new practices. Most of the teachers (71%) in our sample (for whom we have data about enrollment) teach in classes and programs with open enrollment policies; only 16 teachers teach in closed enrollment situations.[58] However, enrollment policy was not related to either amount or type of change.

State in which participant worked (Connecticut, Maine, or Massachusetts)

The number of teachers completing the professional development in each state was roughly the same (MA=26, CT=29, ME=28). We hypothesized that the differences in delivery and professional development systems among the states might contribute to

---

[58] "Rolling enrollment" was defined in the questionnaire as classes or programs where students may enter only at specified times (i.e., once a month).

differences in teacher change, but this was not the case: there were no significant differences in either type or amount of change related to state in which the participant lived.

Access to resources (i.e., access to own classroom, desk, resource room, photocopier, materials, etc.)

We hypothesized that teachers who work in programs with better facilities and more resources would be better supported to change. Neither facilities nor resources demonstrated a significant relationship to either measure of change.

Program working on the same issue (learner persistence) as part of its program improvement effort

Sixty participants indicated that their program has a process for program improvement. Of those, only 11 indicated that their program was actively addressing learner persistence, and this proved not to relate to amount or type of change, although in the subsample we found that teachers whose programs had not previously addressed the problem of learner persistence *and* where those teachers had access to decision-making did seem to demonstrate more change.

Teachers' perception of leadership in the program

We hypothesized that strong leadership in a program (at least as reported by the teachers themselves) would be a supportive factor for change. We asked teachers a range of questions about how strong they perceived the leadership to be in their program.[59] On a composite of leadership questions, among teachers who completed the professional development, there was no relationship between teachers' view of their programs' leadership and either measure of change, although teachers who viewed their program leadership as weak demonstrated more change.

Perceived freedom to decide what and how to teach

We asked teachers to rate (on a scale of 1–6) how much freedom they had to decide what to teach and how to teach in their classrooms and created a composite score. There was no significant relationship between perceived teaching freedom and either measure of change.

---

[59] Questions included the extent to which teachers felt their directors supported them to make change, rating of overall quality of leadership in the program, and rating of directors' expertise.

Program type

Whether the program the teacher worked in was a community-based organization (CBO), a local education agency (LEA) connected to a school district, a correctional facility, library, homeless shelter, workplace, community college, or other type of program was not associated with change.

For a further explanation of the hypotheses underlying these factors, and the findings of these analyses, please see Appendix D: Additional Information on Factors.

Support from Subsample Data about Important Factors

In the sections above, we presented the most important factors from all the data, across all teachers in the sample. Teachers were more likely to change if they:

- Were motivated to learn about the topic or about theories of good teaching and student success
- Had fewer years of experience in adult education
- First taught in adult education (rather than in K–12)
- Had less formal education
- Attended the professional development for more hours
- Participated in professional development groups rated high quality by researchers
- Participated in professional development groups they (teachers) perceived to be of high quality
- Worked in programs that had not yet addressed the issue of learner persistence *and* where they as teachers had some voice in decision-making
- Received benefits as part of their adult education job
- Received paid prep time as part of their adult education job

To a lesser extent, factors that supported change included access to paid professional development release time, more working hours in adult education, a lower level of commitment to working in adult education, and flexibility in changing the curriculum. Collegiality and coparticipation (when coupled with opportunities for ongoing discussion between and after professional development sessions) were also secondary but still somewhat important factors. Finally, type (model) of professional development did not emerge as a key factor, although different patterns of change were associated with the three different models.

Looking across the entire sample of teachers provided us with one way to identify important factors from the multitude that might affect teachers. For any given teacher, however, these individual, professional development, program and system factors interacted to either prevent change or support it. The stories of the subsample teachers helped us to see how factors like motivation, education, experience, working conditions, and collegiality varied and prevented change in some teachers and supported it in others. By looking at these factors and the experiences of teachers within each type of change, we understood better how such factors interact. Specifically, for three of the four types of change (no or minimal change, thinking change, and acting change), we wanted to know how the absence of important factors might have prevented more change. For the fourth type of change (integrated), the type of change we "preferred" to see as a result of this professional development, we wanted to know how the varying presence of these factors worked, together and separately, to support change.

Factors Related to "No or Minimal Change" in the Subsample

In this section, we discuss the factors that influenced the four subsample teachers who made little or no change. Why didn't they make more changes in thinking and acting, and how did the various factors hinder them? Many of the factors that contributed to lack of change in these four teachers were mirrored in the larger sample: lack of motivation for professional development, poor professional development group quality, more experience in the field, and advanced degrees. Working conditions were also bare bones for this group as a whole:

> *Money is low. There're no perks, no benefits. We're not paid for prep time. I would like to see them make [teaching in adult education] a full-time job. I would like to see fewer of us teaching more hours. We have expressed it and we're always told that this is the way it is.*
>
> —Beth, Wave Three interview

All of these teachers were part time. All were experienced teachers[60] in adult education, and all had master's degrees. Three of the four began their teaching in the K–12 system. They appeared to be satisfied with both their own teaching and their programs, and none came in with a strong motivation to acquire deeper concepts about teaching. They were also all in the lowest-quality groups, with generally poor facilitation and poor group dynamics. Perhaps for this reason, three of the four disliked the professional development, and two were confused about its purpose, not being sure whether they were involved in a national study on learner persistence or on professional development.[61] Coming into the professional development, none of the teachers in this type expressed strong motivation related to the issue of learner motivation, retention, and persistence; their longer experience in the field may have contributed to a feeling that there was nothing new to learn.

> *[In relation to formal professional development] I just don't see anything other than renaming things. I don't see a lot of new ideas. I don't know, maybe I'm just getting hardened to the whole thing. ... I'm being very negative, but I guess I am looking for something, but I don't know what it is.*
>
> —Penny, Wave Three interview

---

[60] The only other part-time experienced teacher in our subsample took more action than these teachers and is therefore included in the "more action than thinking" category, but his actions were not sustained from Wave Two to Three and were limited to his practitioner research. He also didn't change his approach to teaching; his main changes involved a desire to to read more research and (initially) the desire for more collegiality with others (but this desire for collegiality also was not sustained through Wave Three). In some ways, he belongs in the "no or minimal change" group.

[61] At the beginning of the first session of each professional development activity, a member of the research team or a trained proxy gave an orientation about the study to the participants, and we explicitly informed participants that the focus of the NCSALL research was the effectiveness of professional development, not learner persistence.

It was just of minimal interest and importance to me at this point, because I've been in this field a long time. I was a counselor, so I dealt with all those issues. None of it was new to me.

—Elizabeth, Wave Two interview

Their reasons for joining the professional development were either convenience, interest in the model, or the urging someone in their program who advised them to attend. Penny's motivation for attending the professional development was primarily to inform others of what she considered her program's successful individualized instruction format, and, as for several other GED teachers in our sample, since passing the GED test is the sole goal of her program, the content of the professional development (trying to help learners persist) did not seem relevant either:

I'm very confident in what I do which is a terrible way to be because you can always learn. Every year when they ask "what would you like?" I would like a sharing session with everyone in the vicinity. But then, people come to our program and we're the ones with the experience so we end up sharing our ideas and normally rejecting their ideas ... we listen, we try to get something out of it but we end up giving our ideas because they're working for us.

—Penny, Wave One Interview

You can't be terribly creative, you can't do these wonderful things: "oh, let's go out into the community and have a field trip" because you're teaching to the test.

—Penny, Wave Three interview

Elizabeth, having worked as an ABE counselor for nine years before teaching, was a strong "rejecter" of the topic and she wished that the professional development had consisted solely of being mentored on a topic of her own choice. Deirdre was not completely "invested" in the NCSALL Professional Development on learner motivation, seeing it as a lot of work that competed with the other professional development she was attending, and she expressed doubts about the value of practitioner research itself. The poor quality of their groups and their general dislike of the professional development was in line with the finding from the overall sample that both rated and perceived quality of the professional development were associated with type and amount of change. Model did not seem an important factor, although none of the subsample "no or minimal change" teachers attended a multisession workshop.

Factors Related to "Thinking Change" in the Subsample

For these four subsample teachers, we wondered why, if their thinking changed, more action did not accompany it. Motivation seemed to play a role here: the most important common factor (for three of the four teachers) seemed to be a particular need or concern, unrelated to the topic, coming into the professional development. Three of four were dissatisfied with their program or teaching situation and had a strong need not associated with the topic of learner persistence: one had a need for collegiality and rejuvenation; one, a need to be respected as a teacher; another, a need to influence the program administration's negative attitude. In all three cases, the most significant change they experienced was a realization or attitude change directly related to this need or dissatisfaction. The fourth subsample teacher in the "thinking change" type did not seem to feel any particular need or motivation coming into the professional development, either on or off the topic. However, three of the four teachers demonstrating change of this type were confident and satisfied with themselves as classroom teachers coming into the professional development. None of these teachers expressed a strong need to change how they taught or how they addressed learner motivation, and this may be a factor in why there was so little change on the topic. All four had teaching certificates or advanced degrees.

Three of the four taught GED and/or job skills; their teaching was focused on basic skills, predetermined goals, passing tests, and curriculum with a clear vocational focus. Changes in action may have been limited by either their own or their program's inability to focus on learner persistence as part of the curriculum. Also, two of these teachers felt that they had no decision-making power in their program and thus found it difficult to initiate change at the program level.

> *I haven't been heard, no, I have not been heard. I don't feel that I'm listened to. It makes me feel that I am an outsider. I'm pretty powerless. So if you feel powerless, you're not going to try to institute change, are you, on a program level?*
> —Lucy, Wave One interview

Model again did not seem to play an important factor, since all three models of professional development were represented in this type. Although we rated their groups as being mixed in quality (two were high-quality groups, one medium-quality, and one low-quality), the teachers in this group all rated the professional development as high quality; this may be due to the fact that the professional development offered three of these teachers what they wanted off the topic: support within an unsupportive program, connection to other adult education teachers, the opportunity to talk with other teachers about concerns and issues.

> *I enjoyed that group of people [the other participants in the professional development] immensely. There are a lot of new ideas, a lot of enthusiasm that I didn't necessarily feel here in [my state].*
> —Gail, Wave Two interview

> *The staff needs to be supportive of each other, and the situation I was in last year, it was lacking. ... I was encouraged to seek a more positive work setting for myself and it helped build up my self-esteem.*
> —Caroline, Wave Three interview

Factors Related to "Acting Change" in the Subsample

In our subsample, there were four teachers who demonstrated primarily acting change. Our main question here, then, was why these teachers, three of whom were new teachers, did not integrate the actions they took with new knowledge or thinking. The key factor here seemed to be that these teachers were primarily motivated by the need to acquire new techniques they could apply quickly, regardless of content, in their classes. All four teachers in this type liked the professional development; all were in what researchers rated as high- or medium-quality professional development groups, and three of the four participated in the workshop model. Three of four were new teachers who had not taught in K–12. While factors such as being new to the field or to teaching support change, probably explaining why they made the changes that they did, the missing factor seems to be the motivation and skill to tie actions to a theory of good teaching and student success. As teachers just at the beginning stages of developing a philosophy of teaching and learning, they were primarily looking for techniques and confidence (rather than to deepen their concept of teaching) so thinking on the topic was not integrated into a cohesive theory of what adult learners need.

I had a lot of theory in graduate school, which is applicable, and it's helpful and I'm using it, but you can't just keep throwing theory at me and expect me to produce. I can't do it. I have to have something practical. I have to fit it into a framework.

—Brenda, Wave Three interview

I'm looking for a magic thing, but I haven't found it. ... I'm always looking for what can help me, I'm looking for things that could help them [students] more. There's a lot that I don't know.

—Emmanuella, Wave One interview

The three new teachers also worked in programs where the issue of learner persistence had already been discussed within the program, perhaps explaining why program action was limited. Overall, it does not seem that any came to the professional development with a burning need, but, rather, as new teachers, were simply on a path to learn and this was professional development that was offered and available. Their interest in the topic was minimal to moderate. They were more interested in acquiring new teaching techniques that they could use in their classrooms.

As a new teacher, I just felt I was kind of soaking that up as a sponge as much as I could...

—Brenda, Wave Three interview

They [the professional development] give me materials and they give me papers, then I start to teach that way, the way I was supposed to teach it. I'm a copycat ... I'm the kind of person that if you tell me it might help, them I'm going to try it. If it doesn't work, it doesn't work, but I have to try it.

—Emmanuella, Wave Two interview

The fourth, more experienced teacher was only attending because it was convenient and he had a point to prove to his program; when his program was not interested in changing based on the evidence he provided from his practitioner research, he gave up on his change and reverted to his previous teaching style.

The [practitioner] research fell on deaf ears. All I was told is, "Let's continue doing what we're doing." And I said "OK."

—David, Wave Three interview

Factors Related to "Integrated Change" in the Subsample

These five teachers made the type of changed we "preferred," to a greater or lesser extent. We looked at their profiles in order to understand how the factors supported them to change in a way that enabled them to integrate thinking and acting. Many of the important factors played a role for these teachers: strong motivation to learn about the topic and theories of good teaching, programs that had not addressed the topic of learner persistence but were receptive to input from teachers about how they might improve, coparticipation, and opportunities for ongoing collegiality.

The professional development these teachers attended was of high quality, and the teachers perceived it as such. None of the teachers demonstrating this type of change participated in practitioner research: three were in mentor teacher groups, the other two in workshops. Two of the three minimal-to-moderate integrated change teachers missed one of the sessions, and in each case, these were the last sessions, where the focus was on planning and strategizing for further action, perhaps explaining why their change was minimal-to-moderate rather than significant.

All expressed strong motivation, coming into the professional development, to address learner persistence, with a strong recognition of it as a problem. All teachers, for different reasons, expressed a need and desire to find a better, more theoretically based way to teach. Unlike the teachers in the thinking change (who either had no strong need or whose need was related to something outside of teaching, such as collegiality or voice in program decisions) or the teachers in the acting change (whose main need seemed to be different techniques to use in the classroom), the teachers in the integrated type were looking for a way to teach that included all of the theories of what helps learners be successful. The fact that all five teachers lamented their lack of better organizational or curriculum planning skills, which perhaps results from their limited formal training, highlights their awareness of the importance of those skills, as opposed to other teachers in our study who appeared to us to do a limited amount of curriculum planning and appeared unaware of its importance.

> I had no training in teaching. I know that teachers have education; it's essential. I need to know how to put together lessons and how to organize information and put it into the classes. ... How do you present to students in a way they're going to understand? ... There has to be some sort of direction for the students, when they walk in the classroom, of where we are going.
>
> —Esther, Wave Three interview

The structure of the professional development encouraged them to learn from practice, from listening more carefully to their learners. For each, the feedback they got from the learners encouraged them to sustain these practices over time. One difference between these teachers and those who did not demonstrate integrated change seems to be that integrated change teachers changed in their approach to teaching to a degree significant enough to keep them from reverting back to the old way of teaching.

Program structure played an important role in change for these teachers. We identified two program aspects that figured in teacher change: (1) Did the teacher have a voice in program decision-making? and (2) Was the program already working to improve learner persistence? What we saw, at least among the sample of teachers participating in our study, is that program structure and current activities related to the topic played a role in how much teachers could change; specifically, teachers had more opportunities for change when their program was not already taking action to address the problem *and* when the program structure gave them opportunities to suggest change. Where programs were already taking action to improve learner persistence, teachers' change was more limited. Where the teacher wanted to make a change but program philosophy or decision-making structure did not match, change was also limited. In two cases, (Debbie and Pamela), the program structure was either so isolating or so impermeable to input from teachers that the program actions they attempted were rejected, leaving them with only the classroom as an arena in which to make change. Neither teacher had received an orientation as a new teacher nor had been evaluated as a teacher; neither had access to regular staff meetings where teachers were included in decision-making.

> *We're on our own. There's no support. None. ... Maybe that's why ... I gravitated toward mentoring. I was so desperate for some kind of feedback! Am I doing a good job? Isolation is difficult and gets in the way of me learning. I need to be stimulated and I need the ideas of other people. ... I think we need to find out from learners what it is that is holding them back. And that's a program responsibility. I think [poor attendance] is because they're not getting programs that are suiting their needs. ... But I think that whatever they [learners] need in order to make it is not being offered to them.*
> —Pamela, Wave Two interview

Both worked in large, top-down bureaucratic systems where adult education teachers were at the bottom, and their programs rejected the changes they suggested (such as having more teacher workshops or holding a class on a Saturday instead of a weeknight). These two teachers worked in programs where teachers were isolated and had no decision-making power to implement change and where no actions were being taken to address learner persistence.

In another case (Erica), the program was already taking many of the actions that her new knowledge indicated would lead to learners' success and persistence, so she simply joined the program actions already underway. In this case, the teacher had a voice in decision-making but program actions were already underway to support learners' success and persistence.

The two teachers with the most significant integrated change both worked in programs where there was some role for teachers in decision-making *and* where little had been done by the program to address learner persistence. Although the programs varied in the amount of support offered to the teachers, neither program resisted the new directions the teachers took. For example, Meg's first step was to join with her colleagues in the professional development to press the director to institute regular teacher meetings where they could brainstorm strategies to address learner persistence. This effort was successful:

> *We [the teachers in the professional development] couldn't meet the director as a group because of our teaching schedules so each and every one of us went in our different times and said, "Look this is what we're interested in. How can you make this happen?" And he said, "Hey, this is great." So we meet every Friday once a month. He's paying us and providing this on our time.*
>
> — Meg, Wave Two interview

In addition to a program structure and situation that encouraged action, both of the teachers who demonstrated the most significant change participated in mentor teacher groups where all of the other participants were teachers from their own programs.[62] Both had important needs that were met by the specific type of professional development in which they participated. Neither had previously participated in professional development that was ongoing and highly collegial. As a new teacher with virtually no exposure to the field and a significant lack of confidence, Esther needed reassurance; the small size and egalitarian nature of the mentor teacher group provided her with a safe environment, which she identified as the most essential condition to her learning. As a veteran teacher, Meg needed to be challenged, and the mentoring experience gave her just the added nudge she needed to try something new (the mentor is coming to observe the class!). The mentor teacher group marked the first opportunity for teachers from Meg's program to discuss, for an extended period of time, issues important to them.

The two teachers who made the most significant change also appeared to be able to make connections between teachers and learners' realities. Unlike many teachers in our study, these two teachers saw themselves as on par with or equal to learners, thus allowing them to readily make connections between themselves and learners. Both were already predisposed to basing instruction on learners' needs, and both demonstrated an eagerness to expand their theories of teaching to concepts about what helps learners be successful.

> *The most important would be learners become part of the classroom and learners have a voice and a say in whatever goes on in the classroom. For the teacher to really listen. [The professional development] made me realize that students should be able to have the last administrative word on how they should learn and what is important to them, not being told what is best for them.*
>
> —Meg, Wave Three interview

Discussion of Factors That Influenced Change

The data from our study indicate that multiple factors interact to influence teacher change as a result of participating in professional development. Across our sample, change was either supported or hindered by the extent to which these factors applied; for any individual teacher, a combination of individual, professional development, program and system factors interacted to influence the amount and type of change experienced. Overall, we found that teachers changed more if they:

- Had a need to learn about the topic or about teaching in general (theories of good teaching and student success)
- Had fewer years of experience teaching/working in adult education
- Had their first teaching experience in adult education, rather than K–12
- Had a bachelor's degree or less
- Attended the professional development for more hours
- Were in higher quality groups (as rated by researchers *or* as perceived by the participating teacher)

---

[62] All five teachers in Esther's program participated in the professional development although two left the field during the course of the professional development activity and therefore dropped out. In Meg's case, the participating teachers were all from the ABE/ESOL component of her program and all participated for the entire 18 hours.

- Had some decision-making input in programs where learner persistence had not been addressed
- Had access to benefits and paid prep time as part of their adult education job

Secondary but still somewhat important factors that supported teacher change included:

- Access to paid professional development release time
- More working hours in adult education
- A lower level of commitment to continue working in adult education
- Coparticipation in professional development when accompanied by opportunities for ongoing discussion between and after professional development sessions
- Opportunities for collegiality
- Flexibility in changing the curriculum

One of our main hypotheses at the start of the study was that model of professional development would make a difference in teacher change. We found, however, that model of professional development was somewhat but not most important as a factor: there was a trend toward more change among those who attended "reform" models of professional development. Teachers who participated in mentor teacher groups (particularly where the group consisted of teachers from the same program) were just slightly more likely to make "preferred change"; teachers who participated in practitioner research groups were slightly more likely to make more change overall. Higher amounts of overall change were related to more integrated change, demonstrated by mentor teacher group and practitioner research group completers, but these differences were not significant.

There are several possible explanations for why model of professional development was not a more significant factor in our study:

1. The sample was too small, and with greater numbers of teachers, the difference among models would be significant.
2. Features of professional development are more important than model (Garet et al., 2001 also found this), and since all three NCSALL-tested models shared similar features,[63] differences among models were not as pronounced.
3. Factors related to professional development exposure (hours attended) and quality are more important than model, so that any model contributes to change as long as it is well-run, well-designed, and teachers attend for an adequate number of hours.
4. Individual and program or system factors, such as teacher motivation, level of education, and access to benefits, were more important than professional development model in influencing change.

---

[63] Extended exposure over multiple sessions; expectations and support for practitioners to try something new in their classrooms or programs between sessions and bring their experience back to the next session; time for planning what they will do with their new learning; time for participants to share their own experiences and ideas of what worked; use of an inquiry approach to learning about teaching, where teachers were to find out from learners about forces affecting their motivation, and then to act on what they heard.

Further research, perhaps with a larger sample size and comparing models that do and do not use an inquiry approach, might determine which of these (or other) explanations may prove true. It may also be the case that other models of professional development not investigated here are even more powerful, such as program-based teacher inquiry groups studying samples of student work to solve problems of practice, for example.

It was not surprising to us that teachers who attended high-quality professional development (or what they perceived to be high-quality professional development) for more hours also changed more. High-quality professional development, however, wasn't always led by professional facilitators; some of the teachers who had been trained to facilitate delivered professional development that was rated both by us and by participants as high quality.

While it was not surprising that those teachers who attended because they had a strong need to learn (either about the topic of the professional development or about teaching in general) changed more, we see the finding as a reminder that not all teachers attend professional development with a burning desire to learn about the topic the professional development covers. This is where Joyce's (1983) concept of categories of teachers as learners and consumers of professional development (omnivores, active consumers, passive consumers, entrenched, and withdrawn teachers) is supported by our findings, although we would prefer to simplify it to two categories: "settled" teachers and "hungry" teachers.[64] Our research leads us to propose a hypothesis (rather than a finding) about the teachers' dispositions as learners: motivation to attend was a factor in what appeared to be an overall portrait of teachers who were either "settled" or "hungry" to learn. Among our sample, teachers who were more satisfied with their teaching or who had no strong need coming into the professional development (perhaps attending at the request of their director), and did not feel that learner persistence was a problem that they either could or wanted to solve, appeared "settled." Those teachers who had a strong need to address the problem of learner persistence or a need to develop their theories of teaching and student success fit the portrait of "hungry" teachers: they wanted to learn new techniques, new theories, or new ways to address learners' problems in their classrooms and programs. Our impression is that settled teachers were more likely to demonstrate minimal or no change and hungry teachers were more likely to demonstrate integrated change. However, we offer this concept not as a conclusion of our research but as an emerging hypothesis about an individual teacher disposition that might play a role in teacher change. Further research might use this construct of "settled" and "hungry" as a way to characterize teachers' dispositions toward learning and develop data-collection protocols for explicitly researching its role in teacher change.

It appeared that being new to the field, teaching for the first time in this field, and having less formal education made teachers seek techniques or theories about learner persistence, good teaching, or student success. In our study, teachers who had more years of experience in the field of adult education, who began their teaching in K–12, and who had advanced degrees were more likely to seem satisfied with their practice and to demonstrate a stronger commitment to the field. This finding mirrors recent research by Livneh and Livneh (1999) among K–12 school teachers. They found that participation in professional development was

---

[64] Because we did not collect data that would allow us to type teachers either according to Joyce's categories (as far as we know, Joyce did not develop a data-collection protocol for these categories) or as "settled" or "hungry," we do not present this as a formal factor, but rather as a concept for further research.

predicted by (1) high internal motivation to learn, (2) high external motivation to learn (wanted career advancement or to network with others), and (3) lower levels of formal education.

We also discovered that there were teachers who identified an "off the topic" need during the course of the professional development and subsequently developed a motivation to change related to that need. These teachers were dissatisfied with some aspect of their program or working situation (isolation, difficulty with program administration, etc.). Through some aspect of the professional development (typically, sharing with colleagues), these teachers recognized this need, developed their thinking about collegiality or program strengths and weaknesses, and then took action to address the problem. Although such action did not address directly learners' needs or persistence, it was action based on a need they had identified and as such denotes change for those teachers.

Program and system factors regulating teachers' working conditions also influenced teacher change. We defined teachers' working conditions as whether or not they have access to:

1. **Resources.** These include classroom and program facilities, materials, and technology that affect how well teachers are able to do their jobs.
2. **Professional Development and Information.** These factors include opportunities for teachers to acquire the knowledge and information they need, primarily through professional development, and through access to written and electronic materials, that help them better understand their classrooms, their programs, and their field.
3. **Colleagues and Program Directors.** These include opportunities and mechanisms that allow teachers to get feedback from supervisors and talk to peers in their program, their state, and the larger field of adult education.
4. **Decision-Making.** These include opportunities and mechanisms for teachers to participate in improving the quality of services that learners receive, particularly through program policies and practices.
5. **A Well-Supported Job.** These factors include adequate pay; sufficient working hours to complete all of the teaching, program, and other tasks required of them; paid prep and professional development time; and job stability and benefits.

Different programs and adult education systems provided the teachers in our study with varied amounts of access to these working conditions, and certain of these factors more strongly influenced how teachers changed. Our findings indicated that access to decision-making and access to certain aspects of a well-supported job—particularly benefits and paid prep time and (to a lesser extent) more working hours and paid professional development time—affected how teachers changed after participating in professional development. Access to colleagues was an important factor for some of the teachers in our subsample, particularly when they participated in professional development groups where all of the other participants were from their own program. However, access to resources and to professional development and information in general did not emerge as particularly important, at least in relation to the professional development in this study.

Conclusion

We conclude that teachers' pathways to change were neither simple nor linear; change was complex and shaped by interaction among who they were as individuals, the quality and amount of professional development in which they participated, and the features of the programs and systems in which they work. Adult education teachers work within a particular ecosystem of funding, structure, and policies, and these factors intertwine with individual factors and with the professional development they participate in. While we, in this research project, have endeavored to isolate the most important factors in order to propose recommendations for action that states, programs, and professional developers can take to increase the effectiveness of professional development, the reality is that any individual teacher's experience of change is determined by a unique interaction of these factors.

The complex interaction between individual, professional development, program and system factors that influenced how and in what ways teachers change is demonstrated best through two examples: one of a teacher (Penny) who made little change, and one of a teacher (Meg) who made significant change.

Penny's lack of change was influenced by the strong individual factors (lack of motivation to learn about the topic or, for that matter, about anything related to her teaching, and a greater amount of formal education), professional development factors (a dislike of the professional development facilitator, mentor teacher group model, and group in which she participated), and program and system factors (part-time status, a requirement to use a particular curriculum, program structure that emphasized individualized instruction for GED test prep). The interaction of these factors contributed to no real change: her lack of motivation to learn, based on her experience and her satisfaction with the personal teaching style she had developed, interacted with what she considered poor-quality professional development, and led her to reject both the topic and any suggestions the professional development had to offer. Also, since the program's goal was to prepare as many students as possible to pass the GED test, they had adopted a policy of cycling students through workbooks individually, and as such, Penny was not encouraged to care about students who dropped out; both she and her program took the stance that students who didn't persist were not ready to study for the GED, and so they were not concerned about them—other, more motivated students would readily take their place. Penny already felt that their program served students as well as it could, and being only a six-hour-a-week employee with no prep time, she was neither motivated nor supported to try new strategies for improving students' motivation, retention, and persistence. In sum, almost all factors—individual, professional development, and program/system—interacted to contribute to her lack of change.

On the other hand, Meg, who also participated in a mentor teacher group, had multiple factors that supported change. She had a strong motivation to learn, as a teacher who started teaching in adult education/family literacy without a master's degree. She loved the mentor teacher group in which she participated, partially because it was high quality and partially because all of the other participants were teachers in her program. Her program had not addressed learner persistence as an issue but was relatively open to input from both teachers and students; her director was approachable to discuss problems. Meg worked as a full-time teacher with benefits and prep time, so she had the time to seek collegial support to take action in the classroom and program. What she initially learned in the professional development, which both she and the researchers rated as high quality, fueled by her motivation to know more about teaching and serving students, led her to make changes in her classroom in both curriculum and class structure. The fact that other teachers in her program were also participants in the professional development led them together to seek changes at the program level. With a responsive program director, Meg could also encourage her students to suggest changes at the program level. Discussions with the teachers in her program also motivated Meg to talk to teachers outside of her program about working conditions that she sensed influenced teachers' persistence. These multiple factors interacted to support transformational change in both her thinking on and off the topic and her actions at all levels.

Conclusion and Recommendations

For the teachers in our study, change did not occur in a vacuum. How—and how much— a teacher changed was influenced by a complex interaction of factors: who teachers were coming into the professional development, the professional development itself, and the program and system in which teachers worked. While most teachers who participated in the professional development made some change, change was limited among teachers who felt less of a need to learn, who attended professional development that was not of high quality, and/or who worked in programs and situations where they were not supported to change. (Those who dropped out made very little change on average.)

Slightly more than one third of the teachers who completed the professional development changed their thinking as a result of participating in the professional development, but this did not always translate into changes in practice in the classroom and program, and this lack of concrete action was due partly to individual motivation and partly to working conditions and program factors that hindered teachers from taking action. However, about one quarter of those teachers who completed the professional development—particularly those who had less experience in the field and less formal education, who had a strong motivation to learn more about the topic or about theories of teaching and student success, who participated in high-quality professional development groups, and who had access to working conditions that supported change (prep time, benefits, opportunities for sharing with colleagues, a voice in decision-making in the program)—made significant change across multiple roles, and this professional development had a strong effect on them and their practice.

While the small sample size and design of the study limit generalizability of these findings to *all* adult education teachers, we present implications of these findings that are applicable to the teachers, programs, and states that participated in the study. Professional development decision-makers in other states must decide for themselves whether these implications are valid for their own population of teachers, based on the extent to which their teachers and programs resemble those that participated in our study.

The fact that 28% of the 83 teachers who completed the professional development demonstrated little or no change (and 16% of the original 100 teachers dropped out and also demonstrated little change) should be of interest to our field. Eighteen hours of professional development is longer in duration than most opportunities adult education teachers typically have for professional development.[65] When even 18 hours of professional development did

---

[65] Almost one quarter of our sample reported receiving no hours of paid professional development release time in the year prior to our study.

not lead to significant change for about one third of our sample, we need to consider the implications for ensuring that teachers are willing, able, and supported to participate in professional development and use it as a springboard to better practice since, arguably, teachers are the most critical factor in student success. We propose the following recommendations, based on the findings from our study, for policymakers in programs and states, for professional developers, and for teachers themselves to better support teachers so that they are able to make the most of professional development and contribute to the positive differences we seek in students' lives.

Recommendations for Program Directors and States

Improve teachers' working conditions, including access to decision-making in the program

Programs and systems had a big effect on the teachers in our study. Teachers' access to benefits and paid prep time seem to be the most critical. Access to paid professional development release time, more working hours, ongoing discussions and teacher sharing with colleagues during and after participating in professional development, and decision-making in the program also, to a lesser extent, influenced the level of change. The presence of these factors in teachers' jobs made it easier for teachers to learn more and do more as a result of participating in professional development. However, many teachers in our study lacked access to such conditions. Programs and states should consider the costs and benefits of providing such types of support to teachers in their states, not only to enhance the productivity of the professional development they offer but also to decrease teacher turnover within the field.

Pay teachers to attend professional development

Attending more hours of professional development contributed to an increased amount of change. The stipend we gave participants may have played a role in their continued participation: although some participants undoubtedly dropped out because they considered the quality of the professional development to be low, and others dropped out because of illness or new jobs, others said they left because they did not have the time.[66] Eighteen hours of professional development is quite an investment for some state adult education systems that feel they only have the resources to offer an annual one-day conference. It is also quite an investment of time and effort for teachers who may teach only six hours per week. However, if adult education teachers receive payment for the hours they attend professional development as well as the hours they teach, they may attend longer, leading to higher returns from investments in professional development.

---

[66] Although there was no direct and significant relationship between amount of annual paid professional development time and change, there was a positive relationship between paid professional development release time and hours of attendance in the NCSALL Professional Development, which in turn was related to change, suggesting at least an indirect link between supported time and change.

Increase access to colleagues and directors during and after professional development

Teachers felt better supported to make change when they participated with colleagues from their program and also had opportunities to discuss what they learned with others following professional development sessions. Programs should find mechanisms, as part of professional development and as part of teachers' paid jobs, for teachers to share ideas about teaching. Particularly for teachers who feel isolated, program-based professional development may be a model that deserves more thought and more research. As long as the professional development is of high quality and is designed using principles of effective professional development, the convenience of being able to attend professional development in one's own program with other colleagues from the program may support change. Program-based professional development may also allow teachers to work together to suggest action at the program level under conditions where this is not ordinarily encouraged. When teachers have paid opportunities to continue to talk with their colleagues outside professional development sessions, there appears to be an even greater likelihood for integrated change. However, states and programs also need to provide opportunities for teachers to meet colleagues outside of their programs, so that teachers develop a critical sense of their programs' assets and needs and an awareness of being part of the field of adult education.

Establish expectations at the state and the program level that all teachers must continue to learn

Help teachers identify their highest-priority learning needs and provide professional development to match, recognizing that not all change is related to the topic of the professional development. When we recommend setting expectations for continued learning, we are not here talking about certification requirements or formal competencies; our study did not investigate the influence of those on teacher change. However, using the concept of the "settled" teacher, professional developers should realize that some teachers attend professional development without a strong desire to learn more about the topic, about theories of teaching and learning, or about good teaching practice. In our sample, not all teachers viewed this particular professional development as necessary. Some had no strong motivation to be there; they were not driven because they had a problem related to the topic and were essentially satisfied with their teaching and their program. While these teachers may have gained some knowledge on the topic, we did not see much change in them. We are *not* saying that these teachers were not good teachers; we have no data about that. We are saying, rather, that we discovered teachers in our sample who were attending professional development for reasons other than to learn about the topic or to develop their theories of good teaching and student success, and that this was a factor in how much they changed. Some of these teachers did acquire new concepts and benefits unrelated to the topic that affected them positively including: collegiality, knowledge of the broader field, and strategies for how to survive in or change the program within which they worked. Just as adult learners may gain something from education that is as, or more, important to them than reading, writing, or math skills (such as self-esteem, working in teams, goal setting, and so on), we found teachers in our study who gained confidence in their teaching, an awareness of what the "field" of adult education is all about, or a feeling of companionship with other teachers, even if they did not do much to address learner persistence in their classroom or program. These are not inconsequential results from professional development, but there's no reason to believe that they wouldn't also result from professional development on topics that match teachers' learning needs more closely.

The fact that there were teachers participating in the NCSALL Professional Development who did not have a strong need to learn about the topic means that professional developers must strive to provide professional development, in convenient venues, that does address a strong learning need. As we have learned from teaching adult students, needs assessment and identification of priority learning goals take time. It involves more than choosing from a menu of professional development topics. It requires teachers to think about what they already feel they know and don't know, and to look within their classrooms at how their teaching is tied to student learning: where are students struggling and not making as much progress as either they or the teacher would like, and why? These needs should drive the type of learning and professional development a teacher seeks and the type of professional development a program or state offers. Teachers must then be provided access to multiple opportunities for professional development on a broad range of topics, some of which they may not even have considered before.

Perhaps such a "learning assessment process" for teachers would be best offered at the program level; it is easier for programs to know the learning needs of their staff than for the state professional development system. It requires programs, however, to establish teachers' participation in formal processes for both individual teacher improvement and program improvement initiatives, where teachers help identify priority program needs and these priorities, in turn, inform teachers' professional development needs. The fact that a few of the teachers who attended our professional development seemingly did not have a strong need to learn on any topic means that programs and states should figure out how to help all teachers adopt the stance that, despite one's qualifications, experience, or even success as a teacher, all teachers need to maintain an intrinsic motivation to continue learning. The mandate for teachers to "learn more and do better" also suggests that administrators hold themselves to the same expectations.

Recommendations for Professional Developers

Teachers are adult learners, and, like the adult learners they teach, teachers are not all alike: they work in a variety of program and system situations, have different backgrounds, and have a range of approaches and motivations for learning. In each professional development group, we found new and experienced teachers, teachers with more and less formal education, teachers with and without K–12 experience, teachers with and without access to working conditions such as benefits, teachers with and without decision-making power in their programs, and teachers with and without a strong desire to learn about the topic or about theories of good teaching and student success: groups of teachers who attend professional development are indeed "multilevel." These differences influenced how teachers changed as a result of participating in the professional development. What we think we know about the best ways to teach adult learners is probably true for educating teachers, too. Specifically, our research recommends that professional developers pay attention to the following.

Ensure that professional development is of high quality

The quality of the professional development, as rated by us and by the participants themselves, was an important factor influencing change. It wasn't necessary for the professional development to be run by a professional trainer; mentor teachers ran some of the highest-quality groups. We assessed three quality factors: group dynamics, clear facilitation, and design. We didn't assess the relative importance of any of these factors compared to the others, but all three played a role in the quality of the group. The facilitator was a crucial element, and the best facilitators were those who followed the design while making changes that allowed time for addressing participants' concerns as they arose.

Offer a variety of professional development models for teachers to attend

All three models of professional development tested in the study (multisession workshops, mentor teacher groups, practitioner research groups) supported teacher change. However, the finding that none of these models was superior to the others (in terms of supporting teacher change) should not be taken to mean that they would be equivalent in every situation. We built similar design features into all the professional development models we tested,[67] so we cannot provide guidance or assurance about the efficacy of professional development models that don't have these features. In other words, our study sheds no light on whether "training" is as effective as practitioner research, if that "training" is only one session with no follow-up. The subtle differences we found among the models—that teachers completing practitioner research group professional development had slightly higher overall change and that teachers completing mentor teacher group professional development were slightly more likely to demonstrate integrated change—might have been more strongly expressed with a larger sample. Therefore, while there is no reason to reject any of these models as less effective than the others, there is also no reason to suppose that there are no differences among them.

There is, however, every reason to believe that a single model of professional development wouldn't have sufficed for all the teachers in our study, year in and year out. Teachers participated for different reasons, with different levels of experience in the field and in professional development, and so had different reactions to the professional development. These reactions in some cases influenced how long teachers stayed in the professional development and in other cases influenced the change they made afterward. For example, we found that practitioner research groups had a greater number of teachers with more experience in the field, whereas mentor teacher groups had a greater number of teachers who worked fewer hours per week in adult education. This is an indication that teachers may opt to participate in different models based on their experience or situation. No one model of professional development is sufficient for the range of adult education teachers in our field.

---

[67] More than one session, scheduled over time; expectations and support for practitioners to try something out in their classrooms or programs between sessions and bring their experience back to the next session; time for planning what they will do with their new learning; time for participants to share their own experiences and ideas of what worked; emphasis on an inquiry process/cycle of learning and taking action.

Be clear during recruitment for "reform" models of professional development what participation will be like for teachers

Providing enough information about the professional development during recruitment is important, because participants' expectations of the professional development affected group dynamics, and this was especially true for newer, "reform" types of professional development such as mentor teacher groups or practitioner research groups. When participants did not have a clear idea of what they would be expected to do during the professional development, they were confused, and this confusion sometimes annoyed other teachers in the group who were ready and willing to engage in the professional development activities. Adequate information about what to expect from nontraditional forms of professional development would have helped those teachers who were more familiar and comfortable with traditional professional development models, such as workshops, that ask them to learn about the knowledge produced by others rather than produce knowledge of their own.

Help teachers acquire skills to build theories of good teaching and student success

Teachers, especially new teachers, often say that they need new techniques and practical ideas; however, a larger "bag of tricks," while helpful to those "acting" teachers in our study, did not lead to sustained, integrated change. Teachers need to understand *why* to use a particular technique, not just *how* to use it; they need the underlying foundational theory of teaching and learning that will allow them to integrate new thinking with new actions.

Teachers in our study who had the skills and desire to build such theories gained more from professional development, and even those teachers who didn't have the skills but had the desire gained something from the professional development. While we discovered teachers who fit the description of "settled" teachers, in that they did not express a desire to build theories of teaching and learning, we also discovered other teachers who had a desire to refine their theories based on practice, but did not have the skills to do so on their own. They knew they needed some overarching theoretical framework, and some even knew they needed to create this framework through a combination of knowledge and practice, but they didn't know how to go about taking what they had learned in the professional development and building on it through practice and reflection of their own. We found that reflecting critically on one's practice in order to build continually one's theories of teaching and learning was not a skill that some teachers simply acquired by dint of being teachers, and it was also not a certain byproduct of attending a particular professional development model (such as practitioner research) that endeavors to develop reflectiveness. Rather, building theories of good teaching and student success through a process of learning, practice, and reflection is a skill that teachers need to be taught deliberately and consciously. A corollary to this expectation is the recommendation that programs and states should work especially hard to reach new adult education teachers, especially those who are teaching for the first time. Our study demonstrated that these teachers may be more open to change, more apt to act upon what they learn, and more in need of developing theories of teaching and learning. These teachers need the skills to reflect critically on what they learn and tie it to a process of integrated thinking and acting.

Add activities to professional development that help teachers strategize how to deal with the forces that affect their ability to take action

Teachers need support in order to translate their new ideas into practice. Teachers in our study were affected by program and system factors that acted as barriers or supports to taking action based on what they learned in the professional development. Whether the barrier is lack of time to prepare new classroom activities, fear of trying something new within the constraints of curriculum and established program policies, or lack of help from colleagues or director in assessing how well something new worked, teachers need time in professional development to strategize how they will deal with these barriers once back in their program.

We feel that teachers in our sample would have been helped had we created an activity within the final session of the professional development where they could brainstorm what would support them to take action and what would hinder them from taking action. If they had time during the professional development to recognize and then strategize how to overcome common barriers, they might have left the professional development with ideas for increasing supportive factors and reducing hindering factors. Professional development cannot erase the barriers to change that exist in teachers' working contexts, but it can provide time and a platform for teachers to discuss these barriers and strategize how to deal with them on their own.

Recommendations for Teachers

We recognize, as do teachers, that teachers do not always have power to change the working conditions and situations in ways that would support them to get the most out of the professional development. Yet our research findings do support some recommendations for teachers to consider and work toward, together with their colleagues:

Expect high-quality professional development

Facilitators should be well organized and follow a clear plan but be able to adapt the activities in the professional development to your particular needs. Teachers should consider how they best learn and request professional development models that match, being aware that different models have different requirements of them as a participant and learner.

Think clearly about what they want to learn in professional development

Start by looking at students' learning and considering the areas where students and teachers feel they are achieving well and where they are not, and what this means for teachers' teaching. Teachers should work with program and state professional development decision-makers and make their needs known, so that they can attend professional development on topics that will be most relevant to their needs (and which will, consequently, have the greatest impact on learners' achievement).

Recognize the need to develop a philosophy and theory of good teaching and student success

Use professional development activities to help them continually revise, expand, and test that theory as they take action to improve the quality of their teaching. Recognize that no theory will ever be "finished"; as long as teachers teach, there is always something more to learn.

Work to increase opportunities for collegiality and teacher decision-making in their program.

Work with other colleagues to improve working conditions
Advocate for paid prep time, professional development release time, and benefits as part of their adult education job.

Final Thoughts

Many professional development studies in K–12 have investigated how teachers change over time as a result of professional development, but few studies of this type have been conducted in adult education. The important contribution of this study is that it offers, for the first time in the field of adult education, an understanding of the factors that affect how teachers change. A key finding of this study is that teachers change in different amounts and ways as a result of participating in professional development, and that individual, professional development, program, and system factors interact to affect this change. These factors, some of which are unique to adult education, such as lack of prep time and benefits, influence how teachers change and benefit from the professional development in which they participate.

Given that few adult education teachers enter adult education classrooms with formal preparation specifically in teaching adults, professional development becomes more important than ever. As the field moves into an era of stronger accountability, it is important for program directors, professional development leaders, and state staff to understand how such factors support or hinder the improvements in quality that are being promoted at the federal, state, and program level. Programs and states increasingly will expect professional development to prepare teachers to adopt evidence from research in their classrooms and programs, in order to improve outcomes for learners. This study demonstrates that professional development alone, while necessary, is not sufficient to drive changes in practice. Professional development is one tool for change but needs to be offered within a context that supports teachers to make change. While teachers are always the link between professional development and student outcomes, they are never the only influence, and this research draws attention to some of the program and system factors that will need to be addressed in our field for change to happen. This may require those who make decisions about how to structure services for learners to think seriously about devoting more funding to better supporting teachers, at the expense of serving more students.

Our study indicates that models for improvement *do* exist in our field. There are programs in the field worth emulating, programs that find ways to support teachers to attend and make change. There are states that invest in teachers' working conditions in ways (more working hours, paid prep time, benefits) that will also "stretch" their professional development dollars. Certainly there are teachers ready to take advantage of professional development offered.

There is still much we don't know about professional development in adult education, such as the connection between professional development and student achievement among different learner populations. Our study provides information to professional development decision-makers about how to help teachers and programs make the most of the professional development that is offered, and we hope that future research will provide more information about other factors influencing teacher change that we were not able to test here. In the meantime, our field will have to continue to learn from the K–12 research on professional development and from what we can glean from evaluations of professional development activities. What is clear to us from our study, however, is that professional development can play a critical role in improving teachers' knowledge and supporting teacher change in our field, but even the hungriest teachers attending the best designed, highest-quality professional development cannot do it alone.

ACKNOWLEDGMENTS

We would like to acknowledge the help of the following people in conducting this study:

Our research analysis team consisted of Cristine Smith, Judy Hofer, Marla Solomon, and Marilyn Gillespie. Judy Hofer coordinated the qualitative data analysis. Karen Rowe and Cristine Smith coordinated the statistical analysis of quantitative data. The research design team included Cassandra Drennon, Marta Mangan, Alison Simmons, Marla Solomon, Michele Sacerdote, Judy Titzel, Cristine Smith, and Judy Hofer. Gretchen Rossman and Stephen Sireci at the University of Massachusetts also provided advice.

The 15 professional development groups were facilitated by Michelle Sedor, Martha Merson, Tricia Donovan, Deborah Schwartz, Donna Curry, Sara Douglas, Bob Aubrey, Sally Riconscente, Velmar Byrd, Dianne Grenier, and Judy Titzel. Local professional development assistants, who audiotaped each professional development session and took notes, included Alicia Albert, Sharon Klufts, Madeleine Costa, Dona Ditrio, Denise Doherty, Michael Haines, Janice Armstrong, Myra Love, Sandra Mawford, Maryanne Pascone, Patricia Richards, Sharon Ultsch, and Jane Noll. Selina Welborn assisted with data collection in Connecticut. We had assistance from state professional development staff within Connecticut, Maine, and Massachusetts, including: Ajit Gopalakrishnan, Evelyn Beaulieu, and SABES staff (Sally Waldron, Bill Arcand, Diane McMullen, Margaret Farrey, Marcia Hohn, and Maria Gonzalez). Michele Sacerdote and Peter Tamas assisted ably with the analysis of the audiotapes of the groups and our rating of group quality. Jane Noll provided administrative support to the study.

Most of all, we would like to thank the teachers and program directors who participated in the study.

REFERENCES

Adey, P. (1995). *The effectiveness of a staff development program: The relationship between the level of use of innovative science curriculum activities and student achievement.* (ERIC Document Reproduction Service No. ED383567)

American Federation of Teachers. (1995). *Principals for professional development: AFT's guidelines for creating professional development programs that make a difference.* Washington, DC: American Federation of Teachers. (ERIC Document Reproduction Service No. ED389482)

Ancess, J. (2000). The reciprocal influence of teacher learning, teaching practice, school restructuring and student learning outcomes. *Teachers College Record, 102*(3), 590–619.

Arlin, P. K. (1999). The wise teacher: A developmental model of teaching. *Theory Into Practice, 38*(1), 12–17.

Ball, D.L., & Cohen, D.K. (1999). Developing practice, developing practitioners: Toward a practice-based theory of professional education. In L. Darling-Hammond & G. Sykes (Eds.), *Teaching as the learning profession: Handbook of policy and practice* (pp. 3–32). San Francisco: Jossey-Bass.

Bandura, A. (1995). Exercise of personal and collective efficacy in changing societies. In A. Bandura (Ed.), *Self-efficacy in changing societies* (pp. 1–45). Cambridge: Cambridge University Press.

Belzer, A., Drennon, C., & Smith, C. (2001). Building professional development systems in adult basic education: Lessons from the field. In J. Comings, B. Garner, & C. Smith (Eds.), *The annual review of adult learning and literacy*: Volume 2 (pp. 151–188). San Francisco: Jossey-Bass.

Bollough, R. V., Kauchak, D., Crow, N., Hobbs, S., & Stoke, D. (1997). Professional development schools: Catalysts for teacher and school change. *Teaching and Teacher Education, 13*(2), 153–169.

Bridges, W. (1991). *Managing transitions.* Reading, MA: Addison-Wesley.

Burt, M., & Keenan, F. (1998). *Q & A: Trends in staff development for adult ESL instructors.* National Clearinghouse for ESL Literacy Education (NCLE). Retrieved November 18, 2003, from http://www.cal.org/ncle/ DIGESTS/TrendQA.htm

Calderón, M. (1999). Teachers learning communities for cooperation in diverse settings. *Theory Into Practice, 38*(2), 94–99.

Carpenter, T. P., & Franke, M.L. (1998). *Teachers as learners in principled practice in mathematics and science education.* Madison, WI: National Center for Improving Student Learning & Achievement in Math & Science, Principled Practice Research Brief, 2(2), Fall, 1-3.

Crocker, J. (1987, October). *ABE statewide staff development programs: Analysis of program dimensions, characteristics, and contextual factors.* Paper presented at the American Adult and Continuing Education Conference, Washington, DC.

Darkenwald, G. (1986). *Adult literacy education: A review of the research and priorities for future inquiry.* New York: Literacy Assistance Center, Inc.

Darling-Hammond, L. (2000). Reforming teacher preparation and licensing: Debating the evidence. *Teachers' College Record, 102*(1), 28–56.

Darling-Hammond, L., & Ball, D. L. (1997, June). *Teaching for high standards: What policymakers need to know and be able to do.* Paper prepared for the National Education Goals Panel (available at http://www.negp.gov/reports/highstds.htm).

Darling-Hammond, L., & Sykes, G. (1999). *Teaching as the learning profession: Handbook of policy and practice.* San Francisco: Jossey-Bass.

Darling-Hammond, L. & Youngs, P. (2002). Defining "high-qualified teachers": What does "scientifically-based research" actually tell us? *Educational Researcher, 31* (9), 13–25.

Doyle, W., & Ponder, G. (1977). The practicality of teacher decision-making. *Interchange*, *8*(3), 1–12.

Drennon, C. (1994). *Adult literacy practitioners as researchers*. ERIC Digest (ED372663).

Elmore, R. F. (1996). Getting to scale with good educational practice. *Harvard Educational Review*, *66*(1), 1–28.

Elmore, R. F. (2002). *Bridging the gap between standards and achievement: The imperative for professional development in education*. Paper for the Albert Shanker Institute.

Feiman-Nemser, S. (2001). From preparation to practice: Designing a continuum to strengthen and sustain teaching. *Teachers College Record*, *103*(6), 1013–1055.

Ferry, N. M., & Ross-Gordon, J. M. (1998). An inquiry into Schon's epistemology of practice: Exploring links between experience and reflective practice. *Adult Education Quarterly*, *48*(2), 98–112.

Fingeret, H. A., & Cockley, S. (1992). *Teachers learning: An evaluation of ABE staff development in Virginia*. Virginia: Virginia Adult Educator's Research Network.

Foucar-Szocki, D., Erno, S., Dilly, S., Grant, S. P., Hindebrandt, N., & Leonard, M. S. (1997). *We are now in the driver's seat: A practitioner evaluation of the Virginia adult education professional development system*. Charlottesville, VA: Virginia Association for Adult Continuing Education (VAACE).

Fullan, M. G. (1990). Staff development, innovation, and institutional development. In B. Joyce (Ed.), *Changing school culture through staff development* (pp. 3–25). Alexandria, VA: Association for Supervision and Curriculum Development.

Fuller, F., & Brown, O. H. (1975). Becoming a teacher. In K. Ryan (Ed.), *Teacher education: The seventy-fourth yearbook of the national society for the study of education* (pp. 25–52). Chicago: University of Chicago Press.

Gardner, J. (1996). *Professional development which provides an icing on the pedagogical cake*. (ERIC Document Reproduction Service No. ED400589)

Garet, M. S., Porter, A. C., Desimone, L., Birman, B., & Yoon, K. S. (2001). What makes professional development effective? Results from a national sample of teachers. *American Educational Research Journal*, *38*(4), 915–945.

Garmston, R. J. (1997). The teacher is within. *Journal of Staff Development*, *187*(1), 62–64.

Ghaith, G., & Shaaban, K. (1999). The relationship between perceptions of teaching concerns, teacher efficacy, and selected teacher characteristics. *Teaching and Teacher Education*, *15*, 487–496.

Goddard, R. D., Hoy, W. K., & Hoy, A. W. (2000). Collective teacher efficacy: Its meaning, measure, and impact on student achievement. *American Educational Research Journal*, *37*(2), 479–507.

Grossman, P. L. (1992). Why models matter: An approach view on professional growth in teaching. *Review of Educational Research*, *62*(2), 171–179.

Grossman, P., Wineburg, S., & Woolworth, S. (2000). *What makes teacher community different from a gathering of teachers?* Washington, DC: Center for the Study of Teaching and Policy and Center on English Learning & Achievement, Occasional Paper.

Guskey, T. R. (1988). Teacher efficacy, self-concept, and attitudes toward the implementation of instructional innovation. *Teaching & Teacher Education*, *4*(1), 63–69.

Guskey, T. R. (1997). Research needs to link professional development and student learning. *Journal of Staff Development*, *18*(2), 36–40.

Guskey, T. R. (1999). Moving from means to ends. *Journal of Staff Development*, Winter 1999, p. 48.

Guskey, T. R., & Sparks, D. (1996). Exploring the relationship between staff development and improvements in student learning. *Journal of Staff Development, 17*(4), 34–38.

Helsing, D., Drago-Severson, E., Kegan, R., Portnow, K., Popp, N., & Broderick, M. (2001). Three different types of change. *Focus on Basics, 5*(B), 10–14.

Holderness, S. T. (1993). *Empowering teachers to change curriculum and schools: Evaluation of a program*. (ERIC Document Reproduction Service No. ED366496)

Hord, S., Rutherford, W., Huling-Austin, L., & Hall, G. (1987). *Taking charge of change*. Alexandria, VA: Association for Supervision and Curriculum Development.

Huberman, A. M., & Miles, M. B. (1984). *Innovation up close*. New York: Plenum Press.

Imel, S. (2000). *Change: connections to adult learning and education*. ERIC Digest No. 221.

Ingersoll, R. M. (2001). *Teacher turnover, teacher shortages, and the organization of schools*. Seattle, WA: University of Washington Center for the Study of Teaching and Policy, Report R-01-1.

Jones, E. V., & Lowe, J. H. (1985). Adult education staff development: Program research and implementation. *Adult Literacy and Basic Education, 9*(2), 80–86.

Joughin, G. (1992). Cognitive style and adult learning principles. *International Journal of Lifelong Education, 11*(1), 3–14.

Joyce, B. (1983). *The structure of school improvement*. New York: Longman, Inc.

Joyce, B., & Showers, B. (1995). *Student achievement through staff development: Fundamentals of school renewal* (2nd ed.). White Plains, NY: Longman.

Joyce, B., Wolf, J., & Calhoun, E. (1995). *The self-renewing school*. Alexandria, VA: Association for Supervision and Curriculum Development.

Kagan, D. M. (1992). Professional growth among pre-service and beginning teachers. *Review of Educational Research, 62*(2), 129–169.

Kuhne, G., Weirauch, D., & Doyle, D. (1997). *Year one of the Pennsylvania action research network: Impact follow-up study of adult literacy practitioners and adult literacy program supervisors directly involved in 1995/1996 action research projects*. McKeesport, PA: Penn State McKeesport Campus.

Kutner, M., Herman, R., Stephenson, E., & Webb, L. (1991). *Study of ABE/ESL instructor training approaches: State profiles report*. Washington, DC: Pelavin Research Institute.

Kutner, M., & Tibbetts, J. (1997). *Looking to the future: Components of a comprehensive professional development system for adult educators*. Washington, DC: Pelavin Research Institutes, Pro-Net project publication.

Langer, J. A. (2000). Excellence in English in middle and high school: How teachers' professional lives support student achievement. *American Educational Research Journal, 37*(2), 397–439.

Leahy, M. (1986). History and practice of ABE staff development. In *Recommendations for Expanding and Enhancing Adult Education Staff development in Pennsylvania*. Harrisburg, PA: Department of Education.

Lewis, L. (1992). Meaning making and reflective practice. *Adult Learning, 3*(4), 7.

Lewis, L., Parsad, B., Carey, N., Bartfai, N., Farris, E., & Smerdon, B. (1999). *Teacher quality: A report on the preparation and qualifications of public school teachers* (NCES 1999-080). Washington, DC: National Center for Education Statistics, U.S. Department of Education.

Livneh, C., & Livneh, H. (1999). Continuing professional education among educators: Predictions of participation in learning activities. *Adult Education Quarterly, 49* (2), 91–106.

Lortie, D. (1975). *Schoolteacher.* Chicago: University of Chicago Press.

Loucks-Horsley, S., Hewson, P. W., Love, N., & Stiles, K. E. (1998). *Designing professional development for teachers of science and mathematics.* Thousand Oaks, CA: Corwin Press.

Lytle, S., Belzer, A., & Reumann, R. (1992a). *Developing the professional workforce for adult literacy education.* Philadelphia, PA: National Center on Adult Literacy Policy Brief PB92-2.

Lytle, S., Belzer, A., & Reumann, R. (1992b). *Invitations to inquiry: Rethinking staff development in adult literacy education.* Philadelphia, PA: National Center on Adult Literacy Technical Report 92-2.

Magnusson, S., Borko, H., & Krajcik, J. S. (1994). *Teaching complex subject matter in science: Insights from an analysis of pedagogical content knowledge.* (ERIC Document Reproduction Service No. ED390715)

Mazzarella, J. A. (1980). Synthesis of research on staff development. *Educational Leadership,* November 1980, 182–185.

Meyer, L. (1988). Research on implementation: What seems to work. In S. J. Samuels & P. D. Pearson (Eds.), *Changing School Reading Programs* (pp. 41–57). Newark, DE: International Reading Association.

Miles, M. B., & Huberman, A. M. (1994). *Qualitative data analysis: An expanded sourcebook* (2nd ed.). Thousand Oaks, CA: Sage Publications.

National Education Goals Panel Reports (1999). *Teacher education and professional development.* Retrieved November 18, 2003, from http://www.negp.gov/reports/99rpt.pdf

Olson, T. A., Butler, J. A., & Olson, N. L. (1991). *Designing meaningful professional development: A planning tool* (Field Test Version). Portland, OR: Northwest Regional Educational Laboratory. (ERIC Document Reproduction Service No. ED334671)

Ottoson, J. M. (1997). After the applause: Exploring multiple influences on application following an adult education program. *Adult Education Quarterly, 47*(2), 92–107.

Pelavin Research Institute (1996). *Professional development resource guide for adult educators.* Washington, DC: Pelavin Research Institute.

Porter, A. C., Garet, M. S., Desimone, L.D., Yoon, K. S., & Birman, B. F. (2000). *Does professional development change teaching practice? Results from a three-year study: Executive Summary.* Washington, DC: U.S. Department of Education, Office of the Under Secretary, 13 pps.

Richardson, V. (1998). How teachers change. *Focus on Basics, 2*(C), 7–11.

Richardson, V., & Anders, P. L. (1994). A theory of change. In V. Richardson (Ed.), *Teacher change and the staff development process: A case in reading instruction* (pp.199–216). New York: Teachers College Press.

Richardson, V., & Placier, P. (2001). Teacher change. In V. Richardson (Ed.), *Handbook of research on teaching* (4th ed.). Washington, DC: American Educational Research Association.

RMC Research Corporation. (1996). *National evaluation of the Section 353 set-aside for teacher training and innovation in adult education* (Contract No. EA 93064991). Portsmouth, NH: RMC Research Corporation.

Roberts, J. K., Henson, R. K., Tharp, B. Z., & Moreno, N. (2000, January). *An examination of change in teacher self-efficacy beliefs in science education based on the duration of in-service activities.* Paper presented at the annual meeting of AERA, Dallas, TX. (ERIC Document Reproduction Service No. ED438259)

Rosenholtz, S. (1986). Educational reform strategies: Will they increase teacher commitment? *American Journal of Education, 95*(4), 543–562.

Ross, J. A. (1994). The impact of an in-service to promote cooperative learning on the stability of teacher efficacy. *Teaching & Teacher Education, 10*(4), 381–394.

Ross, J. A. (1998). Antecedents and consequences of teacher efficacy. In J. Brophy (Ed.), *Advances in research on teaching* (vol. 7, pp. 49–74). Greenwich, CT: JAI Press.

Rueda, R. (1997). CREDE program showcase: Professional Development. *Talking Leaves, 2*(1), 1–2.

Sabatini, J. P., Daniels, M., Ginsburg, L., Limeul, K., Russell, M., & Stites, R. (2000). *Teacher perspectives on the adult education profession: National survey findings about an emerging profession.* Philadelphia, PA: National Center on Adult Literacy Technical Report 00-02.

Sanders, W.L. and Rivers, J.C. (1996). *Cumulative and residual effects of teachers on future student academic achievement.* Knoxville: University of Tennessee.

Schon, D. A. (1983). *The reflective practitioner: How professionals think in action.* New York: Basic Books.

Sherman, R., Green, K., Taylor, L., & Greenberg, I. (1997). *Inquiry/Research compendium.* Washington, DC: Building Professional Development Partnerships for Adult Educators Project (Pro-Net), Pelavin Research Institute American Institutes for Research.

Short, D. J., & Echevarria, J. (1999). *The sheltered instruction observation protocol: A tool for teacher-research collaboration and professional development.* Santa Cruz, CA: Center for Research on Education, Diversity & Excellence, University of California, Santa Cruz.

Smylie, M. A. (1988). The enhancement function of staff development: Organizational and psychological antecedents to individual teacher change. *American Educational Research Journal, 25*(1), 1–30.

Sparks, D. (1994). A paradigm shift in staff development. *Journal of Staff Development, 15* (4), 26–29.

Sparks, D. (1995). Focusing staff development on improving student learning. In G. Cawelti (Ed.), *Handbook of research on improving student achievement* (pp. 163–169). Arlington, VA: Educational Research Service.

Sparks, D., & Loucks-Horsley, S. (1987). Five models of staff development for teachers. *Journal of Staff Development, 10*(4), 40–57.

Sparks, D., & Loucks-Horsley, S. (1990). Models of staff development. In W. R. Houston (Ed.), *Handbook of Research on Teacher Education.* New York: Macmillan.

Stallings, J., & Krasavage, E. (1986). Program implementation and student achievement in a four-year Madeline Hunter follow-through project. *Elementary School Journal, 87*(2), 117–138.

Stein, M. K., Smith, M. S., & Silver, E. (1999). The development of professional developers: Learning to assist teachers in new settings in new ways. *Harvard Educational Review, 69*(3), 237–269.

Stein, M. K., & Wang, M. C. (1988). Teacher development and school improvement: The process of teacher change. *Teaching & Teacher Education, 4*(2), 171–187.

Stout, R. T. (1996). Staff development policy: Fuzzy choices in an imperfect market. *Education Policy Analysis Archives, 4*(2).

Swafford, J. O., Jones, G. A., Thornton, C. A., Stump, S. L., & Miller, D. R. (1999). The impact of instructional practice of a teacher change model. *Journal of Research and Development in Education, 32*(2), 69–82.

Tibbetts, J., Kutner, M., Hemphill, D., & Jones, E. (1991). *Study of ABE/ESL instructor training approaches: The delivery and content of training for adult education teachers and volunteers.* Washington, DC: Pelavin Research Institute.

Tolbert, M. (2001). *Professional development for adult education instructors: State policy update.* Washington DC: National Institute for Literacy.

Tschannen-Moran, M., Hoy, A. W., & Hoy, W. K. (1998). Teacher efficacy: Its meaning and measure. *Review of Educational Research, 68*(2), 202–248.

Valli, L. (1997). Listening to other voices: A description of teacher reflection in the United States. *Peabody Journal of Education, 72*(1), 67–88.

Wenglinsky, H. (2000). *How teaching matters: Bringing the classroom back into discussions of teacher quality* (A Policy Information Center Report). Retrieved November 18, 2003, from Educational Testing Service Web site: http://www.ets.org/research/pic

Wilson, B., & Corbett, D. (2001). Adult basic education and professional development: Strangers for too long. *Focus on Basics, 4*(D), 25–26.

Young, M. B., Fleischman, H., Fitzgerald, N., & Morgan, M. A. (1995). *National evaluation of adult education programs* (Executive Summary) (Contract No. LC 90065001). Arlington, VA: Development Associates.

APPENDIX A:
PROFESSIONAL DEVELOPMENT MODELS AND OBJECTIVES

The core objectives for each professional development model (as presented to the participants) were:

1. **Knowledge:** *Learn more about the topic.* Develop your theories about the topic of learner motivation, retention, and persistence.
2. **Reflection:** *Be critically reflective about your work.* Learn from your own experience, question assumptions that guide your work, and think about your practice in relation to theories of teaching and learning.
3. **Action:** *Try out new learning.* Take action to address the issue of learner motivation, retention, and persistence in the classroom, in the program, and in the community and/or field of adult basic education.

A specific, additional objective for the practitioner research group model was to learn more about research, and for the mentor teacher group model an additional objective was to learn about peer/mentor observation and coaching.

The specific process we suggested that participants follow in addressing learner motivation, retention, and persistence consisted of five steps for gaining knowledge and taking action, including:

1. Understand the topic better.
2. Discover the forces that support learners in their pursuit of their educational goals.
3. Reflect on what you learned from students and what that means for you and your teaching.
4. Choose a goal to work toward.
5. Identify/create a strategy(ies) for taking action to address the issues you've prioritized.

This process was made explicit in both the workshop and the mentor teacher group model, and the sessions were designed to walk participants through the process over the course of the 18 hours. In the practitioner research model, participants were made aware of the above process through handouts and introduced to the specific process for practitioner research (presented as a cycle), which includes: (1) Identifying a question ("What's going on?"—what are the forces that affect learners' persistence? or "What happens when…"—taking action to address learner persistence); (2) Collecting data to answer the question (What are the forces? or How does the action work?); (3) Analyzing and interpreting the data; and (4) Sharing their findings with others in the group.

We identified and presented to participants six main strategies for addressing learner motivation, retention, and persistence, including:

1. **Safety.** An environment in which learners feel that it is okay to make mistakes, that they are respected for what they know, and they are equally respected and valued in the program, regardless of race, gender, class, sexual orientation, and so on.
2. **Community.** An environment among learners and between learners and staff in which learners feel that they are not alone, that they are needed by others, and that they can work together to solve problems.
3. **Self-efficacy.** A belief (of learners) that they can be successful when attempting new activities as learners, workers, family members, and members of their communities.
4. **Quality of Service.** High-quality instruction, program practices, and structures that are driven by the needs of learners and that are engaging, supportive, and relevant to their daily lives.
5. **Accessibility.** A program structure and system that ensures that all services students need (flexibly scheduled classes, day care, transportation, etc.) are available.
6. **Clarity of Purpose.** The realistic and meaningful goals learners have set for themselves and an understanding of how education will help them achieve such goals.

We suggested five arenas within which they, as classroom teachers and program members, might take action to address learner motivation, retention, and persistence:

1. **Within yourself.** Reflect on how your own experiences might affect how you work with learners (we did this by creating our own problem trees).
2. **Within the classroom.** Work with learners to identify or create activities that help them to increase/decrease their prioritized forces.
3. **With individual learners.** Work with individual learners to address forces that are particular to that individual but are not common to the whole class.
4. **Within the program.** Work with staff to implement program-wide changes (such as an improved orientation process for new learners).
5. **Within the community, society, or the field of adult basic education.** Work on your own or with students in the class to implement changes in these areas.

Specific Nature of Multisession Workshop Model

Three multisession workshops were held as part of this professional development study: one in Maine, one in Massachusetts, and one in Connecticut. Each multisession workshop was led by the same facilitator and included up to 16 participants. In Maine and Connecticut, the multisession workshop was delivered in three six-hour, all-day sessions. In Maine, these three days were spaced roughly one to two months apart, with four months from start to completion (the first workshop day was in July, the second was in September, the third was in October). In Connecticut, the three workshop days were spaced two weeks apart, every other Friday (the first day was in January, the second and third days were in February), with six weeks from start to completion. In Massachusetts, the multisession workshop was delivered in four-and-one-half hour afternoon sessions; these sessions were held over four consecutive Fridays in October (with one month from start to completion).

Specific Nature of the Mentor Teacher Group Model

Six mentor teacher groups (run by six different mentor teachers) were run as part of this professional development study: two groups in Maine, two in Massachusetts, and two in Connecticut. Each group consisted of one mentor teacher and up to five participant teachers. The mentor teacher was not a participant but the facilitator of the group's professional development. Each group met for 10 hours as a group; each participant teacher got eight contact hours one-on-one with the mentor. The configuration of the 18 hours was as follows: the group met first for three hours, followed several weeks later by a second meeting of three hours. Then, over the following two months, each participant met individually with the mentor teacher for a total of four hours (one hour of preobservation conference, two hours of observation in class, one hour of postobservation conference). The group then had a third meeting of two hours. In the two months following the observations, each participant teacher met individually with the mentor teacher for a second observation totaling four hours. Finally, the group had a fourth and last meeting for two hours. Each group set its own schedule of meetings and observations, but most groups ran four to six months from start to completion.

Specific Nature of the Practitioner Research Group Model

Six practitioner research groups were run as part of this professional development study: two groups in Maine, two in Massachusetts, and two in Connecticut. One facilitator ran both groups in Maine, and another facilitator ran both groups in Connecticut. Two other facilitators each ran a group in Massachusetts. Each group included up to seven participant teachers. Each group met for six three-hour sessions, most typically spaced one to two months apart. All groups started in the fall and ended by late spring, with six to nine months from start to completion.

Process of Developing the Models/Intervention

The first step in designing the three professional development models was to review the professional development literature for practical suggestions, based on the research, for designing training, peer coaching, study circles, and practitioner research (also called, in some literature, teacher inquiry). This review, coupled with the professional development experience of the research design team, helped us to identify common features for all of the models (i.e., experiential, multisession, etc.) and particular features for the specific models (i.e., the mentor teacher model should include time for a preobservation and a postobservation feedback session; practitioner research model should include an introduction to different methods of data collection that can be done in classrooms, etc.).

Next, we collected information about the topic of the professional development: learner motivation, retention, and persistence in adult basic education programs. After consultation with NCSALL researchers studying learner persistence (John Comings, Andrea Parrella, and Lisa Soricone), we reviewed the literature (both academic and teacher-generated) on learner persistence. Through this review, we were able to identify theories related to why adult learners drop or stop out and what strategies are thought to be most useful in increasing learner persistence. We also developed definitions for common terminology related to the topic.[68]

With key elements of effective professional development and information on the topic, we developed an outline of the agenda for each of the three models. We then held two group meetings with all of the facilitators to review the outline and begin to flesh out the activities for each professional development model. The initial group meetings were followed by multiple meetings for all facilitators implementing the same model (i.e., all practitioner researchers met three times to plan and review activities for the practitioner research group model; all mentor teachers met twice to plan and review for their model).

In between meetings with the facilitators, the research team developed guides, complete with handouts and readings, on each of the professional development models. These guides included step-by-step instructions for the facilitators about how to facilitate all of the activities in the professional development model they would be implementing.

---

[68] Learner motivation is defined engagement while in class. Learner retention is defined as regular class attendance and continued enrollment in the program until goals are reached. Learner persistence is defined as a positive view of themselves as successful lifelong learners, even if they "stop out" or "drop out" at any given point. The issue of learners persisting in programs, in general, is categorized as "learners continuing to pursue their educational goals."

Criteria for Selecting Facilitators

The criteria for mentor teacher group facilitators included:

- Currently teaching in an adult education program
- Extensive teaching experience in the field of adult basic education required
- Previous experience facilitating professional development (especially peer coaching) desired but not required
- Demonstrated ability to understand the demands of mentoring (i.e., good listening skills, nonjudgmental approach, ability to travel to teacher participants' programs to observe their classes, etc.)

All of the six mentor teachers chosen (two per state) had extensive experience teaching in the field, and four out of the six had previous experience facilitating professional development, but all were recognized within their states as strong teachers with leadership potential.

The criteria for practitioner research group facilitators included:

- Experience as a teacher in the field of adult basic education required
- Previous experience facilitating professional development desired
- Experience either conducting practitioner research oneself *or* facilitating others to do so required

Four facilitators were chosen to run the six practitioner research groups: the facilitators for Maine and Connecticut were able and willing to run both groups in their respective states, while in Massachusetts, two well-qualified facilitators were found, each of whom ran one group. All of the facilitators had previous teaching experience; three of them were also professional development specialists with experience in coaching practitioner researchers, while the fourth was a teacher with extensive experience conducting her own practitioner research.

The criteria for the multisession workshop facilitator was:

- Experience as a teacher in the field of adult basic education required
- Previous experience facilitating professional development required

We found one facilitator who was qualified, willing, and able to conduct the workshop in each state.

All facilitators attended two all-day orientation sessions in the spring and early summer of 1998. At these orientation sessions, facilitators were introduced to the study as a whole and to the topic of learner motivation, retention, and persistence. At these meetings, their input was sought about the design of the models. Once the guides were produced for each model, they were reviewed by each of the facilitators, each of whom received one-on-one assistance before the professional development started. Facilitators also received support from the research team during the course of implementing their professional development.

Facilitators were instructed to follow the guides closely, so that the professional development intervention was as uniform as possible across the states and the groups. However, one of the elements of effective professional development identified in the literature is that the professional development should be geared to the needs of the particular group of practitioners participating. Therefore, facilitators were also encouraged and allowed to make minor adjustments to the length or implementation of the activities (e.g., they might change a small-group brainstorm to a whole-group brainstorm if the group were small for a particular session). These changes were to be made based on the facilitator's sense of the importance to the teacher participants of a changed or lengthened discussion to meet the particular needs of the teachers in the group. However, they were instructed not to skip any of the activities or the handouts. Thus, facilitators were trained to work with the research team to strike a balance between the needs of the research (for conformity to the model) and the principles of effective and real professional development (for adaptation of the model to the specific group of participants). Overall, this balance was achieved, with the fewest adaptations needing to be made to the multisession workshop; the most to the practitioner research groups.

APPENDIX B: DEFINING TEACHER CHANGE

Our goal in designing and conducting the NCSALL Professional Development with teachers, regardless of model, was the same: to provide the best quality professional development, based on principles of effective professional development from the research and from our experience, that would help teachers learn and take action on the topic of learner motivation, retention, and persistence (LMRP).

The main focus of our study was "teacher change." "Change" is defined as differences in thinking and acting. "Preferred change," in this study, was change in which the participant acquired knowledge of the topic, took action to find out about forces affecting LMRP from his or her own learners, acquired knowledge of strategies for addressing those forces, made a plan to take action to address forces relevant to his or her own learners, then took action to address the forces (within self, within class, within program, outside of class with individual learners, or within field); in short, the participant achieved the three objectives of the professional development.

Preferred change is action based on knowledge gain—what we call "integrated" change—rather than knowledge not connected to action, or action not connected to knowledge. "No change" is lack of evidence of either knowledge gain or action taken. "Negative change" is rejection of the issue as a problem that should concern the teacher.

The professional development analysis team identified the following criteria for determining change according to outcomes (which are defined as differences in thinking and action between Wave One and Wave Three that can be attributed to participation in the professional development), on and off the topic.

Criteria for Change (Based on Objectives of the Professional Development)

Changes in Thinking
(Also includes beliefs, attitudes, perceptions, feelings, etc.)

1. On Topic

   a. Learned about the topic (understanding the complexity of barriers and supports, changing attitudes toward importance of knowing who learners are, or broadening instruction based on learners' needs)
   b. Learned strategies for addressing LMRP

2. Off Topic

   a. Gained general teaching knowledge (why to use new technique or approach, not related to LMRP)
   b. Became aware of, reflected on, or critically analyzed the weaknesses or strengths of:

      i. The community within which they or learners live
      ii. Their program
      iii. The field of adult basic education
      iv. How they best learn (including the type of professional development they prefer)

   c. Learned strategies (tools) for research
   d. Expressed importance of collegiality in program or in field

Changes in Action
1. On Topic

   a. Took action to find out about their own learners and the forces affecting their LMRP

      i. With individual learners: Took informal action outside class (e.g., called learners at home to find out why they were absent)
      ii. Within classroom: Took action informally inside classroom (e.g., added time to chat with learners within class time) or took action formally inside classroom (used a technique or made curriculum change)

   b. Took action toward addressing LMRP (based on what they learned from their own learners):

      i. With individual learners: Took informal action outside of class
      ii. Within classroom: Took formal or informal action inside of class

     iii. Within program: Took action in program to improve own classroom and/or overall program

     iv. Within field: Took action related to LMRP (offered professional development on the topic to others outside their program)

     v. Within self (changing own behavior toward learners)

2. Off Topic

    a. Made a general teaching change (used a new technique, without intention to affect LMRP)

    b. Made a program change (initiated a policy or structural change [e.g., increased collegiality], without intention to affect LMRP)

    c. Made a learning change (used a new approach to own learning or professional development, without intention to affect LMRP)

    d. Made a field change (contribution to field or community, offered professional development off topic, research about field)

Coding for Change

Through coding of the open-ended responses to all three waves of questionnaire (for the 101 respondents for whom we had at least two waves of data), we were able to gauge change in a number of thinking and acting arenas. Altogether, there were 17 different areas of change. These corresponded to the criteria listed above for changes in thinking and acting, on and off topic (took general teaching action, learned about the topic). Ten of the 17 areas related to changes in thinking; 7 related to changes in acting; 12 related to changes in thinking and acting off the topic; 5 related to thinking and acting on the topic.

Two of the research team members read all of the open-ended responses for each person in the study, then made a judgment about whether the respondent had made no, minimal, moderate, or significant change in that area. If it was not possible to make a clear judgment about the level of change, the respondent was given a code of "too vague to judge" for that area. After coding all of the respondents' answers for each of the 17 different areas, the two research team members compared their answers and reviewed any that had been coded differently by the two coders. Sometimes this entailed lengthy discussions and review of the answers for each respondent, with "too vague to judge" being the preferred default. Quantitative scores for change were derived by assigning a "0" score to no change, "1" to minimal, "2" to moderate, and "3" to significant change for each of the 17 areas of change. The rationale for scoring in each area is as follows:

- **Minimal** = a one-shot action; change in thinking that was limited to one or two new concepts or strategies
- **Moderate** = several one-shot actions or one small action that was sustained over time; several concepts or strategies that were sustained for a short period of time
- **Significant** = one big action or many actions sustained; multiple concepts that were sustained over time

This allowed us to see not only overall change, but also to separate the scores for participants according to thinking only, acting only, on the topic, and off the topic. The total possible score for each category was:

- Thinking on topic: 0–3
- Thinking off topic: 0–27
- Acting on topic: 0–12
- Acting off topic: 0–9
- Overall: 0–51

Coding for Type of Change

Criteria we used to determine in which category a teacher would be placed:

1. The **amount of change** in either thinking or acting relative to teachers' baseline (whether thinking changed a little or a lot, as evidenced by their responses to questions about concepts on the topic; whether they took a little or a lot of action, compared to the action they were taking at baseline).
2. Whether **action was "integrated" with thinking**; i.e., how much teachers understood *and* undertook the process of change (understanding topic, finding out from learners, choosing strategy to address the issue based on what learners had said, taking action to address, reflecting upon the outcome of their action) and integrated it with a cohesive theory of what adult learners need to succeed.
3. The **number of arenas in which change occurred** (as learner, teacher, program member, and/or member of the field).
4. Whether **change was sustained** until Wave Three (one year after professional development was completed).

Validity of Coding

Self-reported questionnaire data has its limitations (as it is not directly observed over time); respondents may underreport by filling out the questionnaire sparsely, or they may overreport, by claiming actions when none were taken. However, we were able to use the examples of the 18 subsample participants, having both questionnaires and interview data to compare, and estimate the amount of under- or overreporting that would be likely to occur in the sample as a whole. Coding of open-ended questionnaire data was done by code # (rather than name) so subsample participants' questionnaires were coded just like all other questionnaires. Afterward, we were able to check their overall amount of change and type of change (based on what they wrote only in the questionnaires) against what we knew of them from the more in-depth qualitative data. In two thirds of the cases, their questionnaire data (and thus scoring of change) was true to the type and amount of change we knew of them from in-depth information. In one case, a subsample participant reported more in her questionnaire than we learned from the interview (overreporting), but all of the remaining subsample participants were cases of underreporting (where, by the sparseness of their answers, they underreported changes in thinking and action we know them to have made). For example, one teacher was typed as "acting change" based on qualitative data but was coded as "no change" based on questionnaire; another was typed as "acting change" qualitatively but was coded as "thinking change" based on questionnaire. These six cases of under- and overreporting happened across professional development models and states. Therefore, the amount of change for the whole sample may be somewhat more than the scores based on the questionnaires in approximately one third of the cases. While we would prefer to wrongly assume less rather than more change, it bears remembering that it is likely that more changes in thinking and acting might have been visible if actual observation had occurred. This points out one of the weaknesses of questionnaires as a data-collection method for determining change over time.

APPENDIX C: CRITERIA FOR RATING GROUP QUALITY

The rating of overall quality of group dynamics was based on six criteria, the extent to which:

- Participants were looking for the correct answer, versus looking for the "truth" or testing assumptions (looking for outside guidance versus reflection)
- Participants talked only to the facilitator, versus talking with each other
- One person dominated the conversations, versus participants taking turns talking
- Conversation was dull or lethargic, versus conversation being animated, energetic, and positive (i.e., participants were engaged)
- Participants asked for clarification of materials, exercises, or activities (i.e., they are confused), versus participants indicating they were clear about expectations
- The group experienced turbulence in attendance, versus all participants attending regularly

The rating of quality of facilitation was based on five criteria, the extent to which the facilitator:

- Acted mainly as a source of knowledge ("a sage on the stage"), versus acting as a facilitator of participants' learning (i.e., to what extent did the facilitator ask questions that drew out the participants' knowledge and ideas)
- Was "fishing" for the right answer (asking closed-ended questions), versus probing for comprehension and understanding (asking open-ended questions)
- Talked, versus the participants talked
- Used the manual as a script versus used it as a guide
- Commented on the fact that there was a guide to be followed, versus internalized the guide

Three criteria were used to evaluate the integrity of the model, the extent to which:

- The activities presented in the guide were not covered (versus all activities were covered to some extent)
- The scheduling of activities was problematic
- Participants mentioned that the NCSALL study interfered with their experience (a research effect)

APPENDIX D: ADDITIONAL INFORMATION ON FACTORS

Before conducting the study, we developed a set of hypotheses, gleaned from the professional development literature and from our experience in the field of adult basic education, about the individual, professional development, and program or system factors that were most likely to support or hinder the type or amount of change teachers demonstrate:

Individual Factors

- Reason/motivation to attend the professional development
- Years of experience in adult education
- Venue of first teaching experience (K–12 or ABE)
- Level of formal education
- Level of professional development consumption
- Belief in purpose of literacy instruction
- Type of teaching (ABE, ESOL, etc.)
- Teaching situation (one-on-one, small class, large class)
- Teaching experience in K–12
- Belief that knowledge about the learner is important
- Age of teacher
- Level of commitment to working in adult education

Professional Development Factors

- Amount (hours) of participation in professional development
- Quality of professional development (as perceived by participants)
- Quality of professional development group (as rated by researchers)
- Model of professional development
- "Coparticipation" in professional development (with colleagues from own program)

Program or System Factors

- Required use of curriculum
- Program situation (decision-making in the program)
- Access to benefits
- Access to prep time
- Number of hours teacher works each week in adult education
- Amount of paid professional development release time
- Enrollment policy
- Program concurrently working on same issue (learner persistence)
- State in which participant works
- Program type
- Teachers' perception of leadership in program
- Perception of freedom to decide what and how to teach
- Opportunities for collegiality
- Access to resources

Individual Factors

Reason for Attending Professional Development

Our hypothesis was that teachers without a strong motivation to learn would change less, and we concluded that this hypothesis was supported. Teachers in this sample who responded to a question about their primary reason for attending the professional development (n=87) reported a variety of reasons for attending the professional development: 30% to learn more about the topic; 22% to participate in a particular model of professional development; 20% to learn more about teaching in general; 8% because their director asked them to attend; 5% because they wanted to be part of the research study; and the rest because they wanted Continuing Education Units (CEUs), thought the facilitator would be good, a colleague was attending, or wanted to meet other teachers. The qualitative data also supports the finding that teachers had a variety of motivations for attending the professional development, and that an interest in the topic of learner persistence was not the primary reason for the majority of teachers who participated. We don't doubt that the professional development being part of a research study probably affected the motivation of the 5% who said they wanted to participate in the research.

In Wave One, we asked teachers to rate (on a scale of 1–6) to what extent they considered learner motivation, retention, and persistence to be a priority topic, compared to other topics on which they had sought or would seek professional development. The mean score for the sample was 5.07 (SD =.89), which indicates a strong interest; on the other hand, it was not a score of six across the board, indicating that some of the teachers in our sample had other topics of equivalent or greater importance to them. Across the whole sample, a stronger existing motivation related to this topic was not associated with any measure of change. However, we had much richer information from the subsample teachers on the question of motivation to attend the professional development, and within the subsample we saw a definite pattern: teachers who had reasons for wanting to attend other than to learn about the topic or about teaching (e.g., director urging, convenience, CEUs, interest in professional development model) more often demonstrated limited or nonintegrated change. The teachers who demonstrated integrated change expressed strong motivations, coming into the professional development, to solve the problem of learner dropout or a strong desire to learn more about teaching. The connection between motivation and type of change was strong enough in the subsample that we identify it as an important factor influencing change.

Years of Experience in Adult Education

Our hypothesis was that teachers who have been teaching longer in this field have a greater depth of knowledge (which is perhaps connected to weaker motivation to learn on any given topic), and so may change less. We found that the hypothesis was supported among completers, for both amount of change ($r=-.245$, $p=.028$, $n=81$) and for type of change, as seen in Table 19 below:

Table 19: Type of Change by Years of Experience in Adult Education (Completers only, n=81)

Type of Change	n	Mean Years of Experience	SD
No or minimal	21	13.19	6.104
Nonintegrated	40	7.65	6.963
Integrated	20	8.35	5.869
Totals	*81*	*9.26*	*6.833*

$F=5.27$, $p<.01$

In our subsample, the pattern was supported: four out of four of the "no or minimal" change teachers, two out of four of the "thinking change" teachers, one out of four of the acting change, and two out of five of the integrated change teachers had more than three years of experience in the field of adult education. Although the sample size is small, we conclude that teachers in our sample who completed the professional development and who had been teaching for more years in the field were less likely to demonstrate greater overall change and change in a preferred direction; however, years of experience made no difference in whether a dropout exhibited change.

Venue of First Teaching Experience

We were not surprised to find that most teachers (69%) in our sample began their teaching career in a nonadult education venue. We hypothesized that a teacher who first started teaching in the adult education field, rather than in K–12, would be more likely to change as a result of participating in professional development, because they would be looking more for ideas and confirmation that they were in fact doing a good job as a teacher. We found support for this hypothesis: among those who completed the professional development ($n=81$), teachers whose first teaching experience was in adult education had a mean overall amount of change of 10.9 ($n=25$, $SD=7.82$), compared to teachers who first taught in K–12 or another venue, who had a mean amount of change of 7.86 ($n=56$, $SD=4.62$), and this difference was significant (one-way ANOVA $F=4.87$, $p=.031$). Type of change was also significantly different by venue of first teaching experience, as presented in Table 20.

This finding was supported among subsample teachers, where three of the four "no or minimal change" teachers started teaching in K–12 but three of the five "integrated" change teachers began their teaching in adult education.

Table 20: Type of Change by First Experience Teaching
(Completers for whom we have data, *n*=81)

First Teaching Experience	n	Type of Change			
		No Change	Non-Integrated	Integrated	Totals
ABE	25	5	9	11	25
K–12 or other	56	16	31	9	56
Totals	*81*	*21*	*40*	*80*	*21*

χ^2=7.26, *df*=2, *p*<.05

Level of Formal Education

Research in K–12 on teacher quality (as defined by more years of formal education completed and certification) indicates that more formal education is related to higher student achievement (Darling-Hammond and Sykes, 1999); however, we do not know whether having an advanced degree (in any field) is related to change as a result of participation in professional development. However, based on the belief that teachers with more formal education have better-developed philosophies of education and theoretical schema upon which to "hang" new learning, we hypothesized that more formal education overall would be related to more change and to change in a preferred direction.

In our questionnaire, we asked teachers their highest level of formal education completed; we did not, however, ask them what field their degree was in. We found that formal education was negatively and significantly correlated with amount of change: those with a bachelor's degree or less had a mean overall amount of change of 10.69 (*n*=45, *SD*=6.47); teachers with a master's degree or more had an overall amount of change of 6.24 (*n*=38, *SD*=4.13), and this difference was significant (one-way ANOVA *F*=13.37, *p*<.001). Type of change was significantly related to level of formal education, as presented in Table 21 below:

Table 21: Type of Change by Level of Formal Education
(Completers for whom we have data, n=83)

Level of Education	n	Type of Change			
		No Change	Non-Integrated	Integrated	Totals
Bachelor's or less	45	6	25	14	45
Master's or Above	38	17	15	6	38
Totals	*83*	*23*	*40*	*20*	*83*

χ^2=10.45, *df*=2, *p*<.01

The subsample supported the rejection of our hypothesis, since all of the four teachers who fell into the "no or minimal" change type had master's degrees, but three of the five teachers who demonstrated "integrated change" did not have a master's or a teaching certificate.

Level of Professional Development Consumption

We hypothesized that practitioners who are regular consumers of professional development might be more likely to demonstrate change as a result of our professional development. This was not the case. Level of professional development consumption (as gauged by the amount of professional development they attended in the year before and the year after attending our professional development, on all topics) was not related to type or amount of overall change. Participants in our study may also have sought out and participated in other professional development on the topic of "learner persistence" before, during, or after participating in the NCSALL Professional Development on the same topic. We asked participants, in each wave, to tell us how many workshops, conferences, study circles, and other types of professional development (including reading on their own) they had done *on* the topic of learner persistence. Fifty-six out of the 106 practitioners in our study indicated that they had received no other professional development on the topic, other than their participation in the NCSALL Professional Development, either before, during, or in the year after participation. Table 22 shows the breakdown of attendance in other activities on the topic before and after the NCSALL Professional Development.

We used a z-score average of all other participation to get a score for the amount of other professional development they received on the topic. The data indicate that attending other professional development on the topic was not associated with amount or type of change.

Table 22: Participation in Other Professional Development on the Topic of LMRP

LMRP Activites	Year Prior to NCSALL Professional Development (n=30)	Year AfterCSALL Professional Development (n=2)
Attended workshops	15%	12%
Read on own	21%	15%
Attended conferences	8%	12%
Participated in curriculum development projects	7%	35%
Participated in study or sharing groups	27%	30%
Peer coached	10%	20%
Attended lectures	24%	20%
Participated in practitioner research projects	17%	20%
Attended college courses	7%	10%

Belief in Purpose of Literacy Instruction

The hypothesis here is that those teachers who believe in a broader purpose of literacy, beyond acquiring reading, writing, and skills, may be more likely to adopt new thinking and strategies for keeping students in the program. This hypothesis was not supported, based on asking participants in the Wave One questionnaire what they believed to be the primary purpose of literacy instruction. We asked teachers what they think the primary purpose of literacy instruction is, with the choices being (a) "helping learners develop basic skills (reading, writing, speaking) or accomplish specific tasks (e.g., getting a GED, filling out a check)" *or* (b) "helping learners develop the ability to use literacy in their own lives or work toward social change (e.g., writing health brochures for their own community, working to change welfare laws.)" The responses indicate that most teachers (65%) believe that the purpose of literacy is the acquisition of basic literacy skills. However, this factor was not related to either amount or type of change.

Type of Teaching (ABE, ESOL, GED)

We had no strong hypothesis that what type of adult learner a teacher taught was related to change, but we felt it was important to collect this data because an ESOL, GED, or ABE teacher may approach teaching in different ways. We do not consider the data collected on this question to be strong, given the difficulty of framing the question. While it would seem as if such a question is simple to ask, in reality, many teachers in this field often teach multiple types of learner populations and learners at different levels. This occurs whether or not teachers are working in two different programs or only one program. We asked teachers to tell us the primary type of teaching they currently do, with choices including (a) "ABE/literacy (reading 0–4 level)," (b) "preGED (reading 5–8 level)," (c) "GED/Adult secondary education preparation," (d) "ESL/ESOL," or (e) "other" (which included "vocational education," "family literacy," etc.). After piloting, we also added an option to choose (f) "an equal combination of ABE/literacy, preGED, and/or GED," since many teachers indicated that they often teach equal numbers of classes at several levels. The results indicated that there was a range of different types of teaching, so we combined teachers who completed the professional development into four categories[69] in order to increase cell sizes: (1) 0–8 level ($n=14$), (2) GED ($n=19$), (3) ESOL ($n=21$), and (4) equal combination of ABE, preGED, GED and other ($n=25$).

We found that type of teaching was not associated with either amount or type of change among those who completed the professional development (for whom we have data).

Teaching Situation

This factor relates to whether a teacher teaches (or tutors) an individual student, a small group or class, or larger classes. Teachers were asked to state whether they provided one-on-one tutoring with either one individual or with different individuals during drop-in sessions, or whether they teach classes of different sizes (2–10 students, 11–20 students, 21+ students, or other). Because cell sizes were small in each of these categories, we coded teachers into three categories: (1) one-on-one teaching or tutoring, (2) small class (2–10 students), or (3) larger class (11+ students). In our sample, 14 teachers reported that they teach one-on-one or provide individual instruction; 33 teachers report that they teach small classes of less than 10 students; and 27 teachers report that they teach classes with more than 11 students.[70] There were no significant differences, nor any discernible trend, between overall amount of change or type of change by teaching situation.

Teaching Experience in K–12

We hypothesized that those who had not been teachers in K–12 might change more, based on the idea that all of their teaching experience was in adult education and so they

---

[69] We used the primary type of teaching that teachers indicated on their Wave One questionnaire, when they began the professional development, rather than Wave Three, since some teachers had stopped teaching by that time.

[70] Five teachers report that their teaching situation is "other," but they either provided no explanation or their explanation (e.g., "family literacy") indicated that they did not understand the question.

might be "hungrier" for professional development. While teachers who had been K–12 teachers had a lower mean amount of change (8.08 out of 30 [n=52, SD=4.91]) than teachers who had never taught in K–12 (10.10 out of 30 [n=29, SD=7.32]), this difference was not statistically significant. Having never been a teacher in K–12 was also not related to type of change.

Age

We had no hypothesis about the relation between age and change, and we almost didn't ask it of teachers, but then decided to add the question to the Wave Three questionnaire upon the advice of our research design team. Of teachers who completed the professional development, there were 18 teachers between the age of 26–40; 21 teachers between 41–50; and 39 teachers 51 and over. Teachers' age was not significantly related to any dependent variable of change.

Belief that Knowledge about the Learner is Important

Our professional development presented a strategy for addressing learner persistence that suggested discovering the forces affecting persistence among learners. Therefore, we hypothesized that teachers who had a stronger belief that knowing one's learners well is important would demonstrate more change. The premise of this hypothesis is that teachers' belief that it is part of their role to know learners or that students' needs and goals should drive curriculum would be associated with more change in this particular study, where the topic and focus was helping learners persist. We asked teachers to what extent (on a scale of 1-6) they felt it was part of an adult education teachers' role to know about learners' lives, goals, and uses of literacy in everyday life. Their rating was not associated with any measure of change.

We also hypothesized that the extent to which a teacher identifies with or sees herself as relatively equal to learners and the extent of the teachers' ability to apply what is true for self to learners would be important factors. However, we could not find a way to accurately or validly assess such attitudes in the questionnaire, so we tested this hypothesis only minimally through our data on the subsample teachers. We felt that three of the four teachers who demonstrated "no or minimal change" expressed distance between themselves as teachers and the learners with whom they work. While a few other teachers in the sample—teachers who did make change in a preferred direction—also expressed "distanced" views of learners, those teachers with the most significant change expressed strong attitudes of equality and respect for learners. Since we did not collect information from the larger sample (via the questionnaire) about teachers' attitudes toward students, it is difficult to do more than hypothesize that these are dispositions which, at least in relation to the topic of learner motivation, retention, and persistence, contribute to greater change in addressing the issue.

We hypothesized that if the curriculum teachers used was driven by students' needs and goals, teachers would change more, taking action to address learner persistence through their curriculum. We also asked them what they felt "drives" their instruction: tests that students are required to take, directors' priorities, students' needs or goals, or required curriculum or competencies. The majority of teachers (68 out of 96) said that students' needs, goals, and issues are the most important factors in driving their curriculum; 10 teachers reported that required curriculum or competencies drive their curriculum; tests are the driving curriculum factor for 15 teachers; and 3 teachers indicated it was their director or other factor (unexplained) that set the course. There was no significant association between either measure of change and whether the teacher reported that instruction was driven by students' needs or by other factors.

Professional Development Factors

Hours of Participation in NCSALL Professional Development

The first hypothesis related to professional development factors was that attending the professional development for more hours would lead to more change. This hypothesis was supported, with more hours of participation (from 0–18 hours) positively and significantly associated with both overall amount of change ($r=.25$, $p<.05$) and type of change, as shown in Table 23 below:

Table 23: Mean Hours of Participation by Type of Change
(Dropouts and completers, $n=95$)

Type of Change	n	Mean Hours of Participation	SD
No or minimal	32	13.641	5.5402
Nonintegrated	42	16.333	2.7262
Integrated	21	15.667	3.2590
Totals	*95*	*15.279*	*4.1313*

$F=4.25$, $p<.05$

Teachers who completed at least two thirds of the professional development experienced more change than dropouts or those who did not participate at all; for those who attended at least two thirds (12 hours), the number of hours above that was not significant to amount or type of change. The significant difference was between the "no change" group and the "nonintegrated change" group ($p=.019$). Differences between the "integrated change" group and either "no change" or "nonintegrated change" were not significant.

Quality of the NCSALL Professional Development (as Perceived by Participants)

The second hypothesis was that the quality of the professional development, as perceived by the participants, would be related to type and amount of change. In other words, the higher the participants rated the professional development quality, the more likely they would be to make changes as a result of it. To test this hypothesis, we asked participants a series of questions, using Likert scales (1=weak or low quality, 6=strong or high quality) about how they would rate the overall quality of the NCSALL Professional Development in which they participated. We also asked them to rate particular elements of the professional development, such as facilitator/presentation, group dynamics, length of the activity, session organization, and readings/materials.

Table 24 below shows the aspects asked about and the mean scores for the sample in descending order.

These scores indicate, overall, a favorable response to the professional development on learner motivation, retention, and persistence. There were no significant differences in rating of the professional development across states and models among those who completed it.

Table 24: Ratings of Key Aspects of the NCSALL Professional Development

Aspects of NCSALL Professional Development	n	Mean	SD
View of quality of facilitator	91	5.27	.76
View of quality of readings	90	4.94	.89
View of interaction with other participants	91	4.92	1.00
View of structure or design of sessions	91	4.82	.97
View of opportunity to meet over time	88	4.41	1.36

Teachers were also asked to rate the extent to which the NCSALL Professional Development affected them in various ways, again using a six-point scale (1="didn't affect me at all," 6="strongly affected me"). Table 25 below presents their perspective on the influence of the professional development on them:

Table 25: Participants' Rating of How the NCSALL
Professional Development Affected Them

How Professional Development Affected Them	n	Mean	SD
Validated what they already knew	92	4.50	.85
Added to their knowledge on topic	92	4.46	1.1
Increased their confidence in how to teach	92	4.24	1.2
Increased number of colleagues	91	3.65	1.4
Changed their way of thinking about teaching	92	3.54	1.2
Changed their way of thinking about students	92	3.46	1.4
Transformed their practice	91	3.43	1.2

No significant differences were found in how participants from different states and different models felt the professional development had affected them. There was also no significant difference between top and bottom mean score listed here. However, we see a pattern: participants felt the professional development affected them more strongly in their knowledge of the topic (the top two aspects in the table) than it affected their thinking and practice (bottom three aspects). This finding is supported by participants' responses to another six-point scale question: to what extent did participation in the NCSALL Professional Development affect the way you conduct classes (1="not at all," 6="to a great extent")? The means from both Wave Two and Wave Three on this question are almost identical: Wave Two mean is 3.69 (n=76, SD =1.318), and Wave Three mean is 3.64 (n=84, SD =1.229). These responses are very close to the mean for how much participants, in Wave Three, felt that the professional development had transformed their practice (3.43), indicating that participants' self-evaluation is that the professional development affected their thinking more than their actions.

In addition to the questions above, we also coded teachers' open-ended explanations for why they rated the professional development as they did. Table 26 below outlines their responses:

Table 26: Perceptions of Specific Aspects of the NCSALL Professional Development (Completers and dropouts, *n*=95)

Factor	Number Of Participants Who Mentioned At All(Out Of 95)	Percent Whose Comments Were Only Positive	Percent Whose Comments Were Only Negative	Percent Whose Comments Were Both Positive and Negative
Facilitator	72	72%	3%	1%
Professional development model	74	52%	10%	17%
Readings	40	40%	1%	1%
Sharing with other practitioners	77	75%	3%	3%

These findings indicate that the quality of the facilitator and the opportunity to share with other practitioners were the two most important factors in how positively they felt about the professional development, and the professional development model in which they participated was the most important factor for those who felt negatively about the professional development. Of the nine participants who made a negative comment about the model, one participated in the workshop model, two participated in the mentor teacher group model, and six participated in the practitioner research group model.

We averaged 13 different Likert-scale responses to the 13 questions we asked about the quality of the professional development (Kronbach-Alpha reliability = .89), and used this combined average (a number between 1 and 6) as a measure of each subject's perception of the high quality of the NCSALL Professional Development. Teachers' perception of the quality of the professional development was positively and significantly correlated with overall amount of change (r=.25, p<.05, n=81). Their perception of quality was also positively and significantly associated with the type of change they demonstrated. Table 27 below presents the findings for teachers' perception of the quality of the professional development.

The significant difference among groups was between the "no change" type and the other two types.

Correlations also show that years working in adult education field (r=-.26, p<.05) and years teaching adult education (r=-.23, p<.05) were both significantly and negatively correlated with the teachers' perception of the quality of the professional development, indicating that the longer the participant had been working and teaching in the field, the less she or he liked the professional development.

Rated Quality of the Group

Of the 15 groups, researchers rated six as high quality, four as medium quality, and five as low quality.[71] Although there was a definite trend toward high-quality groups having

---

[71] Please see Appendix C for a complete description of the process of rating the professional development groups.

higher mean overall change, the difference in amount of change among groups by quality was not significant. The mean overall amount of change among those who completed in the high-quality professional development groups (n=42) was 9.6 (SD=6.3), compared to a mean of 9.0 (SD=5.6) for teachers who completed in the medium-quality groups (n=25) and a mean of 5.6 (SD=4.7) for teachers who completed in the low-quality groups. One-way ANOVA indicates that the difference among groups is not significant.

Table 27: Type of Change by Teachers' Perception of Professional Development Quality (Completers for whom we have complete data, n=81)

Type of Change	n	Mean Combined Quality Score	SD
No or minimal	21	3.90	.71
Nonintegrated	40	4.57	.63
Integrated	21	4.43	.68
Totals	*81*	*4.37*	*.68*

F=8.05, df=2, p<.001

However, the quality of the group was positively and significantly correlated to type of change among those who completed the professional development, as demonstrated in Table 28 below.

Table 28: Type of Change by Quality of Professional Development Group (Completers for whom we have data, n=83)

Quality of Group	n	Type of Change			
		No Change	Non-Integrated	Integrated	*Totals*
Low Quality	16	10	4	2	*16*
Medium Quality	25	4	15	6	*25*
High Quality	42	9	21	12	*42*
Totals	*83*	*23*	*40*	*20*	*83*

χ^2=12.6, df=4, p<.05

These findings indicate that higher quality of facilitation and group dynamics were associated with more preferred type of change (integrated change). There was a trend toward higher overall amounts of change among completers from the high-quality groups, but this trend was not statistically significant.

Interestingly, there was not a significant relationship between the actual quality of the group (as rated by the researchers) and teachers' perceived quality of the group. Regardless of the actual quality, teachers rated it about the same: completing teachers in the lowest-quality groups (n=16) gave their professional development a mean rating of 4.11 (out of 6, on the z-score rating for 13 rating variables); teachers in medium-quality groups (n=25) gave their professional development a mean rating of 4.59; and teachers in the highest-quality groups (n=40) gave their professional development a mean rating of 4.33. Since both actual quality and perceived quality were associated with type of change, but not with each other, it is an indication that teachers in our study experienced professional development differently from one another and, in some cases, differently from how we as researchers rated it.

Type (Model) of Professional Development

Although all three models were designed to be of the highest quality, and all three offered sustained exposure (18 hours over three–six different sessions) with encouragement to try activities and take action between sessions, the mentor teacher group and practitioner research group models offered slightly more one-on-one support to help teachers make direct changes in their classrooms and programs. Therefore, we hypothesized that professional development models that offer more intensive one-on-one support to make changes (mentor teacher group, practitioner research) would result in more change, and that teachers participating in the mentor teacher groups and practitioner research groups would demonstrate more change overall and more change in a preferred direction (toward more integrated change) than would teachers in workshops. Conversely, since workshops include many hands-on activities and modeling of different training techniques by workshop facilitators, we hypothesized that workshop participants would make more general teaching changes than would practitioner research participants and mentor teacher group participants, so we expected to see more change off the topic among teachers who participated in the workshops.

Neither amount nor type of change was significantly related to model of professional development. Amount of change was highest among practitioner research group teachers who completed the professional development (n=24); their mean amount of change was 9.7 (SD=7.7). Mentor teacher group completers (n=24) had a mean amount of change of 9.3 (SD=6.7), and workshop completers (n=35) had a mean amount of change of 7.5 (SD=3.5). Differences among groups were not significant (one-way ANOVA F=1.088, p=.342). Type of change was also not significantly related to which of the three professional development models teachers participated in (if they completed), as seen in Table 29 below.

Table 29: Type of Change by Professional Development Model (Completers only, n=83)

Professional Development Model	n	Type of Change			
		No Change	Non-Integrated	Integrated	Totals
Workshop	35	8	20	7	35
Mentor teacher group	24	7	10	7	24
Practitioner research group	24	8	10	6	24
Totals	*83*	*23*	*40*	*20*	*83*

χ^2=2.1, df=4, p=.717, not significant

Even though model of professional development was not significantly related to change, we saw different patterns of change among models; a larger sample size might have produced significant differences, but that is a question for future research. In each model, "nonintegrated" change (thinking or acting change) was most common, and the most preferred type of change (integrated change) was equal among groups.

However, the trend in percentages indicates that more teachers who completed the workshops (as compared to participants in the other two models) made nonintegrated change. Although there was no significant difference among models, those teachers who participated in mentor teacher groups and practitioner research groups demonstrated more overall change. In fact, no workshop completer had an "overall amount of change" score over 15 (in a range of 0–30), whereas four mentor teacher group participants and five practitioner research group participants had scores between 16 and 30. While this pattern would seem to uphold the hypothesis posed about the greater effectiveness of more in-depth, supportive professional development, the lack of significant differences among groups prevents us from accepting that hypothesis fully.

Being in Professional Development with Others from the Same Program ("Coparticipation")

All of the information we have on this variable is presented in the body of the report.

Participating in a Model of Professional Development Preferred by Teacher

We hypothesized that teachers who participated in a professional development model that was their top preference might gain more from the professional development. Since teachers were not randomly assigned to a professional development model, nor did they in all circumstances (because of geography) have a choice of models, they might have been participating in a model that wasn't their first choice. Teachers were asked, in the Wave One questionnaire, filled out before starting the professional development, whether they would prefer to participate in a workshop, a mentor/peer teaching group, or a practitioner research group, allowing us to determine whether there was a "match" between the type of professional development they preferred and the type in which they actually participated. The results indicate that participating in the type of professional development preferred by the teacher was not significantly related to either amount or type of change, as can be seen in Table 30 below.

Table 30: Type of Change by Match of Preferred Model
with Actual Model (Completers only, $n=83$)

Match of Preferred Model with Actual Model	n	Type of Change			
		No Change	Non-Integrated	Integrated	Totals
Match	45	16	20	9	45
No match	38	7	20	11	38
Totals	83	23	40	20	83

$\chi^2=3.2$, $df=2$, $p=.207$, not signficant

In the final questionnaire, we again asked teachers to tell us what model of professional development they now preferred, giving them four choices: (1) single-session workshop or training, (2) multiple session workshop or training, (3) peer coaching or mentoring, and (4) practitioner research or inquiry group. We then looked at the means for overall amount of change and type of change by final preference for professional development and found that the model they preferred after completion was significantly related to amount of change. Those completing teachers who preferred mentor teacher groups as professional development ($n=8$) had higher mean amount of change (12 out of 30, $SD=4.2$), than teachers preferring practitioner research (mean amount of change=10.7, $n=18$, $SD=5.7$), teachers preferring multiple-session workshops (mean amount of change= 8.2, n=26, SD=4.5), with teachers preferring single-session workshops having the lowest mean amount of change (mean amount of change=6.5, n=18, SD=4.8), and this difference was significant (one-way ANOVA F=2.73, df=3, p=.051).

However, preference for type of professional development model was not related to type of change, as seen in Table 31 below.

Table 31: Type of Change by Final Preference for Professional Development Model (Completers for whom we have data, n=70)

Model Preferred (Wave Three) n		Type of Change			
		No Change	Non-Integrated	Integrated	Totals
Single-session workshop	18	8	6	4	18
Multiple-session workshop	26	5	17	4	26
Peer/mentor coaching	8	0	5	3	8
Practitioner research	18	5	6	7	18
Totals	70	18	34	18	70

χ^2=11.33, df=6, p=.079, not significant

It is interesting that those who preferred peer coaching or mentoring and those who participated in the mentor teacher groups had the highest means for overall amount of change; however, the numbers are small and not significant.

Program or System Factors

Required Use of Curriculum

In some programs, teachers were required to use a specific curriculum (developed by the program or by the state). In other programs, teachers developed their own curriculum. Our hypothesis was that teachers who had the ability to develop their own curriculum would make more changes than teachers who were required to use an established curriculum. To test this hypothesis, we asked teachers whether or not they were required to use a curriculum. Fifty-six (about 58%) of the teachers were not required by their program or state to use a curriculum. Among those who completed the professional development, 44 teachers said they were required to use a curriculum; their mean amount of change was 8.36 (SD=6.4). Thirty-five teachers were not required to use a curriculum; their mean amount of change was 8.6 (SD=4.3). This difference was not significant. Being required to use a curriculum was not significantly related to type of change, as shown in Table 32 below.

However, twice as many completing teachers who demonstrated integrated change reported that they were not required to use a curriculum, and patterns in our subsample strongly indicated that those teachers who teach to the GED test were much less likely to demonstrate change in a preferred direction. Therefore, we think that being required to use a curriculum may have some influence on teacher change. Although we did not characterize it as one of the most important factors, it is worthy of further research.

Program Situation

All of the information we have on this variable is presented in the body of the report.

Access to Benefits

Whether or not teachers received benefits as part of their adult education job was part of a configuration of factors we investigated, based on the hypothesis that teachers working under better conditions would be in a better position to take action. The configuration of working condition factors included access to paid prep time, paid professional development release time, more working hours, benefits, and stability on the job. (We did not ask about salary.) We discovered that access to benefits was related to type of change but not to overall amount of change: teachers completing the professional development (for whom we have this data) who did receive benefits as part of their adult education job had a mean overall amount of change of 9.3 ($n=35$, $SD=6.8$), whereas teachers who did not receive benefits had a mean overall mount of change of 8.4 ($n=34$, $SD=4.5$), and this difference was not significant (one-way ANOVA $F=.508$, $df=1$, $p=.48$). In particular, access to benefits seemed to be an important factor supporting more integrated change.

Table 32: Type of Change by Required Use of Curriculum (Completers for whom we have data, $n=79$)

Policy on Use of Program or State Curriculum	n	Type of Change			
		No Change	Non-Integrated	Integrated	Totals
Required	35	8	21	6	35
Not required	44	14	18	12	44
Totals	70	22	39	18	79

$\chi^2=2.88$, $df=2$, $p=.24$, not significant

Access to Prep Time

Teachers with paid prep time should be better supported to make changes in thinking and acting. Among completers for whom we have data about prep time, paid prep time was significantly related to type of change but not overall amount of change. Although completing teachers with paid prep time have a higher mean overall amount of change, differences between teachers with and without prep time were not significant. However, Table 33 below shows that prep time was related to more integrated change:

Table 33: Type of Change by Access to Prep Time (Completers for whom we have data, $n=78$)

Access to Prep Time	n	Type of Change			
		No Change	Non-Integrated	Integrated	Totals
Received paid time	38	11	14	13	38
Do not receive paid time	40	10	25	5	40
Totals	78	21	39	18	78

$\chi^2=6.7$, $df=2$, $p<.05$

Number of Working Hours

Teachers who work more hours or work full time in the field of adult education may be more motivated to make change and have more time and support to take action based on what they learned from the professional development. This hypothesis was not supported statistically, in either amount or type of change: the 61 part-time teachers who completed the professional development had a mean amount of change of 8.9 (SD=6.2) while the 21 full-time completers had a mean amount of change of 7.9 (SD=5.2), and this difference was not significant (F=.433, df=1, p=.51). Type of change was also not related to full- or part-time status among those who completed the professional development, as seen in Table 34.

Table 34: Type of Change by Full-Time/Part-Time Status
(Completers for whom we have data, n=82)

Job Status	n	Type of Change			
		No Change	Non-Integrated	Integrated	Totals
Full Time	21	6	8	7	21
Part time	61	17	31	13	61
Totals	82	23	39	20	82

χ^2=1.5, df=2, p=.482, not significant

The mean hours of working time among those 20 teachers who demonstrated integrated change is 25.4 hours per week (SD=11.8); the mean number of hours per week for those 39 teachers who demonstrated thinking or acting change is 22.2 hours (SD=11.2), and mean working hours for the 23 teachers who demonstrated no change was 24.1 hours (SD=10.6). This difference was not significant (one-way ANOVA F=.589, df=2, p=.56). However, all teachers in the subsample who demonstrated no or minimal change taught part time. Part-time status was also significantly related to dropping out of the professional development.

Amount of Paid Professional Development Release Time

All of the information we have on this variable is presented in the body of the report.

Enrollment Policy

Closed enrollment should support change. Open or rolling enrollment may hinder change because if the teacher is constantly grappling with new students, then she or he may not have as much time, energy, or freedom to adopt new practices. The type of enrollment was not a significant factor related to amount of change among those teachers who completed the professional development (one-way ANOVA F=.022, df=2, p=.979, n=72). Enrollment policy was also not related to type of change, as seen in Table 35 below.

Table 35: Type of Change by Enrollment Policy in Teacher's Program
(Completers for whom we have data, *n*=72)

Enrollment Policy	n	Type of Change			
		No Change	Non-Integrated	Integrated	*Totals*
Open	11	3	5	3	*11*
Rolling	8	2	4	2	*8*
Closed	53	14	28	11	*53*
Totals	*72*	*19*	*37*	*16*	*72*

χ^2=.314, *df*=4, *p*=.989, not significant

Program Concurrently Working on Same Issue

We hypothesized that, if the program the teacher works in was simultaneously working to improve learner persistence, this would lead to greater teacher change. When programs are addressing an issue by changing structures or policies, teachers may be more motivated to learn about the topic (affecting knowledge gain) or to take action on the topic (affecting acting). Therefore, on the first questionnaire, we asked participants whether their program also had a process for program improvement ("Does your program choose at least one issue each year on which to work towards program-wide improvement?") and, if so, what issue their program was addressing that year. Sixty participants indicated that their program has a process for program improvement. Of those, only 11 indicated that their program was actively addressing learner persistence. Among teachers who completed the professional development and for whom we have complete data on this variable (*n*=80), 47 said their programs had a process for program improvement, and of these 47, 9 indicated that the improvement issue in their program was the same as the professional development (learner persistence). These numbers are too small for valid statistical analysis, but there was no relationship between program improvement issue and either measure of change.

Table 36: Type of Change by Program Improvement Issue
(Completers whose programs choose an issue each year, *n*=47)

Program Improvement Issue	n	Type of Change			
		No Change	Non-Integrated	Integrated	Totals
Same as PD (Learner persistant)	9	1	6	2	9
Not same as PD	38	13	17	8	*38*
Totals	47	14	23	10	47

χ^2=2.02, *df*=2, *p*=.364, not significant

State in which Participant Worked

Since the states in which the study was conducted had different delivery systems and professional development systems, we hypothesized that there might be some differences in change among participants from the three states. However, neither amount nor type of change was related to state of residence among teachers who completed the professional development[72]: Mean overall amount of change was highest in Maine (*M*=9.7, *n*=28,

---

[72] Dropping out was not related to state.

SD=6.8), followed by Massachusetts (M=8.8, n=26, SD=6.6) and Connecticut (M=7.5, n=29, SD=4.3), but differences in mean were not significant by state (one-way ANOVA F=1.02, df=2, p=.364). There was also no difference in type of change by state, as Table 37 indicates.

Massachusetts teachers were approximately evenly split by type of change, while Maine and Connecticut shared a trend: greater numbers of teachers in each of these states demonstrated thinking or acting change.

Table 37: Type of Change by State (Completers only, n=83)

State	n	Type of Change			
		No Change	Non-Integrated	Integrated	Totals
Conneticut	29	8	16	5	29
Maine	28	5	16	7	28
Massachusets	26	10	8	8	26
Totals	*83*	*23*	*40*	*20*	*83*

χ^2=5.52, df=4, p=.238, not significant

Program Type

Whether the teacher worked in was a community-based organization (CBO); a local education agency (LEA); a program connected to a school district, corrections facility, library, homeless shelter, workplace, or community college; or other type of program was not associated with more change. Since most teachers worked in either a CBO or an LEA, we regrouped the teachers into three program types: (1) CBO, (2) LEA, and (3) Other, which included all of the other categories. Program type was not related to amount of change: completing teachers from CBOs had a higher mean amount of change (M=9.7 out of 30, n=21, SD=8.5) than did teachers from LEAs (M=8.2, n=46, SD=4.9) or other types of programs (M=8.6, n=16, SD=4.6), but the difference was not significant (one-way ANOVA F=.427, df=2, p=.654). Similarly, there was no relationship between type of program and type of change among completing teachers, as seen in Table 38 below:

Table 38: Type of Change by Type of Program
(Completers for whom we have data, n=83)

Program Change	n	Type of Change			
		No Change	Non-Integrated	Integrated	*Totals*
CBO	21	9	6	6	*21*
LEA	46	10	25	11	*46*
Other	16	4	9	3	*16*
Totals	*83*	*23*	*40*	*20*	*83*

χ^2=4.99, df=4, p=.288, not significant

Teachers' Perception of Leadership in the Program

In the K–12 literature, strong leadership is often associated with effectiveness of professional development. Using answers from teachers in our sample about their perception of leadership within their program, we developed a composite for a leadership variable (with a mean on a range of 1 to 6, 1=perceived weak leadership and 6=perceived strong leadership).

Among teachers who completed the professional development, there was no relationship between amount of change and perception of leadership (r=-.196, p=.076, n=83). Type of change was also not related to leadership (one-way ANOVA F=1.60, df=2, p=.208) among teachers completing the professional development: teachers who made no or minimal change rated their program leadership higher (M=5.3, SD=1.04, n=23) than did teachers who made nonintegrated change (M=5.0, SD=1.1, n=40) or teachers who made integrated change (M=4.7, SD=1.2, n=20). Interestingly, however, the trend and relationship is in the negative direction; those who viewed their program leadership as weaker made more change, perhaps an indication that either teachers have more autonomy to make change when leadership is weak or that a perception of strong leadership precludes teachers from making change.

Teachers' Perception of Their Freedom to Decide What and How to Teach

The hypothesis here was that teachers who felt they had more freedom to make decisions about how they teach would take more action to make changes in their classroom or program. We asked teachers (using a scale of 1–6) to rate how much freedom they have to decide what to teach and how to teach in their classrooms, then we averaged those two ratings. Among teachers who completed the professional development, amount of change was not related to perceived classroom decision-making (r=-.069, n=79, p=.55). Type of change was also not related to perception of freedom to make classroom decisions about what and how to teach: mean scores for teachers in all three types of change were 5.1 (n=79), so the difference was not significant (one-way ANOVA F=.051, p=.95).

Opportunities for Collegiality

We hypothesized that teachers who feel they have more opportunities to meet, share, or talk with colleagues, either inside or outside of the program, would feel more supported to change, but more collegiality was not associated with more change. We asked teachers several questions about their level of collegiality (the opportunities they have for meeting and sharing with other teachers), then formed a z-score for collegiality overall. Collegiality was not associated with amount of change (r=-.046, p=.71, n=71), nor with type of change (no change teachers' Z-score=-.79, SD=3.2, n=16; nonintegrated change teachers' Z-score=.50, SD=4.9, n=35; integrated change teachers' Z-score=-.70, SD=2.7, n=20), and these differences were not significant (one-way ANOVA F=.841, df=2, p=.44).

We also asked teachers how many times a year, within their program, teachers meet to share ideas for teaching (not just talking about parking policies or paperwork). For completing teachers, the average number of times per year was 6.5 (SD=10.7, n=80).

Interestingly, the mean for teachers who demonstrated integrated change was lower (M=3.9, SD=4.6, n=20) than teachers who demonstrated no change (M=6.9, SD=7.8, n=20) and teachers who demonstrated nonintegrated change (M=7.5, SD=13.8, n=40), but this difference was not significant (one-way ANOVA F=.799, df=2, p=.453).

Access to Resources

We hypothesized that teachers who work in programs with better facilities and more resources would be better supported to change. In the Wave Three questionnaire, we listed a number of different types of program resources (access to own classroom, own desk, copy machines, resource rooms, computers, appropriate-size furniture for adult students, appropriate heating and cooling, etc.), and asked teachers to tell us if these were "available" or "unavailable" in their programs. We then developed a single averaged score for each teacher for overall access to resources. For those teachers who completed the professional development, access to more resources was not associated with amount of change ($r=-.120$, $n=76$, $p=.304$), nor with type of change: teachers who demonstrated no or minimal change had a mean access to resources of 10.1 ($n=19$, $SD=2.6$), teachers who demonstrated nonintegrated change had a mean of 9.2 ($n=37$, $SD=2.5$), and teachers who demonstrated integrated change had a mean of 9.7 ($n=20$, $SD=1.9$). These differences were not significant (one-way ANOVA $F=.831$, $df=2$, $p=.44$). We also asked teachers to rate (on a scale of 1–6) how strong they felt their program facilities were; this rating was not related to either type or amount of change.

Multiple Regression Analyses

We also ran three different analyses to determine which variables might most strongly predict change of the following types:

- Amount of overall change
- Any change at all, dividing the sample into two groups: (1) those who made no or minimal change, and (2) those who made any change: thinking, acting or integrated
- More preferred change, removing those who made no change and dividing those who made any change into two groups: (1) those who made integrated change, and (2) those who made thinking or acting change

Based on our theoretical model, we identified 19 potential variables to be considered for our multivariate analysis.

To Identify the Key Predictors for Amount of Change

We first looked at the correlation results and then conducted multivariate analysis tests based on these results. The bivariate correlations showed us the strength of the associations between the predictors and the outcome variables. Any variable with a correlation probability of .15 or better was included in our initial model. Although many variables were not strongly correlated with the dependent variable, we left them in the initial model because they were considered important variables to control for, and we wanted to include any variables that might have suppression effects.

Using these restrictions, nine variables were included in the preliminary model: quality of the NCSALL Professional Development groups, education, first experience teaching in adult education, years of experience, commitment, perceived quality of professional development, participation in other professional development on the topic, access to resources, and number of hours attended NCSALL Professional Development. Only three variables in the model were significant:[73] education, commitment, and number of hours attended NCSALL Professional Development. Of the three predictors, education is the strongest predictor of change; those teachers with a bachelor's degree or less were more likely to demonstrate higher amounts of change than those teachers with a master's or doctoral degree. Some of the variance is also explained by the exposure to the intervention (number of hours attended the professional development), since those teachers who showed more change were those who participated more fully in the NCSALL intervention. Finally, teachers who reported they have less desire to stay in the field demonstrated more overall change.

Variable Categories		Variables
Professional Development	1.	Model (workshop, mentor teacher group, practitioner research group)
	2.	Quality of professional development group (as rated by research team)
	3	Quality of professional development (as rated/perceived by participants)
	4	Number of hours attended the NCSALL Professional Development
Individual	5.	Level of education
	6.	Commitment/desire to stay in the field
	7.	Venue of first teaching experience (adult education or K–12)
	8.	Years of experience in adult education
	9.	Level of professional development consumption (general)
	10.	Level of other professional development on topic of learner motivation, retention, and persistence
Program/System	11.	State (Connecticut, Massachusetts, Maine)
	12.	Type of program
	13.	Required to use a curriculum
Working Conditions	14.	Receive benefits
	15.	Receive paid preparation time
	16.	Access to resources
	17.	Hours worked per week
	18.	Hours paid professional development release time per year
	19.	Level of interaction with colleagues

To Identify the Key Predictors for "Preferred" Change

We removed those participants who did not change at all ($n=36$), and compared only those with integrated change ($n=22$) to those with nonintegrated (thinking or acting) change ($n=43$). The two variables that most predicted change in a preferred direction (integrated change) in our study were whether teachers received benefits and whether teachers' first teaching experience was in adult education. For teachers who changed at all, those who received benefits[74] as part of their adult education job were five times more likely to demonstrate integrated change. Also, those teachers whose first teaching experience was in adult education, rather than in K–12, appeared more apt to change both thinking and acting as a result of participating in this professional development. Education was not a predictor of whether teachers made the more "preferred" type of change.

---

[73] This model is significant ($F=11.1$, $df=3$, $p<.001$). These three variables explain 27.5% of the overall variance.

[74] Benefits were also strongly correlated with type of program (those who work in CBOs were more likely to receive benefits as part of their adult education job), but program type itself was not a strong predictor of change.

In: Adult Education: Issues and Developments
Editors: P. N. Blakely, A. H. Tomlin, pp. 175-204

ISBN: 978-1-60456-272-9
© 2008 Nova Science Publishers, Inc.

Chapter 3

THE DEVELOPMENT OF KNOWLEDGE STRUCTURES IN ADULTHOOD

Gabriel Bukobza[*]
School of Education,
Tel Aviv University
Israel

ABSTRACT

This study examined the ways by which individuals construe knowledge in adulthood. 80 participants between the ages of 17-70 were interviewed regarding their personal knowledge of self and culture. Content analysis of the interviews revealed four fundamental structures of knowledge, or *epistemes*, that consistently appeared in both domains. These were named Monolithic-Monoformal, Relativistic-Relational, Dialectical-Deconstructive, and Integral-Inclusive. The results suggested that these epistemes can be positioned along a developmental trajectory that is continuous and spiral. The implications of the findings to the areas of self, culture, post formal cognition, and wisdom are discussed.

Keywords: *epistemology, adult development, post formal, self conceptualization, cultural conceptualization, monolithic monoformal, relativistic relational, dialectical deconstructive, integral inclusive, spiral development.*

The things people know and the ways by which they obtain and organize that knowledge change throughout life. Different developmental periods generate appropriate epistemological principles which purpose it is to perceive, organize, and interpret information and experience. During infancy the world is discovered primarily through movements and sensations of the body; later on in life, people rely more heavily on words and symbols to explore and

---

[*] E-mail: Bukobza@gmail.com; T: 972-97483686; 17 borochov St. Apt 4, Ra'anana 43434 Israel.

understand reality (Inhelder and Piaget, 1958). The epistemological set of principles utilized by an individual to know the world is presently referred to as a person's *episteme*, and will be the focus of the following investigation.

Epistemes were studied in the past – under different names - from philosophical, scientific, cultural, linguistic and psychological standpoints. Foucault (1970/1966; 1972/1969), who coined the term 'episteme', used it in his analysis of scientific and cultural discourse. According to his view it the episteme represents the set of relations that define the conception of knowledge during a particular historical period. It consists of preconditioned systems of regulations that unite at a given moment the discursive practices that generate scientific and cultural knowledge.

This episteme may be suspected of being something like a world-view, a slice of history common to all branches of knowledge, which imposes on each one the same norms and postulates, a general stage of reason, a certain structure of thought that the men of a particular period cannot escape – a great body of legislation written once and for all by some anonymous hand. (Foucault, 1972/1969; p. 191).

Pepper (1942) examined various systems of philosophy and science that form the basis for corroborated knowledge statements. He categorized them into four fundamental groups or 'world hypotheses'. These he named Formalism, Mechanism, Contextualism, and Organisicm, and argued that each functions as an independent epistemological framework that organizes information about the world in a coherent, consistent and unique manner. Subsequently, knowledge derived by a particular world hypothesis is markedly distinct in its meaning from knowledge derived by a different hypothesis.

In psychology, it was the seminal work of Piaget (1952/1936; 1954/1937), which empirically assessed epistemological frameworks in the individual knower. Piaget was a Developmental Structuralist (Piaget, 1970), who believed that scientific knowledge is the most refined and valid form of human knowing. Accordingly, his empirical efforts focused on the development in individuals of an episteme that generates scientific reasoning. Researchers following Piaget often chose to focus on other epistemic facets of the individual knower. They examined the ways by which people order knowledge and ascribe meaning (Belenky et al, 1986; Commons and Richards, 2002; Kegan, 1982; Miller, 1994; Perry, 1970), instances where epistemic beliefs and identities intertwine (Fowler, 1981), principles that determine the formation and reformation of beliefs (Kruglansky, 1989), and methods used by individuals to construct reasoned arguments (Kuhn, 1991), or solve sophisticated problems (King and Kitchener, 1994). Epistemic patterns and principles were further related to psychological phenomena such as moral reasoning (Nisan, 1995; Nisan and Applebaum, 1995), ego identity (Cook-Greuter, 1999; Loevinger, 1976), scholastic achievements (Schommer, 1990; 1993), and issues in the theory of mind (Burr and Hofer, 2002).

Based on this previous work it is presently postulated that an episteme consists of systematic operations, regulations, and methods that perceive, process, order, and present knowledge in an intelligible way. The episteme is a system for constructing knowledge, and it is therefore suggested that it shares general qualities with other knowledge systems (Kuhn, 1970; Pepper, 1942). Consequently, it is assumed that the episteme is a cognitive formation that follows a certain rational and hence has *internal logical coherence*; it interprets information and thus offers an *explanation* to occurrences in the world and a meaning to personal experience; it has *implications* for attitudes and behavior in daily life; and it varies in *degrees of complexity*.

Development of the Epistemes in Adulthood, and the Question of Complexity

Piaget's theory postulated that as life unfolds cognitive maturation and environmental support contribute to the construction of a formal-symbolic epistemological system, which is reliable, functional, and adaptive (Flavell, 1963; Moshman, 1999). It further argued that the abilities of thinking abstractly and using logic and deduction - which mature at late adolescence - mark the peak and the endpoint of mental development. Presumably, further permutations using these skills are possible along the life course, but the basic structural cognitive apparatus of the mind remain at a constant equilibrium from that point onwards. When this equilibrium does change in late adulthood, it is usually the result of cognitive decline rather than a sign of new growth patterns (Denney, 1982).

Others contended, however, that meaningful transformations in systematic ways of knowing could potentially occur in the post-adolescent years, beyond or alongside formal operations (Cavanaugh et al, 1985; Chandler and Boutilier, 1992; Edelstein and Noam, 1982; Kegan, 1982; 1994; King and Kitchener, 1994; Kitchener and King, 1981; Labouvie-Vief, 1982; 1992; Perry, 1970; 1981; Richards and Commons, 1984; Riegel, 1973; 1975; Sinnott, 1981; 1998). Perry (1970), for example, suggested that mature adult reasoning involves awareness and use of relativism, doubt and change, combined with the ability to commit to chosen alternatives. Several other theorists have described a dialectical stage of cognitive development that substituted formal operations with a contextual, contradictory, and changing system of knowing (Basseches, 1980; 1984; Broughton, 1975; Kramer, 1983; Riegel, 1973).

This array of studies suggested that the mind has the potential to develop highly complex cognitive networks, which cannot be explained based on formal thinking alone. The degree of complexity in those studies was determined by how well defined and inter-connected the relations between the epistemic principles in the network were. Complexity was assumed to increase with the number of factors and interactions that contributed to the process of interpreting information. Changes in the epistemic framework were considered to be of a developmental nature if and only if they transformed a working system of organizing knowledge into a sub-system or a component in a more complex system (Edelstein and Noam, 1982; Souvaine et al., 1990). This methodology produced a hierarchy of knowing systems wherein each advanced system enveloped a previous mature system and added to it a new level of explanation and meaning. Thus, in Perry's (1970) model relativism was considered a more advanced position than dualism and in Riegel's (1973) model dialectical thought was assumed to be more progressed than formal operations.

Limitations of Previous Models and Aims of the Present Study

The psycho-epistemological literature consists of different models that portray the trajectory of post-formal epistemic growth during adulthood. However, although the numbers and names of stages or levels they present varies, it is possible to identify basic recurring patterns in the developmental changes they depict (Burr and Hofer, 2002; Moshman, 1999).

The starting point for most models is an *objectivist* and *absolutist* episteme, which is a dualistic system for organizing knowledge. This episteme evaluates knowledge statements in an absolute manner as either true and right or false and wrong. True knowledge is considered irrefutable, certain, and eternally stable and the individual is strongly committed to it. Any other form of knowledge is considered completely false and is discarded with. At a more progressive level a *subjectivist* and *relativistic* episteme is depicted. This is a dynamic and versatile system for organizing knowledge claims, which forms a clear relation between elements of knowledge and the subjective perspective of the individual holding them. Furthermore, it acknowledges the legitimacy of different perspectives in the world and understands the idea of truth as uncertain, open to refutation, and constantly changing. The final episteme presented in these models is *meta-subjective* and *evaluative*. This is a system that draws from both objective and subjective worldviews, to form a reflective and critical mental construction. It proposes no claim for an absolute truth, and instead advocates a systematic process of evaluation and justification of knowledge statements.

From reviewing these patterns it is possible to outline certain limitations in past research and theory. First, in a similar way to Piaget's views these models consider rational-scientific knowledge to be the most esteemed form of human knowing attainable. The focus and endpoint of these trajectories consistently depicts a calculated, reasoned and individuated knower, who fundamentally uses means of logical operations in order to construe meaning. As a result, the appropriateness of these models to the understanding of non-scientific knowledge systems is found lacking. So, for example, the way knowledge is being processed and constructed in a system based on faith or creativity is not accounted for. Religious, mystical, meditative, bodily, aesthetic, musical, a-logical, paradoxical, dialogical, relational, collectivistic, and alternative states of consciousness and thinking are neglected. Though these types of knowledge contents have been articulated in philosophical (Adorno, 1990/1966; Marcuse, 1954; Gebser, 1985/1949), theological (Rosenzweig, 1985/1921; Tillich, 1951), artistic (Storr, 1972), as well as psychological writings (Broughton and Freeman-Moir, 1982, Kohlberg and Ryncarz, 1990; Lomranz, 1998; Wilber, 2000), they do not permeate these models. This is a cardinal point since these types of thinking and knowing represent highly complex epistemological levels which have led to some of the most profound creations of the human mind.

A second point is that psycho-epistemological studies that did focus on other orders of thinking were not comprehensive in their efforts. For instance, Basseches' (1984) original work on dialectical thought did not clearly separate between relativistic and dialectical mental operations. Koplowitz's (1984; 1990) unitary stage of thought was well defined, but was not examined empirically in different contextual settings. In a similar way, Fowler (1981) wrote of an epistemic level of universalizing faith but could not find evidence for its existence in the interviews he conducted.

A third lacuna in past models is that most were examined empirically in only one domain, though they claimed to describe structural cognitive attributes. This presents a problem since such highly complex epistemes may be affected by contextual factors and should therefore be studied across more than one domain. Moreover, some researchers claimed that epistemological qualities are domain specific (Mansfield and Clinchy, 2002; Schommer, 1994), and this makes the need for cross-domain research even more pertinent.

Finally, most models of epistemic growth are based on a sequential linear developmental structure which has an initial point of beginning and a clear point of termination (Commons and Richards, 2002; Fischer, 1980; Fowler, 1981; Inhelder and Piaget, 1958; King and Kitchener, 1994; Perry, 1970). They tend to start with a certain basis and gradually advance in a systematic and linear manner along the hierarchical trajectory until a final point where development halts. Though the problems associated with a linear and hierarchical view of development are known (Fischer and Bidell, 1998; Vygotsky, 1978), empirical non-linear models of epistemological growth are scarce.

In summary, previous models did not properly define or differentiate between advanced levels of epistemic development. In addition, they were sometimes limited in the empirical tests they conducted. The present study aims to address some of these issues. The following three empirical questions are posed to meet this purpose:

(1) What are the different epistemes adults use in order to cognize and order knowledge?
(2) Are the epistemes domain specific?
(3) How do the epistemes relate to age, level of education and gender?

Empirical Examination of the Epistemes

The episteme is an abstract and implicit mental organization, which needs to be examined in an empirical setting. Psycho-epistemological research in the past used different settings to learn about individuals' patterns of knowing. Epistemic probing appeared in the form of scientific assignments (Inhelder and Piaget, 1958), moral dilemmas (Gilligan, 1982; Kohlberg, Levine, and Hewer, 1984), learning experiences (Baxter-Magolda, 1999; Perry, 1970), religious beliefs (Fowler, 1981), perceptual skills (Peng and Nisbett, 1999), and direct questioning (Basseches, 1976; Broughton, 1975; King and Kitchener, 1994; Miller, 1994; Schommer, 1990). In interviews using hypothetical or abstract questions it was often acknowledged that participants experienced difficulties that were related not to low performance levels, but to their encounter with unfamiliar material that was irrelevant to their lives (Chandler, Boyes and Ball, 1990). A concrete and clear stimulus that is taken from the person's inventory of life experiences was therefore recommended.

In accordance with this conclusion two real-life domains were chosen for the present investigation, namely the personal conceptualizations of self and culture people hold. Both were chosen since they exist as multi-layered mental systems that are laden with experience and meaning. Though not everyone is gifted with a sharp awareness of such matters, still, most people are able to discuss them on a basic level. Another advantage of working with such concepts is their similarity to ill-structured questions (King and Kitchener, 1994) that can be understood and presented from various perspectives. This allows for a high degree of flexibility in the interview process and gives the interviewee room for expression.

Self-Conceptualization

Self-conceptualization (SC) is a personal epistemological scheme (Brim, 1976; Bukobza, 2007), or a theory regarding the self (Epstein, 1973). It contains within it traits, values, images and memories about the self, as well as emotions and evaluations. The SC controls the elaboration, interpretation, and ordering of information and activity relevant to the self, and provides incentives, standards, plans, rules, and scripts for personal and social behavior (Campbell, et al., 1996; Damon and Hart, 1982; Epstein, 1973; Markus and Wurf, 1987; see also Baumeister, 1998; Levin, 1992; Linville and Carlston, 1994; Yardley and Honess, 1987).

A vast and highly heterogeneous literature dealing with the characteristics of self and self-conceptualizations exists. One group of researchers presented evidence showing that the knowledge components of the SC are plural, versatile (Gergen, 1991; Greenwald and Pratkanis, 1984; Harter and Monsour, 1992; Higgins, 1987; Sande et al., 1988), and inconsistent (Ewing, 1990; Hampson, 1997; 1998; Harter and Monsour, 1992; Lifton, 1993; Neisser, 1988). This group generally claimed that the structure of the SC is dynamic (Markus and Wurf, 1987), consists of several distinct principles (Hermans, 1996; Linville, 1987), which co-exist in different levels of integration and differentiation (Donahue et al., 1993), and different levels of clarity and coherence (Campbell, et al., 1996).

Another group of researchers reached different findings that can be summarized by Baumeister's (1998) succinct remark that the need for consistency is a powerful motivating force in self construction and presentation. This line of research suggested that the SC is characterized by a high degree of stability and congruence across different contexts (Funder, 1983; Schroeder, 1983; Sheldon et al., 1997).

In yet another line of research the development of SC along the life cycle was analyzed. Damon and Hart (1982) wrote in their comprehensive study that SCs go through significant changes in the years between infancy and adolescence. The main transformation in this period is from a bodily-focused SC to a psychological one which includes personality traits, self-reflection, and an inclination to conceptual integration of distinct facets to one unitary system. Harter and Monsour (1992) found that around the time of mid-adolescence there is a gradual increase in the differentiation of the self which elicits experiences of conflict resulting from collisions between contradicting traits. However, in accordance with Damon and Hart's (1982) research they additionally found that towards the end of adolescence the conflict is resolved as a result of cognitive maturation allowing for reconciliation between opposing sides of the SC.

Cultural-Conceptualization

Culture-conceptualization (CC) is a personal *weltanschauung* (Jensen, 1997) or a theory of knowledge about an individual's culture and cultural identity (Phinney, 1989). It is the part in the epistemological matrix stemming from the relation between an individual and a cultural group, including the emotional significance that is attributed to this relation (Phinney, 1990), and the commitment that comes with it (LaFromboise et al., 1993). The CC includes collective meanings, values, norms, ethics, laws, ideas, thoughts, and behaviors (Geertz, 1984; Harris, 1999) which assist the person in understanding social reality and lay guidelines for action in it. In other words, they provide a model of reality together with instructions of how to behave in that reality (Kuper, 1999). The cultural information, interacting with genetic information, provides one with physical and symbolic tools with which to adapt to the social-ecological world.

In a multi-cultural environment, or whilst moving between cultures, individuals confront different worldviews than those they grew up with in their original habitat. The direct and longstanding contact with foreign systems that generates an adaptive change in thought and behavior is known as acculturation (Berry, 1988; Moghaddam et al., 1987; Sayegh et al., 1993). The complex process of acculturation affects the individual's CC; it may strengthen the original CC a person had or alternatively reshape and transform it as happens in assimilation, alternation, multiculturalism and integration (Berry, 1988; Berry et al., 1986; LaFromboise et al., 1993; Moghaddam et al., 1987; Sayegh et al., 1993; Wurzel, 1988).

CCs are often time studied through the ethnic prism – by looking at people's self-definitions, emotions and motivations in regard to their affiliation with a certain ethnic group (Dien, 2000; Phinney, 1989, 1990, 2000; Phinney and Chavira, 1992; Tzuriel and Klein, 1977; Zak, 1976). These studies show that the cultural-ethnic identity develops through a process that begins with low interest and involvement and proceeds to a phase of search and examination, and finally to a commitment to one stabilized identity. Conscious commitment to a cultural identity gives the individual a feeling of purpose and fulfillment (Dien, 2000; Phinney, 1990), enhances self-esteem (Phinney and Chavira, 1992), and may help to protect from mental stress (Berry, 1988).

This brief summary of SCs and CCs exposes the multifarious forms that they can take; the present investigation presumes that these are all reflections of a deep epistemic system, and hence that identifying the components of that system will generate a better understanding of the explicit representation of SCs and CCs.

METHOD

Participants

Eighty participants were drawn from four different age groups representing the span of adult life. Each group consisted of 20 individuals, and was evenly divided by gender. The range and means of the age groups were 17-22 years (M age = 19 yrs, 11 months), 26-32 years (M age = 28 yrs, 7 months), 37-47 years (M age = 40 yrs, 4 months) and 56-70 years (M age = 59 yrs, 10 months). The first two age groups represented the years of emergent adulthood where one's identity is in its formative stages (Arnett, 2000; Erikson, 1968). The next two groups sampled individuals in their mid-life and in the mature adulthood ages, to cover a large a part as possible of the adult years. In addition participants' educational background was recorded resulting in 3 groups of education level (high-school, undergraduate degree, graduate degree). Previous research has shown that a positive correlation exists between age, education, and epistemological level (King and kitchener, 1994). The participants were recruited from different contexts, professions, and walks of life, in order to increase the heterogeneity of the sample.

The Interview and its Coding

Participants discussed their SC and CC in a semi-structured quasi-clinical interview. This is an indirect method of investigation that focuses on a specific overt topic, while aiming to uncover mental principles that underlie it (Kegan, 1982; Kitchener et al., 1989; Kohlberg, Levine, and Hewer, 1984; Perry, 1970; Piaget, 1967). In this method the interviewer asks questions about a certain knowledge domain, in order to understand how this domain is constructed in the mind of the person.

Following a stimulus in the form of self-report in the SC section, and cultural dilemmas in the CC section, participants were asked to reason about their personal conceptualizations in each of the two domains. The interview consisted of an invariable battery of questions, on which the interviewer was free to improvise according to the nature of the interview. Interviews were recorded and fully transcribed.

The interviews were content analyzed based on seven epistemological principles that are discussed elsewhere (Bukobza, 2007). The principles all stemmed from basic queries about the state of knowledge statements and units of meaning. These include questions such as is the knowledge system clear and consistent, how does knowledge in the system get verified and corroborated, does the system openly communicate with other systems, what is the reaction to foreign or refuting information, and so on. Some of these questions have appeared in various forms in psycho-epistemological research of the past (Chandler, Lalonde and Sokol, 2000; King and Kitchener, 1994; Piaget, 1970; Pepper, 1942; Perry, 1970; Ross, 1989). They all commonly strive to uncover the implicit ways in which knowledge is constructed and organized (Kelley, 1955; Medin, 1989). This is a traditional method in psycho-epistemological research (Belenkey, 1986; King and Kitchener, 1994; Kohlberg, Levine, and Hewer, 1984; Koplowitz, 1984; 1990; Perry, 1970), in which interview content is sorted into categorical 'pigeonholes' – basic predefined concepts of interpretation (Holsti, 1969). The following seven categorical principles were used in this investigation, : Consistency – Inconsistency, Fixedness – Dynamics, Form preservability – Transformation, Singularity – Plurality, Context independent – Context dependent, Other independent – Other dependent, Epistemic apparatuses.

All interviews were carried out, analyzed and scored by the author. In addition, two assistants were trained to use the coding system, and they scored half of the interviews. The SC and CC sections were separated for each interview before coding began, in order to yield independent scores for each domain. Coders were blind to age, educational level or gender of the participants, as well as to their score on the corresponding part of the interview. Inter-rater reliability between the three coders had an alpha value of 0.72 ($p>0.005$).

The epistemic score for each category depended on the reasoning used by participants to explain the epistemological principle at stake. An elaborate example of this process shall be given in the results section. The final score for the whole interview was based on the aggregate scores given for all categories, and on the rater's comprehensive evaluation. Because participants did not always exhibit an ideal and whole epistemic stance, a grid system was used (Kegan, 1982). Coders could score an interview as representing a complete episteme, or a transitional one. The transitional epistemes divided into two groups. In the first, a dominant epistemic orientation was identified together with weak but significant expressions of another episteme. The second group consisted of cases with mixed orientations where it was impossible to decide on the dominant-subordinate relations. For statistical analysis purposes the results of the content analysis were transformed into numeric figures using an existing scale (Perry et al, 1986).

RESULTS

The Different Epistemes

Content analysis of the interviews yielded four distinct and independent epistemes that underlie the conceptualizations of both self and culture. These were named Monolithic-Monoformal, Relativistic-Relational, Dialectic-Deconstructive, and Integral-Inclusive. In what follows the four epistemes will be illustrated to give a detailed picture of each. This will be carried out using two epistemic principles in order to exemplify the method of analysis and to outline differences in complexity between the epistemes. The first principle, Consistency vs. Inconsistency, will be presented in the SC context, and the second, Other-independent vs. Other-dependent, will be presented in the CC context. In each of the following excerpts the pseudonym of the participant is given, together with her or his gender, age, and educational level.

Consistency vs. Inconsistency in the SC Context

Monolithic-Monoformal Episteme

Yafit, Woman, 54 years old, has a Bachelor degree.

> Q: You say that there are no contradictions in your self-portfolio. Could you explain that?
> A: I'm not pessimistic, but I'm also not optimistic. It's not a matter of having both traits, but of standing somewhere in the middle. I don't have these contradictions. I don't think that I have contradictory traits that make me behave one time like this and the other time like that. When I say that I'm stable that's exactly what I mean: stability is stability.
> Q: You put down that you are cheerful, warm, and friendly. Don't you have the opposite traits to these?
> A: No.
> Q: And what if the situation you're in changes? Will you still be warm and friendly?
> A: Yes. This will never change.

Yafit reported a SC that included the following 12 traits: Friendly, cheerful, warm, direct, flexible, patient, serious, self-controlled, stable, realistic, planned, introvert. Her self-profile did not include any antinomies; she exhibited an understanding for contradictions, but chose to describe herself in a congruous way.

Yafit mentioned that for her "stability is stability". This is an interesting statement as it is a reflection of the law of identity in Aristotle's formal logic, which claims that 'A is A'. According to that law every object in reality is perfectly identical to its image and cannot be any different without consequently refuting itself. Yafit's words followed that logic in two manners: First by their syntax structure, since the form of her sentence mirrored the rule 'A is A'. Second by their content, since she proclaimed her internal stability and by that declared the unchanging nature of her consistent knowledge system.

In the final part of this excerpt the interviewer tried to establish the level of internal coherence in Yafit's SC. She was presented with two challenging questions that could potentially disrupt the law of identity her SC adheres to. In the first question Yafit was asked if she had any qualities that were opposite to the ones she described. In the second question she was asked whether she would still have a consistent portfolio if situational conditions changed. Yafit responded to both questions in the negative, and hence showed that she really did not have any opposing traits and that her consistency was independent of environmental factors.

This excerpt was coded as an example of high internal consistency and coherence. Yafit's SC was devoid of polarity, negation and oppositions and it did not alter following changes of location or time.

Relativistic-Relational Episteme

Galya, Woman, 28 years old, has a Bachelor degree.

> Q: You've outlined some contradictory traits in your description. Can you explain to me how is it that you have these contradictions inside you?
> A: I believe that different situations bring out different things in you. I can behave in a particular way when I'm with certain people and in a certain place, and then in other circumstances I might behave differently. I'm not some unified whole of a person that will always react the same. Often my behavior is influenced by external situations that are beyond my control. I can find myself traveling in India and there my behavior will be completely different. When you travel you find yourself in foreign places that have ways unfamiliar to you, especially if you come from the Western world. And then in those places you are something else. You react differently. You externalize unfamiliar aspects of yourself. And this also works for how I am in a relationship with my partner, or how I am when I'm at work.

Galyas's overall SC had 34 traits, which included 10 antinomies. She divided the latter to the following pairs: stable-unstable, individualistic-social, considerate-demanding, light hearted – anxious, confident-indecisive.

Galya acknowledged that her SC had inconsistent traits and attributed them to the influence of varying situational circumstances. She explained that she wasn't a "unified whole" that always reacted in the same manner, but was susceptible to the influence of outside factors. Her self was presented as a complex structure encompassing a wide range of traits, which manifested themselves according to the changing environment.

In the excerpt Galya is quoted to have said, "you are something else". This sentence carries great significance since its logical implication is that the self can have more then one interpretation and meaning. Asserting that 'you=something else' means that the basic logical law of identity has been undermined; 'A' is no longer identical with 'A', as 'A' may now be something else, like 'B' for example. Contrasting it with Yafit's saying that "stability is stability", a basic difference may be identified between the two epistemic constructs. Whereas the MM episteme is committed to consistency and to the law of identity, the RR episteme is internally inconsistent and consciously divided into contradictory parts.

Galya had as many self-aspects as the number of situations she encountered; these included different locations in the world, social environments, and human relationships. The plurality of Galya's self was represented by a diversified and inconsistent episteme that is made from separate and distinct parts. This is an example of RR episteme, and the excerpt was coded accordingly.

Dialectical-Deconstructive Episteme

Gideon, Male, 28 years old, has a Masters degree 3.

Q: You described yourself as possessing contradictions. How do they relate to one another?

A: Well, all these terms that we use are laden with so much meaning, and who knows if both of us share the same idea about what they really mean. Lets see. I'm serious in the social sphere where I go by the rules of society etc, and then there are situations where I find myself laughing, acting crazy, and going wild. But here it is: In these moments of acting ridiculous, I feel that to a certain extent I'm actually extremely serious. I might be frivolous or act foolishly but there'll be a feeling of profound seriousness too. What I'm saying is that in what looks like a very serious moment there is also something that is routine, carefree, and extremely not serious. And it works also the other way around – in those situations where I break from the serious circle there is still a very serious element at work.

Gideon attributed 19 traits to himself, 11 of which were contradictory. He lined these up in the following manner: Individualistic-social, serious-daring-frivolous-sudden-unstable, cynic-stormy-cheerful-optimistic. In reasoning about the contradictory traits Gideon first said that different contexts make him behave in different ways. This is a RR justification, which asserts that behavior is relative to relevant circumstances. But as he carried on Gideon exposed another level of meaning in his episteme. He described the reciprocal relationship that is formed between his opposing traits; they are related to one another, yet they also inter-penetrate and influence each other. Every trait is affected and to a certain extent constituted by other traits. Furthermore, a trait that usually appears in one context is able to abandon its prescribed location and immigrate to another, where it interacts with a different trait – an interaction that influences both traits. For instance, the meaning of 'frivolous' is not closed-up to the contradictory messages of 'seriousness', and vice versa – inside the 'frivolous' trait there is a channel that is accepting elements antithetical to its own core meaning.

This is a specific dialectical relation that is hereby termed 'connected contradiction', in which oppositions are consciously juxtaposed against one another resulting in an epistemic tension that cannot be reconciled by logic. In such a case every element of knowledge is defined and experienced from its position in a dissonant relation with another element which refutes it. Connected contradictions may lead to a feeling of deep and powerful understanding and experience of knowledge, and they often appear in elevated states of creative thought (Storr, 1972). This feeling reaches its peak when the individual is able to hold several contradictory elements at the same time, without attempting to separate them into different contexts in a RR manner or cancel out their sharp polarity in a MM way. In a subsequent part of the interview Gideon described further such a relation.

Q: Can you be both serious and frivolous at once?

A: Its obvious that I can have each of these traits separately. But to have frivolous seriousness – yes. Absolutely. I can say it's true even in relation to the same object in question. Let's say I went through a specific experience and later I reflect upon it – there is the sudden experience which is not so serious or deep, and then there is a serious state. And... ah...yes. Yes. For example, when you're going through an experience and at the same time you are aware that you are in the experience. So that awareness – It's not always like this but I know that it's possible – that awareness makes everything magnificent and significant in the serious meaning of the word. You're both in the experience and at the same time you're examining it from the outside. It's like you're dismantling a fundamental core of the world. In these situations I suddenly feel something unexpected; a side that is very light and carefree. I feel at the same moment that I'm both light and also that I'm digging something very deep and very serious. So yes, it can absolutely happen.

Gideon demonstrated his ability to grasp in his mind opposing momentums and to create a connected contradiction of 'awareness' and 'experience' or of 'seriousness' and 'frivolousness'. This experience encompasses meanings of lightness that are related to being frivolous, together with meanings of seriousness and reflection. These are states of great significance, and Gideon claimed that in them he felt like he was deciphering something very fundamental about the world. This exemplifies how the act of knowing can become more powerful when units of knowledge that used to be separate are put forth in a direct and reciprocal manner. Both of these excerpts were coded as DD due to their emphasis and use of contradictions and inconsistency.

Integral-Inclusive Episteme

Ze'ev, Male, 50 years old, has a Bachelor degree.

> Q: You included in your portfolio all the traits that appeared in the original list. Can you please explain that?
> A: Yes. When you become aware of who you are, and when you decide to work to improve yourself, you strive to unite all the powers that you have. In other words you become spiritual. When you do that you discover something that might surprise you – that almost all things exist in you already. So I'm an extrovert, and I'm active; I'm talkative and disciplined, and I'm certainly social; I'm calm, naïve, trusting, excited and daring. All the things in that list and more are me.
> Q: And traits that are considered contradictory – what do they lead to?
> A: In the past it meant conflict. I remember the feeling of bifurcation, internal struggle and conflict. But today it's different. When I was young, or lets call it inexperienced, I was an absolutist and this was a core trait of mine. But I used this core trait in a uni-dimensional, unequivocal, unrealistic and shortsighted way. But today this quality of living things in an absolute way is expressed in a more open and inviting manner. I'm open to others and I listen to them. I'm more balanced and I take other components in. So I'm still an absolutist, but my construction is more stable and unified and is made from many more parts.

When Ze'ev described his SC he pointed out that all traits have the potential to accurately represent him. He paid attention to the fact that some traits were in opposition to others, but that did not prevent him from including them in his description. His reasoning was that the entire range of traits could be attributed to a super-structure or a meta-concept such as 'uniting all powers' or being 'spiritual'. This common structure encompassed all differences and contradictions, and united them into an integral whole.

Ze'ev admitted that holding different contradictory elements did contribute to a state of conflict in the past, but his present episteme was able to reconcile between the various forces and create a balanced equilibrium. The result was that the dynamic and dissonance-arising state caused by conflicting oppositions was replaced by a new, harmonious state of congruence and consistency.

The fact that Ze'ev was able to hold so many contradictory elements under one conceptual umbrella meant that he had an II epistemic structure. It is important to note at this point that the II episteme does not reach consistency through negating or ignoring contradictory elements as does the MM episteme, but through subjecting them to a more comprehensive and totalistic order.

Other-Independent – Other-Dependent in the CC Context

Monolithic-Monoformal Episteme
Yossi, Male, 20 years old, has a high school diploma.

> I'll send my children to a Jewish school abroad because I want them to be Jewish. I don't really care about other alternatives. Other ways of life are irrelevant to me. I want to be Jewish. This is the existential system of my life. And even if you prove to me in the most convincing way that tomorrow the world is going to end, I still will raise Jewish. And since this is what I want, and only this, then I have to act and give them a Jewish education. You may ask why I insist so much about this, and I'll answer you – I don't know why, all I know is that this is what I want.

Yossi preferred the Jewish way of life to any other. He disregarded and rejected foreign cultural models. In epistemic terms his MM episteme adhered to one meaning system, which he assumes to be totally reliable and undisputed. Unfamiliar systems were seen as false or irrelevant, unless they could be subjugated to the original one. Yossi was aware that there are plenty of cultural options in the world, but he didn't wish to be exposed to any of them, and chose to give his children a homogeneous education. This is an example of an absolute commitment to one's original culture, and a MM independence from other cultural forms.

Relativistic-Relational Episteme
Anat, Woman, 37 years old, has a Bachelor degree.

> A: I would like my children to feel comfortable in their social world, to interact with other people, and not to feel alienated or estranged. I don't want them to form a secluded Israeli or Jewish group within the school. On the other hand I wouldn't want them to forget their Judaism. So I would send them to a regular American public school, and in the afternoon to Jewish classes or to Sunday school.
> Q: And what do you generally think about the exposure to a different culture?
> A: I value it. I think it's a good and positive thing. It helps you develop your personality both intellectually and emotionally. Its good to know that there are other forms of life on this planet. It teaches you many things, and personally it really fascinates me. (...) The only way it might confuse you is if you take things from it that you're not happy with. What you need to do is to look at those other people and cultures and learn from them. But you don't have to necessarily adhere to their ways or become like them. I stick to what I have and I try to learn from others.

In Anat's mind acquiring different cultural knowledge is interesting and beneficial. She opted to get exposed to unfamiliar knowledge and constructed an other-dependent meaning system. Nevertheless, Anat perceived the new knowledge as belonging to a different system, which is separated from her own. She acknowledged the importance of learning or experiencing foreign norms and values, but placed them at a distance from her main cultural system. She did not exhibit a wish to reconcile the differences between the worlds, nor did she want to let one world influence the other.

Anat's excerpt is an example of the RR episteme; she is a type of person who views all ways of life as equal in value and validity, and places her own beliefs in *dependent relation* to them. Her episteme is structured in a way which keeps each cultural form secluded in its own context, without the possibility of mutual influence and change.

Dialectical-Deconstructive Episteme

> *Tahel, Woman, 30 years old, has a Bachelor degree.*

> A: I think that encountering contradictory values from different cultures is a good thing. Why? Because it allows you to be in the same place but different; because it brings you choice. Knowing that things are different somewhere else may make life more difficult because then you'll have to make difficult choices. You might feel confused and messed up, and maybe incomplete. But you need to know that the mess in your mind is caused by your expanding horizons. You finally know how much you don't know, and things that you do know get an extra level of depth. For example, I might not accept all the different Jewish movements and schools, but I know that they inject Judaism with more content and more life. It becomes a much richer entity because of them. Now some ideas may be radical enough to change the original form of Judaism, but I think that it's better that way then with a narrower perspective that doesn't allow for any change at all. It's better to have it different and rich then similar and narrow.

Tahel encouraged dependence on unfamiliar cultural knowledge and accepted the changes that might accompany such relationship. Foreign knowledge for her is a source for growth and enrichment, even if it leads to an increase in the level of epistemological chaos and uncertainty. She embraced the plurality of different cultural forms and made an effort to simultaneously fulfill as many aspects of them as possible. Tahel exemplified the dialectical preference for dynamic interactions with other knowledge systems in her belief that her culture can envelope opposing ideas without trying to synthesize them into a singular and unified form.

Integral-Inclusive Episteme

> *Dalit, Woman, 27 years old, has a Masters degree.*

> A: One circle of belonging is the family, or local culture, or your religion. And another circle of belonging is the world. The closer the circle is to you, the more time and thought, study and depth you will give to it. But you must never ignore the circle of the world, even if it looks far away. You are still and always will be a son of Earth. A son of your time, and a son of humanity. The final aim I have is to reach a unity. In the end we are all one. We are a multitude, which forms a unity. We need to reduce the multitude into something singular. The more interaction with the world and the more learning you have, the more you understand that the basis for all religions is one. The idea behind all religions is one. That's why I'll teach my children about everything. Everybody believes in something. Even if you're going from Tel-Aviv to Haifa, you believe you'll eventually get to Haifa. If you had no belief, you wouldn't go. Now the religious person worships God, but each one worships some kind of God, even if that God is a tree, nature, it doesn't matter. And the God at the end is one. (…) And then you realize that everything you see is the fragmentation of that One into thousands of small components that show themselves to you in their multiplicity, sometimes in oppositions and conflict and sometimes not. I understand that these ideas clash with the world of concepts as we know it, but once you live with that unity you merge with all that comes to you and then there is no good and bad and duality but one love for everything.

Dalit interpreted the multitude of elements that make up reality as being the abundant reflection of a deeper unity. According to her epistemic lens, every phenomena or occurrence in reality stems from a fundamental source and can be explained by it. However, other explanatory or interpretive systems are completely ignored by her. Since she viewed everything through one particular Meta-system or core concept, she could not form relations with other potential systems. Dalit is unable to perceive anything as alien; she perceived even those things that might be experienced as foreign as necessary parts in the integrated order of things. Accordingly, this excerpt was coded as representative of II episteme, which is independent of other knowledge.

Distribution of the Four Epistemes in the Sample

Participants' scores were collapsed to 7 basic groups representing the 4 complete and the 9 transitional epistemes of the original scale. The following diagrams display the distribution of epistemes for the SC and CC, respectively.

Diagram 1 shows that in the SC context 16% of the participants presented a MM episteme, 40% were RR, 16% DD, and 9% II. Overall 81% or participants had a complete and whole episteme as opposed to 19% who showed patterns belonging to more than one epistemic orientation. In the CC context (diagram 2) 20% of participants were of MM episteme, 40% were RR, 12.5% were DD, and 15% were II. 87.5% of participants in the CC context were found to possess a whole episteme, and 12.5% were in a transitional position.

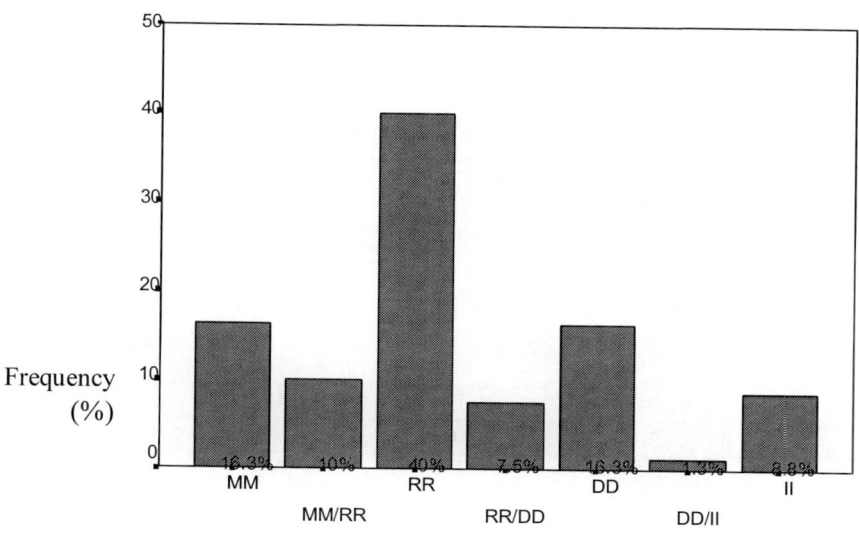

Epistemic score

Diagram 1. Frequency distribution for epistemic scores in the SC context.

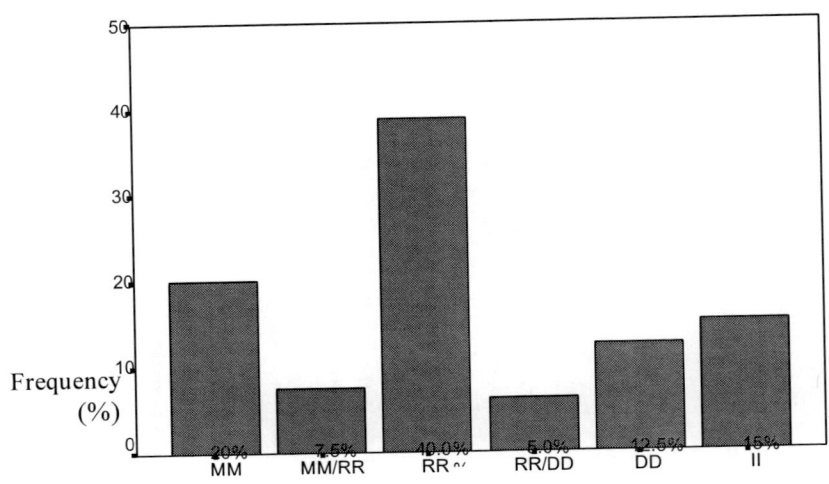

Epistemic score

Diagram 2. Frequency distribution for epistemic scores in the CC context.

Domain Specificity of the Epistemes

A paired sample t test revealed that the difference between epistemic scores in the two domains for the entire population was insignificant, $t = -0.453$, n=80. Further, there was a strong correlation between the SC and CC scores, $r(80) =0.705$, $p<0.001$. This relation was expressed in yet another way; 53 participants (66.3% of population) received an epistemic score in one domain that was identical or not different in more than one grade than their score in the second domain. These results indicate that participants exhibited a high degree of consistency across the two domains. The cross-domain correlation was positive for all age groups but was stronger for the two older groups, as can be seen in table 1. The relationship remains positive in each age group but is dramatically higher in the two older groups.

Table 1. Correlations between SC and CC epistemic scores for each age group

	17-22 yrs	26-32 yrs	37-47 yrs	56-70 yrs
r	0.423	0.362	0.752[**]	0.781[**]
n	20	20	20	20

[**]$p<0.01$.

Relations between the Four Epistemes, Age, Level of Education and Gender

Age groups. An ANOVA test for age groups yielded a significant difference in SC scores $F(2,76)=3.723$, $p<0.01$, and in CC scores $F(2,76)=3.87$, $p<0.01$. Tukey post-hoc tests indicated that the mean epistemic scores for the youngest age group (17-22 yrs) were significantly lower ($p<0.05$) than the scores for the two middle age groups (26-32 and 37-47 yrs) in both domains. However, the mean score for the youngest group was not significantly different than the mean score for the eldest one (56-70 yrs) in both domains. Yet, the similarity in the mean scores of the youngest and eldest age groups does not tell the whole story. In the SC domain 90% of the participants in the young group had a MM or RR score, and only 10% had a RR/DD or DD score. In the oldest group however there was more diversity: 65% were MM or RR, 15% were RR/DD or DD, and 20% were II. In the CC domain 100% of young participants were MM or RR, as opposed to 70% MM or RR, 5% DD, and 25% II of the elder participants. The significance of these findings will be outlined in the discussion section.

Educational groups. An ANOVA test for education groups yielded a significant difference in SC scores $F(2,74)=6.259$, $p<0.005$, and CC scores $F(2,74)=5.128$, $p<0.01$. The Tukey post-hoc test showed that the least educated group had markedly lower mean scores than the other two groups in both domains ($p<0.01$).

Gender. Independent t test revealed no significant gender differences in both domains.

Table 2. t tests for gender differences in epistemic SC and CC scores

	Women	Men	t	Sig	n
SC	X=1.43, sd=4.23	X=1.93, sd=4.58	0.921	NS	80
CC	X=4.26, sd=1.61	X=4.68, sd=1.86	1.071	NS	80

DISCUSSION

This research examined the ways by which adults construe personal knowledge about their self and culture. It identified four distinct epistemes that organize knowledge in both contexts. In what follows the four epistemes will be presented in detail to give an elaborate picture of each, based on the empirical results obtained from the interviews. The internal *logos* or central *rational* of each episteme will first be delineated, followed by a specific principle-based description of the episteme. The '*logos*' refers to a constitutive force or a teleological meaning, which works at the genetic core of the knowledge system. It is related to concepts such as 'root metaphor' (Pepper, 1942), or 'primordial symbol' (Ellwood, 1980), which determine the character of the knowledge system. The *logos* guides the different principles in the same direction, and this constitutes a particular type of an episteme. Each episteme then has a distinct method for interpreting and understanding reality. In this process the *logos* determines the form which in turn determines the function. Thus, what began as prescriptive logos ends up as a complex system of organizing knowledge which functions in an idiosyncratic manner in giving meaning to the world. It directs assumptions about reality, interprets information, and assigns significance to experiences in a unique way. Distinct epistemes do not extract the same meaning from a given experience; they tend to pull away from one another to oppose and contradict each other. Hence, the ability to share an identical way of looking at the world, or otherwise hold completely antinomic views, is dependent upon the epistemic lenses that individuals wear.

Monolithic-Monoformal (MM) Episteme

The MM episteme is based on the *formal monologic*; this logos assumes that there is a fundamental, stable, and a-historic matrix or framework that can determine the truth of all concepts and theories (Bernstein, 1988). This assumption leads to a belief in the existence of an absolute and universally valid system of knowledge, which is logical and rational.

The MM episteme has a consistent and coherent form. It is characterized by a very low tolerance to contradictions and oppositions. Internal or external forces that negate it are ignored, repressed or reconciled, and are not considered a part of the system in their contradictory state. The episteme strives to sustain a balanced and equilibrated condition, which avoids situations of paradox and inconsistency. It is a fixed entity, which is guided by the assertion that its components are true and valid, and therefore do not need to be reflected upon, discussed, or be open to criticism. This is an identical, non-changing formation, which preserves its form despite outside occurrences and influences. Its properties are all constant, since they are believed to be part of a harmonious and absolutely true system. The episteme has a singular form, which is concise and undifferentiated. Divisions and fragmentations are unified through a process of reduction to a crystallized core. The generation of multiplicities and pluralities that are not included in this basic core is restricted. This formation is context-independent; it retains a one-and-the-same appearance in all circumstances, in the same way a logical necessity or a reasoned truth do not alter with a change in context. The construction of this episteme rejects foreign knowledge and is independent of it. The personal known has precedence over the unknown other, and is considered right and superior. Assertions belonging to different belief systems are seen as strange, alien, mistaken, and false. Finally, the MM episteme adheres to a dominant way of knowing that is considered reliable. Other ways can be used as long as their results are consistent with the acceptable form of acquiring knowledge.

Relativistic-Relational (RR) Episteme

The RR episteme is based on the *meta-formal multilogic*; this logos assumes that different orders of meaning exist in the world and their truthfulness is contingent and relative to subjective mentalities, cultural consequences, historical forces, conceptual frameworks and the like (Bernstein, 1988; Mandelbaum, 1982; Williams, 1972). It hence constructs a diversified knowledge system that can make sense of these different orders. Each separate order on its own acts as a MM construction and obeys the formal rules of logic and rationality, but overall the whole system is multiple, relative, and relational.

The RR episteme has an inconsistent and incoherent form. It acknowledges its own versatility and the lack in consistency that results from having many facets. It attributes its own contradictions to differential differences in performance that result from changes in location, time, language, relations with others, etc. However, within the same framework or relationship this episteme has no inconsistencies, since its relative contexts are separated and each keeps an internal balanced state. The RR formation exists in a state of relative motion. It holds that self-knowledge is contingent on the conditions of discourse; since the conditions are dynamic the knowledge they produce is dynamic too, and the episteme is subsequently set in motion. Distinct areas in the episteme can keep their own constancy since they have some autonomy, but the system as a whole has multiple sides and is therefore never at rest. The structure of the RR episteme is subjected to relative transformations; it goes through changes and reformations when the conditions of knowledge change, and when its relations to other systems of knowledge change. This is a plural and fragmented formation; it is composed of many components, facets, and sub-systems, which function as related units in the episteme. These cannot be reduced or generalized to a core center without losing their peculiar character. The RR formation is context-dependent. Its parts are contingent on the particular context in which they were created, and cannot be stretched beyond that context. This episteme is accepting of and dependent on foreign knowledge. Being relational means being influenced and directed by the connections one has with others: other people or other referential systems of significance. Hence, this episteme values information and knowledge from other sources, and views them as relevant and meaningful to its own identity. Moreover, it uses different methods to gather information about the world, since every method has its own contextual validity. This methodology additionally means that the value of knowledge is limited to the ways by which it was constructed and verified.

Dialectic-Deconstructive (DD) Episteme

The DD episteme is based on the *dialectalogic*; this logos assumes that knowledge systems are susceptible to interruptions and refutations, that the meanings they possess are paradoxical and volatile, and that their identity is in constant flux. It deconstructs the regular structures of signs and systems, exposing their internal dynamics, their non-identical features, and their ever-changing character (Adorno, 1990; Marcuse, 1954). It aims to constitute a diversified knowing system that can accommodate cases of paradox, contradiction and irrationality, side by side with instances that abide by the rules of traditional logic.

The DD formation is radically inconsistent as it emphasizes the multitude of opposing elements that exist in mutually dependent relationships. These oppositions dwell inside the system without aspiring to achieve a non-contradictory end-state (Tolman, 1981; 1983). This episteme breaks open its own structure and fragments its constitutive elements through a process of constant negation that uncovers the "untruth of identity" (Adorno, 1990; p. 5). It consists of antinomic elements, and lacks a unifying line or theme. The conflicted elements form complex relations: they collide, inter-penetrate, and influence one another. This is an episteme set in perpetual motion; nothing in it is fixed for more than a short while. Its parts and the relation they form with other parts are dynamic and active, and their movement proceeds in unpredictable patterns. The DD episteme is in a mode of constant transformation and therefore never ceases to alter between different shapes. Change rather than form is its guiding rule. Its identity is never the same, as it sheds old skins and wraps itself with new ones regularly. The identity of the present is deconstructed and replaced by another, which will also be replaced in due time. It is a plural form composed of multiple components and systems. Its parts are influenced by the conditions of particular contexts, but they are also able to cross contexts and to penetrate novel surroundings. Moreover, meaning from one context is not isolated from other contexts, and significant bits of knowledge flow between different locations of meaning. Characters and elements from various systems form bonds and relations that are interactive, reciprocal, oppositional, and constitutive. Hence, an element derived from one system can influence other elements in other systems. This diversity cannot be gathered into distinct categories, and thus cannot be summed up or reduced to specific forms. The DD episteme possesses no motivating drive to bring its own multiplicity under one conceptual roof; on the contrary, there is a force in operation that disperses known categories and relocates them under many roofs or under no roofs at all. Its parts strive to remain in their heterogeneous existence, and not to be channeled into a uniform oneness of any kind. This episteme is dependent on foreign and opposing facts and figures. The boundaries of the episteme are open and function like a diffusive membrane, which can be penetrated and acted upon by elements from other systems. Finally, it uses multiple sources of knowing, which are all inter-dependent. This leads to an accumulation of conflicting results, which are all embraced though not integrated by the DD system.

Integral-Inclusive (II) Episteme

The II episteme is based on the *translogic*; this logos assumes that there is one great Order of reality, which includes within it all the different forms of order and non-order that can be said to exist. It aims to constitute a knowing system that will give a unitary and transcendent meaning to the diverse forms reality takes. In contrast to the MM form which stems from a similar assumption, the II is driven by the belief that all available knowledge including that which is paradoxical or contradictory to it must be accounted for by its own frame of meaning. It works to reconcile between multiple, non-identical systems of meaning in order to fuse them into a unitary, all-inclusive, integrated, and absolute structure (Lovejoy, 1960/1936; Wilber, 2000; Wilson, 1998).

In the II episteme an edifice is constructed from previously differentiated and incompatible elements. The new formation includes some or all of the properties of the original components set in a new, synthetic web of relations. The II episteme is consistent and coherent; it contains a plurality of contradictory parts and oppositely charged momentums, but it is able to cohesively gather them into a comprehensive narrative, theory, or conceptual equilibrium. This is a fixed formation; it has an awareness of the processes of movement and of the dynamics of knowledge, yet it holds that all motion is part of a large body of meaning that is perennially constant. It emphasizes the stillness that lies in the deep order of things, and claims that it can be perceived and known from a global and unlimited perspective. The II episteme does not go through changes in its identity. It encompasses many minor adjustments and alterations, but its overall identity is certain and immutable. It is also a singular episteme: All the systems, sub-systems, and properties that are embraced by it are woven into an all-including Meta-structure. Further, the II is context independent, since it assumes that its own knowledge is completely valid beyond the particular context of its acquisition. Nevertheless, the contribution of each context to the construction of the complete edifice is recognized. This entity is therefore not dependent on time or space, and it may exist in the same form under any possible context, locality or perspective. The II is independent of other factors or voices, since it holds its truth-value to be undisputed. However, unlike the MM episteme it does not reject unknown or foreign knowledge, but instead integrates it to its preexisting conceptual structure. Finally, this episteme assumes that all ways of knowing belong to one general and overriding method which is without fault.

Cross-Domain Consistency of the Epistemes

Psycho-epistemological studies tend to assume that the ways of knowing people have are general and valid beyond the particular context of examination (Basseches, 1984; Commons and Richards, 2002; Kegan, 1994; King and Kitchener, 1994). These studies have been largely influenced by Piaget's structural-developmental model that claimed universal validity (Inhelder and Piaget, 1958). Others criticized this belief, arguing that knowing always takes place in particular contexts and in relation to specific topics that must be taken into account in determining cognitive abilities (Dewey, 1933; Vygotsky, 1978).

The epistemes in the present study were examined in two distinct domains, and so it was possible to test for domain specificity. The results showed that a high degree of correlation exists between self and culture scores, and that no significant difference differentiates between them. In addition, 2/3 of the interviewees received a score in one domain, which was identical or not different by more then one unit of score to their score in the second domain. These results suggest that the epistemes are not domain specific, and that the logic that guides the processes of knowing works in a similar fashion across at least two different contexts.

An intriguing finding in this area was that this consistency grew stronger with age; for example, the correlation for the two young age groups was averaging 0.39 and was not significant, as opposed to the average for the two older groups which was 0.77 and significant. This might indicate that in late adolescence and early adulthood the epistemes are still in a dynamic state of formation (Harter and Monsour, 1992). As years go by a more stable equilibrium is established, and a higher degree of epistemic generalization across domains can be achieved.

The Development of the Four Epistemes

A fundamental issue in the investigation of a psychological concept is its developmental character. The studies of Baldwin, Piaget, Vygotsky, Werner, Kohlberg, Perry, Loevinger, Kegan, Commons and others revealed that psychological structures develop in a hierarchical way. In development each new stage encompasses the qualities of previous stages, and adds to them a new set of elements, functions, and relations.

The present research was cross-sectional and not longitudinal, and therefore any discussion about development is purely suggestive. Having said that, both the theoretical model and evidence from the interviews suggest the possibility of epistemic development. This can be exemplified by looking at the DD episteme in relation to the MM and RR ones. The MM acknowledges one order of knowledge that is coherent, consistent and constant. The RR episteme discovers other valid kinds of orders that are each coherent, consistent, and constant. The DD acknowledges the first order, as well as the new ones revealed by the RR. Moreover, it recognizes the interactive and reciprocal relationship between the orders. In addition to that, it is able to interpret orders that are incoherent, inconsistent, and in perpetual flux, which the first two epistemes cannot comprehend. It further perceives the elements of self-negation that each system carries within it, and their constitutive relations with other elements inside the system. The DD therefore holds more cognitive tools that enable it to understand information and more elaborate ways by which to organize it. These added abilities make for a more a complex way of knowing the world.

The classical definition of development calls for a strong correlation between chronological age and progression in the complexity of the psychological variable (Broughton, 1975). In the present research the correlation between age and level of complexity was very low (r=0.12 and r=0.14 for SC and CC, respectively). Nevertheless, another result that is taken into account in assessing development is the differences in scores between different age groups. In this study, the overwhelming majority of participants from the youngest age group had either MM or RR epistemes in both domains. In the next two age groups there were more instances of DD and II epistemes, and the oldest age group consisted of 25% MM in both contexts, 20% II in the SC and 25% II in the CC.

These results show that some relation between age and epistemic complexity does exist; the frequency of more complex epistemes goes up with the progression in age. This is consistent with other studies that showed that advanced ways of knowing and thinking are more apparent in older populations (King et al, 1983; Kitchener and King, 1981; Kramer and Woodruff, 1986). Based on these findings it may be suggested that epistemological development in adulthood is not determined by age; however, with the progression of time the probability of it happening increases.

The Shape of Development: The Continuous Spiral Model

In contrast to most psycho-epistemological models, which depict a sequential linear developmental structure (Commons and Richards, 2002; Fischer, 1980; Inhelder and Piaget, 1957; King and Kitchener, 1994; Kohlberg, Levine and Hewer, 1984; Perry, 1970), the present model suggests that epistemic growth progresses in a continuous spiral way. The meaning of this is twofold: First, if development is continuous then no episteme, including the Integral-Inclusive, marks the endpoint of potential growth of the knowledge system. Second, if development is spiral and not linear then advanced positions along the trajectory share the exact same structural form with previous ones. This is indeed the case with the MM and II epistemes; both of these epistemes are characterized by a unitary, stable, consistent and coherent organization of knowledge. The II episteme does encompass many more sub-systems of knowledge than the MM episteme, but it ultimately constructs a singular Meta-system that has the same structural traits as the latter system. Its content is therefore richer and its explanatory value much higher, but its epistemological formation is identical with the one the MM episteme has.

This means that the initial position in the developmental trajectory is similar to the last one, and that the most developed epistemic form is not different in its structure from the least developed one. The two positions differ in the breadth of their perspective, but from a formal-epistemological standpoint they are located in the same place.

The singular and coherent formation of the II episteme has another crucial significance for development. Since it is structurally identical to the MM episteme, it is prone to the effects of higher-ordered forms of relativism and dialectics. In this manner further transformations of the episteme are forced, and more advanced forms of RR, DD, and II epistemes evolve. This can be seen in diagram 3 which shows how a second-order RR episteme lies beyond the first-order II episteme. In similar fashion more advanced forms of DD and II epistemes exist further ahead. Since the structure of the MM and II epistemes is identical, the dynamic spiral later consists only of RR, DD, and II structures. It is this relationship between the epistemes that makes the entire developmental model continuous and spiral.

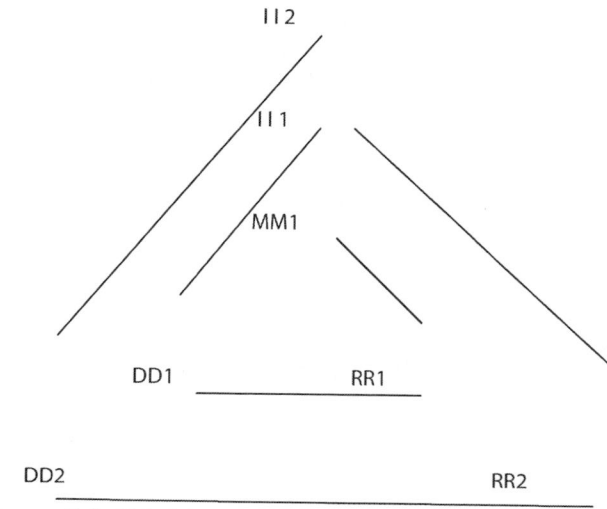

Diagram 3. The Continuous Spiral Model.

Importance of the Present Research

The findings from the research may contribute to several areas of study. In the field of psycho-epistemology they support the growing understanding of the different and complicated facets of the adult's system of knowledge. This research suggests that four types of different epistemes inhabit the adult's mind, and that they develop along a continuous spiral trajectory. In the field of post-formal and post-conventional thought, the results reveal the heterogeneity of advanced ways of thinking. The epistemes that develop beyond the MM formation show more complexity than in formal operational thought. They use cognitive abilities that encompass and transcend hypothetico-deductive operations, and are therefore able to successfully respond to complicated problems and challenges. The DD and II epistemes in particular are further related to the concept of wisdom (Baltes and Staudinger, 2000; Labouvie-Vief, 1990), since they actualize the abilities to comprehend the significance of relativity and relations, to recognize and allow for diversity and contradictions, and to attain the most complicated mental unifications and integration.

Limitation of the Present Investigation

The four epistemes in the current model were constructed according to seven fundamental principles. The principles that were selected therefore determined to a large extent the type of epistemes that were eventually constructed. A relevant question here is why were those principles selected and not others, and were those principles exclusive.

The seven factors were selected since they deal with fundamental issues of organizing knowledge. However, it can be argued that alternative issues exist and therefore other principles could have been used. Potential issues that were not addressed here include the certainty of knowledge, the reaction to knowledge from authority, and the systematic use of questions and doubt. Future research might wish to expand the usage of epistemic issues and principles in order to reach a more comprehensive epistemological picture.

Another criticism deals with the level of generalization of the epistemes. The present study examined individuals' conceptions of self and culture. It is proper to question whether the conclusions from these contexts can be generalized to other areas of meaning making. The strong relation between the SC and CC indicates that a consistent cognitive structure might exist, but there is a need for further research in order to strengthen this finding.

BIBLIOGRAPHY

Adorno, T. W. (1990). *Negative Dialectics*. London: Routledge and Kegan. (Original published 1966).

Baltes, P. B., and Staudinger, U. M. (2000). Wisdom: A meta-heuristic (pragmatic) to orchestrate mind and virtue towards excellence. *American Psychologist, 55(1)*, 122-136.

Basseches, M. A. (1976). *Beyond Closed-System Problem-Solving: A Study of Meta-Systematic Aspects of Mature Thought*. Unpublished Ph. D. thesis, Harvard University.

Basseches, M. (1980). Dialectical schemata: A framework for the empirical study of the development of dialectical thinking. *Human Development, 23*, 400-421.

Basseches, M. (1984). *Dialectical Thinking and Adult Development*. Norwood, NJ: Ablex.

Baumeister, R. F. (1998). The Self. In D. T. Gilbert, S. T. Fiske, and G. Lindzey (Eds.), *The Handbook of social Psychology, Vol. 1.* (pp. 680-740). McGraw-Hill.

Baxter-Magolda, M. B. (1999). The evolution of Epistemology: Refining contextual knowing at Twentysomething. *Journal of College Student Development, 40(4)*, 333-344.

Belenky, M. F., Clinchy, B. M., Goldberger, N. R., and Tarule, J. M. (1986). *Women's Ways of Knowing: The Development of self, Voice, and Mind*. New York: Basic Books.

Berlin, I. (1957). *The Hedgehog and the Fox: Tolstoy's View of History*. New York: The New York American Library. (Original published 1953).

Bernstein, R. J. (1988). *Beyond Objectivism and Relativism: Science, Hermeneutics, and Praxis*. University of Pennsylvania Press.

Berry, J. W. (1988). Acculturation and psychological adaptation: A conceptual overview. In J. W. Berry, and R. C. Annis (Eds.), *Ethnic Psychology: Research and Practice with Immigrants, Refugees, Native Peoples, Ethnic Groups and Sojourners* (pp. 41-52). Amsterdam: Swets and Zeitlinger.

Berry, J. W., Trimble, J. E., and Olmedo, E. L. (1986). Assessment of acculturation. In W. Lonner, and J. W. Berry (Eds.), *Field Methods in Cross-Cultural Research* (pp. 291-324). Newbury Park, CA: Sage.

Brim, O. G. (1976). Life-span development of the theory of oneself: implications for child development. In H. W. Reese (Ed.), *Advances in Child Development and Behavior, Vol. 2* (pp. 241-251). New York: Academic Press.

Broughton, J. M. (1975). *The Development of Natural Epistemology in Adolescence and Early Adulthood*. Unpublished Ph. D. thesis, Harvard University.

Broughton, J. M., and Freeman-Moir, D. J. (Eds.). (1982). *The Cognitive- Developmental Psychology of James Mark Baldwin: Current Theory and Research in Genetic Epistemology*. Norwood: Ablex.

Bukobza, G. (2007). The epistemological basis of the self. *New Ideas in Psychology*, in press.

Burr, J. E., and Hofer, B. K. (2002). Personal epistemology and theory of mind: Deciphering young children's beliefs about knowledge and knowing. *New Ideas in Psychology, 20*, 199-224.

Campbell, J. D., Trapnell, P. D., Heine, S. J., Katz, I. M., Lavallee, L. F., and Lehman, D. R. (1996). Self-concept clarity: Measurement, personality correlates, and cultural boundaries. *Journal of Personality and Social Psychology, 70(1)*, 141-156.

Cavanaugh, J. C., Kramer, D. A., Sinnott, J. D., Camp, C. J., and Markley, R. P (1985). On missing links and such: Interfaces between cognitive research and everyday problem-solving. *Human Development, 28*, 146-168.

Chandler, M. J., and Boutilier, R. G. (1992). The development of dynamic system reasoning. *Human Development, 35*, 121-137.

Chandler, M. J., Boyes, M., and Ball, L. (1990). Relativism and stations of epistemic doubt. *Journal of Experimental Child Psychology, 50*, 370-395.

Chandler, M. J., Lalonde, C. E., and Sokol, B. W. (2000). Continuities of selfhood in the face of radical development and cultural change. In L. P. Nucci, G. B. Saxe, and E. Turiel (Eds.), *Culture, Thought, and Development.* (pp.65-84). Mahwah, NJ: Lawrence Erlbaum.

Commons, M. L., and Richards, F. A. (2002). Four Postformal stages. In J. Demick (Ed.), (pp. 199-219). *Handbook of Adult Development*. New York: Plenum.

Cook-Greuter, S. R. (1999). *Postautonomous Ego Development: A Study of its Nature and Measurement*. Unpublished Ph. D. thesis, Harvard University.

Damon. W., and Hart, D. (1982). The development of self-understanding from infancy through adolescence. *Child Development, 53*, 841-864.

Denney, N. W. (1982). Aging and cognitive changes. In B.B. Wolman (Ed.), *Handbook of Developmental Psychology*. (pp. 807-827). NJ: Prentice-Hall.

Dewey, J. (1933). *How We Think: A Restatement of the Relation of Reflective Thinking to the Educative Process*. Boston: D. C. Heath. (Original published 1910).

Dien, D. S. (2000). The evolving nature of self-identity across four levels of history. *Human Development, 43*, 1-18.

Donahue, E. M., Robins, R. W., Roberts, B. W., and John, O. P. (1993). The divided self: Concurrent and longitudinal effects of psychological adjustment and social roles on self-concept differentiation. *Journal of Personality and Social Psychology, 64(5)*, 834-846.

Edelstein, W. and Noam, G. (1982). Regulatory structures of the self and 'postformal' stages in adulthood. *Human Development, 25(6)*, 407-422.

Epstein, S. (1973). The self-concept revisited, or a theory of a theory. *American Psychologist, 28*, 404-416.

Ewing, K. P. (1990). The illusion of wholeness: Culture, self, and the experience of inconsistency. *Ethos, 18(3)*, 251-278.

Fischer, K. W. (1980). A theory of cognitive development: The control and construction of hierarchies of skills. *Psychological Review, 87(6)*, 477-531.

Fischer, K. W., and Bidell, T. R. (1998). Dynamic development of psychological structures in action and thought. In W. Damon (Series Ed.) and R. M. Lerner (Vol. Ed.), *Handbook of*

Child Psychology: Vol. 1: Theoretical Models of Human Development. (pp. 467-561). New York: Wiley.

Flavell, J. H. (1963). *The Developmental Psychology of Jean Piaget.* N. J.: Van Nostrand.

Foucault, M. (1970). *The Order of Things: An Archeology of the Human Sciences.* New York: Pantheon Books. (Original published 1966).

Foucault, M. (1972). *The Archaeology of Knowledge and the Discourse on Language.* New York: Pantheon Books. (Original published 1969).

Fowler, J. W. (1981). *Stages of Faith: The Psychology of Human Development and the Quest for Meaning.* San Francisco: Harper and Row.

Funder, D. C. (1983). The "consistency" controversy and the accuracy of personality judgments. *Journal of Personality, 51(3),* 346-359.

Gebser, J. (1985). *The Ever-Present Origin.* Athens: Ohio University Press. (Original published 1949; part 2 published 1953).

Geertz, C. (1984). From the native's point of view: On the nature of Anthropological understanding. In R. Shweder and R. Levine (Eds.), *Culture Theory: Essays on Mind, Self, and Emotion.* (pp. 123-136). Cambridge University Press.

Gergen, K. J. (1991). *The Saturated Self.* New York: Basic Books.

Gilligan, C. (1982). *In a Different Voice: Psychological Theory and Women's Development.* Cambridge: Harvard University Press.

Greenwald, A. G., and Pratkanis, A. R. (1984). The Self. In R. S. Wyer, and T. K. Srull (Eds.), *Handbook of Social Cognition, Vol. 3* (pp. 129-178). Hillsdale, NJ: Erlbaum.

Hampson, S. E. (1997). Determinants of inconsistent personality descriptions: Trait and target effects. *Journal of Personality, 65(2),* 249-290.

Hampson, S. E. (1998). When is an inconsistency not an inconsistency? Trait reconciliation in personality description and impression formation. *Journal of Personality and Social Psychology, 74(1),* 102-117.

Harre, R. and Gillett, G. (1994). *The Discursive Mind.* London: Sage.

Harris, M. (1999). *Theories of Culture in Postmodern times.* AltaMira Press.

Harter, S., and Monsour, A. (1992). Developmental analysis of conflict caused by opposing attributes in the adolescent self-portrait. *Developmental Psychology, 28(2),* 251-260.

Hermans, H. J. M. (1996). Voicing the self: From information processing to dialogical interchange. *Psychological Bulletin, 119(1),* 31-50.

Higgins, E. T. (1987). Self-discrepancy: A theory relating self and affect. *Psychological Review, 94(3),* 319-340.

Holsti, O. R. (1969). *Content Analysis for the Social Sciences and Humanities.* Reading: Addison-Wesley.

Inhelder, B., and Piaget, J. (1958). *The Growth of Logical Thinking from Childhood to Adulthood.* New York: Basic Books.

Jensen, L. A. (1997). Different worldviews, different morals: America's culture war divide. *Human Development, 40,* 325-344.

Kegan, R. (1982). *The Evolving Self: Problem and Process in Human Development.* Cambridge: Harvard University Press.

Kegan, R. (1994). *In Over Our Heads: The Mental Demands of Modern Life.* Cambridge: Harvard University Press.

Kelley, G. A. (1955). *The Psychology of Personal Constructs, Vol. 1.* New York: Norton.

King, P. M., and Kitchener, K. S. (1994). Developing Reflective Judgment: Understanding and Promoting Intellectual Growth and Critical Thinking *in Adolescents and Adults*. San Francisco: Jossey-Bass Publishers.

King, P. M., Kitchener, K. S., Davison, M. L., Parker, C. A., and Wood, P. K. (1983). The justification of belief in young adults: A longitudinal study. *Human Development, 26,* 106-116.

Kitchener, K. S., and King, P. M. (1981). Reflective judgment: Concepts of justification and their relationship to age and education. *Journal of Applied Developmental Psychology, 2,* 89-116.

Kitchener, K. S., King, P. M., Wood, P. K., and Davison, M. L. (1989). Sequentiality and consistency in the development of reflective judgment: A six-year longitudinal study. *Journal of Applied Developmental Psychology, 10,* 73-95.

Kohlberg, L., Levine, C., and Hewer, A. (1984). The current formulation of the theory. In L. Kohlberg (Ed.), *Essays on Moral Development, Vol. 2: The Psychology of Moral Development.* (pp. 212-319). San Francisco: Harper and Row.

Kohlberg, L., and Ryncarz, R. A. (1990). Beyond justice reasoning: Moral development and consideration of a seventh stage. In C. N. Alexander, and E. J. Langer (Eds.), *Higher Stages of Human Development: Perspectives on adult growth.* (pp. 191-207). New York: Oxford University Press.

Koplowitz, H. (1984). A projection beyond Piaget's formal-operations stage: A general system stage and a unitary stage. In M. C. Commons, F. A. Richards, and C. Armon (Eds.), *Beyond Formal Operations: Late Adolescence and dult Cognitive Development.* (pp. 272-295). New York: Praeger.

Koplowitz, H. (1990). Unitary consciousness and the highest development of mind: The relation between spiritual development and cognitive development. In M. L. Commons, C. Armon, L. Kohlberg, F. A. Richards, T. A. Grotaer, and J. D. Sinnott (Eds.), *Adult Development: Models and Methods in the Study of Adolescent and Adult Thought; Volume 2.* (pp. 105-111). New York: Praeger.

Kramer, D. A. (1983). Post formal operations? A need for further conceptualization. *Human Development, 26,* 91-105.

Kramer, D. A., and Woodruff, D. S. (1986). Relativistic and dialectical thought in three adult age-groups. *Human Development, 29,* 280-290.

Kruglansky, A. W. (1989). *Lay Epistemics and Human Knowledge: Cognitive and Motivational Bases*. New York: Plenum.

Kuhn, D. (1991). *The Skills of Argument*. Cambridge University Press.

Kuhn, T. (1970). *The Structure of Scientific Revolutions*. University of Chicago Press.

Kuper, A. (1999) *Culture: The Anthropologists' Account*. Cambridge: Harvard University Press.

Labouvie-Vief, G. (1982). Dynamic development and mature autonomy: A theoretical prologue. *Human Development, 25,* 161-191.

Labouvie-Vief, G. (1990). Wisdom as integrated thought: Historical and developmental perspectives. In R. J. Sternberg (Ed.), *Wisdom : Its Nature, Origins, and Development.* (pp. 52-83). New York: Cambridge University Press.

Labouvie-Vief, G. (1992). A neo-Piagetian perspective on adult cognitive development. In R. J. Sternberg, and C. A. Berg (Eds.), *Intellectual Development.* (pp. 197-228). Cambridge University Press.

LaFromboise, T., Coleman, H. L. K., and Gerton, J. (1993). Psychological impact of biculturalism: Evidence and Theory. *Psychological Bulletin, 114(3)*, 395-412.

Levin, J. D. (1992). *Theories of the Self*. Washington: Hemisphere.

Lifton, R. J. (1993). *The Protean Self: Human Resilience in an Age of Fragmentation*. New York: Basic Books.

Linville, P. W. (1987). Self-complexity as a cognitive buffer against stress-related illness and depression. *Journal of Personality and Social Psychology, 52(4)*, 663-676.

Linville, P. W., and Carlston, D. E. (1994). Social cognition of the self. In P. G. Devine, D. L. Hamilton, and T. M. Ostrom (Eds.), *Social Cognition: Impact on Social Psychology*. (pp. 143-193). San Diego: Academic Press.

Loevinger, J. (1976). *Ego Development: Conceptions and Theories*. San Francisco: Jossey-Bass.

Lomranz, J. (1998). An image of aging and the concept of Aintegration. In J. Lomranz (Ed.), *Handbook of Aging and Mental Health: An Integrative Approach*. (pp. 217-250). New York: Plenum Press.

Lovejoy, A. O. (1960). *The Great Chain of Being: A Study of the History of an Idea*. New York: Harper and Row. (Original published 1936).

Marcuse, H. (1954). *Reason and Revolution: Hegel and the Rise of Social Theory*. New York: The Humanities Press.

Mansfield, A. F. and Clinchy, B. M. (2002). Toward the integration of objectivity and subjectivity: Epistemological development from 10 to 16. *New Ideas in Psychology, 20*, 225-262.

Markus, H., and Wurf, E. (1987). The dynamic self-concept: A social psychological perspective. *Annual Review of Psychology, 38*, 299-337.

Medin, D. L. (1989). Concepts and conceptual structure. *American Psychologist, 44(12)*, 1469-1481.

Mandelbaum, M. (1982). Subjective, objective, and conceptual relativism. In J. W. Meiland, and M. Krausz (Eds.), *Relativism: Cognitive and Moral*. (pp. 4-61). University of Notre Dame Press.

Miller, M. E. (1994). World Views, ego development, and epistemological changes from the conventional to the Postformal: A longitudinal perspective. In M. E. Miller, and S. R. Cook-Greuter (Eds.), *Transcendence and Mature Thought in Adulthood*. (pp. 147-179). Lanham: Rowman and Littlefield.

Moghaddam, F. M., Taylor, D. M., and Lalonde, R. N. (1987). Individualistic and collective integration strategies among Iranians in Canada. *International Journal of Psychology, 22*, 301-313.

Moshman, D. (1999). *Adolescent Psychological Development: Rationality, Morality, and Identity*. Mahwah, NJ: Erlbaum.

Neisser, U. (1988). Five kinds of self-knowledge. *Philosophical Psychology, 1(1)*, 35-59.

Nisan, M. (1995). Moral balance: A model for moral choice. In W. M. Kurtines, and J. L. Gewirtz (Eds.), *Moral Development: An Introduction*. (pp. 475-492). Needham Heights: Allyn and Bacon.

Nisan, M. and Applebaum, B. (1995). Maintaining a balanced and respectable identity: Moral choice in late adulthood. In G. Ben-Shakhar, and A. Lieblich (Eds.), *Studies in Psychology in Honor of Solomon Kugelmass*. (pp. 139-152). Jerusalem: The Magnes Press.

Peng, K., and Nisbett, R. E. (1999). Culture, dialectics, and reasoning about contradiction. *American Psychologist, 54(9)*, 741-754.

Pepper, S. C. (1942). *World Hypotheses: A Study in Evidence*. Berkeley: University of California Press.

Perry, B., Donovan, M. P., Kelsey, L. J., Paterson, J., Statkiewicz, W., and Allen, R. D. (1986). Two schemes of intellectual development: A comparison of development as defined by William Perry and Jean Piaget. *Journal of Research in Science Teaching, 23(1)*, 73-83.

Perry, W. G. (1970). Forms of Intellectual and Ethical Development in the College Years: A Scheme. New York: Holt, Rinehart and Winston.

Perry, W. G. (1981). Cognitive and ethical growth: The making of meaning. In A. Chickering (Ed.), *The Modern American College*. (pp. 76-116). San Francisco: Jossey-Bass.

Phinney, J. S. (1989). Stages of ethnic identity development in minority group adolescents. *Journal of Early Adolescents, 9(1)*, 34-49.

Phinney, J. S. (1990). Ethnic identity in adolescents and adults: Review of research. *Psychological Bulletin, 108(3)*, 499-514.

Phinney, J. S. (2000). Identity formation across cultures: The interaction of personal, societal, and historical change. *Human Development, 43*, 27-31.

Phinney, J. S., and Chavira, V. (1992). Ethnic identity and self-esteem: An exploratory longitudinal study. *Journal of Adolescence, 15*, 271-281.

Piaget, J. (1952). *The Origins of Intelligence in Children*. New York: International University Press. (Original published 1936).

Piaget, J. (1954). *The Construction of Reality in the Child*. New York: Basic Books. (Original published 1937).

Piaget, J. (1967). *Six Psychological Studies*. New York: Vintage Books. Piaget, J. (1970). *Genetic Epistemology*. Columbia University Press.

Piaget, J. (1980). *Experiments in Contradiction*. University of Chicago Press. (Original published 1974).

Richards, F. A., and Commons, M. L. (1984). Systematic, Metasystematic, and cross-paradigmatic reasoning: A case for stages of reasoning beyond formal operations. In M. C. Commons, F. A. Richards, and C. Armon, (Eds.) *BeyondFormal Operations: Late Adolescence and Adult Cognitive Development*. (pp. 92-119). New York: Praeger.

Riegel, K. F. (1973). Dialectic operations: The final period of cognitive development. *Human Development, 16*, 346-370.

Riegel, K. F. (1975). Toward a dialectical theory of development. *Human Development, 18*, 50-64.

Ross, M. (1989). Relation of implicit theories to the construction of personal histories. *Psychological Review, 96(2)*, 341-357.

Rosenzweig, F. (1985). *The Star of Redemption*. University of Notre Dam Press. (Original published 1921).

Sande, G. N., Goethals, G. R., and Radloff, C. E. (1988). Perceiving one's own traits and other's: The multifaceted self. *Journal of Personality and Social Psychology, 54(1)*, 13-20.

Sayegh, L., and Lasry, J. C. (1993). Immigrants' adaptation in Canada: Assimilation, acculturation, and orthogonal cultural identification. *Canadian Psychology, 34(1)*, 98-109.

Schommer, M. (1990). Effects of beliefs about the nature of knowledge on comprehension. *Journal of Educational Psychology, 82(3)*, 498-504.

Schommer, M. (1993). Epistemological development and academic performance among secondary students. *Journal of Educational Psychology, 85(3)*, 406-411.

Schommer, M. (1994). Synthesizing epistemological belief research: Tentative understanding and provocative confusions. *Educational Psychology Review, 6(4)*, 293-319.

Schroeder, D. J. (1983). The adjective generation technique: Consistency of self-description in psychiatric patients. *Journal of Personality, 51(4)*, 631-639.

Sheldon, K. M., Ryan, R. M., Rawsthorne, L. J., and Ilardi, B. (1997). Trait self and true self: Cross-role variation in the big-five personality traits and its relations with psychological authenticity and subjective well-being. *Journal of Personality and Social Psychology, 73(6)*, 1380-1393.

Sinnott, J. D. (1981). The theory of relativity: A Metatheory for development? *Human Development, 24*, 293-311.

Sinnott, J. D. (1998). *The Development of Logic in Adulthood: Postformal Thought and its Applications*. New York: Plenum.

Souvaine, E., Lahey, L. L., and Kegan, R. (1990). Life after formal operations: Implications for a psychology of the self. In C. N. Alexander, and E. J. Langer (Eds.), *Higher Stages of Human Development* (pp. 229-257). Oxford University Press.

Storr, A. (1972). *The Dynamics of Creation*. New York: Atheneum.

Tolman, C. (1981). The metaphysic of relations in Klaus Riegel's 'Dialectics' of human development. *Human Development, 24*, 33-51.

Tolman, C. (1983). Further comments on the meaning of 'Dialectics'. *Human Development, 26*, 320-324.

Tzuriel, D., and Klein, M. M. (1977). Ego identity: Effects of ethnocentrism, ethnic identification, and cognitive complexity in Israeli, Oriental, and western ethnic groups. *Psychological Reports, 40*, 1099-1110.

Tillich, P. (1951). *Systematic Theology, (Vol. 1)*. University of Chicago Press.

Vygotsky, L. (1978). *Mind in Society*. Cambridge: Harvard University Press.

Williams, B. (1972). *Morality: An Introduction to Ethics*. New York: Harper and Row.

Wilber, K. (2000). *Integral Psychology: Consciousness, Spirit, Psychology, Therapy*. Boston: Shambhala.

Wilson, E. O. (1998). *Consilience: The Unity of Knowledge*. New York: Vintage Books.

Wurzel, J. S. (1988). *Toward Multiculturalism: A Reader in Multicultural Education*. Yarmouth: Intercultural Press.

Yardley, K., and Honess, T. (Eds.). (1987). *Self and Identity: Psycho-Social Perspectives*. New York: John Wiley and Sons.

Zak, I. (1976). Structure of ethnic identity of Arab-Israeli students. *Psychological Reports, 38*, 239-246.

In: Adult Education: Issues and Developments
Editors: P. N. Blakely, A. H. Tomlin, pp. 205-216

ISBN: 978-1-60456-272-9
© 2008 Nova Science Publishers, Inc.

Chapter 4

LEARNING STYLES AND HIGHER EDUCATION: NO ADULT LEFT BEHIND

Karen Burke and Laura Shea Doolan

ABSTRACT

A basic premise of this chapter is that the quality of teaching in many colleges and universities is perceived as unacceptable. Additionally, in higher education, teaching and learning practices need to be vastly improved to meet the needs of its diverse learners. The world of higher education and the world in which higher education plays a significant role are changing. With these premises as a backdrop this chapter will address the theory, practice, and research on the Dunn and Dunn Learning-Style Model. The authors will suggest specific strategies to identify and accommodate college students' individual learning styles.

INTRODUCTION: A COLLEGE SCENARIO

A good student approaches the professor, Dr. Morrissey, and wants to hand to her his 10 pages of a paper he is writing, which is not due for another two weeks. Dr. Morrissey is laden with papers from another course, which must be graded by tomorrow. She tells the student that she knows he is a very good writer and not to worry, but hand in his work when it is due. He thanks her, but turns away with a frustrated look on his face. Why?

Perhaps, it is because, sociologically, the student's learning style is authority oriented and, emotionally, his learning style is highly motivated, or he may require a need for structure. How can one tell? Only a valid and reliable assessment of the students' learning style correctly will reveal his strengths.

What "is" Learning Style?

Learning styles are the different ways individuals begin to concentrate, process, internalize, and remember new and difficult information (Dunn and Dunn, 1999). When people *use*, rather than ignore their natural styles, they learn more, more quickly, and with less frustration than they do when trying to use someone else's style. St. John's University's Center for the Study of Learning and Teaching Styles' website (www.learningstyles.net) provides ample evidence of documentation. This website includes 800 studies conducted with the Dunn and Dunn Model by researchers at more than 120 different institutions of higher education.

Although researchers have defined the concept in different ways (Canfield and Lafferty (1970), Dunn and Dunn (1978), Entwistle and Ramsden (1983), Hill (1981), Hunt (1971), Kolb (1981), Schmeck, Ribich, and Ramanaiah (1977), and Witkin (1976)) each developed models that documented the many alternative ways in which individuals approached, internalized, and processed information. The differences are enormous between Learning-Style Models that are:

- Comprehensive and those that include only one or two variables on a bi-polar continuum;
- Founded on a strong research base and those without one;
- University- or professional-organization based and those that reflect a single individual's endeavors;
- Implemented locally and those that are implemented nationally and internationally;
- Commercial and those that are not;
- Represented by schools that can be visited for observational purposes and those that are not; and
- Representative of individual concerns and those that are not responsible to an organizational hierarchy (Dunn, 2004).

Any attempt to summarize the Dunn and Dunn Model (see Figure 1) runs the risk of oversimplification. Nevertheless, certain fundamental characteristics can be cited.

How the Environment Affects Learning

Learning-style strengths are affected by *where* individuals prefer to learn. Thus, in a college classroom you will find students who need to learn in an *environment* that is very different from where others need to learn. While concentrating, students react differently to the immediate instructional environment--sound versus silence; bright versus soft lighting; warm versus cool temperatures; and formal versus informal seating (Dunn and Griggs, 2000).

College professors must allow accommodations so that all students will be provided the necessary space that complements their environmental learning-style preferences. By altering their study areas some students will choose to work in formal areas--desks, chairs, and tables; while other students will choose informal areas--couches, rugs, soft chairs, etc. Within the areas of higher education classrooms, adaptations can be made for sound preferences, lighting needs, and temperature controls.

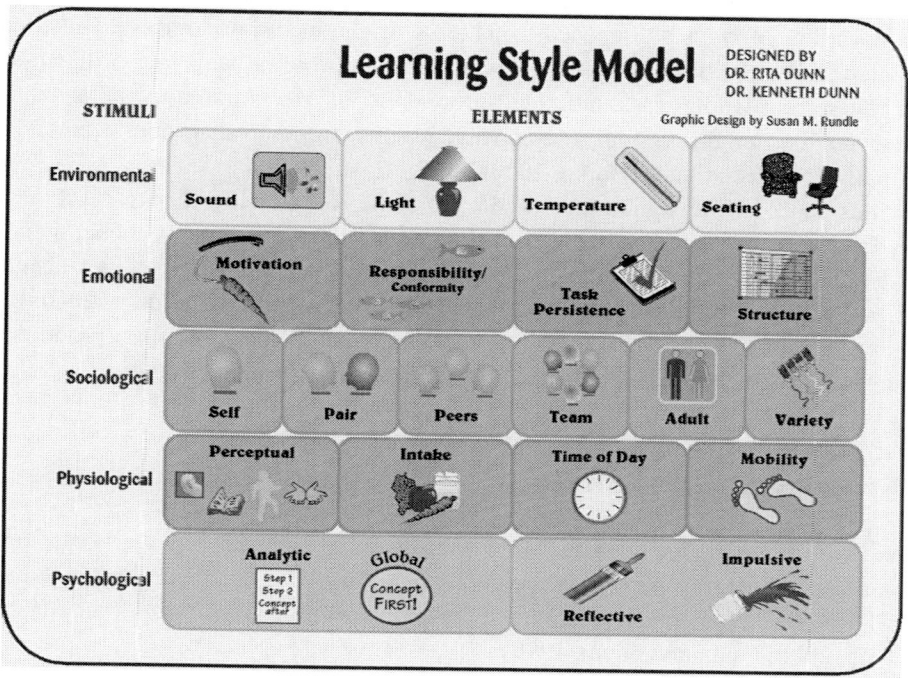

Figure 1. Dunn and Dunn Learning-Styles Model; Reprinted with permission from the authors.

How Emotions Affect Learning

For many, motivation is strongly linked to how well they achieve. In a college classroom you will have young adults who just *enjoy* learning new and difficult material; it makes them feel accomplished! Others strive for good grades because they want their teachers', parents', or friends' approval. When students are interested in *what* they are learning, they become increasingly motivated (Dunn, Burke, and Whitley, 2000).

Persistence refers to each person's ability to stay with a task until it is accomplished whereas responsibility is more closely related to the emotional needs of some to do what others have told them they should. Students who enjoy doing the *opposite* of what they should do are called *nonconformists*. These rarely respond well to authoritative adults. A nonconforming college student must be (a) spoken to in a mutually respectful manner, (b) given an explanation why something is important to the teacher, and (c) given *choices* of how to complete an assignment (Dunn, Burke, and Whitley, 2000).

These students also differ in their need for structure. Some want a great deal of direction and feel best when they know what is required and how to proceed. Such students appreciate specific directions and models to follow. Those who prefer less structure enjoy doing things *their* way (Dunn, Burke, and Whitley, 2000). The classroom professor must provide activities and assignments that offer options.

How Sociological Preferences Affect Learning

Students prefer to learn alone, with peers, with either a collegial or authoritative adult, and/or in a variety of ways as opposed to patterns or routines. For some students, learning requires interaction, and discussion can play an important role in achieving problem-solving expertise. Therefore, whole-class and small-group settings are important. Rather than using large-group lectures or discussions exclusively, teachers need to incorporate other formats such as small-group techniques (Burke, 2000a).

Activities should be designed that encourage some to work together to reach a desired outcome. Tasks can be shared or decided in such a way that teamwork is encouraged. These alternative approaches to instructional events should be mixed and matched in a fashion that exemplifies the varied nature of the learners and the learning process (Burke, 2000a). When given knowledge of their sociological strengths, students will become more productive and more highly achieving than when required to learn in their nonpreferred style.

How Physiology Affects Learning

Individual's *physical beings* affect how they learn and are part of their learning style. Thus, some are affected by perceptual strengths (auditory, visual, tactual, and/or kinesthetic strengths), time-of-day energy levels, intake (snacking while concentrating), and/or mobility needs (Dunn, 2000; Dunn and Dunn, 1999).

Tactual learners absorb new and difficult information most easily by handling and manipulating instructional materials; kinesthetic learners absorb complex information through active involvement and experiences. Students who do not perform well in traditional classrooms tend to be only tactual and/or kinesthetic.

Lecture methods and lessons focusing solely on the textbook are not appropriate for a majority of students. Many students' learning styles dictate a need for exploration and further investigation through simulations, manipulatives, models, role-playing, and computers. Teacher- and student-led demonstrations can provide material for open and directed discussions. Professors often find that kinesthetic activities and tactual resources allow individual students to expand their understanding and interest (Burke, 2000b).

Physiological preferences also include time-of-day, need for intake, and mobility desires. Some students concentrate better in the early or late morning, whereas others do not focus well until afternoon; some are lethargic all day and first become energetic at night. There are students who learn more when they are eating or drinking; others only can nibble or snack after studying when they relax. Most professors expect college students to be able to sit still and pay attention (Dunn and Dunn, 1999). Despite that expectation even some college students will need to move about from one part of the room to another or they will lose a lot of their ability to think; others do not need to move about at all.

How Processing Affects Learning

Analytic thinkers begin to process information or work in a step-by-step sequence. They keep at a task until they have learned what they need or want to, or have accomplished what they set out to do. Global thinkers initially process information by thinking of everything related to what they need or want to learn. They do take many breaks but, eventually, focus on the most relevant information and complete the task (Dunn, Burke, and Whitley, 2000). Both types of processing--analytic and global--are good, but the students who have one style, as opposed to the other, learn very differently from each other (Dunn, Bruno, Sklar, and Beaudry, 1990; Dunn, Cavanaugh, Eberle, and Zenhausern, 1982).

Does Addressing Students' Learning Styles Matter?

In higher education, teaching and learning practices need to be vastly improved to meet the needs of its diverse learners (Claxton and Murrell, 1988). The world of higher education and the world in which higher education plays a significant role are changing (Knight, 2004). In many colleges and universities, services provided to students, such as writing workshops for English language learners, how-to-study seminars, and so forth, are in increased demand. Many learners are enrolled in such programs to meet the requirements to maintain an adequate Grade-Point Average (GPA), and to remain in and graduate from their school. Without such services, many students would falter and, perhaps, not graduate, which could have negative consequences on their future life-long learning and earning power.

As learning becomes more complex, students often depend upon faculty to assist them with the numerous challenges they face. Often times, it is not just those who provide special services, but the course instructors themselves who are being sought out to help students understand the content presented in class. Hence, the tendency for instructors to concentrate on the use of traditional lecture methods to cover the content, many times, can aggravate students' difficulties with learning (Travis, 1996). However, addressing students' learning styles has helped faculty and administrators better assist all students during their higher education experience (Claxton and Murrell, 1988, Dunn and Griggs, 2000). As one undergraduate Native Scholar Program Recipient stated, "Learning style was the stepping-stone to college, and I would have been dismissed from it without that knowledge. I want to be a teacher, and I will use learning style because it makes sense" (Shea Doolan, 2004).

RESEARCH ON LEARNING STYLE AND IMPROVEMENT IN COLLEGE STUDENTS' LEARNING

One hundred and forty-six studies conducted by researchers at 47 institutions of higher education have described the construct of learning style as defined by Dunn and Dunn (2000) and the effects of using style-responsive instructional strategies with adults. Of those, 61 investigations specifically addressed college students. Of that group, no study (see Table 1) failed to identify the diversity that exists among students' unique learning styles (www.learningstyles.net). The Dunns' model is based on a diagnostic and prescriptive approach. After an individual's learning style has been identified, complementary teaching strategies are designed to be congruent to that student's strengths.

Table 1. Research on the Dunn and Dunn Learning-Style Model in Higher Education

Researcher University/Date	Subject Examined	Aspect Examined
Clay, J. E.Alabama A and M University,1984	GPA	High vs. Low Achievers' Learning Styles
Vazquez Arce, W The Union for Experimenting Colleges and Universities, 1985	Various	Learning Style Descriptions
Napolitano, R.A. St. John's University, 1986	Psychology	Structure
Lam-Phoon,S. AndrewsUniversity, 1986	N/A	Cultural and Gender Differences
Clark-Thayer, S. Boston University, 1987	Mathematics	Achievement and Homework
Bailey, G. K. The University of Southern Mississippi, 1988	N/A	Hemisphericity and Environmental Preferences
Dunn, R., Deckinger, E.L., Withers, P. and Katzenstein, H. St. John's University, 1988	Business	Achievement
Cook, L. University of Florida, 1989	General Education	Learning-Style Awareness
Dunn, R., Bruno, J Sklar, R. I. and Beaudry, J. St. John's University, 1990	Mathematics	Processing Style and Hemisphericity
Nelson, B., Dunn, R Griggs, S.A., Primavera, L Fitzpatrick, M., Bacilious, Z., and Miller, R. St. John's University, 1993	Across the-board GPA	Achievement and Retention
Lenehan, M C., Dunn, R., Ingham, J., Murray J. B., and Signer, B. St. John's University, 1994	Anatomy Physiology Bacteriology	Nursing Students' Achievement and Anger
Kennedy, M.D. Florida State University, 1995 Teaching and Learning Styles	Tennis	Matching and Mismatching
Miller, J. St. John's University, 1997	Diagnostic Medical Sonography	PLSs* versus Traditional Lessons Achievement and Attitude
Tendy, S. M. St. John's University, 1998	Group Exercise	Perceptual and Leadership Sociological Preferences
Boyle, R. A., and Dunn, R. St. John's University, 1998	Law	Learning Styles and Homework and Achievement
Bovell, C. St. John's University, 2000	Multidisciplinary	Learning Styles of Non-Traditional College Students
Dolle, L. St. John's University, 2001		Legal ResearchPLSs* versus Traditional Lessons Achievement and Attitude
Jenkins, C. The University of Mississippi, 1991	Generic Freshman Studies	Learning Style Preferences

Note. *PLSs are Programmed Learning Sequences that are a learning–style responsive method. (*Research on the Dunn and Dunn Model*, 2004).

Researchers stated more than three-fifths of learning style was biological; less than two-fifths was developmental (Restak, 1979; Thies 1979, 1999-2000). It is this sociological and biological uniqueness of each individual that makes one person learn differently from another. Information about style can help faculty become more sensitive to the differences students bring to the classroom (Claxton and Murrell, 1988; Dunn and Griggs, 2000) and assist in improving students' academic performance and attitude (Dunn and Griggs, 2004).

Population and Sample

The authors of this chapter conducted a research study in a relatively small urban college in New York that offers an undergraduate teacher education program. This recently revised program awards a Bachelor of Arts degree and fulfills the necessary requirements for four New York State certificates in education.

The students in this investigation included the total enrollment in the introductory Child Development course (CS 101) during the fall 2003 semester. Participants were 57 freshmen enrolled in the Bachelor of Arts degree in Elementary and Special Education. Only full-time college freshmen comprised the sample.

Instrumentation

The *Productivity Environmental Preference Survey* (PEPS) (Dunn, Dunn, and Price, 1996) was administered to each student in the course. The PEPS is a measurement of the learning-style preferences of adults. The measure consists of 100 dichotomous questions that elicit self-diagnostic responses relating to 18 discrete learning-style elements on a 5-point Likert scale. The Ohio State University's National Center for Research in Vocational Education reported that the PEPS had "established impressive reliability and face and construct validity" (Kirby, 1979, p.72).

Procedures

The purpose of this investigation is to explore the question: *What are the tendencies of learning-style preferences among college freshmen students in a small urban college?* It was hypothesized that although there will be a wide range of learning-style preferences among these college freshmen (Dunn and Griggs, 2003), it will be determined that there are distinct learning-style preferences among these freshmen.

Permission to conduct this research was obtained from the Academic Dean and supported by an Institutional Faculty Grant. A meeting to explain procedures was held with the faculty at a regularly scheduled Department Meeting. The Dunn and Dunn Learning Style Model was introduced by a certified learning-style researcher, and the PEPS (Dunn, Dunn and Price, 1996) was administered to 57 full-time college freshmen attending a private, metropolitan college--including males and females of various ethnic and socioeconomic backgrounds.

There were two presentations provided in one morning with approximately one half of the participants in each group. The presentation was given in lieu of their regularly scheduled class. After the collection of the PEPs, the surveys were analyzed and participants received their learning-style profiles along with an extensive study guide based on their personal learning style. This information also was shared with the department faculty.

Descriptive and inferential statistics were utilized to analyze students' responses to each of the 21 learning-style variables. For this exploratory study, percentages, differences in the means, and standard deviations were used for summary statistics.

Findings

The majority of freshmen did not have strong preferences for all but three of the learning-style elements. First, the overwhelming majority of freshmen (75.4%) expressed a strong preference for working in a well-structured academic setting with no ambiguity regarding what was expected of them as college students. Less than a fourth of the group (22.8%) did not indicate a preference in this area, while only 1.8% expressed a preference for determining their own scholastic structure.

Secondly, the majority of freshmen preferred to work in the afternoon (56.1%) or the evening (38.6%). Only 8.8% of the students preferred morning and 12.3% preferred the late morning. Thus, to maximize learning potential, students preferred to be taught later in the day--the time when most of them are involved in recreational activities or part-time employment.

Thirdly, a large percentage (54.4%) preferred to snack while studying or learning new information, while 8.8% indicated that they waited to snack until after the work was completed.

While the majority of students did not have preferences on the remaining elements of learning style, differences did emerge for many students when low and high ends of the range were reviewed. For example, a large percentage (38.6%) preferred to work alone versus 8.8% who preferred to work with peers. Nonetheless, a strong 29.8 % preferred having an authority figure present while only 3.5% were comfortable without this support. Further, only 5.3% preferred a variety of social groupings.

These sociological preferences are worthy of note since 28.1% identified themselves as non-conforming in terms of responsibility. Further, only 10.5% rated themselves as high in persistence and 14% indicated they were motivated to learn.

Students presented some strong preferences for the environment in which new and difficult information were presented and studied. Almost one third (31.6%) of the students preferred to work in an informally designed environment that included relaxed seating provisions as opposed to 5.3% who preferred working at traditional desks. Also relative to the preference for informal seating, 35.1% of the students expressed a strong need for mobility during the course of study while only 1.8% preferred to remain in place until the learning assignment was concluded. Although most students did not have a preference for background sound while learning, not a single student preferred absolute quiet when learning! In fact, 31.6% of the students had a preference to learn new and difficult information through an auditory presentation.

Research Discussion

College freshmen want the professor to provide explicit rules for carrying out assignments and, thus, for securing high grades. Transferring freshmen from high school settings and parental supervision into environments where they are expected to make frequent personal and academic choices for the first time can be devastating. The need for structure regarding learning expectations may reflect a desire to lessen vagueness at a time when ambiguity is high.

Time management, college expectations, grades, personal responsibilities, and length of assignments amalgamate to make these students feel a need for structure. Do these college freshmen *want* structure or do they *need* it to survive? Could it be that we for the most part teach students how to respond to what the professor wants? If the answers to these questions are confirmatory, we need to scrutinize how we are preparing students for the future and how we are training teachers to teach. Structure limits the number of options available to a student and requires a compulsory form of learning, responding, or demonstrating achievement.

In light of the findings of this study, we also should reexamine the conventional practice of scheduling freshmen classes early in the morning under the assumption that that is when students are most alert. The diversity of students' preferences for learning during different periods of the day has been verified by this research. Standardized tests also should be administered at the student's best time. Separate administrations should be arranged in the early morning, afternoon, and evening for those with extreme preferences.

Although several of the learning-style elements failed to reach significance for students as a group, their importance to the individual cannot be dismissed, because how a person prefers to learn is uniquely specific to the individual. This study proposes that teaching freshmen education majors about their own learning styles might be a practical way to empower these future teachers with knowledge that will help them succeed academically. Not only is this knowledge going to support personal learning improvement and academic achievement but it is transferable to their knowledge about the learning styles of the students they will teach in the future.

Hence, teachers, "who know both their subject matter and how to teach it to diverse learners . . ., will . . . change [students'] lives" (Berry, Hoke, and Hirsch, 2004, pp. 688-689); and these effective, qualified teachers are crucial for improving pupils' achievement (Rebell and Hunter, 2004). In this context, future teachers will be successful and proficient managers of their own learning *and* those they teach by addressing the learning-style of all.

What do the college students think about learning-style instruction? Thirty of thirty-eight students enrolled in another education foundations course responded similarly to this pupil:

> I think college professors should accommodate for students' learning styles because . . . a person achieves the most when taught through his or her learning style. [A] college education may be the highest level of education that students receive. It requires us to absorb many facets of knowledge, and this can be very difficult. If we are taught through our learning style, maybe this task will not be so difficult and we can accomplish things much better.

Another stated, ". . . not every person learns in the same manner, and by giving students the option to produce work through their best modality would allow them to produce and hand in their best work."

A few students thought it might be difficult for professors to accommodate all learning-style needs. However, others stated that, if college budgets allowed, classrooms should include some softer seating, light accommodations, and professors could provide assignment options for the nonconforming students and include auditory, visual, tactual, and kinesthetic projects to meet course requirements.

PARADIGM SHIFTS IN THE COLLEGE CLASSROOM

A paradigm shift is taking place in college teaching. Minor modifications in instructional practices will not solve the current problems in higher education. Teaching success in today's world requires a totally new approach.

The old paradigm of college education views teaching as the transfer of faculty knowledge to passive students with little acknowledgement of who they are as individuals in the learning process. The new paradigm of college education views teaching as helping students construct their knowledge in an active way through their strengths and talents. Quality is assured by motivating students to exert extraordinary effort to learn, grow, and develop. This is largely done through knowing your students learning styles, knowing your students personally, and being committed to their intellectual growth and general well-being.

Many faculty members consider the old paradigm the only alternative. They have no vision of what could be done instead. For such instructors it may be helpful to review Hans Christian Andersen's tale of The Emperor's New Clothes. An emperor invested substantial time and money in order to be well-dressed. One day, two dishonest men arrived at court. Pretending to be weavers, they claimed that they were able to create garments so fine that they were not visible to people who were either unfit for the office that they hold, or stupid. The weavers were supplied silk, gold thread, and money, all of which they kept for themselves while pretending to weave the emperor's new clothes.

When the weavers announced that the clothes were ready, the emperor sent a succession of trusted ministers to see them. Not wanting to appear unfit for office or stupid, they all reported that the new clothes were lovely. Finally, the emperor himself went to examine the clothes, which were so heartily praised by his subordinates. Although he saw nothing, he proclaimed, "Oh! The cloth is beautiful! I am delighted with the clothes!"

On the day of the great procession, the emperor disrobed, put on his "new clothes," and marched through the kingdom. Never before had any of the emperor's clothes caused so much excitement! Then a small child said, "But the emperor has nothing on at all!" The child was not yet constrained by the forces that silenced the adult crowd and caused them, despite what they saw, to agree with their superior's false judgment.

This story is an example of events that all too often occur in colleges. Not wanting to appear unfit or stupid, faculty members conform to the current consensus about instruction and are afraid to challenge the methods so widely used. The tradition of the old paradigm continues with the pretense that all is well.

CONCLUSION

The problem of college student attrition and achievement has troubled educators for more than 60 years. Many studies have been conducted to investigate the possible causes of the problem. Researchers have studied the demographic factors, examined personality characteristics, investigated interpersonal dimensions, and constructed causal models. Although research provided important information, their descriptive findings presented limited data and did not isolate specific factors to which interventions could be targeted.

Academic performance is thought to be the single most important factor contributing to attrition. Unfortunately, when utilized, the academic approach to retention programs focused on remediation rather than the students' individual learning-style characteristics and the differences in how they processed and retained academic knowledge. Many independent researchers have reported that identifying individuals' learning-style strengths was the first step towards improving their academic achievement (Dunn and Griggs, 2004; *Research on the Dunn and Dunn Model, 2003*).

The overall goal of all higher education institutions and their faculty is to educate students (*Goals 2000: Educate America Act,* 1996). However, in many institutions, between one third and one fourth of entering freshmen *drop out* and are not graduated, thus failing to fulfill their professors', their parents', and their own career and life goals. One of the reasons for so many students' inability to be graduated may be the lack of professorial awareness of how differently students in the same course learn. Therefore, it may be derived from this research that college professors, like Dr. Morissey, need to identify students' learning-style preferences AND implement learning-style methodology into their own teaching repertoire.

REFERENCES

Berry, B., Hoke, M., and Hirsch, E. (2004). The search for highly qualified teachers. *Phi Delta Kappa, 85*, pp. 684-689.

Burke, K. (2000a). Math education, learning styles, and the standards: The winning tri-mathlon. *Impact on Instructional Improvement,* Association of Supervision and Curriculum Development, *29*(2), 13-19.

Burke, K. (2000b). Chapter 9: A paradigm shift: Learning-style intervention in undergraduate education. In Rita Dunn and Shirley Griggs, *Practical Approaches to Using Learning Styles in Higher Education.* Westport, CT: Greenwood Publishing Group.

Canfield and Lafferty (1970). *Learning Styles Inventory.* Detroit: Humanics Media (Liberty Drawer).

Claxton, C. S., and Murrell, P. H. (1988). *Learning styles.* Retrieved February 5, 2004 www.eduref.crg/plweb-cgi/obtain.pl ERIC Digest NO: ED 301143.

Dunn, R. (2000). Capitalizing on college students' learning styles: Theory, practice, and research. In R. Dunn and S. A. Griggs (Eds.), *Practical Approaches to Using Learning Styles in Higher Education,* (pp. 3-18). Westport, CT: Bergin and Garvey.

Dunn, R., Bruno, J., Sklar, R.I., and Beaudry, J. (1990, May/June). Effects of matching and mismatching minority developmental college students' hemispheric preferences on mathematics scores. *Journal of Educational Research, 83*(5), 283-288.

Dunn, R., Burke, K. and Whitley, J. (2000). What do know about learning style? A guide for parents of talented children. *Parenting for High Potential,* June, 8-13.

Dunn, R., Cavanaugh, D., Eberle, B., and Zenhausern, R. (1982). Hemispheric preference: The newest element of learning style. *The American Biology Teacher, 44,* 291-294.

Dunn, K. and Dunn, R. (1978). *Teaching students through their individual learning styles: A practical approach.* Englewood Cliffs, NJ: Prentice-Hall.

Dunn, R., and Dunn, K., (1999). The complete guide to the learning-styles inservice system. Boston: Allyn and Bacon.

Dunn, R., Dunn, K., and Price, G. E. (1984, 1986, 1989, 1990, 1991, 1993, 1996, 2000, 2001, 2002). *Productivity Environmental Preference Survey.* Lawrence, KS: Price Systems.

Dunn, R., and Griggs, S. A. (Eds.). (2000). *Practical approaches to using learning styles in higher education.* Westport, CT: Bergin and Garvey.

Dunn, R., and Griggs, S. A. (Eds.) (2004). *Synthesis of the Dunn and Dunn learning style model research: Who, what, when, where, and so what?* NY: St. John's University Center for the Study of Learning and Teaching Styles.

Entwistle, N., and Ramsden, D. (1983). *Understanding student learning.* London, England: Croon-Helm.

Goals 2000: Educate America Act (April, 1996). Increasing student achievement through state and local initiatives. Retrieved February 16, 2004. *http://www.ed.gov*

Hill, J. (1981). *The educational sciences: A conceptual framework.* West Bloomfield Hills, MI: Oakland Hill Educational Sciences Foundation.

Hunt, D. E. (1971). *Paragraph completion method.* Toronto, Canada. Ontario Institute for Studies in Education.

Kirby, P. (1979). *Cognitive styles, learning style, and transfer skill acquisition (Information series No 195).* Columbus, OH: The Ohio State University, National Center for Research in Vocational Education.

Knight, J. (2004). Internationalization remodeled: Definition, approaches, and rationales. *Journal of Studies in International Education, 8*(1), pp. 5-31.

Kolb, D. A. (1981). Experiential learning theory and the learning style inventory: A reply to Friedman and Stumpf. *Academy of Management Review, 6*(2), 289-296.

Rebell, M. A., and Hunter, M. A., (2004). Highly qualified teachers: Pretense or legal requirement. *Phi Delta Kappa, 85,* pp. 690 - 696.

Restak, R. (1979*). The brain: The last frontier.* New York, NY: Doubleday.

Schmeck, R. R., Ribich, F. D., and Ramanaiah,N. (1977). Development of a self-report inventory for assisting individual differences in learning processes. *Applied Psychological Measurement, 1*(3), 413-431.

Shea, L. J. (2004). A historical analysis of the international learning styles network and its impact on instructional innovation. Lampeter, Ceredigion, United Kingdom: The Edwin Mellen Press.

Thies, A. (1979). A brain-behavior analysis of learning style. In J. Keefe (Ed.), *Student learning styles: Diagnosing and prescribing programs* (pp. 55-61). Reston, VA: National Association of Secondary School Principals.

Thies, A. (1999-2000). The neuropsychology of learning styles. *National Forum of Applied Educational Research Journal, 13*(1), 50-62.

Travis, J. E. (1996). *Models for improving college teaching.* Retrieved February 5, 2004 www.eduref.org/plweb-cgi/obtain.pl ERIC Digest NO: ED 403810.

Witkin, H. (1976). Cognitive style in academic performance and in teacher relations. In S. Messick (Ed.), *Individuality in learning,* (pp.173-192). San Francisco: Jossey-Bass.

In: Adult Education: Issues and Developments
Editors: P. N. Blakely, A. H. Tomlin, pp. 217-229
ISBN: 978-1-60456-272-9

Chapter 5

TEACHING ADULT LEARNERS THROUGH A LEARNING STYLES APPROACH: AN ANECDOTAL REFLECTION ON 44 YEARS OF TEACHING EXPERIENCE

Bill Purkiss

ABSTRACT

Exploring selected events and themes developed over forty-four years of teaching at a number of educational levels, the chapter discusses the movement from an intuitive approach to learning styles-based teaching, into one that reflected a studied and strategized approach to learning styles. Comparing the teaching theories of Viola Spolin and David Kolb, it shows how the explorational techniques utilized in teaching theatre proved to be a perfect entrée into a more academic discipline and its traditional classroom. Also discussed are the ways in which forms of student diversity are positively addressed in the learning styles-based classroom.

The way we process the possibilities of each new emerging event determines the range of choices and decisions we see. The choices and decisions we make, to some extent, determine the events we live through, and these events influence our future choices. Thus, people create themselves through their choice of the actual occasions they live through. . . . Human individuality results from the pattern or 'program' created by our choices and their consequences. (Kolb, 1984, p. 64)

INTRODUCTION

As teachers, we have access to a wealth of information about the pupils we instruct. At the community college level, this writer's area of experience and expertise, we have a tremendous amount of background concerning each student we teach. Each student's history has been gathered, covering approximately twelve years of schooling. These histories reflect the relative success each student has encountered, his/her areas of apparent academic strength and potential, age, race, and gender. They include some information about the student's socio-economic condition, his/her assessed abilities in communication and calculation, and finally, some norm-referenced predictions as to just how well this student might do in the post secondary environment. With all this information, however, the sad truth is that a large portion of each group of students we encounter either fail to accomplish or meet only a small amount of the goals that they initially establish for themselves in the higher educational academic *milieu*. Where does the root of the failure lie, and what kinds of strategies might be utilized in order to positively engage these students in the learning process?

The reader should immediately take note of the fact that this piece is not a scholarly treatise that attempts to empirically prove a specific point of exploration. It is not an attempt to lay down a new rule or guidepost in the theory of learning. Rather, this is a reflection on over forty years of practicum, scholarly reflection, and interdisciplinary teaching experience as they relate to the utilization of learning styles theory in my own classroom. It is my hope that some of my reminiscences might in some way aid teachers inexperienced with learning styles theory to make their own connection with and integration of learning styles into their own professional endeavors.

AN INTUITIVE APPROACH TO LEARNING STYLES

My career in teaching began as an instructor at the high school level, teaching literature and theatre. Moving to the arena of the community college after four years, my focus was sharpened into a career as a theatre professor. While teaching theatre, I became aware of a very interesting phenomenon. I found that theatre departments tend to be filled with students who often are initially considered by institutional standards to be less than academically capable and are seemingly unfit and certainly unprepared for the college or university classroom. The reading levels were generally quite low, often down at the eighth-grade level, math and science levels were even lower, and the capacity and curiosity for abstract conceptualization appeared to be non-existent. They were most often very gregarious, energetic young people who had somehow come to the conclusion that being a serious student was not in their cards. However, after becoming involved in a theatre production, acting class, or even technical assignments in the preparation of dramatic presentations, these students would often display much higher abilities and even mastery of the basic skills needed for a pursuit of a college education and would many times go on to work in other disciplines with unexpected and unexplained success.

Why did it seem to be that students who would run away as fast as they could at the mere suggestion of reading *King Lear*, would suddenly become able and intelligent apologists for the play, the Bard, and all that goes with a comprehensive understanding of the Shakespearean experience once they were placed in a situation wherein they would help to make it into a tangible living experience? What was the magic that brought these "incapable" students into the realm of competency across a broad range of both literary and theoretical subjects? Students would be seen on campus arguing the issues of the play, the interpretation of parts, and the juxtaposition of societal and often scientific issues between the dramatic moment and real life. How did this happen? Was it simply maturation and the enculturation process they would undergo as they spent more and more time on the college campus, or was there more going on that created this greater acuity and competency? I suggest that it was much, much more.

During much of my early, pre-doctoral career, I had no clue concerning the answer to the above question. For the most part, my work in theatre tended to be based more on intuitive processes, including improvisation and collaboration, than on rigid or impositional processes. For me, the adage that I would live and work by was simply that there was a reason that the activity was called "a play" and not "a work, a hard, or a difficult." The theatre classroom is one in which students and teachers should "play" together in the pursuit of the life truths that are locked in the black and white abstraction that is a written drama. When my students and I embarked on a mission of actualization that was *Hamlet, Evita, A Streetcar Named Desire,* or *Man of La Mancha,* to name only a few of the more than a hundred plays that I directed, the rule was to engage in improvisation, play and discovery, rather than strict adherence to theory, structure, and intellectual purity. The amazing thing, however, was that the theory, structure and intellectual impulses of the piece ultimately became manifest in both the presentation and in the consciousness and cognitive processes of the students involved.

DESTROYING THE "MYSTERY" IN LEARNING

I found that finding deeper truths in the literature lay in the release of the tension that was born of judgment and overbearing control by the teacher/director, the seeming font of knowledge, out of whom all truths traditionally seemed to flow. We did play, but as small children play. We played with energetic abandonment and a sense of freedom, rather than restriction. Watch the difference in little children when two options are placed before them. When given the order to clean up their bedroom, they tend to become sullen, tired, and unengaged, however, when given the opportunity to go play, they suddenly become energetic, filled with inspiration, and deeply engaged. Somehow, in my student's process of play, there was a release that took place, setting the students free to explore, openly diving into some often obtuse and deeply subtle conceptual material, doing so mainly because it "felt" more like play than it did serious "academic inquiry." There was no threat, no fear of failure in the process. My job was transformed from the "holder of the mysteries," as is so often the assumed role of the professor in the academic *milieu,* becoming rather a partner in the explorational pursuit of a common goal. I was the person who did possess information that the students needed, but instead of my informing them that they needed this information, they would demand it from me as it became clear to them that it was a necessary tool to continue on to this exciting and enjoyable goal they had committed to accomplish.

An example of such an explorational pursuit of a common goal would be when I directed an experimental production of *Romeo and Juliet.* In planning for the production, the decision had been made to create the piece without extensive scenery or costumes. The idea was to utilize the techniques of pantomime and imagination, rather than actualizing the physical environments to be played. For many of the scenes, this process provided little challenge, but the balcony scene was especially tricky. By its very title, "the balcony scene," there is a need for two stories for the actors to work from, and the environment of a medieval courtyard had to be presented in some way for the scene to be realized. When we came to that moment in the script, I simply stated that somehow we had to find this balcony and courtyard, and then we discussed the challenge as a group of actors and technical support persons. A supply of pictorial materials dealing with such things as period architecture, balconies, and gargoyles was sitting beside the rehearsal area. It became clear from our group reading of the scene and viewing some of the pictures in the resource materials, that somehow, Juliet had to be above Romeo at the first of the scene, he had to climb up to her level in the middle, and then climb back down to finish the scene. The students were separated into small "discovery" groups, in which the problem of the physical scene would be explored. Looking perhaps, more like a cheerleading squad, rather than a cast of players, they began lifting a "designated Juliet" in each of the groups. After a given time for such exploration, each group shared its findings with the rest of the cast and crew.

Ultimately, it was a technical crew member who found the answer to lifting Juliet, by employing a small, hand-held platform that would rest upon the shoulders of four large male actors. And it was an actor, one who searched the books for an exciting picture of Medieval balconies and gargoyle decorations, who found the answer to the rest of the scene. This actor proposed that the four men who carried Juliet would slowly let her down as Romeo approached, and they would turn, kneel, and assume the kneeling position of gargoyles he had found in the research. Romeo would then climb up over the four men and be with Juliet on her level. It was done without any real scenery being built, and the audience was, in the end of it all, thrilled to have the picture created for them through their imagination. The process had moved from simple play and exploration to what was an imaginative rendition of the period environment called for in the play. All this was done by the students with minimal assistance or directed activity on my part. They became the articulators of authentic, period Shakespeare by the use of play, experimentation, and self-directed research. The necessity of the theoretical and historical material needed to actualize the piece emerged as clearly to them in their work as would the need for a specific tool be obvious to a craftsman repairing something in one's house.

A New Teaching Style

Getting students to perform such activities requires a very clear teaching style. In the theatre, a teacher must be skilled in the development of a creative ensemble. The object of such work is to produce a working company of actors who have no fear of exploration toward a goal, and who are led to set aside individual, ego-driven goals for a more compelling group oriented objective. Perhaps the finest teacher of ensemble-based theatre that I have ever encountered was Viola Spolin. Ms Spolin was the co-founder of the performance group, "Second City," in Chicago, and she was the creator of the landmark text, *Improvisation for the Theatre: A handbook of teaching and directing techniques* (1985). In the introduction to her book, she presented a credo for teachers of acting, but ultimately a challenge to all teachers who wish to teach in a manner that utilizes learning style methodologies to create the widest possible range of engagement for their students, with the sum effect being the broadest level of learning having taken place. As she put it:

> We learn through experience and experiencing, and no one teaches anyone anything. This is as true for the infant moving from kicking to crawling to walking as it is for the scientist with his equations.

If the environment permits it, anyone can learn whatever he or she chooses to learn; and if the individual permits it, the environment will teach him or her everything it has to teach. 'Talent' or 'lack of talent' has little to do with it.

Intuition is often thought to be an endowment or a mystical force enjoyed by the gifted alone. Yet all of us have known moments when the right answer just came' or we did 'exactly the right thing without thinking.' Sometimes at such moments . . . when a person functions beyond a constricted intellectual plane, he or she is truly open for learning. . . .

A way is needed to get to intuitive knowledge. It requires an environment in which experiencing can take place, a person free to experience, and an activity that brings about spontaneity. (p. 3)

A few moments should be taken to reflect on Ms Spolin's salient points, and how they connect to learning styles. To my knowledge, Viola never wrote a treatise dealing with learning in the general sense, nor did she ever meet or interact with learning styles theorists like David Kolb. She concentrated her published comments on the specific process of teaching acting. However, when one looks at what she espoused, the concepts tend to parallel the tenets brought forth by David Kolb and others who spoke about experiential learning. When she spoke of an "environment in which experiencing can take place, a person free to experience, and an activity that brings about spontaneity," she alluded to the same kind of environment that Kolb spoke of when he suggested that ". . . experiential learning theory (embodies) a holistic integrative perspective on learning that combines experience, perception, cognition, and behavior (Kolb, p. 21)." He went on to say in a way not unlike Spolin, "Immediate personal experience is the focal point for testing the implications and validity of ideas created during the learning process. When human beings share an experience, they can share it fully, concretely, and abstractly (Ibid.)."

As I read both Kolb and Spolin, I saw that both spoke of the learning dynamic as being an ongoing process that combines the reflections of previously gained knowledge with the integration of new experience and concept. Kolb said that:

Everyone enters every learning situation with more or less articulate ideas about the topic at hand. We are all psychologists, historians, and atomic physicists. It is just that some of our theories are more crude and incorrect than others (p.28).

As the earlier quote by Spolin demonstrates, she parallels Kolb with the statement that:

We learn through experience and experiencing, and no one teaches anyone anything. This is as true for the infant moving from kicking to crawling to walking as it is for the scientist with his equations.

If the environment permits it, anyone can learn whatever he or she chooses to learn; and if the individual permits it, the environment will teach him or her everything it has to teach.

Both Spolin and Kolb maintained that students come to us with a storehouse of knowledge that has been gained in a number of ways. It may not be formally structured as the discipline might ultimately demand, and it might not in any way utilize the semantic or linguistic formulas of the discipline to describe the known phenomena, but still, usable and functional knowledge exists prior to when we first encounter these students.

Adjusting for Differences

Given the assumption of such insight, however, the teacher, must consider that though these students may have knowledge, it is quite possible, really quite probable, that the knowledge is different, and perceived and acted upon with great variance from student to student. The known challenges we face today with cultural, age-oriented, gender-based, economic driven and sexual orientation diversity in perception and actualization, are in themselves staggering. The ability to create an ensemble of collaborative learners is perhaps more challenged today than ever before. The major issues seem to lie in how we bring that previously gained, diverse working knowledge into some kind of confluence with an ordered discipline, making further, more structured examination and learning possible, and how do we bring together students with such potentially different storehouses and action modes of conceptual material?

To me, the central problem encountered in the attempt to address the above challenges is found in the long-standing traditions established at the post secondary level. Where pedagogy and classroom learning strategies have long been the subject of elementary and secondary school agendas, the post secondary arena has languished, rather bathed in the *milieu* of the lecture. For the college or university academician, a major challenge to be faced in teaching at that level has been the expressed need for a proper sense of rigor and theoretical engagement that seemed only to be accomplished through the lecture mode. One year prior to my retirement, I was elected by my peers to be the "Faculty Lecturer of the Year" at Chaffey. This is one of the most prestigious honors to be given any faculty member, and I deeply appreciated the acknowledgement. However, the very title of the award, faculty "lecturer," reinforces the sense of traditional importance that has been placed upon the transference of information (and presumably learning) through the lecture process. College teachers, above all others, are expected to be and therefore to show themselves, as the great font of knowledge. To suggest less is seen as academic weakness. Historically, the reigning assumption has been that lectures, lectures that are fat with facts, statistics, and data, are the positive driving force in a powerful college education. The student has by tradition, been relegated to the position of having to make sense of the lecture, take notes effectively, hold questions until the end (as if that were really practical), and then be able to either answer questions in some form of true/false or "multiple guess" format, or write an intelligent essay based upon what he or she had gleaned from the professor's message. Thus it is that some of the weakest teaching that occurs at all levels of the learning pyramid often takes place in the college or university classroom. I and other teachers with similar goals as mine have had to immediately address this tradition or never be able to make progress toward the utilization of student learning styles in my classroom.

Facility Issues

Another challenge to the process of setting up a classroom for learning styles based teaching is the fact that a college professor's room is rarely his or her own. Often, the teacher will teach the same class in a number of different venues with each presenting a new and difficult set of roadblocks to learning. Differences in classroom configuration, technology, acoustics, and climate control can make the exact same classroom experience seem totally unrelated to itself when presented in two such diverse environments. The opportunity to set up a room that will be only yours to use is veritably nonexistent at the post secondary level. For me, a system had to be established that made the utilization of learning styles in the college classroom feasible. It had to be mobile, self-contained, and able to work in a variety of different environments. Unlike the elementary, and to some extent the secondary level of learning in which learning areas, resource centers, activity centers, and reflection/discussion areas are semi-permanent fixtures, in the college classroom, those fixtures simply could not exist in the same way.

In my own teaching career, I found what I believe to be the answer to the troubling traditions and physical realities found in the academic arena of higher education after I left the theatre, went on to Chaffey Community College to become the Dean of Instruction and, following five years as an administrator, returned to the classroom as a communication studies teacher. My change in disciplines provided me with a different venue in which to try the techniques that I had gleaned from teaching in the theatrical environment. Concurrent with my move to Chaffey, I began my doctoral work at the Claremont Graduate School in the field of higher education, with an emphasis on cultural diversity and alternative pedagogies. It was there that a formal understanding and ordering of the intuitive information that I had developed in teaching theatre came to be. The situation also provided me with a ready-made laboratory for the process of bringing together the theory that I was learning with the practices that I had previously developed. The results were more than gratifying.

First of all, it became clear to me that I had to develop a clearer formula or *schema* than I had utilized in my theatre classroom. The idea of play, although a powerful one in that venue, might need some adjustment in order for it to work effectively in a more traditionally "academic" environment. The elements that were most important, however, were those of free exploration, free association, and individual empowerment, rather than hierarchical, authority-driven formats. The schema that worked the most effectively in theatre and that I suspected would from the outset of teaching communication, involved moving from a very general introductory experience to a specific, discipline-defined, and intellectually articulated exploration. I had found while working in the theatre, that an introduction to any learning experience is more powerful if the students are not intimidated or in some way made afraid of the subject to be engaged. My rehearsals always began with some form of game that had some relevance to the goals of the rehearsal, but in the eyes of the students, seemed to simply be fun. So it was that I began each new communication unit of study with some form of open experience that the students could share, but not fear.

A Practical, Style-Based Example

When introducing Jungian personality styles, for example, I selected four scenes from current movies, in which I was able to identify persons with close to archetypal personality style qualities. I would not introduce the scenes as being important elements of the unit, however. I played a game with the students. Utilizing the popular theme of dating to hook student interest, I broke the class into small groups and asked them to pretend that a character who performed in the scene I was going to show them was someone that they knew. Additionally, they had a best friend who had been asked out on a date by that character in the scene and who wanted to know as much about the character as they could before they went out on the date. I directed them to consider that their friend had asked them to describe the character to them, as to "just what kind of a person is he/she?" The small group was then to gather together a list of adjectives that would describe the character to their friend. After a short time, they were then to put the group's adjectives on the blackboard for all to see. This activity was repeated four times with each situation being based upon the students developing some adjectives to help their friend have a better idea of this character who had asked them out on a date. What came forth was a list of non-theoretical but accurate descriptions of the Jungian archetypal models. Following this informal and seemingly innocuous "game," I then introduced the Jungian model as a theoretical construct. The students got it every time! The level of understanding they demonstrated was astonishing.

One could say that, of course a discipline like communication lends itself to such an exercise, but this would never work in the math and sciences classroom. I have to disagree. While acquiring my doctorate, the greatest hurdle I knew that I faced was the Statistics class. I have always had a strong fear of mathematics and really, all things abstract. My doctoral advisor said to me that I certainly could do qualitative work rather than quantitative, but we both would know that I had ducked out of my real challenge. To me, it was the kiss of death. I enrolled in the statistics class, and the first day, the teacher, David Drew, lined us all up against one wall. We were asked to stand from the tallest person on one side, progressing by height difference to the shortest person at the other. He then proceeded to show us what an average was. He gave one person a calculator, and the person moved along the line and input each person's height. The person then divided the total by the number of people in the line. As one might expect, the average height rested between two people in the line. No one was "average." Suddenly, I knew I was home. This man gave us experiences before he gave us theory. He provided open experiences, gave us opportunities to see the phenomena could be replicated, and then, after solidifying the linguistic and theoretical structure of the concept being taught, he gave us problems to solve. It worked, and I ended up doing quite well in the class. I am sure that with some creative play consciousness and a desire to engage on a style-based level, any math or science teacher could successfully use this technique.

Here then, is the formula that I utilized to great success in my classes. First an open, seemingly unimportant experience, followed by a secondary experience that allowed the students to see that there was more to the experience than a singular phenomenon. Following these two experiences would come an introduction to the language and theoretical framework of the unit, and last, an experimental unit in which the students utilized the theory in some physical, real-world situation. Continuing the Jungian example, following the opening scenes, I shared a second set of scenes, in which the students could recognize the similarities of some characters to ones in the first set of scenes. After that, I would administer the Jungian model developed by David Kiersey, and the students would learn their particular personality style letters. I prepared a brief description of each of the sixteen personalities as identified in the Kiersey sorter, and gave it to the students when they finished taking the test and scored it. They were intrigued by how well this experience identified their personal style. They wanted to know how it worked. We then had a lecture discussion along with assigned reading concerning the Jungian model, followed by another set of scenes in which the students would gather in small groups and identify the characters by identifying each one's four letter style. They would then share with the class both their findings, and the defense of their choice on the basis of the theoretical model. Together, we would develop a list of questions that could suggest to an interviewer what personality style traits a person they would encounter might possess. Finally, the students would go out of the class in pairs and interview other students on campus and attempt to identify these stranger's styles. Ultimately, an essay examination would be administered, in which I asked the students to individually identify a new set of movie character's styles in a totally new set of scenes and to defend their choices based upon Jungian theory.

Teaching Via the Circle of Learning

If one looks at that example and then considers the circle of learning style qualities listed in Kolb, one finds that my Jungian exercise closely follows that model. Kolb speaks of the first and most universal learning quality as "concrete experiential" learning. It is the learning we first encountered as infants. We experience something, and we learn based upon the nature of the experience and the ultimate effect that it has had on our consciousness. Kolb, of course, describes this form of learning as "grasping via apprehension." (p. 42) The open experience at the beginning of the unit was absolute concrete experiential learning. The students only worked with what they were openly and collectively experiencing. There was no fear or negative reaction because the moment seemed to be only fun and without a heavy academic "load."

The second part of the experience, seeing a second set of scenes, presents what Kolb calls "reflective observation," or "divergent knowledge." (Ibid.) In this area of learning, the student finds more examples of a phenomenon, realizing that the first experience was not unique or anachronistic, but a recognizable quality, concept, or repeatable phenomenon. In this mode, the important step is to recognize the replicable experience, and that it is a quality that one can identify again and again.

The third step in the exercise was to identify and formalize the theory and semantic of the experience. In this moment, an agreement is made between the teacher and student that in order for us to be able to commonly discuss the different qualities that we have individually identified and described, we will use the language of the theory, and that our anecdotal descriptions have a place in a theoretical structure. This learning quality is described by Kolb as "abstract conceptualization," or "grasping via comprehension." (Ibid.) After this experience, only the common language and structural matrix of the theory would be used to discuss the phenomena.

Finally, the last step of the circle and the exercise involved the students going forth into real world situations and utilizing the theoretical framework, followed by an essay examination on the material. This situation is described by Kolb as "active experimentation," or "convergent" and "accommodative" knowledge. In this area, exploration and experimentation are the ruling factors. The students must go forth into the world and identify their own sources of study of the theoretical foundation, followed by a consolidating experience of an examination in which they must not only identify the stylistic elements, but also develop a defense for their choices.

I found that pursuing engagement with my students by utilization of this circle of learning created a viable learning experience for my classes. It provided me with a map for my preparation that never failed me. It also was a much more enjoyable and creative environment in my classes. Students were much more attentive, unafraid to engage with the lesson or me, and they were much more empowered to take on their education rather than be driven by me.

An Added Diversity-Based Dividend

A major dividend that my process provided for my classes was the answer to the issue of cultural diversity and relevance of examples in class. As said earlier in this chapter, we are living in a time of enormous challenge by the recognition of cultural diversity as a primary driving force in education today. When I was a young student, and when I was a new teacher, the issue of diversity of culture, gender, age, sexuality, or socio-economic difference was never dealt with. First of all, our culture was much more segregated than it is today. There was a majority culture of white males, and the driving force was that of white perspective. Over the period of sixty years at the end of the 20th and the beginning of the 21st centuries, an enormous change has taken place in our culture. We are a culture that has mixed its differences to a very great degree. The educational challenge comes from the realization that in earlier times, an example could usually be given by the teacher that would be understood by the students, as the teacher would usually come from the same cultural impulse as his/her students. When I went to school, my teachers were all white, and so were my fellow students. Additionally, the ruling impulse was male, so all images and examples tended to be male-dominated. Today, our classrooms are a veritable salad of different culture, ethnicity, gender and socio-economic difference. Where the past utilization of examples and concepts in a class could possibly be tailored to the unified cultural background of the class, today, no such unity exists. Any example or idea put forth by a teacher runs a real risk of irrelevance or total lack of understanding for a large portion of the students in the class. The area of culture alone provides much difficulty because of the difference in meaning and importance that different groups place on experience in the world. Hence, the beginning of each unit with a shared, unqualified experience provides the students with something common to reflect upon. They may have different ways of viewing the phenomenon, but commonalities found in a shared experience are much easier to identify than they would be in some abstract reference that an instructor might present. When we speak of an experience, the person hearing creates his or her own specific, culture-bound image of what we have said. When the experience is real, concrete, and there for them to have, but in common with the other students, a richness of dialogue develops, along with the identification of common insights.

Teaching to Style or Teaching in Style?

A final consideration on my process of addressing student learning styles in my classes revolves around the question of whether to teach to student's individual styles, or to try to engage students in a broader personal learning process. In this process, they might at the onset of my class be individually invested in a particular learning style, and then as the class moves forward, be able to successfully navigate the learning experience of other and to them, more challenging styles. I think that higher education must move in a direction that goes forward, beyond either elementary or secondary educational models. In those models, an emphasis is often placed on students learning from their own personal style and connecting with persons of like style for purposes of study and class action. According to Rita Dunn (1996) in her short book, *How to Implement and Supervise a Learning Style Program* (ASCD, p.26), elementary and to an extent, secondary level students are focused on their personal learning style and learning requirements, and are often encouraged to study and learn according to their individual learning styles. College students by contrast, are taught in a more traditional venue that only rarely acknowledges different learning styles, usually investing in an afore-mentioned uniform delivery system that revolves around the lecture format.

The question that surrounds teaching the college student who is usually a more mature student, lies in whether the major impulse of the class should be stressing the individual learning idiosyncrasies of each student, or to as best as possible, get each student to begin to learn from all four quadrants of the style wheel? My choice was to pursue the latter course, attempting to take all the students around the wheel of style, involving them all in a holistic encounter with style. I perceived that the situation that these students generally would face when they moved out into the non-academic world demanded that they be free to experience openly and learn from it, to be able to gather research and supporting proof that the experience is not just an anachronism, identify and freely relate to the theoretical structure and the language of an issue, and to competently and confidently explore new experiments that utilize previously established paradigms, and when appropriate, challenge those paradigms. Additionally, I chose to personally and pedagogically challenge what I considered to be a myth about traditionally "higher learning" styles versus more balanced forms of stylistic learning strategies. I firmly believe that all students need to learn more holistically.

Addressing first the idea that many in higher education hold that the highest form of learning involves that of the abstract conceptual learner; I simply do not accept that premise. Colleges and especially universities tend to pride themselves in the inundation of students in logical forms and experimental models. Often the idea of "rigor" simply means a stricter sense of formulaic language and abstract models. I have no problem with this sense of rigor. However, college students are placed in situations in the "real world" that involves them in forming judgments that require more than the ability to simply deal with theory and abstract modeling. I believe that we often do our students a great disservice by simply directing them into primarily abstract models. When critics of academia speak of a need for "common sense," I believe that they are referring to the ability to deal with the world in very concrete and experimental ways that go beyond the restrictions of theory and abstraction. Recent movements in to the area of "service learning," in which students are sent forth into the community to do curriculum-based volunteer work are attempts at injecting that sense of experience into the college curriculum. However, I strongly felt that the use of experience, both simple and complex should regularly be part and parcel of every classroom learning matrix, rather than relegated to an adjunct experience beyond the core curriculum.

I found in much of my teaching and relationship with other teachers, that there is a sense of holding more abstract conceptual students back when they are placed in a situation of concrete experience, collaborative learning, or active experimentation. If the student can grasp the concept, then the rest is not needed. More traditionally oriented professors contend that styles-driven pedagogical models are only for those students who are "slower," or less capable of learning. Often colleagues consider such strategies to be a process of coddling or watering-down the curriculum. I intensely disagree. In my time in the classroom I observed that students with different learning styles brought things to the classroom that had the capability of broadening the perspective of different concepts. Instead of watering-down the curriculum, it became richer by the different processes of inquiry. Where the concrete-experiential students might have difficulty in dealing with an intellectual construct, the abstract-conceptual students would often have a measure of difficulty with actually getting in and doing or experiencing a concept in action. I found it to be extremely important that students ultimately be able and willing to enter the learning environment at whatever point on the wheel that the particular situation presented. This requires that students develop a process of "strategic learning," as described by Riding and Rayner (1998). They speak of a process that "will lead [the student] to the development of a strategy of translating learning material into the preferred mode where this is possible." (p. 79) Riding and Rayner go on to speak of a learner developing a "repertoire of learning strategies – a cognitive tool-kit." (Ibid.)

A Second Example

A powerful example of this transformative experience in which students actively utilized the full circle of learning styles came in a book review assignment that I regularly used in both my gender communication and intercultural communication classes. I firmly believe in enriching a class offering with outside reading. Additionally, it seems to me that, in this age of computers, cyberspace, and graphic visual extravagance, that much of the joy of reading has been lost to many in the younger generations. I selected a set of six brand new writings dealing either directly or indirectly with the course curriculum and allowed the students to select one of the books to read. However, I would set a limit as to how many people could sign up for any individual book. The idea was to set up first reading teams and then teaching teams. The groups would set up reading assignments for themselves, covering a certain number of pages in the book for each meeting that they had. After all the students in the group had read the book, they were then challenged to "teach" the book to the rest of the class. The assignment was not to create a "report" with posters and presentational material that basically demonstrates that the individuals in the group had read the book. Instead, their assignment was to create an environment that facilitated the other students learning the concepts presented in the book. My judgment of the "teachers" would be based upon how effectively they singly and as a group, communicated the material to the other students. The only requirement of the rest of the class was that they be there to learn from the presenting group. This was free learning. The "students" didn't need to take notes or to hold on to the material after the class experience. The amazing thing is that they did. The student teachers had powerful engagement in the books that they read and taught. Instead of simply a written book report that often would be forgotten once it was complete, for the most part, these students kept the material and the concepts that they explored and many times would see me years after taking the class and be able to tell me about the book and its insights.

The results of the reading assignment were astounding. First of all, the students charged with teaching the material felt compelled to create all manner of visual and tactile materials to accompany their presentation. They prepared study guides for the other students that briefly took the students through the book that they were teaching. And finally, the students charged with learning the material were totally engaged in the book and the teachers, actively taking part in discussions concerning the content and the inferences presented. It was exciting and it was a powerful learning styles directed assignment. Regularly, students came away from my class either borrowing a book that they had been introduced to by their fellow students, or actually buying the book.

CONCLUSION

In my view, the students that I worked with went away from my classes with a sense of empowerment that allowed them to work with both the abstract and the concrete models of learning. They felt comfortable seeking extra information in the form of divergent knowledge, and the ultimate excitement came in the experimental quadrant of the wheel, or the accommodative knowledge, when they physically stepped out into the college or community and actively utilized the conceptual model in a real world situation. The classroom was committed to a spirit of play and exploration rather than drudgery and discipline, but the students worked and with a high level of discipline. It was a self-imposed rather than teacher imposed level of discipline. Additionally, and to my real pleasure, the students worked in cadres that reflected the great diversity in the population that now populate our colleges and universities. Most of all, they succeeded at a much higher rate than students did prior to my insertion of learning styles strategies.

This has been an admittedly anecdotal series of reflections concerning a forty-four year career in teaching. I have left teaching, not because I have tired of it, but because I do not care if I ever attend another faculty meeting, curriculum council, or faculty senate gathering. If I could have merely spent my time interacting with students, I might never have left the profession. I can say that the last years of my teaching were some of the most enjoyable and productive that I ever had. I firmly believe that my involvement with learning styles theory and strategies through my work in theatre, and the willingness to explore with it in a more traditionally academic discipline made it so. Facing up to the challenge of a more universal engagement through styles strategies is exciting and daunting at first. But in the end, it is far more fulfilling and successful than any other strategy that I have experienced. I challenge all teachers to take the step of entering and playing in the arena of learning styles-based strategies. I would urge them to take the risk of laying down the burden of being the font of knowledge and join in the joint exploration of their discipline with student colleagues. They just might find it to be as fulfilling and successful as I did.

REFERENCES

Dunn, R. (1996). *How to implement and supervise a learning style program.* Alexandria, Virginia: Association for Supervision and Curriculum Development (ASCD).

Kolb, D. A. (1984). *Experiential learning: experience as the source of learning and development.* Englewood Cliffs, New Jersey: Prentice Hall.

Riding, R., and Rayner, S. (1998). *Cognitive styles and learning strategies: Understanding style differences in learning and behaviour.* London: David Fulton Publishers.

Spolin, V. (1985). *Improvisation for the theatre: A handbook of teaching and directing techniques.* Evanston: Northwestern University Press.

In: Adult Education: Issues and Developments
Editors: P. N. Blakely, A. H. Tomlin, pp. 231-251

ISBN: 978-1-60456-272-9
© 2008 Nova Science Publishers, Inc.

Chapter 6

THE FIELD DEPENDENCE/FIELD INDEPENDENCE LEARNING STYLES: IMPLICATIONS FOR ADULT STUDENT DIVERSITY, OUTCOMES ASSESSMENT AND ACCOUNTABILITY

Blue Wooldridge and Melanie Haimes-Bartolf

ABSTRACT

In this chapter the authors define and describe the Field Independence-Dependence (FI/FD) Cognitive Learning Style as developed by Herman Witkin. The evolution of FI/FD is described and discussed, along with significant research findings. Special emphasis focuses on research that demonstrate individual differences in students, and that suggest alternative instructional strategies for maximizing the achievement of learning outcomes. The chapter suggests that the integration of the results of such research into instructional design and delivery demonstrates the willingness of instructors to be held accountable for their efforts.

INTRODUCTION

How individuals learn, that is a person's learning style, has been the subject of learning style theory over the last fifty years. Most of the research in this area has focused primarily on perception or cognition with little attention, until the 1970s, toward practical applications (Streufert and Nogami, 1989). It was during that time that researchers involved in education and training demonstrated links between the design and alignment of training to individual teaching and learning styles, to successful training programs (Knowles, 1973). Since then, many studies also suggest that optimum student achievement occurs when the students' learning styles and the teacher's instructional methods are aligned (Terrell, 1976; Bertini, 1986; Davis, 199_; Moallem, 2003; Pithers, 2001; Saracho, 2003).

Unfortunately, learning style research has remained largely academic due to the nature of learning itself. Individual differences in learning preference, strategy, style, cognitive strategy and style, and confusion among the constructs themselves present a formidable venture for individualizing the design, development, and delivery of instruction across many instructional environments. But, recently more interest in learning style research has resurfaced, particularly for two reasons: the implications for closing the achievement gap between white and minority students and for outcomes-based assessments and accountability (Burke and Dunn, 2002). Educators believe that research in this area may help to improve academic achievement, and thus retention and graduation rates in schools. Instruction that improves achievement also helps to support particular pedagogical strategies and supports teachers who are required to account for their students' learning.

Furthermore, in the workplace, some researchers contend that understanding diverse learning styles may ultimately improve efficiency and productivity in industries and corporations (Adler, 2002; Hickcox, 1995). Application of learning styles in professional and organizational training, particularly for management training and development, has generally emphasized the individual (Boyatzis and Kolb, 1995; Lord and Maher, 1989; Streufert and Nogami, 1989). But, some studies have analyzed learning styles at the organizational level, and focus on the importance of transactional learning between individuals and the organization for more seamless development and productivity (Easterby-Smith, 1997; Hayes and Allinson, 1998; Swieringa and Wierdsma, 1992). In the current analysis, what remains relatively unchallenged is the assumption, supported by research, that if instructional materials and strategies are designed to accommodate different learning styles, then the outcomes of learning, as well as learning itself, are improved for most individuals (Canino and Cicchelli, 1988; McLoughlin, 1999; Smith, 2002).

Back in 1979, Keefe, in his identification and analysis of several learning concepts, recognized the bipolar learning style of field dependence/independence as among those learning style theories that were especially appropriate to the improvement of learning outcomes, particularly in terms of predictability. Of all the many learning style models that have evolved over the last thirty years including, Dunn and Dunn's Learning Styles (1978), Howard Gardner's Multiple Intelligence Theory (1983), Kolb's Learning Styles (1984), and Grasha's Learning Style Scales (1996), to name just a few, field dependence/independence still remains the most researched of all the learning style concepts (Pithers, 2002; Wooldridge, 1995). Witkin, himself, viewed field dependence/independence as a dynamic theory and was excited at the prospect of applying field dependence/independence in innovative ways based on contingent and incremental knowledge. Witkin believed that "field-dependence theory is still very much in evolution" and was certain that "it will appear quite different in the future under the impetus of newly emerging evidence" (Witkin and Goodenough, 1981, p. x). In this context, the purpose of this chapter is to examine the evolving applications of field dependence/independence learning theory and to suggest ways in which new ideas in this learning style theory may improve learning for a diverse student population and assessment outcomes in positive ways.

FIELD DEPENDENCE/INDEPENDENCE: ESSENCES AND EVOLUTION

According to Keefe (1979), field dependence/independence measures the degree to which an individual uses "an analytical as opposed to a global way of experiencing the environment" (Keefe, 1979, p. 9). Field dependent individuals engage a global organization of the surrounding field, and perceive parts of the field as fluent. In contrast, field independent learners discern discrete parts of the field, distinct from the organized background. On the one hand, field dependent learners depend on cues and structure from their environment and then make the learning process contingent on their experience in that environment. Field dependent learners tend to have short attention spans, are easily distracted, and prefer casual learning environments. In addition, field dependent learners choose instructional situations that elicit their feelings and experiences. Field dependent persons are also more socially oriented, less achievement-oriented and less competitive, than field independent individuals (Wooldridge, 1995). In sum, and particularly relevant to education in a global society shrunken by technology, "...field dependent individuals are interpersonally oriented and rely heavily on external stimuli. This motivates them to look toward others for reinforcement of opinions and attitudes" (Wooldridge, 1995, p. 51).

On the other hand, field independent individuals, overall, are more analytical and independent than field dependent learners. In addition, these learners are characterized by their analytical approach and abilities to problem solving. These analytical learners tend to be more independent, more intrinsically motivated, and task-oriented in their learning processes than field dependent individuals. Field independent learners are also more focused and disciplined learners, and they are characterized by a longer attention span and a greater contemplative disposition than are field dependent learners. Thus, field independent individuals depend more on internal than external cues, and prefer formal learning environments conducive to their competitive and achievement-oriented learning style (Witkin et al., 1971; Witkin et al., 1977; Witkin and Goodenough, 1981; Wooldridge, 1995). Furthermore, Wooldridge (1995) reports in his review of the literature that field dependent individuals require more structure in terms of objectives and planned activities in human relations training, lecture outlines, or in the "inherent organization of the task material itself," (Wooldridge, 1995, p. 52), than do field independent learners. This appears to be true regardless of the amount of material learned. At the same time, these studies also indicate that field dependent learners, in contrast to their counterparts, "...prefer less structured learning environments such as discussion or discovery" (Wooldridge, 1995, p. 52).

The development of the concept of field dependency all started with the question: "How important are visual cues in perceiving the vertical direction of space?" (Goodenough, 1986, p. 5). In general, people know which way is up on the basis of information they receive from the visual environment around them. A room, for example, is filled with many vertical objects which correspond to the true upright in space. In addition, we make reference to sensations from within the body, as the body continuously adjusts itself to the downward pull of gravity in maintaining upright posture and balance (Witkin et al., 1977, p. 2). The answer to the question posed above was determined by creating a conflict between visual and gravitational cues.

One method for creating this conflict is the Rod and Frame Test (RFT) (Witkin and Goodenough, 1981). In this test, a luminous square frame is presented to the subject in a completely darkened room. The frame can be rotated about its center clockwise or counterclockwise. Pivoted at the same center is a luminous rod which also can be tilted clockwise or counterclockwise, independently of the frame. Frame and rod, presented in tilted positions, are all the subject can see in the dark room. The subject's task is to adjust the rod to a position where it is perceived as upright, while the frame around it remains in its initial position of tilt (Witkin et al., 1977).

A second test that was developed to determine the roles of the visual and bodily standards in perception of the upright is the Body-Adjustment Test (BAT). In this test, the object of perception is the body itself, and the key is how people determine the position of their bodies in space.

> The subject is seated in the chair which can be tilted clockwise or counter-clockwise; the chair is projected into the small room which can also be tilted clockwise or counterclockwise, independently of the room. After the subject is seated, the chair and room are brought to prepared tilted settings, and the subject is then asked to adjust the chair to a position where he experiences it as upright. From this account it is not difficult to see that the body-adjustment situation and the rod-and-frame situation are in fact structurally similar. In each there is an item—rod or body—surrounded by a visual field—frame or room—and the question is to what extent the perception of the item is determined by the surrounding framework. (Witken et al., 1977, p. 5).

Witkin et al. (1977) describe vast differences among individuals when they participated in the body-adjustment and the rod and frame tasks. Some people perceive their own bodies as upright when they are fully aligned with the surrounding tilted room. In some cases, someone tilted as much as 35 degrees, and if he is aligned with the room, will claim that he is perfectly straight. Likewise, some individuals would state that a rod (in the RFT) which is tilted 30 degrees is perfectly upright if the frame is also tilted 30 degrees in the same direction. There are others who adjust the rod more or less close to the upright regardless of the position of the surrounding frame.

These research findings led to the development of a different terminology for describing these phenomena. "The concept that contrasting modes of establishing the upright reflected primary reference to the external field or to the body made 'field dependent' and 'field independent' appropriate designations for these modes" (Witkin and Goodenough, 1981, p. 14). Field dependency was defined as a bipolar personality dimension that assesses an individual's tendency to rely on the visual field or the body itself as a cue for locating the upright. FD was defined as a personality measure, not a measure of ability (Linn and Kyllonen, 1981). Witkin was searching for a value-neutral dimension of individual differences. "Field-dependent people evidently differ from field-independent people in how they perceive the upright, rather than in how accurately they perceive the upright" (Goodenough, 1986, p. 11). The finding was that people differ dramatically in degree of field dependence. "Witkin discovered that individual differences in the effects of visual cues are not merely errors of method People showed remarkable self-consistency in degree of field dependence across many tests of orientation perception" (Goodenough, 1986, p. 6).

Further research linked the ability to locate the upright to other perceptual capabilities, including "success in locating camouflaged or embedded figures" and "a new interpretation of the field dependence construct" that "provided a new and much more convenient assessment method" (Goodenough, 1986, p. 7). In the Embedded Figure Test (EFT) the subject is shown a simple figure and then required to find it in a complex design that is so patterned that each component of the simple figure is made part of a clear-cut, sub-whole of the pattern; the simple figure is thereby effectively hidden:

To locate the simple figure it is necessary to break up the organized pattern so as to expose the figure. It was found that subjects who had difficulty separating the sought-after simple figure from the complex design were the ones who could not easily keep body or rod separate from or frame in the orientation tests—in other words, were the ones who were field dependent. Conversely, people who were field independent in the orientation tests found it easy to overcome the influence of the organized complex design in locating the same figure within it. (Witkin and Goodenough, 1981, p. 15).

Later, a reference test was developed by Oltman, Raskin, and Witkin (1971) to facilitate group testing for cognitive style. In this Group Embedded Figure Test (GEFT), subjects are asked to locate a previously seen simple figure embedded within a larger, more complex figure. "The test is scored on the basis of the total number of simple forms correctly traced. Scores may range from zero to eighteen" (MacNeil, 1980, p. 355). Persons with lower scores are said to be field dependent. Field-independent individuals have scores approaching eighteen. MacNeil reviewed much of the relevant research on this topic and concluded that researchers assumed that the cut-off point between FI's and FD is somewhere between twelve and thirteen (MacNeil, 1980).

Witkin (Witkin and Goodenough, 1981) came to view field dependence as a dimension of autonomy, or "self-non-self" differentiation expressed in upright perception and in social functioning such that field dependent people "characteristically rely more on information that is perceived to come from the world of objects and people around them" (Goodenough, 1986, p. 11). By the early 1960's, the concept of field independence had been redefined as the capacity to overcome or analyze an embedding context in perceptual functioning (Witkin et al., 1962), and "(I)dividual and even group administered versions of the Embedded-Figures Test became readily available and economical tools for use in measuring independence." Consequently, the Embedded-Figures Test eventually replaced the tests of upright perception and research on field dependence escalated (Goodenough, 1986, p. 8).

Field Dependence/Independence-Its Relation to Cognitive Style

The development and analysis of the field dependent/independent construct demonstrates Witkin's desire to investigate its origins in terms of how it is influenced culturally, genetically, physiologically, and in terms of personality and social dynamics, and attests to the complexity of this concept: "It is a major aim of the cognitive-style theorists to seek unifying themes that cut across traditional areas of research on human behavior." Witkin recognized in field-dependence theory "a common conceptual framework" (Witkin and Goodenough, 1981, p. 101). Toward this end, Sigal (1991) addresses several questions concerning "reconceptualizations" of field dependence theory and development (Sigal, 1991, p. 387). The first question Sigal asks is how is field dependence defined? In *Origins of Cognitive Style* (Witkin and Goodenough, 1981), Witkin describes field dependence as a cognitive style and vice versa. According to Sigal, this is akin to fishing in muddy waters, because cognitive style and intelligence are inherently difficult concepts to define and thus field dependence becomes mired in the murkiness of these constructs. To support this argument, Sigal contends that "style" "is an overarching concept that refers to the notion that individuals display consistencies in modes of functioning in a variety of behavioral situations." (Sigal, 1991, p. 388). Thus, in this view, field dependence/independence is only one kind of behavioral consistency in a collection of other cognitive styles that also expose this type of consistency. Furthermore, if the construct itself is not clear, then the measurement of the construct is also questionable. Sigal believes that procedures used to assess field dependence /independence actually measure related, but different cognitive characteristics. Finally, Sigal argues that the term consistency itself has multiple definitions. For example, consistency may refer to a particular skill or talent, or it may describe a pattern of behavior that is the same across several different tasks as distinct from the qualitative nature of the outcome (process versus product).

Allinson and Hayes (1996) consider cognition as a continuum of styles and conclude that, "Interest now (centers) on how far individuals are analytical or intuitive in their cognitive style." In addition, the authors consider the degree to which "it is possible to integrate the two and develop a whole brain approach and whether or not this can be assisted by training or education." (p. 132). This perspective includes and is consistent with Sternberg's (1998) view of learning style as a fluid construct, such that learners adapt their learning style to particular situations.

Related to this question are two more fundamental and often debated issues in the cognitive/learning style literature; is field dependence a measure of intelligence or talent? Does field dependence indicate ability or preference? Sigal believes that regression analyses might provide some answers to the first question in terms of separating "...general intelligence or analytic intelligence from field independence" (Sigal, p. 389), but he feels that the answer to the second question is still tentative. Sigal summarizes the complexity of these interrelated concepts and measurements in the following argument:

> Ability as reflected in the field-independence research seems tied to a competence model, a skill in disembedding. Such a skill is necessary for performance on many intelligence test items (Guilford, 1967; Thurstone, 1938; Wechsler, 1939). If considered as an ability, then there is reason to assume that this ability can vary from low to high. If this is the case, it poses problems differentiating style as an ability compared to preference. If preference is the construct of choice, then variation in preference refers to variation in intensity of commitment to a perspective, but may or may not interfere with competent functions. If on the other hand, field dependence is an ability, then it follows that it is difficult to untangle it from general intelligence—also an ability or set of abilities employed in the performance of tasks. (Sigal, 1991, p. 390).

Sigal (1991) concludes his reflections concerning the nature of field dependence by suggesting that field dependence is really a "pseudo-cognitive phenomenon" (p. 390) that is a collection of behaviors that are reclaimed from cognitive ability. These patterns of behaviors then determine an individual's mode of "...organizing and categorizing the environment." (Sigal, 1991, p. 390). The implications of this analysis are that perhaps in observing field dependence or field independence, we are actually measuring a panoply of an individual's interacting characteristics contingent on not only the task itself, but also on the circumstances surrounding the task performance; "I ask: If field dependence is not intelligence, is intelligence field dependence?" (Sigal, 1991, p. 391).

Field Dependence/Independence Psychometric Studies

After a review of the research on field dependence/independence, MacNeil (1980) suggested that scores between 12 and 13 on the GEFT differentiate field dependent from field independent individuals. The measure was designed to reveal a respondent's "general tendency to function at a more differentiated or less differentiated" level (Witkin et al., 1971). The psychometric ratings generally for Witkin's tests were strong for reliability and good for validity (Hickcox, 1995).

A study by Lusk and Wright (1981) focused on instrumentation, as a threat to internal validity, on the Group Embedded Figures Test. The authors demonstrated in a previous study that a learning effect took place between the two sections of the Group Embedded Figures Test (GFT). The results supported the authors' hypothesis that the scores attained on the section worked first would be smaller (few embedded figures identified) than those attained on the subsequent section worked (more embedded figures identified). Hence practice may improve an individual's score on the GFT, and if a person is labeled field dependent or field independent.

Field Dependence/Independence: Implications for a Diverse Student Population

A recent report by the Educational Testing Service forecasts that African American, Hispanic, and Asian/Pacific Islander will account for 80 percent of the increases in undergraduates by the year 2015. Minorities as a group will increase their combined share of the undergraduate population from 29.4 to 37.2 percent. The percentage of African American undergraduates will change only marginally—from slightly less than 13 percent to slightly more than 13 percent. A 73 percent increase in the number of Hispanic American undergraduates from 1995 to 2015 will make Hispanics the country's largest college-going minority, accounting for about one in six undergraduates. Over the same time period, an 86 percent increase in the enrollment of Asians will make this group comprise more than 8 percent of the undergraduate student population (Carnevale and Fry, 2000). The same report states that some of the rise in undergraduate numbers by 2015 will be comprised of mature students, age 35 and older. Analysis projects that older students will account for about 31 percent of the projected 2.6 million rise in undergraduate enrollments. During 1999-2000, there were 151 associate degrees awarded to women for every 100 associate degrees awarded to men. By mid-decade, this ratio is projected to rise to 167 women per 100 men and by 2009-2010 the ratio is projected to rise to 173 women per 100 men.

The U.S. Department of Education projected undergraduate enrollments by gender in two and four-year post- secondary institutions. In the fall of 1999, there were 128 women enrolled in such college programs for every 100 men. By 2010, the Department of Education projects that the female/male enrollment ratio will rise above 138 (U.S. Department of Education, The Condition of Education, 2002, p. 130). The construct of Field Dependence/Independence learning styles provides special insight for this projected change in the demographics of the college student population. Wooldridge (1994, p. 378) points out "field independence is not equally distributed across all population groups." Females, blacks, and Hispanics generally appear to be more field dependent than are Asian or White male Americans. However, Allen and Cholet (1979) estimated that gender accounts for less than 15 percent of the variance in field-dependence scores.

However, several other studies refute Witkin's conclusion that males tend to be more field-independent than females, and many studies are simply inconclusive concerning gender differences. Witkin attributed the gender difference to several factors, including hereditary and cultural. In addition, Witkin describes field dependence-independence as a stable characteristic of individuals. In his studies, which compared males and females in practice situations, although the scores of both sexes improved, there was still a definite difference between males and females and their relative field dependence (Johnson, Flinn and Tyer, 1979). These researchers report in their investigation the effect of practice and training in spatial skill scores from male and female drafting, mathematics, and liberal arts students on the Embedded Figures Test. The authors conclude from their study that gender differences reported in previous research, using the Embedded Figures Test might actually reflect differences in previous experience and population. Carter and Loo's (1980) conclusion in their study of psychometric data of the GEFT, is consistent with this notion. These researchers suggest that large differences in mean performance on the GEFT among data from Witkin et al. (1971), Renna and Zenhausern (1976), and Oltman, Raskin, and Witkin (1971) may be due to the effects of different populations and contexts. Thus, these factors may have some important implications in scores for males and females. Mykytyn (1989) supports this observation in a study conducted by administering the GEFT to 48 finance specialists. In this study, Mykytyn indicates the lack of significant gender-related differences and an increase in field *dependence* for subjects with more than the average experience in the organization. De Sanctis and Dunikoski (1983), in their study using the GEFT to evaluate business students, advise other researchers to consider the validity of the GEFT with regard to populations that are different from the norming population. This is because De Sanctis and Dunikoski report no gender differences, contrary to previous research, including Witkin's own validity information. The authors suggest that the lack of gender differences in their population may have been due to their sample of business school subjects, which may be more homogeneous and field independent than the liberal arts students of Witkin's norming group. This conclusion appears to challenge the notion that as a group there are more differences between men and women than individual differences among men and women and so disputes gender as a factor in field dependence/independence. In qualified support of this view, Chin (1998) takes exception to the highly "value-laden," (p. 75) terms that Witkin uses to describe gender differences concerning field dependence-independence. Chin cites developmental data to support the idea that gender differences in field independence actually measure gender differences in visual-spatial abilities. Chin contends that field dependence-independence tests actually assess spatial abilities, rather than cognitive modes of learning. The author believes that this is a relevant consideration in view of Witkin's biased descriptive terms for field dependent females.

The field dependence/independence learning style construct also has special insights for the instruction of adults in general. The volume of literature on the adult learner has reached a consensus on two of their common characteristics-their capacity for self-directed learning and their need for a supportive interpersonal learning environment (Knowles, 1973). However the field dependence construct challenges any learning orientation that assumes a high degree of learning style congruence between learners.

Those adults who tend towards field-independence will have a relatively well-developed capacity for some aspects of self-directed learning-their analytical ability will enable them to conceptualize the various components of a learning task, to put order into disorganized elements of a learning field, and to be aware of their own needs and strengths as they progress towards meeting goals. On the other hand, those adults who tend towards field dependence will be relatively lacking in these skill (Joughin, 1992, p. 13).

Field Dependence/Independence: Instructional Implications

A major field of interest to researchers has been to relate the field-dependent/field-independent styles of learning to the design and delivery of educational/ training experiences. This study will now present descriptions of some of this research that describes the implications of field dependency for the design of human-relation training (HRT), learning from a lecture, relationship between learning style and recall, the relationship between learning style and learning high- and low-structured information from a lecture, the relationship of learning styles and study technique, and learning styles and memory.

The Relationship of the Field-Dependent Continuum and Human Relations Training

Recognizing that the effectiveness of human relations training (HRT) varies with the type of participants, Mezoff (1982) sought to explain why one kind of HRT may be effective for some people but unproductive for others. Research has shown that certain people are more amenable to HRT than others. "Typically, wide differences are seen in the extent to which individual members 'take to' the sensitivity-training experience" (Harrison, 1966, p. 518). Mezoff points out that: "Research in education and psychotherapy suggests that cognitive style variables can account, in part, for the differential effectiveness of various educational and therapeutic programs (1982, p. 16).

Mezoff first differentiated HRT along the dimension of structured-unstructured. He suggests that HRT is structured and that "Structured training takes place with specific learning goals and objectives determined in advance by the training staff," including "the sequence, timing, and pace of the activities throughout the program," such as "role plays, simulation games, micro-counseling, and video-feedback training (p. 15)." He goes on to suggest that unstructured HRT is participant-controlled. Much of the learning is "processed" during or after the events of the training. "The purest example of unstructured HRT is the T-group (also known as sensitivity training)" (Mezoff, 1982, p. 15). Mezoff then reviewed the considerable literature on FI for two purposes: (1) to understand interpersonal behavior in the HRT setting better, and (2) to hypothesize the relationships that might make for successful or unsuccessful matches between participants of varying cognitive styles and HRT programs with varying degrees of structure. This review of the literature led Mezoff to conclude that for most circumstances structured HRT is more appropriate than unstructured HRT, since unstructured HRT seems to be systematically biased against individuals with FD learning styles. Furthermore, groups that are heterogeneous in cognitive styles have distinct advantages, since they allow group members to observe examples of behaviors they might try to develop in themselves. Human relations trainers must recognize that their interventions are likely to be differentially effective with persons of different learning styles. "What is effective for an FD trainee may be ineffective for an FI (or vice versa)" (p. 29). Human relations trainers should try to compensate for a trainee's stylistic weakness. "For example, FI's tend not to focus on interpersonal interactions. The trainers, therefore, should continually make explicit references to this domain so that FI's will remain alert to it and focus on it" (p. 30). Mezoff concludes by observing: "we infrequently modify our training designs to accommodate the perceptual or cognitive styles of our participants" (p. 30). The tentative conclusions of this study are of most importance to public administration faculty that utilize these types of instructional strategies and are more attune to individual differences.

THE RELATIONSHIP OF FIELD-INDEPENDENCE-DEPENDENCE AND LEARNING FROM A LECTURE

Frank (1984) believes that discovering "specific processing differences between field-dependent and field-dependent students" has powerful potential in guiding the development and implementation of "classroom strategies that capitalize on the characteristics of the different styles of students" (p. 677). He suggests that one area of investigation that might uncover specific ability differences is the relationship between cognitive style and the effectiveness of study technique. Witkin and Goodenough (1981) suggest that field-independent individuals have greater ability to break up an organized field into its basic elements and provide structure for an ambiguous stimulus complex. Such skills should be extremely useful in academic settings where students are frequently required to take notes. The purpose of the Frank study was to assess the extent to which FI and FD learning performance benefits from note-taking under increasing degrees of external structural support. In addition, exploratory analyses were conducted in an effort to detect differences in the kind of notes taken by field-independent and field-dependent students while listening to a taped lecture (Frank, 1984). Frank concludes that: "The typical classroom procedures in which teachers lecture and students take notes may favor the performance of field-independent students over field-dependent students" (Frank, 1984, p. 677). Thus, he suggests, instructors may want to provide students with additional organizational aids while lecturing, perhaps through outlines or a handout. "By clearly presenting the structure of the lecture, the teacher may be able to help the performance of the field-dependent student without hindering the performance of the field-independent student" (Frank, 1984, p. 677). An alternative would be to provide field-dependent students with structured training explicitly designed to enhance note-taking skills.

COGNITIVE STYLE, STUDY TECHNIQUE AND RECALL AND RECOGNITION

Annis and Davis (1978) point out that although there has been an increasing emphasis in instructional research on the techniques used by students in their efforts to learn from written material, there still is a great deal of disagreement regarding the most effective study technique to use in studying an assignment. Students put a great deal of effort and a lot of faith into commonly-used study methods, which include reading only, underlining, formal outlining, marginal notes, and note-taking; yet there has been very little systematic research on the effectiveness of these study methods. "That which has been done has yielded inconsistent results with little support for any particular study technique" (Annis and Davis, 1978, p. 175). These authors feel that this might be due to the fact that students have been arbitrarily assigned to study conditions without any concern for the student's preferred method of study. In addition, previous studies have neglected the effects of different cognitive styles on the effectiveness of various study techniques. The purpose of the Annis and Davis study was to ". . investigate the effect of the variables of study technique (read, underline, or notes), preference for study technique (preferred or non-preferred), review (review or no review), and cognitive style (field independent or field dependent) on tests of recall and recognition (p. 176)."

The experimental design consisted of three levels of study technique (read only, read and underline, read and take notes), two levels of preference (preferred or non-preferred), two levels of review (review or no review), and two levels of cognitive style (field- independent or field-dependent). The findings indicated that FI subjects using a non-preferred study technique with no review scored significantly better than FD students using a non-preferred study technique with no review. None of the other FI/FD comparisons reached significance. However, of the four possible conditions, FI students scored higher on the examination than did FD. The one exception was that FD students using a preferred study technique with no review scored better than FI students under the same conditions. The authors conclude "The results of the preference by review by cognitive style interaction indicate a tendency for field-independent subjects to score better than field-dependent subjects except when assigned to use both a less effective preferred study technique and no review (Annis and Davis, 1978)."

FIELD DEPENDENCY, OUTLINE CONDITION AND STRUCTURE INFORMATION FROM A LECTURE

As Ward and Clark (1987) point out: "In recent years research in cognitive styles has begun to focus on the relationship between individual differences in cognitive style and performance on educationally relevant tasks" (p. 259). Research indicates that under normal learning and instructional conditions, FI individuals perform better than FD students on a wide variety of different learning tasks. It has been suggested that this superior performance exists, because FI individuals display an active analytic approach to learning by seeking to abstract and use the organization of structured learning material and by seeking to impose their organization on ambiguous or loosely-structured material (Witkin and Goodenough, 1981). If FI's higher performance is due to their superior cognitive restructuring skills, perhaps providing external structural support to FD, individuals may allow them to compensate for poor restructuring skills and minimize performance differences between students of these two cognitive types. The research conducted by Ward and Clark (1987) was designed to investigate the effect of a structural outline on FD and FI students' learning and retention of structurally-important and less-important information from a videotaped lecture.

Subjects were first measured as to their field independence-dependence and then assigned to either an outline or no-outline condition. The basic instructional material was a twenty-minute videotape on the topic of bird migration. A hierarchical outline of the lecture was created. Information was considered of high structural (HS) importance if it specified a main topic or subtopic in the lecture. Information was considered of low structural (LS) importance if it specified a detail of a main topic or subtopic. Ward and Clark (1987) found that an outline contributed significantly to FD and FI participants' recall of HS and LS information, but the absence of an outline was detrimental to FD subjects. In this case, FI subjects had better recall of HS information than did FD subjects, but FD and FI subjects had the same recall of LS information. Furthermore, FD and FI participants revealed no differences in their recall of either HS or LS information when aided by an outline (p. 264).

EFFECT OF COGNITIVE STYLE AND LEARNING PASSAGE ORGANIZATION ON STUDY TECHNIQUE

Annis (1979) hypothesized that if field-independent persons are better than field-dependent persons at structuring material, it would seem likely that they would be better at focusing on and remembering material of high structural (HS) importance regardless of whether they were taking notes or reading only. In this study, it was shown that FI students scored better than the FD students in completing sentences of high structural importance regardless of whether the passage was organized or unorganized. The reason postulated for this superior performance was that FIs ".. actively abstracted general principles and mediating concepts from the passage," but "field-dependent students are more likely" to use "the characteristics of the learning task" instead of "analyzing or imposing their own structure on it" (Annis, 1979, p. 624).

LEARNING AND MEMORY OF FIELD INDEPENDENT-DEPENDENT INDIVIDUALS

A study by Davis and Frank (1979) was undertaken in response to findings by Goodenough (1986) who suggested that the difference between field-dependent and field-independent people is *how* the learning or memory process occurs rather than in how *effective* that process is. This study discusses alternative explanations that emphasize developmental differences and differences in efficiency of performance between FI's and FD's.

Experiments were conducted concerning two types of memory, short-term memory and free recall. In the experiment with short-term memory, field-independent individuals were found to be more efficient than field-dependent individuals under conditions of high information load and when sources of potential interference were present. "In the case of free recall learning, the evidence reviewed indicated that the chances of field-independent individuals displaying superior recall increases as the inherent organization of the task material decreases" (Davis and Frank, 1979, p. 477).

FIELD DEPENDENCE AND SHORT-TERM MEMORY

Berger and Goldberger (1979) examined the relationship between field dependence and short-term memory. These researchers predicted that, relatively, field-independent individuals would perform better on short-term memory tests in which a large amount of interference is assumed to be present than would individuals who are more field-dependent. The findings supported this hypothesis and are consistent with the understanding of field independence as the ability to focus attention on the relevant aspects of a field. "In summary, the findings of the present study seem to give strong support to the conceptions of field independence as involving the ability to attend selectively and the tendency to be task-oriented" (Berger and Goldberger, 1979, p. 96).

COGNITIVE AND INSTRUCTION STYLE: THE LEARNING PERFORMANCE OF UNDERGRADUATE STUDENTS

Not all research findings support differential responsiveness to treatment by field-independent and field-dependent students. It had been suggested that optimal learning occurs when the instructional style of the teacher is matched to the particular strengths of the learner's cognitive style (Witkin et al., 1977). MacNeil (1980) investigated the relative effects of two different instructional styles: "discovery" in which general concepts are verbalized and taught as the *final* step in the instructional sequence. The discovery style also includes "a low degree of instructor guidance, and an emphasis on student-centered presentation methods, such as discussion, role-playing, self-paced workbook exercises, and group problem solving." In contrast, the "expository" strategy verbalizes generalizations in the *initial* step of instruction, and conversely uses "a high degree of instructor guidance, and an emphasis on teacher-centered presentation methods, especially lectures" (p. 355). The research question explored whether or not the learning performance of students differing in cognitive styles would be significantly affected by a particular style of instruction. "The results obtained from this study revealed that differential effects did not occur" (MacNeil, 1980, p. 357). However, MacNeil suggests that one possible explanation for the lack of significant interaction might have been the nature of the subject matter chosen for the unit of instruction. MacNeil points out that in other research that supported the "matching" theory, the educational topic used was a unit of mathematics (a subject area that stresses analytical skills). "Thus, it may be postulated that the difference in the nature of the subject matter used in these various investigations has affected the conclusions reached" (MacNeil, 1980, p. 358).

MacNeil's study falls under the heading of Aptitude-Treatment-Interaction (ATI) research (Cronbach et al. 1977). Advocates of this approach recommend that researchers try to find aptitudes that interact with variations in instructional treatment and to design instructional treatments to fit particular aptitudes of groups of students. As mentioned above, there have been several studies successful in finding that ATI's have used the cognitive style of field dependence/ independence as an aptitude variable (Adams and McLeod, 1979). McLeod, Carpenter, McCornack, and Skvarcius (1979) investigated the relationship between FI/FD and expository and discovery instructional style."The results support the hypothesis that field-independent students will perform best when allowed to work independently, whereas field-dependent students perform best when given extra guidance" (Adams and McLeod, 1979, p. 348).

Rollock (1992) evaluated whether certain learning conditions could bring out effects of style as distinct from ability. The purpose of Rollock's study was to determine whether field dependent students' achievement could be higher than field independent students on a test of freshly-learned material when learning required social awareness. Rollock concluded from his study that field dependent students performed better than did their field independent colleagues under learning conditions in which interpersonal skills were required.

This brief summary of only a few of the thousands of studies that have discussed the educational implications of the field independence/dependence dimensions of learning styles clearly demonstrates that different instructional techniques are required for effective instruction of students at each of the polar extremes of this dimension.

IMPLICATIONS FOR ENHANCING STUDENT LEARNING OUTCOMES

As Cronbach and Snow state (1977, p. 1):

> Since learners differ, the search for generally superior methods should be supplemented by a search for ways to fit the instruction to each kind of learner. One can expect interaction between learner characteristics and instructional method. Where these exist, the instructional approach that is best on the average is not best for all persons.

There are many ways to relate the field dependent/independent styles of learning to instructional methodologies. One approach is to categorize the instructional methodologies into degrees from formal/unambiguous to informal/ambiguous learning environments. This dichotomy is particularly important, since research has shown that field dependents and field independents react differently to these two learning situations (Mezoff, 1982). In light of the characteristics of field-dependent students already described, field dependents would prefer discussion or discovery modalities in which they can interact with others, while field independent students like a lecture format in which they can take in the information autonomously. Based on these descriptions, one would suspect an informal training environment would be the most effective for the global-learner whereas the formal environment would be the most effective learning environment for the analytical-oriented student. Research has indicated, however, that there are some very important exceptions to this conventional wisdom. In a structured learning environment, there appears to be no difference between the amount of material learned by either the global relational or the analytical learner. However, when the material to be learned lacks clear inherent structure therefore requiring that the learner provide organization as an aid to learning, field-dependent persons are likely to have greater difficulty as compared to field independent students. This apparent need on the part of field dependents for structure in order to facilitate the learning process leads to several strategies for effective instruction. For example, in a class having field-dependent students which might prefer discussion, effective instruction would require questions or a list of suggested topics to guide the discussion. Or, if the instructor is using case studies as the teaching method, the instructor should provide the field dependents with questions to focus their discussion. Likewise, the characteristics of the learning style of field-independent students require some specific attention from an astute instructor. Field-independent individuals do not seek out external feedback; thus, a field-independent student, while working alone on a project, might be going completely down the wrong track and not recognize this until after the assignment has been completed. In an ongoing class project, perhaps the instructor could require progress reports and monitor those to insure that the field-independent student has perceived the correct method for responding to the assignment.

Since field-dependent people are particularly interested in the social aspects of their surroundings, it is obvious such people are better at learning material with social content. Thus, if a course activity required the learning of socially-related material, the instructor could assume the field-dependent students would learn the material quite readily. On the other hand, it was shown while field-independent students are not particularly sensitive to social material, once being alerted they are to look out for certain social related facets of the learning experience, they will learn the material just as well as the field-dependent student will. Thus, an observant instructor is apt to see that sufficient clues are provided in a socially-oriented learning situation to assist the field-independent student learning process.

The motivation for learning, apparently, is also extremely important in the degree to which field-dependent and field-independent people learn. To some degree, perhaps contrary to conventional wisdom, evidence suggests that field-independent persons tend to learn more than field-dependent persons when the motivation is completely intrinsic. However, when there are external rewards for learning, whether material or non-material in nature, there is no difference in how much learning takes place. Recognizing this difference, the instructor might want to make sure there are extrinsic rewards available to stimulate the field-dependent learner.

There is one common theme running through the literature on field independence/dependence research reviewed in this study (Mezoff, 1982; Murphy, 1982; Frank, 1984; Witkin and Goodenough, 1981; Annis and Davis, 1978; Ward and Clark, 1987; Annis, 1979; Davis and Frank, 1979; Berger and Goldberger, 1979; Adams and McLeod, 1979; McLeod, Carpenter, McCornack and Skvarcius, 1979; Witkin et al., 1977). Field-dependent participants require more structure than field-independent participants in order to achieve the same level of learning. Whether this structure is manifested through a presentation of objectives and planned activities in human relation training (Mezoff, 1982), through structured lecture outlines (Frank, 1984; Ward and Clark, 1987), or in the inherent organization of the task material itself (Davis and Frank, 1979), its existence appears to remove any difference between the amount of material learned. This finding is ironic since, as the literature reviewed indicated, the field-dependent learner prefers less structured learning environments such as discussion or the discovery mode.

FIELD DEPENDENCE/INDEPENDENCE: IMPLICATIONS FOR FACULTY ACCOUNTABILITY

Faculty at institutions of higher education currently work in environments that demand accountability. There are few ways to respond to these demands more compelling than to show key stakeholders how serious faculty are about identifying strategies for enhancing student learning. Knowles (1973), among others, points out that understanding how a person learns is a major requisite for a successful educational program. Studies have shown that identifying a student's learning style and then providing appropriate instruction in response to that style can contribute to more effective learning (Claxton and Murrell, 1987). Thus it behooves today's faculty to be aware of important student learning styles and how to design and deliver instruction in response to them.

Faculty development activities, such as workshops, seminars, and similar activities can be useful in helping faculty better understand the concepts behind learning styles and how an understanding of these concepts can lead to an improvement in students' learning.

This insight is important for more than understanding how to modify course design and delivery as suggested in the previous section. Research has indicated teachers are more likely to use instructional methods that are congruent with their cognitive learning style. Wu (1968, as quoted in Bertini, 1986) for example, found that more field-dependent student teachers in social studies ranked discussion as more important to the practice of good teaching than lecture, which was favored by more field-independent instructors. "A discussion approach…emphasizes social interaction" and "gives the student more of a role in structuring the classroom situation" (Bertini, 1986, p. 95). After summarizing the relevant literature reviewing research on the relationship between instructors' cognitive styles and their preferred instructional methods, Bertini concluded that "field-dependent and field-independent teachers have different teaching preferences syntonic with their own personal styles" and consequently they may demonstrate "different patterns of actual teaching behavior in the classroom" (1980, p. 96).

This natural tendency might have special significance for public administration faculty, since the research findings of this study showed many of the subjects had undergraduate preparation in the "Social Professions," and these subjects were significantly more field-dependent than students with other undergraduate preparation. Assuming public administration faculty approximate this distribution, one could infer a significant number of public administration faculty are field-dependent. Combining this hypothesis with the findings that instructors have teaching styles that are congruent with their own personal styles, it could be concluded that there might be a large number of classroom situations where field-dependent public administration faculty are using low or non-structured teaching methods with field-dependent students. The research findings described in the previous section, however, suggest that such teaching methods/student characteristics combinations place the field-dependent student at a disadvantage.

In addition to increasing the sensitivity of the field-dependent faculty member to the possible dysfunctional consequences of the congruent instructional style on field-dependent students, both field-independent and field-dependent faculty need to be made aware of how teacher/student matching or mismatching of learning styles can lead to bias in assessment. DiStefano (1970, as described in Bertini, 1986) found when teachers and students had similar cognitive styles they tended to describe each other in positive terms, not only in personal but intellectual characteristics as well. "Teachers often believe that students whose cognitive styles match theirs are smarter than those whose styles are different from theirs. They say that the former are more intelligent, more logical, and more successful as students" (Bertini, 1986, p. 97).

These findings should also be of interest to field-independent faculty members having their instructional effectiveness assessed by a class with a high percentage of field-dependent students.

CONCLUSION

Guild and Garger stated that "Style is the most important concept to demand attention in education in many years (and) is the core of what it means to be a person" (1985. p. viii). Of all the learning styles developed (Keefe, 1979, Wooldridge, 1995) field independence-dependence appears to have the most potential for the improvement of the educational experience.

What insights has research on this important learning style contributed to the improvement of the instructional process? First, in a field-dependent mode of perceiving, perception is strongly dominated by the overall organization of the surrounding field, and parts of the field are experienced as "fused." In a field-independent mode of perceiving, parts of the field are experienced as discrete from the organized ground. Moreover, as this chapter has pointed out, these differences have important learning implications since they also reflect differences in interpersonal orientation, attention span, comfort with different degree of structure of the learning situation, competitiveness, and attention span.

Next, this learning style dimension is not equally distributed among the student population. Research has suggested sex, as well as ethnic/racial differences in Witkin's dimension of field independence/dependence. Students might also differ in their responses in light of their undergraduate major.

Finally, research suggests that instructional effectiveness can be enhanced by responding to the field independence/dependence learning style of an individual student. However, not as some learning style researchers (Dunn, Dunn and Price 1978) have suggested, by providing instruction in a form that is congruent with the student's preference, but rather by selecting instruction methods in light of research on this particular style. There is one common theme running through the literature on field independence/dependence research reviewed in this study. Field dependent participants require more structure than field independent participants, in order to achieve the same level of learning. Moreover, research on the field dependence learning style construct raises serious questions about some of the most cherished assumptions of "andragogy."

In October 1990, an article in the *Chronicle of Higher Education* stated that: "For teaching to gain prestige in higher education, faculty members must make pedagogy a subject of scholarly debate" (Watkins, 1990, p. A11). This article goes on to quote Lee S. Shulman, a professor of education at Stanford University, as saying: "Teaching will be considered a scholarly activity only when professors develop a conception of pedagogy that is very tightly coupled to scholarship in the disciplines themselves" (p. A11). Commanding a professional base of knowledge of subject matter with knowledge of how to teach it effectively to others is the primary purpose of classroom research (Cross, 1990). "Classroom research is the careful, systematic, and patient study of students in the process of learning" (Cross, 1990, p. 2). It has as its goal making teaching more professional, based on understanding, insights, knowledge, and skill. This goal is congruent with Ernest L. Boyer's observation that: "The time has come for us to inquire much more carefully into the nature of pedagogy. It's the most difficult and perhaps the most essential work in developing future scholars" (Watkins, 1990, p. A12). Although there have been many false starts, there is no better time than the present during present accountability trend in education to make the concept of different learning styles mandatory in instructional research and classroom pedagogy.

The prominence of the field independence/dependence learning style has clearly not been overstated. As Messick (1986), of the Educational Testing Service, once said, "I once heard a noted perceptual psychologist remark that (although) cognitive styles were exciting concepts," they were also long on promise and short on delivery. But, such was not the case for field dependence-independence, for which "its early promise has been fulfilled, and its potential continues to offer sample collateral for exciting forays. That, we owe to Herman Witkin. That is his intellectual legacy" (p. 117).

REFERENCES

Adams, V. M., and McLeod, D. B. (1979). The interaction of field dependence/independence and the level of guidance of mathematics instruction. *Journal for Research in Mathematics Education, 10*, 47-55.

Adler, N. J. (2002). *International dimensions of organizational behavior* (4th ed.). Cincinnati, OH: South-Western College Publishing.

Allen, M. J., and Cholet, M. E. (1979). Strength of association between sex and field dependence. *Perceptual and Motor Skills, 47*, 419-421.

Allinson, C. W. and Hayes, J. (1996, January). The cognitive style index: A measure of intuition-analysis for organizational research. *Journal of Management Studies, 33*(1), 119-135.

Annis, L. F., and Davis, J. K. (1978). Study techniques and cognitive style: The effect on recall and recognition. *Journal of Educational Research, 71*, 175-178.

Annis, L. F. (1979). Effects of cognitive style and learning passage organization on study technique effectiveness. *Journal of Educational Psychology, 71*, 620-626.

Berger, E., and Goldberger, L. (1979). Field dependence and short-term memory. *Perceptual and Motor Skills, 49*, 87-96.

Bertini, M. (1986). Some Implications of field dependence for education. In Bertini, M.,Pizzamiglio, L., and Wapner, S. (Eds.). *Field dependence in psychological theory, Research, and application: Two symposia in memory of Herman A. Witkin..* Hillsdale, NJ: Lawrence Erlbaum Associates.

Boyatzis, R. E. and Kolb, D. A. (1995). From learning styles to learning skills: The executive skills profile. *Journal of Managerial Psychology, 10*(5), 3-17.

Burke, K. and Dunn, R. (2002). Learning style-based teaching to raise minority student test scores: there's no debate! *The Clearing House, 76*(2), 103(4).

Canino, C., and Cicchelli, T. (1988). Cognitive styles, computerized treatments on mathematics achievement and reaction to treatments. *Journal of Educational Computing Research, 4*(3), 253-64.

Carnevale, A. P., and Fry, R.A. (2000). *Crossing the great divide: Can we achieve equity when generation Y goes to college?* Princeton, NJ: Educational Testing Service.

Carter, H. and Loo, R. (1980). Group Embedded-Figures Test: Psychometric data. *Perceptual and Motor Skills, 50*, 32-34.

Chin, E. L. S. (1998, Winter). The influence of a distance-learning environment on students' field dependence/independence. *The Journal of Experimental Education, 66*(2), 149-161.

Claxton, C. S. and Murrell, P. H. (1987). *Learning styles: Implications for improving educational practices*. (ASHE - ERIC Higher Education Reports, 1987; No. 4) Washington, DC: Association for the Study of Higher Education.

Cronbach, L. J., and Snow, R.E. (1977). *Individual differences in learning ability as a function of instructional variables*. Final Report. Stanford, CA: Stanford University School of Education.

Cross, K. P. (1990, May). *The current status of classroom learning*. Paper presented at the meeting of the National Conference on College Teaching and Learning. Jacksonville, FL.

Davis, J. K., and Frank, B. M. (1979). Learning and memory of field independent-dependent individuals. *Journal of Research in Personality, 13*, 469-479.

Davis, J. K. (1991). Educational implications of field dependence-independence. In S. Wapner and J. Demick (Eds.), *Field dependence-independence cognitive style across the life span* (pp. 149-175). Hillsdale, New Jersey: Lawrence Erlbaum Associates.

De Sanctis, G. and Dunikoski, R. (1983). Group embedded-figures test: Psychometric data for a sample of business students. *Perceptual and Motor Skills, 56*, 707-710.

Dunn, R., and Dunn, K. (1978). *Teaching students through their individual learning style*.Englewood Cliffs, NJ: Prentice-Hall.

Easterby-Smith, M. (1997). Disciplines of organizational learning: Contributions and Critiques. *Human Relations, 50*(9), 1085-1113.

Frank, B. M. (1984). Effect of field independence-dependence and study technique on learning from a lecture. *American Educational Research Journal, 21*, 669-678.

Gardner, H. (1983). *Frames of mind*. New York: Basic Books, Inc.

Goodenough, D. R. (1986). History of the field dependence construct. In M. Bertini, L.Pizzamiglio and Seymour Wapner (Eds.), *Field dependence in psychological tTheory, Research, and applications: Two symposia in memory of Herman A. Witkin.*. Hillsdale, New Jersey: Lawrence Erlbaum Associates, Publishers.

Guild, P. B., and Garger, S. (1985). *Marching to a different drummers*. Alexandria, VA:Association for Supervision and Curriculum Development.

Guilford, J. P. (1967). *The nature of human intelligence*. New York, NY: McGraw-Hill.

Grasha, A. F. (1996). *Teaching with style: A practical guide to enhancing learning by understanding teaching and learning styles*. Pittsburgh: Alliance Publishers.

Hale-Benson, J. E. (1982). *Black children: Their roots, culture, and learning styles*. Baltimore: Johns Hopkins University Press.

Harrison, R. (1966). Cognitive change and participation in a sensitivity training laboratory. *Journal of Consulting Psychology, 30 (6), 51-520*.

Hayes, J. and Allinson, C. W. (1998, July). Cognitive style and the theory and practice of individual and collective learning in organizations. *Human Relations, 51*(7), 847-872.

Hickcox, L. K. (1995). Learning styles: A survey of adult learning style inventory models. In R.R. Sims and S. J. Sims (Eds.). *The importance of learning styles: Understanding the implications for learning, course design, and education* (pp. 25-47). Westport, Connecticut: Greenwood Press.

Johnson, S., Flinn, J. M., and Tyer, Z. E. (1979). Effect of practice and training in spatial skills on embedded figures scores of males and females. *Perceptual and Motor Skills, 48*, 975-984.

Joughin, G. (1992). Cognitive style and adult learning principles. *International Journal of Lifelong Education*, 11, 3-14.

Keefe, J. W. (1979). Learning style: An overview. In J. W. Keefe (Ed.) *Student learning styles: Diagnosing and prescribing programs*. Reston, VA: National Association of SecondarySchool Principals.

Knowles, M. (1973). *The adult learner: A neglected species*. Houston, TX: Gulf Publishing.

Kolb, D. A. (1984). *Experiential learning: Experience as the source of learning and development*. New Jersey: Prentice Hall, Inc.

Linn, M., and Kyllonen, P. (1981). The field dependence-independence construct: Some, one or none. *Journal of Educational Psychology, 69* (2), 261-273.

Lord, R. G., and Maher, K. J. (1989). Cognitive processes in industrial and organizational psychology. In Cooper, C. L. and Robertson, I. T. (Eds.). *International Review of Industrial and Organizational Psychology* (pp. 49-92). New York, NY: John Wiley and Sons.

Lusk, E. J. and Wright, H. (1981). Notes on learning the Group Embedded Figures Test. *Perceptual and Motor Skills, 53*, 370.

MacNeil, R. (1980). The relationship of cognitive style and instructional style to the learning performance of undergraduate students. *Journal of Educational Research, 73*, 354-59.

McLeod, D. B., Carpenter, T. P., McCornack, R. L., and Skvarcius, R. (1979). Cognitive style and mathematics learning: The interaction of field independence and instructional treatment in numeration systems. *Journal for Research in Mathematics Education, 9*, 163-174.

McLoughlin, C. (1999). The implications of the research literature on learning styles for the design of instructional material. *Australian Journal of Educational Technology, 15*(3), 222-241.

Messick, S. (1986). Herman Witkin and the meaning of style. In M. Bertini, L. Pizzamiglio and S. Wapner (Eds.), *Field dependence in psychological theory, research, and applications: Two symposia in memory of Herman A. Witkin.*. Hillsdale, New Jersey: Lawrence Erlbaum Associates, Publishers.

Mezoff, B. (1982). Cognitive style and interpersonal behavior: A review with implications for human relations training. *Group and Organization Studies, 7*(1), 13-34.

Moallem, M. (2003). Applying learning styles in an online course. *Academic Exchange Quarterly, 7*(4), 209(6).

Murphy, K. (1982). Field-dependent and field-independent students: Implications and strategies for teaching public administration. Proceedings of the Fifth National Conference on Teaching Public Administration. Boston, MA: Suffolk University.

Mykytyn, P. P., Jr. (1989, Winter). Group embedded figures test (GEFT): Individual differences, performances, and learning effects. *Educational and Psychological Measurement, 49*(4), 951-959.

Oltman, P. K., Raskin, E., and Witkin, H. A. (1971). *Group embedded-figures test*. Palo Alto,CA: Consulting Psychologists Press.Pithers, B. (2001). An aspect of vocational teachers' cognitive style: Field dependence-field independence. *Australian and New Zealand Journal of Vocational Education Research, 9*(2), 47-60.

Pithers, B (2002). Cognitive learning style: A review of the field dependent-field independent approach. *Journal of Vocational Education and Training, 54*(1), 117-32.

Renna, M. and Zenhausern, R. (1976). The Group Embedded-figures Test: Normative data. *Perceptual Motor Skills, 43*, 1176-1178.

Rollock, D. (1992). Field Dependence/independence and learning condition: An exploratory study of style vs. ability. *Perceptual and Motor Skills, 74,* 807-818.

Saracho, O. N. (2003). Matching teachers' and students' cognitive styles. *Early Child Development and Care, 173*(2-3), 161-73.

Sigal, I. E. (1991). The cognitive style construct: A conceptual analysis. In Wapner, S.and Demick, J. (Eds.). *Field dependence-independence: Cognitive style across the life span.* (pp. 385-397). Hillsdale, NJ: Lawrence Erlbaum Associates.

Smith, J. (2002). Learning styles: Fashion fad or lever for change? The application of learning style theory to inclusive curriculum delivery. *Innovations in Education and Teaching International, 39*(1), 63-70.

Sternberg, R. J. (1998). *Thinking styles.* New York: Cambridge University Press.

Streufert, S. and Nogami, G. Y. (1989). Cognitive style and complexity: Implications for I/O Psychology. In C. L. Cooper and I. T. Robertson (Eds.), *International review of industrial and organizational psychology 1989* (pp. 94-143). Hillsdale, New Jersey: Lawrence Erlbaum Associates.

Swieringa, J. and Wierdsma, A. (1992). *Becoming a learning organization: Beyond the learning curve.* Reading, MA: Addison-Wesley Publishing Company.

Terrell, W. R. (1976). Anxiety level modification by cognitive style matching. *Community/Junior College Research Quarterly, 1,* October/December, 13-24.

Thurstone, L. L. (1938). *Primary mental abilities.* Chicago, IL: University of Chicago Press.

United States Department of Education (2002). *The Condition of Education.*

Ward, T. J. and Clark, III, H.T. (1987). The effect of field dependence and outline condition on learning high-and low-structure information from a lecture. *Research in Higher Education. 27*(3), pp. 259-272.

Watkins, B. T. (1990). Two-year institutions under pressure to ease transfers. *Chronicle of Higher Education,* A11-A12.

Wechsler, I. S. (1939). *A textbook of clinical neurology with an introduction to thehistory of neurology* (4th ed.). Philadelphia, PA: W. B. Saunders Company.

Witkin, H. A., Dyk, R. B., Faterson, H. F., Goodenough, D. R., and Karp, S. A. (1962). *Psychology differentiation.* New York: Wiley.

Witkin, H. A., Oltmann, P. K., Raskin, E., and Karp, S. A. (1971). *A manual for the embedded figures tests.* Palo Alto, CA: Consulting Psychologists Press.

Witkin, H. A., Moore, C. A., Goodenough, D. R., and Cox, P. W. (1977). Field dependent and field independent cognitive styles and their educational implications. *Review of Educational Research, 47,* 1-64.

Witkin, H. A., and Goodenough, D. R. (1981). *Cognitive styles: Essence and origin.* New York: International University Press.

Wooldridge, B. (1994). Changing demographics of the workforce: Implications for the use of technology as a productivity improvement strategy. *Public Productivity and Management Review, Vol. XVII,* (4), 371-386.

Wooldridge, B. (1995). Increasing the effectiveness of university/college instruction: Integrating the results of learning style research into course design and delivery. In R. R. Sims and S. J. Sims (Eds.). *The importance of learning styles: Understanding the implications for learning, course design, and education* (pp. 49-67). Westport, Connecticut: Greenwood Press.

In: Adult Education: Issues and Developments   ISBN: 978-1-60456-272-9
Editors: P. N. Blakely, A. H. Tomlin, pp. 253-270   © 2008 Nova Science Publishers, Inc.

Chapter 7

EVIDENCE ON THE IMPACT OF ADULT UPPER SECONDARY EDUCATION IN SWEDEN

Anders Stenberg[*]

Swedish Institute for Social Research (SOFI), Stockholm
University, SE-10691 Stockholm, Sweden

ABSTRACT

This chapter gives a brief survey of the literature on earnings effects of adult education at upper secondary level in Sweden (AE) and presents new estimates based on more detailed information than previous studies. The data concern all individuals born in 1970 and residing in Sweden from 1988 to 2001. One third was at some point registered in AE and among them 44 per cent went on to higher education. Regression results indicate that credits equal to one year of AE increase annual earnings by five per cent. The positive returns are mainly associated with vocational studies such as health related subjects and computer science while general subjects like Mathematics, Swedish or English are linked to insignificant estimates. Of those that went on to higher studies, the payoff to another year of education is essentially similar between individuals with and without AE prior to enrolment. The results thus imply that AE works well as a preparation for higher education but individuals who have no interest in further studies should choose vocational courses.

1. INTRODUCTION

The economics field of research has remained relatively passive as the interest in comprehensive adult education has increased during the last two decades. This is troublesome as lifelong learning is often described, in political as well as academic discourses, as a potentially powerful tool to improve productivity and employability of the low-skilled. The lack of research is all the more puzzling bearing in mind that countries such as France and the

---

[*] Email: anders.stenberg@sofi.su.se.

UK have substantially lower fractions with completed upper secondary level schooling compared with several Eastern European countries, the Scandinavian countries or the US (OECD, 2006). The scarcity of studies may partly reflect that adult education is seldom directed towards formal education but instead tend to concern vocational or firm-specific training. If this is the case, Sweden is an exception as it already in 1969 became mandatory that each municipality should offer adult education at compulsory and upper secondary level. Municipal institutes known as *Komvux* have since been responsible for providing the service.

The numbers enrolled at Komvux varied around 110,000 until in the mid 1990s when there was a strong increase in participation. From 1998 to 2001 there were more than 300,000 enrolees annually, making it similar in size to the upper secondary education for youths! This development was largely a consequence of an extraordinary recession that hit Sweden a few years earlier when unemployment rates rocketed from 1.7 per cent in 1990 to 8.2 per cent in 1993. From that year, the government funded the municipalities to provide extra seats at Komvux, earmarked for unemployed individuals. The financial support corresponded to around 20 per cent of the total costs of Komvux in 1994 and 30 per cent in 1996. It increased further to around 50 per cent from the autumn of 1997 when the government launched the so called Adult Education Initiative (*Kunskapslyftet*, AEI). This gradual increase in the adult education sector was matched with an enlarged access to study allowances for adult students. With the AEI, the special grant for education and training, UBS, was introduced. It meant that participants eligible for unemployment insurance (UI) were offered a year of full-time studies at Komvux with a relatively generous grant equal to the level of their UI benefits. This had a massive impact on the numbers enrolled.

The possibilities to carry out follow up studies of Komvux upper secondary education in Sweden (henceforth, AE) have been favourable since 1979 when register data of individual transcript records first started to be collected. The data include information on e.g. course participation, course subject, course credits, course grade or a reported interruption. However, the transcripts are fairly complex and time consuming to arrange and it was not until after the turn of the century, subsequent to the huge increase of AE, that empirical evaluations started to emerge. The studies so far have not used the detailed data on specific courses but instead reported participation in AE with indicator variables (0/1) which signal (semester-wise) whether an individual is "registered" or "not registered" at Komvux. Of course, it does not necessarily provide a good measurement of the amount of AE conducted. Instead, this practice appears as one of several candidate explanations for the rather mixed earnings effects of AE which have been presented. Axelsson and Westerlund (2005) as well as Stenberg and Westerlund (2007) reported positive effects while the results in Albrecht et al. (2004) were insignificant and Ekström (2003) found them to be partly negative. Another shortcoming of these studies is that individuals who continue from AE to higher studies have been excluded from the analyses. If AE participants differ in their performance at university and/or in their earnings impact of the studies, it could have important implications for policy. Educational choices may for instance improve with age as individuals learn about the labour market with experience. However, hypotheses are usually posed in the opposite manner, presuming the performance of AE participants to be weaker than average. This is thought to arise if e.g. AE is of insufficient quality as preparation for university studies (Heckman and LaFontaine 2006, and Boesel et al. 1998, both on the GED in the US), if adults experience more family- work and/or other commitments, if the returns to education decrease with age (Ekström 2003, Light

1995, Monks 1997) or if AE individuals tend to pursue education due to bleak employment prospects (Stenberg, 2007a, and Stenberg and Westerlund, 2007).

The purpose of this chapter is to present empirical results of the earnings effects of course credits actually accomplished at AE. Estimates are also reported on whether individuals in higher studies, with and without a prior registration in AE, differ in their achievements at university and/or in their subsequent earnings. The analyses are based on all individuals born in 1970 and residing in Sweden from 1988 to 2001. Around one third was (until 2001) at some stage enrolled in AE and of those 44 per cent continued to higher education.

The plan of the chapter is to describe the Swedish educational system and the role of AE in the next section. This is followed by an account of the economics research on adult education in Sweden and some related studies on community colleges in the US. Section four contains descriptive statistics of the data while section five provides the empirical strategies and results. [1] Section six briefly discusses costs and benefits to the society and section seven concludes.

2. ADULT EDUCATION IN THE SWEDISH EDUCATIONAL SYSTEM

The Swedish educational system is based on a compulsory school of nine years, usually conducted from the age of seven to fifteen. Upper secondary school then follows, which until 1996 was two or three years depending on individual program choice. Two year programs were typically vocational and displayed strong gender patterns in enrolment, e.g. males were overrepresented in construction, house-painting and electronics while nursing attracted females. Three year programs consisted of theoretical studies intended to prepare for tertiary education. In the mid 1990s, a reform of the upper secondary school extended the two-year programs into three years. The purpose was that everyone with an upper secondary diploma would be eligible for university studies.

Eligibility for tertiary education entails a general admission requirement which roughly corresponds to a three year upper secondary diploma. Individuals aged above 24 may also fulfil the general admission requirement through four years of work experience and passing grades in Swedish and English at upper secondary level. In some cases, depending on the type of education, there are specific requirements. Many of the programs offered at university level have more applicants than there are seats. The sorting process of the applicants is partly regulated and always conditioned on the general admission requirement. At least one third of the seats must be offered to those with the highest grade point averages (GPA) from upper secondary school. Another third of the seats must be offered to those with the highest score on the Swedish Scholastic Aptitude Test (*Högskoleprovet*), which is voluntary and similar to the SAT in the US. In Sweden, formal education is free of charge at all levels. An important part of the picture is also that when enrolled in post-secondary education or adult education, most individuals receive some form of study allowance consisting of about $850 in monthly financial support. One third of it is a grant and the rest is a government loan with favourable reimbursement conditions.

---

[1] For the interested reader, a more comprehensive account of issues related to methodology and presentation of the data is given in the working paper version of this study, Stenberg (2007b).

Komvux offers courses at three different levels. Compulsory school courses constitute about 10 per cent of the supply while some 85 per cent participate at upper secondary level. The remainder is in supplementary courses (vocational post-secondary education) or, from 1997, in introductory courses which were intended for adults who were reluctant to re-start schooling. Concerning courses at upper secondary level, persons with a prior compulsory school or two year upper secondary school enrol to improve their formal qualifications. Individuals with a three year upper secondary school also often enrol; either to complete one or more subjects that were missing from their curricula to fulfil the (general) admission requirement or to slightly re-direct their education. From 1997, it also became permissible to improve grades that were already passed in order to enhance the possibility of gaining access to tertiary education.

3. Evaluations of Adult Education in the Economics Literature

There is a substantial economics literature devoted to the study of the "wage premium" to another year of schooling for youths (see Card, 1999 for an extensive survey). The results have indicated wage increases of slightly below 5 per cent in Sweden and between 8 and 11 per cent in the US. The set-up in several of these studies resembles social experiments and they have thereby generated a certain consensus among economists about their credibility. Evaluations of educations otherwise suffer from an inherent uncertainty in that it is impossible to observe an individual as "educated" and "not educated" at the same moment in time. If participants are more productive also without the education, the estimated causal effects of education risk to be exaggerated. On the other hand, if higher foregone earnings deter more productive individuals from enrolment, the effects are underestimated.

Interestingly, the above mentioned estimates for youths are relatively close to the ones that have been obtained with non-experimental data. Studies on AE with a non-experimental set-up might in this light appear as rather uncomplicated. However, when the educational choice concern AE, rather than education for youths, additional selection mechanisms come into play. If the program is available year after year, as is usually the case, individuals will continuously "self-select" whether to participate, postpone or do without AE. It means individuals with identical characteristics, who enrol and/or complete AE at different points in time, may well experience different program effects. The motivation to enrol in AE is also more differentiated among adults compared with youths. While one group actively pursues AE to complete an upper secondary diploma, possibly also to later enrol in higher studies, there are other groups that enrol in AE as part of a labour market measure for the unemployed or merely to "consume" education, i.e. as part of their leisure. In the absence of some sort of randomization in the enrolment process, which controls for systematic differences between participants and non-participants, a common way of taking selection into account is to use income measures observed before the education and create so-called difference-in-differences estimates. The studies on AE referred to below are all based on methods closely related to this concept.

Swedish studies evaluating AE have mostly concerned participants enrolling in the autumn of 1997 when the Adult Education Initiative was launched as a large scale measure for the unemployed. To this end, Albrecht et al. (2004) used a random sample of the Swedish population consisting of 200,000 individuals. Participants in AE as well as control group members were drawn from this sample and conditioned to fulfil six restrictions on e.g. age, education, gender and country of birth. The change in annual earnings between 1994 and 2000 was used as outcome variable and they found no effects of AE on earnings. A critique against this study is that their data restrictions made the sample sizes of AE participants very small, in most cases below 100 individuals.

Stenberg (2007a) compared participants in the AEI with enrolees in a vocational program called Labour Market Training (LMT). Put differently, the study compares the earnings effects of general human capital and specific human capital. The enrolees in the AEI were defined as those registered at Komvux and eligible for the special grant for education and training UBS, i.e. participants primarily arriving from open unemployment (84 per cent according to the Report from the government SOU 1998:51).[2] Those who enrolled in the AEI in 1997 were, as the schooling year was ongoing, offered an extension of their right to receive the special grant UBS with another year and thus prolong their AE. The participants in the AEI can therefore be divided into four categories based on the number of semesters they were registered. The largest numbers participated two or four semesters but there is no group of males or females that consists of less than 1,000 individuals.

Figure 1 and Figure 2 show the male and female earnings trajectories of these groups from 1991 to 2003. The wage paths reveal only minor differences pre-program but LMT stands out with higher earnings post-program until in 2002 or 2003 when individuals with two and/or three semesters in the AEI catch up. The impression of a lower earnings impact of the AEI is confirmed by empirical estimates, 22 per cent lower for males and 6 per cent lower for females. The results also point towards weaker outcomes of those enrolled four semesters compared with two or three semesters, implying that some AEI participants may have remained in AE to "avoid" the labour market. Plausibly, it was a side effect of the special grant UBS which made the opportunity costs for studying low. However, the comparison between general and specific human capital is not challenged by this as LMT participants had a financial scheme similar to UBS.

The major conclusion of this study is that vocational (or specific) training on average outperforms comprehensive (or general) training as a measure against unemployment. A drawback is, of course, that one can not conclude whether either LMT and/or the AEI had a beneficial effect on earnings as these are not compared to the alternative of "no program".

Axelsson and Westerlund (2005) compared the earnings effects of the AEI both with a group enrolled in LMT and with individuals that continued in open unemployment in the autumn of 1997. Those in open unemployment were conditioned not to later have enrolled in Komvux or LMT. Figure 3 shows the annual earnings from 1990 to 2002 of their samples. The average post-program earnings of the AEI exceed the trajectory of those in open unemployment and regression estimates on annual earnings in 2002 indicate that participation in the AEI is associated with an earnings premium of almost 10 per cent. However, there was no positive effect of the AEI participants if registration only occurred one semester. Also, the impact on earnings of LMT was found to be approximately 10 per cent higher than that of the AEI.

---

[2] This definition is used in all the below studies which concern participants in the AEI.

Stenberg and Westerlund (2007) studied long-term unemployed who enrolled the AEI. Long-term unemployment was defined as being in the unemployment registers all days in 1996 and in 1997 and having registered zero earnings in both years. The results show a strongly positive earnings effect, on average 14 per cent for males and 23 per cent for females. There are again no significantly positive effects for individuals registered only one semester. Insignificant effects were also found for males with four semesters in the AEI. A more careful analysis of this group revealed that it was overrepresented in regions with low levels of employment and the estimation method could not adequately correct this imbalance. Still, it seems a reasonable interpretation that some participants choose to remain in the AEI as their prospects of finding a job were conceived as bleak. This is reminiscent of the result on individuals with four semesters in Stenberg (2007a), particularly visible in Figure 1.

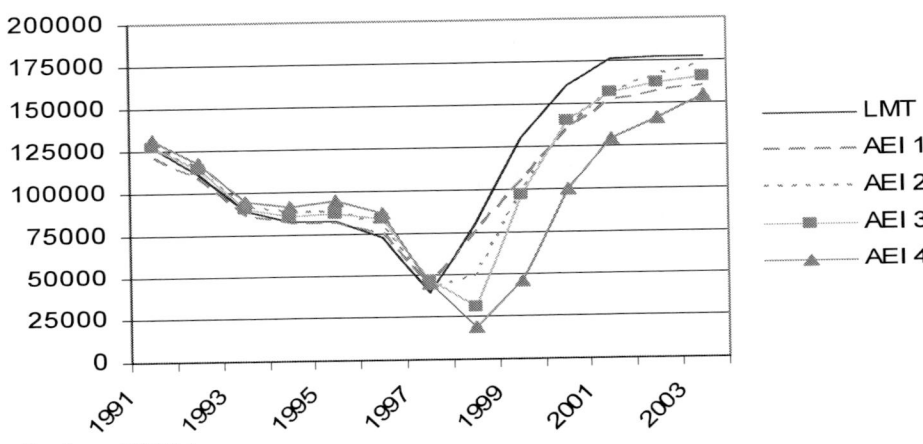

Source: Stenberg (2007a).

Figure 1. Male wage earnings trajectories 1991-2003.

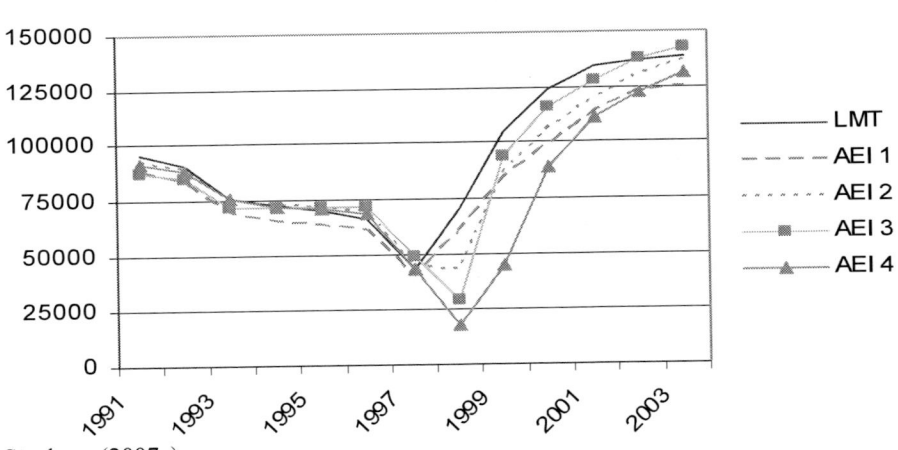

Source: Stenberg (2007a).

Figure 2. Female wage earnings trajectories 1991-2003.

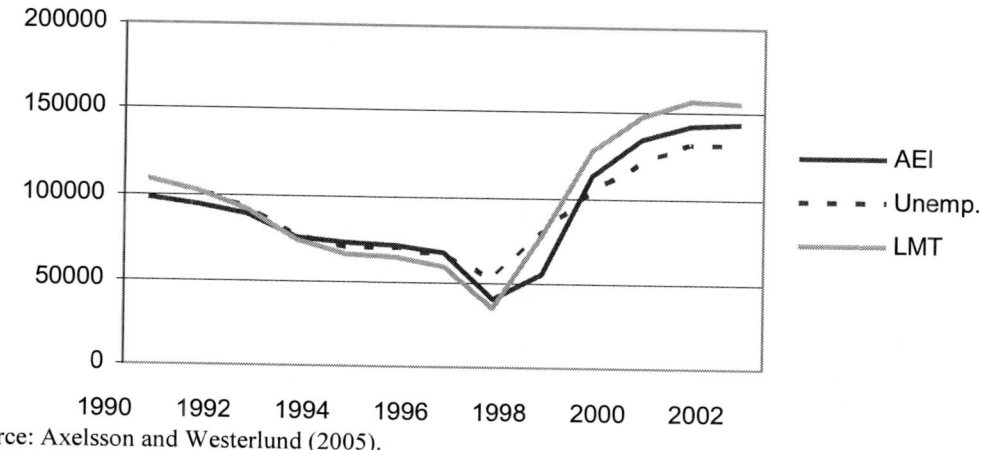

Source: Axelsson and Westerlund (2005).

Figure 3. Wage earnings trajectories 1990-2002.

Ekström (2003) studied participants in AE registered at some stage between 1988 and 1993, using annual earnings in 2000 as outcome variable. It is an interesting study as it is the only one so far which does not focus on a sample that enrolled in 1997 or later. The findings indicate that males born in Sweden experienced a *negative* earnings effect, minus 3 per cent for 25-42 year olds and minus 6 per cent for 43-55 year olds. No significant effects were found for foreign born males or for females born in Sweden while foreign born females displayed positive effects of 9 per cent.

As mentioned, the studies referred to above use indicator variables (0/1) to distinguish between individuals "registered" and "not registered" in AE in a certain semester. This leaves out important information concerning the course credits completed, course subjects, grades etc. Before turning to the presentation of the returns to AE credits in Sweden, let us look briefly at the research in the US on adult education. It is in fact based on records of course credits attained, considering foremost post-secondary education at community college (e.g. Light, 1995, Monks, 1997, Leigh and Gill, 1997, Jacobson et al., 2005, see also Grubb 2002 for a survey). The most ambitious study is arguably Jacobson et al. (2005) which concerns a sample of workers in Washington State who were laid off at some point between 1990 and 1994. Information from detailed transcript records of credits accomplished at community college is combined with quarterly earnings, which cover the period 1987 to 1995. They find credits corresponding to one year of full time studies to increase earnings by 7 per cent for males and 13 per cent for females, but with a large variation in the estimated returns depending on the subjects studied. Courses labelled "technical" render returns of up to 30 per cent while human sciences are associated with zero effects. If one would like to compare the magnitude of these results with the Swedish context there are a number of caveats, even disregarding the fact that one partly compares different educational levels. First, the course contents differ as community college to a large extent offer vocational training. If vocational training is linked to higher returns, as found in Axelsson and Westerlund (2005) and Stenberg (2007a), one would expect the payoff to studies at community college to be more positive. A higher payoff is also implied by other factors such as a less generous financial support to adult students in the US compared with Sweden and that there is a larger dispersion in the US labour force in terms of skills in literacy and mathematics (Adult Literacy Survey in OECD and Statistics Canada, 1995). Even so, the above estimates are an interesting reference point as we now turn to a more detailed account of the first Swedish study which considers the number of credits attained in AE at Komvux.

4. DATA

The cohort born in 1970 consists of roughly 107,000 individuals who resided in Sweden during the period 1988 – 2001. In 1990, the highest attained level of education was compulsory school for 13 per cent of the cohort while 48 per cent had a two year upper secondary school. Participation in AE is naturally most interesting for these two groups with short educations. Among them, the shares registered in AE (at some point until 2001) are 27 per cent of the males and 48 per cent of the females. The fractions are relatively high also in the group with a three year upper secondary school. In all, 25.6 per cent of the men and 43.3 per cent of the women have a registration in AE. The timing of participation is highly influenced by the improved financial conditions during the 1990s; both for the municipalities to offer seats at Komvux and for individuals to get access to loans and grants when in AE. In 1998, the peak in participation occurred as 10 per cent of the cohort was registered at Komvux (almost half of them received the special grant UBS). The intensity of the studies was also influenced by the policies; the average number of courses per individual doubled from 1992 to 1997 and the average number of course credits tripled during the same period.

Most of the AE participants fit in to one of two categories; a first category seeks to improve their formal qualification at upper secondary level and a second category uses AE as a stepping stone to higher education. Methodologically, it is a very different task to explore educational effects of AE if an individual continues to higher education or not (further discussed in section 5). The analyses which follow will therefore keep them separate.

4.1. Individuals with no Registration in Higher Education

The descriptive statistics in this section concern the part of the sample that was never registered in higher education (until 2002). This restriction affects various groups of the sample very differently. Of those with compulsory school or a two year upper secondary school, 12 per cent and 18 per cent are excluded respectively, while the same applies to 67 per cent of those with a three year upper secondary school.

To further adapt the data for the empirical analysis, those registered in AE after 1999 are excluded to allow for observations of earnings post-AE. Another constraint is that AE participants at least once must have an earnings level exceeding SEK 20,000 prior to enrolment.[3] This is to avoid absurdly high percentage increases post-program. For the comparison group (without AE), the condition is set that every individual should have at least four observations with annual wage earnings in excess of SEK 20,000. The purpose is to exclude those who mainly stay outside the labour force. The remaining sample consists of 49,675 individuals of whom 24.8 per cent have at least one registration in AE.

---

[3] Approximately USD 2,500.

Each AE participant is in the following associated with his or her number of course credits accumulated up and until the autumn of 1999. Credits of a course are only given if the grade is at least three (on a scale from one to five) or from 1993/94 Pass, otherwise the credits of that course are set to zero. The number of course credits will then be a better measure of the added human capital of the individual. If one follows Skolverket (2000), a year of full time studies correspond to 500 credits but there are no records of such changes in the formal educational level.

Table 1 presents the sample frequencies with and without AE, across gender and educational levels prior to enrolment. The AE participants are divided into five groups based on their accumulated course credits at upper secondary level. Among them, the fraction with zero credits is rather high, around 25 per cent. The supply of courses is very broad but traditional subjects such as Swedish, English or mathematics attract more than half of the enrolees. The median number of courses is 13 in the group with a prior compulsory school, ten if a two year upper secondary level and six if a three year upper secondary level.

One way to depict annual earnings before, during and after AE is to focus on individuals who participated at approximately the same period of time. Figure 1 (males) and Figure 2 (females) describe average earnings for individuals registered in AE for the first time in the autumn of 1997 and not later than the spring semester of 1999. Using a short window of this kind makes it possible to discern patterns more clearly and in this case one can also single out individuals with UBS, i.e. enrolees who in the majority of cases were unemployed prior to AE. The drawback is that the number of observations becomes limited so the trajectories are only presented for those with a prior two year upper secondary school. As expected, the individuals with UBS had an overall low earnings level before 1997. The AE participants without UBS have higher earnings both before and during their studies, indicating a stronger attachment to the labour market and less intensity in their studies. Post AE, their earnings level is also above that of the control group.

Table 1. Individuals at some point attending upper secondary AE across various educational levels (in 1990)

Males/Females	Compulsory		2-year upp. sec.		3-year upp. sec.	
	M	F	M	F	M	F
Not participated	3,505	1,747	16,339	7,837	3,192	3,157
Zero credits	262	345	868	922	229	417
1-250	315	360	1,290	1,421	427	835
251-500	179	295	582	969	98	192
501-1000	131	297	391	801	61	123
1001-1500	33	111	83	191	10	20
1501-	3	11	11	31	2	0
Median no of credits	125	252	101	207	60	60
Total number of ind.	4,427	3,165	19,564	12,172	4,019	4,744

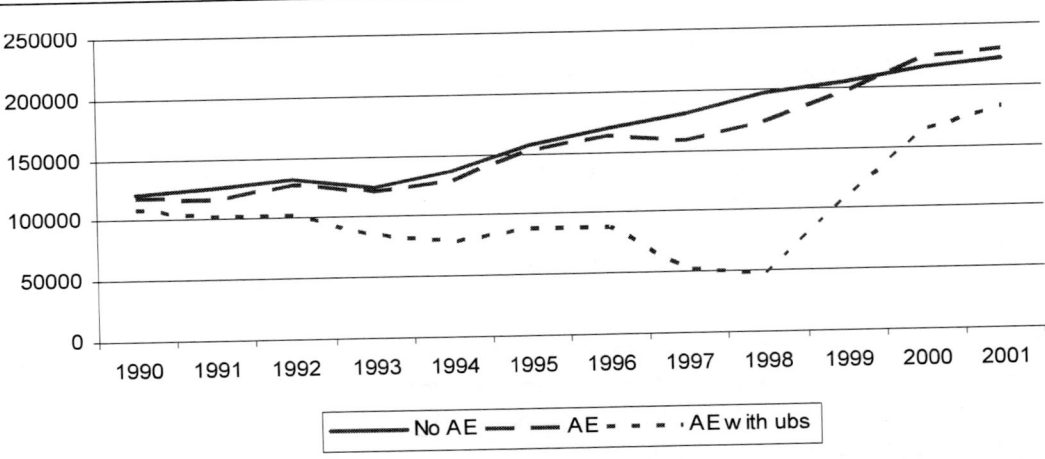

Note: Number of observations in AE are 111 with no UBS and 201 with UBS. Annual wage earnings expressed in SEK 2001 values.

Figure 4. Males with two-year upper secondary school; earnings 1990-2001, AE sample registered from the autumn of 1997 until 1999.

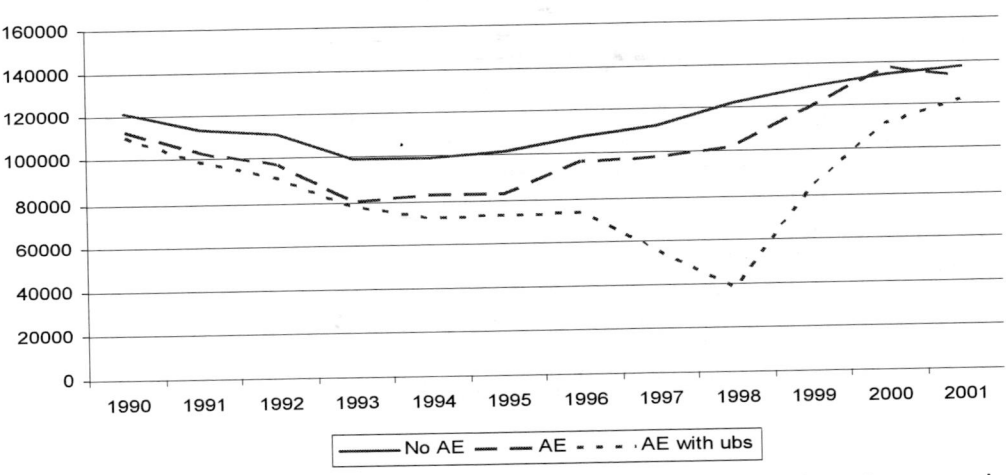

Note: Number of observations in AE are 134 with no UBS and 412 with UBS. Annual wage earnings expressed in SEK 2001 values.

Figure 5. Females with two-year upper secondary school; earnings 1990-2001, AE sample registered from the autumn of 1997 until 1999.

4.2. Individuals Registered in Higher Education

The fraction of AE participants who continue to tertiary education is slightly higher than that of the cohort in general, 44 per cent compared with 36 per cent. Conditioning on regis-tration in higher education, comparisons can be made between individuals with and without AE in terms of accomplished higher studies and/or annual earnings following their completion.

Table 2. Average annual wage earnings (thousands of SEK) in 2002 across years of completed higher education

Years in higher education	Males				Females			
	No AE		AE		No AE		AE	
Totalt	343.7	(8161)	288.3	(2933)	198.0	(7789)	184.4	(4595)
> 1 year	302.4	(.094)	249.0	(.156)	177.6	(.076)	157.2	(.141)
1 years	315.1	(.168)	277.7	(.178)	210.4	(.097)	175.0	(.107)
2 years	322.2	(.165)	286.7	(.159)	162.6	(.254)	163.7	(.202)
3 years	341.0	(.238)	282.3	(.307)	197.7	(.338)	185.4	(.402)
4 years	384.1	(.284)	336.2	(.171)	234.2	(.194)	241.1	(.129)
5 years	405.2	(.020)	365.6	(.020)	255.1	(.025)	262.6	(.016)
≥ 6 years	348.8	(.031)	336.2	(.007)	257.7	(.016)	208.9	(.003)

Note: The sample includes individuals with positive wage earnings in 2002, registered for the first time in higher education before 1998 and for the last time not later than 2000. Further, observations are excluded if a missing value is reported for education attained in 2001, for grade point averages from upper secondary school or whether the individual is foreign born.

The description of wage earnings in 2002 is made without individuals registered in studies after 2000 and without those who in 2002 had zero annual earnings.[4] The sample of AE participants is then reduced by 32 per cent, foremost due to participation in education after 2000, and 19 per cent of the non-AE individuals are excluded. Table 2 shows the average annual earnings across different educational attainments (as measured in 2001). The classification follow the principle that individuals have completed at least the stated number of years of higher education. An exception to this rule is in the group with one year which include individuals with "more than a semester" of studies. If one assumes Table 2 to reflect the actual number of years of accomplished college, the average is 2.62 for those with no prior AE and 2.21 for those with AE. The fractions with at least four years are markedly lower among individuals with AE who instead are over-represented in the groups with three years and less than one year.

The yearly earnings are in general lower for groups with AE, even though this pattern is slightly irregular for females. A natural cause for lower earnings among AE individuals is of course that they have completed their education at a later date, and had a shorter time to establish themselves on the labour market. This is clearly detectable in the data. For example, the fraction of the sample registered in studies after 1997 is 41 per cent among those with AE compared with 24 per cent of the non-AE individuals.

Somewhat unexpectedly, the female group with one year of studies display average earnings that are higher than those with two years and the progress looks weak also for those with three years. At least partly, this reflects different career choices. Women with two years are concentrated to a few educational choices with approximately 40 per cent directed towards teaching at preschool level or recreational activities and 20 per cent in nursing. These professions are strongly connected to the public sector which offers safe employment conditions, has a compressed wage structure and a relatively high share of part-time

---

[4] Wage earnings are only interesting if individuals have completed their university education. Records of registration at komvux are available until 2001 and for higher education until 2002. This is why individuals are followed a year longer here than in the preceding section.

employees. Males display a more stable relation between the years of studies and earnings and their choices of study are far more dispersed across educations than for females. Of the males with two years of higher education, 27 different study directions are represented by more than 1 per cent while for females, the corresponding number is twelve. A similar but less extreme pattern can be discerned among those with three years.

5. ESTIMATIONS AND RESULTS

The empirical section follows the structure of the descriptive part and separates individuals with and without a registration in higher education. First, estimates are presented evaluating the effects of AE course credits on yearly earnings. This is followed by an analysis of individuals registered in tertiary education and whether those with and without AE differ in terms of the probability of accomplishing four years of higher education and/or in their annual wage earnings following completion of their studies.

Before the presentation of the empirical results, it is important to stress the intrinsic methodological dilemma of self-selection in evaluation studies mentioned in section 3. As it is impossible to observe an individual in two states at the same time, with and without the education, a reference group is needed. When analysing the impact of AE on earnings, the sample restrictions will assure that the reference groups always share the same educational level prior to enrolment in AE. The regressions are based on panel data, i.e. data which makes it possible to follow individuals over time and generate difference-in-differences estimates. These results take into account time-consistent differences between individuals and also consider changes over time which are equal to all individuals. However, when the analysis concerns those registered in higher education, it becomes more problematic to observe earnings before education as many individuals continue straight from upper secondary school to university. For this reason, the cross-section of annual earnings in 2002 is used, and the grade point average from upper secondary school controls for otherwise unobservable individual characteristics.

5.1. Individuals with no Registration in Higher Education

The estimates in this section are based on a regression model of the logarithmic value of annual wage earnings 1990-2001. A key explanatory variable is the attained number of AE course credits, which in the regressions below is divided by 500. The coefficient in front of it will thereby reflect the percentage effect on earnings from one year of AE. Table 3 presents these estimates. The parameter values vary strongly depending on educational level prior to enrolment in AE, indicating a five percent earnings increase for individuals with a two-year upper secondary school but three times higher for males with a prior compulsory school. Course credits acquired by individuals with a prior three-year upper secondary school are more complicated to interpret as they to a large extent may concern improvements in grades and/or a re-direction of earlier studies. The estimated effects are negative for males and positive for females.

To check that the positive effects are not an artefact of increases from low income levels, results are also reported from samples where AE participants are conditioned to have earnings exceeding SEK 100,000 at least once both before and after AE enrolment. The coefficient values then increase in three of the first four columns.

Table 3. Estimation results of a year in adult education, defined as Credits attained / 500

Dependent variable: log annual wage earnings 1990-2001						
	Compulsory school		2-year upper secondary		3-year upper secondary	
Males/FemalesM	F	M	F	M	F	
Total sample	.148***	.097***	.051***	.051***	- .059*	.083***
	(.0303)	(.0254)	(.0141)	(.0138)	(.0348)	(.0322)
N^{TOT} / N^{AE}	4427/923	3165/1419	19564/3226	12172/4336	4019/827	4744/1587
Earnings	.128***	.102***	.076***	.095***	- .074*	.015
> 100000	(.0326)	(.0306)	(.0150)	(.0156)	(.0383)	(.0369)
N^{TOT} / N^{AE}	4101/597	2411/664	18803/2464	10793/2956	3715/523	4080/923
With UBS	.066	.065**	.012	.049***	- .110	.126*
	(.0430)	(.0320)	(.0189)	(.0177)	(.0764)	(.0732)
N^{TOT} / N^{AE}	3676/171	2179/432	16946/606	9174/1336	3222/30	3213/56

*** Significant at the 1 % level.
** at the 5 % level.
* at the 10 % level.
Note: N^{TOT} / N^{AE} report total number of individuals and the number with AE.

The effects of AE on earnings reasonably work both through an increase in the probability of finding employment and through an increase in wages. Antelius and Björklund (2000), using data from the Swedish Level of Living Survey, found that when conditioning all observed annual earnings to be above SEK 100,000 the estimates of (youth) educational attainment on annual earnings were similar to estimates on hourly wages. When this is applied here, there is no coefficient that is significantly different from zero, implying that the positive effects in Table 3 essentially work through employment increases rather than wage increases.

The estimates of the enrolees in AE with UBS are insignificant for males. This is at odds with the evaluations of the AEI referred to in section 3 which show positive effects. It may be related to the fact that the regressions above assume a proportional payoff in the number of course credits, but that UBS-individuals partly have decreasing returns, i.e. that individuals with a large number of course credits tend to *not* experience an earnings increase (as reported in Stenberg, 2007a, and Stenberg and Westerlund, 2007). This appears less to be the case among females who, presumably, more often searched for work in the public sector.

One way to proceed with the results reported in Table 3 is to relax the assumption of a proportional payoff to course credits by introducing binary variables indicating different interval numbers of credits. Results from such regressions (not displayed) imply that individuals who study less than 250 credits, i.e. the equivalent of one semester of full time studies, do not experience an earnings payoff from AE.

Table 4. Payoff to AE participants with a prior two-year upper secondary school, conditioning on passes in various subjects

Dependent variable: log annual wage earnings 1990-2001	Males	S.E.	N^{AE}	Females	S.E.	N^{AE}
Maths (M)	- .020	(.0188)	987	- .010	(.0200)	1,401
Swedish (S)	- .001	(.0200)	821	- .025	(.0195)	1,501
English (E)	.016	(.0190)	957	- .031	(.0198)	1,545
M S E	- .044[*]	(.0237)	457	- .042[*]	(.0236)	859
Natural sciences	- .002	(.0249)	616	- .018	(.0255)	863
Computer science	.030[*]	(.0162)	1,095	.054[***]	(.0157)	1,755
Human sciences	.064[*]	(.0366)	170	- .022	(.0338)	409
Health, nursing	.130[***]	(.0311)	176	.136[***]	(.0195)	768
Social sciences	.005	(.0162)	1,312	.053[***]	(.0148)	2,308
Vocational	- .008	(.0261)	345	.002	(.0346)	350

[***] Significant at the 1 % level.
[**] at the 5 % level.
[*] at the 10 % level.
Note: Standard errors within parentheses. N^{AE} report the number of AE participants.

It is also possible to make a rudimentary check of how different subjects studied influence the estimated returns. Table 4 presents results from regressions where AE individuals are conditioned to have a passing grade in various subjects or subject categories. Due to the loss of observations, this is only performed for those with a prior two year upper secondary school. The subject categories are based on the names of the courses and admittedly somewhat arbitrary. Nevertheless, a pattern that emerges is that the positive effects are almost exclusively linked to the categories "health, nursing" and "computer sciences". Most notably, subjects providing general knowledge such as Swedish, English and mathematics, usually thought of as highly important to the labour market performance, are associated with (negative) coefficients that are not significantly different from zero. The results imply that the benefit from general AE is primarily to provide preparation for higher studies. A possible interpretation is that general education has a weaker payoff to groups of individuals from the lower half of the income distribution. In the economics literature, it is sometimes argued that general knowledge is a complement to specific knowledge, i.e. that it enhances the ability to take in firm-specific knowledge (Borghans and Golsteyn, 2005, and Gathmann and Schönberg, 2006) but the results in Table 4 do not support such indirect effects of general knowledge. However, when interpreting the insignificant parameters one should keep in mind that they do not necessarily imply zero returns to AE. If participation in AE entails reduced work experience and/or less intense search for jobs, a zero return would entail negative estimates.

The main result presented in this section is that there is a positive earnings impact of AE course credits. It may partly reconcile the conflicting evidence from earlier studies which have approximated the human capital investment in AE by the number of semesters registered. For example, participants in Ekström's sample were registered in AE in 1993 at the latest. A good guess is that the average number of credits then was considerably lower than a few years later when the financial conditions for studying were more generous. A reservation concerning the results is related to the age of the sample studied (20-31 years old). It is an open question whether age is of importance for the estimated effects. Numerous studies find that beneficial effects decrease with age (Light, 1995, Monks, 1997, on community college in the US and Ekström, 2003 on AE in Sweden). However, Jacobson et al. (2005) report no differences between age groups and Stenberg and Westerlund (2007) find signs of the returns to increase with age. Öckert (2001) finds older students in tertiary education in Sweden to have a lower probability of completing their studies but once they do complete them, their payoff is if anything higher than average.

5.2. Individuals Registered in Higher Education

Let us now continue the analysis by examining whether individuals with and without AE before tertiary education differ in terms of the probability of completing four years of college and/or in the impact on annual wages of higher education. Such differences may arise e.g. if Komvux provides a poorer preparation for higher studies than upper secondary education for youths or if higher education among adults is used as a manner of avoiding the labour market when the probability of finding job is relatively low. Each regression in this section includes the grade point average from upper secondary school to control for systematic differences between AE and non-AE-individuals.

The probability of completing at least four years of higher education is measured by creating a variable which takes the value one if the number of years in education is four or higher, otherwise zero. A logit regression model examines if the probability of this value being one differs between individuals with and without AE. The sample consists of individuals who had started their higher studies in 1997 at the latest. The results (not displayed) imply no differences between male individuals with and without AE but females with AE are found to have a lower probability to complete four years of studies. The results are partly worrying as they raise the question whether AE is of insufficient quality as a preparation for higher studies, but the insignificant results of males contradict this hypothesis. An alternative explanation is that the regression model does not properly catch the responsibility for household work which is possibly larger for females with prior AE compared with the reference group.

The next step is to investigate whether individuals with and without AE differ in their annual earnings after completion of higher education. Table 5 displays results from regressions where the dependent variable is the logarithmic value of annual wage earnings in 2002. The sample is conditioned not to have been registered in education after 2000. Included among the explanatory variables is the number of studying years. This variable assumes values from zero to six (in accordance with Table 2). The coefficients associated with this variable indicate how annual earnings increase for each additional year of higher studies, i.e. by 8.2 per cent for males and 5.1 per cent for females. To discern whether these estimated returns differ for AE individuals, an interaction term is used which is "years of studies" multiplied with one if the individual has been in AE, otherwise zero. However, there are no differences in the returns implied as the parameters are not significantly different from zero at a five per cent level.

Table 5. Wage earnings regression on individuals with registration in higher studies

Dependent variable: Log annual wage earnings in 2002	Males	Females
Years of studies	$.082^{***}$	$.051^{***}$
	(.0072)	(.0108)
AE * yrs of studies	$-.013^{*}$	$-.011$
	(.0072)	(.0106)
N	7,511	9,025
Adj R^2	.073	.043

*** Significant at the 1 % level.
** at the 5 % level.
* at the 10 % level.
Note: Explanatory variables include dummies indicating foreign born, children living at home in 1999, transfers received in 1999 from unemployment insurance, sick-leave, pensions, adult education grants and binary variables indicating year of exam 1991-1999.

This can be analysed further by using binary variables for each accomplished year of studies (not displayed). It relaxes the restriction of a proportional payoff, i.e. that the returns must be identical for each additional year of education. The overall impression of insignificant differences in the returns is maintained except in the groups with one year or less where the annual earnings are significantly lower among AE individuals. This result holds for both men and women. A possible explanation is that the groups with AE more often are dropouts from longer educational programs. Their added human-capital would then be of limited value as it lacks important complementary knowledge never acquired. Another interpretation is that AE individuals have an overall weaker attachment to the labour force which prevents them from using a short college education to be promoted at a current workplace. Also, it can not be excluded that AE participants to a larger extent use education as a means to avoid the labour market where their probability of finding work may be low.

6. ECONOMIC EFFECTS ON THE SOCIETY

Now, one may wonder whether the public investments made in AE are beneficial not only to the individuals but also to the society as a whole. Costs and benefits to the society can be calculated by comparing the estimates of AE on earnings with the costs incurred by teacher salaries, the use of premises and foregone earnings of the participants in AE. When executing such calculations of costs and benefits for the part of the sample that did not continue to higher education, it is found that AE covers its costs within six or seven years. For those that continued to higher education, the AE is beneficial to the society within ten years if one uses an implicit payoff to AE *per se* that is equal to the estimates found in Table 3. Of course, these calculations are based on an incomplete list of costs and benefits as there are a number of immeasurable values of education such as increased (or decreased) self-esteem and spill-over effects on peers and colleagues of the AE participant in terms of democratic values and productivity. Enhancing the employment prospects of one group may also come at the cost of some other group, so called crowding out effects, something which would exaggerate the positive effects from the society's point of view.

7. CONCLUSION

The results of this study show that the equivalent of one year of full time studies in adult upper secondary education in Sweden renders very different returns depending on the level of education prior to enrolment. The preferred estimates concern those with a prior two year upper secondary school and indicate positive effects of around five per cent. Various versions of the regressions further imply that the effects primarily stem from employment effects rather than increased hourly wages. There are no effects if the studies amount to less than one semester and the positive effects are mainly driven by individuals who studied health-related subjects or computer sciences. More general subjects such as Swedish, English and mathematics are not associated with any positive returns. Among those who continued to university, the returns to years of education for individuals with and without AE appear as roughly similar but AE participants had lower payoffs if the studies amounted to less than one year. The results also show that females with AE have a lower probability of completing four years of higher studies. However, a more generalized interpretation of this result seems shaky as it does not hold for males.

REFERENCES

Albrecht, J.W., van den Bergh, G. and Vroman, S.B. (2004): The knowledge lift: The Swedish adult education program that aimed to eliminate low worker skill levels, IFAU Working Paper 2004:17, Uppsala.

Antelius, J. and Björklund, A. (2000): How Reliable are Register Data for Studies of the Return on Schooling? An examination of Swedish data. *Scandinavian Journal of Educational Research* 44(4): 341-355.

Axelsson, R. and Westerlund, O. (2005): Kunskapslyftets effekter på årsarbetsinkomster – Nybörjare höstterminen 1997. *Umeå Economic Studies 647.*

Boesel, D., Alsalam, N. and Smith, T.M. (1998): *Educational and Labor Market Performance of GED Recipients.* US Dept of Education, Washington, DC.

Borghans, L. and Golsteyn, B. (2005). Human Capital Accumulation over the Life-Cycle: Reasons for and Costs of Learning at a Later Age. Mimeo, Maastricht University.

Card, D. (1999): The causal effect of education on earnings. In O.A. Ashenfelter and D. Card (eds): *Handbook of Labor Economics*, Vol 3. Amsterdam: North-Holland.

Ekström, E. (2003): *Essays on Inequality and Education.* Avhandlingsuppsats, Economic Studies 76, Uppsala Universitet.

Gathmann, C. and Schönberg, U. (2006). How General is Specific Human Capital? *IZA Working Paper* 2485.

Grubb, N.W. (2002). Learning and earning in the middle, part I: national studies of pre-baccalaureate education. *Economics of Education Review* 21, 299-321.

Heckman, J. and LaFontaine, P.A. (2006): Bias Corrected Estimates of GED Returns. *NBER Working Paper* 12018.

Jacobson, L.S., LaLonde, R.J. och Sullivan, D.G. (2005): The Returns to Community College Schooling for Displaced Workers. *Journal of Econometrics* 125, 271-304.

Leigh, D.E. and Gill, A.M. (1997). Labour Market returns to Community Colleges: Evidence for Returning Adults. *Journal of Human Resources,* 334-353.

Light, A. (1995): The Effects of Interrupted Schooling on Wages. *Journal of Human Resources* 30(3): 472-502.

Monks, J. (1997): The Impact of College Timing on Earnings. *Economics of Education Review* 16(4): 419-423.

OECD (2006). Education at a glance. OECD, Paris.

OECD and Statistics Canada (1995). *Literacy, Economy and Society. Results of the First International Adult Literacy Survey,* OECD and Statistics Canada, Paris.

Skolverket (2000): Lyft eller bredd? Utbildningsnivåer före och efter studier i kommunal vuxenutbildning/Kunskapslyftet läsåret 1997/98 (Dnr 1999:633):

SOU 1998:51. Vuxenutbildning och livslångt lärande. Situationen inför och under första året med Kunskapslyftet. *Reports of the Government Commission,* Ministry of Education and Science, Stockholm.

Stenberg, A. (2007a): Comprehensive Education or Vocational Training for the Unemployed? *International Journal of Manpower* 28(1), 42-61.

Stenberg, A. (2007b): Does Adult Education at Upper Secondary Level Influence Annual Wage Earnings? *IFAU Working Paper 2007:9,* Uppsala.

Stenberg, A. and Westerlund, O. (2007): Does Comprehensive Education Work for the Unemployed? *Labour Economics,* forthcoming.

Öckert, B. (2002): Do University Enrollment Constraints Affect Education and Earnings? *IFAU Working Paper* 2002:16, Uppsala.

In: Adult Education: Issues and Developments
Editors: P. N. Blakely, A. H. Tomlin, pp. 271-354

ISBN: 978-1-60456-272-9
© 2008 Nova Science Publishers, Inc.

Chapter 8

ADULT LEARNERS IN HIGHER EDUCATION: BARRIERS TO SUCCESS AND STRATEGIES TO IMPROVE RESULTS

Elaine L. Chao[1], Emily Stover DeRocco[2] and Maria K. Flynn[3]

[1] U.S. Department of Labor
[2] Employment and Training Administration
[3] Office of Policy Development and Researc

This series presents research findings and analyses from papers prepared by research contractors, staff members and individual researchers. Manuscripts and comments from interested individuals are welcome. All correspondence should be sent to:

ETA Occasional Papers Office of Policy Development and Research Frances Perkins Building, Room N5641 200 Constitution Avenue, N.W. Washington, D.C. 20210

JOBS FOR THE FUTURE seeks to accelerate the educational and economic advancement of youth and adults struggling in today's economy. JFF partners with leaders in education, business government, and communities around the nation to: strengthen opportunities for youth to succeed in postsecondary learning and highskill careers; increase opportunities for lowincome individuals to move into familysupporting careers; and meet the growing economic demand for knowledgeable and skilled workers.

For more than a decade, EDUVENTURES has been the most trusted and influential name in education market research, consulting services, and peer networking. Our clients include senior administrators and executives from leading educational institutions and companies serving the K12, higher education, and corporate learning markets, as well as decisionmakers in government agencies and the investment community.

FUTUREWORKS is a consulting and policy development firm that helps its clients design and build the strategies and institutions that promote sustainable, skillbased, regional economic growth. Core competencies are rooted in deep knowledge and wide experience in linking sound theory to effective practice in economic and workforce development, postsecondary education, and civic improvement.

This report was prepared for the U.S. Department of Labor, Employment and Training Administration, Office of Policy Development and Research by Jobs for the Future. Since contractors conducting research and evaluation projects under government sponsorship are encouraged to express their own judgment freely, this report does not necessarily represent official opinion or policy of the U.S. Department of Labor.

This report was prepared under Contract No. DOL AF125370000230 from the U.S. Department of Labor. The views expressed herein do not necessarily reflect the policies or opinions of the U.S. Department of Labor.

Jobs for the Future
Richard Kazis
Eduventures
Abigail Callahan Chris Davidson Annie McLeod
FutureWorks
Brian Bosworth Vickie Choitz John Hoops

ACKNOWLEDGEMENTS

The authors would like to thank the U.S. Department of Labor's Employment and Training Administration for its support of this research project. In particular, we would like to thank the following individuals for their support, expertise, and enthusiasm for this project, for funding this research, and for their continued advice and expertise: Maria Flynn; Mary Ann Donovan; Wayne Gordon; and Roxie Nicholson. Many thanks to several colleagues at Jobs for the Future for their insights and advice: Marlene B. Seltzer; Heath Prince; and Jerry Rubin. Our appreciation also goes to Marc S. Miller for his careful and timely editing. Orson Watson, a consultant to JFF, conducted valuable research and contributed greatly to the research and early drafting of sections of this report

PREFACE

Jobs for the Future—with its partners Eduventures and FutureWorks—was asked by the U.S. Department of Labor to synthesize the research literature on the challenges facing adult learners in higher education today and emerging strategies for increasing the number of adults over 24 who earn college credentials and degrees. This synthesis is meant to provide perspectives on key issues facing adults as more and more of them see the need for higher education credentials, not just for shortterm training. The project has two phases: first, this document, which is a broad, synthetic overview of the issues; and second, a more indepth exploration of particular highvalue topics that will be agreed upon by the partners and department personnel.

Powerful economic, demographic, and market trends are reshaping the landscape of higher education, particularly for adults. Moreover, it is wise to ask how these trends might affect its key constituencies: employers who depend on increasingly highly skilled employees for their competitive success and growth; job seekers who need more than high school credentials to succeed in the economy; and workers who may have to, or want to, transition to new careers.

If there is one overarching "takeaway" from this survey, it is that traditional higher education programs and policies—created in an era when the 18to 22yearold, dependent, fulltime student coming right out of high school was seen as the core market for higher education—are not welldesigned for the needs of adult learners, most of whom are "employees who study" rather than "students who work."

This first paper looks at the nature of the obstacles that adult learners face in trying to earn credentials with labor market value, the promise of innovative practices that target adult learners, and changes in institutional and governmental policies that might help more adults earn higher education credentials. The paper is divided into five sections that explore the following:

1. *Supply and demand dynamics*: The changing nature of adult access to and success in higher education and the response of different segments of the higher education industry;
2. *Accessibility*: Ways in which traditional delivery systems create barriers for adult learners and how these barriers might be overcome though innovative programming design and delivery;
3. *Affordability*: Obstacles to adult success in higher education that are a function of student financial aid and institutional funding policies and practices—and strategies that can make aid and adequate funding more accessible to adult learners;
4. *Accountability*: Accountability systems in higher education and how they would have to change to make adult outcomes more visible and better drive improvement in how well college programs serve adult learners; and
5. *Recommendations*: A plan for addressing adult learners' needs in higher education, addressing each of the major topics in this report: accessibility, affordability, and accountability.

Each section begins with a brief set of talking points summarizing the main findings and their implications. The research and policy literature is reviewed. Promising innovations are mapped. Their implications for improving college access and success for adult learners are highlighted.

During the second phase, Jobs for the Future and its partners will undertake additional research on knowledge gaps that were identified in the process of preparing this overview. Possible topics for phase II analysis include assessments of: higher education capacity to serve significantly greater numbers of adult learners and the factors that will shape capacity and the supply/demand balance in the coming years; faculty quality and preparation in programs and fields where adult learners are concentrated in higher education; and the implications of changing patterns of collegegoing for employer engagement in the design of curricula, provision of workbased learning experiences, financing of adult collegegoing, and involvement in the design of and reliance upon improved accountability measures.

SECTION I.
ADULT LEARNERS IN HIGHER EDUCATION: TRENDS IN DEMOGRAPHICS, INSTITUTIONAL GROWTH, AND GAPS IN SERVICE

Talking Points

This paper examines barriers to higher education success facing nontraditional, adult learners and identifies promising strategies for overcoming these obstacles.

- *Adult learners over age 24 currently comprise about 44 percent of U.S. postsecondary students, but many millions more need postsecondary credentials to succeed economically.*
- *The practices and policies of the higher education system continue to favor traditional, financially dependent, 18to 21yearold high school graduates who enroll full time.*

The transformation of the world economy increasingly demands a more highly educated workforce with postsecondary skills and credentials.

- *Today's adults need higher levels of academic and technical knowledge to remain employable in an information and service economy characterized by frequent job and career change.*
- *Adults with postsecondary credentials earn significantly more than those with just a high school education—and the gap has widened.*
- *Job categories with the fastest expected growth in the next decade require postsecondary education; those with the greatest expected decline require only onthejob training.*

The United States runs the risk of being hobbled economically by an adult population that is insufficiently qualified to meet the demands of the modern workplace.

- *Over 60 percent of the U.S. population between the ages of 25 and 64 had no postsecondary education credential in 2004.*
- *Demographic shifts are expected to worsen the gap between qualifications and job demands, creating a shortage of 9 million qualified workers by 2014.*
- *Higher education must look more closely at how to raise the skill levels of the current workforce; the economy cannot depend solely on future graduating high school students.*

The adult learner market is large and has great potential to grow.

- *Growing numbers of adults are participating in postsecondary and workrelated courses; as many as 37 million more adults are interested but unable to participate.*
- *Projections assume a slower growth rate for 200510 for students over age 25 in college credential programs than for traditional 18to 21yearolds, despite the predicted gap in the labor market.*

Adult learners face significant challenges in seeking postsecondary credentials and degrees.

- *The vast majority of adult learners are financially independent, work part time or full time, have dependents, and must juggle many responsibilities with school.*
- *Adults have lower postsecondary persistence and completion rates than traditional students.*
- *Understanding the unique needs of adult learners is critical to designing higher education systems and policies that support this population and promote their success.*

Some types of higher education providers are more responsive than traditional institutions to adult learner needs and interests.

- *Institutions that offer shorter programs and vocational and technical degrees and certificates are most popular with adult learners.*
- *Community colleges and forprofit institutions have been particularly aggressive in creating programs and policies to address the needs of adult learners.*
- *The flexibility and convenience of online education makes it particularly attractive to adult learners and a fastgrowing segment of the postsecondary market.*

The U.S. higher education system can—and must—do a much better job of improving adult learner access and success.

- *The remaining sections of this paper examine the areas of accessibility, affordability, and accountability for opportunities to better align the higher education system with the needs of adult learners and the employers who hire them.*

INTRODUCTION

No longer is the financially dependent, 18yearold high school graduate who enrolls full time the "typical college student." More than half of today's postsecondary students are financially independent; more than half attend school part time; almost 40 percent work full time; 27 percent have children themselves (NCES 2002). More and more adults are looking for ways to upgrade and expand their skills in an effort to improve or protect their economic position. Many are ending up in credential or degreegranting programs in colleges and universities.

However, today's higher education institutions—twoand fouryear, public and private— are failing to serve adult learners well. For too many adults who want to earn postsecondary credentials, the traditional structure and organization of higher education pose significant barriers to access and, particularly, to persistence and success.

This paper examines the obstacles facing nontraditional, adult learners—and points to emerging strategies for overcoming the barriers that keep too many adults on the sidelines of college learning. This paper argues that traditional higher education institutions can do a much better job of serving adults. Huge numbers of adults—over seven million individuals over 25 years of age—are enrolling in both twoand fouryear institutions. However, the mismatch between adult learners' needs and the organizational, funding, and accountability systems in higher education must be addressed—in practice and in policy—if adult learners are to routinely find higher education institutions responsive and effective.

As the convening of the Secretary of Education's Commission on the Future of Higher Education demonstrates, there is growing national concern about the effectiveness and responsiveness of higher education. High and rising college costs, weak and uneven student outcomes, limited institutional accountability for results— these are all receiving significant new attention at the national, state, and institutional levels. Too often, those who debate these challenges and their solutions give short shrift to the needs and the potential market of adult learners, falling back into an outdated conception of higher education as dominated by younger, fulltime learners. The costs of this approach—both to adults who want to upgrade their skills and to our economy that desperately needs more and betterskilled adult workers— are tremendous. The purpose of this paper is to look at higher education from the perspective of the more than seven million adults enrolled in college degree and credential programs and the many millions more who need, and are trying to secure, skills and credentials that can help them succeed economically and make a more positive contribution to society.

CHANGING WORKPLACES PUT MORE EMPHASIS ON EDUCATION

The transformation of the world economy over the past several decades has put a premium on an educated workforce. The industrial economy of the early 20th century that created remunerative work for unskilled labor has given way to an information and service economy that demands higher levels of academic and technical knowledge, as well as other skills such as good communication and problemsolving abilities.

A more fluid and volatile global economy is characterized by more frequent job and career change, which is an important factor in the growing demand for continual learning and skill enhancement.[1] During the late 1990s, about one of every five large U.S. employers downsized its workforce. In addition, more than a third reported simultaneously creating jobs in one division while shedding jobs in another (National Governors Association 2002). To

---

[1] Job tenure for men has dropped significantly in recent decades, from 5.9 years per job to 5.0 between 1982 and 2000. At the same time, job tenure for women has increased. The trends for women appear to be a function of the rise of the percentage of women in the labor force since the 1970s.

remain employable in such an environment, workers continually need to learn new skills and adapt rapidly to new job roles.

THE ECONOMY REWARDS SKILLS AND CREDENTIALS

The ability to access education and training is critical to current and future generations of adult workers seeking higher wages and a better quality of life. Unlike previous generations for whom a high school or General Education Degree (GED) diploma provided a ticket to a livingwage job, the bar has been raised for today's adults. Postsecondary degrees and certificates have become critical even for workers in the lower and middle tiers of the labor market.

A recent analysis of Census data on labor market participation in Louisiana (prior to Hurricane Katrina), conducted by the National Center for Higher Education Management Systems, found a significant disparity in labor market participation by educational attainment. Only 37 percent of those with less than a high school diploma were competing in the labor market, compared to 60 percent of those with a high school diploma and 80 percent of individuals with an Associate's degree or higher (U.S. Census Bureau 2002).

The earnings premium for postsecondary credentials is also significant. In 2003, the median earnings of an American worker with only a high school diploma was $30,800, 38 percent less than the $48,800 median for those with a Bachelor's degree. (See figure 1.) The significant positive return to increasing one's education is evident at all levels of educational attainment. It has only grown over time. Whereas in 1975, a worker with a Bachelor's degree could expect to make 1.5 times the salary of a worker with only a high school diploma, this ratio had increased to 1.8 by 1999 (Day and Newburger 2002).

The value of a postsecondary credential for future employment and earnings is expected to rise. For example, the three job categories projected by the Bureau of Labor Statistics to be among the 10 fastestgrowing through 2014 (as measured by total number of new and vacant positions) and pay a median annual salary over $29,000 (approximately the federal lower living standard income level for a family of four) all require postsecondary credentials (Hecker 2005). Similarly, 15 of the 20 occupations predicted to grow the fastest (in terms of percentage growth in new and vacant positions) require some form of postsecondary education, while nine require a Bachelor's degree or better. All 20 jobs expected to suffer the greatest decline in openings by 2014 require only onthejob training (U.S. Bureau of Labor Statistics 2005).

DEMOGRAPHIC TRENDS WILL WORSEN THE GAP BETWEEN LABOR MARKET NEEDS AND EDUCATIONAL ATTAINMENT

At the same time that postsecondary credentials are becoming more critical for economic and labor market success, demographic changes are working against any automatic rise in postsecondary attainment for the adult population as a whole. As the predominantly white and comparatively welleducated baby boom generation moves toward retirement, there will be fewer young people moving into the labor force to take their place. In addition, because younger age cohorts in this country are more racially and ethnically diverse and have greater representation from groups that have historically not been wellserved in either K12 or postsecondary education, educational attainment rates are likely to drop, at just the time when the economy needs them to rise.

Source: Education Pays 2004, College Board.
Figure 1. Median Earning by Level of Education, 2003.

By 2020, the proportion of whites in the workforce between the ages of 25 and 64 is expected to have dropped 19 percentage points to 63 percent, down from its 1980 level of 82 percent. During the same period, the percentage of Hispanic residents aged 2564 will nearly triple from 6 percent to 17 percent, and the proportion of African Americans in the U.S. population will grow by almost a third (National Center for Public Policy and Higher Education 2005). (See figure 2.) In Texas, a state with very fastgrowing Hispanic population, the state demographer projects that the state will have more Hispanic than Anglo residents by the year 2020 (Murdock 2004).

This demographic shift will have a direct impact on the educational attainment of the U.S. workforce—unless higher education institutions break with their historic patterns of access and completion. According to 2000 Census data, whites are twice as likely as African Americans and three times as likely as Hispanics/Latinos to earn a Bachelor's degree. The racial gap in educational attainment has actually grown since 1980. Between 1980 and 2000, the percentage of workingage Hispanics/Latinos with Bachelor's degrees rose three percentage points to 11 percent and that of African Americans rose 6 percentage points to 15 percent. During the same period, the Bachelor's degree attainment rate for whites jumped a full 10 percentage points (National Center for Public Policy and Higher Education 2005). If these current patterns continue, the result will be a significant erosion in the average education level of the U.S. workforce. The percentage of the workforce with less than a high school diploma may grow by nearly 15 percent over the next 20 years, accompanied by decreases in the fraction of the population that will have earned higherlevel credentials and degrees (Kelly 2005).

The implications for the nation's economy are troubling. Assuming no change in the racial/ethnic educational attainment gap over time, the National Center for Public Policy and Higher Education (2005) projects a loss of $395 in annual personal income per capita between 2000 and 2020—a decrease of 2 percent compared to a 41 percent increase between

1980 and 2000. This expected decrease would carry broad implications, given its impact on individual purchasing power, tax revenues, and the demand for public services. In Texas, where more than half of all Hispanic adults over 25 years of age have less than a high school diploma, the state demographer projects a drop in baccalaureate attainment from 18 to 13 percent of the adult population by 2040, contributing to a projected decline in average household income of between 10 and 15 percent—unless educational attainment rises significantly (Murdock 2004).

The U.S. runs the very real risk of being hobbled economically by an adult population that is insufficiently qualified to meet the demands of the modern workplace. Estimates suggest that by 2014 the U.S. labor force will experience a shortage of 9 million collegeeducated workers: excess openings will exist for 3 million Associate's degree holders, 4 million Bachelor's degree holders, and 2 million advanced degree holders (Employment Policy Foundation 2004).

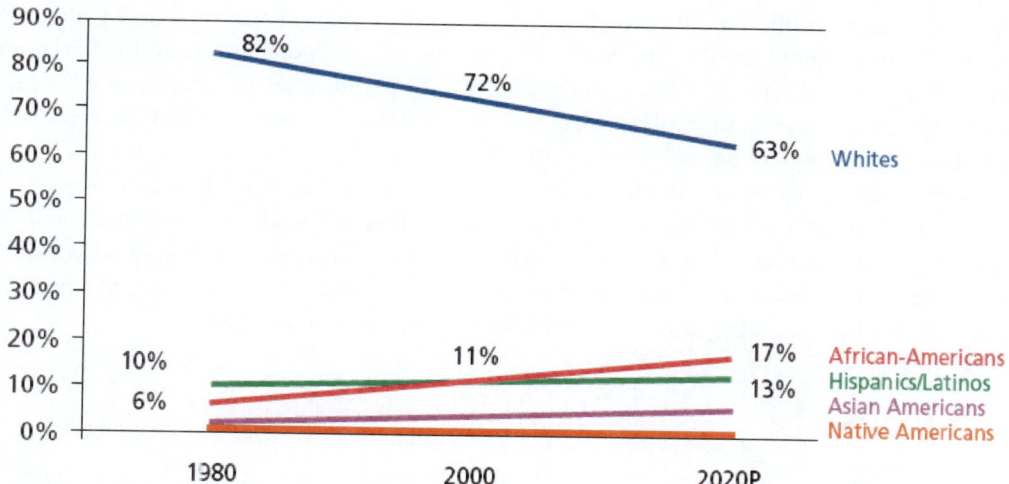

Source: U.S. Census Bureau as reported in National Center for Public Policy and Higher Education, 2005.

Figure 2. U.S. Population by Race/Ethnicity, 1980 to 2020 Projected.

The inescapable reality is that the combination of rising skill requirements and changing demographics makes it essential that the nation look to better meeting the needs of its adult workers for skills and credentials—now. The solution does not lie solely with educating the next generation: the state of Washington has estimated that the number of adults with either a high school diploma or less or a need for ESL instruction is equal to the number of high school graduates projected for the next ten years from the state's secondary schools. The U.S. must find a way to raise the skill levels of the current workforce so that adults with limited abilities will be able to succeed in jobs requiring higher levels of literacy, technological knowhow, and problemsolving capabilities.

ADULT LEARNERS ARE A HUGE MARKET FOR HIGHER EDUCATION—AND THEY ARE DEMANDING SKILLS AND CREDENTIALS

According to data from the U.S. Census Bureau (2004), over 60 percent of the U.S. population between the ages of 25 and 64 in 2004 had no postsecondary education credential. *(See figure 3.)* That is about 65 million people over 25 years of age (Bosworth and Choitz 2002).

Growing numbers of working adults have responded to clear economic signals that they will need more education and training to do well in today's economy. The National Household Education Survey has found consistent increases over the past few decades in the number of adults participating in some form of postsecondary education or training and taking workrelated courses. The number of adults engaging in *any* form of adult education increased from 58 million in 1991 to 90 million in 1999, a remarkable rise in a decade's time (Bosworth and Choitz 2002). In 2003, 33 percent of the population over 25 reported participating in workrelated courses (defined by the Department of Education as courses on narrow topics, delivered in concentrated courses, usually in nonaccredited postsecondary institutions)—up from 24 percent in 1999. *(See figure 4.)*

Many more adults would like to participate in workrelated courses than currently do. An analysis by FutureWorks of the 1995 National Household Education Survey indicated that there may be as many as 37 million adults who are interested in workrelated adult education but unable to participate; 27 percent of working adults in the survey had not participated in workrelated education in the prior 12 months (Bosworth and Choitz 2002).

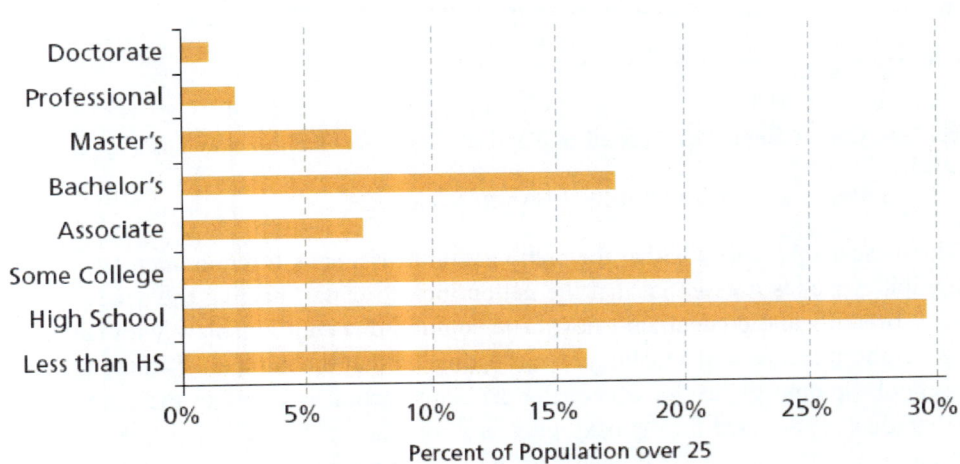

Source: U.S. Census Bureau, 2004.
Figure 3. Educational Attainment of Adults over 25 Years of Age.

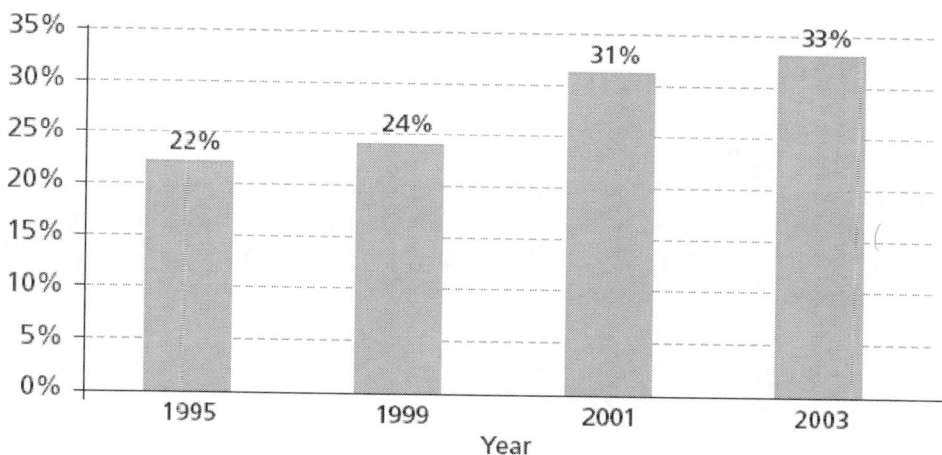

Source: NCES, Participation in Adult Education for WorkRelated Reasons, 20022003; NCES, The Condition of Education Indicator 8; Eduventures analysis.

Figure 4. Percent of Population Over 25 Participating in Workrelated Education.

Adult enrollments in college credential programs have also risen, though more slowly. The percentage of the population over age 25 enrolled in colleges and universities and seeking a degree or certificate grew from about 12 percent in 1970 to about 18 percent in 2002, an increase of 50 percent (NCES 2004). In recent decades, enrollment of adults over age 24 in college credential programs has grown far faster than that of younger students. In 19992000, 7.1 million individuals age 24 or older comprised 43 percent of all undergraduate enrollment, up from 28 percent in 1970 (Berker, Horn, and Carroll 2003).

This trend appears to be shifting. The U.S. Department of Education's projections of annual growth in postsecondary students of different age ranges for the next five years assume a slowing of the growth rate for students over 25 years of age. *(See table 1.)* While the rate of growth from 20002005 was higher for adult students 25 years and older than for the traditional 1821 year olds, the predicted rates through 2010 are lower and insignificant relative to the need.

Table 1. Compound Annual Growth Rate of Higher Education Enrollments by Age, 2000–2010

Age Group	Compound Annual Growth Rate (2000-2005)	Projected Compound Annual Growth Rate (2005-2010)
18 and 19 years old	1.0%	1.9%
20 and 21 years old	2.6%	2.2%
22 to 24 years old	3.7%	1.5%
25 years old and greater	2.8%	1.3%

Source: NCES, 2004.

ADULT LEARNERS HAVE DIFFERENT NEEDS AND FACE DIFFERENT BARRIERS THAN TRADITIONAL STUDENTS

Adult learners face significantly different challenges to completing an education program than students who enroll in college immediately after high school, depend on their parents financially, and work part time or less while in school. A 1998 study by Mathematica Policy Research found four consistent and powerful barriers to further education for working adults (Silva et al. 1998):

- *The lack of time to pursue education;*
- *Family responsibilities;*
- *The scheduling of course time and place; and*
- *The cost of educational courses.*

These obstacles pose challenges to both access to college credential programs and to persistence and success, particularly for students who work full time and attend college part time.

In a 2002 report, *Nontraditional Undergraduates*, the National Center for Education Statistics defined nontraditional students as students with any of seven characteristic risk factors:

- *Delayed enrollment in postsecondary education beyond the first year after high school graduation;*
- *Parttime attendance;*
- *Financial independence from parents;*
- *Fulltime work;*
- *Having dependents (other than a spouse);*
- *Being a single parent; and*
- *No high school diploma (or GED).*

Students who fit only one of these characteristics were labeled "minimally nontraditional," those who fit two or three were "moderately nontraditional," and those with four or more were "highly nontraditional."

In the academic year 19992000, only 27.4 percent of undergraduates met none of these risk factors and could be categorized as traditional students. Just about the same percentage, 27.7 percent, were found to be highly nontraditional. Slightly more—28 percent—were identified as moderately nontraditional and 16.6 met the criteria for minimally nontraditional (Choy 2002). *(See figure 5.)*

Over half of nontraditional students in 2000 were financially independent. Just under half attended college part time, and 46 percent had not enrolled in college directly after high school. Parttime enrollment was significantly more common for students who reported working full time, with 73 percent doing so. Figure 6 summarizes the percentage of all students who reported each of the nontraditional characteristics (Choy 2002).

Although not all nontraditional students are adults (many 1821 year olds meet at least one of the seven criteria), all adult college students are by definition nontraditional. Financially independent, working full time, with dependents and family responsibilities to juggle, and back in school after an extended time out—adult learners are at great risk of not achieving their postsecondary education goals. Over 40 percent of highly and moderately nontraditional students indicated in a survey that work had a negative effect on their grades. More than half also reported that working harmed their ability to schedule classes and register for the number of classes they desired (Choy 2002).

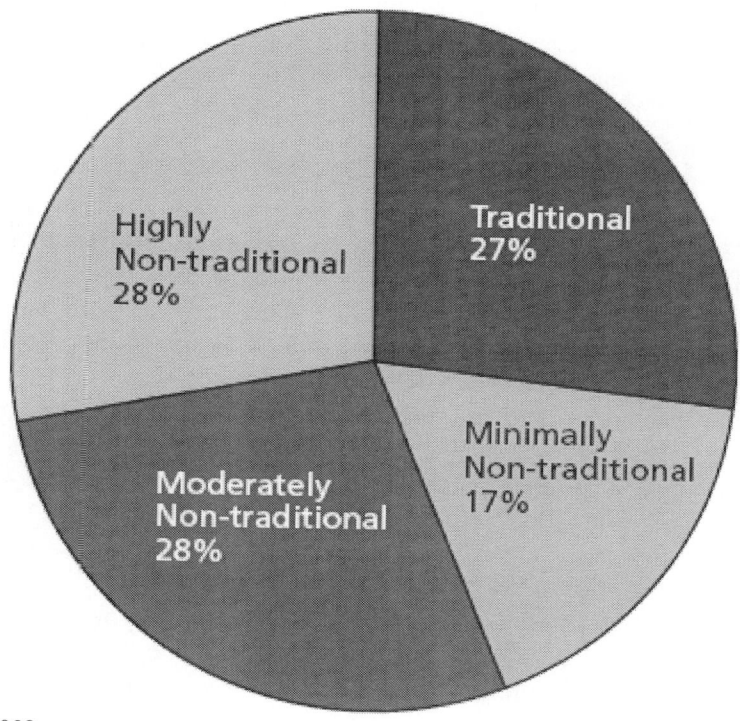

Source: Choy 2002.
Figure 5. Distribution of Students by Traditional/Nontraditional Status, 19992000.

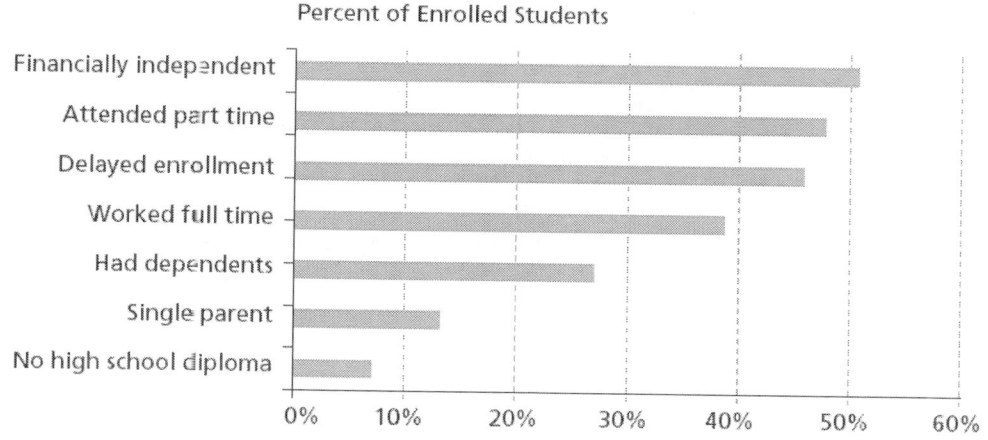

Source: Choy 2002.
Figure 6. Percent of Undergraduates with Nontraditional Characteristics, 19992000.

A recent study took a close look at adult undergraduates who both work and attend college—about 82 percent of the population of adults age 24 and older enrolled in postsecondary education (Berker, Horn, and Carroll 2003). This study contrasted the characteristics and college experiences of two groups: *students who work*, i.e., individuals who saw themselves as students first, working to help pay expenses; and *employees who study*, individuals who see themselves as workers first, taking college programs to help them improve their job prospects or for other reasons. In 19992000, a significant majority— about two out of three working college students—saw themselves as employees first and students second. Among both groups, getting a degree or credential was their primary goal. Among employees who study, about a third had enrolled because their job required them to seek additional education.

"Employees who study" tend to be older, work more, attend school less, and have family responsibilities, compared to their peers whose primary activity was being a student. They tend, therefore, to be more likely to have multiple risk factors associated with moderately and highly nontraditional students. According to this research, 68 percent of working adults who identified themselves as employees who study in 19992000 were at substantial risk of not completing their postsecondary program, by virtue of their being both employed full time and studying only part time (compared to only 18 percent of students who work).

Indeed, adults who are working full time and studying part time have trouble completing their programs. Six years after beginning postsecondary studies, 62 percent of these adult learners had not completed a degree or certificate and were no longer enrolled, compared to 39 percent of students who work. Employees who study were at particular risk of leaving postsecondary education in their first year with no credential, compared to only 7 percent of students who work (Berker et al. 2003).[2]

These findings are consistent with those of the NCES study of nontraditional students, which found that nontraditional students are considerably less likely to complete their program. Three years after enrolling in a community college, nearly half of nontraditional students had left school without a degree, compared to only onefifth of traditional students. Similarly, a sixyear study of students enrolled at fouryear colleges and universities found nontraditional students with at least two risk factors completed at a rate of less than 15 percent, compared to 57 percent of traditional students (Choy 2002).

SOME TYPES OF INSTITUTIONS ARE MORE RESPONSIVE TO ADULT LEARNERS THAN OTHERS

While adult learners face significant barriers to access and success, some segments of postsecondary education have been more responsive to their needs and interests. Not surprisingly, given the preponderance of adult learners who are looking for maximum labor market benefit from shorter courses, institutions that grant vocational and technical certificates and degrees are attracting the largest numbers of adult learners, rather than

---

[2] Persistence in the first year is the challenge: differences in rates of attrition between the two groups of adult college students were similar after the first year.

traditional four year baccalaureate institutions. A study of Census Bureau data indicates significant increases in adult attainment of shorterterm degrees in the past 20 years:

- *From 1984 to 1996, the number of adults with vocational certificates more than doubled, from 1.8 percent of the population to 4.2 percent.*
- *During the same period, the number of adults with Associate's degrees nearly doubled, from 3.4 percent to 6.1 percent.*
- *The growth in vocational and Associate's degrees easily outpaced the increase in baccalaureate attainment, which grew about 33 percent.*

The absolute number of adult learners who are benefiting from this growth in vocational certificates and Associate's degrees remains small—particularly compared to the attrition rates of adult learners from college credential programs. However, these data point to a clear trend among adult learners. Given their schedules and other obligations, adult learners demonstrate a preference for institutions and programs that are shorter and more vocational in nature. This is evident in the patterns of enrollment of traditional and nontraditional undergraduates in higher education presented in table 2.

In broad terms, the U.S. higher education system can be segmented into three categories. (See figure 7):

- *Traditional Public and Private Four-Year Institutions;*
- *Community Colleges (public two-year); and*
- *For-Profit/Proprietary.*

While each of these segments serve the working adult population, they vary in their approach and focus. Two—community colleges and forprofit institutions— have been far more aggressive in trying to meet the particular needs of adults who want to earn college credentials. That strategy is evident in the number of adults who have turned to these institutions for their college credential programs in the past 10 to 20 years.

Table 2. Percentage Distribution of Undergraduates According to Type of Institution Attended, 1999–2000

Student Status	Public, less than 2 year	Public, 2-year	Public, 4-year	Private not-for-profit, less than 4-year	Private not-for-profit, 4-year	Private, for-profit
Total	0.7	44.9	33.4	0.8	14.9	5.2
Traditional	0.2	17.3	52.1	1.0	27.3	2.2
Minimally non-traditional	0.5	39.3	41.0	0.9	13.5	4.7
Moderately non-traditional	0.9	55.5	27.2	0.6	8.6	7.1
Highly non-traditional	1.2	64.2	17.2	0.8	10.1	

Source: NCES: nces.ed.gov/programs/coe/2002/analyses/nontraditional/tables/tab03.asp.

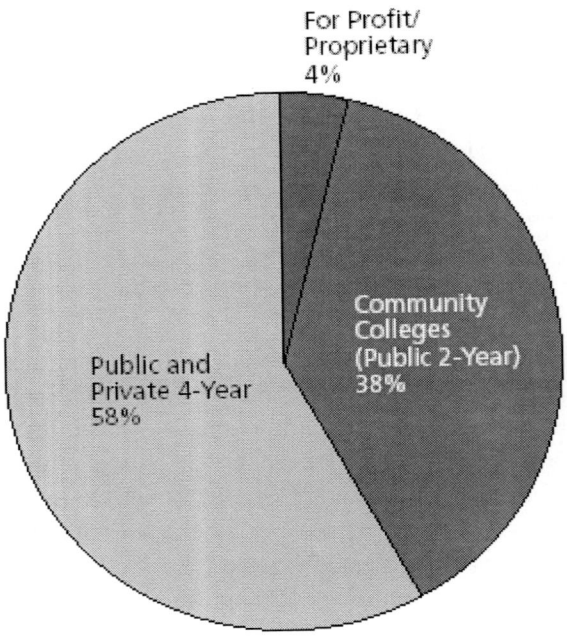

Source: NCES 2004, Table 172.
Figure 7. Postsecondary Undergraduate Enrollment by Type of Institution, 2002.

Traditional Public/Private, Fouryear Institutions Use Continuing Education to Serve Adult Learners

Public and private fouryear colleges and universities have persisted over the past decades as the predominant providers of higher education, serving over 10 million students in 2002 (NCES 2004). Twothirds of these students enroll in public institutions, which offer statesubsidized tuition substantially lower than that of private colleges and universities.

Many public and private fouryear institutions also offer courses and degree programs to less traditional populations through schools of continuing education. While some schools offer Bachelor's degree completion options, many cater to existing professionals interested in graduatelevel degrees and certificates. Although schools of continuing education serve adult learners, the adults who have enrolled have not traditionally been drawn from the atrisk segments of the undereducated. In fact, an Eduventures (2006) survey at a range of schools of continuing education across the U.S. found that the average household income for current students was about $70,000, and more than 70 percent of survey respondents held a Bachelor's degree or above. Moreover, these students are often supported by employer tuition reimbursements.

Community Colleges Serve Largest Portion of Adult Learners

Community colleges enroll more than 6 million students in credit programs each year (along with another 5 million students in noncredit courses) at 1,157 institutions across the nation. Community colleges are very popular with adult and other nontraditional students for a number of reasons: their relative low cost; their mission to serve less academically prepared and lowerincome students; their flexibility in scheduling where and when courses are offered; their occupational and technical skill focus and close ties to local employers. In 2001, over 2.6 million people aged 25 and over enrolled in public twoyear institutions, comprising 44 percent of total community college enrollment. An additional 13 percent of community college students were aged 22 to 24, meaning that more than half of community college attendees are older than the traditional college student (NCES 2004). Parttime students outnumber fulltime students by 62 to 38 percent. Black, Hispanic, Asian and Native American students are all overrepresented in community colleges compared to their enrollment in fouryear colleges and universities.

The popularity—and responsiveness—of community colleges to nontraditional and adult students can be seen in the distribution of different groups of traditional and nontraditional students in their institutions. *(See figure 8.)* The more nontraditional the student, the more likely that he or she will attend a community college.

Forprofit Colleges Serve as a Benchmark for Institutions Looking to Better Serve Adult Learners

Forprofit institutions have been a fixture in American higher education for years, but investment by public companies with access to the capital needed to fund extensive marketing campaigns has raised the public's awareness of these schools in the past decade. This segment of higher education is small: about 770,000 students were served in 2005, according to Eduventures estimates. It has been growing rapidly, though: forprofit postsecondary education companies generated $15.4 billion in revenue in 2004, up 14.3 percent from the prior year, with about twothirds of this growth attributed to increases in enrollment (Eduventures 2004).

This postsecondary segment has been particularly responsive to the adult learner population. Eduventures attributes the rapid growth of forprofit institutions *(see figure 8)* to differentiated offerings that allow for accelerated completion with flexible scheduling and to careeroriented programs tailored to the needs of specific labor markets (Eduventures 2004). These characteristics are exactly those that adult learners are seeking to complete their education. Harris Nesbitt estimates that 56 percent of students attending forprofit institutions are over the age of 24, compared to only 30 percent of those at private and public nonprofits, confirming the appeal of forprofits to the adult learner (Silber and Fisher 2005).

Analysts are predicting that the kind of growth experienced by the forprofit sector in the past decade will decelerate, as competition increases and other factors come into play (Harris Nesbitt 2006).[3] Regardless of the exact trajectory of this segment of the higher education market, two generalizations can be drawn. First, the sector appeals to adult learners, the market that it has explicitly targeted. Forprofit institutions have the potential to play a critical role in helping adult learners advance and succeed. Second, although the forprofit sector is

---

[3] Policymakers and others have been concerned by the emergence of sometimes overzealous and occasionally fraudulent recruiting and/or financial aid practices. These very real excesses are not adversely affecting overall growth of the sector. Nor should the practices of unscrupulous operators overshadow the value delivered by legitimate and ethical institutions.

small and will continue to serve particular narrow industry and skill niches, the sector wields significant power relative to its size as a benchmark of responsiveness and flexibility in serving adults that institutions in other, larger sectors (e.g., twoand fouryear public institutions) might emulate. In designing more effective practices to serve adult learners, the innovative approaches of forprofit institutions point the way for other postsecondary institutions and systems to follow.

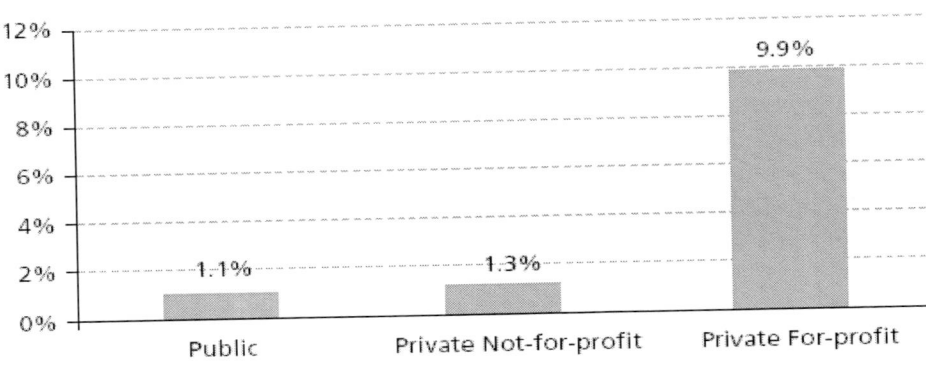

Source: U.S Department of Education, NCES, Condition of Education, 2004.
Figure 8. Compound Annual Growth Rate for Postsecondary Institution Segments, 19922002.

Online Programs Hold out Particular Promise for Adult Learners

Online education is an important innovation in higher education design and delivery that is changing higher education products and services in forprofit and notforprofit, public and private, institutions. Online education has shown significant growth, particularly with adult learners, and appears to have great potential for helping more institutions serve adult learners more effectively.

Online education programs and courses can be found in all higher education segments. It represents a new, flexible medium in which the needs of adult learners may be met. The growth of online learning has been dramatic. Enrollment in courses delivered *entirely* on line increased by nearly 250 percent in the three years from 2002 to 2005. Eduventures estimates that 1.2 million unique students were enrolled in postsecondary programs delivered entirely on line in 2005, a 28 percent increase over the previous year. This number is expected to continue to increase so that, by early 2008, one of every ten postsecondary students will be participating in online distance learning (Edventures, 2005d).

The stature of online education is increasing with key stakeholders. A recent survey by Eduventures found that over 62 percent of employers considered online education equal to or better than facetoface instruction (Eduventures 2005). In a survey of prospective students aged 18 and older, more than threefourths of respondents said that they would consider a fully online program (Eduventures 2005c).

Older potential students are particularly interested in online provision. Over 80 percent of potential students over 25 years of age reported they would consider an online program, compared to 48 percent of respondents 18 to 25 years old (Eduventures 2005c). The increased interest by adults is most likely attributable to the flexibility and convenience offered by online programs. For example, students do not need to live near a college campus or commit the time to commuting, parents can complete coursework while their children are asleep without paying for childcare, and workers with unpredictable schedules can complete their coursework at a different time each week.

THE WAY FORWARD: STRATEGIES FOR BETTER ADDRESSING THE NEEDS OF THE ADULT LEARNER

This section has described the challenge of raising educational attainment in the U.S. and the critical importance of addressing the needs and demands of adult learners, the vast majority of whom work, have family and other responsibilities, and find it hard to free up time and dollars to attend school intensively. We have shown that a large proportion of this population wants to raise their skill and education levels and that they are finding ways to enter higher education, particularly as parttime or shortduration students in institutions that are better set up to serve this population's particular needs. This section has also highlighted the difficulties that adult learners face in persisting in their programs, completing them, and achieving their educational goals. The costs of this attrition and failure—for adults who want education, the employers who need better skilled workers, and the society that bears the costs of this inefficiency—are too high.

In the remaining sections, we take a close look at areas where changes in the practices and policies that shape how postsecondary institutions and adult learners interact could have a powerful impact on improving adult learner access and success. We focus on three areas:

Accessibility: How program structure and delivery in traditional higher education disadvantages working adults—and what can be done to make institutional offerings more adultlearner friendly, more flexible, and easier to move through quickly.

Affordability: How current patterns of student financial aid and institutional funding reinforce the disadvantages that face adult learners, particularly working adults who attend school part time—and how the biases against adult learners can be mitigated.

Accountability: How current enthusiasm for greater accountability in higher education threatens to create and intensify institutional incentives that favor enrollment of traditional students over adult learners—and take institutional attention away from reforms that can address adult student needs more effectively; also, what an accountability system geared to meeting adult students' needs might look like.

The research presented here begins to set out an agenda for further research and action to address this critical challenge from multiple perspectives. Each section begins with a set of "talking points" that summarize the main findings from our review of the literature. The examples and models we highlight in this paper tend to reflect the experience of community colleges and forprofit institutions. This reflects our own knowledge base and our research experience; it is also is an acknowledgement of the importance of these institutions to new directions in serving adult workers efficiently and effectively.

This paper is a broad review of the literature and available research. We look forward to working with the Department to identify mutually agreeable, highvalue topics for further research and analysis.

SECTION 2.

ACCESSIBILITY: GREATER FLEXIBILITY AND MORE ACCELERATED LEARNING OPTIONS ARE NEEDED FOR ADULT LEARNERS

Talking Points

Adult learners have much different needs than traditional college students and face many challenges as they seek postsecondary credentials.

- *Adult learners are more likely to work full time and have family responsibilities that compete for their time, energy, and financial resources.*
- *Adult learners want to minimize the amount of time they spend in class while maximizing the economic payoff of their effort.*

The inability of the higher education system to meet these needs is a significant barrier to access and success for many adult learners.

- *Traditional higher education institutions are organized in ways better suited to younger, traditional students who are more likely to attend full time, work less, and have greater flexibility in terms of time and other commitments.*
- *As a result, adult learners have more trouble staying in college and earning credentials than do more traditional students.*

Public and private institutions that target adult learners seeking postsecondary credentials emphasize alternatives to the inflexibilities built into traditional higher education institutions. Flexible and accelerated program schedules and designs

- *Postsecondary institutions are increasingly offering more flexible schedules, such as weekendonly classes, accelerated vacation programs, online instruction, and critical support services during nontraditional hours.*
- *Some institutions offer multiple entry, exit, and reentry points, including more frequent start times throughout the year.*
- *An area with great promise is the shortening and modularizing of curricula and the offering of interim credentials linked to career advancement.*
- *Some community colleges are improving developmental education by offering basic skills and English language instruction in workrelated contexts and occupational certificate programs.*

"Adultfriendly" instructional methods

- *Forprofit institutions and many college occupational programs are emphasizing adultfocused teaching methods with applied learning models and "practical" curricula that tap into adult experiences in work and life.*
- *New partnerships with employers are helping to integrate jobrelated content and teach what students need to advance in their careers.*

Easier transitions and transfer across institutions

- *Many individual institutions are creating systems that make it easier to move between noncredit and credit courses and programs.*
- *Articulation agreements between institutions help students know in advance which courses will receive credit at their new school; statewide agreements can help smooth turf battles.*

Government and institutional policies created during a different era in higher education are impeding the expansion of models designed to meet adult needs. Program innovations are pushing against powerful traditions of how higher education does business—and point the way toward how the sector's organizational and business models must evolve.

- *Alternative financial aid programs should be considered for adult learners, whose preference for flexible schedules and shorter course offerings often prevent them from qualifying for traditional aid.*
- *Innovative adult learning programs that base credentialing on demonstration of competency rather than on credit hours challenge traditional funding systems based on fulltimeequivalent enrollments; more study is needed of the implications of this shift from institutional to learner convenience.*
- *Credit transfer policy must adapt to balance adult learners' need for greater flexibility in credit accumulation with legitimate concerns about academic quality.*
- *The expansion of technology use has the potential to standardize course content while customizing instructional delivery, freeing up resources for more effective supports to help students stay in school and succeed; more study is needed of this promising new area.*

INTRODUCTION

Adult learners are more likely than traditional students to work full time and have family responsibilities that compete for their time, energy, and financial resources. Where and when classes are available become critically important criteria for deciding where to enroll. The ability to access needed classes and skills quickly is another calculation driving students' choices of schools and programs—and their decisions about whether to enroll in any postsecondary program.

Adult learners—particularly the most economically vulnerable and those most in need of additional credentials to advance in the labor market—use a simple calculus. They ask: How can I maximize the economic value of my time in school while minimizing the amount of time I have to spend in classes? They are looking for flexibility, convenience, and accelerated progress to skills and credentials that pay off, as well as better odds for completion.

Adult learners, many of whom have weak academic preparation, have much lower persistence and completion rates than more traditional and younger students. According to a 2003 General Accounting Office study, about twothirds of lessthanhalf time enrolled adults who began postsecondary certificate and degree programs in 19951996 did not complete a certificate six years later and were no longer enrolled in postsecondary education. The characteristics that make adult learners "nontraditional"—delayed entry into postsecondary education; independent financial status; fulltime employment—also make them more vulnerable to getting derailed and not achieving their educational goals.

Two sets of postsecondary institutions appear to be taking more aggressive steps to serve adult learners more effectively: community colleges and the forprofit colleges that cater explicitly to adult learners. This is certainly true for the most vulnerable and needy adult learners—those with lower incomes, poorer academic preparation, and fewer learning options. According to the National Center for Education Statistics, two thirds of "highly nontraditional" adult learners (those with four or more nontraditional characteristics) are concentrated in public, twoyear community colleges. In the last decade, as noted in Section 1, the forprofit proprietary sector has grown rapidly in enrollments, revenue, and credentials granted.

If more higher education institutions are to adapt to this critically important market, they will have to rethink institutional practices that make it difficult for nontraditional adult learners to find appropriately flexible learning programs. Public policy will need to adapt as well, so that institutions can more easily respond to adult learners' needs.

Fortunately, the past decade has been one of significant innovation and change within segments of higher education interested in competing for adult learners, among twoand fouryear, public and private, forand nonprofit institutions across the country. In this section, we:

- *Outline key challenges and barriers facing adult learners in higher education;*
- *Describe specific institutionallevel innovations and promising practices that can improve outcomes for adult learners; and*
- *Suggest challenges and solutions that require significant and thoughtful innovation beyond the capacity of individual postsecondary institutions, at the level of state and federal policy, if new practices and delivery frameworks are to have an impact at significant scale.*

CHALLENGES AND BARRIERS FACED BY ADULT LEARNERS

The challenges facing adult learners trying to upgrade skills, earn needed credentials, and advance to further education and/or in the labor market can be grouped into three categories:

- *Program structure and duration that make access and persistence difficult;*
- *Pedagogy and supports that do not meet adult learner needs; and*
- *Alignment of institutions and of courses and transferability of credits that slow progress to credentials.*

Program Structure and Duration that Make Access and Persistence Difficult

Twoand fouryear colleges, excluding perhaps the most selective fouryear institutions, have long tried to serve students who work by offering "night school" classes outside the traditional ninetofive business day. This recognition of many students' need for flexibility enabled institutions to tap a broader market. In the current environment, the need for flexibility has grown well beyond the scheduling of daytime courses in the evening.

Given their diversity, adult learners require a menu of flexible options for: when, where, and how courses and programs are offered; how long it takes to complete a class or a program; how easily students can move into and out of classes and programs as their schedules change; and how they can shorten the time it takes to learn sufficient basic skills to succeed in occupational or academic programs.

Inflexible Schedules and Difficult to Access Locations

Adult learners trying to fit education into schedules dominated by work and family obligations need to be able to take courses at night, on weekends, in intensive blocks of vacation time, and in other varied schedules. They need access to courses at workplaces, in their neighborhoods, or at convenient satellite campuses, not just in main campuses that may be many miles away.

Long Course and Program Duration

Adult learners are particularly challenged by inflexibilities built into many multipleyear programs and courses of study that lead to credentials. Twoyear programs, for most adult learners, are that in name only: about 78 percent of firsttime, fulltime community college students do not complete a twoyear course of study within even three years (and this data do not include the majority of community college students who attend part time) (Bailey et al. 2005). Taking six or seven years to complete is not uncommon. For adults who want a credential indicating that they have learned new skills, perhaps skills their employers want them to demonstrate, shorterduration programs of study or programs broken into smaller "chunks," each with an intermediate credential, would be quite attractive.

Inflexible Entry, Exit and Reentry

Many parttime adult learners attend college intermittently, picking up credits or upgrading particular skills whenever they have the time. Traditional degree programs are not designed to stretchout completion over a longer period of time and have their often varied courses add up to a certificate or degree in the end. Openentry, openexit policies that enable adult students to drop out of a course and return in another term, picking up where they left off, without having to repeat the entire course, can be critical to an adult learner's ability to successfully complete certification and degree programs (Cook and King 2005).

Precollegiate Education: Where Many Adults Enter— and Stop

Many working adults enroll in postsecondary programs that can improve their career and income potential—only to find that they lack basic skills necessary to take even introductory degreecredited courses. As a legacy of an often substandard secondary education, these adult students must first complete one or more noncredit "developmental" English and math skills classes. Approximately 40 percent of all community college students are required to take at least one remedial course (McCabe 2000). Many adult learners start even further back on the educational ladder—in adult basic education courses geared to those with less than eighthgrade reading, writing, and math skills. Many from immigrant families start in English as a Second Language courses and programs.

Although such courses are designed to be a door into postsecondary education (and there is sufficient evidence that students who lack collegelevel reading and math skills are unlikely to complete occupational or academic college degrees), they function for many students as the wall that keeps them from earning college credentials. Unable yet to take the classes that brought them to college, timeconstrained adults can get frustrated, lose motivation, and give up. It is not surprising that fewer than half of all developmental education students complete their programs and move on to forcredit work (Kazis and Liebowitz 2003).

Pedagogy and Supports that Do Not Meet Adult Learner Needs

Another set of obstacles to adult learners' success is the lack of instruction and support that can engage them and put and keep them on a path to success. These are important challenges facing institutions that are geared more to teaching younger, traditional students.

Teaching Methods
Traditional postsecondary instructional methods tend toward "chalk and talk" lectures and textbooks that assume the student to be passive, with little experience or expertise to bring to the learning relationship. The instructor defines what, how, and when learning takes place. For adult learners, these traditional teaching methods can not only demean and infantilize them, but they do not acknowledge the reallife experiences and knowledge that the students bring to class. For many lowincome adult learners, traditional pedagogical approaches replicate the very techniques that did not work particularly well for them in high school. Adult learners benefit from active engagement in defining the learning program and approach, from methods that tap their experience base as workers and in other aspects of life, and from learning that is structured in ways that align with work settings—in teams, group discussions, emphasizing skill practice, use of technology, and use of case method to elicit lessons (Knowles 1970).

Adultfocused Academic and Social Supports
Because adult learners typically have spent a significant amount of time away from the classroom, they often require additional supports to succeed. This is especially true of lowincome, minority, and firstgeneration collegegoing adults, many of whom attended weak high schools that prepared them inadequately for college success. In fact, adult learners need as much help as, if not more than, their younger cohorts. They frequently need nonacademic advice and assistance: for example, finding dependable child care is one of the biggest challenges confronting adult learners, particularly at the lowerincome levels.[4] Adult learners

---

[4] In 1999, 55 percent of all adult students and 59 percent of lowincome adult students had dependent children. Fewer than 30 percent of postsecondary institutions offer oncampus child care. Institutions that offer child care have important gaps in services—child care is intended for institutions' employees, many child care centers have

also need a range of academic supports and services, such as tutoring, financial aid advising, and personal counseling—available on and offcampus, during and outside of traditional business hours, from paid staff and peers. Particularly important for adults who are trying to navigate their way to a credential is quality career counseling.

Poor Alignment of Learning Institutions and Systems that Limit Adult Worker Choices and Progress toward Credentials

On its Web site, the KnowledgeWorks Foundation reports the plight of a fairly typical adult worker in Ohio: call him Ken Thomas. Ken is a custodian at a wellknown Ohio manufacturing facility, who decided that he wanted to be a draftsman to increase his salary. After earning his drafting certificate at a nearby adult career center (while working full time), Ken realized that he made even less money than before. Setting his sights higher, Ken checked out the engineering technician program at his local technical college, but he was told that none of his credits were transferable, despite the fact that he had taken many of the same courses through his drafting certificate program. Defeated, Ken returned to being a custodian.

Like Ken, adult learners want to earn credentials as quickly as they can. Frequently, though, the dominant organizational model of higher education—individual institutions that create and offer their own programs, with little crossinstitutional collaboration or sharing of resources—creates barriers to achieving that goal:

- *Within comparable segments of higher education (e.g., fouryear institutions), transferability of credits earned from one institution to another is uncertain and can set students back as they try to get credit for prior experience and courses.*
- *Across different levels, this becomes more problematic: community college courses are frequently rejected for credit by fouryear institutions; technical classes are rejected when students want to switch into different programs.*
- *Credits earned at forprofit institutions are routinely rejected for credit by traditional private and public nonprofit colleges.*
- *In addition, disconnects between noncredit and credit programs within twoyear institutions, and between adult education providers and postsecondary institutions exacerbate the inflexibility that constrains adult students:*
- *A worker might enroll in a noncredit course at a community college, then continue on in a credit program, only to find that he must repeat similar material for credit.*
- *A new immigrant might take an ESL class at a communitybased organization but then find that the material taught did not align with the progression at the local community college.*
- *A returning veteran might seek credit for skills learned in the military, but is frustrated by institutional inflexibilities regarding prior learning outside traditional institutions.*

As individuals become more mobile and freer to choose among geographic regions, labor market sectors, and educational institutions, students (and policymakers) are beginning to demand that our educational institutions and systems become less isolated, more interconnected,

---

limited capacity and do not offer care during lateevening and weekend classes, or have age restrictions that allow toddlers but not infants or older children.

with greater transparency to the learner. Repeating course work unnecessarily and negotiating institutional bureaucratic obstacles can be powerful disincentives for adult learners. The need for strategies that recognize the outcomes of learning undertaken in different contexts, and that ensure that credit is more readily transferable, has become increasingly important.

How Innovative Postsecondary Institutions are Responding to Adult Learner Needs

Adult learners pose some fundamental challenges to the organizational model of traditional higher education. Yet the growth in demand for higher education among adults of many different skill and educational attainment levels is driving many institutions—in the public and private, forprofit and nonprofit sectors—to seek a larger share of this market.

Lessons from the Forprofit Sector
An entire industry has emerged in response: forprofit proprietary colleges and universities devoted exclusively to serving the needs of working adults have been rapidly expanding and flourishing. The sector is small in relation to all of higher education: 3 to 5 percent of all postsecondary education students enroll in forprofit institutions, while only 10 percent of the entire forprofit industry possesses the regional accreditation that enables them to compete with traditional universities. Because of their limited range of course offerings tightly linked to students' skill and career aspirations in a small number of business and technical fields, direct competition with community colleges is likely to remain limited (Bailey et al. 2003). However, these schools are making significant inroads—and appear to be having great success—serving adults within their targeted markets.

Data from the 1990s indicate that forprofit twoyear institutions account for a much higher share of completion of degrees and certificates than they do of enrollments: their emphasis on credentials and completion pays off (Berg 2005).[5] Even with fees higher than public community colleges, forprofit models are surprisingly effective with minority, adult, and firstgeneration students. Of the top 100 institutions conferring degrees on people of color, the top producer of minority B.S. degrees in engineeringrelated technologies was ITT Technical Institutes of California, while the number two and three institutions conferring B.S. degrees in computer and information services on African Americans were Strayer College and DeVry University—all forprofit institutions (Berg 2005).

Moreover, proprietary colleges provide a road map to the kinds of changes in organizational model that will be needed across higher education if adult learners are to be better served. Here are some of the innovations that distinguish these institutions (Bailey et al. 2003):

---

[5] These data must be interpreted cautiously. Many of the schools with the highest rates of completion are not accredited by regional bodies, raising issues of quality. In addition, forprofit students are in school fulltime, many at their employers' expense, for particular certificates, while community college students are attending part time.

- *Focused offerings targeted to meet specific career needs of adult learners.*
- *Curriculum and course content that are standardized and developed centrally, making it possible for students to take courses at different campuses of the same institution or find the same course taught at different times at different campuses.*
- *Use of technology to deliver instruction on line and in combination with classroom instruction.*
- *Faculty hiring decisions that are biased toward applicants with industry experience and an appreciation of applied learning (in addition to an education credential in their field).*
- *Instructional methods that are handson and practical.*
- *Integration of some general education courses with occupational content, and delay of general education courses until after students have started their technical program.*
- *Aggressive and integrated marketing strategy that links admissions, financial aid, assessment, advisement, and registration.*
- *Employment focus that emphasizes counseling and placement and tracking of employment outcomes.*
- *Flexible scheduling with frequent entry and exit options.*
- *Accelerated time to degree as a priority, with shorter course lengths.*
- *Datadriven assessment of student learning and program value to students.*

Like any new and fastgrowing industry, the forprofit college industry is vulnerable to wide variations in quality and outcomes, as well as to fraud and exploitation of students (Dillon 2005). There is a need for policies that can mitigate the excesses without constraining the very real strengths of this sector (Sperling and Tucker 1997). But the power of their redesign of education is significant. As one University of Phoenix administrator notes, "We're really fulfilling a need for what has been an almost forgotten segment of the population: adults" (Berg 2005).

Responses from Traditional Institutions

Like the forprofit sector, twoand fouryear colleges are also responding to the new demand for more flexible and accelerated models of adult learning. Nearly 60 percent of colleges and universities articulate some type of commitment to serving adult students in their mission statements or strategic plans (Cook and King 2005). "Traditional" colleges and universities with a majority 18to 22yearold population offer special programs targeted toward adult learners, such as support services, night and weekend classes, and distance education. Community colleges—for which the adult market is a critically important part of their mission and business strategy—are making particularly aggressive efforts to incorporate some of the approaches evident in the forprofit world into their more comprehensive and complex institutional culture.

Similarly, selectivity in admissions among forprofits means that a segment of the adult population with very low basic skills will be referred to adult education providers and not admitted.

In the following pages, we present some novel and promising solutions to the dominant inflexibilities built into more traditional higher education institutions. We look at innovations in:

- *Availability and duration of courses and programs;*
- *Instructional strategies for adults;*
- *Use of technology for online learning; and*
- *Alignment of institutions and systems.*

While the innovations we highlight are certainly not restricted to community colleges, they are more commonly found in these institutions. For this reason (as well as the nature of our own expertise), we have used community college examples to illustrate the following approaches.[6]

More Fexible Structure and Duration of Courses and Programs

To address adult learners' needs for flexible delivery of learning, innovative postsecondary institutions are following a path similar to that of forprofit schools, when feasible: more varied and flexible schedules; easier and more individualized entry and exit options; and restructuring of twoyear degree programs into shorter, credentialgranting modules that roll up into the full degree.

Flexible Scheduling Options
Nearly 70 percent of all higher education institutions now have course offerings that allow students to complete a degree by taking classes exclusively on nights and weekends. However, this meets just part of the need for scheduling flexibility. Many adults do shift work at night or have better child care options during the day, and find traditional daytime classes a better fit. In response to these challenges, postsecondary institutions are increasingly offering adults:

- *Classes that meet one night a week instead of two or three;*
- *Classes that meet on weekends only;*
- *Accelerated program options that enable adult learners to squeeze learning into available chunks of time;*
- *Courses and curriculum formats that are fully or partially selfpaced;*
- *Distance learning and online options that do not require a physical presence of all students in the same place.*

---

[6] We are unable to characterize the extent to which the practices we describe have diffused through either twoor fouryear institutions. It is safe to say that there is widespread experimentation with new approaches to organizing and delivering instruction in ways that are more flexible. However, as with so many innovations, the challenge is in introducing not just a pilot or a boutique program, but also to rethink institutional practice so that specific innovations are more broadly available and are part of a more concerted effort to address the needs of large numbers of potential or existing students.

Institutions are also beginning to offer critical support services such as career counseling, library services, and administrative functions at nontraditional times. Many schools provide such services on line, along with some forms of instruction and tutoring on a 24hour basis.

Sinclair Community College in Dayton, Ohio, which has a large population of shift workers, has focused on flexibility in scheduling. In some programs, courses are offered at times convenient to all three work shifts, including midnight to 7:00 a.m. Sinclair also offers flexible times for students to access educational support. Faculty are required to hold office hours that are convenient to all shifts, some as late as 3:00 a.m.

Flexible Entry, Exit and Reentry

Some postsecondary institutions have come up with strategies to offer adult learners a menu of more flexible ways to enter and exit individual courses, programs and institutions. For example, a degree program can offer clearly defined, but varied, starting points for students who need Englishlanguage or basic reading, writing, and math skills, or for students who are ready for collegelevel work but lack experience in the occupational or technical field they are entering. For adult students with more experience and skills than a traditional undergraduate, some colleges grant credit for previous knowledge, enabling them to enter programs at a more advanced point in the curriculum. The Council on Adult and Experiential Learning has been a pioneer for decades in the use of models for assessing prior learning and granting college credit for experience (CAEL 2005).

For students who return to school to acquire a skill set for employment purposes, some institutions create nontraditional exit points other than established degree or certificate programs. In these programs, students are given interim certificates that indicate completion of a particular cluster of classes. This certification allows students to get the skills they need without having to take courses that are less immediately relevant. It provides "stepping stones" that are recognizable to employers and other educational institutions.

In acknowledgement of the dynamic career and family lives of adult learners, some institutions are beginning to provide flexible entry and exit points for an entire course of study, allowing students who drop out to return to the same course in another semester and pick up where they left off.

City College of San Francisco, a public twoyear institution with nine campuses, has long been the city's designated provider of adult and vocational education. One out of three students begins in noncredit, developmental courses, and more than 22,000 students speak English as their second language. CCSF established an "open entry, open exit" policy whereby students can drop out of a course and return in another term, picking up where they left off, without having to repeat the entire course.

Modularized Curricula and Certification

An important innovation with promise for adult learners involves enabling students in credential programs to earn certificates or degrees in more manageable "chunks" of time. This may involve either less total time in classes or shorter, sequenced modules that yield interim credentials recognized by employers and linked to career advancement. Such models make it easier for adult learners to maximize credits and credentials during the times they can afford to be in school.

Modularization frequently involves breaking existing credential programs into segments that combine existing courses in new ways. In an effort to address adult motivation, modules typically put the technical skill classes upfront, move general education requirements into later modules, and emphasize career development early so that students understand possible and ultimate pathways. Wellconstructed efforts to shorten and modularize offerings are attentive to the skills employers value, provide interim credentials employers value, and roll up into longerterm credentials that allow for further education and economic advancement. They also tend to emphasize assessment of skills through competency attainment.

In some fields, such as information technology, welldefined career ladders exist, linked to industryrecognized certificates. In others, it is necessary to secure agreements with local employers and industry associations so that they will recognize completion of a particular sequence of courses in a longterm credential program as a milestone for career advancement.

Portland (OR) Community College is a leader in efforts to modularize the curricula and credentialing pathways for occupational programs. PCC first redesigned its Machine Manufacturing Technology Associate's degree and certificate programs into an articulated sequence of open entryopen exit modules. Courses are organized around skill sets identified and validated by employers. Completion of modules is through demonstration of mastery of performance outcomes linked to industry standards—and recognized by interim certificates. Modules are designed to roll together into a longterm credential. This model, which includes career planning early in the sequence and general education courses nearer the end, is also used in accounting and facilities management.

Redesign of Precollegiate Education

Modularization and structural strategies for accelerated progress are also important in the organization and delivery of developmental education, required of students who are not yet ready for collegelevel academic success. Restructuring developmental education into shorter and more integrated pathways to credit programs is critically important if adult learners are to persist to completion. Key elements of some promising new strategies in use among some community colleges include:

- *Integrating developmental skills instruction into occupational certificate programs, rather than requiring completion of developmental education before entering the skills program;*
- *Teaching developmental skills within a workrelated context, tied to a course of study that leads to higherwage employment in high demand sectors;*
- *Partnering with the noncollege adult basic education system to create a bridge from their programs into college credential programs;*
- *Offering basic skill instruction to entrylevel workers at worksites through distance learning and online technology; and*
- *Accelerating progress through developmental education courses by increasing use of selfpaced learning, tied to skill assessments that pinpoint weaknesses and target instruction to them, so students need only a few weeks' refresher.*

Community College of Denver has revamped its developmental education courses to emphasize accelerated mastery of basic skills. An intensive GED lab for welfare recipients makes it possible for students with seventhgrade skills to earn a high school equivalency credential in four months rather than well over a year. Individualized learning targets what a student needs to learn to pass each of the five GED test sections, with a concurrent focus on testtaking and critical skills. The college's CNA (Certified Nursing Assistant) to LPN (Licensed Practical Nurse) program enables working adults at the lowest developmental math level to gain the skills they need to enter the LPN degree program in 24 weeks, compared to the 45 weeks of a traditional developmental education sequence (Goldberger 2006).

More Adultappropriate Pedagogy

Adult-Focused Teaching Methods

The Council on Adult and Experiential Learning (2005) has developed a set of principles of effectiveness for serving adult learners in higher education. CAEL emphasizes the need for multiple methods of instruction—including experiential and problembased methods—for adult learners in order to connect curricular concepts to useful knowledge and skills. Of particular power are methods that recognize learners' individual differences and that model the kind of learning that is expected at work (CAEL and ACE 1993). In many proprietary programs, students are typically organized into learning teams, enabling them to incorporate work experience into their classes. Learning objectives are clear and there are many opportunities for assessment of both student learning and teaching quality.

According to the administrator at one forprofit technical college:

> [Our] approach is different because of how we teach. [We] provide an education for students who are not that theoretically oriented to mathematics but who want to pursue a career in technology. Due to these students' particular orientation, they do best in a handson environment. . . . We do have theory here, but we try to make the theory easier to understand through the use of lots of experiments [labs]... Students look through our curriculum and they see lots of labs and they say, "Oh, I can learn from labs" (Bailey et al. 2003).

In keeping with this more practical orientation, forprofit colleges and many innovative occupational programs in twoand fouryear colleges rely on instructors who are also practitioners and have experience in their field. In forprofit institutions, while introductory general education courses are usually taught as standalone courses, secondlevel "gen ed courses" and some electives—such as Motivation and Leadership; Professional, Business, or Technical Writing; Technology and Ethics—are frequently integrated with career classes (Bailey et al. 2003).

Contextualized Learning that Takes Advantage of Work Setting and Needs

The adult education field stresses the importance of contextualized learning, which sets course instruction within meaningful academic, real life, and occupational contexts. This approach enables learners to see more clearly the relevance of their education by tying learning to tangible, more immediate, results in terms of job performance and opportunity.

To do this well, postsecondary institutions work closely with employers who are looking for workers with particular skills or want to upgrade the skills of their existing workers. Postsecondary institutions are beginning to form strategic partnerships with individual employers and employer associations so they can design curricula, projects, lessons, and assessments that maximize the institution's ability to integrate jobrelated content into instruction, build on learners' jobrelated knowledge and motivations, and organize instruction to help students learn what they need to move forward in their future careers.

Partnerships between colleges and employers are strengthening the ties between adult education and labor market outcomes by:

- *Enabling postsecondary institutions to keep abreast of and adapt to changing employer and industry demands;*
- *Recruiting nontraditional practitioner instructors with experience and contacts in the field of study, broadening their role beyond teacher to include career mentor;*
- *Offering adult student internships and externships to ground their learning in the context of work;*
- *Delivering instruction at workplaces when employers request it;*
- *Revising curriculum and program content to promote contextualization of developmental education, particularly in occupational and skills programs; and*
- *Making it easier for working adults to fit college credential coursework into their busy schedules.*

Genesis Health Care Systems, the largest extended care provider in Massachusetts, and WorkSource, Inc., a labor market intermediary, are partnering with a consortium of community colleges to operate a career advancement program designed to help entrylevel workers in CNA, housekeeping, and dietary positions move on tracks toward betterpaying LPN and RN jobs in two parts of the state. This program is made possible by the state's Extended Care Career Ladder Initiative, designed to meet an acute nursing shortage in the longterm care industry and provide interagency funding for career ladder pathways. The partnership provides intensive career counseling and case management to incumbent employees and facilitates access to education and training. The "Campus on a Campus," on site at Genesis's Agawam facility, provides a range of education and training, including an LPN degree program. Employees meet with career counselors to set career advancement goals and begin to map an education plan to reach those goals (Goldberger 2006).

The Power of Technology to Increase Flexible Access and Accelerate Progress

At the heart of most innovative approaches to increase postsecondary accessibility for adult learners is the power of new information and education technologies. The Internet, email, and videoconferencing create the opportunity for learning to proceed in virtual rather than physical space, in asynchronous schedules, within more mediarich environments, and with connections to workplaces that might otherwise be more limited.

As noted in Section 1, the rise of the Internet has made online distance learning a significant presence in American postsecondary education. By early 2008, one of every ten postsecondary students are likely to be participating in their education via online distance learning (Eduventures 2005d).

The diffusion of online courses and programs is likely to accelerate: in March 2006, in a budget bill, Congress passed a provision eliminating the "50 percent rule." Instituted in 1992 in the wake of fraud investigations of online institutions, this rule had required colleges to deliver at least half their courses on a campus to qualify for federal student aid. A waiver program created in 1998 allowed exemptions for a few dozen colleges with online programs. Enrollments at eight colleges jumped 700 percent in six years (Dillon 2006).

The spread of online education—individual courses combined with traditional classroom courses or wholly online programs—greatly increases the options available. An extra course might be taken on line to complement a classroom course, making it easier to gain credits and advance. An online program might make it possible for a working adult to participate in higher education at night, on weekends, or from varied locations.

The Center for Academic Transformation has shown that the redesign of college courses using instructional technology can also improve quality, reduce cost, and result in higher completion and persistence rates. A project to redesign large enrollment courses at both twoand fouryear public institutions found that redesign that used technology for online tutorials, continuous assessment and feedback, ondemand support, increased interaction among students, and clear milestones for learning found a 10 to 20 percent decrease in the dropfailurewithdrawal rates and higher course completion rates, compared with traditionally taught courses at the same institutions. At the same time, redesign is able to reduce the costs of delivery of largeenrollment classes and expand access to new populations (Twigg 2005).

Alignment of Institutions and Systems

A student who is trying to squeeze the maximum amount of value from a short stint in higher education can ill afford setbacks, particularly those that end up costing time and money because one institution does not recognize learning from courses taken elsewhere. For adult learners, the disconnects between institutions in a given education sector—and across sectors—can be the toughest obstacle to overcome and the most deflating aspect of trying to advance educationally and economically. As noted above, these problems are varied: they exist between noncredit and credit programming within a single institution; academic and occupational courses, within an institution or across them; precollegiate adult education and college creditgranting programs; two and fouryear institutions; and between forprofit and more traditional institutions.

Individual institutions can—and many do—address some of these obstacles to smooth and speedy student progress. They can:

Create Career Pathway Models that Make It Easier to Move from Credit to Noncredit Programs within an Occupational Area

Career pathways are efforts to create clear road maps of how entrylevel individuals, usually adults, can navigate a sequence of precollege and collegelevel technical and other courses that prepare them for advancement in a particular industry or occupation. Negotiated through partnerships that include employers, adult basic education providers, and postsecondary institutions, career pathways smooth the transitions that enable adults to accelerate the earning of credentials that employers seek in fields such as information technology, allied health, hospitality, and early childhood education (Fitzgerald 2006).

Align Credit and Noncredit Courses and Divisions Better

Many adult learners find their way to college initially in a noncredit course that they or their employer might want them to take. This can lead to an interest in moving into a credit program. Colleges can make this transition easier in a number of ways, such as better counseling and advising for noncredit students and clear pathways from noncredit offerings into credit programs. Some schools offer the same course in a credit and noncredit format, with credit students having more assignments and requirements, but with noncredit students having the ability to opt for credit at the end of the course by taking a test on the course material (Alssid et al. 2002).

Negotiate Articulation Agreements among Institutions in a Region to Accept Courses in Particular Programs for Credit

These agreements are common in higher education, particularly between twoand fouryear institutions (and between high schools and colleges), so that students who transfer will know which courses that they take will be given what kind of credit from the school they move into. These agreements can be important tools in helping students get the most out of courses they have taken at different institutions (Jobs for the Future 2004).

Ultimately, though, flexibility and accelerated learning demand action at a level above that of individual institutions and consortia of regional providers and employers. State policy is a critical arena in this regard. For example, state policy can help smooth some of the institutional discontinuities and turf battles that often catch adults in the middle. Take the case of articulation agreements: states with more centralized public higher education systems, such as North Carolina and Florida, have developed a number of statewide articulation agreements. Florida, by having statewide course numbering and curricula, makes it easier for students to know whether their courses will be transferable to other institutions in the state.

Or consider how states fund noncredit versus credit programs. In a number of states, including Oregon, credit and noncredit courses are funded at the same reimbursement rate by the state. This minimizes the tendency to focus all the attention on traditional courses and encourages more innovation and less of a divide between divisions within higher education institutions. The impact of equal funding is significant. In Washington State, which does not fund noncredit courses in the state community college FTE formula, noncredit courses account for 3 percent of the community college FTE. In neighboring Oregon, in 19992000, 32 percent of the total FTE generated by Oregon community colleges was noncredit (Warford 2002).

Kentucky has tried to minimize the discontinuity between noncredit and credit courses by helping students secure credit for developmental courses taught in the state's adult education system. The state has also turned a significant number of noncredit courses in its community college and workforce system into credit offerings by adjusting curriculum and learning expectations to align with both college and employer standards.

BEYOND INSTITUTIONAL INNOVATION: IMPLICATIONS FOR SYSTEMS AND POLICY

The key to serving adult learners is providing them with opportunities to earn workrelated postsecondary credentials with a maximum of flexibility, speed of mastery, and useful learning. Market forces have led both forprofit and more traditional learning providers to seek new ways to serve this vibrant market more effectively.

However, as the adult higher education market evolves, new models are bumping up against rigidities not just in institutional practice, but also in the rules, regulatory frameworks, and other policies that shape institutions and their behavior.

We are at the beginning of complex debates and battles over how these rules and policy frameworks—at the state and federal level, but also in longstanding accountability mechanisms like accreditation—must change to accommodate adult learners and their particular needs (while sustaining strengths that have developed over time in serving more traditional students). The outcome of these debates and policy battles will play a significant role in determining how well the existing higher education systems and institutions ultimately will respond to adult learner needs.

The kinds of flexible delivery systems and innovative program structures described above raise a number of very serious challenges to the organization and business models of traditional higher education that must be addressed thoughtfully.

More Flexible Program Length and Scheduling: Can Financial Aid Systems Adjust?

As the next section explains, federal and state student financial aid is far more easily accessed by traditional and fulltime students than adult learners, who typically attend school part time. As instructional delivery becomes more flexible, competencybased, and customized to student needs, the "fit" between financial aid rules and student coursetaking patterns weakens. If planners and policymakers are not careful, flexible scheduling can make it more difficult for students to qualify for financial aid and to access aid across various smaller modules or "chunks" of a program, particularly if those segments do not explicitly constitute a credential program when reassembled as a whole package. This mismatch constrains institutions' interest in and ability to experiment with shorter and accelerated programs and courses. As the next section suggests, alternative aid programs that are a better fit with adult learning realities might be needed.

Competency Assessment: Can Proficiencies be Reconciled with Credit Hours?

Innovative adult learning programs—particularly those that are responsive to student needs for acceleration and employer interest in particular technical or workrelated skills—frequently base progress and credentialing on demonstration of specific competencies. Courses are designed in shorterthansemester chunks. Students earn credentials—whenever they are ready—by showing mastery of content or skills on selfpaced exams, through performance assessment and other methods, not for completing a certain number of credit hours.

These models pose a challenge to the structure, organization, and business model that dominates traditional higher education, which is primarily funded on the basis of Full Time Equivalent enrollments in courses of specific length. As learning becomes more centered on adult students' needs and experiences, organizational and finance models built around standardized course duration may need to change, so they are better aligned with the notion that adult learning will occur when the adult learner has the time, not when the institution has prearranged it (Bonk and Kim 2004). The full implications of the emerging shift from institutional routine and convenience to a flexible customerresponsiveness are only beginning to be understood.

Transfer of Credits: Can Greater Flexibility and Access be Balanced with Academic Quality Concerns?

About 60 percent of undergraduates enroll in courses at more than one institution during their college career, according to U.S. Department of Education researcher Clifford Adelman (2004), a proportion that has risen from 40 percent in 1970.[7] This growing tendency to take courses at multiple institutions makes the ability to transfer credits increasingly important for adult learners. Larger forprofit institutions like the University of Phoenix use standardized curricula and course content: Phoenix can offer the same course across its many campuses without any questions about consistency and comparability (Berg 2005b). However, traditional institutions have long protected their right to accept or reject courses and credits from other institutions, in the name of academic standards. (They also want to protect revenue, which can be threatened by more fluid transfers of credits across institutions.) A number of states, such as Florida, have recently standardized course numbering and learning content, to make it easier for courses to be assessed as to the transferability of credits. However, private colleges are frequently more resistant; and in states where public higher education is decentralized, individual institutions typically retain the power to accept or reject credits from another institution. The transferability of credits is particularly difficult for students taking occupational courses and sequences. Transferability between forprofit and traditional higher education institutions is similarly fraught.

The balance between different public purposes needs to be addressed carefully, but headon. Those who view credit transfer primarily as an academic issue see the current practice of casebycase faculty review of course and program standards as a critical protection of instructional quality. Those who see transfer primarily as an accessibility issue focus on the need to promote flexible accumulation of learning and credits to meet the realities of adult enrollment patterns (Eaton 2005).

---

[7] While coursetaking at multiple institutions has risen, the patterns vary for different groups. The vast majority of students who start their education at a fouryear institution, particularly traditional age students, finish their degree at the school where they started. They may be taking courses elsewhere, but they have not transferred or been "mobile" students. For adult students and for students who begin at twoyear institutions, mobility is much more of an issue.

The question is: how can transfer policy advance both goals? How our nation—its states, regional and program accreditation bodies, and institutions—responds to this complex challenge will have a great impact on adult learners' ability to pursue coherent, yet flexible, learning paths toward higher education credentials and valuable skills.

Technological Innovation: Would Adult Learners Benefit from More Standardized Instruction and More Customized Support Services?

The rapid expansion of technology use in higher education, particularly in forprofit institutions but also in more traditional institutions, raises huge questions for the future structure and organization of higher education—and for the traditional conceptions of how instruction and learning are delivered. In a provocative essay, Dewayne Matthews, senior research director at the Lumina Foundation for Education, argues that "[b]ecause of telecommunications and inexpensive computing power, the content of the college curriculum is rapidly becoming universally available at little or no cost to the consumer" (Matthews 2005). Content is becoming a commodity and traditional college classroom delivery is no longer the most efficient delivery method. Matthews argues that value will increasingly come not from the creation of content, but from its packaging and delivery to meet the specific needs of particular groups of individuals.

If content costs can be reduced, this can free up resources for customization of delivery methods—to workplaces, nontraditional venues, or in the home. It can also free up resources for more effective and powerful supports for students—academic supports such as counseling, tutoring, mentoring, and advising, as well as social supports that can help students find services they need to stay in school. As content becomes more standardized, the valueadded of institutions might be their ability to support students so they persist, complete, succeed, and move on to meet their personal goals.

The implications are significant. Greater attention to the demands of particular niche markets, such as groups of employers in particular industries or groups of students with particular basic or technical skill needs, will be critical to the longterm viability of many higher education institutions. In that environment, learner outcomes will become the coin of the realm. As the accountability section below argues, the measure of effectiveness will have to be in the payoff in the labor market and in access to future further education and credentials. The competitive edge (and perhaps the relative investment of resources) may shift away from the development of course content to its packaging in a rich system of delivery options and support systems.

SECTION 3.

AFFORDABILITY: NEW STRATEGIES OF STUDENT AID AND INSTITUTIONAL FINANCING ARE NECESSARY TO SUPPORT THE NEEDS OF ADULT LEARNERS

Talking Points

Federal financial aid policies disadvantage working adults who struggle to balance the conflicting demands of work, family, and college enrollment

- *Federal education loans are available only to students attending half time or more. Working adults are seldom able to maintain this pace of enrollment for more than one or two semesters.*
- *Pell grants are technically available even to lessthanhalftime students, but the eligibility formula does not allow these students (as opposed to students who are halftime or more) to count living expenses or other indirect costs as part of the cost of education.*
- *The practice of determining Pell eligibility based on the previous year's income penalizes working adults seeking to return to school following layoffs and sharp reductions in income.*
- *Pell grants cannot be used for nondegree or noncredit programs that might otherwise be attractive to working adults who want to improve specific jobrelated skills.*
- *Requirements to demonstrate "satisfactory progress" toward completion can be a barrier for those working adults who can take only one or two courses at a time; the twosemestersperyear limit can be a problem for those trying to accelerate their way through programs.*
- *Even though working adults strongly prefer intensive, shortterm programs, Pell grants pay only for programs provided over a traditional 15week basis with a minimum of 16 credit hours.*
- *Pell grants can be used for distance learning programs only if they lead to a degree; oneyear or shorter certificate programs otherwise attractive to adults are not eligible.*
- *New (1998) federal tax credits are not much help to working adults. Less than 20 percent of the credits (which totaled $6.3 billion in 2003) are going to working adults.*
- *Of the two tax credits, the generous one—the Hope Scholarship—is only available to families of more traditional students (halftime or more). The Lifetime Learning Tax Credit that was intended for working adults is much less generous and is irrelevant for millions of working adults whose lack of postsecondary education forces them into lowpaying jobs where tax credits are not useful.*

State student aid polices generally follow federal eligibility rules, severely limiting aid to lessthanhalftime students.

- *A majority of the states provide no grant aid to lessthanhalftime students.*
- *A few states have more liberal, needbased formulas that do not disadvantage students based on enrollment intensity.*
- *A few states provide grants to students in shortterm, intensive, nondegree programs that would not be eligible under Pell.*
- *Almost all states have very early aid application deadlines (March or April preceding the fall semester of intended enrollment) that disadvantage adults whose work and family obligations discourage longterm planning.*

Federal workforce development programs—TANF and WIA—can sometimes pay for postsecondary study, but eligibility requirements and program restrictions pose sharp limitations.

- *Some states aggressively utilize TANF resources (including state MOE funds) for postsecondary study.*
- *Less than 40 percent of WIA funds are used for education and training.*
- *Proposed new "Career Advancement Accounts" offer strong promise to boost postsecondary studies by the WIAeligible population.*

State institutional financing methods discourage programming that would be better suited to the needs of working adults.

- *The shift toward tuition support and away from state support disadvantages those working adults with limited resources and those not eligible for financial aid.*
- *FTEbased funding formulations can make parttime adult students less attractive to colleges.*
- *State funding seldom supports noncredit coursework that is otherwise attractive to employers and their workers.*
- *The gap between "workforce development" and "academic" programs is widening.*

In order to meet the needs of adult learners, state and federal governments should undertake a systemic redesign of student aid policies. Specific new directions to help working adults afford the postsecondary credentials they need for economic success might include:

- *Recognizing more adequately in Pell grant distribution formulas the educational costs facing working adults and their interest in yearround study.*
- *Using aid policies to encourage shortterm, intensive programs and innovative delivery mechanisms that will help underprepared working adults rapidly acquire postsecondary credentials with immediate labor market impact.[8]*
- *Providing federal loans, subsidized for the most needy, for working adults who have demonstrated their commitment and capacity for postsecondary study but are unable to complete college on a half time or more basis.*
- *Encouraging states to apply their aid programs to working adults in ways that complement federal support.*

---

[8] As seems feasible in the DOLproposed new "Career Advancement Accounts."

- *Modifying the Lifetime Learning Tax Credit (LLTC) to offer working adults parity with the more generous credits available for traditional students through the Hope program.*
- *Making the LLTC credits available to lowincome working adults though new "refundability" provisions similar to those of the Earned Income Tax Credit.*

INTRODUCTION

From the original enactment of the federal Higher Education Act in 1965, federal and state student aid and institutional financing policies have been designed primarily for traditional students—dependent adolescents who enroll full time in residential institutions immediately after high school graduation and pursue traditional programs with traditional classroom models of program delivery. As described in Section 1, such students are a declining minority of postsecondary enrollment in both community colleges and fouryear colleges (NCES 2002).

Most adults attempting postsecondary education have jobs and families and are unable to enroll on a fulltime or even a halftime basis, especially over the 15week semester model of traditional postsecondary education. Those who lack any postsecondary education and therefore need it the most (about 60 percent of working adults over age 24 have no credential beyond high school) tend to be employed in lowwage jobs that do not offer employer supports or the time flexibility to pursue traditional postsecondary opportunities. Yet because aid eligibility is based not just on need but also on enrollment intensity, adult learners frequently find that they are ineligible for student aid or that they can receive only nominal amounts.

State institutional financing models offer little financial incentive to colleges to serve these parttime, working adult students. Funding formulas that are based on fulltime enrollment equivalency advantage those colleges that have mostly fulltime students and discourage better attention to the needs of working adults. While working adults do not necessarily require more expensive support than traditional students, it often costs the college more to educate two halftime students than one fulltime student (MDRC 2003). In addition, federal and state aid policies and statebased institutional financing systems have tended to discourage compressed and accelerated programming that would better meet the scheduling needs and learning styles of many working adults (FutureWorks 2002).

If we are to respond more effectively to the challenges of a 21st century economy, where the good jobs require credentialed postsecondary skills and where competitive businesses need better educated workers, postsecondary financing and student aid policies must change to better serve those 65 million working adults who have no postsecondary credentials.

A Quick Primer on Federal Student Aid

The federal government provides student aid for postsecondary education in the form of grants, loans, and tax credits.[9] The grant programs and some of the loan programs require a demonstration of financial need. To determine their eligibility for needbased aid, students and their families supply detailed financial information using a uniform process known as the Free Application for Federal Student Aid (FAFSA), from which the Department of Education calculates the Expected Family Contribution (EFC). Schools estimate their Cost of Attendance (COA), subtract the EFC, and then work with the student to at least partially bridge the gap with grants, loans, and workstudy as appropriate.

Grants

Under the federal Higher Education Act (HEA), there are two types of grants available to students who can demonstrate financial need.[10] The Federal Pell Grant is by far the largest program. In 200304, 5.1 million students received an average award of $2,466, for a total of $12.7 billion. The maximum grant is now set at $4,050 and the minimum award is $400. The Federal Supplemental Educational Opportunity Grants (SEOG) are awarded to undergraduate students with exceptional financial need. In 200304, 1.2 million students received an average award of $615 for a total of $760 million.

SEOG awards range between a minimum of $100 and a maximum of $4,000. Both Pell and SEOG grants are available to students regardless of enrollment intensity, but the determination of need for lessthanhalftime students differs from the calculation for those who are halftime or more.

Loans

There are three federal student loan programs under the HEA—the small "Perkins Loan" program for students with exceptional need who are enrolled full or part time and two larger "Stafford Loan" programs for students who are enrolled at least half time.[11] The Federal Stafford Direct Loans come from the U.S. Department of Labor and are delivered through the schools and repaid to the schools. The Federal Family Education Stafford Loans come from a bank, credit union, or other private lender and are repaid to the lender or its collection agent.

---

[9] Most colleges and universities also participate in the federal workstudy program, which provides parttime jobs to fulltime or parttime students. Adult students usually work already and rarely are in a position to benefit from the workstudy program.

[10] There are some federal grants available through nonHEA programs, including tuition assistance for activeduty armed forces personnel, Reserve Officers Training Corps members, and education and training payments for veterans and dependents. There are also Americorps national service grants, a variety of small programs for Native Americans, and modestly funded NSF and Health Service grants for graduate studies. In 200304, these grants amounted to about $3.7 billion.

[11] There is an additional program, the PLUS Loans, available without subsidy for parents of dependent undergraduates who are enrolled at least half time, up to the amount of need minus other aid. In 200304, the interest rate for loans in repayment was 4.17 percent and about $7.1 billion was loaned. In addition, there are a few small and highly targeted loan programs for health professionals available through HHS.

In 200304, about $1.2 billion was loaned under the Perkins program, and about $48.4 billion was loaned under the two Stafford programs. While the Perkins loans cannot exceed the unmet need of the student, the *unsubsidized* Stafford loans do not require a demonstration of need. However, students who have financial need after counting all other grant awards may receive a *subsidized loan* up to the amount of that need. Under these subsidized Stafford loans, the federal government will pay the interest while the student is enrolled at least half time for the first six months after the student leaves school (or reduces enrollment intensity to less than half time) and during any period of deferment. Interest on the Perkins loan is set at 5 percent. Interest on the Stafford Loans changes yearly; in 200405 it was 3.37 percent for loans in repayment. There are annual and total limits that a student may borrow under the Stafford Loan programs, as outlined in the chart below. (See table 3.)

Table 3. Annual and Total Limits to Student Borrowing under Stafford Loan Program[12]

	Dependent Undergraduate Student	Independent Undergraduate Student	Graduate and Professional Student
1st Year	$2,625*	$6,625	$18,500 for each
2nd Year	$3,500**	$7,500	$18,500 for each
3rd and 4th Year (each)	$5,500	$10,500	
Maximum Debt at Graduation	$23,000	$46,000	$138,500 (includes undergraduate loans)

*As of July 1, 2007, this will increase to $3,500.
** As of July 1, 2007, this will increase to $4,500.

The prohibition against federal loans, subsidized or unsubsidized, for lessthanhalftime enrollment does not mean that many working adults taking only a few courses at a time do not borrow; it simply means that they must borrow from highercost, private sources. In fact, for all categories of students, private, bankbased borrowing is growing at a very rapid pace. From just less than $1.3 billion in 199596, private borrowing increased to almost $10.6 billion by 200304 (College Board 2004). This data may not capture much private lending that is not certified by or directly received by a college or university, and it does not include credit card debt (ACE 2004). While there is little hard data about private college debt incurred by working adults, research suggests that independent students who maintain their own households rely more heavily on credit card debt to finance college expenditures than their younger, dependent peers (ACE 2004).

Tax Credits

There are two major tax credit programs— the Hope Scholarship and the Lifetime Learning Tax Credit (LLTC)—established under the Taxpayer Relief Act of 1997 that directly offset the cost of postsecondary education for eligible families.[13] Both programs are tied to similar family income levels; the credits begin to phase out at modified adjusted gross

---

[12] The Deficit Reduction Act of 2005, signed by the President on February 8, 2006, will increase the interest rates on all these federal loans, probably effective on July 1, 2006. However, because of technical inconsistencies in the act, the Department of Education will have to clarify these new rates by administrative ruling.

[13] Federal tax laws also permit a variety of taxadvantaged college savings plans (*i.e.*, Section 529 savings plans, education IRAs, and penaltyfree IRA withdrawals) that are not discussed here.

income levels above $43,000 for single filers and above $87,000 for joint filers. They phase out fully at income levels above $53,000 and $107,000, for a single return and a joint return, respectively. Unlike the Earned Income Tax Credit, these programs are not *refundable*; that is, the taxpayer must have tax liability equal to or greater than the amount of the credit for which they may qualify. Lowincome families and individuals may not have enough income to qualify for the credits.

The Hope Scholarship provides a tax credit of up to $1,500 for each of the first two years of postsecondary education. Depending on family income, tax filers can claim a credit equal to 100 percent of the first $1,000 and 50 percent of the next $1,000 spent on qualified expenses (limited to tuition and fees and net of any grants received) for themselves and/or any (each) of their dependents. Students must be pursuing a formal academic credential, and they must attend at least half time to qualify. Because eligible costs almost always exceed $2,000 for halftime or more attendees, most fully incomeeligible taxpayers are almost always able to obtain the full amount of the Hope credit.

The LLTC allows students (or taxpayers claiming the students as dependents) who are studying beyond the first two years of undergraduate coursework, or those taking courses on a lessthanhalftime basis, to claim a credit of 20 percent on the first $10,000 of tuition and fee expenses (net of grants received) up to a maximum credit per taxpayer (family) of $2,000. Those claiming the LLTC need not be pursuing a recognized credential. Fulltime or morethanhalftime students frequently have eligible expenses approaching or even exceeding $10,000. Lessthanhalftime students, especially those attending public community colleges, would almost certainly not incur tuition and fee costs that would result in a substantial credit.

In 2001, 7.4 million taxpayers received $5.2 billion in credits—44 percent of those taxpayers received $3.1 billion in Hope credits, 52 percent received $1.7 billion in LLTC credits, and an additional 5 percent of them received $.47 billion in benefits from both programs. About 35 percent of the credits went to households with annual adjusted gross incomes below $30,000. The mean credit for Hope recipients in 2001 was $969 and the mean for LLTC recipients was $432. Filers who received the credit for their own/spouse's expenses but did not indicate on their tax return that they were primarily students (that is, they indicated an occupation other than student) received less on average—$881 mean for the Hope and $361 mean the LLTC.

BARRIERS TO FEDERAL HIGHER EDUCATION ACT FINANCIAL AID FOR WORKING ADULTS

In its 2002 report *Held Back: How Student Aid Programs Fail Working Adults*, FutureWorks determined that there were about two million independent students enrolled in postsecondary institutions who worked full time, considered themselves *employees* rather than *students*, and had dependent children (Bosworth and Choitz 2002). Of these, almost half (47 percent) were enrolled on a lessthanhalftime basis. (As might be expected, only 15 percent of these fulltime working adults with dependents were enrolled full time.) Of those enrolled lessthanhalftime, 28 percent earned less than 200 percent of the federal poverty level for a family of four, a family income level that would almost certainly make dependent students Pelleligible. However, only 7.7 percent of them received any federal, state, or institutional aid. Only 3.3

percent of them received Pell grants (they received an average award of $813); 1.7 percent received state aid; and just less than 3 percent received institutional aid. Because they were lessthanhalftime students, none of these lowincome students were eligible for federal loans.

However, the limited, almost negligible, participation of working adults in the Pell program is not a simple matter of eligibility *per se*; rather it is a consequence of how the aid is calculated and the kind of programs for which it may be applied. There are several ways that the Pell formula negatively affects lessthanhalftime working students.

Indirect Education Expenses

The Pell formula calculates the Cost of Attendance differently for students attending half time or more versus those attending less than half time. For students attending half time or more, the formula counts both direct expenses—tuition, fees, books and supplies, dependent care expenses, and transportation—and indirect expenses—most importantly, room and board, but also student loan fees, studyabroad programs, and even the cost of obtaining a computer. Lessthanhalftime students can count only the direct expenses, specifically not including room and board, towards their costs of attending school. As a result, the real costs of attending school are underestimated for lessthanhalftime students; they are not awarded a proportional share of what they received when attending fulltime, but typically receive less, or no aid at all. This creates a student aid "cliff" for those who were attending half or full time but are sometimes forced to drop down to quartertime status for a semester. This is especially true for students attending lowcost institutions, whose indirect costs for rent and food often exceed direct costs such as tuition and fees.

An Illinois study found that a majority of lessthanhalftime students in any semester actually attend half time or more for the rest of their college careers, averaging 7.6 credits per term. They drop down to lessthanhalftime because of interruptions in child care, transportation problems, or conflicting work schedules. Eliminating aid for these students causes significant problems: it discourages them from continuous enrollment and decreases their likelihood of persistence and completion (Center for the Study of Education Policy and the Illinois Student Assistance Commission 2004).

The Deficit Reduction Act of 2005 permits room and board costs for lessthanhalftime students to be included in their Cost of Attendance, using the current statutory room and board requirements. However, the use of a room and board cost allowance for these students is limited to not more than three semesters. This change became effective on July 1, 2006.

Lack of satisfactory progress

Postsecondary institutions have the discretion to deny Pell aid to students based on a lack of "satisfactory progress" toward completion. Most schools establish both qualitative and quantitative standards that typically include a minimum grade point average and the steady accumulation of credits toward completion. For working adults who might be forced by job or family considerations to drop out for a semester, and who in any case often enroll lessthanhalftime, these standards can constitute a tough barrier. Two or three underaverage grades in succession, or feeling forced to drop a course and then not being able to "doubleup" the next semester, can quickly jeopardize aid eligibility. Even with decent grades, working students enrolled part time may not be able to keep up a pace of enrollment that allows them to make what their college deems satisfactory progress in their program. As a result, they may be denied Pell aid.

Sudden Changes in Income

Eligibility and need for federal financial aid are calculated according to the previous year's income. This presents a special problem for dislocated workers who might otherwise be inclined to enroll quickly in programs leading to new skills and new job opportunities. While most colleges give their financial aid administrators discretion to allow estimates of currentyear income to be used under special circumstances, suddenly dislocated workers unaccustomed to navigating the complexities of postsecondary education bureaucracies are often too quickly discouraged by apparent regulatory constraints to ask for special consideration.

The Twosemester Limit

Pell grants are available for only two semesters each year. Working adult students who enroll on a lessthanhalftime basis for the two regular semesters are forced to make do without aid or to sit out the summer even if they are prepared to take one or two courses. (Fulltime students who wish to accelerate their path toward completion are hampered by this regulation as well.) Further, even if students only receive a Pell grant for one term, they are eligible to receive a Pell grant for the summer term only if their summer enrollment status is fulltime.

Nondegree and Noncertificate Programs

In order to be eligible for Pell funding, individuals must be considered "regular students." This criterion requires that students be enrolled in programs leading to a degree or certificate. However, many working adult students enroll in school in order to obtain jobspecific skills; they do not intend to pursue a degree or formal academic certificate. Frequently they enroll in vocationally and occupationally focused noncredit courses that are offered through continuing education departments at times that fit their work schedule better than forcredit courses. Often these students are seeking skills and knowledge that would help them pass an industrycertified examination leading to an industryrecognized certification. These certifications have been quite popular for several years in computer hardware service and repair and in software applications, but they also include specific training applicable to such diverse occupations as automotive service, health and nutrition, electrical installation and repair, real estate sales and management, welding, and appliance repair. These students are not considered regular students and therefore would not be eligible under Pell to receive a grant to help them with their skill development.

Program Eligibility

Nontraditional students, such as working adults, frequently find it difficult to attend college in traditional schedule formats because of competing demands of work and family. Postsecondary institutions could respond to these students' needs by breaking longer college programs into shorter modules or compressing longer programs into shorter, more intensive formats that can be completed as students have time. However, such modules or compressed programs can be ineligible for financial aid because of their shorter length. Pell's "eligible program" criteria stipulate that Pelleligible students must attend courses that meet for a minimum number of total hours. Federal student aid regulations require that in order to be Pelleligible, programs must provide at least a 15week program that offers 600 clock hours, 16 semester or trimester hours, or 24 quarter hours. Shorter programs that offer a minimum of 300 clock hours over a 10week program may be eligible for federal loan participation, but not for Pell grants.

Because concerns about aid eligibility tend to drive program structures, most colleges do not provide shortterm, forcredit courses that require fewer than the mandated minimum hours, even though they may help workers develop job skills quickly. Programs available on a noncredit basis are not eligible for federal aid.

Limits on Distance Learning

Pell also places restrictions on correspondence and online courses, including denying Pell eligibility for correspondence courses that lead to a certificate, as opposed to a degree. These restrictions limit the potential of promising new approaches to reach students for whom traditional instruction is not accessible.

WORKING ADULTS AND THE LIFETIME LEARNING TAX CREDIT

When the two federal tax credits for postsecondary education were first introduced in the Taxpayer Relief Act of 1997, it was suggested that they would complement each other by targeting different groups of students. The Hope Scholarship was intended to make traditional postsecondary education more affordable to the children of middleincome families by offering a $1,500 tax credit for each of the first two years of college. Available for only two years, and of full consequence only to families with at least a few thousand dollars of federal tax liability,[14] it explicitly favors families of dependent students attending colleges and universities on a fulltime basis. It requires at least halftime study and supports only pursuit of a conventional academic degree or certificate.

The Lifetime Learning Tax Credit was targeted more explicitly at helping working adults develop careerbuilding skills. It is not limited to two years; it does not require halftime enrollment; and it does not require pursuit of an academic degree or certificate. On the other hand, it is also available to more traditional students— those in their junior or senior year of college and those pursuing graduate studies.

A 2004 report by FutureWorks concluded that working adults were not gaining as much benefit from the LLTC program as was hoped at its introduction. First, according to the 2001 Household Education Survey, most students simply did not even know of the education tax credits—only 17 percent of working adults without a Bachelor's degree had heard of either Hope or LLTC (Choitz, Dowd, and Long 2004). On the other hand, it appears that of those who do file for the LLTC, most do appear to be working adults. About 80 percent of those who claim the LLTC claim the credit for their own or their spouse's educational expenses, and of those 82 percent did not indicate "student" as their occupation.

However, the amount of credit these working adult taxpayers actually received was very modest—on average, they claimed just $361 in 2001 (the most recent year for which research has been done). Those who sought the LLTC on behalf of a dependent received an average of $536 in credits, the same amount as those who claimed it on their own behalf but listed their occupation as "student." Effective credits under Hope appear to be much higher. Taxpayers who claimed Hope for a dependent received an average of $1,104, while those who claimed it for themselves or their spouses received an average of $936.

In 2001, the Hope and LLTC resulted in about $5.2 billion in tax credits. Less than 20 percent of that amount appears to have gone to working adults pursuing education or training (Choitz et al. 2004). The total tax credits have climbed over the past few years to about $6.3 billion in 2004, but it seems unlikely that the share of the credits going to working adults has increased beyond that found in 2001.

This underscores another fundamental issue in the impact of the tax credits on working adults: most of the tax subsidy goes to middleincome rather than lowincome families. This is as true for LLTC as it is for Hope. Only 36 percent of those "nonstudent" taxpayers claiming the 2001 LLTC for themselves or their spouse reported adjusted gross incomes below $30,000, and only 17 percent had incomes below $20,000.

There are two reasons for this skewed impact. First and most obviously, the majority of working adults who might benefit most from the tax credit programs (those with no previous postsecondary education) do not enroll at least half time and are therefore ineligible for Hope. Second, even if they can manage half time or more enrollment intensity and qualify for Hope, their limited taxable income makes these credits much less relevant. Finally, to the extent they seek benefits only under the LLTC, the tax credits are far less generous and are still reduced by their limited tax liability.

STATE STUDENT AID PROGRAMS

Statefinanced undergraduate grant aid programs have increased consistently in current dollar terms over the past several years, from about $2.9 billion in 199495, to over $5.7

---

[14] A fourperson family with one student needs at least $18,000 of income to have any tax liability, and it would need income of about $32,000 to realize the full benefit.

billion in 200304. Non needbased grants increased rapidly, doubling as a share of that total and now constituting about $1.5 billion. Still, the needbased programs alone increased over 100 percent in that 10year period. In addition to these grants, states provided another $1.2 billion in loans, loan forgiveness, workstudy, tuition waivers, and other nongrant programs in 200304. All the states have some form of direct student aid and some are quite large—in 200304, 18 states had grant programs of over $100 million, 11 of those were over $200 million, and six were over $300,000.

On the basis of needbased grant dollars per undergraduate fulltime equivalent (FTE), New York had by far the largest program in 200304, allocating $1,094 per FTE. The average among all the states was $378. New Jersey, Pennsylvania, and Illinois also spent more than twice that national average. However, on the basis of grant expenditures as a percentage of total higher education expenditures, South Carolina led the states, followed by Vermont, New York and Georgia, all at more than twice the national average.

It might be hypothesized that because the states are more directly or more immediately influencing the changing economic circumstances of working adults in need of postsecondary education, the statebased student aid programs would demonstrate greater diversity of program structure and more attention to the financial needs of nontraditional students. In its 2002 study, FutureWorks did find a number of state programs offering direct aid to nontraditional, working adult students. Only two states (Illinois and Virginia) had established special programs to focus directly on the lessthanhalftime students. However, six other states had created special programs for parttime students for which lessthanhalftime students were eligible, and a number of other states did not discriminate on the basis of enrollment intensity in their general aid programs.[15]

Most states determine the level of their award by using the same needs determination procedures as are used in the Pell program, often with the same unfortunate consequences for lessthanhalftime adults, whose room and board costs are not included. However, a few states were found to have more liberal, needbased formulas that allowed working adults to qualify for more aid by counting living expenses, child care, and transportation costs. While most states simply follow the federal guidelines for determining eligible programs (length of program, contact hours, etc.), FutureWorks found that several states provided grant awards to students in shortterm, intensive, nondegree programs that would not be eligible under Pell.

On the other hand, FutureWorks also found that early financial aid application deadlines imposed a significant barrier for working adults. Commonly, applicants for state aid (and institutional aid) must complete and submit the required federal forms by March or April before the fall semester in which the student would enroll. Such deadlines do not work well for working adults, whose work and family schedules seldom encourage such longrange planning. As a result, aid grants for most states tend to go to traditionalaged students and fulltime enrolled students and are less likely to be awarded to nontraditional students (St. John and Tuttle 2004).

In 200304, 11 states surveyed by the National Association of State Student Grant and Aid Programs reported that they provided statefinanced loans to undergraduates. Most of these programs require halftime attendance, but a few states provide loans to students taking only one threecredithour course.

---

[15] The states are Delaware, Michigan, New York, Ohio, Vermont, and West Virginia (Bosworth and Choitz 2002).

Federal Workforce Development Programs: TANF and WIA

The federal *Temporary Assistance to Needy Families (TANF)* program assists states to move people off public assistance and into work. TANF requires that each state engage at least 50 percent of assistance recipients in "work activities." The legislation provides that vocational training is an allowable work activity, but limits training to 12 months and forbids states from allowing more than 30 percent of the work participation requirements to be met by individuals in vocational training or attending high school.

Under TANF, states must supplement to match federal funds with at least 75 percent of what they had been spending for welfare when TANF was enacted in 1996. This required state expenditure is known as the states' Maintenance of Effort (MOE). The TANF law permits states to spend from their MOE for education and training without being limited to the 30 percent of work participation requirement or the 12month length of program requirement. States are also permitted to reduce their 50 percent work participation requirements by the percentage that they have reduced their welfare caseload since TANF was enacted in 1996.

States may define "vocational education" to include academic programs offered at postsecondary institutions, but the 12month limitation usually precludes enrollment in degree programs, even at the Associate level. Therefore, most TANF recipients in postsecondary programs are participating in onesemester or twosemester programs, typically resulting in a certificate rather than a degree. A few states use their MOE funds to effectively waive that 12month limit for some individuals, enabling them to complete a degree (MDRC 2001).

These restrictions on the use of TANF resources only for shorterterm programs have had the effect of inducing some community colleges to develop alternative and more flexible programs and delivery models. In a few states (California, Washington, and Oregon), TANF funds were allocated to community colleges specifically to design shorter classes and training programs, increasing weekend and evening offerings and developing tighter linkages with the regional labor market to help assure that completers would find their way quickly to good jobs. Some of these new programs are reserved for the TANF population and, because of their length and contact hours, they would not meet the requirements of the Pell grants or Stafford loans. In other cases, however, innovations that serve TANF eligible individuals also help other working adults by offering modularized and carefully sequenced programs that can lead to a degree but also have labor market value in "chunks" short of a degree (MDRC 2001).

Reliable data about the number of adults participating under TANF in postsecondary vocational training or degreeoriented programs is not readily available. Analysis of TANF spending indicates that combined state (MOE) and federal funding for education and training activities was about $494 million in 2003, the most recent year for which data is available (CLASP 2005).

The *Workforce Investment Act (WIA)* of 1998 guides federal workforce investments, including those for job training, adult literacy, and vocational rehabilitation. In addition to other major provisions that establish a system of state and local planning, provide for universal access to employment and career development services, and facilitate intensive services (assessment, job readiness, case management) to dislocated and disadvantaged youth and adults, WIA also provides training for eligible individuals by certified education/training providers through the use of Individual Training Accounts or vouchers. States decide who will be eligible for ITAs. WIA requires that lowincome and public assistance recipients be given priority for service, but states have broad flexibility to set priorities or to allow local boards to set priorities.

Due to the decentralized administration of WIA, there is little information available on training activities, and especially on training outcomes. A 2005 GAO report examining data from 2003 concluded that about $929 million was expended on training by local boards for training programs enrolling about 416,000 individuals, 323,000 of those in occupation programs. (This GAO estimate is controversial. According to the U.S. Department of Labor, about 200,000 people complete WIAfunded training annually.) According to the GAO, only about 38 percent of the funds that were available through local boards to services to WIAeligible individuals were spent on training (GAO 2005). Of course, in addition to these funds the Department of Labor has provided over $3 billion of WelfaretoWork grants and a wide variety of other competitive grants to Workforce Investment Boards and their local partners over the past several years.[16]

The Department of Labor has proposed a new approach to funding training for WIAeligible individuals. It proposes to consolidate four major funding streams—the WIA Adult, Dislocated Worker, Youth, and Employment Service Programs—into one single grant to states. The states would be required to allocate at least 75 percent of their grants to individuals in need of education and training. DOL estimates that about 800,000 people would receive these "Career Advancement Accounts." The maximum amount of an account would be $3,000 for one year, and the accounts could be renewed for one additional year. The remaining funds would be used to provide core employment services and related activities at OneStops and for administrative costs. The President's 2007 budget proposes about $3.4 billion to fund these accounts and employment services.

DOL proposes that these accounts would be available to adults and outofschool youth entering or reentering the workforce or transitioning between jobs and to incumbent workers in need of new skills to remain employed or to move up career ladders. States would have flexibility to establish additional criteria for eligibility priorities. Unlike the case with Department of Education programs, use of these funds would not be limited to postsecondary institutions certified by the Secretary. Rather, the states would be allowed to establish eligibility for participation and accountability standards for those providers. To the extent that Pelleligible individuals used their account for Pelleligible education, the career advancement funds would supplement, not replace Pell funds. However, these funds might be expected to spur the development of specialized programs not now eligible under Pell or other federal grants or loans. They would be available for individuals studying less than half time and for programs of less than 10week duration.

---

[16] The GAO report was unable to determine average expenditures per participant due to the multiplicity of programs and conflicting definitions. There were many different kinds of providers used: community colleges and secondary school vocational centers were frequent providers, but many boards also authorized training by communitybased organizations, private training firms, and proprietary schools. The GAO found that most of the 600 local workforce boards had established time limits and dollar limits for WIAfinanced training; these limitations varied widely. According to the GAO, it was not possible to determine how many individuals received academic degrees or certificates or industryrecognized certifications.

INSTITUTIONAL FINANCING FOR POSTSECONDARY EDUCATION

Two issues in institutional funding dominate discussion of postsecondary education finance: (1) the total amount of funding for higher education; and (2) the expression of public policy priorities in funding decisions—i.e., what dollars are available to invest in education and what the public should get for its investment. Each factor has distinct impact on higher education's capacity to provide services to adult students; collectively, they shape the access to and success in postsecondary education for working and lower income adult students.

The Overall Flow of Revenues to Higher Education and Impacts on Adult Students

Three categories of revenue provide support for public higher education institutions: state institutional finance allocations, tuition, and other funds (including federal and private). Tuition and state institutional financing are inversely related: as state allocations have fallen (or failed to keep pace with costs) tuition costs have risen. In general terms, tuition costs are determined by subtracting the amount of institutional funding from the total costs of education. Institutional financing for postsecondary education in the United States comes from appropriations and allocations of state funds. State funding for the general operating costs of postsecondary education is far larger than revenue from federal funds. Most federal dollars for postsecondary education generally flow through financial aid and loans to students, who then use these funds for tuition. Some federal funds are provided in the form of restricted grants to institutions for specific purposes, such as research or facilities. Other revenues to colleges and universities come from philanthropic sources and may or may not be for restricted purposes.

States derive an overall budget and appropriation for higher education based on calculations of what's possible, given tax revenues, and shaped by the operating needs in the postsecondary system. In general, states decide the amount of support to education using allocation formulae and assumptions of base costs in twoyear colleges, fouryear colleges, and research universities. The most important factor in any formula is the number of fulltime students or fulltimeequivalent students enrolled at an institution; this factor is then adjusted by a range of others, including a measure of base costs, increases, special services, and special programs (Jones 2003; Center for Community College Policy 2000). The two important characteristics of institutional financing are the methods of calculating funding (based on enrollments such as FTE formulas) and the impact of trends in declining amounts of funding over time.

According to State Higher Education Executives Organization, as higher education FTE enrollments increased from about seven to ten million students between 1980 and 2004,[17] educational appropriations per FTE declined from about $6,100 in 1980 to $5,750 in 2004. This is the lowest level of per FTE funding since 1983, and down from a high of nearly

---

[17] FTE, or fulltime equivalency enrollment, is a standard unit of measure for most postsecondary reimbursement or allocation calculations. It is, of course, a smaller number than total postsecondary enrollment, which in 2004 was just over 14 million.

$6,900 in 2001, for a sharp threeyear decline of nearly 17 percent.[18] It is true that state funding for education grew considerably in dollar amounts during this 25year period, but the increases were eclipsed by growth in the number of students and in the costs of higher education. Between 2001 and 2004, total postsecondary revenues per FTE remained almost flat, but enrollment grew by 11.8 percent and costs increased by 10.3 percent (Lingenfelter, Wright, and Bisel 2005). In community colleges, state appropriations (not including local tax allocations) accounted for an average of nearly 44 percent of the major sources of revenue in 1981, but by 2003 this proportion amounted to 33 percent (NCES 2004).

Although there is considerable variation by state, legislated funds for higher education declined during the last economic recession and are not recovering as quickly as their cyclical history would predict. In absolute terms, state financing for higher education fell by $2.5 billion in just two years, from 2002 to 2004, and several states cut education budgets by more than 10 percent (Kane and Orszag 2004).

State spending on education is highly cyclical, but longterm trends of higher education's share of state expenditures show consistent decline. Higher education's share of state's general fund spending fell from 15 percent in 1987, to 12 percent in 1998 (Zumeta 2005). Other meanstested or mandated expenditures (notably, Medicaid and corrections) create unavoidable demands on state funds, and these may now be crowding out more discretionary allocations of funds to education (Jones 2003).

Declining appropriations of funds relative to steadily increasing education costs leads to tuition hikes. Stateappropriated funds now make up a smaller proportion of total per student costs than in the last 15 years, as tuition increases shift the cost of education from public funds to individual obligations (and student financial aid). However, there are often political and social constraints on how much tuition is allowed to increase in public colleges. In general, tuition increases in public institutions do not completely replace losses of state allocations. This inevitably results in both an overall decline of resources available to the institution and more requirements on students and their families to finance, through loans and grants to cover tuition, a higher proportion of costs of attendance.

Tuition revenue as a proportion of higher education revenue is now at its highest levels and has risen more quickly than any other source of education revenue. Between 1980 and 2000, higher education tuition increased by 117 percent, while state government expenditures rose by 24 percent (National Center for Public Policy and Higher Education 2003). In 2004, higher education tuition stood at 36 percent of total revenue per FTE, compared to 26 percent in 1991. While community college tuition still averages less than $2,000 a year, it has risen 33 percent between 1992 and 2002 (National Center for Public Policy and Higher Education 2003). Recent trends in tuition financing show that families at all income levels are accumulating more educational debt relative to total income in order to pay for education, and the composition of student financial aid packages is shifting toward a higher proportion of debt rather than grants or needsbasedaid. Student aid grants have declined from 52 percent of financial aid packages in 1981, to 39 percent in 2001 (National Center for Public Policy and Higher Education 2004).

How states finance postsecondary education has several implications for adult student access and participation in higher education. The following points are not exhaustive but do

---

[18] These figures are in 2004 constant dollars.

identify some of the critical impacts on adult students, and lower income adult students in particular.

FTEbased Funding Formulations Can Make Parttime
Adult Students Less Attractive to Colleges

The funding formulas that states use to calculate the flow of support to higher education are shaped idiosyncratically by legislative politics, institutional history, and policy influences that accumulate over time. Most states utilize a funding formula to determine either an overall appropriation for postsecondary funding or an allocation (between institutions) of already appropriated funds in consolidated higher education funding. Despite the variety of formulas and factors considered in the equations, nearly all funding formulas include fulltimeequivalent enrollments as the overwhelmingly determinant feature of funding determination (Center for Community College Policy 2000). The greater the number of students enrolling in higher education programs, the greater the amount of revenue flowing to the institutions.

Fulltimeequivalencybased funding formulas can place pressure on colleges to promote enrollment growth at the expense of services that support student retention, persistence, and completion. Thus schools may focus on frontloading new enrollments and may lose many enrollees because of a lack of investment in appropriate support services and advising. This can have a sharp impact on nonresidential adult students, who often depend on ancillary support to sustain their education. For adults, who are often parttime students, the services that promote persistence and completion and help them to manage work, family, and education demands are particularly important. Adult students report the centrality of services around obtaining financial aid, advising, and special programs to aid them as important in helping them manage their education and stay enrolled (MatusGrossman 2004).

Reliance on enrollments as a source of revenue tends to diminish the revenue value of adult students to an institution. Because over half of all adult students participate in education less than half time, it typically takes more adult students than traditional students to comprise a population of FTE students (Cook and King 2005). Under FTE funding formula, there is an implicit value for traditional students over adult students; traditional students may simply be more valuable to schools and cost less to enroll and maintain than adult and lowincome adult students (Carnevale and Deroschers 2004). Schools may thus devote greater support for marketing, information, and supportive services to enroll traditional students.

Declining State Funding for Education Discourages
Smart Programming for Working Adults

Downward pressures on state allocations for general operations strain the capacity of institutions to sustain critical services or to offer innovative services upon which adult students depend. Declines in operational support limit an institution's capacity for growing innovative curricula targeted to adult students, supporting the remediation that many require, or investing in new educational delivery methods that better fit the learning styles and constraints of working adults.

Promising directions in educational delivery, such as compressed curricula, hybridized course structures, and accelerated degree programs can benefit adult students in community colleges by making it more feasible and efficient to schedule classes, attend at convenient times, and complete a degree. Over the short run, however, such programs require developmental expenses and increase costs due to additional services (e.g., additional student advising time or different hours for the financial aid office). Without a mechanism to account for these additional development costs in the funding formula, colleges now have a disincentive to either invest in or offer the services.

Shifting the Proportions of Overall Costs to Tuition Revenue Penalizes Working Adults Who Face Greater Barriers to Aid Eligibility

The overall financial cost of education in the form of tuition to individuals is a major barrier to many moderate and lowincome adults (MatusGrossman 2004). Shifting proportionately more costs toward tuition to compensate for declines in institutional funding may create a complex impact on the ability of adult students to participate in education. Broadly, it makes attending college more difficult for all adult students, but for different reasons depending on their socioeconomic status. Working adults with moderate family incomes are sensitive to total tuition costs because they may be outside of the limits for maximum needsbased financial aid. They bear more of the direct cost of tuition increases. At community colleges, working adult students, whose incomes would disqualify them for grants and whose lessthanfulltime enrollment may make them ineligible for full financial aid, may be forced to choose between maintaining family supports and covering tuition, even with marginal increases in tuition costs.

Lower income adult students, on the other hand, depend more heavily on financial aid programs and loans than any other group of students. These lower income students often express considerable reluctance to take on sizeable debt, though there is not a clear picture of what an unacceptable debt level threshold might be (MatusGrossman 2004). Thus, increased reliance on tuition and financial aid for adult students may discourage some working adults from enrolling or completing their education, and may, for lower income adults, pose unacceptable levels of debt.

Public Policy Priorities through Postsecondary Finance

As the perception of the economic role of higher education in contributing to economic development and the preparation of a skilled workforce has evolved, appropriations and allocations of public funds now come with more explicit expectations of results and outcomes. Some states now use performance measures to shape the allocation of funds toward public policy priorities, such as occupational preparation or contributions toward economic development and job growth. Some attention is now being paid to higher education efficiency, and there is much more focus on performance outcomes such as graduation rates, reducing the time to graduate, and degrees attained.

As more attention is given to performance measures and to shaping educational policy through financial allocation mechanisms, there is a greater need for understanding the differential impact of these mechanisms on different groups of students. In particular, the mechanisms must clearly reflect the goals, and reflect an accurate understanding of, who is obtaining education and how they get it.

It is especially important to grasp the changing characteristics of community colleges and to distinguish these from other parts of higher education. Community colleges, which enroll the majority of adult students and the large majority of lower income adults, have recently received much attention as key partners in a continuum of public higher education, from the K12 system through universities. Community colleges across the country have grown rapidly over the past 15 years, and this itself presents a complicated picture of demographics and demands on the institution. For example, the average age of a community college student has fallen from 29 years old to 27 years old, but adult students over age 25 represent the largest increase in community college enrollments and are now 40 percent of enrollments (College Board 2005).

As part of the workforce needing to increase skills and retrain and reeducate themselves in a globally competitive world, and as part of a group whose basic skills are seen as inadequate and whose educational attainment is too low, adult students are seen as a vast pool of potential students who need postsecondary education for good jobs in the economy (Cook and King 2005; Center for Community College Policy 2003; Carnevale 2004).

Broadly speaking, institutional financing for higher education and for community colleges in particular has not adapted financing mechanisms or finance policy to support this new vision for adult students and lower income adults (Lingenfelter and Voorhees 2003; Bailey and Mingle 2003). Some of the newer trends toward accountability in state financing actually work against offering more effective services for adult students. For instance, reducing timetograduation rates may make supporting parttime students, many of whom will be adults, a nowin proposition for colleges. Community colleges are straining to accommodate growth and to find ways of adapting to new adult students who seek postsecondary education, but in general the structures of educational finance have not.

State financing mechanisms for higher education no longer match the realities of student experience, especially the influx of adult students and especially in community colleges. As state financing policy changes, it should consider ways to better reflect both the ways students now obtain their education and the new ways that higher education can provide that education. This entails both an overhaul of the formula on which funding allocations are made and additional clarity in specifying and then supporting the missions of higher education. The following points address mismatches between state financing mechanisms for community colleges (where the large majority of adult students and lower income adults enroll in higher education) and the tasks confronting this sector as it seeks to fulfill educational demands.

State Funding Seldom Supports "Noncredit" Coursework

Only a handful of states, including North Carolina, Pennsylvania, Oregon, Kentucky, Mississippi, and Maryland, fully include noncredit and continuing education courses in FTE calculations and therefore in institutional financing calculations (Center for Community College Policy, 2000; Wang and Clowes 1994; Kaufman 1994).[19] A few other states, like Arizona, Illinois, and New Jersey, provide partial funding for noncredit courses or for some noncredit programs. Most provide no significant institutional funding for noncredit courses.

---

[19] No states fund hobby, avocational, or recreational, noncredit classes.

Yet, in community colleges, noncredit enrollments now account for nearly half of the courses offered and are the fastest growing segment of community college courses (Meyer 2002). Many adults enter postsecondary education through noncredit courses offered through workforce development or continuing education programs. Continuing education courses constitute a growing area of professional development and career development courses; these are important to adults for gaining technical skills, career building capacity, and gaining workforce credentials.

Including noncredit offerings in the calculations for institutional financing would provide incentives for schools, especially community colleges, to incorporate these courses more fully into the mainstream organization of academic educational programs and provide incentives to close the gap between many credit and noncredit courses in critical occupational fields such as information technology. This, in turn, would reflect the ways that many people, especially adults, now gain education and could help link interests in specific skill development courses or credential courses to degree programs. In other words, it could help create a more seamless pathway from job training to full degrees and be of particular benefit to adult students (and their employers). Funding noncredit courses commensurate with credit courses also would build incentive for colleges to learn new ways of delivering education (i.e., customized training, distance education, and accelerated courses that often utilize innovative curricula to target learning for specific audiences and types of learners).

Current Institutional Financing Policies Tend to Weaken and to Separate Workforce Development Programs from the Basic Operations of Higher Education

In the 1970s and 1980s, most community colleges established business and industry training divisions to offer largely customized training programs to employers and noncredit occupational or technical courses to the public. Nearly all of these divisions were selfsupporting and dependent on "sales revenue" or grantfunded contracts. In some colleges, these became profit centers and revenue streams for their colleges. In many colleges, these areas became the location that carried out publicly funded training programs (WIA, TANF, etc.) as well as the more entrepreneurial efforts in new, occupationally oriented education and in aligning services to economic development needs (Spaid and Parsons, 1987; Wang and Clowes, 1994; Center for Community College Policy 2000). Today, these divisions are most commonly known as Workforce Development Divisions or Workforce and Economic Development Offices.

A historical legacy of the development of these divisions within a community college structure is the ongoing division between academic programs and workforce development. The former is still the basis of accreditation, financial aid eligibility, and enrollments that in turn are the basis for calculation of FTE. Workforce development divisions are largely sales revenue driven or grant dependent. Grant dependence is unstable; grantsdriven services rightly focus on meeting the funding criteria but not on developing a stable platform of services.[20]

---

[20] Ironically, the workforce development departments are the main areas where employers have a say in the design of educational services to the workforce. In fact, some community colleges point to their workforce development programs as the "industry responsive" or "industry driven" components of their services. The effect of this is to let the traditional academic, degreebased programs off the hook for industry responsiveness. A clear institutional financing policy on workforce development would help end the isolation of academic programs from industry.

These workforce development programs are often inefficient instruments for carrying out a state's economic development and workforce development policies because they are simply not well integrated into an institution's educational framework. Yet, many adult education and adult services are delivered through (if not consigned to) the workforce divisions of community colleges, and in many community colleges there is little communication between workforce development programs and academic programs. This usually means that a skill development course delivered through a workforce development program will have no connection to or will not bear credit toward a degree.[21] However, the overwhelming evidence on the impact of higher education on incomes shows that the most consequential gains in income accrue to those who achieve formal postsecondary certificates and degrees and not just coursework or a collection of courses. Achieving increases in the educational attainment of adults that has meaning for the economy and for workers means developing ways of helping adults gain degrees.

If states do seek to establish educational policy priorities and performance goals for adult students and services, then the continuing division between workforce development and academic programs will have to be bridged. One incentive to create this bridge is to build in ongoing institutional support for meeting workforce development goals, incorporating these goals into the basic foundation (that is, degreebased occupational education) of community colleges.

NEW DIRECTIONS

The primary conclusion that emerges from this necessarily limited description of postsecondary student aid and institutional financing is that these financing systems simply do not work for working adults. These systems were built to promote postsecondary access for traditional students; they do not support the educational needs of working adults who face an economy that rewards postsecondary credentials and punishes the underprepared.

The Commission on the Future of Higher Education should encourage federal and state governments to begin a systemic redesign of student aid policies—not to reduce support for traditional students in need, but rather to offer more direct assistance to working adults and to use financing policies to foster innovations in program design and delivery. Important places to begin might include the following:

1. Recognizing more adequately in Pell grant distribution formulas the educational costs facing working adults and their interest in yearround study.
2. Using aid policies to encourage shortterm, intensive programs and innovative delivery mechanisms that will help underprepared working adults rapidly acquire postsecondary credentials with immediate labor market impact.[22]

---

[21] For example, until recently the information technology curricula that led to certifications in Microsoft, Novell, or Cisco systems were by and large delivered as noncredit courses and did not—without what amounted to an internal articulation agreement—count toward credit in an academic computer science program.

[22] As seems feasible in the DOLproposed new "Career Advancement Accounts."

3. Providing federal loans, subsidized for the most needy, for working adults who have demonstrated their commitment and capacity for postsecondary study but are unable to complete college on a halftime or more basis.
4. Encouraging states to apply their aid programs to working adults in ways that complement federal support.
5. Modifying the Lifetime Learning Tax Credit (LLTC) to offer working adults parity with the more generous credits available for traditional students through the Hope program.
6. Making the LLTC credits available to lowincome working adults though new "refundability" provisions similar to those of the Earned Income Tax Credit.

SECTION 4.

ACCOUNTABILITY: EFFORTS TO MONITOR QUALITY AND DRIVE IMPROVED OUTCOMES MUST INCORPORATE MEASURES OF ADULT LEARNER SUCCESS

Talking Points

The current debate over whether—and how—to develop accountability systems to assess and increase the effectiveness of higher education has failed to address adult learners and their needs.

- *Accountability measures are intended to provide meaningful ways to assess program quality and to help institutions and systems improve by identifying strengths and weaknesses.*
- *Most public accountability discussions and measures center on traditional, fulltime students, even though higher education outcomes are weaker for adult learners.*
- *Four key groups—students, employers, institutions, and federal and state policymakers—share an interest in better adult learner outcomes but have different priorities.*

Existing federal, state, and institutional accountability systems demonstrate little power to monitor outcomes or drive improvement for adult learners.

- *Little publicly available information exists to answer adult learner questions about employment outcomes, earnings potential, or return on education investment when choosing a postsecondary institution.*
- *Many employers are frustrated with the quality of job candidates, but have had little practical involvement in designing better accountability systems.*
- *IT certifications are an example of how occupational assessment can mutually benefit both students and prospective employers.*
- *Institutional accountability is managed through a peerreview accreditation process that puts variable emphasis on student learning outcomes.*

- *Occupational, programspecific accreditation bodies overseen by industry or trade groups with specific training and resource requirements better serve adult learners.*
- *Many higher education institutions express concern that overly simplistic metrics and reporting systems will fail to drive improvement and will further polarize key stakeholders.*
- *The most common higher education accountability measure is the IPEDS graduation rate reported to the federal government; this data does not include parttime or transfer students, who make up the vast majority of adult learners.*
- *The federal government does not require institutions to report labor market participation, employment, or earnings data that would be relevant for adult students.*
- *State accountability policies tend to emphasize enrollment, but new pressures are leading to greater attention to student outcomes. However, the particular interests and needs of employers and adult learners are rarely integrated into accountability systems.*

Proposed federal legislation provides a starting point for better aligning higher education accountability efforts with the needs of adult learners.

- *Proposals to strengthen accountability in the Higher Education Act would provide online tools for students to research and compare institutions and get more accurate information about college costs and financial aid.*
- *The legislation also would include parttime and transfer students in the calculation of graduation rates, a positive step to incorporate adult learners.*

To be truly effective for adult learners, accountability systems should include:

- *Measures of enrollment, progress, and completion of degreeseeking, parttime students;*
- *Disaggregation of outcomes by age and other characteristics of nontraditional students;*
- *Outcomes that incorporate industry credentials and licensure exams as well as educational credentials; and*
- *Employment and earnings outcomes that capture adult learners' economic gains.*

Additional research and analysis is needed before policymakers will be able to design accountability systems that meet adult learners' needs. Areas for further attention include:

- *The study of existing programmatic accreditation processes to determine how promising approaches can be replicated, and what kinds of new approaches might help address the growing demand for such evaluation;*
- *Incorporating lessons from employer methods of measuring skills and learning into design of accountability systems that acknowledge the range of occupational programs that adults choose;*

- *Development of state data systems that can report economic as well as educational outcomes, including longitudinal tracking to capture the effect of different kinds of precollege and collegelevel credential programs;*
- *Finding ways to engage all of the key stakeholders of adult postsecondary education—and to represent the variety of perspectives within each group—in future discussions of accountability design and implementation.*

INTRODUCTION

Accountability in higher education has become a heated and divisive issue. Conflict over whether and how to assess—and increase—the quality of higher education programs has been building, as both the costs and value of obtaining postsecondary skills and credentials have been rising. Fueling the debate is growing evidence about two areas of significant concern—high rates of attrition from college credential programs and doubts about the quality of student learning in higher education institutions. In a world where higher education is the key to economic selfsufficiency, better ways to assess results— and to improve performance—are critical. But in an industry where accountability has historically been weak and institutional autonomy strong, a shift to more effective accountability systems will not come without further debate, conflict, trial and error, and, ultimately, cooperation among the various stakeholders for whom higher education is a critical investment.

These issues are receiving increased attention as the Secretary of Education's Commission on the Future of Higher Education holds public hearings and solicits public comment. Supporters of increased accountability decry the lack of evidence currently available to help judge the impact colleges have on individual students, particularly given the amount of money that the federal government, states, and students spend on higher education each year. Others are skeptical of what they consider simplistic approaches to accountability that fail to take into account the complexity of missions, market niches, and students served at different postsecondary institutions. In recent testimony to the Commission, Paul Lingenfelter, president of the State Higher Education Executive Officers, acknowledged the growing polarization in the field when he noted, "Current accountability practices frequently reflect worry, frustration, and pique, more than confident, welldesigned strategies for improvement. At its worst, current practice is a tool for placing blame on others and deflecting blame from oneself."

From the perspective of adult learners and those working to serve them better, the current interest in accountability is both welcome and frustrating. It is welcome because, as we have shown in this paper, higher education outcomes are weaker for adult learners than for traditional students and improvement is sorely needed. At the same time, it is frustrating because in most discussions of accountability, adult learners remain largely invisible. Deliberations proceed as if the 27 percent of college enrollments who are "traditional" 18to 21yearold, dependent, fulltime students comprise an overwhelming majority of learners. They make little acknowledgement of the unique needs and interests of adults.

A striking example is the 2005 report of the National Commission on Accountability in Higher Education, *Accountability for Better Results*, a very thoughtful and rich argument for improved accountability sponsored by the State Higher Education Executive Officers. The report does a terrific job of explaining why clearer goals, better measures, and more effective use of data on student and institutional outcomes are critically important to the future of higher education and the U.S. economy. However, while the report presents powerful evidence on inequities in postsecondary outcomes for various subpopulations—minorities, lowincome, and firstgeneration students—adult learners are never mentioned and the kinds of steps that might help improve their outcomes remain underdeveloped.

This section describes the ways in which higher education stakeholders, including students, employers, and policymakers, currently assess the effectiveness of postsecondary education. We then analyze opportunities for improving these processes for adult learners— and offer some general principles that should guide the future development of accountability metrics and systems to help improve outcomes for this important population.

EXISTING ACCOUNTABILITY SYSTEMS DO LITTLE FOR ADULT LEARNERS

Accountability systems are intended to provide meaningful ways to assess program quality and to help institutions and systems improve by identifying strengths and weaknesses. In recent years, following on the heels of the accountability movement in K12 education, higher education policymakers and leaders have been evaluating the need to improve postsecondary accountability mechanisms and measures. Four distinct groups have a shared interest in better outcomes in higher education, though their priorities and concerns vary:

- *Students. Students, both traditional and nontraditional, are the primary consumers of higher education— and their tuition rates, loans, and other costs are rising.*
- *Employers. Employers rely on higher education institutions to supply much of their workforce, at the entry, technician, professional, and managerial levels. They may be seen as the secondary customer for higher education's products.*
- *Institutions. Institutions have a clear stake in demonstrating to consumers, employers, and policymakers that their students benefit from their services. They also want to show other institutions that their courses are of sufficient quality and their credits should be transferable.*
- *Federal and state policymakers. Federal and state policymakers provide funds for higher education operations and student financial aid. Policymakers at both levels of government are growing increasingly interested in measuring higher education results as budgets are squeezed by rising health care and other entitlement costs.*

At present, existing accountability systems address the interests and needs of each of these groups in only limited ways. Most important, from the perspective of adult learners, they have demonstrated little power to monitor outcomes or drive improvement in postsecondary programs serving adults.

MOST CONSUMER INFORMATION ABOUT HIGHER EDUCATION FOCUSES ON TRADITIONAL STUDENT NEEDS

Prospective college students rely on a variety of commercial products when evaluating postsecondary institutions to attend. College guides that present comparative data about individual institutions (e.g., *U.S. News* and *World Report's* "America's Best Colleges") are the bestknown example. However, these products, which include information on everything from academic offerings to campus social life, target traditional students looking for a residential, fulltime college experience. No commercial products geared for adult learners exist.

Compared to traditional students, who are more likely to attend a fouryear private institution and value academic reputation, availability of financial aid, and affordable cost most highly, adult learners place greater emphasis on flexible access to courses and future employment opportunities when making a college enrollment decision. (See table 4.)

Unfortunately, there is little publicly available information that addresses the primary concerns of adult learners, especially related to employment outcomes, future likelihood of earning enough to repay student loans, and return on their education investment. This huge gap in the public's ability to evaluate institutional performance as it relates to adult learners' needs poses another serious obstacle to adults making quality choices about their further education.

Table 4. Prioritized Ranking of Enrollment Factors

Rank	Undergraduate Adult Students	Rank	Traditional Students
1	Academic reputation	1	Academic reputation
2 (tie)	Availability of evening/weekend courses	2	Financial aid
2 (tie)	Future employment opportunities	3	Cost
4	Campus location	4	Personalized attention prior to enrollment
5	Personalized attention prior to enrollment	5	Size of institution

Source: NoelLevitz 2005.

EMPLOYERS PLAY A LIMITED ROLE IN ACCOUNTABILITY SYSTEMS, DESPITE DEPENDENCE ON GRADUATES

Employers are among the most vigorous proponents of the need for better education and training, up and down Recent growth in the number of certifications awarded in the labor market. They are visible in local, state, and the information technology field demonstrates one area national debates about higher education and the access to where employers have sent clear signals to workers about human capital that their firms require. However, they are the credentials that have high labor market value. *(See* frequently on the sidelines when specific accountability *figure* 9.) The development of IT certifications illustrates and improvement strategies are developed. Beyond their how occupational assessment can be mutually beneficial hiring decisions, employers tend to have few direct ways to both students and prospective employers. to signal their interests and priorities in higher education accountability systems.

When it comes to hiring decisions, employers in many industries continue to struggle to find effective methods for evaluating recent college graduates. One proxy some employers use to guide their judgments about program quality and student qualifications is industry certification. Certification assures employers that individuals have completed a course of study that has taught them particular skills or knowledge, which they can apply to a specific workforce role.

Recent growth in the number of certifications awarded in the information technology field demonstrates one area where employers have sent clear signals to workers about the credentials that have high labor market value. *(See figure 9.)* The development of IT certifications illustrates how occupational assessment can be mutually beneficial to both students and prospective employers.

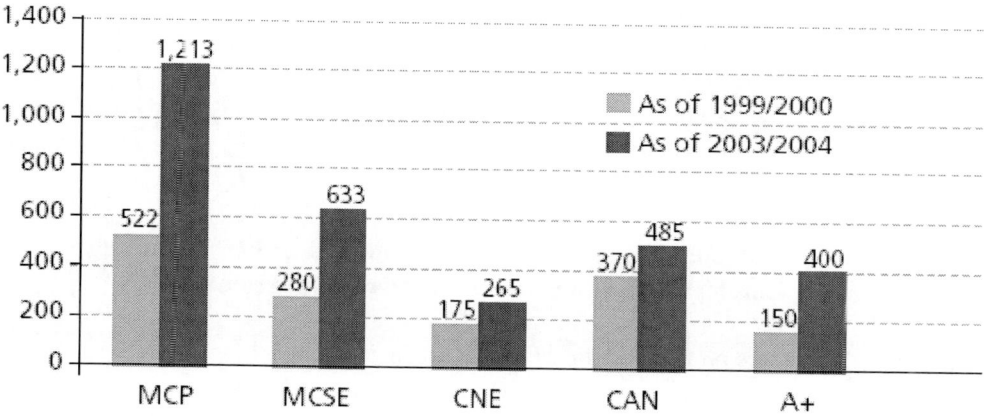

Source: University Continuing Education Association 2004 .
Figure 9. Total IT Certifications Awarded to Date, Selected Certificate Types.

Other industries have well developed occupational assessments of this kind, particularly in health care, but also in technical fields such as automotive service and construction. However, employer reliance on these certifications is spotty. The field of business, the most common undergraduate major in two- and four-year higher education, offers no such system of assessing work-readiness of program completers. In many industries, employers are left to rely on little more than program brand reputation or long-term relationships with certain postsecondary institutions.

Many employers are clearly frustrated with the quality of job candidates available today. Much of that frustration has been channeled into efforts to improve K12 education in communities from which they hire. Recent Eduventures research identifies the priority concerns of U.S. employers regarding education and training outcomes at the postsecondary level. Above all, employers want to know whether, after a learning and development opportunity, a particular person will be able to do a particular job well. (See table 5.)

Ultimately, employers need to be more active in demanding better accountability from higher education—and in helping to develop new accountability metrics of value to the modern workplace. Otherwise, they will remain relatively weak players in the arena of higher education improvement—despite the importance of improvement to their longterm prospects.

Institutional accountability is managed primarily through the accreditation process. Accreditation is a peer review that may be completed by either a private agency or a government body with the goal of ensuring "that education provided by institutions of higher education meets acceptable levels of quality" (U.S. Department of Education). Institutions are required to maintain their accreditation status through ongoing reviews that may occur on a programspecific or institutionwide basis. These reviews serve to "approve" an institution's programs based on how the institution compares to its peers and established standards.

Over the past decade, the regional bodies that govern accreditation procedures have begun to place greater emphasis on student outcomes in their standards; they were fairly silent on the subject through much of the 20th century. However, accreditation is a process that respects institutional autonomy and grants great latitude in the setting of priorities. Institutions set their own goals and then do a selfstudy and peer evaluation of whether they are meeting those goals and how they can improve their efforts. They are not required to pay particular attention to improving student outcomes. According to the association of accrediting agencies, "Accrediting organizations have frequently acknowledged student learning outcomes as an important dimension of quailty—and in many cases, have actively built or adopted new review standards and criteria to address it. But the particular 'stances' that they have adopted vary widely" (Ewell 2001).

Table 5. Outcome Measures Employers Value Most in Evaluating Employee Learning and Development Programs

1	Workforce proficiency (the ability to do the job well)
2	Operational efficiency (the ability to do the job efficiently)
3	Regulatory compliance (improved knowledge of regulatory requirements)
4	Changes in employee commitment to the organization (improved commitment)
5	Changes in employment motivation (increased employee motivation)
6	Learner satisfaction (with the learning program)
7	Time-to-competency (speed of learning new skills)

Source: Eduventures 2005.

For adult learners—and their employers—the programspecific accreditation bodies may be more relevant. These organizations assess the quality of specific educational programs, typically occupational, such as nursing and other allied health fields. The process is typically overseen by an industry or trade association and features specific requirements to ensure that students receive sufficient training and have access to appropriate resources. This oversight is designed to ensure that program graduates are adequately prepared to enter the workforce.

Postsecondary institutions have varied internal approaches to improving quality and trying to help their students/customers achieve their educational and career goals. Recent research indicates that many institutions' primary strategic objectives align with the goal of improving the number and the readiness of their graduates (See objectives 1, 4, 5, and 6 in table 6.)

However, institutional commitment to improvement is very different from public accountability for student learning, credential attainment, employment and earnings, or success in further education. Institutionlevel resistance to pressures for greater accountability combines a natural resistance to curtailment of autonomy and a desire to minimize comparisons with other institutions with a legitimate concern that the rush to more metrics and requirements will result in overly simplistic prescriptions that will do little to drive improvement.

Moving too quickly does run the risk of further polarizing institutional leaders, policymakers, employers, and students—without contributing to better outcomes.

Unfortunately for adult learners, this polarized positioning of competing interests does little to focus attention on their needs or how to improve services for them. Indeed, the current debate runs the risk of further marginalizing the interests of this significant constituency in higher education. Consider the College Learning Assessment that the Council for Aid to Education has developed to measure students' critical thinking, analytic reasoning, and written communication skills. The exam is currently available to institutions on a voluntary basis.

Supporters have argued that this kind of standardized test is necessary to determine student learning outcomes in postsecondary institutions, while critics fear that standardized testing of college learning is too simplistic to be an effective tool given the diversity of institutions and curricula that make up higher education in this country. The CLA may or may not be a good idea, but its relevance for adult students is not yet being considered. For example, would this test be appropriate for adults who are pursuing occupational credentials? Or would it be more appropriate for those who take full general education sequences? These questions are not part of the current national debate on measuring student learning outcomes.

Table 6. Strategic Objectives of Senior Higher Education Administrators

1	Improve student learning outcomes
2	Attract/retain faculty
3	Improve fundraising
4	Improve retention rates
5	Improve use of data for strategic decision support
6	Increase enrollment
7	Enhance productivity of faculty and administrators

Source: Eduventures, 2005b.

FEDERAL ACCOUNTABILITY REQUIREMENTS ARE POORLY SUITED FOR ADULTS

The most ubiquitous accountability metric in higher education is the graduation data reported to the federal government. Since 1999, all postsecondary institutions that are eligible to participate in Title IV loan and grant programs have been required to report their annual graduation rate for fall semester cohorts of firsttime, fulltime students in degree programs. (The mandate was part of the Student Right to Know and Campus Security Act amendments to the Higher Education Act.) Fouryear colleges calculate the number of students who graduate within six years, while community colleges calculate a threeyear rate.

However, this common accountability tool is largely irrelevant for comparisons of quality or outcomes for adult learners. The methodology for calculating this graduation rate does not include parttime students or transfer students, who make up a huge proportion of adults furthering their education (American Association of State Colleges and Universities 2002).[23] Rather, it focuses on results for just a fraction of the nation's postsecondary population. In New Mexico, for example, only 8 percent of the 74,000 enrollments in the state's community colleges in the fall of 2004 were firsttime, fulltime students.

The federal government requires institutions to submit additional data, besides graduation rates. All institutions receiving Title IV grants must report information about a variety of institutional characteristics, including:

- *Basic characteristics: tuition, enrollment, and other student expense data (e.g., room and board fees);*
- *Completions: level of degree, field of study, and demographic data for each student who earns a credential;*
- *Enrollment: number of fulltime and parttime students by degree level, gender, and race/ethnicity; and*
- *Financial aid: number of students receiving financial aid, including student demographics and various types of aid (e.g., grants, loans, etc.).*
- *Operational information: selected data including staff and salary information*

From the perspective of adult learners, it would be critical to include measures of labor market participation, employment, and earnings of graduates as well. However, there is no federal requirement for connecting education and employment data or for reporting employmentrelated outcomes.

Here is another example of how the diversity of institutions that serve adults demands careful consideration of accountability metrics and reporting standards. Many institutions—specifically the proprietary career colleges that serve a large population of adult learners—report data only on an aggregate basis, rather than breaking it down campus by campus. As a result, adult learners find it difficult to get basic information about a particular career college campus or location.

PROPOSED FEDERAL LEGISLATION ADDRESSES NONTRADITIONAL ADULT LEARNER NEEDS

In 2005, the House leadership proposed several measures designed to strengthen federal accountability systems in the Higher Education Act. H.R. 609, which was introduced but has

---

[23] This data is gathered through the Graduation Rate Survey, conducted by the National Center for Education Statistics.

not been acted upon, includes proposals that would make it easier for students to gather critical information about postsecondary institutions and would include adult learner data in some accountability metrics. The legislation is a starting point for better aligning higher education accountability efforts with the needs and interests of adult learners. One particularly promising proposal would include parttime and transfer students in the calculation of graduation rates. Other proposals include:

- *Providing students and families with online tools to research and compare institutions;*
- *Increasing the transparency of college cost, price, and financial aid;*
- *Raising public awareness of available information, especially for nontraditional students; and*
- *Making more information available on the number of transfer and parttime students, and including them in relevant calculations.*

STATE ACCOUNTABILITY SYSTEMS INCREASINGLY TRACK MORE THAN ENROLLMENTS, BUT THEY ARE SLOW TO ADDRESS ADULT LEARNERS AND ECONOMIC METRICS

Almost every state in the nation claims to have some form of accountability system (Wellman 2003). The State Higher Education Executive Officers Web site lists accountability reports and plans for about 40 states (*www.sheeo.org*). The starting points are the accountability metrics reported to the U.S. Department of Education. However, states use that information in many different ways, and to different extents, to inform funding decisions. They also use more than graduation rate data in oversight and improvement roles.

By and large, because of the way in which funding formulas are constructed for public higher education, enrollment is the metric that states are most intent on collecting and tracking. Colleges are reimbursed by the state for enrollments; not surprisingly, reporting of enrollments is quite well developed.

Economic, fiscal, and other pressures are now driving states to consider strengthening their accountability systems for higher education. And a number of states have made expanded their accountability systems to address student outcomes more directly—and to address economic impacts of higher education in the state. However, particular consideration of adult learners and accountability metrics that address their progress through higher education are rare.

Almost two dozen states have begun to set overall goals for their higher education systems in the areas of attainment and completion. A smaller number of states— seven—have set specific attainment and/or completion goals for minority, lowincome, or other populations. Some, though not all, are also putting in place mechanisms for tracking progress. According to a recent Jobs for the Future report, approximately half of all states have "specified measurable goals for increasing the proportion of their population with a postsecondary education, including specific benchmarks and a specific timeframe for achieving the goals" (Collins 2006). (See table 7.) While these goals are not necessarily formally linked to postsecondary accountability systems, identifying specific goals is a necessary first step in linking actual results with desired outcomes.

The report did not identify any goals that were disaggregated by age or that specified outcomes for adult learners.

Kentucky is one state that has begun to investigate how its higher education system is faring relative to its projected labor market needs for skilled and wellrounded college graduates. Kentucky has as one of its key accountability questions: "Are college graduates prepared for life and work in Kentucky?" (Kentucky Council on Postsecondary Education 2006).

Kentucky estimates that it will need up to fifteen years to nearly double the number of residents ages 2564 with at least a fouryear degree. Kentucky has also identified specific occupations/fields where future need is critical if the state is to remain economically competitive. From this process, the state has allocated $1 million per year to "recruit, mentor and place minorities and women in engineering programs" (Kentucky Council on Postsecondary Education 2006).

Table 7. Statewide Numerical Goals for Student Access and Success Number of States

Enrollment: States with at least one enrollment goal	20
Retention: States with at least one retention goal	10
Graduation: States with at least one graduation goal	19
All: States with at least one enrollment, retention, and graduation goal	10

Texas is also building a comprehensive higher education accountability system focused on increasing education attainment for key population segments, in order to "preserve the state's standard of living" (Collins 2006). Texas has a clear plan called *Closing the Gaps* that specifies targets for increased enrollment and degree completion of individuals from different population subgroups in the state by 2015. While the plan does not specify targets for adult students, it will be difficult for the state to meet its goals without addressing adult learners more effectively in higher education.

Texas and Kentucky are both tying their accountability systems and priorities to higher education gains—and to employer and economic demand. Much work remains to be done in this area, in these two states and certainly in others, if state accountability systems are to embrace and address the interests of both adult learners and the states' employers, who want to see a greater supply of credentialed, quality employees.

Initial Thoughts on Strengthening Accountability Systems—from Adult Learners' Perspective

It would be premature at this early stage in the discussion of accountability for adult learners to propose a specific set of goals and metrics that would focus attention on the quality of education and training they are receiving and the benefits accruing to them from college participation. However, it is possible to identify broad principles that should guide the development of accountability systems in higher education to ensure they are flexible enough to be relevant to adult learners and the programs they care most about. An adultfocused higher education system would:

- *Encourage greater postsecondary participation among adult learners to support their employment and career goals and employer interest in skill upgrading;*
- *Promote student success from enrollment to degree completion in order to reduce high attrition rates for adult learners; and*
- *Connect students with employers in their fields and with routes into the labor market in order to maximize the economic gains of working adults and those who employ them.*

An accountability system that monitors and accelerates achievement of these goals would feature priority statements that explicitly acknowledge the importance of serving adult learners. In order to be successful, the system must address each step in the adult learner's path, from postsecondary enrollment through completion to participation in the labor force. Such a system would specify metrics for institutional performance and student outcomes that take into account adult learners' distinctive patterns of college attendance and encourage colleges to be more effective in helping adult learners earn credentials. Key metrics must include measures of employment and earnings over time as well as credential and educational gains, such as:

- *Measures of enrollment, progress, and completion of degreeseeking, parttime students;*
- *Disaggregation of outcomes by age and other characteristics of nontraditional students;*
- *Outcomes that incorporate industry credentials and licensure exams as well as educational credentials; and*
- *Employment and earnings outcomes that capture adult learners' economic gains.*

Much more research and analysis is needed before policymakers will be able to design accountability systems that better address adult learners' needs—and drive improvement in adultlearner programming. Some areas requiring further attention include:

STRATEGIES TO STRENGTHEN PROGRAM ACCREDITATION

Existing programmatic accreditation processes should be studied to determine how promising approaches can be replicated and what kinds of new approaches might help address the growing demand for this type of quality control in both public and private higher education systems. Research should also consider how programmatic and institutional accreditation processes can be better aligned to promote flexible movement across programs and institutions.

APPROACHES TO MEASURING STUDENT SKILLS AND LEARNING

Employers play an important role in some credential programs in helping shape ways to evaluate whether students possess the competencies needed in new hires or whether workers have the ability to adjust to new technologies and responsibilities. Policymakers should incorporate lessons from the best of these efforts—employer roles in standardsetting, providing workplace practicums and designing performance assessments—to help them create accountability systems that acknowledge the range of occupational programs that adults choose. As accountability debates turn to what are the best ways to determine how much students are learning, through standardized exams or other means, the perspectives of both employers and adult learners themselves can help provide a broader range of options to consider.

WAYS TO STRENGTHEN DATA SYSTEMS IN ORDER TO REPORT ECONOMIC AS WELL AS EDUCATIONAL OUTCOMES

State governments have been at the forefront of developing new data and accountability systems. Some states— such as Florida, Washington, and Texas—have made progress in determining employment outcomes by linking databases to connect higher education outcome data with unemployment insurance system data. Much additional work is needed in this arena so that longitudinal tracking of postsecondary students can capture the effect of different kinds of precollege and collegelevel credential programs on educational and economic outcomes.

STRATEGIES FOR ENGAGING ALL KEY STAKEHOLDERS IN ACCOUNTABILITY DISCUSSIONS AND DEVELOPMENT

Designing an accountability system that meets the needs and interests of adult learners will require careful construction. All of the key stakeholders need a seat at the table, including higher education leaders from all types of institutions—public and private, nonprofit and forprofit. State and federal policymakers should also be involved. Above all, representatives of different kinds of employers must step up to argue for a system that better meets their needs and to help design its contours. Finally, adult learners themselves should participate. Just as adult instruction should incorporate adults' knowledge and experiences, so too should the design of systems intended to help them achieve their goals for a better education, a better career, and a better life.

SECTION 5.
RECOMMENDATIONS: A PLAN FOR ADDRESSING ADULT LEARNERS' NEEDS IN HIGHER EDUCATION

INTRODUCTION

This paper has shown the critical importance of improving adult access to and success in higher education for the economic wellbeing of the nation, employers and workers alike. While some postsecondary institutions have responded creatively to the needs of adult learners, the shift toward a more adultfriendly system remains far too slow. The challenge of making it easier for working adults to succeed in college credential programs requires explicit attention and a carefully tailored strategy. It is not enough to hope for improvement as a byproduct of increasing college success for traditional, younger students.

Such an effort will require commitment and action from employers, educational institutions, and adult learners themselves. But policymakers have a significant role to play, as well. At both the federal and state levels, policymakers can take important steps to create conditions and supports that encourage commitments to developing the affordable, flexible, and responsive postsecondary programs working adults need.

For this reason, we recommend here a policy plan for increasing the number of working adults pursuing and earning postsecondary credentials. The plan addresses the three major topics of this report—accessibility, affordability, and accountability—as well as employer engagement, which affects each of the other areas. While our analysis of the challenges facing adult learners in higher education highlighted many issues meriting attention, this section presents the top priorities for immediate action. Each would require significant levels of both cooperation and funding, but without them, systemic change in higher education that would dramatically improve outcomes for adult learners will be unlikely.

These recommendations, summarized here, are outlined in detail below:

- *Develop federalstate partnerships to promote and test innovative approaches to increasing adult access to and success in higher education.*
- *Update federal student financial aid programs to stimulate and support the postsecondary education of working adults.*
- *Create a national system to track and report individual adult student outcomes over time.*
- *Establish research and development programs to encourage employer engagement in the postsecondary education of working adults.*

RECOMMENDATION 1: DEVELOP FEDERALSTATE PARTNERSHIPS TO PROMOTE AND TEST INNOVATIVE APPROACHES TO INCREASING ADULT ACCESS TO AND SUCCESS IN HIGHER EDUCATION

Except for the funds it provides for student financial aid, the federal government has little influence over the structure or programming of postsecondary education. State governments oversee and fund these institutions, and therefore states must be important partners in any effort to make postsecondary systems more amenable to working adults. Nonetheless, the federal government can play a critical role, working closely with states and offering financial incentives that jumpstart the process.

Specifically, the federal government should partner with states to create Innovation Partnerships that: 1) test new approaches for increasing adult access to and success in higher education; and 2) scale up promising strategies. There is no shortage of innovative ideas for better meeting the needs of adult learners. A number of postsecondary institutions in the nonprofit and forprofit sectors target working adults by offering flexible and accelerated programs, adultfriendly instructional methods, and easier transitions within and across institutions. Their successes point the way toward a system that would encourage, not block, adults in their efforts to earn postsecondary credentials, despite the difficulties of juggling work, school, and family obligations. They also highlight how institutional, system, and public policy might better support such innovations.

The new federalstate Innovation Partnerships would be propelled by a competitive grant program, offering federal matching funds to states interested in testing some of these varied approaches to helping their adult learners complete higher education credentials more quickly and successfully. The partnerships would focus on any area of higher education policy where change is likely to improve results for adults, including governance, financing, programming, licensing, and accreditation.

This would be a timelimited "research and development" investment by the federal government, designed to leverage state innovation and investment to serve a critical student population. States would not have to participate, but the incentives would be available only to states that, in partnership with their higher education systems, submit clear proposals for multiyear activities to test and expand approaches to increase adult learner access and success.

Key features of the Innovation Partnerships should include:

- *A sharp focus on improving results for working adults, as measured by credential completion, the strengthening of performance measures, and system reform to expand and sustain innovations statewide;*
- *Strong employer involvement in all levels, from state oversight to local partnerships with educational institutions;*
- *A dollar-for-dollar match from participating states;*
- *One year planning grants, followed by annual, formulabased implementation grants (for a maximum of five years total);*
- *Databased management for the implementation grants, against clear, annual progress goals; and*

- *Waiver authority where needed for institutions and postsecondary systems that wish to research specific learning and programming needs of adult students and test strategies that can increase their access to and success in postsecondary credential programs (e.g., adjusting FTEbased funding formulas for innovative efforts to provide education for hardtoserve populations).*

RECOMMENDATION 2: UPDATE FEDERAL STUDENT FINANCIAL AID PROGRAMS TO STIMULATE AND SUPPORT THE POSTSECONDARY EDUCATION OF WORKING ADULTS

It is essential to rethink how the federal and state governments provide financial aid to adult students. Aid programs designed for fulltime, traditional students, while slowly being updated for the modern educational experience, remain sorely out of touch with the needs of working adults. Many adult learners do not qualify for financial aid because they cannot sustain a morethanparttime school schedule, or they are eligible to receive only a few hundred dollars in aid each year. This prevents many lowincome adults from accessing or completing postsecondary education. Working adults need a student aid system that matches their needs, and more must be done more quickly to improve it. Such a redesign must not reduce support for traditional students in need but rather offer more direct assistance to adult learners.

Two priorities emerge from the research. First, the federal government should continue to update the Pell Grant program and revisit restrictive rules of the federal student loan programs. At the same time, the federal government should energetically pursue the expansion of education tax credits and deductions, which are a promising alternative to complex, burdensome traditional grant and loan programs. In fact, the U.S. government is already delivering more and more student aid through the tax code, including credits and deductions for spending on tuition and fees in the current tax year and for saving toward college in the future. This method of delivery works particularly well for working adults, who pay taxes and who—unlike most traditional students—can benefit from offsets to their tax liability.

Updates to the Pell Grant and federal student loan programs should include these features:

- *Create a "year round" option for Pell Grant recipients: Many students—especially parttime, working adult students—must attend yearround in order to graduate within a reasonable timeframe. However, Pell Grants are limited to two semesters per academic year. Allowing students to receive Pell funding yearround promises to increase their persistence and, ultimately, their ability to complete degrees.*
- *Repeal the "tuition sensitivity" provision of Pell Grants: This provision stipulates an automatic reduction in aid*

for students attending lower cost institutions, such as community colleges, where adults often make up most of the student body. This disproportionately harms working adult students, especially those whose low incomes force them to attend lowcost colleges.

- *Allow use of "current year income" to determine Pell Grant allocations: Many working adult students would benefit from easing the rigid adherence to using a student's prioryear income on the Free Application for Federal Student Aid to determine the amount of aid the student will receive. Many adults enroll in postsecondary education because they are displaced from a job and no longer enjoy their former income. Streamlining the FAFSA to consider the current year's income—at least for students in these types of special circumstances— would provide a significant benefit for these students.*
- *Expand loan eligibility to parttime students: Current federal policy limits student loans to those who enroll at least half time. However, most working adults consistently attend less than half time or vary their enrollment intensity. The federal government may be able to improve persistence and completion rates by expanding student loans to students who are committed to postsecondary study but are unable to consistently enroll half time or more.*

Amendments to the Hope Scholarship and Lifetime Learning Tax Credits should include these provisions:

- *Increase the percentage of "qualified educational expenses" allowed under the Lifetime Learning Tax Credit: Increasing the percentage from 20 percent to 50 percent (while capping the total credit at an appropriate level) would mean that financial aid covers more of the real costs of attending a postsecondary institution.*
- *Expand the definition of "qualified expenses" for both the Hope Scholarship and Lifetime Learning Tax Credit: Including room and board, books, supplies, equipment, transportation, and child care as "qualified expenses" would target the costs that burden working students the most. It also would bring the credits in line with current student aid rules, thereby reducing some of the confusion surrounding the student aid programs.*
- *Allow the Lifetime Learning Tax Credit to be applied on a "per student" basis: Current rules allow only one credit per family. Changing the policy—which would put it in line with the Hope guidelines—would help families with two generations of students in college, and it would simplify the credits for filers.*
- *Make both the Hope and Lifetime Learning Tax Credits "refundable": This would allow tax filers to keep the full amount of the credits, including any amount beyond their tax liability. This would provide a necessary boost for lowincome working adults who need postsecondary education the most to help them climb out of poverty, but get stuck in a "Catch 22": they earn too much to qualify for student aid but too little to incur a tax liability. Therefore, they receive no benefit from the education tax credits.*

RECOMMENDATION 3: CREATE A NATIONAL SYSTEM TO TRACK AND REPORT EDUCATIONAL AND EMPLOYMENT OUTCOMES FOR ADULT LEARNERS OVER TIME

Higher education accountability systems were designed with traditional, fulltime students in mind and fail to meet adult learner needs. The federal government can play a significant role in creating tracking systems for adult learners that better capture not only educational outcomes but also the economic and employment outcomes that are important to them. This would help adults make informed decisions about where to seek higher education. It would also enable policymakers to more accurately assess the impact of higher education spending and to plan institutional and system improvements.

However, the federal government must proceed carefully, so that the ability of states and institutions to use data for decision making and improvement is maximized in the shift to a national system.

Some proposals for amending the Higher Education Act would provide a starting point for better alignment of higher education accountability efforts with the needs of adult learners, such as including parttime and transfer students in the calculation of graduation rates and providing online tools for students to research and compare institutions. However, even if these win approval from Congress, much more change will be needed. Metrics for a comprehensive, adultfocused accountability system also would include: measures of enrollment, progress, and completion of degreeseeking, parttime students; disaggregation of outcomes by age and other characteristics of nontraditional students; outcomes that incorporate industry credentials and licensure exams in addition to educational credentials; and employment and earnings outcomes that capture adult learners' economic gains.

The federal government can take two important steps to improve the ability of higher education data and accountability systems to reflect the progress of adult learners. First, it should create a national, longitudinal, student record system that includes working adults and can disaggregate their progress. Second, it should promote statelevel higher education accountability systems that contain richer information on adult learners and their educational and economic successes.

The U.S. Department of Education should move toward a national, longitudinal, unit record system for tracking all postsecondary students that would include[24]:

- *The ability to distinguish among students enrolled at different intensities—fulltime or parttime, as measured by number of creditor clockhours enrolled;*
- *The ability to distinguish among students seeking all types of postsecondary education—certificates, degrees, and noncredit education;*
- *The ability to follow students as they combine courses and programs from a variety of educational providers;*
- *Disaggregation of student populations and their outcomes by age, ethnicity, employment status, and other demographic characteristics to create a better picture*

---

[24] For more information on how a national unit record system might be structured and managed to support improvement and state and institutional decision making, see Florida Community Colleges and Workforce Education, KnowledgeWorks Foundation, and North Carolina Community College System (2006).

of the entire higher education population, and the hardtosee adult learner population in particular; and

- *Integration with other education and employment data systems, so that individual K12 education records and unemployment insurance history are also accessible.*

It is clear that there are political sensitivities around this recommendation. Not long ago, intense opposition from various constituencies (certain groups of colleges, state data offices, privacy advocates, and others) caused a proposal for a national system to be shelved. However, several states—including California, Washington, Oregon, and Texas—have made significant progress in the mechanics and design—and effective use—of such systems. Any movement toward a national unit record system can and should work closely with these lead states and learn from their experience and expertise. This is particularly important if data on students and their outcomes are to be helpful in decision making to improve results. States need access to student data regularly and quickly to inform decisions about funding and policy priorities. If a national student unit record data system is created, the federal government must make a strong commitment to provide states and institutions with easy access to data for decision making.

THE FEDERAL GOVERNMENT SHOULD ENCOURAGE AND SUPPORT STATE HIGHER EDUCATION ACCOUNTABILITY SYSTEMS THAT INCLUDE LABOR MARKET OUTCOMES, AS WELL AS EDUCATIONAL OUTCOMES

Institutions and public accountability systems should report not just on credential completion rates but also on employment and earnings outcomes for those who enter and complete their programs of study. A number of states do this by integrating educational data systems with the employment and earnings data reported through the unemployment insurance system. Federal funding and other policies should promote and support this integration so that it is more readily available information in more states.

RECOMMENDATION 4: ESTABLISH RESEARCH AND DEVELOPMENT PROGRAMS TO ENCOURAGE EMPLOYER ENGAGEMENT IN THE POSTSECONDARY EDUCATION OF WORKING ADULTS

Despite the occupational focus of most postsecondary graduates, few educational institutions and postsecondary policies engage employers—the demand side of the labor market—beyond a limited advisory capacity. It is rare for these institutions to involve employers deeply in designing curricula, importing information and materials from the workplace into the classroom, providing student internships and other types of work experiences merged with course activities, providing faculty externships, and delivering classes in the workplace. Likewise, federal and state policies fail to fully leverage employer involvement in targeted financing for credentialed education and skill development of working adults who lack postsecondary credentials.

Encouraging deeper engagement of employers in all aspects of postsecondary education could result in tremendous benefits for students, employers, and the educational institutions themselves. However, research to document existing practices or what works is limited.

For this reason, the federal government should undertake two sets of research and development activities to learn more about and better leverage employers in higher education. First, it should research current practices in employer involvement in postsecondary program design, delivery, and financing. Second, it should invest in the seeding and testing of promising practices in employer engagement, with the goal of promoting successful strategies for broad adoption.

Research to understand current practice in employer involvement in postsecondary education should include:

- *Benchmarking the extent of intensive employer involvement in postsecondary curriculum design, faculty development, and program delivery: A scan of how colleges and universities engage employers would help to establish this benchmark and uncover "pockets" of innovation whose lessons can help guide future employer activity and supportive policy.*
- *Basic research on employer financing of postsecondary education: Current estimates of what employers spend vary wildly because they are based on select sample surveys. One area of research that would be particularly helpful is on employer tuition assistance programs. Reinstating and expanding IRS reporting requirements for "section 127" filers would help tremendously in understanding how these investments are made and who benefits from them.*
- *State efforts to better leverage employer investment: For example, some states provide tax credits to companies that invest in education and skill development of workers. However, little is known about how widely used these policies are, which companies claim them, or which workers benefit. A better understanding of an employer's return on investment could help shape the expansion of such credits to other states.*

THE PROMOTING OF PROMISING PRACTICES IN EMPLOYER ENGAGEMENT SHOULD PROVIDE STRONGER INCENTIVES FOR EMPLOYER PARTNERSHIPS

At the institutional level, the incentives to engage employers in postsecondary improvement are weak. A grants program—perhaps a partnership among business, private philanthropy, and government—could help institutions and their employer stakeholders expand their partnerships and ultimately institutionalize new ways of collaborating. It could promote and advance innovations—in curriculum design and delivery, the use of workplaces as learning places, and employer financing of employee education costs—that could have a lasting impact for adult learners, their employers, and the economy.

REFERENCES

ACE Issue Brief. 2004. *Federal Student Loan Debt: 1993 to 2004*. Washington, DC: American Council on Education.

Adelman, Clifford. 2004. *Principal Indicators of Student Academic Histories in Postsecondary Education 19722000*. Washington, DC: U.S. Department of Education.

Allen, Elaine I. and Jeff Seaman. 2005. *Growing by Degrees: Online Education in the United States*. Wellesley, MA: The Sloan Consortium.

Alssid, Julian et al. 2002. *Building a Career Pathways System*. New York: Workforce Strategy Center.

American Association of State Colleges and Universities. 2002. *Accountability and Graduation Rates: Seeing The Forest and the Trees*. Washington, DC: Author.

Arone, Michael. 2004. "State Spending on Colleges Drops Over All for the First Time in 11 Years." *Chronicle of Higher Education*. January 8.

Bailey, Alice Anne and James R. Mingle. 2003. *The Adult Learning Gap: Why States Need to Change Their Policies Toward Adult Learners*. Denver, Colorado: Education Commission of the States.

Bailey, Thomas et al. 2003. *ForProfit Higher Education and Community Colleges*. CCRC Brief No. 16. New York: Community College Research Center, Teachers College, Columbia University.

Bailey, Thomas et al. 2005. *Is Student RightToKnow All You Should Know?* CCRC Working Paper No. 2. New York: Community College Research Center, Teachers College, Columbia University.

Bailey, Thomas, Davis Jenkins, and Tim Leinbach. 2005. *Is Student Success Labeled Institutional Failure? Student Goals and Graduation Rates in the Accountability Debate at Community Colleges*. CCRC Working Paper No. 1. New York: Community College Research Center, Teachers College, Columbia University.

Baum, Sandy and Kathleen Payea. 2004. *Education Pays 2004*. New York: College Board.

Bell, Julie Davis, Cheryl D. Blanco, Jacqueline E. King, Paul E. Lingenfelter, and David A. Longanecker. 2003. *Integrating Financial Aid and Financing Policies: Case Studies from Five States*. Report prepared for the Western Interstate Commission for Higher Education. Boulder, CO: WICHE.

Berg, Gary A. 2005a. *Lessons from the Edge: ForProfit and Nontraditional Higher Education in America*. Westport, CT: Praeger.

Berg, Gary A. 2005b. "Reform Higher Education with Capitalism?" *Change*. May/June.

Berker, Ali, Laura Horn, and C. Dennis Carroll. 2003. *Work First, Study Second: Adult Undergraduates Who Combine Employment and Postsecondary Enrollment*. Washington, DC: U.S. Department of Education, Institute of Education Sciences.

Berkner, Lutz, Laura Horn, and Michael Clune. 2000. *Descriptive Summary of 199596 Beginning Postsecondary Students: Three Years Later*. Washington, DC: U.S. Department of Education, National Center for Education Statistics.

Berkner, Lutz, Shirley He, and Emily Forrest Cataldi. 2002. *Descriptive Summary of 199596 Beginning Postsecondary Students: Six Years Later*. Washington, DC: U.S. Department of Education, National Center for Education Statistics.

Bonk, Curtis J. and KyongJee Kim. 2004. *Future Directions of Blended Learning in Higher Education and Workplace Learning Settings*. San Francisco: John J. Wiley and Sons.

Bosworth, Brian and Victoria Choitz. 2002. *Held Back: How Student Aid Programs Fail Working Adults*. Arlington, MA: Futureworks, LLC.

Bosworth, Brian and Victoria Choitz. 2004. *Title X: A New FederalState Partnership in Higher Education for Working Adults in the 21st Century*. Arlington, MA: Futureworks, LLC.

Burgdorf, Barry D. and Kent Kosta. 2005. *Eliminating Complexity and Inconsistency in Federal Financial Aid Programs for Higher Education Students: Towards a More Strategic Approach*. Unpublished Paper, University of Texas.

Carnevale, Anthony P. and Donna M. Deroschers. 2004. "Benefits and Barriers to College for LowIncome Adults." In *Low Income Adults in Profile: Improving Lives Through Higher Education*. Washington, DC: American Council on Education, Center for Policy Analysis.

Center for Community College Policy. 2000. *State Funding for Community Colleges: A Fifty State Survey*. Denver, CO: Education Commission of the States.

Center for the Study of Education Policy and the Illinois Student Assistance Commission. 2004. *Summary and Recommendations from Symposium on Financing Higher Education: Putting Illinois in the National Context*. Bloomington, IL: Illinois State University.

Choitz, Victoria and Rebecca Widom. 2003. *Money Matters: How Financial Aid Affects Nontraditional Students at Community Colleges*. New York, NY: MDRC.

Choitz, Victoria, Laura Dowd, and Bridget Terry Long. 2004. *Getting Serious About Lifelong Learning*. Arlington, MA: FutureWorks, LLC.

Choy, Susan. 2002. *Nontraditional Undergraduates*. Washington, DC: U.S. Department of Education, National Center for Education Statistics.

Chronicle of Higher Education. 2004. Survey of Public Opinion on Higher Education. FebruaryMarch.

Collins, Michael. 2006. *By the Numbers: State Goals For Increasing Postsecondary Attainment*. Boston: Jobs for the Future.

Committee for Economic Development. 2005. *Cracks in the Education Pipeline: A Business Leader's Guide to Higher Education*. Washington, DC: Committee for Economic Development.

Cook, Bryan and Jacqueline E. King. 2004. *Low Income Adults in Profile: Improving Lives Through Higher Education*. Washington, DC: American Council on Education, Center for Policy Analysis.

Cook, Bryan and Jacqueline E. King. 2005. *Improving Lives Through Higher Education: Campus Programs and Policies for LowIncome Adults*. Washington, DC: American Council on Education, Center for Policy Analysis.

Council for Adult and Experiential Learning and the American Council on Education. 1993. *Adult Degree Programs: Quality Issues, Problem Areas, and Action Steps*. Chicago: CAEL.

Council for Adult and Experiential Learning. 2005. *Serving Adult Learners in Higher Education*. Chicago: CAEL.

Day, Jennifer Cheesman and Eric C. Newburger. 2002. *The Big Payoff: Educational Attainment and Synthetic Estimates of WorkLife Earnings*. Washington, DC: U.S. Census Bureau

Dillon, Sam. 2005. "Closing of College Shadows Candidate for Governor," *New York Times*. November 17.

Dillon, Sam. 2006. "Online Colleges Receive a Boost from Congress," *New York Times*. March 1.

Eaton, Judith. 2005. "Transfer of Credit: Taking a Fresh Look or Continuing the Controversy?" *Inside Accreditation with the President of CHEA*. 1:4. November 4. Accessed February 26, 2006 at http://www.chea.org/ia/IA_110405.htm.

Eduventures. 2004. *Postsecondary Learning Markets and Opportunities 2004*. Boston: Eduventures, LLC.

Eduventures. 2005. *Developing Effective Channels to Corporate and Government Markets, Part I*. Boston: Eduventures, LLC.

Eduventures. 2005a. *Employer Policies and Practices for Learning and Development*. Boston: Eduventures, LLC.

Eduventures. 2005b. *Higher Education Survey on Leadership, Innovation and Technology*. Boston: Eduventures, LLC.

Eduventures. 2005c. *Assessing Consumer Attitudes toward Online Education*. Boston: Eduventures, LLC.

Eduventures. 2005d. *Online Distance Education Market Update 2005: Growth in the Age of Competition*. Boston: Eduventures, LLC.

Eduventures. 2006. *Assessing Consumer Demand for Adult, Continuing, and Professional Education, Part I*. Boston: Eduventures, LLC.

Employment Policy Foundation. 2004. *NinthAnnual Workplace Report: The American Workplace 2004*. Washington, DC: Employment Policy Foundation.

Ewell, Peter. 2001. *Accreditation and Student Learning Outcomes: A Proposed Point of Departure*. CHEA Occasional Paper. Washington, DC: Council for Higher Education Accreditation.

Fitzgerald, Joan. 2006. *Moving Up in the New Economy: Career Ladders for U.S. Workers*. Ithaca, NY: ILR Press

Florida Community Colleges and Workforce Education, KnowledgeWorks Foundation, and North Carolina Community College System. 2006. "A National Unit Record Data System: State Experience Can Strengthen this Proposal." Statement to the Secretary's Commission on the Future of Higher Education. August 7.

Goldberger, Susan. 2005. *From the Entry Level to Licensed Practical Nurse: Four Case Studies of Career Ladders in Health Care*. Boston, MA: Jobs for the Future.

Hecker, Daniel. 2005. "Occupational Employment Projections to 2014." Monthly Labor Review Online. Bureau of Labor Statistics. 128(11):70101.

Hersh, Richard H. 2005. "What Does College Teach?" *Atlantic Monthly*. Accessed February 26, 2006, at www.theatlantic.com/doc/20511/measuringcollegequality/2.

Horn, Laura. 1996. *Nontraditional Undergraduates, Trends in Enrollment From 1986 to 1992 and Persistence and Attainment Among 1989–90 Beginning Postsecondary Students*. NCES 97–578. Washington, DC: Government Printing Office.

Institute for Higher Education Policy. 1996. *Life After Forty: A New Portrait of Today's— and Tomorrow's— Postsecondary Students*. Washington, DC: Author.

ISAC Research Reports. 2001. *Initiative to Aid Illinois Adult Learners*. Springfield, IL: Illinois Student Assistance Commission. Summer.

Jasnick, Scott. 2006. "The Abandonment of Community Colleges." *Inside Higher Ed.* www.insidehighered.com/news/2006/01/16/cc

Jobs for the Future. 2004. *Breaking Through: Helping LowSkilled Adults Enter and Succeed in College and Careers.* Boston: Author.

Jones, Dennis, et al. 2003. *Policies in Sync: Appropriations, Tuition, and Financial Aid for Higher Education: A Compilation of Commissioned Papers.* Boulder, CO: Western Interstate Commission for Higher Education.

Jones, Dennis. 2003. *"Financing in Sync: Policy Brief: Policy Insights.* Boulder, CO: Western Interstate Commission for Higher Education.

Kane, Thomas J. and Peter R. Orszag. 2004. *Financing Public Higher Education: Short Termand LongTerm Challenges.* Washington, DC: Ford Policy Forum, Brookings Institution.

Kaufman, Rhoda S. 1994. "State Funding for Community College Noncredit Continuing Education Courses." *Catalyst.* 24(2). Richmond, VA: Virginia Polytechnic Institute.

Kazis, Richard and Marty Leibowitz. 2003. *Changing Courses: Instructional Innovations That Help LowIncome Students Succeed in Community College.* New York: MDRC.

Kelly, Patrick J. with Lumina Foundation for Education. 2005. *As America Becomes More Diverse: The Impact of State Higher Education Inequality.* Boulder, CO: National Center for Higher Education Management Systems.

Kentucky Council on Postsecondary Education. 2006. Accessed February 27 at: http://www.cpe.ky.gov.

Knowles, Malcolm S. 1970. *Modern Practice of Adult Education: Andragogy Versus Pedagogy.* Chicago: Follett Publishing Company.

Lingenfelter, Paul and Richard A. Voorhees. 2003. *Adult Learners and State Policy.* Denver, CO: State Higher Education Executive Officers and Chicago, IL: Council for Adult and Experiential Learning.

Lingenfelter, Paul E., David L. Wright, and Tara Bisel. 2005. *State Higher Education Finance FY 2004.* Boulder, CO: State Higher Education Executive Officers.

Matthews, Dewayne. 2005. "Toward a New Way of Thinking: Quality, Productivity, and College Costs." In Dickeson, Robert, ed. *Course Corrections: Experts Offer Solutions to the College Cost Crisis.* Indianapolis: Lumina Foundation for Education.

MatusGrossman, Lisa and Susan Gooden, et al. 2002. *Opening Doors: Students' Perspectives on Juggling Work, Family and College.* New York: MDRC.

MatusGrossman, Lisa and Susan Tinsley Gooden. 2001. *Opening Doors to Earning Credentials: Impressions of Community College Access and Retention from LowWage Workers.* New York: MDRC.

McCabe, Robert H. 2000. *No One to Waste: A Report to Public Decision Makers and Community College Leaders.* Washington, DC: Community College Press.

Michelau, Demaree K. 2003. *Tuition and Fees Policies in the Nation's Public Community Colleges.* Boulder, CO: Western Interstate Commission for Higher Education.

Murdock, Steve. 2004. *The Texas Challenge in the TwentyFirst Century: Implications of Population Change for the Future of Texas.* PowerPoint presentation.San Antonio: The Institute for Demographic and Socioeconomic Research, College of Business, University of Texas at San Antonio.

National Center for Education Statistics. 2002. *NonTraditional Graduates. Digest of Educational Statistics.* Washington, DC: U.S. Department of Education.

National Center for Education Statistics. 2004. *Digest of Educational Statistics*. Washington, DC: U.S. Department of Education.

National Center for Education Statistics. 2000. "National Household Education Surveys Program 1991, 1995, and 1999: Adult Education Survey." Washington, DC: U.S. Department of Education.

National Center for Public Policy and Higher Education. 2002. *Losing Ground: A National Status Report on the Affordability of American Higher Education*. San Jose, CA: Author.

National Center for Public Policy and Higher Education. 2004. *Losing Ground: A National Status Report on the Affordability of American Higher Education—Update, 2004*. San Jose, CA: Author.

National Center for Public Policy and Higher Education. 2005. *Income of U.S. Workforce Projected to Decline If Education Doesn't Improve*. San Jose, CA: Author.

National Education Association Research Center. 2003. *Why are College Prices Increasing and What Should We Do About It? Update*. 9(5). Washington, DC: National Education Association.

National Education Association. 2006. "Financing Higher Education: A Crisis in State Funding." *Higher Education*. http://www2.nea.org/he/fiscalcrisis/index.html

National Governors Association. 2002. *Assisting LaidOff Workers in a Changing Economy*. Issues Brief. Washington, DC: Author. *New York Times*. 2006. "Proof of Learning in College." February 26.

Noel Levitz. 2005. *2005 National Student Satisfaction and Priorities Report*. Accessed March 8, 2006 at www.noellevitz.com/Papers+and+Research/Research/Res earchLibrary/2005+National+Satisfaction+Report.htm.

Public Policy Associates, Inc. 2004. *Lifelong Learning Accounts Demonstration Interim Report One*. Report prepared for the Council for Adult and Experiential Learning. Lansing, MI: Author.

Reed, Sally. 2005. "Lifelong Lessons: Barriers Remain, Especially Financial Ones." *Lumina Foundation Focus*. Winter. Indianapolis, IN: Lumina Foundation for Education.

Reed, Sally. 2005. "Lifelong Lessons: Learning for Life," *Lumina Foundation Focus*. Winter. Indianapolis, IN: Lumina Foundation for Education.

Rooney, Kathryn. 2002. *Profile of Undergraduates in U.S. Postsecondary Institutions: 1999–2000*. Washington, DC: U.S. Department of Education, National Center for Education Statistics.

Scarafiotti, Carol. 2005. "Dreams Detoured: Community Colleges, A Vital and Affordable Resource, Also Feel the Pinch." *Lumina Foundation Focus*. Fall. Indianapolis, In: Lumina Foundation for Education.

Silber, Jeffrey and Avram Fisher. 2005. *Education and Training*. New York: Harris Nesbitt.

Silber, Jeffrey and Avram Fisher. 2006. *The Report Card*. New York: Harris Nesbitt.

Silva, Tim, Margaret Calahan, and Natalie LacirenoPaquet. 1998. "Adult Education Participation Decisions and Barriers." *Review of Conceptual Frameworks and Empirical Studies*. Washington, DC: U.S. Department of Education, National Center for Education Statistics.

Sperling, John and Robert Tucker. 1997. *ForProfit Higher Education: Developing a World Class Workforce*. New Brunswick, NJ: Transaction Books.

St. John, Edward P., et al. 2004. *Expanding College Access: The Impact of State Finance Strategies*. Indianapolis, IN: Lumina Foundation for Education.

St. John, Edward P. and Tina J. Tuttle. 2004. *Financial Aid and Postsecondary Opportunity for Nontraditional Age, PreCollege Students: The Roles of Information and the Education Delivery Systems.* Bloomington, IN: Indiana University.

State University of New York/Albany. 2000. "Financing Higher Education in New York State." *Higher Education Policy Brief, 012000.* Albany, NY: State Department of Education.

Twigg, Carol A. 2005. *Increasing Success for Underserved Students: Redesigning Introductory Courses.* Saratoga Springs, NY: National Center for Academic Transformation.

U.S Census Bureau. 2002. Public Use Microdata Samples (Based on the 2000 Decennial Census). Accessed at: www.census.gov/population/www/cen2000/ pums.html

U.S. Census Bureau. 2004. *American Community Survey.* Accessed at http://www.census.gov/acs/www/

U.S. Department of Education. 2006. Integrated Postsecondary Education Data System. Accessed February 27, 2006 at: http://nces.ed.gov/ipeds/AboutIPEDS.asp.

U.S. Department of Education. 2006. Financial Aid for Postsecondary Students: Accreditation in the United States. Overview of Accreditation. Accessed February 27, 2006 at: http://www.ed.gov/admins/finaid/accred/accreditation.ht ml#Overview.

U.S. Department of Education. 2005. "Secretary Spellings Announces New Commission on the Future of Higher Education." Press Release. Accessed February 27, 2006 at: http://www.ed.gov/news/pressreleases/2005/09/09192005.html.

U.S. General Accounting Office. 2003. *Federal Student Aid.* Washington, DC: Author.

U.S. General Accounting Office. 2003. *Federal Student Aid: Expanding Eligibility for Less Than Halftime Students Could Increase Program Costs, But Benefits Uncertain.* GAO03905: Highlights of GAO03905. Washington, DC: Author.

University Continuing Education Association. 2004. *Lifelong Learning Trends.* Washington, DC: Author.

Wang, Shaoli and Darrel A. Clowes. 1994. "Financing Community Services and Continuing Education: An Historical Review." *Catalyst.* 24(2). Richmond, VA: Virginia Polytechnic Institute.

Warford, Larry. 2002. *Lifelong Learning: A Funding Priority.* Phoenix, AZ: League for Innovation.

Wellman, Jane. 2003. *Statewide Higher Education Accountability: Issues, Options, and Strategies for Success.* Washington, DC: National Governors Association.

Wiley, John D. 2006. *SelfRegulation: Past, Present, and Future.* Address to Council on Higher Education Accreditation Annual Conference, San Francisco: January 24. Accessed March 14, 2006 at: http://chancellor.wisc.edu/CHEAtalk.html.

Zumeta, William. 2005. "Higher Education Funding: Stagnation Continues; Financial Restructuring Underway." *National Education Association 2004 Almanac of Higher Education*

INDEX

A

academic performance, 3, 8, 204, 211, 216
academic settings, 240
academic success, 17, 300
access, 2, 10, 17, 20, 27, 28, 30, 46, 56, 65, 66, 86,
  96, 100, 111, 112, 114, 116, 117, 123, 125, 127,
  129, 130, 131, 132, 167, 171, 172, 217, 254, 256,
  260, 273, 275, 276, 277, 278, 282, 284, 287, 289,
  290, 291, 292, 293, 299, 302, 303, 305, 307, 319,
  321, 322, 327, 332, 334, 341, 342, 343, 346
accessibility, 273, 275, 302, 306, 341
accountability, 29, 34, 136, 232, 245, 247, 273, 274,
  275, 276, 289, 305, 307, 320, 325, 328, 329, 330,
  331, 332, 334, 335, 336, 337, 338, 339, 340, 341,
  345, 346
accounting, 237, 300
accreditation, 296, 305, 307, 326, 328, 329, 334,
  339, 342, 353
acculturation, 181, 198, 203
accuracy, 66, 200
achievement, viii, 9, 16, 32, 33, 36, 37, 41, 44, 89,
  135, 137, 139, 140, 142, 156, 213, 214, 215, 216,
  231, 232, 233, 244, 248, 339
action research, 38, 140
activities, 3, 26, 28, 29, 30, 32, 33, 34, 37, 39, 41, 43,
  45, 47, 48, 49, 50, 53, 56, 58, 59, 60, 63, 66, 67,
  68, 69, 74, 75, 76, 82, 83, 84, 86, 89, 90, 96, 105,
  106, 109, 115, 123, 134, 135, 137, 141, 142, 144,
  145, 146, 148, 152, 153, 157, 164, 207, 208, 212,
  220, 233, 239, 245, 246
adaptation, 9, 148, 198, 203
adjustment, 199, 223, 234
administration, 4, 5, 11, 19, 20, 43, 50, 89, 119, 127,
  240, 246, 250, 320
administrators, 3, 4, 5, 6, 7, 10, 29, 35, 38, 42, 48,
  51, 56, 86, 132, 209, 272, 315, 335

adolescence, 177, 180, 195, 199
adolescents, 203, 310
adult learning, 21, 26, 41, 48, 57, 98, 138, 140, 249,
  291, 297, 305, 306
adult literacy, 54, 63, 82, 83, 140, 141, 319
adult population, 274, 277, 279, 285, 297
adulthood, viii, 175, 177, 181, 195, 196, 199, 202
affect, 6, 7, 8
African American(s), 11, 237, 278, 296
afternoon, 145, 187, 208, 212, 213
age, vii, 1, 4, 7, 11, 54, 56, 102, 159, 179, 181, 182,
  183, 190, 195, 196, 200, 201, 218, 222, 226, 228,
  237, 254, 255, 257, 267, 274, 275, 276, 278, 279,
  280, 281, 284, 287, 288, 295, 306, 310, 325, 329,
  338, 339, 345
agent, 311
aging, 202
aid, 5, 6, 12, 13, 14, 15, 17, 20, 33, 218, 244
Alabama, 210
alternative(s), viii, 22, 32, 34, 48, 177, 178, 187, 197,
  206, 208, 214, 223, 231, 240, 242, 257, 267, 290,
  305, 319, 343
ambiguity, 212, 213
amendments, 336
American Educational Research Association, 141
American Federation of Teachers, 31, 138
Amsterdam, 198, 269
analytical framework, 90
andragogy, vii
annual, 22
annual review, 138
ANOVA, 56, 64, 68, 80, 100, 155, 156, 163, 164,
  166, 167, 168, 170, 171, 172, 190, 191
anxiety, 9, 21, 37, 251
applied research, 29
appreciation, 5, 94, 107
aptitude, 243
argument, 236, 330
Aristotle, 183

Arizona, 325
armed forces, 311
articulation, 304, 327
assessment, 12, 21, 34, 85, 91, 132, 205, 232, 234, 246, 297, 300, 301, 303, 306, 319, 328, 333
assets, 131
assignment, 45, 207, 212, 213, 228, 241, 245
assimilation, 181
association, 160, 223, 248
assumptions, 3, 4, 34, 38, 45, 77, 85, 143, 152, 191, 247, 321
Athens, 200
attachment, 261, 268
attention, 10, 19, 132, 136, 186, 208, 231, 233, 243, 245, 247, 276, 289, 304, 307, 310, 318, 324, 325, 329, 330, 332, 334, 335, 338, 339, 341
attitudes, 1, 30, 36, 39, 42, 43, 44, 46, 81, 90, 139, 149, 159, 176, 233
authenticity, 204
authority, 42, 198, 205, 212, 223, 343
autonomy, 38, 171, 193, 201, 235, 330, 334, 335
availability, 332
average earnings, 261, 263
averaging, 195, 314
awareness, 40, 60, 73, 74, 82, 83, 88, 90, 91, 92, 94, 107, 122, 131, 177, 179, 185, 186, 194, 215, 244, 287, 337

B

baby boom, 277
background information, 41
balanced state, 192
barriers, 8, 9, 20, 21, 40, 60, 67, 79, 82, 83, 88, 111, 135, 149, 273, 274, 276, 282, 284, 292, 295
basic needs, 9
beginning teachers, 44, 140
behavior, 33, 62, 150, 176, 180, 181, 184, 185, 216, 221, 236, 239, 246, 248, 250, 305
behaviour, 229
belief systems, 67, 192
beliefs, 35, 38, 39, 44, 46, 67, 102, 142, 149, 176, 179, 188, 199, 204
benchmarks, 337
beneficial effect, 257, 267
benefits, 27, 28, 30, 32, 52, 56, 65, 74, 95, 96, 97, 100, 110, 112, 117, 118, 125, 127, 128, 129, 130, 131, 132, 136, 154, 167, 173, 240, 254, 255, 268
benign, 69
bias, 66, 246
Bible, 11
birth, 257
black, 219

blame, 73, 86, 92, 330
blocks, 293
body, 9
bonds, 193
borrowing, 228, 312
brain, 91, 216, 236
brainstorming, 58
breakdown, 157
buffer, 202
burning, 121, 126
business, 4, 5, 92, 238, 249
business model, 6, 291, 305, 306

C

calculus, 291
California, 142, 203, 296, 319, 346
campaigns, 287
campus climate, 6, 12, 13
Canada, 202, 203, 216, 260, 270
candidates, 328, 333
career counseling, 295, 299, 302
career development, 300, 319, 326
Carter, 238, 248
case study, 8, 83, 84
cast, 220
category a, 151
category d, 182
CBO, 117, 170
CE, 312
cell, 66, 80, 158
Census Bureau, 277, 279, 280, 285, 349, 353
certainty, 198
certificate, 7, 43, 100, 156
certification, 34, 37, 39, 51, 131, 156, 333
changing environment, 184
chaos, 188
character, 2, 223
Chicago, 139, 141, 201, 203, 204, 220, 251, 349, 351
child care, 10
child development, 198
childcare, 289
childhood, 304
children, vii, 17, 84, 187, 188, 199, 215, 219, 249, 268, 275, 289, 294, 313, 316
Cincinnati, 248
class size, 36
classes, 2, 6, 11, 14, 16, 17, 18, 19, 44, 52, 76, 77, 83, 85, 89, 90, 93, 110, 115, 120, 122, 144, 147, 158, 161, 187, 213, 224, 225, 226, 228, 229, 283, 290, 291, 293, 294, 295, 297, 298, 299, 300, 301, 303, 319, 323, 325, 346
classification, 263

classroom management, 44
classroom practice, 26, 33, 37, 91
classroom teachers, 27, 77, 120, 144
clients, 271, 272
coding, 64, 65, 70, 78, 150, 182
coffee, 82
cognition, viii, 175, 202, 221, 231, 236
cognitive abilities, 195, 197
cognitive ability, 236
cognitive development, 22, 177, 199, 201, 203
cognitive process, 219
cognitive research, 199
cognitive style, 45, 235, 236, 239, 240, 241, 243, 246, 248, 249, 250, 251
cognitive tool, 195, 228
coherence, 39, 48, 176, 180, 183, 184
cohort, 2, 14, 17, 20, 260, 262
collaboration, 35, 47, 142, 219, 295
collateral, 248
college campuses, 2
college students, viii, 8, 205, 208, 209, 212, 213, 215, 227, 282, 284, 287, 290, 293, 294, 296, 332
colleges, vii, viii, 2, 6, 10, 23, 205, 209, 214, 229, 255, 275, 276, 281, 284, 285, 286, 287, 289, 290, 292, 293, 295, 296, 297, 298, 299, 300, 301, 302, 303, 304, 306, 309, 310, 311, 313, 315, 316, 319, 320, 321, 322, 323, 324, 325, 326, 327, 330, 336, 339, 343, 346, 347
collisions, 180
Columbia University, 203, 348
commitment, 4, 10, 27, 47, 84, 95, 96, 97, 101, 102, 105, 117, 125, 126, 142, 153, 172, 236
commitments, 5, 10, 20, 68
commodity, 307
communication, 6, 20, 47, 218, 223, 224, 228, 276, 327, 335
communication skills, 235
community(ies), vii, 7, 8, 22, 35, 46, 53, 61, 70, 73, 76, 77, 83, 84, 85, 87, 88, 117, 119, 138, 139, 143, 144, 145, 149, 150, 157, 170, 217, 218, 227, 229, 255, 259, 267, 272, 284, 285, 287, 289, 290, 292, 293, 294, 295, 296, 298, 300, 302, 304, 310, 313, 319, 320, 322, 323, 324, 325, 326, 327, 336, 343
community service, 88
competence, 44, 47, 236
competency, 218, 291, 300, 334
competition, 287, 296
competitive, 233
competitiveness, 247
complement, 266, 303, 309, 316, 328
complementary teaching, 209

complexity, 9, 149, 176, 177, 183, 196, 197, 202, 204, 235, 236, 251, 330
compliance, 31, 334
components, 83, 180, 181, 186, 188, 192, 193, 194, 239, 326
composition, 54, 66, 322
comprehension, 152, 204, 225
computer(s), 18, 171, 208, 228
computing, 307
concept, 22
conception, 31, 176, 247, 276
conceptual model, 229
conceptualization, 175, 179, 180, 201, 218, 225
concrete, 81, 129, 179, 225, 226, 227, 229
conditioning, 265, 266
conduct, 10
confidence, 60, 82, 84, 88, 91, 94, 105, 121, 124, 131, 161
confidence interval, 105
confidentiality, 10, 69
configuration, 112, 145, 167, 222
conflict, 65, 180, 186, 188, 200, 233
conformity, 148
confusion, 69, 134, 232, 344
Congress, 303, 345, 350
congruence, 38, 180, 186, 238
Connecticut, 26, 29, 52, 54, 55, 56, 68, 115, 137, 145, 146, 147, 170, 173, 249, 251
consciousness, 178, 201, 219, 224, 225
consensus, 214, 238, 256
consent, 10
Constitution, 271
constraints, 50, 135, 315, 322, 323
construct validity, 211
construction, 177, 178, 180, 186, 192, 194, 199, 203, 255, 333, 340
consulting, 271, 272
consumer(s), 6, 21, 43, 126, 157, 331
consumption, 46, 95, 97, 102, 153, 157, 173
content, vii, 1, 4, 12, 17, 34, 35, 38, 39, 44, 49, 53, 77, 83, 87, 119, 120, 141, 143, 209, 228, 245
content analysis, 182
context, vii, 1, 4
contextualization, 302
control, 10, 40, 44, 73, 82, 85, 108, 172, 184, 199, 219, 222, 257, 261, 267, 339
control group, 257, 261
cooling, 171
cooperative learning, 142
coping, 22
corporations, 232
correlation(s), 12, 64, 101, 102, 172, 181, 190, 195, 196

costs, 130, 254, 255, 257, 268, 276, 289, 303, 307, 308, 309, 310, 313, 314, 318, 320, 321, 322, 324, 327, 329, 330, 331, 344, 347

counseling, 8, 9, 22, 239, 295, 297, 299, 302, 304, 307

course content, 259, 291, 297, 306, 307

course design, 246, 251

course work, 296

coverage, 30

covering, 217, 228, 324

creativity, 178

credentials, 272, 273, 274, 275, 276, 277, 278, 279, 285, 290, 291, 292, 293, 294, 295, 296, 299, 300, 304, 305, 307, 309, 310, 326, 327, 329, 330, 332, 333, 335, 339, 341, 342, 345, 347

credibility, 42, 256

credit, 2, 11, 286, 291, 295, 296, 299, 300, 303, 304, 306, 308, 311, 312, 313, 316, 317, 326, 327, 344

crime, 18

critical thinking, 335

criticism, 42, 192, 198

crowding out, 268, 322

CSF, 299

cues, 233, 234

cultural, 1, 222, 223, 226, 238

culture, viii, 3, 5, 35, 36, 38, 42, 44, 46, 47, 139, 175, 179, 180, 183, 187, 188, 191, 195, 198, 200, 226, 249, 297

curiosity, 218

curriculum, 12, 28, 36, 38, 42, 45, 48, 52, 53, 63, 83, 84, 85, 86, 95, 96, 97, 113, 117, 120, 122, 125, 128, 129, 135, 137, 140, 149, 154, 157, 159, 166, 173, 227, 228, 229, 251, 298, 299, 301, 302, 304, 307, 347

curriculum change, 149

curriculum development, 157

customers, 5, 23, 334

cyberspace, 228

cycles, 38

cycling, 128

D

data analysis, 80, 137, 141

data collection, 30, 52, 55, 66, 137, 146

dating, 223

DD, 186, 189, 191, 193, 195, 196, 197

death, 9, 224

debt, 14, 312, 322, 324

decision-making, 27, 28, 30, 46, 74, 86, 95, 96, 97, 110, 111, 116, 117, 120, 122, 123, 125, 127, 129, 130, 132, 136, 139, 154, 171, 345, 346

decisions, viii, 32, 40, 63, 66, 111, 122, 136, 171, 217, 291, 297, 321, 333, 337, 345, 346

deduction, 177

defense, 224, 225

definition, 196, 257

delivery, viii, 3, 11, 48, 115, 143, 169, 227, 231, 232, 239, 246, 248, 251, 273, 288, 289, 291, 292, 298, 300, 303, 305, 307, 309, 310, 319, 323, 327, 343, 347

demand, 209, 219, 221, 245, 247, 271, 273, 276, 279, 295, 296, 297, 300, 304, 329, 338, 339, 346

demographic change, 277

demographic characteristics, 12, 345

demographic data, 6, 336

demographic factors, 214

demographics, 6, 11, 21, 46, 237, 251, 279, 325, 336

dendritic cell (DC), 22

dependent, 27, 62, 64, 159, 172, 233, 234, 235, 237, 238, 239, 240, 241, 242, 243, 244, 245, 246, 247, 249, 250, 251

dependent variable, 27, 62, 64, 159, 172, 267

depression, 202

desire(s), 6, 17, 50, 66, 69, 84, 85, 86, 91, 102, 118, 122, 126, 131, 132, 134, 155, 173, 208, 213, 224, 235, 335

development policy, 143

developmental change, 177

deviation, 68

Dialectical-Deconstructive,, viii

differentiation, 180, 199, 235, 251

diffusion, 303

dimensions, 12

direct cost(s), 314, 324

direct observation, 41

discipline, viii, 3, 16, 217, 221, 222, 223, 224, 229

discontinuity, 304

discourse, 176, 192

dispersion, 259

disposition, 126, 233

dissatisfaction, 17, 119

distance education, 3, 11, 297, 326

distance learning, 288, 300, 302, 308

distribution, 189, 190, 246, 266, 287, 309, 327

diversity, viii, 11, 142, 191, 193, 197, 209, 213, 217, 222, 223, 226, 229, 231, 293, 318, 335, 336

dividends, 20

division, 48, 276, 326, 327

dominance, 14

dualism, 177

duration, 19, 32, 39, 40, 41, 129, 142, 292, 298, 306, 320

E

earning power, 209

earnings, viii, 253, 254, 255, 256, 257, 258, 259, 260, 261, 262, 263, 264, 265, 266, 267, 268, 269, 277, 328, 329, 335, 336, 339, 345, 346

ears, 46, 55, 63, 99, 121, 155, 172

Eastern Europe, 254

eating, 208

economic(s), 1, 218, 222, 226, 253, 255, 256, 266

economic development, 324, 326, 327

economic growth, 272

ecosystem, 128

education expenditures, 318

education/training, 319

educational attainment, 263, 265, 277, 278, 289, 296, 325, 327

educational background, 46, 47, 181

educational institutions, 272, 295, 299, 341, 342, 346, 347

educational policy, 324, 327

educational practices, 249

educational process, 3, 4, 6, 8, 20

educational programs, 268, 326, 334

educational services, 3, 6, 326

educational system, 255

educators, 1, 8, 26, 43, 48, 52, 57, 73, 93, 140, 141, 214

effective, 3, 8, 16, 19

efficiency, 232, 242

ego, 176, 202, 220

Eisenhower, 39

elaboration, 179

electives, 301

electronic materials, 127

elementary (primary) school, 84

email, 10, 18, 19, 302

emotion(s), 8, 179, 181

employability, 253

employees, vii, ix, 1, 264, 271, 273, 284, 294, 302, 313, 338

employment, 2, 5, 6, 7, 212, 255, 258, 263, 265, 268, 269, 277, 292, 297, 299, 300, 319, 320, 328, 329, 332, 334, 335, 336, 339, 340, 345, 346

employment status, 345

empowerment, 223, 229

encouragement, 106, 164

enculturation, 218

energy, 38, 43, 115, 168, 208, 290, 291

engagement, 146, 220, 222, 225, 228, 229, 274, 294, 341, 347

England, 26, 28, 29, 53, 67, 216

English, 25, 29, 50, 53, 54, 88, 139, 140, 209

enrollment, 2, 4, 14, 19, 39, 48, 97, 115, 146, 168, 211, 237, 281, 282, 285, 287, 289, 303, 306, 308, 309, 310, 311, 312, 314, 315, 317, 318, 319, 321, 322, 323, 324, 329, 332, 335, 336, 337, 338, 339, 344, 345

enthusiasm, 120, 272, 289

environment, vii, 1, 3, 4, 6, 8, 16, 18, 20, 21, 34, 41, 46, 112, 124, 144, 180, 184, 206, 212, 218, 219, 220, 221, 223, 225, 228, 233, 236, 238, 244, 248, 277, 293, 301, 307

environmental factors, 184

episteme(s), viii, 176, 178, 179, 182, 184, 185, 186, 187, 188, 189, 191, 192, 193, 194, 195, 196

epistemology, 139, 175, 197, 199

equality, 159

equilibrium, 177, 186, 194, 195

equipment, 344

equity, 248

ERIC, 22, 137, 138, 139, 140, 141, 142, 215, 216, 249

erosion, 278

ESL, 88, 138, 140, 143, 158, 279, 295

ETA, 271

ethics, 44, 180

ethnic groups, 204

ethnicity, 11, 226, 336, 345

ethnocentrism, 204

evaluation, 15, 43, 48, 75, 84, 86, 139, 142, 143, 161

evening, 2, 9, 23, 212, 213, 293, 319, 332

evidence, 38, 40, 81, 89, 92, 94, 96, 121, 136, 138, 148, 178, 180, 195, 206, 232, 242, 245, 266, 294, 327, 330, 331

evolution, viii, 34, 198, 231, 232

excuse, 93

exercise, 23, 224, 225

expectations, 9, 12, 20, 28, 42, 44, 69, 84, 93, 125, 131, 132, 133, 134, 152, 213

expenditures, 312, 318, 320, 322

experimental design, 241

expertise, 116, 208, 217, 272, 294, 298, 346

experts, 32, 34, 45

exploitation, 297

exposure, 47, 59, 106, 124, 125, 164, 173, 187

extra help, 85

extrinsic rewards, 245

extrovert, 186

eyes, 223

F

face-to-face interaction, 50

facilitators, 59, 62, 66, 69, 70, 126, 133, 146, 147, 148, 164

factor(s), 1, 3, 4, 5, 9
factual knowledge, 40
faculty, 3, 4, 5, 6, 7, 8, 9, 10, 14, 17, 18, 19, 20, 23, 209, 210, 211, 214, 215, 222, 229, 240, 245, 246, 247
failure, 9, 218, 219, 289
faith, vii, 1, 3, 4, 11, 178, 241
families, 7
family, 2, 7, 9, 10, 14, 15, 20, 82, 85, 92, 93, 103, 128, 144, 158, 188, 254, 277, 283, 284, 289, 290, 291, 293, 299, 308, 309, 312, 313, 315, 316, 317, 318, 323, 324, 342, 344
family income, 312, 313, 324
family literacy, 82, 85, 93, 103, 128, 158
family members, 144
family support, 324
fat, 222
fear, 86, 135, 219, 220, 223, 224, 225, 335
federal, 29, 48, 136
federal funds, 319, 321
federal government, 48, 309, 311, 312, 329, 330, 335, 336, 342, 343, 344, 345, 346, 347
federal grants, 311, 320
feedback, vii, 1, 19, 20, 34, 38, 41, 58, 59, 60, 69, 82, 122, 123, 127, 146, 239, 245, 303
feelings, 10, 45, 60, 149, 233
female(s), 11, 54, 211, 237, 238, 249, 255, 257, 258, 259, 260, 261, 263, 264, 265, 267, 269
Field Independence-Dependence (FI/FD) Cognitive Learning Style, viii, 231
finance, 238
financial barriers, 8
financial support, 254, 255, 259
fishing, 152, 235
flexibility, 14, 66, 104, 113, 117, 179
flight, 9
Florida, 210
fluid, 236
focusing, 8, 20, 208, 242
food, 9, 314
Ford, 351
forgetting, 67
forgiveness, 318
formal education, 27, 34, 37, 43, 54, 63, 64, 95, 97, 100, 101, 117, 126, 128, 129, 132, 153, 156, 254, 255, 261
fragmentation, 188
framework, 49, 52, 90, 121, 134, 216, 224, 225, 234, 235
framing, 158
France, 253
fraud, 297, 303
free, 39, 52, 53, 219, 221, 223, 227, 228, 242

free association, 223
free recall, 242
freedom, 28, 95, 97, 115, 116, 154, 168, 171, 219
frustration, 16, 206, 330, 333
fulfillment, 181
funding, 31, 39, 48, 74, 77, 128, 136, 272, 273, 276, 289, 291, 302, 304, 309, 315, 319, 320, 321, 323, 324, 325, 326, 337, 341, 343, 346
fundraising, 17, 335
funds, 3, 309, 319, 320, 321, 322, 323, 324, 331, 342
furniture, 171

G

GAO, 320
gauge, 41, 43, 52, 60, 62, 64, 75, 101, 102, 150
gender, 39, 63, 144, 179, 181, 182, 183, 191, 218, 222, 226, 228, 237, 238, 255, 257, 261, 336
gender differences, 191, 238
gene, 5, 243, 287
general adaptation syndrome, 9
general education, 297, 300, 301, 335
general intelligence, 37, 236
general knowledge, 266
generalization, 195, 198
generation(s), 192, 204, 228, 248, 277, 279
genetic information, 180
geography, 53, 67, 165
Georgia, 49, 318
gifted, 179, 221
global economy, 276
goals, 4, 6, 7, 8, 9, 38, 39, 46, 50, 57, 63, 75, 84, 88, 89, 120, 132, 144, 146, 159, 215, 218, 220, 222, 223, 239, 283, 289, 292, 302, 307, 324, 327, 331, 334, 337, 338, 339, 340, 342
goal-setting, 75, 83, 89, 131
God, 188
gold, 214
governance, 342
government, 7, 22, 48, 254, 255, 257, 271, 272, 309, 311, 312, 322, 327, 329, 330, 331, 334, 335, 336, 340, 342, 343, 344, 345, 346, 347
government expenditure, 322
GPA, 209, 210, 255
grades, 36, 207, 212, 213, 255, 256, 259, 264, 283, 315
Grant, 139, 211
grants, 20, 260, 268, 308, 309, 311, 313, 314, 315, 316, 318, 319, 320, 321, 322, 324, 334, 336, 342, 347
gravity, 233
Green, Carole, 7, 22, 49, 142

growth, 2, 17, 44, 52, 81, 83, 139, 140, 177, 178,
    188, 196, 201, 203, 214, 272, 273, 274, 275, 277,
    281, 285, 287, 288, 296, 322, 323, 324, 325, 332,
    333
growth rate, 275, 281
guidance, 133, 152, 243, 244, 248
guidelines, 138, 180, 318, 344

H

habitat, 180
Haifa, 188
hands, 37, 39, 164
Harvard, 139, 143, 198, 199, 200, 201, 204
health, viii, 5, 43, 68, 69, 77, 87, 88, 110, 157, 253,
    266, 269, 304, 311, 315, 331, 333, 334
health care, 5, 331, 333
health education, 43
health problems, 68
heat, 84
heating, 171
height, 224
heterogeneity, 8, 181, 197
HHS, 311
high school, vii, 4, 6, 14, 54, 90, 140, 187, 212, 218,
    273, 274, 275, 277, 278, 279, 282, 294, 301, 304,
    310, 319
higher quality, 104, 124, 163
higher-order thinking, 37
hiring, 297, 333
Hispanic(s), 11, 55, 237, 278, 279, 287
Hispanic population, 278
history, 27, 217
holistic, 4, 6
homework, 69
homogenous, 5
House, 248, 336
household income, 279, 286
households, 312, 313
human behavior, 235
human capital, 257, 261, 266, 332
human development, 204
human sciences, 259
humanity, 3, 188
Hurricane Katrina, 277
hypothesis, 4, 26, 30, 98, 99, 100, 101, 104, 105,
    108, 109, 110, 111, 113, 126, 154, 155, 156, 157,
    158, 159, 160, 165, 166, 167, 168, 171, 176, 237,
    243, 246, 267
hypothetico-deductive, 197

I

ideas, 37, 38, 42, 43, 44, 72, 81, 83, 86, 87, 90, 96,
    99, 108, 109, 111, 115, 118, 119, 120, 123, 125,
    131, 133, 134, 135, 152, 155, 171, 221, 232
identification, 132, 203, 204, 226, 232
identity, 74, 176, 180, 181, 183, 184, 193, 194, 199,
    202, 203, 204
idiosyncratic, 191
illusion, 199
images, 179, 226
imagination, 219, 220
implementation, 30, 37, 38, 139, 140, 141, 142, 148,
    240, 330, 342
implicit knowledge, 41
in situ, 227
incentives, 42, 180, 289, 326, 342, 347
incidence, 109
income, 256, 265, 266, 277, 278, 286, 293, 308, 313,
    315, 317, 321, 322, 323, 324, 325, 327, 344
income distribution, 266
independence, 6, 8, 187, 232, 233, 235, 236, 237,
    238, 239, 242, 243, 244, 245, 247, 248, 249, 250,
    251, 282
independent variable, 39
India, 184
Indiana, 22
indication, 71, 74, 80, 92, 106, 133, 164, 171
indicators, 15, 37, 70, 115
indirect effect, 266
individual characteristics, 54, 264
individual differences, viii, 216, 231, 234, 238, 240,
    241, 301
individual students, 56, 76, 208, 330
individualism, 38
individuality, viii, 217
individualized instruction, 89, 119, 128
induction, 34
industry, 273, 288, 296, 297, 300, 302, 303, 326,
    329, 330, 333, 334, 339, 345
infancy, 175, 180, 199
infants, 225, 295
inferences, 228
influence, 2, 3, 5, 10
information, 5, 11, 50, 70, 103, 117, 127, 143, 153,
    210, 216, 241, 242
information processing, 200
Information System, 5, 11
information technology, 300, 304, 326, 327, 332,
    333
informed consent, 10
infrastructure, 15
injury, iv

innovation(s), 10, 33, 35, 42, 139, 140, 142, 216, 288, 292, 299, 304, 305, 307, 342, 347, 350, 353
input, 43, 84, 122, 123, 125, 128, 147, 224
insertion, 229
insight, 46, 79, 222, 237, 246
inspiration, 219
instruction, 19, 20, 21, 33, 40, 44, 52, 67, 73, 86, 89, 92, 95, 97, 102, 119, 124, 128, 141, 142, 144, 149, 153, 157, 158, 159, 213, 214, 232, 238, 243, 244, 246, 247, 248, 251, 279, 288, 290, 294, 297, 298, 299, 300, 301, 302, 307, 316, 340
instructional design, viii, 2, 231
instructional materials, 208, 232
instructional methods, 231, 246, 290, 294, 342
instructional practice, 143, 214
instructional skills, 49
instructors, viii, 3, 12, 16, 17, 19, 50, 51, 52, 138, 143, 209, 214, 231, 240, 246, 301, 302
instruments, 327
insurance, 52, 110, 254, 268, 340, 346
Integral-Inclusive, viii
integration, viii, 38, 40, 180, 181, 197, 202, 218, 221, 231, 346
integrity, 62, 153
intellectual development, 203
intelligence, 37, 235, 236, 249
intensity, 236, 260, 261, 309, 310, 311, 312, 317, 318, 344
intentionality, 4
interaction(s), 19, 20, 22, 47, 50, 60, 77, 88, 128, 129, 161, 173, 185, 188, 203, 208, 240, 241, 243, 244, 246, 248, 250, 267, 303
interdisciplinary teaching, 218
interest, 7, 17, 29, 41, 57, 83, 89, 92, 93, 98, 119, 121, 129, 154, 208, 223, 232, 239, 246
Interest, 236
interest rates, 312
interference, 242, 243
internal consistency, 184
internal validity, 237
internet, 18, 302
interpersonal interactions, 240
interpersonal skills, 244
interpersonal support, 21
interpretation, 4, 65, 179, 182, 184, 218, 234, 258, 266, 268, 269
interpreting, 67, 144
interval, 105, 265
intervention(s), 16, 41, 47, 146, 148, 173, 215
interview, 10, 12, 17, 19, 53, 62, 63, 69, 76, 81, 83, 84, 85, 86, 87, 88, 89, 90, 91, 92, 93, 109, 118, 119, 120, 121, 122, 123, 124, 151, 179, 181, 182, 185, 225

intrinsic motivation, 132
introvert, 183
intrusions, 3
intuition, 248
investment, 14, 48, 130, 266, 272, 287, 307, 321, 323, 328, 330, 332, 342, 347
investment of time, 130
isolation, 60, 74, 127, 326
Israel, 175
issues, 5, 8, 11, 16, 73, 74, 85, 86, 90, 92, 102, 109, 119, 120, 124, 144, 159, 218, 222, 236

J

job performance, 301
job skills, 91, 120, 316
job training, 2, 319, 326
jobs, 7, 28, 30, 35, 50, 51, 56, 86, 96, 112, 113, 127, 130, 131, 266, 276, 277, 279, 302, 308, 310, 311, 319, 320, 325
Jones, Bill, 31, 41, 43, 140, 143
judgment, 9, 73, 77, 80, 150, 201, 214, 219, 228, 272
justice, 201
justification, 178, 185, 201

K

King, 2, 5, 7, 8, 23, 176, 177, 179, 181, 182, 195, 196, 201, 218, 293, 297, 323, 325, 348, 349
knowledge, 3, 4, 5, 8, 17, 19

L

labor, 254, 256, 257, 259, 260, 261, 263, 266, 267, 268, 273, 275, 276, 277, 279, 284, 287, 291, 292, 295, 302, 307, 309, 319, 327, 329, 332, 333, 336, 338, 339, 346
labor force, 276, 277, 279, 339
labor force, 259, 260, 268
labor market(s), 254, 256, 261, 263, 267, 287
lack of confidence, 124
language, 81, 83, 87, 88, 192, 209, 224, 225, 227, 290, 299
language skills, 83
laptop, 18
Latinos, 278
laughing, 185
laws, ix, 158, 180, 271, 312
layoffs, 308
LEA, 84, 85, 117, 170

lead, 7, 8, 9, 36, 43, 45, 79, 104, 123, 130, 134, 160, 169, 185, 186, 228, 246, 293, 304, 308, 316, 319, 346

leadership, 36, 46, 47, 95, 97, 111, 116, 141, 147, 154, 170, 210, 336

learner support, 83

learning disabilities, 85

learning environment, vii, 1, 4, 5, 8, 16, 20, 21, 34, 228, 233, 238, 244, 245, 248

learning outcomes, viii, 138, 231, 232, 328, 334, 335

learning process, 3, 8, 45, 83, 208, 214, 216, 218, 221, 226, 233, 244, 245

learning skills, vii, 248

learning styles, viii, 205, 208, 209, 213, 214, 215, 216, 217, 218, 221, 222, 226, 227, 228, 229, 231, 232, 237, 239, 244, 246, 247, 248, 249, 250, 251, 310, 323

learning task, 45, 239, 241, 242

Learning-Style Model, viii

legal, 216

legislation, 176, 319, 329, 337

leisure, 43, 256

lending, 312

lens, 189

lesson plan, 83, 85

library services, 299

life course, 177

life cycle, 180

life experiences, 179

life span, 249, 251

lifelong learning, vii, 50, 253

lifestyle, 9

likelihood, 48, 131, 314, 332

limitation, 66, 67, 319

linear model, 179

links, 139, 199, 231, 297

listening, 69, 85, 122, 147, 240

literacy, 25, 54, 63, 66, 67, 82, 83, 85, 87, 93, 95, 97, 102, 103, 114, 128, 138, 139, 140, 141, 153, 157, 158, 159, 259, 279, 319

literature, viii, 18, 30, 31, 32, 33, 34, 36, 39, 44, 45, 46, 47, 51, 52, 59, 60, 62, 95, 146, 148, 153, 170, 177, 180, 218, 219, 233, 236, 238, 239, 245, 246, 247, 250, 253, 256, 266, 272, 273, 289

living standard, 277

loans, 20, 260, 308, 309, 311, 312, 314, 318, 319, 320, 321, 322, 324, 328, 331, 332, 336, 344

local community, 77, 295

Local Education Agency, 57

local educational agencies, 53

location, 14, 18, 19, 63, 99, 184, 185, 192, 326, 332, 336

London, 198, 200, 216, 229

longitudinal study(ies), 38, 49, 201, 203

Los Angeles, 23

Louisiana, 277

love, 188

M

Maine, 26, 29, 52, 54, 55, 56, 68, 115, 137, 145, 146, 147, 169, 170, 173

male, 11, 220, 226, 237, 238

males, 211, 226, 238, 249, 255, 257, 258, 259, 260, 261, 264, 265, 267, 269

management, vii, 1, 4, 10, 11, 12, 15, 16, 17, 22, 44, 90, 213, 216, 232, 248, 251, 300, 302, 315, 319, 342

manners, 183

manufacturing, 295

market(s), 3, 7, 11, 143, 254, 256, 257, 261, 263, 266, 267, 268, 271, 272, 273, 275, 276, 277, 284, 287, 291, 292, 293, 295, 296, 297, 302, 305, 307, 309, 319, 327, 329, 330, 332, 333, 336, 338, 339, 346

market forces, 305

market value, 273, 319, 332, 333

marketing, 287, 297, 323

marketing strategy, 297

Maryland, 325

Massachusetts, 26, 29, 52, 54, 55, 56, 68, 115, 137, 145, 146, 147, 170, 173, 302

mastery, 218, 300, 305, 306

mat, 21

mathematics, 138, 141, 215, 224, 238, 243, 248, 250, 259, 261, 266, 269, 301

matrix, 65, 180, 192, 225, 227

maturation, 177, 180, 218

mean, 12, 71, 81, 99, 104, 106, 111, 155, 160, 161, 163, 169

meanings, 180, 186, 193

measurement, 211, 236, 254

measures, 9, 10, 27, 62, 72, 75, 233, 256, 274, 324, 328, 331, 336, 339, 342, 345

media, 85

median, 55, 68, 261, 277

Medicaid, 322

memory, 239, 242, 243, 248, 249, 250

men, 26, 53, 176, 214, 220, 237, 238, 260, 268, 276

mental development, 177

mentor, vii, 25, 26, 29, 34, 45, 53, 56, 58, 60, 66, 68, 69, 70, 74, 83, 84, 85, 86, 90, 92, 106, 107, 108, 109, 110, 122, 123, 125, 128, 133, 134, 144, 145, 146, 147, 162, 164, 165, 166, 173, 302, 338

mentoring, 32, 34, 35, 39, 44, 49, 58, 123, 124, 147, 165, 166, 307

messages, 185
metamorphosis, 6
metaphor, 191
methodology, 52, 215
Mexico, 336
Microsoft, 327
migration, 242
military, 295
mind-body, 22
Ministry of Education, 270
minority(ies), 39, 203, 215, 232, 237, 248, 294, 296, 310, 331, 337, 338
minority students, 232
missions, 325, 330
Mississippi, 210, 325
mobility, 23, 43, 208, 212, 306
modeling, 164, 227
model(s), vii, viii, 10, 25, 26, 27, 28, 29, 30, 31, 32, 33, 34, 35, 42, 52, 53, 54, 56, 57, 58, 59, 60, 61, 66, 67, 68, 69, 72, 74, 77, 95, 96, 106, 107, 108, 110, 115, 117, 119, 120, 125, 126, 133, 134, 135, 136, 139, 142, 145, 146, 147, 152, 153, 161, 164, 165, 166, 173, 177, 178, 179, 187, 196, 205, 206, 207, 208, 210, 211, 215, 224, 226, 227, 229, 232, 249, 289, 290, 291, 296, 297, 299, 305, 306, 310, 319
modules, 298, 299, 300, 305, 316
momentum, 38
money, 18, 49, 118, 214, 295, 303, 330
monitoring, 16, 37
Monolithic-Monoformal, viii
mood, 10
Moore, Dennis, 251
moral reasoning, 176
morning, 208, 211, 212, 213
motion, 192, 193, 194
motivation, 7, 17, 23, 26, 27, 36, 42, 43, 44, 46, 47, 57, 58, 61, 62, 70, 72, 73, 74, 75, 76, 79, 81, 84, 85, 86, 88, 91, 92, 93, 94, 96, 98, 99, 101, 102, 109, 111, 117, 118, 119, 120, 121, 122, 125, 126, 127, 128, 129, 131, 132, 143, 144, 146, 147, 148, 153, 154, 155, 159, 161, 173, 207, 245, 256, 294, 300, 334
motives, 3, 10
movement, viii, 46, 193, 194, 217, 331, 339, 346
multiculturalism, 181
multiple factors, 26, 30, 124, 128
Multiple Intelligence Theory, 232
multiple regression analysis(es), 100, 101, 102, 104, 105, 112
multiplicity, 188, 194, 320
multivariate, 172

N

nation, 271, 278, 279, 287, 307, 336, 337, 341
national, 15, 21, 31, 37, 48, 49, 51, 118, 139
National Center for Education Statistics (NCES), 2, 4, 5, 6, 7, 22, 23, 44, 140, 275, 281, 282, 284, 285, 286, 287, 288, 292, 310, 322, 336, 349, 350, 351, 352
National Education Association, 352, 353
Native American(s), 287, 311
needs, 4, 6, 8, 9, 10, 17, 18, 20, 21
negative consequences, 209
negative experiences, 93
neglect, 23
negotiating, 296
nervous system, 5
network, 2, 43, 47, 127, 140, 177, 216
networking, 271
neuropsychology, 216
New England, 26, 28, 29, 53, 67
New Jersey, 229, 249, 250, 251, 318, 325
New Mexico, 336
New York, 22, 23, 138, 140, 141, 142, 198, 199, 200, 201, 202, 203, 204, 211, 216, 249, 250, 251, 318, 348, 349, 350, 351, 352, 353
New Zealand, 250
next generation, 279
niche market, 11, 307
Normative, 250
North Carolina, 304, 325, 345, 350
Notre Dame, 202
nurses, 23
nursing, vii, 1, 9, 11, 19, 23, 255, 263, 266, 302, 334
nutrition, 85, 315

O

objectives, 3, 58, 61, 79, 80, 92, 94, 106, 143, 148, 149, 233, 239, 245
objectivity, 202
observations, 59, 62, 65, 145, 260, 261, 262, 263, 266
OECD, 254, 259, 270
online learning, 3, 288, 298
openness, 47, 67
opportunity costs, 257
Oregon, 43, 85, 304, 319, 325, 346
organ, 108, 115, 176
organism, 9
organization(s), 42, 49, 53, 54, 105, 117, 140, 160, 170, 179, 196, 206, 232, 233, 238, 241, 242, 244,

245, 247, 248, 249, 251, 276, 295, 300, 305, 306, 307, 320, 326, 334

organizational behavior, 248

orientation, 17, 32, 35, 90, 118, 123, 144, 145, 147, 182, 189, 222, 234, 235, 238, 247, 301

outliers, 114

outline, 30, 94, 146, 241, 251

OVAE, 48, 51

overload, 7

oversight, 334, 337, 342

overtime, 73

P

Pacific Islander, 237

packaging, 307

pairing, 34

paradigm shift, 1, 34, 142, 214, 215

parameter, 264

parenthood, 6

parents, 42, 207, 215, 232, 289, 311

Paris, 270

participation, 23, 32, 37, 39, 43, 44, 47, 49, 53, 61, 63, 66, 68, 69, 71, 77, 80, 81, 82, 84, 94, 95, 96, 104, 126, 130, 132, 134, 141, 148, 153, 156, 157, 160, 161, 172, 249

partnership(s), 23, 290, 301, 302, 303, 341, 342, 347

passive, 126, 214, 253, 294

pathways, 128, 300, 302, 303, 304

pedagogy, vii, 38, 222, 247

peer review, 334

peers, 37, 40, 43, 127, 208, 212, 222, 268, 284, 295, 312, 334

Pennsylvania, 1, 49, 140

pension plans, 30

pensions, 268

percentile, 36

perception(s), 9, 12, 21, 23, 68, 86, 95, 97, 105, 106, 116, 139, 149, 154, 162, 170, 171, 221, 222, 231, 234, 235, 247, 324

performance, 3, 8, 13, 15, 16, 17, 18, 37, 38, 41, 62, 179, 192, 204, 211, 215, 216, 220, 236, 238, 240, 241, 242, 243, 250, 254, 266, 300, 301, 306, 324, 327, 330, 332, 339, 340, 342

permit, 312

personal, vii, viii, ix, 5, 6, 7, 8, 9, 10, 13, 18, 43, 44, 45, 86, 89, 91, 128, 138, 175, 176, 179, 180, 182, 191, 192, 203, 211, 213, 221, 224, 226, 246, 271, 278, 295, 307

personal goals, 8, 307

personal histories, 203

personal learning, 211, 213, 226

personal problems, 10, 89

personal styles, 246

personality, 38, 180, 187, 199, 200, 204, 214, 223, 224, 234, 235

personality characteristics, 215

personality traits, 180, 204

perspective, 17, 22

philanthropy, 347

philosophy, 28, 33, 38, 121, 123, 135

physical environment, 219

physiology, 22

planning, 40, 44, 48, 122, 125, 133, 141, 219, 300, 309, 318, 319, 342

pleasure, 229

plurality, 184, 188, 194

polarity, 184, 185

polarization, 330

policy(ies), 7, 42, 48, 52, 61, 70, 76, 88, 95, 97, 115, 127, 128, 135, 138, 139, 140, 141, 143, 150, 154, 167, 168, 169, 171

policymakers, 28, 29, 31, 32, 130, 138, 295, 305, 328, 329, 331, 335, 339, 340, 341, 345

politics, 23, 323

poor, 44, 69, 86, 91, 93, 118, 119, 123, 128, 241

population, 2, 3, 4, 5, 6, 7, 8, 9, 10, 11, 13, 14, 17, 20, 51, 129, 190, 211, 229, 232, 237, 238, 247, 257, 274, 275, 277, 278, 279, 280, 281, 284, 285, 287, 289, 297, 299, 309, 319, 323, 331, 336, 337, 338, 342, 346, 353

population group, 237

portfolio, 183, 184, 186

positive correlation, 102, 181

positive feedback, vii, 1, 19

positive relationship, 130

posture, 233

poverty, 313, 344

power, 44, 120, 123, 132, 135, 209, 279, 288, 297, 301, 302, 306, 307, 328, 331

predictability, 232

predictors, 101, 172

preference, 89, 165, 166, 188, 212, 215, 232, 236, 241, 247, 285, 291

preschool, 263

president, 330

pressure, 92, 251, 323

prestige, 247

primacy, 3

primary, 3, 14, 17, 33, 42, 47, 49, 56, 68, 69, 77, 78, 88, 94, 98, 103, 154, 157, 158, 226, 234, 247

priorities, 40, 49, 65, 132, 138, 159

prisons, 57

privacy, 346

probability, 7, 172, 196, 264, 265, 267, 268, 269

probe, 101

problem solving, 34, 35, 40, 46, 199, 208, 233, 243
procedural knowledge, 40
procedures, 20, 89, 211, 236, 240
production, 218, 219
productivity, 130, 211, 216, 232, 251, 253, 268, 335
profession, 5, 138, 142, 229
professional growth, 83, 139
professions, 5, 181, 263
profit, 3, 4, 285
profit margin, 3
program administration, 119, 127
programming, 273, 303, 309, 310, 339, 342, 343
progress reports, 245
proliferation, 2, 3
promote, 6, 9, 10, 49, 142, 272, 275, 302, 306, 323, 327, 339, 341, 345, 346, 347
proposition, 36, 325
protocol(s), 12, 52, 126, 142
psychiatric patients, 204
psychological phenomena, 176
psychologist, 248
psychology, 36, 42, 176, 204, 250, 251
psychotherapy, 239
public administration, 240, 246, 250
public awareness, 337
public domain, ix, 271
public education, 48
public investment, 3, 268
public policy, 321, 324, 342
public policy priorities, 321, 324
public sector, 4, 263, 265
public service, 279
pupil, 48, 213
purchasing power, 279

Q

qualifications, 5, 132, 140, 256, 333
quality control, 339
quality of life, 7, 277
quality of service, 29, 127
quality research, 65
questioning, 179
questionnaire(s), 26, 29, 46, 53, 54, 61, 62, 63, 64, 68, 70, 77, 84, 93, 94, 100, 101, 111, 114, 115, 150, 151, 156, 157, 158, 159, 165, 169, 171

R

research and development (R&D), 33
race, 11, 63, 144, 218, 336
racial, 11

racial differences, 247
rain, 46
range, viii, 7, 12, 25, 34, 39, 41, 48, 50, 53, 57, 61, 71, 90, 107, 116, 132, 133, 158, 165, 170, 181, 184, 186, 211, 212, 217, 218, 220, 235, 286, 295, 296, 302, 311, 321, 329, 340
rating scale, 22
ratings, 19, 65, 101, 105, 171, 237
rationality, 192
reading, 43, 49, 50, 59, 74, 85, 89, 90, 92, 131, 141, 157, 158, 218, 220, 224, 228, 241, 242, 294, 299
real estate, 315
reality, 65, 73, 128, 158, 176, 180, 183, 189, 191, 194, 279
reasoning, 176, 177, 182, 185, 186, 199, 201, 203, 335
recall, 239, 241, 242, 248
recession, 254, 322
recognition, 3, 7, 122, 226, 241, 248, 293
reconcile, 186, 187, 194, 266
reconciliation, 180, 200
recruiting, 17, 287
reduction, 65, 192, 343
reflection, vii, 1, 35, 38, 40, 43, 45, 79, 86, 87, 88, 134, 143, 152, 180, 183, 186, 189, 218, 223
reflective practice, 139, 140
reforms, 46, 47, 289
regional, 49, 272, 296, 304, 307, 319, 334
regression, 100, 101, 102, 104, 105, 112, 236, 257, 264, 267, 268
regression analysis(es), 100, 101, 102, 104, 105, 112
regulation(s), 176, 315, 316
regulatory framework, 305
regulatory requirements, 334
rehabilitation, 319
reinforcement, 43, 233
rejection, 100, 148, 156
relationship(s), 8, 13, 14, 16, 17, 19, 47, 70, 96, 106, 113, 114, 116, 130, 137, 139, 140, 163, 169, 170, 171, 184, 185, 188, 190, 192, 193, 195, 197, 201, 227, 239, 240, 241, 243, 246, 250, 294, 333
Relativistic-Relational, viii
relativity, 197, 204
relaxation, 22
relevance, 223, 226, 301, 335
reliability, 12, 162, 182, 211, 237
religion, 188
religious beliefs, 179
remediation, 215, 323
rent, 9, 314
repair, 315
reparation, 158, 246

report, 2, 22, 29, 39, 48, 57, 69, 93, 114, 140, 158, 165, 167, 168, 216, 228, 237, 238
reputation, 332, 333
research and development, 33
research design, 12, 33, 51, 66, 67, 137, 146, 159
resistance, 9, 335
resources, 18, 30, 31, 32, 42, 76, 86, 95, 97, 116, 127, 130, 154, 171, 172, 173, 208, 290, 291, 295, 307, 309, 319, 322, 334
responding, vii, 1, 4, 6, 17, 85, 213, 245, 247
response, 7, 9, 17, 22
responsibility, 7, 73, 123, 207, 212
responsiveness, 243, 276, 287, 288, 326
restructuring, 33, 138, 241, 298
retention, 6, 7, 8, 9, 16, 22, 26, 51, 57, 58, 61, 70, 72, 73, 74, 75, 76, 79, 81, 82, 84, 86, 89, 92, 98, 101, 109, 111, 118, 128, 143, 144, 146, 147, 148, 154, 159, 161, 173, 215, 232, 241, 323, 335, 338
retirees, 31
retirement, 222, 277
retrieval, 18
returns, viii, 130, 253, 254, 259, 265, 266, 267, 268, 269, 270
revenue, 5, 287, 292, 306, 321, 322, 323, 326
revolutionary, 2
rewards, 245, 327
risk(s), 9, 40, 206, 226, 229, 256, 274, 279, 282, 283, 284, 335
risk factors, 282, 284
role-playing, 208, 243
rolling, 115, 168
routines, 31, 208
Ryan, Jack, 139

S

safety, 6, 12, 13, 18, 85
sales, 315, 326
sample, 26, 27, 30, 51, 52, 53, 54, 55, 56, 57, 61, 62, 63, 64, 65, 66, 68, 71, 72, 75, 77, 78, 80, 94, 95, 96, 98, 99, 100, 101, 102, 103, 104, 105, 107, 108, 110, 111, 114, 115, 117, 118, 119, 122, 124, 125, 126, 129, 130, 131, 133, 135, 139, 151, 154, 155, 158, 159, 160, 164, 170, 172, 181, 190, 211, 238, 248, 249, 257, 259, 260, 261, 262, 263, 264, 265, 266, 267, 268, 347
sample survey, 347
sampling, 51, 66
satellite, 293
satisfaction, 3, 6, 9, 10, 12, 13, 14, 16, 17, 18, 19, 20, 21, 22, 23, 128, 334
saturation, 10
savings, 312

scarcity, 254
scheduling, 86, 153, 213, 282, 287, 293, 297, 298, 299, 305, 310
schema, 100, 156, 223
scholarship, 3, 247
scholastic achievement, 176
Scholastic Aptitude Test, 255
school culture, 36, 47, 139
school work, 15
schooling, 85, 217, 254, 256, 257
science, viii, 11, 37, 39, 137, 138, 141, 142, 176, 218, 224, 253, 266, 327
scientific knowledge, 176, 178
scores, 12, 15, 17, 19, 36, 37, 70, 107, 150, 151, 152, 160, 161, 165, 171, 182, 189, 190, 191, 195, 196, 215, 235, 237, 238, 248, 249
search, 47, 181, 215, 244, 266
searches, 18
searching, 234
second language, 88, 299
secondary, 25, 29, 53, 90, 117, 158, 218, 222, 223, 224, 226, 237
secondary education, 25, 29, 53, 90, 158, 226, 254, 255, 256, 259, 267, 269, 293
secondary schools, vii, 279
secondary students, 204
secular, 3
security, 6, 12, 13, 18
seeding, 347
selecting, 14, 247
selectivity, 297
self, 7, 8, 9, 34, 35, 36, 38, 39, 40, 43, 44, 45, 51, 61, 66, 69, 84, 94, 108, 120, 131, 139, 140, 142, 148, 150, 159, 161, 211, 216, 220, 223, 229, 234, 235, 238, 239, 243
self-concept, 9, 139, 180, 199, 202
self-confidence, 84, 94
self-consistency, 234
self-control, 183
self-definition, 181
self-efficacy, 36, 44, 45, 142
self-esteem, 7, 120, 131, 181, 203, 268
self-identity, 199
self-knowledge, 192, 202
self-reflection, 180
self-reports, 38, 39, 61, 66
self-understanding, 199
senate, 229
sensations, 175, 233
sensitivity, 239, 246, 249, 343
series, ix, 2, 8, 88, 105, 160, 216, 229, 271
service provider, 88

services, 3, 5, 6, 8, 9, 10, 12, 13, 14, 15, 16, 17, 18, 20, 21, 22, 25, 53, 74, 127, 136, 144, 209

sex, 247, 248

sexual orientation, 144, 222

sexuality, 226

shape, 273, 289, 305, 321, 324, 340, 347

shaping, 324

shares, 176, 260

sharing, 8, 28, 58, 77, 82, 84, 91, 109, 114, 115, 119, 127, 129, 130, 157, 171, 295

shelter, 117, 170

sheltered instruction, 142

short run, 324

shortage, 274, 279, 302, 342

short-term memory, 242, 243, 248

shoulders, 220

sign(s), 177, 193, 228, 267

signals, 280, 332, 333

silk, 214

similarity, 179, 191

simulation, 239

sites, 11, 16

skill acquisition, 216

skills, vii, 2, 5, 7, 8, 28, 34, 35, 37, 38, 43, 49, 50, 83, 86, 88, 91, 102, 120, 122, 131, 134, 147, 157, 177, 179, 199, 218, 240, 241, 243, 244, 248, 249, 259, 274, 275, 276, 277, 279, 290, 291, 292, 293, 294, 295, 297, 299, 300, 301, 302, 305, 307, 308, 310, 315, 316, 317, 320, 325, 326, 329, 330, 333, 334, 335

SN, 11

social awareness, 244

social behavior, 180

social change, 102, 157

social environment, 184

social group, 212

social life, 332

social network, 2

social psychology, 42

social relationships, 47

social roles, 199

social support, 307

society, 139, 145, 185, 233, 255, 268, 276, 289

socioeconomic background, 36, 211

socioeconomic status, 324

software, 64, 315

solvency, 15

sorting, 255

South Carolina, 318

species, 22, 250

specific knowledge, 266

specificity, 195

spectrum, 27, 78, 80, 92

speed, 305, 334

spontaneity, 221

SPSS, 64

stability, 112, 127, 142, 167, 180, 183, 184

staff, 3, 4, 12, 16, 17, 18, 20, 26, 35, 36, 37, 39, 48, 50, 51, 57, 58, 59, 66, 82, 87, 91, 120, 123, 132, 136, 137, 138, 139, 140, 141, 142, 144, 145, 239

staff development, 35, 36, 37, 39, 48, 137, 138, 139, 140, 141, 142

staffing, 63

stages, 121, 177, 181, 195, 199, 203

stakeholders, 32, 33, 245, 288, 329, 330, 331, 340, 347

standard deviation, 68, 212

standard error, 266

standard of living, 338

standardized testing, 335

standards, 39, 46, 53, 138, 139, 180, 215, 218, 234, 300, 304, 306, 314, 320, 334, 336

state aid, 310, 314, 318

State Department, 353

state innovation, 342

state oversight, 342

statistical analysis, 137, 169, 182

statistics, 2, 18, 23, 140, 212, 222, 224, 255, 260

stereotypes, 8

stigmatized, 8

stimulus, 5, 179, 182, 240

strain, 323

strategies, viii, 10, 32, 38, 40, 42, 45, 47, 58, 60, 61, 62, 70, 73, 79, 81, 85, 89, 93, 96, 101, 111, 123, 128, 131, 142, 144, 146, 148, 149, 150, 157, 202, 205, 209, 218, 222, 227, 229, 231, 232, 240, 244, 245, 250, 255, 272, 273, 274, 276, 296, 298, 299, 300, 330, 333, 342, 343, 347

strength, 10, 16, 82, 94, 102, 172, 217

stress, 3, 6, 7, 8, 9, 12, 16, 20, 21, 22, 23, 37, 181, 202, 264

stressor(s), vii, 1, 3, 4, 5, 7, 8, 9, 10, 11, 15, 16, 21

structuring, 242, 246

student achievement, 32, 33, 36, 37, 41, 44, 137, 139, 140, 142, 156, 216, 231

student characteristics, 246

student motivation, 17

student populations, 4, 345

student retention, 323

student teacher, 228, 246

subgroups, 338

subjective well-being, 204

subjectivity, 202

subsidy, 311, 317

summaries, 64

summer, 147, 315

supervision, 43, 213
supervisors, 50, 127, 140
supply, 220, 256, 261, 273, 311, 331, 338
support services, 10, 74, 290, 297, 299, 323
support staff, 18
suppression, 172
surprise, 186
survey, 10, 11, 12, 13, 14, 16, 211, 216
survival, 10, 44
Sweden, viii, 253, 254, 255, 256, 259, 260, 267, 269
symbols, 175
sympathetic nervous system, 5
syndrome, 9
synthesis, 32, 40, 64, 272
systemic change, 341
systems, 8, 31, 32, 35, 43, 47, 48, 65, 67, 115, 123,
    127, 128, 130, 138, 169, 176, 177, 178, 179, 180,
    182, 187, 188, 189, 192, 193, 194, 196, 250, 273,
    275, 276, 288, 291, 295, 298, 304, 305, 307, 310,
    327, 328, 329, 330, 331, 333, 336, 337, 338, 339,
    340, 342, 343, 345, 346

T

talent, 221, 236
TANF, 309, 319, 326
targets, 301, 338
task performance, 236
tax credit, 308, 311, 312, 313, 316, 317, 343, 344,
    347
teach to the test, 113
teacher effectiveness, 36, 37, 41
teacher performance, 62
teacher preparation, 37, 138
teacher training, 142
teaching effectiveness, 36
teaching experience, 27, 39, 45, 47, 55, 56, 95, 97,
    98, 99, 100, 112, 124, 147, 153, 155, 158, 173,
    218
teaching quality, 301
teaching strategies, 40, 209
team members, 150
technical assistance, 31, 49
technician, 295, 331
technology, 20, 23, 127, 222, 233, 251, 291, 294,
    297, 298, 300, 301, 303, 304, 307, 326, 327, 332,
    333
Tel Aviv, 175
telecommunications, 307
telephone, 19
television, 85
temperature, 207
Tennessee, 36, 142

tension, 185, 219
tenure, 276
tertiary education, 255, 256, 262, 264, 267
test items, 236
test scores, 37, 248
test-retest reliability, 12
Texas, 278, 279, 338, 340, 346, 349, 351
textbooks, 17, 18, 294
theory(ies), viii, 9, 28, 31, 38, 39, 41, 44, 45, 66, 83,
    88, 89, 92, 121, 134, 135, 138, 141, 151, 176,
    177, 178, 179, 180, 194, 198, 199, 200, 201, 203,
    204, 205, 216, 218, 219, 221, 223, 224, 225, 227,
    229, 231, 232, 235, 243, 248, 249, 250, 251, 272,
    301
thinking, 27, 29, 30, 34, 37, 40, 41, 60, 61, 62, 70,
    72, 73, 74, 75, 77, 78, 79, 80, 81, 82, 83, 84, 86,
    87, 88, 89, 90, 92, 93, 94, 100, 101, 110, 111,
    112, 113, 114, 115, 117, 118, 119, 120, 122, 127,
    129, 134, 148, 150, 151, 152, 155, 157, 161, 164,
    167, 168, 170, 172, 173, 177, 178, 196, 197, 198,
    209, 221, 335
threat, 3, 219, 237
threshold, 324
time frame, 18, 20
time pressure, 8
timing, 64, 239, 260
toddlers, 295
total costs, 254, 321
total revenue, 322
tracking, 297, 330, 337, 340, 345
trade, 329, 334
tradition(s), 214, 222, 223
traditional, vii, 1, 2, 3, 4, 5, 6, 7, 8, 9, 10, 18, 21, 22,
    32, 210
training, 2, 22, 31, 33, 34, 35, 37, 38, 42, 47, 48, 51,
    74, 75, 85, 91, 108, 122, 133, 140, 142, 143, 146,
    164, 165, 213, 231, 232, 233, 236, 238, 239, 240,
    244, 245, 249, 250, 254, 257, 259, 273, 274, 277,
    280, 302, 309, 311, 315, 317, 319, 320, 326, 329,
    332, 333, 334, 338
training programs, 231, 319, 320, 326
traits, 179, 180, 183, 184, 185, 186, 196, 203, 204,
    224
trajectory, viii, 175, 177, 179, 196, 197, 257, 287
transactions, 19
transcripts, 254
transfer, 14
transference, 222
transformation(s), 1, 177, 180, 195, 196, 274, 276
transition(s), 38, 138, 273, 291, 303, 304, 342
transmission, 3
transparency, 296, 337
transportation, 73, 144, 314, 318, 344

treatment, 19

trees, 145

trend, 96, 105, 113, 114, 125, 158, 162, 163, 164, 170, 171, 247, 281, 285

trial and error, 38, 41, 330

triangulation, 66

triggers, 94

true/false, 222

trust, 38

tuition, 14, 15, 18, 286, 309, 311, 313, 314, 318, 321, 322, 324, 331, 336, 343, 347

turbulence, 72, 115, 152

turnover, 31, 46, 51, 54, 74, 82, 86, 130, 140

tutoring, 158, 295, 299, 307

U

U.S. economy, 331

uncertainty, 40, 188, 256

undergraduate, 4, 11, 22, 54, 181, 209, 211, 215, 237, 246, 247, 250, 281, 299, 311, 312, 313, 317, 318, 333

undergraduate education, 215

unemployment, 254, 257, 258, 268, 340, 346

unemployment insurance, 254, 268, 340, 346

unemployment rate, 254

uniform, 66, 148, 194, 227, 311

United Kingdom (UK), 216, 254

United States, 1, 143, 251, 274, 321, 348, 353

United States (US), 1, 143, 251

universities, vii, viii, 1, 2, 3, 6, 10, 23, 35, 205, 209, 227, 229, 276, 281, 284, 286, 287, 296, 297, 311, 316, 321, 325, 347

university community, 7

V

vacuum, 129

validity, 12, 188, 193, 195, 211, 221, 237, 238

values, 20, 39, 40, 179, 180, 187, 188, 193, 262, 264, 265, 267, 268

variable(s),14, 22, 27, 39, 42, 62, 64, 71, 96, 100, 101, 102, 159, 163, 165, 167, 168, 169, 170, 172, 173, 196, 206, 212, 239, 241, 243, 249, 254, 257, 259, 264, 265, 266, 267, 268, 328

variance, 173, 222, 238

variation, 66, 204, 236, 259, 322

venue, 27, 56, 84, 99, 112, 155, 223, 227, 271

Vermont, 318

versatility, 192

veterans, 311

Victoria, 349

videotape, 242

Viola Spolin, viii

Virginia, 23, 49, 139, 229, 318, 351, 353

vision, 35, 93, 214, 325

visual environment, 233

visual field, 234

vital, 4

vocational, ix

vocational education, vii, 91, 158, 299, 319

vocational rehabilitation, 319

vocational training, 259, 319

voice, 20, 86, 87, 96, 97, 109, 110, 111, 117, 122, 123, 124, 129

volunteer work, 227

vouchers, 319

Vygotsky, 179, 195, 204

W

wages, 265, 267, 269, 277

walking, 93, 220, 221

war, 200

Washington, 22, 32, 138, 139, 140, 141, 142, 143, 202, 249, 259, 269, 271, 279, 304, 319, 340, 346, 348, 349, 350, 351, 352, 353

weakness, 16, 82, 222, 240

wealth, 217

wear, 191

web, 194

welding, 315

welfare, 158, 300, 319

welfare law, 158

well-being, 3, 204, 214

White, 11, 55, 140, 237

winning, 215

withdrawal, 10

women, 2, 9, 14, 22, 26, 53, 237, 238, 260, 268, 276, 338

words, 17, 18

work, 8, 14, 15, 16, 18, 20, 26, 28, 30, 32, 34, 35, 38, 40, 41, 44, 46, 47, 49, 51, 52, 69, 74, 76, 84, 87, 88, 89, 91, 92, 93, 94, 111, 112, 113, 116, 119, 120, 121, 126, 128, 131, 132, 134, 135, 136, 141, 143, 144, 145, 148, 157, 159, 168, 169, 171, 173, 205, 206, 208, 212, 213, 218, 219, 220, 223, 224, 227, 229, 243, 245, 247

work activity, 319

workers, 144, 259, 271, 273, 274, 276, 277, 279, 284, 289, 294, 299, 300, 301, 302, 309, 310, 315, 316, 320, 327, 332, 333, 340, 341, 347

workforce, 141, 251

Workforce Investment Act, 319

working conditions, 26, 28, 29, 30, 62, 83, 85, 86, 117, 127, 129, 130, 132, 135, 136
working groups, 49
working hours, 28, 68, 97, 112, 113, 117, 125, 127, 130, 136, 167, 168
workload, 17
workplace, vii, 3, 41, 90, 117, 170, 232, 268, 274, 279, 334, 340, 346
worldview, 14

worry, 205, 330
writing, 34, 49, 50, 84, 131, 157, 205, 209, 294, 299

Y

yield, 20, 182, 299
young adults, 201, 207